Travel Disc[...]

G000024050

**This coupon entitles [...]
when you book y[...]**

RESERVATION SERVICE

Hotels ♦ Airlines ♦ Car Rentals ♦ Cruises
All Your Travel Needs

Here's what you get: *

♦ A discount of $50 USD on a booking of $1,000** or more for two or more people!

♦ A discount of $25 USD on a booking of $500** or more for one person!

♦ Free membership for three years, and 1,000 free miles on enrollment in the unique Travel Network Miles-to-Go® frequent-traveler program. Earn one mile for every dollar spent through the program. Redeem miles for free hotel stays starting at 5,000 miles. Earn free roundtrip airline tickets starting at 25,000 miles.

♦ Personal help in planning your own, customized trip.

♦ Fast, confirmed reservations at any property recommended in this guide, subject to availability.***

♦ Special discounts on bookings in the U.S. and around the world.

♦ Low-cost visa and passport service.

♦ Reduced-rate cruise packages and special car rental programs worldwide.

Visit our website at http://www.travelnetwork.com/Frommer or call us globally at 201-567-8500, ext. 55. In the U.S., call toll-free at 1-888-940-5000, or fax 201-567-1838. In Canada, call at 1-905-707-7222, or fax 905-707-8108. In Asia, call 60-3-7191044, or fax 60-3-7185415.

* To qualify for these travel discounts, at least a portion of your trip must include destinations covered in this guide. No more than one coupon discount may be used in any 12-month period, for destinations covered in this guide. Cannot be combined with any other discount or promotion.
**These are U.S. dollars spent on commissionable bookings.
*** A $10 USD fee, plus fax and/or phone charges, will be added to the cost of bookings at each hotel not linked to the reservation service. Customers must approve these fees in advance. If only hotels of this kind are booked the traveler(s) must also purchase roundtrip air tickets from Travel Network for the trip.

Valid until December 31, 1998. Terms and conditions of the Miles-to-Go® program are available on request by calling 201-567-8500, ext 55.

BAH234

Frommer's® 98

Bahamas

by Darwin Porter
& Danforth Prince

Macmillan • USA

ABOUT THE AUTHORS

Darwin Porter, while still a teenager, began writing about The Bahamas for the *Miami Herald* and has been a frequent visitor ever since. He's seen the country go through good times, bad times, hurricanes, and heat waves. A native of North Carolina, Porter wrote the first-ever Frommer's guide to The Bahamas. In 1982, he was joined by Ohio-born **Danforth Prince,** formerly of the Paris bureau of *The New York Times,* who has co-authored numerous Frommer best-sellers with Porter, including guides to England, Germany, France, and the Caribbean. Together, they share their secrets and discoveries of The Bahamas with you.

MACMILLAN TRAVEL

A Simon & Schuster Macmillan Company
1633 Broadway
New York, NY 10019

Find us online at **http://www.mgr.com/travel**
or on America Online at Keyword: **Frommer's**

ISBN 0-02-861647-2
ISSN 1068-9338

Editor: Suzanne Roe
Production Editor: John Carroll
Design by Michele Laseau
Page Creation by Deb Kincaid, Joy Dean Lee, Dana Davis, Toi Davis, Kathleen Caulfield, Jerry Cole, Dave Faust, Stephanie Hammett and Michelle Croninger
Digital Cartography by Ortelius Design

SPECIAL SALES

Bulk purchases (10+ copies) of Frommer's travel guides are available to corporations, organizations, mail-order catalogs, institutions, and charities at special discounts, and can be customized to suit individual needs. For more information write to Special Sales, Macmillan General Reference, 1633 Broadway, New York, NY 10019.

Manufactured in the United States of America

Contents

6 Grand Bahama (Freeport/Lucaya) 145

7 Bimini, The Berry Islands & Andros 184

List of Maps

An Invitation to the Reader

In researching this book, we discovered many wonderful places—hotels, restaurants, shops, and more. We're sure you'll find others. Please tell us about them, so we can share the information with your fellow travelers in upcoming editions. If you were disappointed with a recommendation, we'd love to know that, too. Please write to:

Darwin Porter/Danforth Prince
Frommer's Bahamas '98
Macmillan Travel
1633 Broadway
New York, NY 10019

An Additional Note

Please be advised that travel information is subject to change at any time—and this is especially true of prices. We therefore suggest that you write or call ahead for confirmation when making your travel plans. The authors, editors, and publisher cannot be held responsible for the experiences of readers while traveling. Your safety is important to us, however, so we encourage you to stay alert and be aware of your surroundings. Keep a close eye on cameras, purses, and wallets, all favorite targets of thieves and pickpockets.

What the Symbols Mean

✪ Frommer's Favorites

Hotels, restaurants, attractions, and entertainment you should not miss or that offer great value.

The following abbreviations are used for credit cards:

AE	American Express	DISC	Discover
CB	Carte Blanche	MC	MasterCard
DC	Diners Club	V	Visa

The following abbreviations are used in hotel listings:

AP (American Plan): Includes three meals a day (sometimes called full board or full pension).

EP (European Plan): This rate is always cheapest, as it offers only the room—no meals.

MAP (Modified American Plan): Sometimes called half board or half pension, this room rate includes breakfast and dinner (or lunch if you prefer).

The Best of The Bahamas

You've come to The Bahamas or Turks and Caicos to relax—not to exhaust yourself searching for the best deals and unique experiences. With this guide in hand, you can spend your vacation in peace and let us do the work. Below you'll find our carefully compiled lists of the most superlative beaches; the best spots for diving, snorkeling, fishing, and sailing; the best hotels (from modest inns to deluxe resorts) for honeymooners, families, and those who want to get away from it all; the best restaurants, nightlife, and gambling—and nearly everything else your heart might desire. We'll even tell you how you can rent your own deserted island.

Since it's very inconvenient to move easily from one island to another, this "best of" list can be an important resource in helping you define your holiday. For our suggestions, we'll island hop from one to another, finding what's good and discarding what isn't. For more information on which island—or islands—you should go to, the destinations that best suit your goals and vacation dreams, refer to "The Islands in Brief" in chapter 2, which explores the various offerings in more detail.

1 The Best Beaches

Good beaches can be found on virtually every island of The Bahamas, although in some cases, you might have to walk, drive, or bicycle a short distance from your hotel or guest house to reach them.

- **Old Fort Beach** (New Providence Island): This beach lies near the relatively unpopulated western tip of the most populous island in The Bahamas. It's the least developed major beach on New Providence Island. Many of its biggest fans are homeowners from nearby Lyford Cay, whose homes are among the priciest in The Bahamas. Least crowded times are weekdays. Windiest times are throughout the winter. Calmest times (best suited for waterskiing) are during the summer. Sands are white, waters are turquoise. See chapter 4.

- **Cable Beach** (New Providence Island): Cable Beach has easy access to shops, casinos, restaurants, water sports, and bars. It got its name when the first underwater cable was laid in 1892, linking it and the Bahamian capital of New Providence to the mainland of Florida. During the 1930s, it enjoyed a certain vogue because of a nearby racetrack. See chapter 4.

- **Cabbage Beach** (Paradise Island): If Las Vegas were a seaside resort, its beaches would resemble Cabbage Beach. The sands are broad (but slope in some places rather steeply) and stretch for at least 2 miles. Palms, sea grapes, and casuarinas line its edge. You get the feeling that many of the sunbathers dozing on the sands are recovering from the previous evening's revels. It's likely to be rather crowded near the megahotels that form the core of Paradise Island, but escapists can find something approaching solitude on the beach's isolated northwestern extension (Paradise Beach), where the only access is by boat or on foot. See chapter 5.
- **Xanadu Beach** (Grand Bahama Island): Grand Bahama Island boasts about 60 miles of sandy shoreline. The most convenient to the resort hotels of Freeport is Xanadu Beach. Shuttle-bus service connects the beach with several nearby hotels. The beach offers at least a mile of white sand and a (usually) gentle surf. It's among the most-visited beaches on the island. If you're looking for more privacy, seek out any of the beaches stretching for many miles in either direction. See chapter 6.
- **Tahiti Beach** (Hope Town, the Abacos): Its isolation at the far end of Elbow Cay island ensures that only a handful of people will ever visit its cool waters and white sands. Access is possible only by foot, by riding a rented bicycle across sand and gravel paths from Hope Town, or by private boat. The Abacos are the sailing capital of The Bahamas, and you'll never lack for boats to carry you there. See chapter 8.
- **Pink Sands Beach** (Harbour Island): This pale pink beach stretches for 3 miles past a handful of low-rise hotels and private villas. When visitors leave the warm waters and pink sands, they can ramble along the streets of a village whose clapboard-covered roofs are pure New England. See chapter 9.
- **Ten Bay Beach** (Eleuthera): This beach was one of the reasons the exclusive and famous Cotton Bay Club was built here. Ten Bay Beach lies a short drive south of Palmetto Point, just north of Savannah Sound. Since the fabled Cotton Bay Club remains closed, the white sands and turquoise waters will be even more idyllic for vacationers. See chapter 9.
- **Saddle Cay** (the Exumas): Most of the Exumas are oval-shaped islands strung end to end like the links of a 130-mile chain. One notable exception is Saddle Cay, whose horseshoe-shaped curve lies near the Exumas's northern tip. Don't even think of getting here except by boat. Once you reach it, however, you'll find an unspoiled setting without a trace of the modern world and lots of other cays and islets for stranding yourself on, shipwreck-style, for a few hours. See chapter 10.
- **Grace Bay Beach** (Providenciales, Turks and Caicos Islands): Its 12 miles of pale sands are the premier attraction of Provo. It's so spectacular that increasing numbers of resorts (including Club Med) have developed along its edge. See chapter 12.

2 The Best Dive Sites

Scuba diving is a year-round undertaking in The Bahamas, where shallow, sunlit seas and thousands of reefs are packed with brilliant underwater life. All of the major islands offer diving excursions, lessons, and equipment rentals. Intermediate and advanced divers can participate in night dives.

- **New Providence Island:** Many ships have sunk near Nassau in the past 300 years; the numerous wrecks are well known to the dive outfitters here. Other attractions are underwater gardens of elk-horn coral and dozens of reefs teeming with underwater life. See chapter 4.

- **Grand Bahama Island:** The island is ringed with reefs, and dive sites are plentiful. What makes the island a cut above many others is the presence of a world-class dive operator, **UNEXSO** (Underwater Explorer's Society; ☎ **242/373-1244**), whose teaching methods are well regarded. See chapter 6.
- **Andros:** The barrier reef off the coast of Andros is the third largest in the world and a famous destination for scuba enthusiasts. Marine life abounds. See chapter 7.
- **Bimini:** Although most outsiders appreciate Bimini for its game-fishing options, its charms are obvious to scuba divers, too. Three miles of offshore reefs attract millions of colorful fish. Its allure also includes the wreck of a motorized yacht, the *Sapona* (owned by Henry Ford), which sank in shallow waters off the coast in 1929. See chapter 7.
- **Eleuthera:** This island contains all the underwater coral and fish a diver would expect, as well as a handful of bizarre underwater experiences, such as the "Current Cut," an exciting underwater gully that carries divers for a 10-minute ride on a swiftly flowing underwater current. A boat retrieves divers at the end. There are also four wrecked ships that lie in less than 40 feet of water. The most unusual of these contains the engine of a steam locomotive that was being transported on a barge in 1865, reportedly after being sold by the American Confederacy to raise cash for its war effort. See chapter 9.
- **Long Island** (the Southern Bahamas): Shallow-water snorkeling is spectacular on virtually all sides of the island, and in deeper waters offshore, teams of experienced divers make regular excursions in underwater cages to feed swarms of mako, bull, and reef sharks. Dive sites abound. See chapter 11.
- **San Salvador** (the Southern Bahamas): Ironically, the life teeming below the seas surrounding this isolated island is more robust than on the dry, salty soil of the island's surface. There are nearly 80 well-known dive sites here, most on the leeward side of the island where the waves are usually the least powerful. The island's largest resort (Club Med; ☎ **800/CLUB-MED** or 242/331-2458) offers a complete array of dive facilities, including a decompression chamber. See chapter 11.
- **Turks and Caicos Islands:** This cluster of islands contains a rich assortment of underwater sites, including sea lanes where boaters and divers often sight whales during April. There's also a collection of unusual underwater wrecks (such as the HMS *Endymion,* which sank during a storm in 1790) and many miles of reefs with every kind of marine life. Off Grand Turk, divers appreciate the many miles of "drop-off" diving, where the sea walls descend rapidly to uncharted depths known as blue holes. The dive sites here are relatively unexplored. See chapter 12.

3 The Best Snorkeling

The Bahamas is among the top places in the world for snorkeling and is unequaled in the Caribbean. The pristine waters offer accessible coral reefs and abundant marine life. Even the tiniest hotel is likely to have equipment on hand. The snorkeling excursions of the following islands tend to be better organized and more frequent than those at islands with fewer tourists. Keep in mind, though, that such outlying islands as Eleuthera and the Abacos offer a wealth of spectacular snorkeling options, as well.

- **New Providence/Paradise Island:** The waters that ring densely populated New Providence Island and nearby Paradise Island are among the most frequently explored in The Bahamas. The action is usually focused around the Rose Island Reefs, a series of well-known underwater wrecks, Gambier Deep Reef, Booby Rock

Channel, and the Goulding Reef Cays. Virtually every resort hotel on the island offers equipment, often with a motorboat ride to the site. See chapters 4 and 5.

- **Grand Bahama Island:** Boats depart from hotel piers at frequent intervals for supervised snorkeling excursions around the island. There are miniflotillas, including glass-bottomed boats; sailboats offering free use of snorkeling equipment; and yachts with everything from dinner cruises to snorkeling junkets. Great dive sites around Grand Bahama Island include the Wall, the Caves, the site of a long-ago marine disaster known as Theo's Wreck, and Treasure Reef.

The best way to go snorkeling off Grand Bahama Island is to hook up with the Underwater Explorers Society (UNEXSO) at Lucaya Beach (☎ 242/373-1244). This is not only the premier facility for snorkeling (also diving) in The Bahamas, but is compared to the very best in the Caribbean. It makes three dive trips daily and takes you to all the best sites. Reef trips, shark dives, wreck decks, and even night dives—UNEXSO knows how to do them all. There's no one better. See chapter 6.

4 The Best Fishing

The Bahamas is the best-known sportfishing region in the world—the waters teem with barracuda, tuna, amberjack, bonefish, wahoo, marlin, tarpon, and kingfish.

- **Bimini:** All kinds of fish seem to flourish in the deep waters around Bimini, but the most sought-after trophy is the marlin, whose image appears on the Bahamian $100 bill. As many as 40 annual fishing tournaments are held every year in The Bahamas, many of which transform Bimini into a mini–Olympic village where fish are hunted by a daunting armada of well-equipped fishing boats. Bimini was novelist Ernest Hemingway's favorite place to fish. See chapter 7.
- **Andros:** The fishing is good everywhere in The Bahamas, but bonefish seem to thrive in the shallow, sunlit waters off Andros Island. It isn't the best-tasting fish in the islands (it's mostly cartilage and bones), but aficionados say that it puts up one of the strongest fights of any fish in the world. Other islands good for bonefishing include Bimini, Walker's Cay, Abaco, Eleuthera, Exuma, and Long Island. See chapter 7.

5 The Best Sailing

Most large hotels in The Bahamas will have small sailboats (especially Sunfish, Sailfish, and small, one-masted catamarans) available for their guests. Windsurfers are also widely available.

- **The Abacos:** Vying with the Exumas as the most perfect sailing area not only in The Bahamas but also in the world, the Abacos are known among yachties for their many anchorages, sheltered coves, and plentiful marine facilities. The sailing tradition in the Abacos dates from the 18th century. Boats of all shapes and sizes can be chartered for a week or longer, with or without a crew. Major charter centers are found at Marsh Harbour and Hope Town. Make arrangements for rentals with **The Moorings** (☎ 242/367-4000) in Marsh Harbour. See chapter 8.
- **The Exumas:** The Exumas are the setting for the famed April Family Island Regatta, the most-attended sailing event in The Bahamas. In winter, Elizabeth Harbour is a mecca for yachties who explore the deserted islands and cays nearby, as well as the secluded bays, safe anchorage harbors, and secret coves. Even in winter, unless the weather turns unexpectedly bad (and usually foul weather days are

short lived), the seas are balmy, the temperatures ideal. Clear skies and smooth waters make for ideal sailing conditions. Yacht magazines praise the Exumas for having the finest cruising areas in The Bahamas. Most marine supply facilities are in George Town, the capital. All of them, including Exuma Docking Services (☎ 242/336-2578), are located at the marina. See chapter 10.

6 The Best Hiking

Hiking is not well organized in The Bahamas the way it is in the States. It's mostly a do-it-yourself thing. Some Bahamians tell us they think "it's a bit mad" to go out and hike under the noonday sun. The best hiking possibilities are found at Grand Bahama Island (Freeport/Lucaya).

- **Lucayan National Park** (Grand Bahama Island): The 40-acre Lucayan National Park offers visitors a view of undisturbed nature that is very far removed from the casinos and cabaret shows. It lies about 25 miles east of Freeport beside the island's main east-to-west traffic artery. The landscape is mostly covered with stunted pines and gnarled palmettos, except for groves of more verdant trees at the entrances to each of the park's caves. The largest cave contains spiral staircases that lead visitors down into a freshwater world inhabited by shrimp, mosquito fish, fruit bats, freshwater eels, and a species of crustacean (*Spelionectes lucayensis*) that has never been found anywhere else in the world. A series of paths in the park leads to diverse flora and fauna, including rare varieties of orchids, sea turtles, hummingbirds, and barn owls. See chapter 6.
- **Rand Nature Centre** (Grand Bahama Island): Lying 2 miles east of the center of Freeport, this is the second-best place on Grand Bahama for hiking. It's a 100-acre pineland sanctuary where you can ramble along forest nature trails taking in the native flora and fauna. Bird-watchers are especially attracted to the area, as wild birds abound. Hiking along the trails, you are likely to see the West Indian flamingo, the national bird of The Bahamas. Or you may spot a tiny Bahama woodstar or a Cuban emerald hummingbird. The nectar of the hibiscus seems to be the latter's favorite food. Raccoons can also be spotted along the trails. They're not native but were brought here during the rum-running days of America's Prohibition era. Perhaps you'll encounter one of three species of native boa constrictors, but move along rapidly if you do. There are some 130 types of native plants to see, including 20 species of wild orchids. Both self-guided or guided hikes are offered. See chapter 6.

7 The Best Golf Courses

Some of the world's most famous golf architects, including Robert Trent Jones Sr. and Dick Wilson, have designed challenging courses in The Bahamas.

- **South Ocean Golf and Beach Resort** (New Providence Island; ☎ 242/362-4391): Set on the underpopulated southwestern side of the island, it's so isolated from the congestion of Nassau that golfers imagine themselves on a remote island. The rolling terrain is hilly and dotted with palm trees. It is superior and more challenging than the other major course on New Providence Island at Cable Beach (see below). From its relatively high elevation, golfers can view a seascape called "Tongue of the Ocean." Designer Joe Lee factored in a quartet of challenging water holes. See chapter 4.

- **Cable Beach Golf Course** (New Providence Island; ☎ 242/327-6000): Set on the low hills of north-central New Providence, this is the oldest golf course in The Bahamas. It was the private retreat of British expatriates in the 1930s. Today, it's owned by the same folks who market the vast casino complexes of Cable Beach and managed by a corporate namesake of Arnold Palmer. This par-72 course features a series of small ponds and water traps and more than 7,000 yards of well-maintained greens and fairways. In spite of its pluses, we still prefer its competitors, the Paradise Island Golf Club and the South Ocean Golf and Beach Resort. See chapter 4.
- **Paradise Island Golf Club** (Paradise Island; ☎ 242/363-3925): Dick Wilson designed this 18-hole, par-72 course. It's not as challenging as its nearest competitor, South Ocean Golf and Beach Resort, but it has its own pitfalls, including the world's largest sand trap and water hazards (the Atlantic Ocean) on three sides. Jack Nicklaus and Gary Player have endorsed this course. For the best vista (good enough to take your mind off your game) play the par-3, 14th hole dubbed "cocoa plum." Here the view of the water is panoramic. See chapter 5.
- **Bahamas Princess Resort and Casino** (Grand Bahama Island; ☎ 242/352-6721): This megaresort offers two different golf courses, the Princess Ruby and the Princess Emerald, both of which are par 72. Terrain is rolling and sandy, a welcome relief from the glitter and asphalt-covered boulevards that flank them. Both of these courses were designed by Dick Wilson, but they're not as challenging as the South Ocean Golf and Beach Resort. See chapter 6.
- **Provo Golf Club** (Turks and Caicos Islands; ☎ 809/946-5991): Its arrival on the arid surface of Provo was a major feat of landscape architecture. The design features a desert-inspired mixture of limestone and sand interspersed with greenery and relatively narrow fairways. The course is categorized as a challenging par 72. See chapter 12.

8 The Best Tennis Facilities

Tennis is a popular sport in The Bahamas, although it is not promoted or pursued as aggressively as in clubs in California or even elsewhere in the Caribbean. The preferred hours of play are early in the morning and in the evening, when it's cooler. If tennis is your passion, consider any of the resorts listed below. And when you're booking your holiday, ask about a tennis package, which some resorts offer; it includes rooms and often meals at discounted rates.

- **Paradise Island:** Paradise Island has the best tennis in The Bahamas—not only the best courts but the best players. If you're a true tennis buff, consider checking into **Club Med** (☎ 242/363-2640), which has the largest court complex on the island, with a total of 20 clay composition courts. Eight of these courts are lit for night games. There are also ball machines, a full staff of instructors who offer expert advice, and an instant-replay TV. More accessible to the general public is the tennis complex at **Atlantis** (☎ 242/363-3000), which has a dozen asphalt courts. Some of these are lit for night games. See chapter 5.
- **Freeport** (Grand Bahama Island): Freeport is the second place to head in The Bahamas if you're a tennis buff. The best complex is at the **Bahamas Princess Resort and Casino** (☎ 242/352-6721), a multimillion-dollar resort featuring golf and tennis. Its 12 tennis courts are state of the art, and 8 are lit for night games. The resort consists of the Princess Country Club and the Princess Tower. The Princess Country Club has 6 hard-surface courts, and the Princess Tower has 3 clay

and 3 hard-surface courts. You don't have to be a guest of the resort to play here, but you should call ahead for a reservation. See chapter 6.

9 The Best Offbeat Experiences

If you've had your fill of soaking up the sun and playing the slot machines, consider one of these adventures.

- **Hopping Aboard a Mail Boat to the Out Islands:** For a unique exposure to Bahamian life, book passage on a mail boat. The Bahamas hires about 30 different mail boats to service at least 17 very remote islands. Itineraries depend on the priorities of the captain and crew and the weather. The mail boats make a real difference in the quality of life for the scattered communities of the archipelago, especially since the mail accompanies deliveries of goats, chickens, hardware, and food staples. Nassau is the embarkation point for every boat in the network. Passage from Nassau to, say, Governor's Harbour on Eleuthera costs about $25 each way and takes about a full day. If you're committed to roughing it, you might be able to commandeer a mattress onboard, depending on the facilities in each of these privately owned boats. For more information, call The **Bahamas Tourist Office** at ☎ **800/422-4262** or the dockmaster at the Nassau piers at ☎ **242/393-1064** for current schedules of mail boat departures. Don't expect luxury, and be prepared to spend lots of time dealing with local (and sometimes bizarre) bureaucracies. See chapter 3.
- **Visiting a Loyalist Town:** There are about a half dozen Loyalist towns scattered throughout the Bahamian archipelago. Each one was founded under difficult circumstances by disgruntled British colonists who did not regard the independence of the United States as a joyful event. Clapboard-sided houses resemble the saltbox cottages of New England, except for the bougainvillea climbing up the porch trellises. Life is gentle, detached from the outside world, and rather charmingly old-fashioned. Many visitors appreciate the Loyalist towns even more after the touristic frenzy of Nassau or Freeport. Suitable choices include Harbour Island, Spanish Wells, George Town, or Marsh Harbour/Green Turtle Cay. See chapters 8 and 9.
- **Sea Kayaking** (the Exumas): Modern sea kayaks are so small they let you experience the movement of the sea up close and personal. Since 1976, several tour operators have led kayak expeditions around the 365 islands and cays of the Exumas. Some tours feature a week of kayaking and camping on remote islands. For more information, contact **Ecosummer Expeditions,** 1516 Duranleau St., Vancouver, B.C., Canada V6H 3S4 (☎ **800/465-8884**). See chapter 10.
- **Getting Marooned on Bowe Cay** (the Exumas): No permanent residents live on sandy, scrub-covered Bowe Cay, which is set offshore from Great Exuma Island. But for a price it can be all yours. Visitors fly to George Town, then climb into a powerboat for a 45-minute ride to three shed-roofed, screened-in cabanas (built in the 1990s, they're the only structures on the island). You'll find the barest of worldly necessities: solar panels that power the lights, a stereo, a small refrigerator, and a freezer. You also get fishing gear, a gas-powered grill, and a two-way radio for emergencies. With the boat transfer from Great Exuma included, Bowe Cay rents for about $1,700 per week for two occupants. If you want to bring a group, the owners can provide tents for up to eight visitors, but the rustic charms of the 200-acre island are best appreciated by two. For information, call ☎ **800/992-0128.**

- **Diving the Wall off Grand Turk** (Turks and Caicos Islands): Some divers have compared this experience to jumping off a cliff top in the Swiss Alps. This is one of the most unusual experiences in the world of scuba diving. Only 300 yards from the shoreline of Grand Turk, the waters suddenly drop to uncharted depths of more than 7,000 feet below sea level. Only experienced divers should attempt this. Along the descent, you'll see colonies of black coral, rare forms of anemone, purple sponges, stunning gorgonia, endless forms of coral, and thousands of fish (with different species at different depths). See chapter 12.

10   The Best Honeymoon Resorts

A resort that's suitable for a honeymoon should offer stunning natural beauty, lots of privacy, and a cheerful, supportive staff. There are dozens of resorts that might fit the bill, but these are our top choices.

In recent times, as wedding ceremonies have become increasingly expensive and complicated, more and more couples are exchanging their vows in The Bahamas. Many resorts will arrange everything from the preacher to the flowers, so we've included some resorts that provide wedding services in the following list.

For more information about the various options and the legal requirements for marriages in The Bahamas, refer to chapter 3, "Planning a Trip to The Bahamas."

- **Sandals Royal Bahamian** (Cable Beach, New Providence Island; ☎ 800/ SANDALS or 242/327-6400): This Jamaican chain is the honeymooners' favorite. It operates a series of couples-only, all-inclusive hotels in the Caribbean, with the largest cluster in Jamaica. Now it's invaded The Bahamas. Enthusiastic members of the staff lend their experience and talent to whatever knot-tying rituals happen to be celebrated on-site. Sandals will provide everything from a preacher to flowers, as well as champagne and a cake. The resort offers a total of 27 secluded honeymoon suites with semiprivate plunge pools. See chapter 4.
- **Nassau Marriott Resort & Crystal Palace Casino** (New Providence Island; ☎ 242/327-6200): If you're bored with the idea of honeymooning in an isolated village, with just you, your loved one, the moon, and the stars, head to this megacomplex of electronic razzmatazz, where bright lights, bright colors, and a mind-boggling assortment of diversions will help you while away your time. See chapter 4.
- **Villas on Coral Island** (Silver Cay, off the coast of Nassau; ☎ 800/328-8814 in the U.S., or 242/328-1036): These units include private plunge pools, Italian marble accents, and lots of space. The setting is a small offshore cay whose ambience encourages couples (especially honeymooners) to disappear inside their villas for entire days at a time. When you want to venture out, you can sample the booming nightlife and casino options of the New Providence mainland. See chapter 4.
- **Graycliff** (Nassau, New Providence Island; ☎ 242/322-2796): It's the only member of the prestigious Relais and Châteaux chain in The Bahamas. Its origins are at least 200 years old, and although many of the accommodations are much newer, each has antique charm. The setting, in a garden in the heart of downtown Nassau, allows greater access to everyday Bahamian life than a megaresort would. See chapter 4.
- **Ocean Club** (Paradise Island; ☎ 800/321-3000 in the U.S., or 242/363-3000): It's elegant, low-key, and low-rise, and feels exclusive. The clientele is likely to include many older couples who might be celebrating second (or third)

honeymoons. The Ocean Club's formal terraced gardens were inspired by the club's founder (an heir to the A&P fortune) and are the most impressive in The Bahamas. See chapter 5.

- **Xanadu Beach Resort & Marina** (Grand Bahama Island; ☎ 242/352-6782): Despite its contemporary exterior, the public rooms of this resort contain many expensive decorative touches that might have been chosen by a reclusive billionaire. And sure enough, the builder of this resort was Howard Hughes, who lived in its penthouse for many years. With some of the best architecture on Grand Bahama Island, it's closely linked to the goings-on of the island's restaurants, beaches, and casinos. The comfortable, contemporary bedrooms are suitable for an extended honeymoon. See chapter 6.
- **Bahamas Princess Resort and Casino** (Grand Bahama Island; ☎ 242/352-6721): Your marriage might have an auspicious beginning at a resort whose architecture includes minarets. Whether you consider it kitsch or old-fashioned fun, there's no escaping the presence of enough diversions to keep your honeymoon whirring along as smoothly as a roulette wheel. Casinos and beach life are only a shuttle-bus ride away. See chapter 6.
- **Green Turtle Club** (Green Turtle Cay, the Abacos; ☎ 242/365-4271): Honeymooners appreciate this resort's winning combination of yachting atmosphere and well-manicured comfort. The setting is small (31 rooms) and civilized in an understated, unflashy way. When you want a change of pace, you can stroll through the clapboard-covered village of New Plymouth. New Plymouth is accessible either by motor launch or, even better, by a 45-minute walk across windswept scrublands, which seem far removed from everything. See chapter 8.
- **Bluff House Club & Marina** (Green Turtle Cay, the Abacos; ☎ 242/365-4247): Its name derives from its position on a low cliff above a beach. The architecture focuses on privacy, with a rustic, seafaring decor that has its own kind of elegance. If you're at all intrigued by the sea, Bluff House is very appropriate. See chapter 8.
- **Stella Maris Resort Club** (Long Island, the Southern Bahamas; ☎ 800/426-0466, 242/338-2051, or 954/359-8236 in Fort Lauderdale): The Stella Maris is the social highlight of Long Island. Sailing is important here, as are diving and getting away from it all. European flair is added by a clientele who hail in many cases from Germany. The island itself is often cited as the most beautiful in The Bahamas. Honeymooners fit into the grand scheme of things perfectly. See chapter 11.

11 The Best Family Vacations

If you've ever traveled with a family, you know that children, especially small or loud children, aren't welcome everywhere. But those hotels that do welcome families with children tend to go all out to make them feel wanted, with everything from playgrounds to baby-sitters.

- **Radisson Cable Beach** (Cable Beach, New Providence Island; ☎ 242/327-6000): A family could opt to never leave the grounds of this resort during their stay. The pool area features the most lavish artificial waterfall this side of Tahiti. The health club at the nearby Crystal Palace can be used by guests and their children, and the list of in-house activities includes dancing lessons. See chapter 4.

- **Radisson Grand Resort** (Paradise Island; ☎ **242/363-2011**): This hotel offers activities for children aged 5 to 13 in its Camp Caribbean. Baby-sitting can be arranged, and older children have free use of bicycles. Also, right on the beach in front of the hotel is a water-sports center that offers banana boat rides for kids. All rooms have balconies. See chapter 5.

- **Atlantis Paradise Island Resort & Casino** (Paradise Island; ☎ **242/363-3000**): This is one of the largest hotel complexes in the world, with some 1,200 rooms, endless rows of shops, and water sports galore. Children—and adults, too—enjoy this 14-acre sea world with water slides, a lagoon for water sports, white sandy beaches, underground grottoes, plus an underwater viewing tunnel and 800 feet of cascading waterfalls. See chapter 5.

- **Pirate's Cove Beach Resort** (Paradise Island; ☎ **242/363-2100**): With 18 stories, this pirate-themed hotel is the tallest in The Bahamas. The pool was inspired by a tropical lagoon, and the bar that dispenses drinks to adults is modeled on a 95-foot pirate ship. There's a day camp for children (Captain Kid's), and even the game room bears the name and accessories of a pirate's den. If parents want to escape from all this saber rattling, there are lots of quiet escape hatches for them, as well. See chapter 5.

- **Bahamas Princess Resort and Casino** (Grand Bahama Island; ☎ **242/352-6721**): Many of its clients come just to gamble and get a suntan, but others bring their children. To divert them, the hotel maintains a pair of playgrounds and a swimming pool inspired by a tropical oasis, and offers children's platters in some of the restaurants. The architecture features lots of "Aladdin and His Lamp" accessories, such as minarets above a decidedly non-Islamic setting. A shuttle bus makes frequent trips to and from the nearest beach. See chapter 6.

- **Castaways Resort** (Grand Bahama Island; ☎ **242/352-6682**): This is a relatively modest resort. The pagoda-capped lobby is set a very short walk from the ice-cream stands, souvenir shops, and fountains of the International Bazaar. Children under 12 stay free in their parents' room, and the in-house lounge presents limbo and fire-eating shows several evenings a month. See chapter 6.

- **Club Med** (Eleuthera; ☎ **800/CLUB-MED**): With 300 rooms, this is the largest hotel on Eleuthera. There's a miniclub for child-minding (which parents can use to escape to the beach for a few hours), a staff that dresses up as clowns during children's parties, and a miniclub where teenagers are taught how to snorkel and sail. At the end of each week, children and adults participate in a circus workshop, with trapeze and trampoline acts, funny costumes, and lots of greasepaint. See chapter 9.

- **Turquoise Reef Resort & Casino** (Provo, Turks and Caicos Islands; ☎ **809/946-5555**): A luxury resort with oversized oceanfront rooms, this hotel aggressively pursues the family trade. This is a very activity-oriented place—it even stages treasure hunts for kids. Baby-sitting can also be arranged. See chapter 12.

12   The Best Places to Get Away from It All

Activity and a fast pace might be the last thing you're seeking in The Bahamas. You may just plain want to escape from the world. Assuming that you don't feel any urgent need to visit a casino or disco, here is a list of practically perfect options.

- **Green Turtle Club** (Green Turtle Cay, the Abacos; ☎ **242/365-4271**): Secluded and private, this mariner's retreat consists of tasteful one- to three-bedroom villas with full kitchens. It opens onto a small private beach with a 35-slip marina, which is the most complete yachting facility in the archipelago. Many rooms open onto poolside, and there's a dining room decorated in Queen Anne style. The hotel is sometimes visited by celebrities. See chapter 8.

- **Dunmore Beach Club** (Harbour Island, off the coast of Eleuthera; ☎ 242/ 333-2200): It's one of the less expensive all-inclusive resorts of The Bahamas. Because of its limited number of accommodations, its atmosphere is akin to a private house party in a New England summerhouse. Each of the dozen or so lodgings is positioned for privacy, and you can escape to the nether regions of the local beach if you're looking to get away from it all. See chapter 9.
- **Club Med** (San Salvador, the Southern Bahamas; ☎ 800/CLUB-MED): This was the first large resort to be built on one of The Bahamas' most isolated islands, site of Columbus's first landfall in the New World. It's unusually luxurious, and unusually isolated, for a typical Club Med. The sheer difficulty of reaching it adds to the get-away-from-it-all mystique. See chapter 11.
- **Fernandez Bay Village** (Cat Island, the Southern Bahamas; ☎ 800/940-1905, or 305/474-4821 in Plantation, Florida): The dozen stone and timber villas of Fernandez Bay Village are the closest thing to urban congestion Cat Island ever sees. The beach bar is suitably raffish and has a thatch roof, evoking the South Pacific. There's only one phone at the entire resort, and your bathroom shower will probably open to a view of the sky. See chapter 11.
- **Meridian Club** (Pine Cay, Turks and Caicos Islands; ☎ 800/331-9154): This cluster of vacation homes is the only real development on an 800-acre island covered with shrubs and low trees. With most of the island devoted to the preservation of bird and animal life, it is truly a drop-out-and-disappear sort of place. Communications with the outside world are deliberately limited, and the only socializing you're likely to find will be with occupants of the island's 30 or so privately owned homes. See chapter 12.

13 The Friendliest Islands

Open-minded visitors with a sense of humor will almost always have a good rapport with locals, regardless of which destination they choose. Remember, however, that islands known for friendliness are usually the smaller ones that don't have much tourism.

- **Elbow Cay/Hope Town** (the Abacos): Access to this town requires a 20-minute boat ride from the airport at Marsh Harbour. Although it's only a short passage across usually calm waters, many visitors imagine that they've gone back a century in time. Bougainvillea flames on picket fences, and a stark lighthouse on the town's highest bluff looks like a scene from a Winslow Homer painting. While not necessarily chatty, the townspeople will greet you with respect and usually look out for your well-being. Most full-time residents are the descendants of 18th-century British Loyalists who fled the North American mainland shortly after the American Revolution. See chapter 8.
- **Harbour Island** (off the coast of Eleuthera): During the 18th century, this town was famous for boatbuilding. Its colonial charm is evident in the rows of handsome clapboard-sided cottages, neat picket fences, and the capital (Dunmore Town), whose populace barely numbers 1,000. People take time to sit out on their verandas, sip a drink, and watch the world go by. Locals are friendly and crime is low. See chapter 9.
- **The Exumas:** Their sheer size (365 tiny islands strung over a distance of 177 miles) and the titanic force of the sea that surrounds them produce a rawboned kind of

grit that encourages neighbors to look out for each other. Residents display a genuine curiosity about outsiders. See chapter 10.
* **Cat Island** (the Southern Bahamas): Life here is slow paced, and during some seasons, flights arrive only two or three times a week. Islanders live by fishing and
cultivating whatever will grow in the thin, sandy soil. A churchgoing ethic on Cat
Island was reinforced here for many years by the presence of legendary monk
Father Jerome Hawes, a semirecluse who almost single-handedly built one of the
most famous abbeys in The Bahamas. See chapter 11.
* **Providenciales/Provo** (Turks and Caicos Islands): It's the most international
island in the Turks and Caicos, with residents who hail from virtually every country of Europe and North America. Blessed with some of the finest beaches in the
western hemisphere, the islanders have a buoyant enthusiasm. See chapter 12.

14   The Best Budget Islands

* **Andros:** It's the largest, least-frequently explored, and most mysterious island
in The Bahamas. About a half dozen hamlets line its edges, each of which offers
very simple accommodations. Food is about as basic as you'll get anywhere,
and often only Bahamian regional items are available. But if you're willing to
go through the inconvenience of getting here, and if all you're looking for is a
beach and some palm trees, Andros is about as cost conscious as you'll ever get.
See chapter 7.
* **Eleuthera:** Because of this island's changing fortunes, hotel and restaurant tabs are
likely to be competitive. Most accommodations are not luxurious, but you might
overlook this if costs are a serious consideration. If you're looking for family-
style lodging, you might opt for any of the simple guest houses that line the island's
long and narrow shores. Among these are Edwina's Place at Rock Sound (☎ **242/
334-2094**) and Hilton's Haven Motel and Restaurant at Tarpum Bay (☎ **242/
334-4231**). See chapter 9.
* **The Exumas:** The entire chain contains only about 3,800 residents, many of
whom grow onions or fish for a living. Unless you charter a boat to take you to
some of the chain's 365 isolated cays (which is an expensive proposition), you'll
spend your time on one of the Exumas's three or four larger islands. George Town
in particular (the largest town in the Exumas) offers several budget options. See
chapter 10.
* **Cat Island** (the Southern Bahamas): The local populace makes its living by
farming and fishing. Hotels are anything but glamorous, and costs are proportion-
ately low. Although Cat Island is the sixth-largest island in The Bahamas, it's
undeveloped, underpopulated, and lined with beautiful white-sand beaches. See
chapter 11.
* **Grand Turk** (Turks and Caicos Islands): Although there are some adequately
comfortable low-rise hotels on the island, it never benefited from the spectacular amount of money that was spent on the development of Provo. See
chapter 12.

15   The Best Nightlife

It's sleepy time in most of the Out Islands (or so-called Family Islands), such as Spanish Wells, Andros, and the Berry Islands. Except for Provo, the serious partyer will
also want to avoid Turks and Caicos.

- **Cable Beach:** Cable Beach has a lot more splash and excitement than Nassau, with which it shares New Providence Island. Wandering around Cable Beach is also a lot safer than exploring the back streets of Nassau at night. Instead of finding that little hot spot, you might get mugged. At Cable Beach, the main attraction is the **Crystal Palace Resort and Casino** (☎ 242/327-6200). Its 800-seat theater is a runner-up to the theater on Paradise Island, but it is also known for its Las Vegas–style extravaganzas. Most of the action spins around the casino (see below), however. There are many cozy bars and nooks as well if you'd like a tranquil, less spectacular evening. See chapter 4.
- **Paradise Island:** Paradise Island is the leader in nightlife in all of The Bahamas. No place else even comes close, including nearby Nassau and Cable Beach. Nearly all of the action takes place at the Atlantis Paradise Island Resort and Casino (☎ 242/363-3000). Its biggest highlight is the Cabaret Theatre, which stages the most spectacular productions in The Bahamas. There are also intimate bars, the biggest casino in The Bahamas, and lots more. One of the best vantage points for a view of both the entrance to the casino and the famous Bird Cage Walk (chief nighttime promenade of Paradise Island) is the Atlantis's cozy Gallery Bar. See chapter 5.
- **Freeport:** This is the only other spot in The Bahamas that is even in the running. In Freeport you can enjoy both casino action (see below) and splashy Vegas- (or at least Reno-) style shows at either the Casino Royale Showroom, in the Bahamas Princess Resort and Casino (☎ 242/352-6721), or the Flamingo Showcase Theatre in the Lucayan Beach Resort (☎ 242/373-7777). For real Bahamian entertainment, however, head for the Yellow Bird Show Club, in the Castaways Resort at the International Bazaar (☎ 809/352-6682). That means conga drums, steel drums, fire dances, glass-eating, and all that good stuff. See chapter 6.

16 The Best Gambling

- **Crystal Palace Casino** (Cable Beach; ☎ 242/327-6200): This is the dazzling place to be after dark along this beach strip. Its gaming room makes you think you're right in the middle of Las Vegas. One of the largest gambling casinos on the islands, it features 750 slot machines, 51 blackjack tables, 9 roulette wheels, 7 crap tables, and a baccarat table. You get some of the best gambling in The Bahamas here, although the Paradise Island casino has more class. See chapter 4.
- **Paradise Island Casino** (in the Atlantis Paradise Island Resort and Casino; ☎ 242/363-3000): It's the biggest and the best. Nothing in The Bahamas—or even in the Caribbean—compares with it. It attracts high rollers from Vegas and Atlantic City, but also the grandmother from Iowa who likes to secretly play the slot machines when her family isn't looking. It's an extravaganza of gloss, glitter, and show biz. The gambling is good, although savvy locals tell us the odds are better in Vegas. You know you're viewed by the house as a high roller on Paradise Island when you're invited to gamble in a *salon privé*. See chapter 5.
- **Princess Casino** (at The Mall in Freeport, Grand Bahama Island; ☎ 242/352-6721): Although this casino ranks third behind Paradise Island and Cable Beach, most of the nightlife in Freeport/Lucaya revolves around this glittering, giant, Moroccan-style palace, one of the largest casinos in either The Bahamas or the Caribbean. You get not only high-stakes and low-stakes gambling, but also Vegas-style nightlife. See chapter 6.

17 The Best Restaurants

For more information on cuisine in The Bahamas, refer to "What's Cookin' in The Bahamas" in chapter 2.

- **Graycliff** (Nassau, New Providence Island; ☎ 242/322-2796): It was once a private home, but now it's also the most elegant restaurant on New Providence Island, with more class, style, and flair than anything found on Cable Beach. Some food critics say it's not what it once was, but they're wrong. The continental cuisine is given added flair and zesty flavor with Bahamian seasonings. Guests rarely question the quality of the cuisine. The only horror is when it comes time to pay the bill. This is the most expensive restaurant in The Bahamas. You get quality cuisine and tantalizing dishes, but you pay dearly for the privilege of dining in such splendor. Someone has to pay for the $8 million wine cellar, which, with 175,000 bottles, is a sight worth seeing. Order from the *carte* carefully if you want your accountant to continue to speak to you. See chapter 4.

- **Sun And . . .** (Nassau, New Providence Island; ☎ 242/393-1205): The only restaurant in the capital that's on a par with Graycliff, and it's a bit cheaper. It's a favorite restaurant of visiting celebrities, a fact that would mean little if it didn't serve top-notch food. (After all, celebrities can go to a lot of bad restaurants.) You cross a drawbridge to enter a soothing world with a fountain and rock pool adding a note of grace. The food is French, with an emphasis on fresh seafood. The sizzling sounds from the kitchen lead to vividly flavored dishes that reveal the hallmarks of a master chef. Whatever you order, try to save room for one of the incomparable soufflés. There is none better this side of France. See chapter 4.

- **The Restaurant at Compass Point** (Love Beach, New Providence Island; ☎ 242/327-4500): This is the only restaurant to join the stellar ranks of the finest in The Bahamas in years, breaking the monopoly held by Graycliff and Sun And . . . . Yes, it's true, it's not as elegant as those two, but it's still up there near the top. Its California/Caribbean cuisine has made it a hot spot for savvy foodies. The menu is not only delicious but innovative, as well, with many dishes influenced by Thailand. Everybody in The Bahamas serves conch, but here it appears with agnolotti, sun-dried tomatoes, and spinach in a tomato-basil cream sauce. Want something new and different? Try a Bahamian makki roll with conch, mango, and cucumber served with wasabi and pickled ginger. See chapter 4.

- **Café Martinique** (Paradise Island; ☎ 242/363-3000): Opposite the Atlantis, this longtime favorite remains this expensive island's best choice for dishes prepared with continental flair and flavor. Even James Bond dined here in the movie *Thunderball,* and that secret agent knew about food, or at least his creator, Ian Fleming, did. The setting is faux *fin de siècle,* and this former private home overlooks a lagoon. Paradise Island has lots of pretty settings for restaurants, but not all places serve good food. This one does. The chefs create refined dishes based on top-quality ingredients. It's expensive but worth it. Its Sunday brunch is the best on the island. See chapter 5.

- **Villa d'Este** (Paradise Island, also at the Atlantis; ☎ 242/363-3000): This is the finest Italian restaurant on Paradise Island, with nothing in Nassau to top it either. The setting is gracious, tasteful, and Old World, but it's the food that keeps them calling for reservations. All the old favorites are here, including veal parmigiana and fettuccine Alfredo as fine as you are likely to be served in Rome. Fresh herbs add zest to many dishes. The pasta dishes are particularly succulent. See chapter 5.

18 The Best Shopping

U.S. citizens are allowed to leave The Bahamas with $600 worth of goods untaxed.

- **Nassau:** This is the place to be if you were born to shop. Its merchandise is wider in scope, more varied, and more appealing than that of its nearest competitor, Freeport. The best bargains are found in perfumes, watches, and china and crystal—sometimes 30% to 50% off stateside prices. The best place to find china and crystal gifts is **Treasure Traders** on Bay Street (☎ 242/322-8521), which offers the biggest selection in The Bahamas—all the big names from Waterford to Orrefors. For perfumes, **The Perfume Shop** (☎ 242/322-2375) at the corner of Bay and Frederick streets, is the place to go. For the best buys in jewelry, try either **Little Switzerland** (☎ 242/322-8324) along Bay Street or **John Bull** (☎ 242/322-4253) at the corner of Bay and East streets. See chapter 4.
- **The Plait Lady** (The Regarno Building, Bay Street and Victoria in Nassau; ☎ 242/356-5584): Everybody heads to the famous Straw Market in Nassau for straw souvenirs, but Clare Sands, the so-called "Plait Lady," will tell you that many of Nassau's Straw Market items are made in Taiwan. If you check carefully, you'll find out she's right. For centuries, Bahamians have been famous for their straw wares, and the products sold at The Plait Lady are 100% genuine. You'll also get the best selection of Bahamian handcrafts here. See chapter 4.
- **Androsia Batik** (Small Hope Bay, Andros Town; ☎ 242/368-2020): Although located on one of the remotest islands in The Bahamas, this is a first-rate shopping mecca. The batiks are made using age-old waxing techniques and adopt island motifs in their designs, including lobsters or sea-grape leaves. The dresses, swimwear, fabrics, pants, and shirts are among the smartest fashions on the islands, each hand painted and hand signed. Of course, if you can't get to Andros to purchase these brilliant fabrics, you'll find Androsia Batiks in various outlets in Nassau and Freeport. See chapter 7.

2 Getting to Know The Bahamas

The Bahamas (that's with a capital "The") is one of the most geographically complicated nations of the Atlantic. It's a coral-based archipelago comprising more than 700 islands—hundreds more if you count the rocky outcroppings that have damaged the hulls of countless ships since colonial days.

Made of more than 100,000 square miles of dry and sometimes barren land, the archipelago comprises The Bahama islands and also, in the south, the Turks and Caicos islands, which maintain a separate government. Most of the population is centered on New Providence Island (Nassau/Cable Beach) and Grand Bahama Island (Freeport/Lucaya). Paradise Island, the most heavily developed tourist complex, lies directly off Nassau and is reached by a causeway.

The 760-mile-long chain of islands, cays, and reefs that make up The Bahamas stretches from Grand Bahama Island, whose western point is 75 miles almost due east of Palm Beach, Florida, to Great Inagua, southernmost of The Bahamas, which lies about 60 miles northeast of Cuba and less than 100 miles north of Haiti. *Cay* (pronounced *key*) is the Spanish word for small island.

Sandy beaches, fishing (some of the best in the world), boating, nearly perfect weather (even though these islands are in the often stormy Atlantic Ocean), and accessibility to the U.S. mainland put this archipelago on the world tourist map. The Bahamas lies right off the Florida coast. In one 20- to 30-minute plane ride, you can flee the congestion of Miami and land on Bimini.

The Bahamas is ideal for both quick 4- or 5-day jaunts and longer vacations, if you'd really like to island hop and see as much as you can.

In the 1940s, when the duke and duchess of Windsor ruled The Bahamas (after he'd renounced the British throne), the islands were considered exclusive. Beginning in the 1960s, that reputation changed. Today the islands lure people from all walks of life, whether they want a $500-a-day luxury resort or prefer to rough it for $50 a day on one of the little-visited Out Islands.

1 The Natural Environment

With more than 700 islands and some 2,000 cays, The Bahamas is spread over 100,000 square miles of the Atlantic Ocean and is home to countless natural attractions, including underwater reefs that stretch from the Abacos in the northeast 760 miles to Long Island in the southeast.

The Bahamas is the largest oceanic archipelago nation in the tropical Atlantic Ocean, with miles of crystal clear waters rich in fisheries and other marine resources. Although New Providence Island is heavily populated, the rest of the Out Islands, including Grand Bahama Island, have relatively small populations. Unlike Puerto Rico, Jamaica, Barbados, and other Caribbean island nations, The Bahamas has large areas of undeveloped natural land. The islands also have the most extensive ocean hole and limestone cave systems in the world.

The approximately 900 square miles of coral reefs in The Bahamas includes the third-largest barrier reef in the world, located off the coast of Andros. The reef is rich with diverse marine life, including green moray eels, cinnamon clownfish, and Nassau grouper. The Bahamas was one of the first Caribbean countries to outlaw long-line fishing, realizing it was a threat to the country's ecology.

Another act of Parliament, the Wild Birds Protection Act, was passed to ensure the survival of all bird species throughout The Bahamas. Great Inagua Island is home to more than 60,000 pink flamingos, Bahamian parrots, and a large proportion of the world population of reddish egrets. These birds live in the government-protected 287-square-mile Inagua National Park.

The islands of The Bahamas are home to more than 1,370 species of plant life and some 13 species of mammals, mainly bats. Other mammals include wild pigs, donkeys, raccoons, and the Abaco wild horse. Whales and dolphins, including the humpback and blue whales and the spotted dolphin, are found in the seas around the various islands.

Ecotourism highlights of The Bahamas include:

- **Bahamas National Trust:** The headquarters, which is home to one of the finest collections of wild palms in the western hemisphere, is located in Nassau at The Retreat on Village Road (☎ **242/393-1317**). Guided tours are conducted Tuesday through Thursday at 11:45am and by appointment. Volunteers at The Retreat can also help arrange visits to the national parks on the various islands, the best of which are previewed below. The Bahamas National Trust administers 12 national parks and protected areas covering more than 240,000 acres.
- **Inagua National Park:** Located on Great Inagua Island in the Southern Bahamas, this park is internationally famous as the site of the world's largest colony of wild West Indian flamingos. In Bahamian dialect, these birds are sometimes called *fillymingos* or *flamingas*.
- **Union Creek Reserve:** This 7-square-mile enclosed tidal creek on Great Inagua serves as a captive breeding research site for giant sea turtles, with special emphasis on the endangered green turtle. In the distant past, the sea waters around Green Turtle Cay in the Abacos teemed with prehistoric-looking green turtles. However, because they were a valuable food source, they were overhunted and their population greatly diminished.
- **Exuma Cays Land and Sea Park:** This park is the first of its kind anywhere on the planet and a major attraction of The Bahamas. The 22-mile-long, 8-mile-wide natural preserve encompasses 175 square miles of sea gardens with spectacular reefs, flora, and fauna. Inaugurated in 1958, it lies some 22 miles northwest of Staniel Cay or 40 miles southeast of Nassau and is accessible only by boat. The Exumas is one of the world's most colorful yachting grounds. Its nearest rivals in the Caribbean are the British Virgin Islands and the Grenadines.

The Bahamas

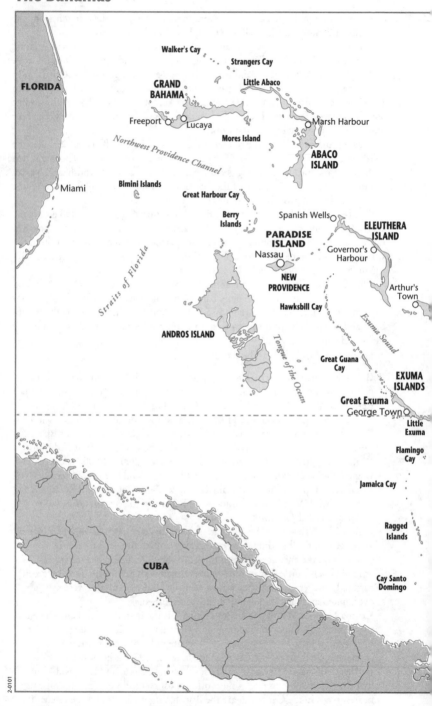

FLORIDA

Walker's Cay

Strangers Cay

GRAND BAHAMA

Little Abaco

Freeport Lucaya

Marsh Harbour

Northwest Providence Channel

Mores Island

ABACO ISLAND

Miami

Bimini Islands

Great Harbour Cay

Berry Islands

Spanish Wells

ELEUTHERA ISLAND

PARADISE ISLAND

Nassau

Governor's Harbour

NEW PROVIDENCE

Straits of Florida

Hawksbill Cay

Arthur's Town

Exuma Sound

ANDROS ISLAND

Tongue of the Ocean

Great Guana Cay

EXUMA ISLANDS

Great Exuma

George Town

Little Exuma

Flamingo Cay

Jamaica Cay

Ragged Islands

CUBA

Cay Santo Domingo

2-0101

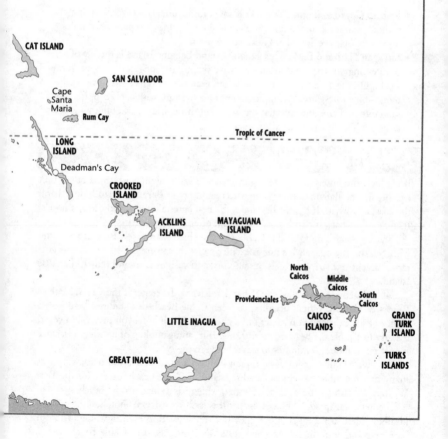

❓ Did You Know?

- Following in the footsteps of Columbus, Ponce de León arrived in The Bahamas searching for the legendary Fountain of Youth, which led to the discovery of Florida and the Gulf Stream.
- The Bahamians earned a comfortable living bootlegging liquor to the United States during the Prohibition era.
- In 1856, about half of the able-bodied men of the colony lived off the ship-wrecking industry.
- Neville Chamberlain, later to fail as prime minister of Great Britain on the eve of World War II, first failed at sisal (fiber) production in The Bahamas.
- In 1940, the Duke of Windsor (formerly King Edward VIII) arrived in Nassau to rule an impoverished colony of 65,000 people after briefly presiding over an empire numbering hundreds of millions.
- In World War II, two young British seamen whose ship had been torpedoed by the Germans south of the Azores sailed an 18-foot "jolly-boat" across 3,000 miles of ocean before reaching the shores of Eleuthera.

- **Pelican Cays Land and Sea Park:** Known for its undersea caves, seemingly endless coral reefs, and abundant plant and marine life, this park lies 8 miles north of Cherokee Sound at Great Abaco Island.
- **Lucayan National Park:** This park on Grand Bahama Island is the site of a 6-mile-long underground, freshwater cave system, the longest of its type in the world. On the 40-acre preserve you'll find examples of the island's five ecosystems—pine forests, rocky coppice, mangrove swamps, whiteland coppice, and sand dunes. Trails and elevated walkways cut through the park, offering visitors a rugged hike to a tranquil white-sand beach.

2 The Islands in Brief

If it's high-rise hotels and glittering casinos you want, along with some of the best beaches in The Bahamas, there is no better choice than **Paradise Island,** directly off the coast of Nassau. It has the best food, the best entertainment, and the best hotels. Its major drawback is that it's expensive and often overcrowded.

Paradise Island's main rival is **Cable Beach,** which shares New Providence Island with Nassau, the capital. It's not as exclusive or chic as Paradise Island, but its glittering beachfront strip of hotels, restaurants, and casinos is second only to Paradise Island.

Cable Beach is often called the Bahamian Riviera. Its center is the **Crystal Palace Resort & Casino.** Often, deciding between Cable Beach or Paradise Island isn't a choice of which island you prefer but a choice of which hotel you prefer. However, it's easy to sample the beaches, cuisine, nightlife, and gambling of both islands, since it only takes about 30 minutes to travel between the two.

But what about **Nassau?** The capital isn't on a great beach and doesn't have as many first-rate hotels as either Paradise Island or Cable Beach, except for the **Best Western British Colonial Beach Resort,** which has a small private beach.

The main advantage of Nassau is that it is less expensive. Its hotels, although not ideally located, are cheaper, and some offer very low prices even in winter. You can base here and commute to the beaches at Paradise Island or Cable Beach. Many nonbeach types also prefer Nassau because it's the seat of Bahamian culture and history. Nassau is also the shopping mecca of The Bahamas. In fact, many Floridians come here just to shop. Paradise Island and Cable Beach have shops, as well, but they can't compare to those in Nassau.

Freeport/Lucaya on Grand Bahama Island is another popular destination for American tourists. It has its pockets of posh (Howard Hughes once holed up here), but Freeport/Lucaya has a lot more tacky development than Paradise Island or Cable Beach. It's also a lot cheaper with just as good a climate, which explains why it attracts hordes of vacationers. Like its rivals Paradise Island and Cable Beach, Freeport/Lucaya offers plenty of opportunities for fine dining, entertainment, and gambling. Grand Bahama Island also offers the best hiking in The Bahamas and has some of the finest sandy beaches. Its golf courses attract players from all over the world, and the island hosts major tournaments several times a year. It also offers some of the best diving in the world and is the home of UNEXSO, the world-famous diving school. Grand Bahama Island is especially popular with families.

After this line-up, the tourist hordes start to diminish. All of the other Out Islands are relatively sleepy. Most of the other islands attract people interested in a particular sport, such as fishing or boating.

NEW PROVIDENCE ISLAND (NASSAU/CABLE BEACH)   It isn't the largest of the Bahamian Islands, yet New Providence is the historic core of the Bahamian nation, with a strong maritime tradition and the largest population of any island in the country. Home to about 125,000 residents, it offers groves of pines and casuarinas; sandy, flat soil; the closest thing in The Bahamas to urban sprawl; and superb anchorages, which are sheltered from rough seas by Paradise Island. New Providence contains the country's busiest airport, hundreds of villas owned by foreign investors, and two concentrations of resort development: Cable Beach and Nassau.

PARADISE ISLAND   It has one of the most colorful histories, and some of the least interesting architecture, of any resort island in the world. Elongated and narrow, its sands and shoals form a seawall for the wharves and piers of Nassau (New Providence Island), which rise across a narrow channel only 600 feet away. Inch for inch, it's probably the most intensely marketed piece of real estate in the world.

Owners of the 685-acre island have included brokerage mogul Joseph Lynch (of Merrill Lynch) and Huntington Hartford, heir to the A&P supermarket fortune. More recent investors have included Merv Griffin. The island today is a carefully landscaped residential and commercial complex with good beaches, lots of glitter, and many diversions. All of these cater to a clientele from around the world, many of whom devote part of each day to the casinos.

GRAND BAHAMA ISLAND   Until the hotel developments of the 1950s, Grand Bahama Island was sparsely populated. The name derives from the Spanish term *gran bajamar* ("great shallows"), which refers to the shallow reefs and sandbars that have, over the centuries, destroyed everything from Spanish galleons to English clipper ships. (Although many of their onboard treasures were pillaged, those in deeper waters are still being found.) Thanks to the tourist development schemes of U.S. financiers such as Howard Hughes, Grand Bahama boasts one of the most industrialized economies and one of the best-developed tourist infrastructures of any island in The Bahamas. It has experienced a more rapid population growth since the 1960s than any other island of The Bahamas. Casinos, beaches, and restaurants are plentiful. Visitors can escape the island's towns and head across casuarina-dotted scrublands to explore the island's isolated western end.

BIMINI   It's one of the smallest islands in The Bahamas and lies close enough to Miami (just 50 miles away) to be distinctly separate from the other islands of the archipelago. Bimini is divided into two islands, whose area totals 9 square miles. The smaller of these, North Bimini, is better developed than South Bimini. The yachts and fishing boats that dock at the island's marinas are among the most luxurious in the western hemisphere. Throughout Bimini, there's a slightly rundown Florida-resort type of atmosphere mingled with some small-town charm. Because of its proximity to the Florida coast, Bimini is also a center for drug-smuggling.

The setting for Ernest Hemingway's *Islands in the Stream,* Bimini attracts big-game fishers. It has only minor appeal to the casual sightseer. But if you'd like to follow in the footsteps of such famous fishers as Zane Grey and Howard Hughes, Bimini is your island. Its sportfishing is among the best in the world. It is also an excellent center for yachting and cruising and offers some of the best scuba diving in The Bahamas.

BERRY ISLANDS   Lying between Nassau and the coast of Florida, these islands, which comprise only about 30 square miles of land, attract devoted yachties and serious fishers. The islands are composed of about 30 islets and cays and rows of barely submerged rocks. Most of the full-time population (about 700 people) live on Great Harbour, the largest island, which measures only 6 by 2$^1/_2$ miles. The islands have extremely limited tourist facilities and are geared mostly to well-heeled fishers, many from Florida. The Berry Islands are a lot classier and far less dangerous than their closest rival, Bimini, which has a large drug problem.

ANDROS   The largest island in The Bahamas (104 miles long and 40 miles wide), Andros attracts divers and fishing enthusiasts, as well as casual sightseers.

The population numbers 8,180, although most of the island is uninhabited and unexplored. Andros is actually two islands, connected by a series of canals and cays called *bights.* The chief towns are Nicholl's Town, Andros Town, and Congo Town. All are accessible by frequent boat and plane connections from Miami and Nassau. Lodgings range from large resorts to small guest houses, which are rather bare and cater mainly to fishers.

Divers from all over the world come here to explore the third-largest barrier reef on the planet. The reef plunges 6,000 feet to a narrow drop-off known as the Tongue of the Ocean. Bonefishing here is among the best in the world. Andros is also known for its world-class marlin and bluefin tuna fishing.

The natural wonders of the island have much to offer nonfishing and nondiving visitors, as well. Known as the "Big Yard," the central portion of Northern Andros is largely a dense forest of mahogany and pine where more than 50 varieties of orchids bloom. Southern Andros boasts a 40-square-mile forest and mangrove swamp—home to a variety of birds and animals, including the Bahamian parrot and the nonpoisonous Bahamian boa constrictor, called "fowl snake." Any hotel can arrange a local guide to show you the attractions.

THE ABACOS   Often referred to as Abaco, this "island" is actually a cluster of islands and islets. With some 650 square miles of land, it is the second-largest grouping in The Bahamas. It is a mecca for yachties and other boaters, who flock here year-round but mainly for The Bahama Cup Regatta held at the Green Turtle Yacht Club in July. (The Exumas is also a favorite with the yachting crowd, and we think Exuma waters are even more beautiful.) For hundreds of years the residents of the Abacos have been boatbuilders, although tourism is now the main industry.

The islands are mainly for the sailing and fishing crowds. Visitors will find everything from luxurious accommodations to rather bare-bones inns. There is more New

England charm here than anywhere else in The Bahamas except on Harbour Island in Eleuthera. Loyalists who left New England after the American Revolution settled here and built clapboard houses with white picket fences, evocative of Cape Cod. The best places to stay to experience the nostalgic charm are Green Turtle Cay, which was patterned after a New England fishing village, and Elbow Cay, which is accessible from Marsh Harbour. Marsh Harbour is home to an international airport and a shopping center, although its hotels aren't as good as those on Green Turtle Cay and Elbow Cay (Hope Town).

Many islands are undeveloped and uninhabited. For the best of both worlds, visitors can stay at resorts on Walker's, Green Turtle, and Treasure cays, and charter a boat to tour the more remote areas.

ELEUTHERA   Long and slender, the most historic of the Out Islands is actually a string of islands that includes Spanish Wells and Harbour Island (a chic destination). The length of the island (110 miles) and the distances between Eleuthera's communities require access via three different airports (Rock South, Governor's Harbour, and North Eleuthera). The first English settlers arrived here in 1648.

The island lies about 60 miles west of Nassau, with which it is linked by frequent air connections. Eleuthera is similar to Abaco. Visitors are drawn to Eleuthera's miles of barrier reef and its secluded beaches. Picket fences and pastel-colored houses evoke a Cape Cod feeling in parts, especially on Harbour Island, where you'll find the best hotels and the best food. The beaches on Harbour Island are famed for their pink sand, tinted that color by crushed coral and shells.

Spanish Wells, another offshore island nearby, has extremely limited accommodations, and the residents—descendants of long-ago Loyalists—aren't as welcoming to visitors.

Head south of these islands and you come to Gregory Town, the pineapple capital of the island chain. A bit farther south is Surfers Beach, one of the best surfing spots in The Bahamas. Several accommodations are available in this sleepy, slightly down-market section of Eleuthera.

The only major resort along the entire stretch of Eleuthera is Club Med at Governor's Harbour. Other inns are more basic.

At the southern end of the island, Rock Sound is in a slump, awaiting the reopening (or not) of the fabled Cotton Bay Club. The now-divorced Prince Charles and Princess Di are long gone, as are all the other rich and famous who used to vacation here. Until this island and the nearby once-exclusive enclave of Winderemere Island get going again, there's little reason to visit. Head for Harbour Island instead.

THE EXUMAS   Just 35 miles southeast of Nassau, this 365-mile-long string of islands and keys—most of them uninhabited—is the great yachting mecca of The Bahamas, rivaling or even surpassing Abaco. There are daily flights from both Nassau and Miami, although the Exumas attract mainly boaters. It's also an ideal vacation spot for beachcombers, as it has many secluded beaches opening onto tranquil cays.

Its center is George Town on Great Exuma. The Exuma National Land and Sea Park, which is protected by The Bahamas National Trust, encompasses much of the coastline. The park is accessible only by boat, but is one of the major natural wonders and sightseeing targets of The Bahamas. The park is filled with undersea life, reefs, blue holes, and shipwrecks. Portions of the James Bond thriller *Thunderball* were filmed at Staniel Cay. The waters aren't just ideal for yachties, but for fishers as well. Each year in April, the interisland Family Island Regatta, a major event on the yachting calendar, is held at George Town. There are a few good inns centered mainly at George Town. Otherwise, you'll practically have the archipelago to yourself.

CAT ISLAND   With an eel-like shape, Cat Island is only a few miles wide and 48 miles long. It's one of the most fertile of the Bahamian islands; most of its residents grow pineapples and tomatoes for a living. Only one road connects the villages that dot the island's surface. The largest village is Arthur's Town, a sunflooded cluster of clapboard and cement buildings that seem to slumber in the salty air.

A sleepy island in the southern Bahamian backwater, Cat Island ranks with Crooked Island (see below) as an escapist's retreat. Most tourists visit for the annual Cat Island Regatta in summer, which attracts some of the top yachties from Florida and The Bahamas. This remote island is difficult to reach with infrequent flights from Nassau. If you're not a boater, the only real reason to visit is for its miles of beautiful and untrammeled beaches. There are a few sights, including the 206-foot Mount Alvernia, the highest point in The Bahamas, but don't expect any grand tourist facilities. There are only a few small resorts and inns.

SAN SALVADOR   Tradition holds that this island was the first landmass Columbus reached during his voyage to the New World in 1492. (Modern scholars disagree.) Rising to heights of 140 feet above sea level, the island boasts fine beaches, a scrub-covered landscape dotted with lakes containing both fresh and brackish water, and a landmass that measures 6 by 12 miles. Its height has always made it a useful navigational aid for mariners negotiating local sea lanes, and for several decades, lighthouses have been maintained to assist them. A single, badly rutted road skirts the island's 35-mile perimeter. Only 500 residents lived here before several new hotels were built (including a Club Med). With its newfound fame and good beaches, the island will probably undergo further development.

LONG ISLAND   Named for its length, this island is 58 miles long. Despite a promising early start (Columbus told the queen of Spain that it was the most beautiful island he'd ever seen), it languishes today in comparative obscurity, a position it shares with Cat Island and Crooked Island. Most of its populace of 4,500 earn a living building boats, fishing, farming, and conducting diving excursions to its spectacular offshore reefs. It's a haven for rugged travelers from as far away as Europe.

The island is inconvenient to reach; there are two minor airports with arrivals from Nassau (but not every day). There's more reason to go than ever before because of the opening of a luxury resort, Cape Santa Maria Beach, with a clubhouse and six cottages set on a strip of white sand. There is also the less-desirable Stella Maris Resort Club. Both offer fishing, boating, windsurfing, and scuba diving.

ACKLINS ISLAND & CROOKED ISLAND   These islands are hard to reach, have very limited tourist facilities, and, as such, appeal to people who want to get away from it all and don't mind the inconveniences. The clear waters offshore offer good snorkeling, and you'll have the fine sandy beaches almost all to yourself. The islands, which encompass about 190 square miles, are populated by a mere 1,000 souls. These residents have a hard time making a living here, and the occasional tourist brings in some much-needed revenue. The islands lie in the remote southern end of The Bahamas, closer to Cuba than to Florida. In 1493 Columbus dubbed the islands the "Fragrant Islands" because of the rich aromas that wafted from them toward his ships. In the 18th century, British Loyalists tried to establish plantations, but they all went bankrupt. Accommodations are available on Crooked Island only.

MAYAGUANA ISLAND   Located between the Bahamian islands and the Caicos, Mayaguana has 110 square miles of land, but only about 600 residents. This combination guarantees long panoramas of scrubland, whose hardy, salt-resistant plants thrive despite the high temperatures that are the norm here throughout the spring, summer, and early autumn. The island's largest settlement is a weather-beaten hamlet on the south coast (Abraham's Bay), which is rarely visited except by mariners. Mayaguana is sometimes a stopover for yachts from Miami headed south. But anyone else contemplating a visit might want to hold off until the island gets a decent place to stay.

INAGUA ISLAND   Set very close to the eastern tip of Cuba, Inagua is the most southerly island of The Bahamas and the third largest in the nation. Its scrub-dotted flatlands are baked white by the sun and the high salt content of the soil. Most of the population of around 1,200 people make their living harvesting salt from marsh areas. Pink flamingos thrive here. Inagua is hard to get to, although there are air links. A handful of simple, no-frill inns provide overnight accommodations, but the island is a little rawboned in terms of places to eat or even get a drink. For the serious birder, however, there is no place like it in The Bahamas or even the Caribbean.

GRAND TURK   Grand Turk is the farthest island from Florida. Ringed by abundant marine life, it totals 9 square miles and houses 4,000 residents. Most of the island's surface is flat, rocky, and dry. Donkeys and cattle often graze beside the rutted roads that crisscross the island. The atmosphere is that of a small town, despite the presence of Cockburn Town, the capital of Turks and Caicos. Grand Turk has a relatively undeveloped tourist infrastructure, although it offers a scattering of inns and hotels. The real tourist island of the Turks and Caicos with first-class hotels is Providenciales (called "Provo" for short). Grand Turk is the second-most built-up island in this small nation, but it's still very sleepy.

The diving here is first class and is what draws most visitors. For tourists not interested in diving, there's not a lot except for Governor's Beach, a long, white strip of sand on the west coast. For many, that's reason enough to visit. There are daily air connections.

SALT CAY   For years most of its income derived from salt harvested from the sunbaked flats on the island's coast. With only 3½ square miles of surface, and very fine beaches, it has experienced a recent influx of mariners and hotel owners. Salt Cay lies 9 miles southwest of Grand Turk; in recent years it has developed a corps of fans. The most famous resort on the island is the Windmills at Salt Cay; others on the island are atmospheric but somewhat scruffy.

NORTH CAICOS   Only a narrow saltwater channel separates it from Middle Caicos. Large, flat, and dotted with mangrove swamps and thriving vegetation, it offers good beaches and excellent bonefishing for the hardy souls who brave the inconvenience of getting here. Only about 1,200 people, scattered amid a quartet of sunbaked villages, make this island their home. Large sections of the island are protected as nature reserves. However, unlike some of the islands of Turks and Caicos, this one is at least blessed with some places to stay, including a resort that opens onto 7 miles of beach.

MIDDLE (GRAND) CAICOS   This is the largest (48 square miles) island of the Turks and Caicos, although, ironically, it's home to only about 300 people. Few of the attempts to colonize the area were ever successful, although archaeologists are often intrigued by the artifacts that remain from long-since-vanished Lucayan Indians, marooned sailors, and stranded slaves. Large sections of the island are marshland favored by aquatic birds and reptiles. Geologists appreciate the island's eerie collection of caves. The island is only now beginning to awaken to tourism, and it remains relatively cut off from the outside world. Unlike the old days, there is at least a place to stay now.

Hemingway in Bimini

It's one of the oddest pieces of real estate in the Atlantic. Less than a few hundred feet wide in many places, with a surface area of only 9 square miles, Bimini has always floated like a magic lure, only 50 miles from some of the most crowded seashores in the United States. Even during the 1930s, it was famous as an alter ego to such stateside islands as Key West. Soaked with liquor during U.S. Prohibition (it served as a depot for outlawed contraband) and widely recognized today as a storage depot for illegal drugs, it's one of the most controversial and raffish islands in the Western Hemisphere.

Thanks to American writer Ernest Hemingway, its raunchy, no-holds-barred lifestyle became known throughout North America.

Hemingway's first boat (the *Pilar*) was a diesel-powered tub he skippered with fellow writer John Dos Passos for the express purpose of reaching Bimini. One of the bloodiest of his many self-destructive acts occurred off the coast of Bimini when, struggling to aim a revolver at the thrashing jaws of a captured mako shark, he accidentally shot himself in both legs. Among his best catches were a 785-pound mako shark and a 514-pound tuna, both captured off the coast of Bimini. Some of his most famous fistfights? On Bimini, one with wealthy publisher Joseph Knapp, another with a series of black contenders who stood to earn $250 if they could stay in the ring with him for three 3-minute rounds. (No one ever collected the money.) Hemingway revised the manuscript of *To Have and Have Not* on Bimini in 1937. The town that inspired his evocative description of the seaport in *Islands in the Stream* was Alice Town, the still-seedy capital of Bimini.

SOUTH CAICOS   The reefs that surround it are treacherous, although Cockburn Town (the island's only port) is the best and largest natural harbor in the Turks and Caicos. Small fishing craft explore and fish in the island's numerous jagged coves. There aren't many acceptable hotels here, except Club Caribe Harbour & Beach Resort. Only about 1,400 residents (clustered around Cockburn Town) occupy this 8½-mile-long island. Much of the interior is scrubland and marshes, home to lots of reptiles and birds. The island's airport accepts short-haul flights (and many privately owned aircraft) from Florida, the Turks and Caicos, and The Bahamas. The beaches of South Caicos are small and unremarkable. Its offshore reef, however, makes the island a worthy goal for divers.

EAST CAICOS   Part of the Caicos archipelago, this island is almost completely uninhabited, with a uniformly low elevation above the sea and a landscape of scrubs and stunted trees. Birds, reptiles, and marine life find it rewarding. Head here only if you have sufficient food and water and love roughing it. The island is accessible only by boat, but many visitors are making trips here because of the 17-mile beach that stretches along the north coast. Some of the boaters who live on Middle Caicos will take passengers over for the day.

PROVIDENCIALES (PROVO)   Its 12-mile beach and undeveloped coastline were a tourist development waiting to happen. In the late 1970s, hotel megaliths such as Club Med poured money into increasingly popular low-rise ecoconscious resorts. Its tourist infrastructure far surpasses anything on Grand Turk. One of the larger islands of the Turks and Caicos, Provo is green but arid, with miles of scrubland and stunted trees covering the island's low, undulating hills. The population of Provo has grown in the last decade to around 6,000 persons, most of whom work in the tourist industry. Their differing nationalities (French, Canadian, German, American, and British) make this one of the most international communities in the archipelago. Many of the investors on the island are from the United States, including the Ludingtons, the DuPonts, and the Roosevelts, and many have built winter homes here or else chosen to retire here. Even Dick Clark owns a house. Whatever the Turks and Caicos have to offer in organized sports is found here. Provo has the nation's only golf course, the best boat tours and sea excursions, and the most organized snorkeling and scuba diving. It also has the best cuisine and the finest entertainment.Everything else in the island nation is still drowsy and early-to-bed.

PINE CAY   Pine Cay is the largest and most visible of the cays that stretch between North Caicos and Provo. Sparsely inhabited, with 800 acres and only about 35 carefully planned private homes under the administration of the Meridian Club, it's a relaxed but expensive enclave of European and North American investors. The island has its own landing strip, its own electrical generators, some remarkably good architecture, and sweeping stretches of beach. Reminders of bygone eras include ruins of Loyalist plantations built in the 18th century and petroglyphs carved by stranded sailors. The landscape is rocky, relatively flat, and arid.

This is a place for high rollers with a lot of dough who like to vacation in style and exclusivity. If you can afford it, awaiting you are $2^1/2$ miles of soft white sand, plus a 500-acre nature reserve. The Meridian Club has a lot more class and style than any of the new and flashier resorts of Provo.

3 The Bahamas Today

If Bill Clinton will forgive us, The Bahamas might be dubbed "the comeback kid." Everyone who watches television seemingly has seen the ad, "It's Better in The Bahamas." The truth is, it wasn't always better. Conditions in the tourist sector, on which much of the economy of the archipelago depends, were growing worse by the year in the 1980s and early 1990s. Ruled by Lynden Pindling, a virtual dictator prime minister, the government was corrupt. Thankfully, after a long and inglorious reign, he was voted out of office in 1992.

When Hubert Ingraham became prime minister, he launched the country on the long road to regain its marketshare of tourism, which under Pindling had rapidly dwindled, as visitors flocked to more hospitable climes. Bermuda, for example, enjoys a long list of repeat visitors, many middle-aged couples having visited the island annually ever since their college days. In contrast, exit polls showed that some first-time visitors vowed never to return to The Bahamas.

Under the notorious Pindling, the government had taken over a number of hotels and had tried to use them as cash cows, without putting money back into the structures. The new prime minister recognized that the government wasn't a hotelier and decided to turn many properties over to the professionals once again.

What the new resort developers found was a deteriorating infrastructure. Some hotels, such as the famed Royal Bahamian on Cable Beach, cost as much as $30 million to renovate before it reopened as a couples only Sandals resort.

By the end of 1996, some $1.5 billion alone had been invested in just Nassau and Paradise Island. Sidewalks were replaced, roads widened, air terminals improved, and an island-wide clean-up campaign inaugurated. Police officers were added to the beat to cut down on a rising crime rate, with tourists often targeted as victims.

Five new or completely renovated hotels and resorts have opened in Nassau and Paradise Island since 1994. The big changeover occurred at the Atlantis on Paradise

Island. Some $125 million had to be pumped into this structure. During his ownership, Merv Griffin let this landmark property decline to the extreme. Arguably, Griffin was a great talk show host, but he bombed as a hotelier, after having taken over the property from Donald Trump, who wisely fled the scene.

By 1995, The Bahamas had their best year, with more than 1.59 million stopover visitors. As the country faces the millennium, figures continue to grow.

Many problems remain. Although some Bahamians are among the friendliest and most hospitable people in the world, certain staff members employed in the tourist industry are downright hostile, an attitude observed by writers for many publications. To counter this, the government is trying to train its citizens to be more helpful, courteous, and efficient. Sometimes this training has taken root; at other times it has fallen on barren ground. Service with a smile is still not assured in The Bahamas.

If there's a downside to the continuing development, it's the emphasis on megahotels and casinos, with less focus on the Out Islands. Although there has been talk, most large resort chains except for Club Med have ignored the Out Islands, letting them slumber in their poverty. Making a living on these inhospitable islands is a daunting task, as the plantation owners of yesteryear could testify. For the most part, the Out Islands are The Bahamas "the way they were." In this case, that evokes the 1950s. Of course, it is the very lack of progress on the Out Islands that attracts the adventurous explorer who shuns megaresorts and glittery casinos, which are at their best on Paradise Island and Cable Beach, and with less sparkle in the Freeport/Lucaya area.

After a long slumber, the government and many concerned citizens of The Bahamas are awakening to ecotourism. More than almost any government in the Caribbean, except Bonaire, the country is trying to protect its natural heritage. If nothing else, they realize it's good for business. Many visitors come to The Bahamas for a close encounter with nature.

Government, private companies, and environmental groups have drawn up a national framework of priorities to protect the islands. One of their first goals was to save the nearly extinct West Indian flamingo. Today, there are nearly 60,000 flamingos living on the Island of Great Inagua. Equally important are programs to prevent the extinction of the green turtle, the white-crowned pigeon, the Bahamian parrot, and the New Providence iguana.

As The Bahamas faces the millennium, the government casts a leery eye at Cuba, wondering what impact its possible reopening to the American market will have on Bahamian tourism.

Unlike Haiti and Jamaica, The Bahamas has remained politically stable. The transition from a poverty-stricken nation under minority white rule to black majority rule has been relatively free of tension, unlike in some other countries, particularly Jamaica. No one knows exactly how the Bahamians made the transition from colonial rule to independence so smoothly, because that has hardly been the case in many other countries. But they did.

You do not see the wretched poverty in Nassau that you do when you fly into Kingston, Jamaica, where it assaults you at every turn. There are a lot of poor people living on New Providence Island, but they mostly live in a section called "over the hill," which few tourists visit.

You'd think that a city so close to the U.S. mainland would be overpowered by American culture. Except for some fast-food eateries, and American music and films, Nassau retains its traditional British overlay.

Freeport/Lucaya on Grand Bahama Island, on the other hand, has become totally Americanized. There is little British aura here, or even a Bahamian tradition. Everything is modern all the way.

The smuggling of drugs remains a serious problem. Because the country is so close to the Florida mainland, it is often used as a temporary depot for drugs from South America. Drugs are smuggled into The Bahamas for later shipment to the Florida mainland. The Bahamas has a long tradition of catering to the illicit habits of U.S. citizens. During the heyday of Prohibition, long before cocaine, marijuana, and heroin were outlawed, many Bahamians grew rich smuggling rum into the United States.

4 History 101

THE EARLY YEARS   Columbus made his first landfall in the New World somewhere in The Bahamas on October 12, 1492. He landed on an island called *Guanahani* by the local inhabitants, Arawak Indians called *Lucayans*. Columbus renamed the island San Salvador. Over the years there has been much dispute as to just which island this was. A long-standing tradition held that the discoverer's first landfall in the New World was a place known as Watling Island. The island was renamed San Salvador to bolster this tradition. Recent research, however, places the first landing on Samana Cay, 65 miles southeast of San Salvador. In 1986, *National Geographic* supported this island as the true Columbus landfall.

The Lucayans Columbus encountered are believed to have come to the islands from the Greater Antilles in about the 8th century A.D. They came seeking refuge from the savage Carib Indians then living in the Lesser Antilles. The Lucayans were peaceful people who welcomed the Spaniards and taught them a skill soon shared with the entire seagoing world: how to make hammocks from heavy cotton cloth.

The Spanish who claimed the Bahamian islands for their king and queen did not repay the Lucayans kindly. Finding neither gold nor silver mines, nor fertile soil, the conquistadors cleared out the population of the islands, taking some 40,000 doomed Lucayans to other islands in New Spain to work mines or dive for pearls.

Ponce de León voyaged here in 1513 looking for the legendary Fountain of Youth. This journey, incidentally, led to the European discovery of Florida and the Gulf Stream—but not the magic fountain. The historian for Ponce de León described the waters of the Little Bahama Bank—just north of Grand Bahama—as *bajamar* (pronounced "*bahamar,*" Spanish for "shallow water"). This seems a reasonable source of the name Bahamas. Other than this, however, there are practically no references for the

Dateline

- **700** Lucayans emigrate to The Bahamas from the Greater Antilles, seeking refuge from the cannibalistic Caribs.
- **1492** Columbus makes his first landfall in the New World, traditionally said to be at San Salvador, although many historians dispute this.
- **1513** Ponce de León searches for the Fountain of Youth and discovers the Gulf Stream instead.
- **1629** England claims The Bahamas, then destitute of population.
- **1640s** First Western settlements are established.
- **1656** New Providence Island (site of Nassau) is settled.
- **1717** King George I orders Captain Woodes Rogers, the first royal governor, to chase the pirates out of Nassau.
- **1776** The fledgling U.S. Navy captures Nassau but soon departs.
- **1782** The British Crown Colony surrenders The Bahamas to Spain, which rules it for almost a year.
- **1783** Spain signs the Treaty of Paris, ceding The Bahamas to Britain.
- **1833** The United Kingdom Emancipation Act frees slaves throughout the British Empire.
- **1861–65** Blockade-running during the U.S. Civil War brings prosperity. Nassau becomes a vital supply base for the Confederacy.

continues

- **1920–33** Rum-running during Prohibition in the United States revives a slumping Bahamian economy. The 1920s are a busy and prosperous time for bootleggers.
- **1933** Repeal of Prohibition causes an economic collapse on the islands.
- **1940** The Duke of Windsor, after renouncing the throne of England, is named governor of The Bahamas as war rages in Europe.
- **1964** Sir Roland Symonette is chosen as the country's first premier. The Bahamas are granted internal self-government.
- **1967** Lynden Pindling, named premier in a close election, begins a long, notorious reign.
- **1968** African-Bahamian rule becomes firmly entrenched.
- **1972** Bahamians vote for total independence from Britain.
- **1973** On July 9, the Union Jack in New Providence is lowered for the last time, ending more than three centuries of British rule.
- **1992** After 25 years, controversial Prime Minister Pindling goes down in defeat. Hubert Ingraham, campaigning against corruption and recession, replaces him.
- **1994** Hotel mogul and entertainer Merv Griffin sells Paradise Island properties.
- **1995** Developers of famed Sun City complex in Swaziland become hotel czars of Paradise Island.

next 135 years to the islands first discovered by Columbus.

THE COMING OF THE ENGLISH   England formally claimed The Bahamas, by then destitute of population, in 1629. No settlement took place, however, until the 1640s, and it resulted from a religious dispute that arose in Bermuda (as it had originally in England). Dissident English and Bermudian settlers sailed to an island called Cigatoo, changed the name to Eleuthera (from the Greek word for freedom), and launched a tough battle for survival. Many became discouraged and went back to Bermuda, but a few hardy souls remained, living on fish, ambergris, and salvage from shipwrecks.

Other people from Bermuda and England eventually followed, and New Providence Island was settled in 1656. Crops of cotton, tobacco, and sugarcane were planted, and Charles Towne, honoring Charles II, was established at the harbor.

PIRATES & PRIVATEERS   The promising agricultural economy was short-lived, however. Several of the governors of The Bahamas during that era were corrupt, and soon the island became a refuge for English, Dutch, and French buccaneers who plundered Spanish ships. The Spaniards repeatedly ravaged New Providence for revenge, and many of the settlers left. Those who remained found supplying the rich pirates a good source of income. Privateers, a slightly more respectable type of freebooter (they had their sovereign's permission to prey on enemy ships), also found the many islets, tricky shoals, and secret harbors of the islands good hiding places from which to stage their attacks on ships sailing between the New and Old Worlds.

Late in the 17th century, the name of Charles Towne was changed to Nassau to honor King William III, who also held the title Prince of Nassau. But the change didn't ease the troubled capital. Some 1,000 pirates still called New Providence their home base.

Finally the appeals of merchants and law-abiding islanders in favor of Crown control were heard, and in 1717 the lord proprietors turned over the government of The Bahamas, both civil and military, to King George I, who commissioned Captain Woodes Rogers as the first royal governor.

Rogers seized hundreds of the lawless pirates. Some were sent to England to be tried, eight were hanged, and others received the king's pardon, after promising thereafter to lead law-abiding lives. Rogers was later given authority to set up a representative assembly, the precursor of today's Parliament. Despite such interruptions as the capture of Nassau by the fledgling U.S. Navy in 1776 (only for a few days) and the surrender of the Crown Colony to Spain in 1782 (which lasted almost a year), the government of The Bahamas since Rogers's time has been conducted in an orderly fashion. The Spanish matter was settled in early 1783 by the Treaty of Paris, when Spain permanently ceded The Bahamas to Britain, ending some 300 years of disputed ownership.

LOYALISTS, BLOCKADE-RUNNERS & BOOTLEGGERS   Following the American Revolution, several thousand Loyalists from the former colonies emigrated to The Bahamas. Some of these, especially southerners, brought their slaves with them and tried their luck at planting sea-island cotton in the Out Islands. Growing cotton was unsuccessful (the plants fell prey to the chenille bug), but by then the former Deep South planters had learned to fish, grow vegetables, and provide for themselves in other ways.

The first white settlers of The Bahamas had also brought slaves with them, but they were freed when slavery was abolished throughout the British Empire in 1834. A fairly peaceful transition was achieved, although it was many years before any real equality between blacks and whites was discernible.

During the Civil War in America, blockade-running brought a transient prosperity to The Bahamas. Nassau became a vital base for the Confederacy, with vessels taking manufactured goods to South Carolina and North Carolina and bringing back cotton. The Union victory ended blockade-running and plunged Nassau into economic depression.

The next real economic boom for the islands was the result of Prohibition in the United States. Just like the blockade runners who preceded them—only with faster boats and more of them—rumrunners churned the waters between The Bahamas and the southeastern United States. From the enforcement of the 18th Amendment in 1920 to repeal of that law in 1933, Nassau, Bimini, and Grand Bahama were used as bases for running contraband alcoholic beverages across the Gulf Stream. Ceaseless battles were waged between the U.S. Coast Guard and this new generation of freebooters. Repeal dealt another shattering blow to the vulnerable Bahamian economy.

THE WAR YEARS   On August 17, 1940, the Duke and Duchess of Windsor arrived in Nassau, following his appointment as governor of the colony. The duke had abdicated as King Edward VIII to marry the woman he loved, the divorced American Wallis Simpson. The people of The Bahamas were shocked that such a once-powerful figure had been assigned to govern their impoverished colony, which was viewed then as a "backwater" of the British Empire. The duke set about trying to bring self-sufficiency to The Bahamas and to provide more employment for its out-of-work population.

World War II healed the wounds left over from the bootlegging days. The Bahamas served as an air and sea way station in the Atlantic. As a result, the country inherited two airports built by the U.S. Air Force. The islands were also of strategic importance when Nazi submarines intruded Atlantic coastal and Caribbean waters. Today, some of the outlying islands house U.S. missile-tracking stations.

THE POSTWAR YEARS   In the years following World War II, party politics developed in The Bahamas as independence from Britain seemed more possible. In 1967 Lynden Pindling won a close election to become prime minister. During the general election of 1972, the Bahamian people voted for total independence. The Bahamas agreed to be a part of the British Commonwealth, presided over by Queen Elizabeth II. Her representative in the future would be a governor-general, a position with mostly symbolic power. In 1992, after years of corruption under Pindling and countless exposés in the *Miami Herald*, Hubert A. Ingraham became prime minister. In office, he has renewed his pledge to promote quality tourism for his nation.

5 Junkanoo & Folklore

JUNKANOO

No Bahamian celebration is as extroverted as the *Junkanoo*. The special rituals originated during the colonial days of slavery, when African-born newcomers could legally drink and enjoy themselves only on certain strictly predefined days of the year. In its celebration, Junkanoo closely resembles Carnival in Rio and Mardi Gras in New Orleans. Its major difference lies in the ornamentation of the costumes and the timing: The major Junkanoo celebrations occur the day after Christmas, a reminder of the medieval English celebration of Boxing Day on December 26, and on New Year's Day.

In the old days, Junkanoo costumes were crafted from crepe paper, often in primary colors, stretched over wire frames. One sinister offshoot to the celebrations was that the Junkanoo costumes and masks were used to conceal the identity of anyone seeking vengeance on a white or on another slave. Locals have more money to spend on costumes and Junkanoo festivals today than they did in decades past. Today the finest costumes can cost up to $10,000 and are sometimes sponsored by local bazaars, lotteries, and charity auctions. More common, however, are the vibrant costumes worn by everyday revelers, whose sensual and humorous participation in the Junkanoo is one of the high points of the Bahamian calendar. The best time and place to observe Junkanoo is New Year's Day in Nassau, when throngs of cavorting, music-making, and costumed figures prance through the streets. Find yourself a good viewing position on Bay Street. Less elaborate celebrations take place at major population centers on the other islands, including Freeport.

For more information about the musical expression of Junkanoo, see "The Music of the Islands," below.

FOLKLORE

Many different factors contributed to the formation of a potent and vital body of myths within The Bahamas. Among the strongest factors were the nation's unusual geography, its noteworthy history, and the often turbulent mingling of cultures. Some tales are a mélange of about a half dozen different oral traditions, including those of England, Africa, France, and neighboring islands of the Caribbean. Storytelling is a fine art, with a tradition that remains the strongest on the Out Islands, where television (and electricity) were introduced only a few years ago.

Obeah, which has been defined as a mixture of European superstitions, African (especially Yoruban) religion, and Judeo-Christian beliefs, retains similarities to the voodoo of Haiti, the Santeria of Cuba and Brazil, and the Shango of Trinidad. Steeped in the mythic traditions of West Africa, it is an important part of Bahamian national heritage.

An obeah practitioner may chant, sing, or go into a trance to communicate with another dimension of reality. The most common method of obeah practice in The Bahamas today involves "fixing" a person with a spell, which can be "cleared" either by another obeah practitioner or by a formal medical doctor. Much more serious is to be "cursed" by an obeah master, the effect of which can be lifted only by that same person. Magic is divided into black and white spheres, with white magic being the more potent and the less evil.

Ghosts or spirits are known as "sperrids," and necromancy—the habit of soliciting communications from the dead—is a ritualistic form of obeah used to get information that can be put either to good or evil use. According to tradition, the sperrids dwell in the fluffy tops of the silk cotton trees that are widespread throughout The Bahamas. This belief probably has its origins in African traditions, where many tribes worship the cotton tree as the abode of the spirits of the dead. Although sperrids wander at will throughout the earth, causing mischief and unhappiness wherever they go, only the obeah man or woman can channel their power.

On some islands (including remote Cat Island), residents believed that a "working witch" could be hired to perform tasks. The most common form of a witch was that of a cat, rabbit, snake, or rat. Folk tales abound about the mythical powers of these witch-animals. Especially fearsome was any short, fat snake with a ribbon tied around it, a sure sign that the reptile was actually a witch in disguise.

Highly secret, as clandestine as you might imagine witchcraft to be within unpublicized covens of New England, obeah is a superstitious undercurrent running through the context of life on some islands. No outsider would be invited to the few ritualized events that might take place.

6 The Music of the Islands

The Bahamas maintains great pride in its original musical idioms, often comparing their vitality to the more famous musical traditions of Jamaica, Puerto Rico, and Trinidad. Other than the spirituals whose roots were shared by slaves in colonial North America, by far the most famous musical products of the archipelago are *Goombay* and its closely linked sibling, *Junkanoo.*

GOOMBAY   Goombay music is an art form whose melodies and body movements are always accompanied by the beat of goatskin drums and, when available, the liberal consumption of rum. Goombay is a musical combination of African tribal heritage (especially that of the Egungun sect of the Yoruba tribe) mingled with Native American and British Colonial influences. Although its appeal quickly spread to other islands, such as Bermuda, the traditions of Goombay remain the strongest in The Bahamas.

The most outlandish expressions of Goombay occur the day after Christmas (Boxing Day), especially in Nassau on Bay Street. Dancers outfit themselves in masquerade costumes whose bizarre accessories and glittering colors evoke the plumage of jungle birds. Once dismissed by the British colonials as the pastime of hooligans, Goombay is now the most widespread and broad-based celebratory motif in The Bahamas, richly encouraged by the islands' political and business elite. Goombay musicians and dancers are almost always male. Men and boys from the same family pass on the rhythms and dance techniques from generation to generation. Goombay signifies at the same time the Bantu word for "rhythm" as well as a specific type of African drum.

Today, Goombay has a gentle, rolling rhythm, a melody produced by either a piano, a guitar, or a saxophone, and the enthusiastic inclusion of bongos, maracas, and rhythm ("click") sticks. Lyrics, unlike the words that accompany reggae, are rarely politicized, dealing instead with topics that might have been referred to in another day as "saucy."

Over time, the sounds of Goombay would be commercialized and adapted into the louder and more strident musical form known as Junkanoo. Nearly all resort hotels that offer entertainment feature either Goombay or Junkanoo music.

JUNKANOO   Until the 1940s, Junkanoo referred almost exclusively to yuletide processions during which elaborate costumes were paraded down the main streets of towns accompanied solely by percussion music (see "Junkanoo & Folklore," above). During the days of slavery, Christmas was the most important of the four annual holidays granted to slaves, and the one that merited the most exuberant celebrations. The rhythms of Junkanoo, understandably, soon became hypnotic, growing with the enthusiasm of the spectators and the uninhibited movements of the dancers. Essential to the tradition were the use of traditional goatskin drums, cowbells, and whistles.

Around World War II, a series of Bahamian musicians fleshed out the percussion rhythms of the yuletide Junkanoo parade with piano, electric bass, and guitar accompaniment. This sparked the beginning of its development into what is today the most prevalent musical form in The Bahamas.

Today, Junkanoo music is to The Bahamas what reggae is to Jamaica. In other words, you can't miss hearing the music. All hotels and resorts, and even some restaurants, offer this music as part of the evening's entertainment. Some musical groups even call themselves "Junkanoo." It's a lot safer hearing this music in resorts or hotels than it is wandering the back streets of Nassau at night looking for some local club. If you do the latter, you could get mugged.

7 What's Cookin' in The Bahamas

There *is* a bona fide Bahamian cuisine, but you'll have to leave the first-class hotels to find it. In Nassau, for example, head to such old-time favorites as the **Traveller's Rest** or the **Bahamian Kitchen** for an authentic "taste of The Bahamas" (see chapter 4). On Grand Bahama Island you'll have to look even harder to find typically native dishes. They're best at **Fatman's Nephew** (see chapter 6). If you'd like to eat authentic Bahamian food, look for the word BAHAMIAN in caps under the restaurant reviews. When you see the word INTERNATIONAL, know that this is typical fare likely to be offered anywhere, especially at a resort in Florida.

Once you reach the Out Islands, eating Bahamian food is often the only way to go. In some of the remote places, it's the only type of cuisine offered. Of course, the major restaurants have continental chefs, but in many places, especially at the little local restaurants previewed in this guide, you eat as the Bahamians eat.

Cuisine, sad to say, is not one of the most compelling reasons to come to The Bahamas. You can fare much better on the mainland, especially in Florida. Except for some notable exceptions (see "The Best Restaurants" in chapter 1), many restaurants serve fairly routine international fare of the "surf and turf" variety. Local fish and shellfish consists mainly of grouper and conch. When we tour the Out Islands, we often get one or the other every night. More exotic fish is often flown in frozen from Miami.

Except for some homegrown chicken, such as poultry raised on the island of Eleuthera, most meat and poultry also arrive frozen from the U.S. mainland.

The best restaurants are in Nassau, Cable Beach, Paradise Island, and, to a lesser extent, Freeport/Lucaya. The Out Islands are not famed for their cuisine. It's pretty much local fare, or an international dish or two if the hotel is more upmarket. That doesn't mean you can't eat satisfactorily in The Bahamas. You can. But chances are you won't be writing any cookbooks or collecting recipes for the meals you are served.

THE CUISINE

SOUP Bahamian fish chowder can be prepared in any number of ways. Old-time Bahamian chefs tell us that it's best when made with grouper. To that they add celery, onions, tomatoes, and an array of flavorings that might include A-1 sauce (or Worcestershire, or both), along with thyme, cooking sherry, a bit of dark rum, and lime juice.

Increasingly rare these days, turtle soup was for years a mainstay of the Out Islands. Turtle soup and other turtle dishes still appear on some local menus despite their status as endangered species. However, if you have alternatives, it would be better to choose another dish.

CONCH   The national food of The Bahamas is conch (pronounced *"konk"*). The firm white meat of this mollusk—called the "snail of the sea"—is enjoyed through-out the islands. Actually, its taste is somewhat bland, but not when Bahamian chefs finish with it. Locals eat it as a snack (usually served at happy hour in taverns and bars), as a main dish, as a salad, or as an hors d'oeuvre.

The Pacific Coast resident will think it tastes like abalone. Conch does not have a fishy taste, like halibut, but it has a chewy consistency, which means that a chef must pound it to tenderize it, the way one might pound Wiener schnitzel. Every cook has a different recipe for making conch chowder. A popular version includes toma-toes, potatoes, sweet peppers, onions, carrots, salt pork or bacon, bay leaf, thyme, and (of course) salt and pepper.

Conch fritters, shaped like balls, are served with hot sauce and are made with finely minced sweet peppers, onions, and tomato paste, among other ingredients. They are deep-fried in oil.

Conch salad is another local favorite, and again it has many variations. Essentially, it is uncooked conch that has been marinated in Old Sour (a hot pepper sauce) to break down its tissues and to add extra flavor. It is served with diced small red (or green) peppers, along with chopped onion. The taste is tangy.

Cracked conch (or fried conch, as the old-timers used to call it) is prepared like a breaded veal cutlet. Pounded hard and dipped in batter, it is then sautéed. Conch is also served steamed, in a Creole sauce, curried, "scorched," creamed on toast, and stewed. Instead of conch chowder, you might get conch soup. You'll also see "conch burgers" listed on menus.

SEAFOOD   The most elegant item you'll see on nearly any menu in The Bahamas is the spiny local lobster. A tropical cousin of the Maine lobster, it is also called crayfish or rock lobster. Only the tail is eaten, however. You get fresh lobster only when it's in season, from the first of April until the end of August. Otherwise it's frozen.

Bahamian lobster, in spite of its cost, is not always prepared well. Sometimes a cook leaves it in the oven for too long, and the meat becomes tough and chewy. But when prepared right, such as is done by the famed Graycliff Restaurant in Nassau, it is per-fection and worth the exorbitant cost.

The Bahamian lobster lends itself to any international recipe for lobster, includ-ing Newburg or Thermidor. A typical local way of preparing it is curried, with lime juice and fresh coconut among other ingredients.

After conch, grouper is the second–most-consumed fish in The Bahamas. It's served in a number of ways, often batter dipped or sautéed, and called "fingers" because of the way it's sliced. The fish is also steamed and served in a spicy Creole sauce. Sometimes it comes dressed in a sauce of dry white wine, mushrooms, onions, and such seasonings as thyme. Because the fish has a mild taste, the extra flavor of the other ingredients is needed.

Baked bonefish is also common, and it's very simple to prepare. The bonefish is split in half and seasoned with a hot pepper sauce (Old Sour) and salt, then popped into the oven.

Baked crab is one of the best-known dishes of The Bahamas. A chef mixes the eggs and meat of either land or sea crabs with seasonings and bread crumbs. The crabs are then replaced in their shells and baked.

You'll also encounter yellowtail, "goggle eyes," jacks, snapper, grunts, and margot, plus many other sea creatures.

POULTRY, MEATS & VEGGIES   A limited number of chickens are raised locally in The Bahamas, especially on Eleuthera. Chicken souse is a popular dish made with chicken, onion, sweet peppers, bay leaves, allspice, and other ingredients left up to a cook's imagination. It's simmered in a pot for about an hour; then lime juice is added and it's simmered a little longer. Pig's feet souse is also a favorite dish.

Goats and sheep are also raised on the Out Islands. "Mutton" on a menu can refer to either meat. It's often curried. Wild boar is caught on some of the islands, and game birds such as ducks and pigeons are hunted. Raccoon stew is also eaten.

Most meats, including pork, veal, and beef, are imported. However, even here, Bahamian cooks show their ingenuity by giving these meats interesting variations. For example, at an Out Island inn, we recently enjoyed pork that had been marinated with vinegar, garlic, onion, celery tops, cloves, mustard, and Worcestershire sauce, then baked and served with gravy. Even a simple baked ham is given a Bahamian touch with the addition of fresh pineapple, coconut milk, and coconut flakes, along with mustard, honey, and brown sugar.

Many vegetables are grown in The Bahamas; others are imported. If it's a cucumber, you can be almost certain it's from one of Edison Key's farms in North Abaco. They not only supply cucumbers to their own country, but it's estimated that they also have captured about 5% of the stateside market. Bahamians also grow their own sweet potatoes, corn, cassava, okra, and peppers (both sweet and hot), among other produce.

PEAS 'N' RICE & JOHNNYCAKE   If mashed potatoes are still the "national starch" of America, then peas 'n' rice perform that role in The Bahamas. Peas 'n' rice, like mashed potatoes, can be prepared in a number of ways. A popular method is cooking pigeon peas (which grow in pods on small trees) or black-eyed peas with salt pork, tomatoes, celery, uncooked rice, thyme, green pepper, onion, salt, pepper, and whatever special touch a chef wants to add. When it's served as a side dish, Bahamians most often sprinkle hot sauce over the concoction.

Johnnycake, another famed part of the Bahamian table, dates from the early settlers, who most often were simple folk and usually poor. They survived mainly on a diet of fish and rice, supplemented by johnnycake, a pan-cooked bread made with butter, milk, flour, sugar, salt, and baking powder. (Originally it was called "Journey Cake," which was eventually corrupted to johnnycake.) Fishers could make this simple bread on the decks of their vessels. They'd build a fire in a box that had been filled with sand to keep the flames from spreading to the craft.

DESSERTS   Guava duff is the dessert specialty of The Bahamas, although one cook confided to me, "It takes too long, and we don't like to make it anymore unless there's a special call for it."

The dessert, which resembles a jelly roll, is made with guava pulp that has been run through a food mill or sieve. Nobody seems to agree on the best method of cooking it. One way is to cream sugar and butter and add eggs and spices such as cinnamon and cloves, or nutmeg. The flour is made into a stiff dough and mixed with the guava pulp, which is then placed in the top of a double boiler and cooked over boiling water for hours. It can also be boiled or steamed, and there are those who insist it should be baked. Guava duff is served with hard sauce (a blend of butter, confectioners' sugar, vanilla, and rum).

Other tasty Bahamian desserts and breads include coconut tarts, coconut jimmie, benne seedcakes, and potato bread.

TROPICAL FRUITS   Bahamians are especially fond of fruits, and they make inventive dishes out of them, including soursop ice cream and sapodilla pudding. Guavas are used to make their famous guava duff dessert, described above. The islanders also grow and enjoy melons, pineapples, passion fruit, mangoes, and other varieties.

Their best-known fruit is the papaya, which is called pawpaw or "melon tree." It's made into a dessert or a chutney, or eaten for breakfast in its natural state. It's also used in many lunch and dinner recipes. An old Bahamian custom of using papaya as a meat tenderizer has, at least since the 1970s, invaded the kitchens of North America. Papaya is also used to make fruity tropical drinks, such as a Bahama Mama shake. And if you see it for sale in a local food store, take home some "Goombay" marmalade, made with papaya, pineapple, and green ginger.

RUM, LIQUEURS & SPECIALTY DRINKS   Rum was known to the ancient Romans—it was even known to the ancient Chinese—but it is today mostly associated with the islands stretching from The Bahamas to the Caribbean. Although rum came north from Cuba and Jamaica, the people of The Bahamas quickly adopted it as their national alcoholic beverage. And using their imagination, they "invented" several local drinks, including the Yellow Bird, the Bahama Mama, and the Goombay Smash.

The Yellow Bird is made with crème de banana liqueur, Vat 19 rum, orange juice, pineapple juice, apricot brandy, and Galliano. A Bahama Mama is made with Vat 19, citrus juice (perhaps pineapple, as well), bitters, a dash of nutmeg, crème de cassis, and a hint of grenadine. The Goombay Smash is usually made with coconut rum, pineapple juice, lemon juice, Triple Sec, Vat 19, and a dash of simple syrup.

Nearly every bartender in the islands has his or her own version of planter's punch. A classic recipe is to make it with lime juice, sugar, Vat 19, plus a dash of bitters. It's usually served with a cherry and an orange slice. If you want a typically Bahamian liqueur, try Nassau Royale. It is used to make an increasingly popular drink, the C. C. Rider, which also includes Canadian Club, apricot brandy, and pineapple juice.

3

Planning a Trip to The Bahamas

You can be in The Bahamas sipping a Goombay Smash after only a 35-minute jet-hop from Miami. Travel agents who keep up-to-the-minute schedules and rates can inform you of the latest package deals if you're contemplating either a summer or winter holiday. Fortunately, many of these package deals aren't offered just in the slow season—the summer—but appear frequently throughout the winter, except during the heavily booked Christmas period.

In this chapter we concentrate on what you need to do before you go. In addition to helping you decide when to take your vacation, we answer questions about where to get information and what documents you need to obtain. We also offer sample itineraries, alternative travel options, and tips for special travelers.

1 Visitor Information & Entry Requirements

VISITOR INFORMATION   To obtain information on The Bahamas before you go, see your travel agent or the Bahamas Tourist Office nearest you. In the United States, offices are found in *Chicago* at 8600 W. Bryn Mawr Ave., Suite 820, Chicago, IL 60631 (☎ 312/693-1500); in *Dallas* at World Trade Center, 2050 Stemmons Freeway, Suite 116, Dallas, TX 75258 (☎ 214/742-1886); in *Florida* at 1 Turnberry Place, 19495 Biscayne Blvd. 809, Adventura, FL 33180 (☎ 305/932-0051); in *Fort Lauderdale,* Bahamas Out Islands Promotion Board, 1100 Lee Wagener Blvd., Suite 204, Fort Lauderdale, FL 33315 (☎ 954/359-8099); in *Los Angeles* at 3450 Wilshire Blvd., Suite 208, Los Angeles, CA 90010 (☎ 213/385-0033); and in *New York* at 150 E. 52nd St., New York, NY 10022 (☎ 212/758-2777).

In **Canada** there is an office in Toronto at 121 Bloor St. E., Suite 1101, Toronto, ON M4W 3M5 (☎ 416/968-2999).

In **England,** contact The Bahamas Tourist Office, 3 The Billings, Walnut Tree Close, Guildford, Surrey GU1 4UL (☎ 01483/448900).

A good travel agent can be a source of information. If you use one, make sure the agent is a member of the American Society of Travel Agents (ASTA). If you get poor service from an agent, you can write to the **ASTA Consumer Affairs,** 1101 King St., Alexandria, VA 22314 (☎ 703/706-0387).

ENTRY REQUIREMENTS   To enter The Bahamas, citizens of the United States coming in as visitors for a period not to exceed 8 months only need to bring proof of citizenship, such as a passport, a birth certificate, or a voter registration card. The latter two require a photo ID. Onward or return tickets must be shown to immigration officials in The Bahamas.

The Commonwealth of the Bahamas does not require visas. On entry to The Bahamas, you'll be given an Immigration Card to complete and sign. The card has a carbon copy that you must keep until departure, at which time it must be turned in. Also, a departure tax is levied before you can exit the country (see "Taxes" under "Fast Facts" later in this chapter).

Note: It's good policy to make copies of your most valuable documents, including your passport, before you leave home. Make a photocopy of the inside page of your passport, the one with your photograph. In case of loss abroad, you should also make copies of your driver's license, an airline ticket, strategic hotel vouchers, and any other sort of identity card that might be pertinent. You should also make copies of any prescriptions you take. Place one copy in your luggage and carry the original with you. Leave another copy at home.

CUSTOMS   U.S. Customs   Visitors leaving Nassau or Freeport/Lucaya for most U.S. destinations clear U.S. Customs and Immigration before departing The Bahamas. Charter companies can make special arrangements with the Nassau or Freeport flight services and U.S. Customs and Immigration for preclearance. No further formalities are required upon arrival in the United States once the preclearance has taken place in Nassau or Freeport.

When you return home you may take $600 worth of merchandise duty free if you've been outside the United States for 48 hours or more and have not claimed a similar exemption within the past 30 days. Articles valued above the $600 duty-free limit but not over $1,000 will be assessed at a flat duty rate of 10%. Gifts for your personal use, not for business purposes, may be included in the $600 exemption. Unsolicited gifts totaling $100 a day may be sent home duty free. You are limited to one liter of wine, liqueur, or liquor. One carton of cigarettes can be brought home duty free. U.S. Customs preclearance is available for all scheduled flights. Passengers leaving for the United States must fill out written declaration forms before clearing U.S. Customs in The Bahamas. The forms are available at hotels, travel agencies, and airlines in The Bahamas.

Collect receipts for all purchases made in The Bahamas. *Note:* If a merchant suggests giving you a false receipt, misstating the value of the goods, beware—the merchant might be an informer to U.S. Customs. You must also declare all gifts received during your stay abroad.

If you purchased an item during an earlier trip abroad, carry proof that you have already paid Customs duty on the item at the time of your previous reentry. To be extra careful, compile a list of expensive carry-on items and ask a U.S. Customs agent to stamp your list at the airport before your departure.

If you're concerned and need more specific guidance, write to the U.S. Customs Service, 1301 Constitution Ave., P.O. Box 7407, Washington, DC 20044, and request the free pamphlet *Know Before You Go.*

U.S. Customs Service has launched its home page, designed for the international travel and trade communities, on the Internet's World Wide Web. The site, which contains a variety of information on Customs issues, may be accessed by the Web-surfing public 24 hours per day at **http://www.customs.ustreas.gov**.

Canadian Customs For information on Canadian Customs, write for the booklet *I Declare,* issued by Revenue Canada, 875 Heron Rd., Ottawa, ON K1A OL5. Canada allows its citizens a $300 exemption, and you are allowed to bring back duty free 200 cigarettes, 400 grams of tobacco, 40 imperial ounces of liquor, and 50 cigars. In addition, you are allowed to mail gifts to Canada from abroad at the rate of Can$60 per day, provided they are unsolicited and aren't alcohol or tobacco (write on the package: "Unsolicited gift, under $60 value"). All valuables should be declared on the Y-38 form before departure from Canada, including serial numbers, as in the case of, for example, expensive foreign cameras you already own. *Note:* The $300 exemption can be used only once a year and only after an absence of 7 days.

British Customs On returning from The Bahamas, if you either arrive directly in the United Kingdom or arrive via a port in another EU country where you did not pass through Customs controls with all your baggage, you must go through U.K. Customs and declare any goods in excess of the allowances. These are: 200 cigarettes or 100 cigarillos or 50 cigars or 250 grams of tobacco; 2 liters of still table wine and 1 liter of spirits or strong liqueurs over 22% volume, or 2 liters of fortified or sparkling wine or other liqueurs, or 2 liters of additional still table wine; 60cc/ml of perfume; 250cc/ml of toilet water; and £145 worth of all other goods, including gifts and souvenirs. (No one under 17 years of age is entitled to a tobacco or drinks allowance.) Only go through the Green "nothing to declare" channel if you're sure that you have no more than the Customs allowances and no prohibited or restricted goods. For further details on U.K. Customs, contact H.M. Customs and Excise Office, Dorset House, Stamford Street, London, SE1 9PY (☎ **0171/202-4227**).

2 Money

CASH/CURRENCY Legal tender is the Bahamian dollar (B$1), which is on a par with the U.S. dollar. Both U.S. and Bahamian dollars are accepted on an equal basis throughout The Bahamas. There is no restriction on the amount of foreign currency brought into the country by a tourist. Traveler's checks are accepted by most large hotels and stores, but you may have trouble getting a personal check honored.

A NOTE ON CURRENCY FOR BRITISH TRAVELERS The British pound trades at an average of around 62p = $1 U.S. Stated another way, $1.60 U.S. = £1. The chart below gives a rough approximation of conversion rates you're likely to find at the time of your trip, but confirm before you make transactions.

TRAVELER'S CHECKS Traveler's checks are the safest way to carry cash while traveling. Most banks will give you a better rate on traveler's checks than for cash. Each of the agencies listed below will refund your checks if they are lost or stolen, provided you produce sufficient documentation. When purchasing your checks, ask about refund hotlines: American Express has probably the greatest number of offices around the world.

American Express (☎ **800/221-7282** in the U.S. and Canada) is one of the largest and most immediately recognized issuers of traveler's checks. American Express platinum card holders get traveler's checks issued commission free at American Express offices or through the American Express service number (☎ **800/553-6782**). Gold card holders can get commission-free checks only through the American Express service number; other cardholders pay a commission. No commission is paid by members of AAA provided checks are purchased at AAA offices.

The U.S. Dollar & the British Pound

U.S.$	U.K.£	U.S.$	U.K.£
.25	.16	15.00	9.38
.50	.31	20.00	12.50
.75	.47	25.00	15.63
1.00	.625	50.00	31.25
2.00	1.25	75.00	46.88
3.00	1.88	100.00	62.50
4.00	2.50	150.00	93.75
5.00	3.13	200.00	125.00
6.00	3.75	250.00	156.25
7.00	4.38	300.00	187.50
8.00	5.00	350.00	218.75
9.00	5.63	400.00	250.00
10.00	6.25	500.00	312.50

Other issuers include **Citicorp** (☎ **800/645-6556** in the U.S. and Canada, or call ☎ 813/623-1709 collect from anywhere else in the world) and **Thomas Cook** (☎ **800/223-7373** in the U.S. and Canada, otherwise call ☎ 609/987-7300 collect from other parts of the world), which issues MasterCard traveler's checks. **Interpayment Services** (☎ **800/221-2426** in the U.S. or Canada, or call ☎ 212/858-8500 collect from other parts of the world) sells Visa checks that are issued by a consortium of member banks and the Thomas Cook organization.

CREDIT CARDS & ATM NETWORKS   Credit cards are in wide use in The Bahamas. Visa and MasterCard are the major cards used, although American Express and, to a lesser extent, Diners Club are also popular.

There are a limited number of ATMs within the islands' most cosmopolitan areas. Plus, Cirrus, and other networks connecting automated-teller machines operate in The Bahamas. The busiest one in the country is in Nassau, adjacent to that city's cruise-ship docks, although those within the megaresorts of Paradise Island, Cable Beach, and Grand Bahama Island are also much used, partly because of their proximity to some of the busiest casinos in the country.

You shouldn't even attempt to find an ATM outside these three islands. They simply don't exist, although a well-meaning hotel receptionist on one of them might be able to cash a check for you if you present the proper ID.

Before going, check to see if your PIN number must be reprogrammed for usage in The Bahamas. For locations of Cirrus abroad, call ☎ **800/424-7787.** For Plus usage abroad, dial ☎ **800/843-7587.** ATMs give a better exchange rate than banks, but some ATMs exact a service charge on every transaction.

MONEYGRAMS   Moneygram, 6200 S. Quebec St. (P.O. Box 5118), Englewood, CO 80155-5118 (☎ **800/926-9400**), sponsored by American Express, is the fastest-growing money-wiring service in the world. Funds can be transferred from one individual to another in less than 10 minutes from any of thousands of locations to any thousands of other locations throughout the world.

What Things Cost in The Bahamas	U.S. $
Taxi from airport to Nassau's center (with tip)	20.00
Local phone call on pay phone	.25
Double room at Graycliff (deluxe)	290.00
Double room at British Colonial Beach Resort (moderate)	129.00
Double room at El Greco (inexpensive)	80.00
Continental breakfast in a hotel	10.00
Lunch for one at the Europe (moderate)*	12.00
Lunch for one at the Bahamian Kitchen (inexpensive)*	12.00
Dinner for one at Buena Vista (deluxe)*	44.50
Dinner for one at Green Shutters (moderate)*	25.00
Dinner for one at Pick-A-Dilly at 18 Parliament (inexpensive)*	18.00
Bottle of beer in a bar/hotel	1.75–3.50
Coca-Cola in a cafe or bar	.80–1.35
Rolls of ASA 100 color film, 36 exposures	7.00
Movie ticket	6.50
Show at the Palace Theatre	30.00

Includes tax and tip, but not wine.

There are three Moneygram branches in the **Bank of The Bahamas:** Woodstock Street and Bank Lane, Freeport (☎ **242/352-7483**); Marlborough Street, Nassau (☎ **242/322-1690**); and 50 Shirley St., Nassau (☎ **242/322-1210**).

3 When to Go

CLIMATE   The temperature in The Bahamas varies to a surprisingly slight degree, averaging between 75° and 85°F in both winter and summer, although it can get very chilly, especially in the early morning and at night. The Bahamian winter is usually like a perpetual May.

The Tropic of Cancer crosses the Bahamian archipelago at about the halfway mark, passing through Great Exuma and the northern part of Long Island. Thus, there is some variation between the mean temperatures in the northernmost and southernmost islands, but the climate overall is mild. The Gulf Stream sweeps along the western shores with its clear, warm waters, and the prevailing trade winds blow steadily in from the southeast.

THE HURRICANE SEASON   The curse of Bahamian weather, the hurricane season lasts—officially at least—from June 1 to November 30. But there is no cause for panic. More tropical cyclones pound the U.S. mainland than hurricanes devastate The Bahamas. Hurricanes are, in fact, infrequent in The Bahamas. However, when one does come, satellite forecasts generally give adequate warnings so that precautions can be taken.

If you're heading for The Bahamas during the hurricane season, you can call your nearest branch of the National Weather Service. In your phone directory, look it up under the U.S. Department of Commerce listing. You can also obtain current weather information on many destinations, including The Bahamas, by dialing a toll-charge call (95¢ per minute) from any Touch-Tone phone in the United States (☎ **900/WEATHER**).

Average Temperatures & Rainfall (Inches) in The Bahamas

	Jan	Feb	Mar	Apr	May	June	July	Aug	Sept	Oct	Nov	Dec
Temp. °F	70	70	72	75	77	80	81	82	81	78	74	71
Temp. °C	21	21	22	24	25	27	27	28	27	26	23	22
Rainfall (in.)	1.9	1.6	1.4	1.9	4.8	9.2	6.1	6.3	7.5	8.3	2.3	1.5

HOLIDAYS   Public holidays observed in The Bahamas are *New Year's Day, Good Friday, Easter Monday, Whitmonday* (7 weeks after Easter), *Labour Day* (the first Friday in June), *Independence Day* (July 10), *Emancipation Day* (the first Monday in August), *Discovery Day* (October 12), *Christmas,* and *Boxing Day* (the day after Christmas). When a holiday falls on Saturday or Sunday, stores and offices are usually closed on the following Monday.

THE BAHAMAS CALENDAR OF EVENTS

January

✪ **Junkanoo.** This Mardi Gras–like festival begins 2 or 3 hours before dawn on New Year's Day. Throngs of cavorting, music-making, costumed figures prance through Nassau, Freeport/Lucaya, and the Out Islands. Elaborate headdresses and festive apparel are worn by jubilant men, women, and children as they celebrate their African heritage. Mini-Junkanoos, in which visitors can participate, are regular events. Local tourist offices will advise the best locations to see the festivities.

April

✪ **The Bahamas Family Island Regatta.** Featuring Bahamian craft sloops, these celebrated boat races at George Town in the Exumas began in 1954. Held in Elizabeth Harbour, the races are divided into five separate levels. The regatta program also features a variety of onshore activities including basketball, a skipper's party, and a Junkanoo parade. Call ☎ **800/32-SPORT** for exact dates and information.

May

• **Long Island Regatta,** Salt Pond, Long Island, sees some 40 to 50 sailing sloops from throughout The Bahamas compete in three classes for trophies and cash prizes. Onshore entertainment consists of indigenous "rake and scrap" music, sporting activities, and the sale of native food—all taking place in a carnival-like atmosphere. For more information, call ☎ **242/328-2495.**

June

• **The Goombay Summer Festival** incorporates the sounds of Junkanoo and the rhythm of Goombay in a 4-month, round-the-clock celebration for the enjoyment of summer visitors. The start date of the Goombay Festival varies, so check with The Bahamas Tourist Office nearest you. It begins some time in June.

• **Eleuthera Pineapple Festival,** Gregory Town, Eleuthera. A celebration devoted to the island's succulent pineapple. Featuring a Junkanoo parade, craft displays, dancing, a pineapple recipe contest, tours of pineapple farms, and a "pineathalon"—a ¼-mile swim, a 3½-mile run, and a 4-mile bike ride. For more information, call **The Bahama Tourist Office.**

July
- **Independence Week** is marked throughout the islands by festivities, parades, and fireworks to celebrate the independence of the Commonwealth of The Bahamas, with the focal point being Independence Day, July 10.
- **Regatta Time in Abaco,** a series of five sailboat races taking place in the Sea of Abaco. Participants compete for more than 100 trophies skillfully crafted by local Abaco artisan Pete Johnston. Highlights include nightly entertainment, free cocktail parties, and a grand finale party. For registration forms and more information, write to Regatta Time in Abaco, P.O. Box AB20551, Marsh Harbour, Abaco, or call Dave or Kathy Ralph at ☎ **242/367-2677.**

August
- **Emancipation Day.** The first Monday in August commemorates the emancipation of slaves in 1834. A highlight of this holiday is an early morning "Junkanoo Rushout" starting at 4am in Fox Hill Village in Nassau, followed by an afternoon of "cook-outs," cultural events such as climbing the greasy pole, and the plaiting of the Maypole.

October
- **Discovery Day.** The New World landing of Christopher Columbus, traditionally said to be the island of San Salvador, is celebrated throughout The Bahamas. Naturally, San Salvador town has a parade every year on this day, October 12.

November
- **Guy Fawkes Day.** The best celebrations are in Nassau. Nighttime parades through the streets are held on many of the islands, culminating in the hanging and burning of Guy Fawkes, an effigy of the British malefactor who was involved in the Gunpowder Plot of 1605 in London. It usually takes place around November 5, but check with island tourist offices.

December
- **Junkanoo Boxing Day.** High-energy Junkanoo parades and celebrations are held throughout the islands on December 26. Many of these activities are repeated on New Year's Day (see January, above).

4 The Active Vacation Planner

The more than 700 islands in the Bahamian archipelago—fewer than 30 of which are inhabited—are surrounded by clear waters ideal for fishing, sailing, and scuba diving. (Detailed recommendations and often the costs of these activities are previewed under the individual destinations listings.) The country's perfect weather and its many cooperative local entrepreneurs allow easy access to more than 30 sports throughout the islands. For sports-related information about any of the activities listed below, call ☎ **800/32-SPORT.**

BICYCLE & SCOOTER RENTALS   Most biking or scooter riding is done either on New Providence Island (Nassau) or Grand Bahama Island; both have relatively flat terrain. Biking is best on Grand Bahama Island because it's bigger with better roads and more places to go. Getting around New Providence Island is relatively easy once you leave the traffic congestion of Nassau and Cable Beach. In Nassau many hotels will rent you a bike or motor scooter.

On Grand Bahama Island, bikes can be rented at certain hotels, including Castaways Resort, Bahama Princess Resort and Casino, and Flamingo Beach Resort on Lucaya Beach (see chapter 6, "Grand Bahama," for phones and addresses). You can

also rent motor scooters starting at about $50 per day. The tourist office at Freeport/
Lucaya will outline on a map the best biking routes.

In the Out Islands, roads are usually too bumpy and potholed for much serious
biking or scooter riding. Bike rental places are almost nonexistent unless your hotel
has some vehicles.

FISHING   The shallow waters between the hundreds of cays and islands of The
Bahamas are some of the most fertile fishing grounds in the world. Even waters where
marine traffic is relatively congested have yielded impressive catches. Grouper, billfish, wahoo, tuna, and dozens of other species thrive in Bahamian waters, and dozens of charter boats are available for deep-sea fishing. Reef fishing, either from small
boats or from shorelines, is popular everywhere, with grouper, snapper, and barracuda being the most commonly caught species. Specialists, however, or serious
amateurs of the sport, often head for any of the following points:

Hemingway's old haunt, the island of **Bimini,** is known as the "Big-Game Fishing Capital of the World," where anglers can successfully hunt for swordfish, sailfish,
and marlin. Bimini maintains its own Hall of Fame where many a proud angler has
had his or her catch honored. Annual highlights include the Bimini Billfish Championship in May and the Hemingway Championship Tournament in July. World
records for the size of catches don't seem to last long here, being quickly surpassed.

Walker's Cay in the Abacos and **Chub Cay** in the Berry Islands are famous for
both deep-sea and shore fishing. Some anglers return to these cays year after year.
Grouper, jacks, and snapper are plentiful. Even spearfishing without scuba gear is
common and popular.

Andros is the site of the world's best bonefishing. Bonefish (also known as "gray
fox") are medium-sized fish that feed in shallow, well-illuminated waters. Known as
some of the most tenacious fish in the world, they struggle ferociously against anglers
who pride themselves on using light lines from shallow-draft boats.

Cargill Creek Lodge (☎ 242/368-5129) specializes in fishing adventures off
some of the most remote and sparsely populated coastlines in the country. Andros
Island's annual Bonefish Bonanza is held every October.

Note: Taking sponges or turtles from Bahamian waters is strictly prohibited. The
Ministry of Agriculture, Fisheries, and Local Government keeps a close eye on catches
of crayfish (spiny lobster), and the export of conch meat is prohibited. Stone crab
cannot be caught within two miles off Bimini or Grand Bahama.

FITNESS CLUBS   These exist mainly in the major tourist meccas of Cable Beach,
Paradise Island, and Grand Bahama Island. The best full-service gym in The Bahamas is part of the **Crystal Palace** complex (☎ 242/327-6200), adjoining the
Radisson Cable Beach Hotel. It has state-of-the-art equipment including a
Stairmaster, cardiovascular exercise equipment, whirlpool, steam room, saunas, and
free weights. On Paradise Island, the **Atlantis Paradise Island Fitness Centre**
(☎ 242/363-3000) is the finest choice.

On Grand Bahama Island, the relatively small fitness center at the **Bahamas Prin-
cess Resort and Casino** (☎ 242/352-6721) is open to both guests and nonguests.
Although it has a Universal gym, bicycles, and aerobics, the club at **Clarion Atlantik
Beach** (☎ 809/373-1444), is even better.

GOLF   Since the introduction of golf to The Bahamas in the 1930s, the islands
have lured both stars and duffers in increasing numbers. The richest pickings
areoffered on Grand Bahama Island, home to three courses that have been designated as potential PGA tour stops. The Princess Resort and Casino boasts two
challenging and spectacular courses: the Princess Ruby and the Princess Emerald,

site of The Bahamas National Open. The oldest course on Grand Bahama Island is the Lucayan Park Golf and Country Club, a heavily wooded course with elevated greens andnumerous water hazards designed for precision golf. See chapter 6, "Grand Bahama," for more information, and also refer to "The Best Golf Courses" in chapter 1.

Quality golf in The Bahamas, however, is not restricted to Grand Bahama Island. The Cable Beach Golf Club, part of the Radisson Cable Beach Hotel on New Providence, is the oldest and best-established golf course in the country, although not as good as the South Ocean Beach and Golf Resort in the secluded southern part of New Providence. The widely publicized Paradise Island Golf Club has unusual obstacles—a lion's den and a windmill—which have challenged the skill of both Gary Player and Jack Nicklaus. It also boasts the world's largest sand trap. See chapter 4, "New Providence," for more information, and also refer to "The Best Golf Courses" in chapter 1.

Golf is also available at a course in the Abacos (Treasure Cay). The design is challenging, with many panoramic water views and water obstacles.

HIKING   As mentioned in chapter 1, hiking is not a highly developed or organized sport in The Bahamas. The best hiking is on Grand Bahama Island, especially in **Lucayan National Park,** which spreads across 40 acres and is located some 20 miles from Lucaya. A large map at the entrance to the park outlines the trails. The park is riddled with trails and elevated walkways. The highlight of the park is what may be the largest underground cave system in the world, some 7 miles long. Spiral steps let you descend into an eerie underground world.

Also on Grand Bahama Island, the **Rand Memorial Nature Center** is the second-best place for hiking. It offers some 100 wooded acres that you can explore on your own or else book a guided tour at the entrance. A half mile of winding trails acquaints you with the flora and fauna that call Grand Bahama home, everything from a native boa constrictor to the Cuban emerald hummingbird, whose favorite food is the nectar of the hibiscus.

HORSEBACK RIDING   The best riding possibilities are at **Pinetree Stables** on Grand Bahama Island (☎ **242/373-3600**), which you should call for more information if you're interested. Its beach rides are especially interesting. Both trail and beach rides are offered five times a day, Tuesday through Sunday. Experienced guides will accompany you, and you're given a choice of Western, English, or Endurance saddles. Private lessons, including jumping, can also be arranged.

Virtually the only place on New Providence Island (Nassau) offering horseback riding is **Happy Trail Rides,** Cable Beach (☎ **242/362-1820**), which features both morning and afternoon trail rides and requires a reservation. These tours include transportation to and from your hotel. The trail rides are guided through the woods and along the beach.

Horseback riding is hardly a passion on the other islands.

SAILING   The Bahamas, rivaled only by the Virgin Islands and the Grenadines, is one of the most sought-after yachting destinations in the Atlantic. Its more than 700 islands and well-developed marinas provide a spectacular and practical backdrop for sailing enthusiasts. The miniarchipelago of the Abacos is called "The Sailing Capital of the World." You might think it deserves the title until you've sailed the Exumas, which are even better.

Don't be dismayed if you don't own a yacht. All sizes and types of crafts, from dinghies to blue-water cruisers, are available for charter. Crew and captain are optional.

If your dreams involve experiencing the seagoing life for only an afternoon or less, many hotels offer sight-seeing cruises aboard catamarans or glass-bottom boats, often with the opportunity to snorkel or swim in the wide open sea.

Regattas and races for both sail and power craft are held throughout the year. The Exumas host the Cruising Yacht Regatta in George Town every March and another regatta limited to boats crafted in The Bahamas in April. The Abacos host both the Green Turtle Cay Boating Fling in June and Regatta Week at Marsh Harbour in July. Also important are the Boating Fling at Port Lucaya, Freeport, scheduled in June, and the All-Eleuthera Regatta in August.

The Abacos have many marinas. The best arrangements for boating can be made at **Abaco Bahamas Charters** (☎ **800/626-5690**) and at **The Moorings** (☎ **242/367-4000**). In the Exumas it's difficult to rent boats. Most yachties arrive with their own. However, take a chance and contact **Happy People Marina** (☎ **242/355-2008**) on Staniel Cay.

SCUBA DIVING & SNORKELING   The unusual marine topography of The Bahamas offers an astonishing variety of options for snorkelers and scuba enthusiasts. Throughout the more than 700 islands, there are innumerable reefs, drop-offs, coral gardens, caves, and shipwrecks. In many locations, visitors feel like they are the first human beings ever to explore the site. Andros Island boasts the third-largest barrier reef in the world. Chub Cay in the Berry islands, and Riding Rock, San Salvador, also offer premium spots to take a plunge in an underwater world teeming with aquatic life. The intricate layout of the Exumas includes virtually every type of underwater dive site, very few of which have ever been explored. The Abacos, famous for its yachting, and the extensive reefs off the coast of Freeport are also rich sources for dive sites.

Freeport, incidentally, is home to the country's most famous and complete diving operation, **UNEXSO** (☎ **242/373-1244**). It offers an 18-foot-deep training tank, a diving museum, and the popular "Dolphin Experience," in which visitors are allowed to pet, swim, snorkel, and dive with these remarkable animals.

Since fewer than 30 of the Bahamian islands are inhabited, diving can usually occur in unspoiled and uncrowded splendor. Visitors need not be highly experienced to share in the underwater fun. Most Bahamian resorts offer diving programs for novices, usually enabling a beginner to dive with a guide after several hours of instruction. This is usually conducted either in a swimming pool, with scuba equipment, or from the edge of a beach. A license proving the successful completion of a predesignated program of scuba study is legally required for solo divers. Many resort hotels and dive shops offer the necessary training as part of a 5-day training course. Participants who successfully complete the courses are awarded PADI- or NAUI-approved licenses.

Snorkeling cruises are packaged by **Oceanic Society Expeditions,** Fort Mason Center, Building E, San Francisco, CA 94123 (☎ **800/326-7491** or 415/441-1106). In The Bahamas, research trips involving close encounters with dolphins are organized.

Jean-Michel Cousteau, son of famed oceanographer Jacques Cousteau, recently teamed up with the Out Islands of The Bahamas, American Airlines/American Eagle, and US Divers to create a snorkeling program that emphasizes marine conservation and education. **Jean-Michel Cousteau's Out Islands Snorkeling Adventures,** located in 24 resorts on 9 islands, takes visitors through Bahamian reefs for $240 a trip. The fee includes instruction, three guided tours, snorkeling gear, waterproof ID charts and reference books, and a T-shirt. They even send you a set of snorkeling gear after you've returned home. For more information, contact The Bahamas Out Island Promotion Board at ☎ **800/688-4752,** or 305/359-8099 in Miami.

TENNIS   Most tennis courts are part of large resorts and are usually free during the day for the use of registered guests. Charges are imposed to light the courts at night. Nonguests are welcome, but are charged a player's fee. Larger resorts usually offer on-site pro shops and professional instructors. Court surfaces range from clay or asphalt to such technologically advanced substances as Flexipave and Har-Tru.

New Providence, with more than 80 tennis courts, wins points for offering the greatest number of choices. At least 21 of these lie on Paradise Island. Also noteworthy are the many well-lit courts at the Radisson Cable Beach Hotel. After New Providence, **Grand Bahama** has the largest number of courts available for play—almost 40 in all. The Burger Tennis Classic is held every August at the Bahamas Princess Country Club. Within the Out Islands, tennis courts are available on Eleuthera, the Abacos, the Berry Islands, and the Exumas.

WINDSURFING   On Grand Bahama Island, the best windsurfing is offered by **Bahamas Sea Adventures** at Lucaya (☎ **242/373-3923**). Their kiosk is found on the sands in front of the Clarion Atlantik Beach Resort.

In the Cable Beach area, the best outfitter is **Sea & Ski Ocean Sports** at the Radisson Cable Beach Hotel (☎ **242/363-3370**). In the Out Islands, one of the best bets for windsurfing is the **Ramora Bay Club** on Harbour Island, Eleuthera (☎ **242/ 333-2325**).

Frankly, however, the Caribbean islands, especially Barbados, have better windsurfing than The Bahamas.

ADVENTURE TRAVEL OPERATORS

Ecosummer Expeditions is your best bet if you want to explore the pristine Exumas Land and Sea Park, which is not only the finest in The Bahamas but also surpasses anything in the Caribbean. The area consists of some 365 mostly uninhabited cays, and Ecosummer will take you there on a kayak so you can explore its white beaches and numerous reefs. Sea kayak adventures are diverted with snorkeling, beachcombing, and exploring. A 1-week trip costs $1,345, and a 2-week trip goes for $1,995. Both trips are from George Town, the capital of the Exumas. For more information, call Ecosummer Expeditions, 1516 Duranleau St., Vancouver, BC V6H 3S4 (☎ **800/465-8884** or 604/669-7741).

Another sea kayaking outfit is **Ibis Tours.** They also take you through the Exumas, at $1,020 to $1,350 for an 8-day adventure, depending on the time of year. The trips include guides, all meals, the boat, equipment (including camping gear), and waterproof bags. The kayaks come with sails to shorten travel time and to make paddling easier. To make reservations, contact Ibis Tours at 5798 Sunpoint Circle, Boynton Beach, FL 33437 (☎ **800/525-9411**).

5 Health & Insurance

STAYING HEALTHY   The Bahamas has excellent medical facilities. Physicians and surgeons in private practice are readily available in Nassau, Cable Beach, and Freeport/Lucaya. In the Out Islands, there are 13 health centers. Satellite clinics are held periodically in small settlements by health personnel, and there are 36 other clinics, making a total of 49 health facilities throughout the outlying islands. For the names and telephone numbers of specific clinics, refer to the individual island listings. If intensive or urgent care is required, patients are brought by the Emergency Flight Service to Princess Margaret Hospital in Nassau.

There is a government-operated hospital, Rand Memorial, in Freeport, plus government-operated clinics on Grand Bahama Island. Nassau and Freeport/Lucaya also have private hospitals.

Dentists are plentiful in Nassau, but somewhat less so on Grand Bahama. You'll find two dentists on Great Abaco Island, one at Marsh Harbour, another at Treasure Cay, and one on Eleuthera. Some of the remote islands, especially those in the southern Bahamas, have no dentists at all. Some of the big resort hotels have in-house physicians or can quickly secure one for you. Staffs are also knowledgeable as to where to go for dental care.

At some point during a vacation, most visitors experience some diarrhea, even those who follow the usual precautions. This is often the result of a change in diet and eating habits, not usually from bad or contaminated food and water. Mild forms of diarrhea usually pass quickly without medication. As a precaution, take along some antidiarrhea medicine, moderate your eating habits, and drink only mineral water until you recover. If symptoms persist, consult a doctor.

Vaccinations aren't required to enter The Bahamas if you're coming from a "disease-free" country such as the United States, Britain, or Canada.

Take along an adequate supply of any **prescription drugs** that you need and a written prescription that uses the generic name of the drug, not the brand name.

INSURANCE   Insurance needs for the traveler abroad fall into three categories: Health and accident, trip cancellation, and lost luggage.

First, review your present policies before traveling internationally—you may already have adequate coverage between them and what is offered by credit card companies. Many credit card companies insure their users in case of a travel accident, providing a ticket was purchased with their card. Sometimes fraternal organizations have policies that protect members in case of sickness or accidents abroad. Many homeowners' insurance policies cover theft of luggage during foreign travel and loss of documents—your airline ticket, for instance. Coverage is usually limited to about $500. To submit a claim on your insurance, remember that you'll need a police report.

Some policies (and this is the type you should have) provide advances in cash or transfers of funds so that you won't have to dip into your precious travel funds to settle medical bills.

If you've booked a charter fare, you will probably have to pay a cancellation fee if you cancel the trip suddenly, even if it is due to an unforeseen crisis. It's possible to get insurance against such a possibility. Some travel agencies provide such coverage, and often flight insurance against a canceled trip is written into tickets paid for by credit cards from such companies as Visa or American Express. Many tour operators and insurance agents provide this type of insurance.

Here are some companies offering insurance policies for travelers:

Access America, 6600 W. Broad St., P.O. Box 11188, Richmond, VA 23230 (☎ **800/284-8300,** or 804/285-3300 in the U.S.), offers a comprehensive travel-insurance and assistance package, including medical expenses, on-the-spot hospital payments, medical transportation, baggage insurance, trip-cancellation/interruption insurance, and collision-damage insurance for a car rental. Their 24-hour hot line connects you to multilingual coordinators who can offer advice and help on medical, legal, and travel problems. Varying coverage levels are available.

Wallach and Co., 107 W. Federal St., Middleburg, VA 20118-0480 (☎ **800/237-6615,** or 540/687-3166 in the U.S.), offers coverage for between 10 and 120 days at $3 per day; this policy includes accident and sickness coverage to the tune of

$100,000. Medical evacuation is also included, along with $25,000 accidental death and dismemberment compensation. Provisions for trip cancellation can also be written into this policy at a nominal cost.

Mutual of Omaha (Tele-Trip Company, Inc.), Mutual of Omaha Plaza, Omaha, NE 68175 (☎ **800/228-9792**), offers cruise and tour insurance packages priced from $39 to $59 per person for a cruise or land tour valued at $1,000. Included in these packages are travel-assistance services and financial protection against trip cancel-lation, trip interruption, bankruptcy, flight and baggage delays, baggage loss, accident and sickness, accidental death and dismemberment, missed connection, trip delays, and medical evacuation coverage. Both cruise and tour packages offer the ability to waive preexisting condition limitations. Application for insurance can be made over the phone for major credit card holders.

Travelers Insurance PAK, Travel Insured International, Inc., P.O. Box 280568, East Hartford, CT 06128 (☎ **800/243-3174** or 860/528-7663), offers illness and accident coverage costing from $10 for 6 to 10 days. For lost or damaged luggage, $500 worth of coverage costs $20 for 6 to 10 days. You can also purchase trip-cancellation insurance for $5.50 per $100 of coverage to a limit of $10,000 per person.

INSURANCE FOR BRITISH TRAVELERS   Most big travel agents offer their own insurance and will probably try to sell you their package when you book your holiday. Think before you sign. Britain's Consumers' Association recommends that you insist on seeing the policy and reading the fine print before buying travel insurance.

You should also shop around for better deals. You might contact **Columbus Travel Insurance Ltd.** (☎ **0171/375-0011** in London) or, for students, **Campus Travel** (☎ **0171/730-3402** in London). Columbus Travel will sell travel insurance only to people who have been official residents of Britain for at least a year.

6 Tips for Travelers with Special Needs

FOR TRAVELERS WITH DISABILITIES   Some 30 hotels and resorts in The Bahamas have made provisions for travelers with disabilities that allow full or limited use of the accommodations and facilities, including easy use of dining rooms, nightclubs, pool areas, and the like. Such accommodations can be found in Nassau and Cable Beach, and on Paradise Island, Grand Bahama, the Abacos, Andros, Cat Island, Eleuthera, Great Inagua, Long Island, and Spanish Wells. Some other small hotels, guest houses, and cottages have also made provisions for comfortable stays. Ask your travel agent.

You can obtain a free copy of "Air Transportation of Handicapped Persons," published by the U.S. Department of Transportation, by writing Free Advisory Circular No. AC12032, Distribution Unit, U.S. Department of Transportation, Publications Division, 3341Q 75 Ave., Landover, MD 20785, or calling ☎ **301/ 322-4961.**

For names and addresses of operators of tours specifically for people with disabilities, and other relevant information, contact the **Society for the Advancement of Travel for the Handicapped (SATH),** 347 Fifth Ave., Suite 610, New York, NY 10016 (☎ **212/447-7284;** fax 212/725-8253). Yearly membership dues in the society are $45, $25 for senior citizens and students. Send a self-addressed, stamped envelope. **SATH** will also provide you with hotel/resort accessibility for Caribbean and Bahamian destinations.

For the blind or visually impaired, the best source is the **American Foundation for the Blind,** 11 Penn Plaza, Suite 300, New York, NY 10001 (☎ **800/232-5463** or 212/502-7600), to order information kits and supplies. It acts as a referral source for travelers and can offer advice on various requirements for the transport of and border formalities for seeing-eye dogs.

One of the best organizations serving the needs of people with disabilities (wheelchairs and walkers) is **Flying Wheels Travel,** 143 W. Bridge St., P.O. Box 382, Owatonna, MN 55060 (☎ **800/535-6790** or 507/451-5005), which offers various escorted tours and cruises internationally.

For a $25 annual fee, consider joining **Mobility International USA,** P.O. Box 10767, Eugene, OR 97440 (☎ **541/343-1284** (TDD); fax 503/343-6812). It answers questions on various destinations and also offers discounts on its programs, videos, and publications. Its quarterly newsletter, *Over the Rainbow,* provides information on Bahamian hotel chains, accessibility, and transportation.

FOR GAY & LESBIAN TRAVELERS   Think twice before choosing The Bahamas. Although many gay people visit or live here, the country has very repressive antihomosexual laws. Relations between homosexuals, even if between consenting adults, are subject to criminal sanctions carrying prison terms. Sexual intercourse (either homosexual or heterosexual) in a public place (that would include a beach late at night) is punishable by up to 20 years in prison.

If you would like to make visiting gay beaches, gay bars, or gay clubs part of your vacation, consider traveling to South Miami Beach, Key West, or Puerto Rico instead.

FOR SENIORS   Many discounts are available for seniors, but be advised that you have to be a member of an association to obtain certain discounts.

For information before you go, obtain a copy of *101 Tips for the Mature Traveler,* available from **Grand Circle Travel,** 347 Congress St., Suite 3A, Boston, MA 02210 (☎ **800/221-2610,** or 617/350-7500 in the U.S.). This travel agency also offers escorted tours and cruises for seniors.

Information on travel for seniors is also available from the **National Council of Senior Citizens,** 1331 F St. NW, Washington, DC 20004 (☎ **202/347-8800**). A nonprofit organization, the council charges a membership fee of $13 per couple, for which you receive 11 issues annually of a newsletter and membership benefits, including travel services and discounts on hotels, motels, and auto rentals.

Mature Outlook, P.O. Box 10448, Des Moines, IA 50306 (☎ **800/336-6330**), is a membership program for people more than 50 years of age. Members are offered discounts at ITC-member hotels and will receive a bimonthly magazine. The annual fee of $14.95 entitles its members to free coupons for discounts at Sears. Savings are also offered on selected auto rentals and restaurants.

Golden Circle Travel, 347 Congress St., Boston, MA 02210 (☎ **800/248-3737**), offers escorted tours and cruises to The Bahamas for retired people.

Golden Companions has helped travelers 45 and older find compatible companions since 1987. The organization offers a 6-month introductory membership for $49.95. The $94 annual membership includes free mail exchange, a bimonthly newsletter, *Golden Gateways,* and get-togethers. Newsletter-only subscriptions cost $17.95 for 12 months, or $26.95 for 24 months. For a free brochure, write Golden Companions, P.O. Box 5249, Reno, NV 89513 (☎ **702/324-2227;** fax 702/324-2236). A sample newsletter costs $3.

7 Flying to The Bahamas

Nassau, followed by Freeport, is the busiest and most popular point of entry, with connections on to many of the more remote Out Islands. If you're headed for one of the Out Islands, refer to the "Getting There" section that appears at the beginning of the review of each island chain.

You face a choice of booking a seat on a regularly scheduled flight or on a charter flight, the latter being somewhat cheaper. On a regular flight, you can usually cancel or alter your flight dates without penalty; on a charter you do not have such leeway.

Flight time to Nassau from Miami is about 35 minutes; from New York, $2\frac{1}{2}$ hours; from Atlanta, 2 hours 5 minutes; from Philadelphia, 2 hours 45 minutes; from Charlotte, about 2 hours 10 minutes; from central Florida, around 1 hour 10 minutes; and from Toronto, about 3 hours.

THE MAJOR AIRLINES

From the U.S. mainland, about a half dozen carriers fly nonstop to the country's major point of entry and busiest airline hub, **Nassau International Airport.** Some also fly to the archipelago's second most populous city of Freeport. Only a handful (see below) fly directly to any of the Out Islands.

American Airlines (☎ 800/433-7300) flies to Nassau nonstop from Miami, with more than a dozen daily departures. There is no nonstop flight between New York and Nassau on American. One must fly to Miami and change planes there. American Eagle also offers about 10 daily flights between Miami and Freeport.

Delta (☎ 800/221-1212) has several connections to The Bahamas, including twice-daily nonstop flights from Atlanta. There's also a daily nonstop flight between LaGuardia airport in New York and Nassau. Delta has daily flights (nonstop) to Nassau from both Orlando and Fort Lauderdale. There are also two flights a day between Fort Lauderdale and Nassau and two flights a day between Orlando and Nassau on Comair, a partially owned subsidiary of Delta. Comair also has three flights a day between Orlando and Freeport and four daily flights between Fort Lauderdale and Freeport.

The national airline of The Bahamas, **Bahamasair** (☎ 800/222-4262), flies to The Bahamas from Miami, landing at either Nassau (with five nonstop flights daily) or Freeport (with three nonstop flights daily).

US Airways (☎ 800/428-4322) offers daily direct flights to Nassau from Philadelphia and Baltimore, with a brief stopover in Charlotte, North Carolina.

Canadians often opt for flights to The Bahamas on **Air Canada** (☎ 800/268-7240 in Canada, or 800/776-3000 in the U.S.). Flights are possible on Sunday from Toronto. There's also a Saturday flight in winter from Montréal. Air Canada is the only carrier offering scheduled service to Nassau from Canada.

British travelers opt for transatlantic passage aboard **British Airways** (☎ 0345/222111 toll-free from anywhere in the U.K.), which flies every day nonstop from London's Heathrow to Miami. Sometimes it has two flights a day. From here, a staggering number of convenient connections are available to Nassau and many other points within the archipelago on several different carriers.

FLYING TO THE OUT ISLANDS DIRECTLY FROM FLORIDA   Many frequent visitors to The Bahamas do everything they can to avoid the congestion, inconvenience, and uncertain connections of the Nassau International Airport.

U.S.–based airlines that cater to these needs include: **American Eagle,** an affiliate of American Airlines (☎ 800/433-7300), which offers frequent service from Miami's International Airport to such Out Island outposts as the Abacos, Eleuthera, and the Exumas, and **US Airways** (☎ 800/428-4322), which flies nonstop every day from Fort Lauderdale, Florida, to Eleuthera, usually making stops at both Governor's Harbour and North Eleuthera. USAirways also flies every day from West Palm Beach to the Abacos, stopping in both Treasure Cay and Marsh Harbour.

Pan Am Air Bridges (☎ 800/424-2557) operates 17-passenger amphibious aircraft that take off and land in waters near the company's port-side terminals. From the Florida mainland, nonstop flights for both Bimini and Paradise Island depart from both Miami's Watson Island Airport and Fort Lauderdale's Jet Center Airport. (The airline also offers charter flights to virtually anywhere in The Bahamas.)

CONSOLIDATORS   In their purest sense, consolidators, also known as "bucket shops," act as clearinghouses for blocks of tickets that airlines discount and consign during normally slow periods of air travel. In the case of The Bahamas, that usually means from mid-April to mid-December. Charter operators (see below) and consolidators used to perform separate functions, but many outfits perform similar functions these days.

Tickets are sometimes—but not always—priced at up to 35% less than the full fare. Terms of payment can vary—anywhere, from, say, 45 days before departure to last-minute sales offered in a final attempt by an airline to fill an empty craft. Tickets can be purchased through regular travel agents, who usually mark up the ticket 8% to 10%, maybe more, thereby greatly reducing your discount.

Consolidators abound from coast to coast. Look also for their ads in your local newspaper's travel section.

A good resource is ☎ 800/FLY-4-LESS, a nationwide airline reservation and ticketing service that specializes in finding only the lowest fares.

CHARTER FLIGHTS   Now open to the general public, charter flights offer a cheaper way to visit The Bahamas. Many major carriers offer charter flights to The Bahamas at rates that are sometimes 30% (or more) off the fare of regularly scheduled flights.

There are some drawbacks to charter flights that you need to consider. Advance booking, for example, of up to 45 days or more may be required. You could lose most of the money you've advanced if an emergency should force you to cancel a flight. However, it is now possible to take out cancellation insurance against such an event.

Unfortunately, on the charter flight you are forced to depart and return on a scheduled date. In most cases, unless you've arranged special insurance with the charter operator in advance, it will do no good to call the airline and tell them you're in the hospital with yellow fever! If you're not on the plane, you can kiss your money good-bye.

Since charter flights are so complicated, it's best to go to a good travel agent and ask him or her to explain to you the drawbacks and advantages. Sometimes charters require ground arrangements, such as the prebooking of hotel rooms.

The most visible agent for booking charter flights to The Bahamas is **Nassau/Paradise Island Express,** P.O. Box 3429, Secaucus, NJ 07096 (☎ 800/722-4262). The company contracts for the entire aircraft. No advance booking is required, and there are no restrictions on travel dates. You can stay for a day or as long as you like. Airfare can be sold alone, but about 65% of the company's ticket sales are sold in conjunction with hotel packages at New Providence, Paradise Island, and Freeport/Lucaya.

TRAVEL CLUBS   A club supplies an unsold inventory of tickets discounted in the usual range of 20% to 60%. Some of the deals involve cruise ships and complete tour packages. After you pay an annual fee to join, you are given a hotline number to call when you're planning to go somewhere. Many of these discounts become available several days in advance of an actual departure, although sometimes you have as much as a month's notice. The following are two of the best travel clubs:

Moment's Notice, 7301 New Utrecht Ave., Brooklyn, NY 11204 (☎ **718/ 234-6295**), which charges $25 per year for membership and allows spur-of-the-moment participation in dozens of tours to sunny climes. Although membership is required to participate in the tours, anyone can call the company's hotline (☎ **212/ 873-0908**) to learn what options are available. Most of the company's best-valued tours depart from the Northeast.

Travelers Advantage, 3033 South Parker Rd., Suite 900, Aurora, CO 80014 (☎ **800/TEL-TRIP**) features a 3-month trial offer for $1 and an annual membership fee of $49, and offers members-only vacation packages to some of the most popular destinations at reductions of 5% to 25%. For membership information, call ☎ **800/548-1116.**

8 Cruises

If you have about a week to spare and want to view the islands the way newcomers did in days of yore—from a water's edge view—a cruise might be for you. Except for your initial embarkation, which might be somewhat frazzled, it's slow and easy, allowing you to bypass the sometimes awkward airline connections into The Bahamas from the North American mainland.

Most cruises to The Bahamas last between 3 and 4 days—a length so short that some oft-traveled Floridians refer to them almost as commuter shuttles for escapist weekends in a foreign country. Other cruises stop at Nassau and/or one of several privately owned Bahamian islands for a day at the beach en route to Caribbean ports further south.

A brief summary of cruise lines that offer diversions in The Bahamas is outlined below, but for much more detailed information, and reviews of each of the ships spending significant time in either the Caribbean or The Bahamas, consider picking up a copy of *Frommer's Caribbean Cruises.*

Regardless of the cruise line you opt for, there's a strong possibility that your cruise will depart from the cruise capital of the world, Miami. To a somewhat lesser extent, vessels also depart for Bahamian waters from Port Everglades (adjacent to Fort Lauderdale), Port Canaveral, and in very rare instances, from New York. Because of the emergence of Florida as one of the premier touristic destinations in the world, many cruise-ship passengers combine a 3- or 4-day cruise with visits to Orlando's theme parks, Miami's South Beach, the Florida Everglades, or the Florida Keys and Key West.

How will you arrive at your port of embarkation? Virtually every line afloat offers a fly-and-cruise vacation. Terms vary widely under this arrangement. You spend a week cruising, another week staying at an interesting hotel at reduced prices, and purchase airfare from the major airport nearest your home to your port of embarkation. These total packages cost less (or should!) than if you'd purchased the air, cruise, and hotel portions of your holiday separately. If you want to keep costs at a minimum, ask for one of the smaller, inside cabins when booking space on a cruise ship. If you're the type who likes to be active all day and for most of the night, you need not pay the extra money, which can be considerable, to rent a luxurious suite. Nearly all cabins rented today have a shower and a toilet, regardless of how cramped and confining the bathroom is. If you get a midship cabin, you are less likely to experience severe rolling and pitching.

Most cruises to The Bahamas are of very short duration, rarely exceeding 3 to 4 days. Sometimes the cruise stopover includes a night in Nassau or Freeport (or one in both, depending on the cruise). If you've never been to The Bahamas, consider a cruise to Nassau, where you can also enjoy Paradise Island and Cable Beach on the same visit. It's got better shopping possibilities, better restaurants, and more entertainment than any other site in The Bahamas, including Freeport/Lucaya on Grand Bahama Island.

The best airports to use for one of these "quickie" trips to The Bahamas from Florida are Orlando (for traffic heading to Port Canaveral), Fort Lauderdale (for cruise departures from Port Everglades), and, of course, Miami for departures from the Port of Miami.

Because getting around Freeport/Lucaya or Nassau is relatively easy, and the official shore excursions are dull and sometimes restrictive, it's best to decide what you want to do and then pursue that activity yourself, be it shopping, swimming, snorkeling, or gambling. Water sports are also a major draw and you may wish to join in the fun. See chapter 4 for more details about sports in Nassau, or chapter 6 for information about sports in Freeport/Lucaya.

In Nassau, cruise ships anchor at a trio of piers along Prince George's Wharf. Taxi drivers meet all arrivals and for around $2.50 will transport you into the heart of Nassau, center of most shopping and sightseeing activities. Duty-free shops also lie just outside the dock area, but for that, you'd do better going inside the city's commercial and historic core.

As you disembark, you'll find a tourist information office in a tall pink tower, where you can pick up maps of New Providence Island or of Nassau itself. Free 1-hour walking tours are conducted from here if you'd like an overview of the city, with a guide pointing out historic monuments. Outside this office, an ATM will hook you in with U.S. dollars if your cash is running low and your PIN number is in order.

Here's a rundown of some major cruise lines serving The Bahamas. Most of them, along with the bulk of visitors to The Bahamas, focus either on Nassau or Freeport (or maybe both).

American Canadian Caribbean (☎ **800/556-7450** or 401/247-0955) is an innovative, Rhode Island–based cruise outfit whose shallow-draft, small-scale coastal cruisers have been studied with almost obsessional interest by most of their competitors. They embark on 7- to 12-day excursions through complicated shoals, near Bahamian landmasses where larger ships cannot go. Other territories covered by this no-frills, aggressively unpretentious line include the Panama Canal and the coasts of Central America. The company has been recognized for the quality of its ecological and historical tours by both the National Geographic Society and the Library of Congress. Designed with a shallow draft of only 6 feet, the company's small-scale cruise ships can accommodate 78 to 92 passengers and can land on isolated shorelines without the pier and wharf facilities required for the disembarkation of larger cruise ships. Thanks to a specially designed 40-foot bow ramp, passengers can disembark directly onto the sands of some of the most obscure but pristine islands in The Bahamas—places that you would otherwise have to charter a private yacht to reach.

Cape Canaveral Cruise Line (☎ **800/910-SHIP**). Its only ship, a battered but serviceable survivor of many different owners, is a pro at carrying hard-partying passengers from Cape Canaveral to Nassau for 2-day, 2-night quickie vacations. Don't expect sophisticated amenities and lavish entertainment aboard this line, but in view of the short transit time, and the emphasis most passengers place on visiting the attractions of Nassau, no one seems to mind. Plus, the price of a 2-day Bahamian cruise is about equivalent to what you might have spent partying, drinking, and dining at a series of land-based resorts on the Florida mainland.

Carnival Cruise Line (☎ 800/438-6744 or 305/599-2600) is the boldest, brashest, and most successful mass-market cruise line in the world. However, its major drawback is a somewhat generic, mass-produced cuisine. There's little relief from the gambling, the glitz, and the crowds so if you're the type who likes to retreat to a cozy nook and cranny from time to time, this might not be your cup of rum.

Carnival's best bet for The Bahamas is aboard the *Ecstasy*, a vessel that's been likened to a "Las Vegas at sea." It sails year-round on 3-day loops departing from Miami on Friday and calling at Nassau. The ship is very similar to another Carnival ship, *Fantasy*, which also sails on 3-day loops to Nassau, but departs throughout the year from Port Canaveral. The average on-board age is a relatively youthful 42, although ages range from 3 to 95.

Celebrity Cruises (☎ 800/437-3111 or 305/262-8322) maintains five newly built, medium- to large-sized ships offering cruises of between 7 and 17 nights. The focus of its cruises is on jaunts to such ports as Key West, San Juan, Grand Cayman, Ocho Rios, Antigua, St. Thomas, and Curacao, among others, although in some cases, stopovers at Nassau are thrown in, as well. The niche this line has created is unpretentious but classy, several notches above mass-market, but with pricing that's nonetheless relatively competitive. Accommodations are roomy and well-equipped, and the cuisine is among the best of any of the cruise lines.

Costa Cruise Lines (☎ 800/462-6782 or 305/358-7325), the U.S.–based branch of a cruise line that has thrived in Italy for about a century, maintains hefty to megasized vessels that are newer than those of many other lines afloat. Two of these offer virtually identical jaunts through the western and eastern Caribbean on alternate weeks, departing from Fort Lauderdale. Ports of call during the eastern Caribbean itineraries of both vessels include stopovers in Nassau, as well as in such other ports as St. Thomas, San Juan, and Serena Cay—a private island known for its beaches off the coast of the Dominican Republic. There's an Italian flavor and lots of Italian design on board here, as well as an atmosphere of relaxed indulgence. The ships—*Costa Romantica* and *Costa Victoria*—feature tame versions of ancient Roman Bacchanalia, as well as such celebrations as *Festa Italiana*, and focaccia and pizza parties by the pool.

Disney Cruise Line (☎ 407/566-7000). At this writing, Disney megaships were still being built, with an anticipated launching sometime in 1998. Permeated with a sense of the whimsy and fantasy that propelled Disney into one of the world's biggest entertainment empires, ships will be big, state-of-the-art vessels with lots of Disney razzle-dazzle. Expect lots of Mickey and Minnie Mouse hoopla, a high percentage of parents and grandparents accompanied by their children and grandchildren, and mega-spending on advertising and promotion. Itineraries will begin and end in Port Canaveral, last between 3 and 4 days, and include visits to Nassau and Castaway Cay. The latter of these is a fabulously expensive, privately owned Bahamian island that Disney has upgraded into a state-of-the-art, palm-fringed icon to the power of myth and fantasy.

Dolphin Cruise Lines (☎ 800/222-1003 or 305/358-5122). Its trio of ships base their success on low-cost, relatively unglittery cruises within much-renovated older vessels with somewhat outmoded amenities that are anything but cutting edge.

Nothing is particularly fancy, but no one seems to mind in view of the good values. Cruise bargain-hunters, retirees on a budget, and families with sometimes boisterous children often make up the passenger list. One of the line's ships, *OceanBreeze,* maintains a year-round roster of 3- and 4-day cruises to The Bahamas from either Miami or Fort Lauderdale. Stopovers include Nassau and a small, sandy hideaway that the line refers to as Blue Lagoon.

Holland America Line-Westours (☎ 800/426-0327 or 206/281-3535). This is the most high-toned of the mass-market cruise lines, with eight respectably hefty and good-looking ships. Throughout the winter, three of these vessels include daylong stopovers in Nassau as part of visits of 7 days or more to such mainstream Caribbean ports as San Juan, St. Thomas, St. Maarten, and St. Lucia. They usually offer solid value, with very few jolts or surprises, and an overall sense of squeaky-clean thrift and value. Expect a staid, well-grounded clientele of mature travelers on board who expect (and get) return for their dollar. Late-night revelers and serious party people might want to book cruises on other lines such as Carnival.

Majesty Cruise Line (☎ 800/532-7788 or 305/530-8900). This is a company whose U.S. port of embarkation is almost always Miami and whose one ship (the *Royal Majesty*) was specifically built in 1992 for continuous 3- or 4-day circuits whose outer limits are usually Nassau, Key West, and the coastal resorts of Mexico. About two-thirds of the passengers are from Florida, mostly couples in the 38 to 58 age bracket. Although lots of liquor might be consumed on board, partly as a revenue-raising device, Majesty doesn't officially designate itself as a "party boat." Consequently the atmosphere might teeter between relatively calm and raucous, depending on whoever happens to be on board at the time of your sailing. Despite signs that some of its polish might be wearing off, it's still one of the most stylish choices for a quickie Bahamian vacation. Its strongest points include good value—especially during seasonal promotions—and its expertise in the 3- to 4-day cruise market from the Port of Miami.

In spite of the ship's many strong points, such as its modern design and easy passenger flow, it suffers from a lackluster cuisine and slow service in the dining room.

One note: The *Royal Majesty* is definitely not for smokers. It is, in fact, the least smoker-friendly vessel afloat. The ship became the first major cruise line to feature a nonsmoking dining room. One-fourth of the cabins are designated smoke free. If that weren't enough of a blow to the tobacco industry, *Royal Majesty* even offers on-board "Kick the Habit" seminars.

The ship does not offer first-rate evening entertainment, and you may want to toddle off to bed long before the show is over. The ship tends not to attract the serious party crowd, or those who like to stay up until 2am. If you're into serious beer drinking, and having a rowdy and raucous night at sea, you might prefer a Carnival cruise instead.

Norwegian Cruise Line (☎ 800/327-7030 or 305/445-0866) appeals to all ages and income levels. One of the company's five ships (the small-scale and relatively informal *Leeward*) specializes in 3- and 4-day circuits from Miami that call on either Nassau or Key West, with additional stopovers at NCL's private Bahamian island, Great Stirrup Cay. When full, the ship can seem very crowded, with only four elevators accommodating as many as 950 passengers. Because of its relatively small size, the ship can rock and roll, causing seasickness in some passengers. On the plus side, it's well-conceived for its short cruises, appealing to a wide variety of passengers. Because of its emphasis on sports, it attracts a lot of men in the 24 to 45 age bracket. Activities are routine, but adequate enough for short-time cruises. Dining is not a major reason to sail. NCL's largest ship and corporate symbol (the *Norway*) offers better amenities and services, but features only one Bahamian stopover, the above-mentioned beach island of Great Stirrup Cay. Between ports of call, the line administers a snappy array of on-board activities and party themes.

Premier Cruise Lines (☎ **800/473-3262** or **407/783-5061**), also known as The Big Red Boats, appeals to first-time family cruisers, a growing market that will soon be influenced by the arrival of the Disney megavessels in 1998. Itineraries are quite simple. For the 3-night cruise, *Atlantic* leaves Port Canaveral on Thursday at 5:30pm, spending Friday at Nassau from 10am until 6pm when it sails to Port Lucaya, where it remains from 8am to 6pm Saturday. It then returns to Port Canaveral at 7am on Sunday. For the 4-night cruise, the ship leaves Port Canaveral Sunday at 5:30pm, spends Monday at sea, visits Nassau on Tuesday from 9am until 6pm, then sails for Port Lucaya where it spends Wednesday (from 8am to 6pm). From here, it returns to Port Canaveral, arriving at 7am on Thursday. *Oceanic* does an almost exact replica of the same program, leaving on Friday for the 3-night cruise and on Monday for its 4-night cruise, but with slight variations in its arrival times.

Premier's greatest challenge as a family cruiser will come in 1998 when Disney Cruise Lines, also operating out of Port Canaveral, launches its new ship that will carry 2,400-plus passengers with considerably more razzmatazz than aboard those of Premier.

The Premier Cruise Line package is ideal for family vacations. Its land-sea packages, tied in with a visit to Disney World at Orlando, offer superb values.

There are drawbacks, however. The ships are in their 30s, so no matter how much maintenance is done, the antiquity shows. Although the catered cuisine is good— typical family fare for mid-America—the worst single item is the noise while dining.

Premier tries to create something to entertain everyone, as most mass-market ships do. This is a special challenge, as the passenger list has ranged in age from 2 to 102.

Royal Caribbean Cruise Line (☎ **305/539-6000**) leads the industry in the development of megaships. Most of this company's dozen or so vessels weigh in at around 73,000 tons, are among the largest of any line afloat, and represent a roster of floating hardware that's more impressive than that belonging to many national navies. Marketed as a mainstream, mass-market venue whose components have been fine-tuned through endless repetition, the line encourages a house-party theme that's somehow a bit less frenetic than that found aboard the megaships of some other cruise lines. The company is well-run, and there are enough on-board activities to suit virtually any taste and age level. Though accommodations and accoutrements are more than adequate, they are not upscale, and cabins aboard some of the line's older vessels tend to be a bit more cramped than the industry norm. RCCL deploys one of its most photographed, most publicized ships, *Sovereign of the Seas* (year-round) and its smaller and less legendary *Nordic Empress* (June to August only) for 3- and 4-night cruises to The Bahamas. The 4-night cruises depart from Miami, calling at Nassau, Key West, and a private Bahamian island, Coco Cay, that RCCL has loaded with facilities for beach barbecues and water sports. Three-night loops call at Nassau and Coco Cay, without a visit to Key West.

9 Chartering a Boat

For those who can afford it, this is one of the most luxurious ways to see The Bahamas. On your private boat, you can island-hop at your convenience. Well-equipped marinas are on every major island and many cays. There are designated ports of entry at Great Abaco (Marsh Harbor), Andros, the Berry Islands, Bimini, Cat Cay, Eleuthera, Great Exuma, Grand Bahama Island (Freeport/Lucaya), Great Inagua, New Providence (Nassau), Ragged Island, and San Salvador.

Vessels must check with Customs at the first port of entry and receive a cruising clearance permit to The Bahamas. Carry it with you and return it at the official port of departure.

You should buy *The Yachtsman's Guide to The Bahamas,* which is available from Tropic Isle Publishers. Edited by Meredith H. Fields, this is the only guide covering the entire Bahamas and Turks and Caicos Islands. Copies of the book are available at major marine outlets and bookstores, and by mail direct from the publisher for $34.95, U.S. postpaid: **Tropic Isle Publishers, Inc.,** P.O. Box 610938, North Miami, FL 33261-0938 (☎ **305/893-4277**).

Experienced sailors and navigators, with a sea-wise crew, can charter "bareboat," a term meaning a rental with a fully equipped boat but with no captain or crew. You're on your own, and you'll have to prove you can handle it before you're allowed to take out such a craft. Even if you're your own skipper, you may want to take along an experienced yachtsperson familiar with local waters, which may be tricky in some places.

Four to 12 people often charter yachts varying from 50 to more than 100 feet and split the cost. The Bahamas, as will be pointed out many times, offer some of the most beautiful and romantic cruising grounds in the world, especially around such island chains as the Exumas, the Abacos, and Eleuthera.

Most yachts are rented on a weekly basis, with a fully stocked bar, plus equipment for fishing and water sports. People taking bareboat charters can save money and select menus more suited to their tastes by doing their own provisioning.

Sunsail, 980 Awald Rd., Annapolis, MD 21403 (☎ **800/327-2276**), specializes in yacht chartering from one of its bases in Marsh Harbour, Great Abaco, The Bahamas. Bareboat and crewed yachts between 32 and 56 feet are available from a well-maintained fleet of sailing craft. The charter manager suggests that a 3-month advance reservation (which requires a 25% deposit of the total rental fee) is a good idea for locked-in dates. Clients whose schedules are more flexible usually need only reserve about a month ahead of time. Insurance and full equipment will be included in the rates.

10 Package Tours

If you want everything done for you, and want to save money as well, consider traveling on a package tour. General tours appealing to the average traveler are commonly offered, but many of the tours have a special focus—tennis, golf, scuba, or whatever. The costs of airplane fare, a hotel room, food (sometimes), and sightseeing (sometimes) are combined in one package, neatly tied up with a single price tag. Transfers between your hotel and the airport are often included. Many packages carry several options, including the possibility of low-cost car rentals.

There are disadvantages, too. First, you generally have to pay the cost of the total package in advance. Then, you may find yourself in a hotel you dislike immensely, yet you are virtually trapped there. The single traveler, regrettably, usually suffers, too, since nearly all tour packages are based on double occupancy.

Also, we find that many package deals to The Bahamas contain more hidden extras than they should. The list of "free" offerings sometimes sounds better than it is. Forget about that free rum punch at the manager's cocktail party, and peruse the fine print to see if your deal includes meals and other costly items.

Choosing the right tour can be a bit of a problem. It's best to go to a travel agent, tell him or her what island (or islands) you'd like to visit, and see what's currently offered.

Also, consider hiring the services of **TourScan, Inc.,** P.O. Box 2367, Darien, CT 06820 (☎ **800/962-2080** or 203/655-8091). TourScan researches the best value vacation at each hotel and condo. Two catalogs are printed each year. Each lists a broad choice of hotels on most of the islands of The Bahamas, in all price ranges. Catalogs cost $4 each, the price of which is credited to any TourScan vacation. Prices are based on travel from New York, Newark, Baltimore, Philadelphia, and Washington, D.C., although the company will arrange trips originating from any location in the United States or abroad on request.

Another good deal might be a combined land-and-air package offered by one of the major U.S. carriers. Call **American Fly-Away Vacations** (☎ 800/321-2121); **Delta's Dream Vacations** (☎ 800/872-7786); **TWA Getaway Vacations** (☎ 800/ GETAWAY); and **United Airlines Vacations** (☎ 800/328-6877).

Horizon Tours, 1010 Vermont Ave. NW, Suite 202, Washington, DC 20005 (☎ **888/SUN-N-SAND** or 202/393-8390), specializes in all-inclusive resorts on the islands of The Bahamas, Jamaica, Aruba, St. Lucia, and Antigua.

Club Med, Club Med Sales, P.O. Box 4460, Scottsdale, AZ 85258 (☎ **800/ 258-2633**), has various all-inclusive options throughout the Caribbean and The Bahamas.

Advertising more packages to The Bahamas and the Caribbean than any other agency is **Liberty Travel,** with offices in many states. One base is 4397 N. State Rd. 7, Lauderdale Lakes, FL 33319 (☎ **954/486-2020**).

Frontiers International, 305 Logan Rd. (P.O. Box 959), Wexford, PA 15090 (☎ **800/245-1950,** or 412/935-1577 in Pennsylvania), features fly-and-spin fishing tours of The Bahamas and is a specialist in saltwater-fishing destinations.

FOR BRITISH TRAVELERS   Package tours to The Bahamas can be booked through **Harlequin Worldwide Connoisseurs Caribbean Collection,** 2 North Rd., South Ockendon, Essex RM15 6QJ (☎ **01708/852-780**). This agency offers both air and hotel packages not only to Nassau, but to most of the Out Islands. The company also specializes in scuba diving and golf holidays. Another specialist is **Kuoni Travel,** Kuoni House, Dorking, Surrey RH5 4AZ (☎ **01306/742-222**), offering both land and air packages to The Bahamas, including such destinations as Nassau and Freeport, and also to some places in the Out Islands. They also offer packages for self-catering villas on Paradise Island.

11 Getting Around

If your final destination is Paradise Island, Freeport, or Nassau (Cable Beach), and you plan to fly here, you'll have little trouble in reaching your destination. However, if you're heading for one of the Out Islands, you face more exotic choices, not only of airplanes but also of other means of transport, including a mail boat, the traditional connecting link in days of yore.

As mentioned, each section on one of the Out Island chains has specific transportation information, but in the meantime, we'll give you a general overview.

BY PLANE

The national airline of The Bahamas, **Bahamasair** (☎ **800/222-4262**), serves 19 airports on 12 Bahamian islands, including Abaco, Andros, Cat Island, Eleuthera, Long Island, and San Salvador. Many of the Out Islands have either airports or airstrips, or are within a short ferry ride's distance of one.

BY MAIL BOAT

Before the advent of better airline connections, the traditional way of exploring the Out Islands—in fact, about the only way unless you had your own craft—was by mail boat. This 125-year-old service is still available, but it's recommended only for those who have unlimited time and a sense of adventure. You may ride with cases of rum, oil drums, crawfish pots, live chickens, even an occasional piano.

The boats, 19 of them comprising the "Post Office Navy," under the direction of the Bahamian Chief of Transportation, are often fancifully colored, high sided, and somewhat clumsy in appearance, but the little motor vessels chug along, serving the 30 inhabited islands of The Bahamas. Schedules can be thrown off by weather and other causes, but most morning mail boats depart from Potter's Cay (under the Paradise Island Bridge in Nassau) or from Prince George Wharf. The voyages last from 4^1/$_2$ hours to most of a day, sometimes even overnight. Check the schedule of the particular boat you wish to travel on with the skipper at the dock in Nassau.

Tariffs charged on the mail boats are considerably less than for air travel. Many of the boats offer two classes of passenger accommodations, first and second. In first class you get a bunk bed; in second you may be entitled only to deck space. Actually, the bunk beds are usually reserved for the seasick, but first-class passengers sit in a fairly comfortable enclosed cabin, at least on the larger boats.

For information about mail boats to the Out Islands, contact the **Dockmasters Office** in Nassau, under the Paradise Island Bridge on Potter's Cay (☎ **242/ 393-1064**).

BY TAXI

Taxis are plentiful in the Nassau/Cable Beach/Paradise Island area and in the Freeport/Lucaya area on Grand Bahama Island. These cabs, for the most part, are metered. See "Getting Around" in the section on each island.

In the Out Islands, however, you will not be so richly blessed. In general, taxi service is available at all air terminals, at least if those air terminals are of the status of "port of entry" terminals. They are also available in the vicinity of most marinas.

Taxis are usually shared, often with the local residents. Out Island taxis aren't metered, so you must negotiate the fare before you get in. Cars are often old and badly maintained, so be prepared for a bumpy ride over some rough roads if you've selected a particularly remote hotel.

BY CAR

RENTALS   Some judicious research may reveal that renting a car is less expensive than you might think, especially if you consider the high cost of transportation by taxi or the inconvenience of traveling by bus. Blithe spirits will also appreciate the freedom of reaching that out-of-the-way beach or secluded cove.

Of all the locations in The Bahamas, the airports at Nassau (New Providence Island) and Freeport (Grand Bahama Island) have the most North American car-rental companies. Of course, they compete with a handful of local car-rental companies, some of which may charge a few dollars less.

Most readers prefer to do business with one of the major firms, since they offer toll-free reservation services and, generally, better-maintained vehicles.

Reserving a car in Nassau or Freeport is just a matter of making a toll-free phone call in advance from wherever you live. Renting a car in the Out Islands, however, may be more difficult. If you plan to remain near your hotel, you'll probably be better off just using taxis.

Each of the major firms quotes an unlimited-mileage rate, which varies slightly with the time of year. Each company's system is slightly different, although after the first week the per-day rate is less expensive than the daily rate for rentals of less than a week. Of course, there are extra charges, which the fine print of a rental contract will reveal. These sometimes include a small refueling service charge, which applies if the renter returns the car with less fuel than when he or she originally rented it. More important, a renter is able to arrange additional insurance in the form of a *collision damage waiver* (CDW). Without the waiver, depending on the company, a renter is liable for the first several hundred dollars' worth of damage to the car in the event of an accident. If the waiver is purchased, the driver waives all financial responsibility in the event of an accident. The amount of liability varies from company to company. If in doubt, we suggest you purchase the waiver. Some credit card companies offer their cardholders free rental-car insurance if the driver uses the credit card to pay for the rental and declines the rental agency's CDW; check with your credit card company to find out the extent of coverage and if coverage is offered when renting in the Bahamas.

Each company has a different age limit for its drivers. All require a minimum age varying from 21 to 25, and some won't rent a car to anyone over 70. Underage drivers can sometimes rent from an agency upon payment of a substantial cash (not credit card) deposit. Of course, a valid driver's license must be presented when the rental contract is issued.

For more information about rentals in Nassau or Freeport, you can call the international departments of **Budget Rent-a-Car** (☎ 800/472-3325), **Hertz** (☎ 800/654-3001), and **Avis** (☎ 800/331-2112). Budget rents only in Nassau.

If you'd like to deal with local agencies, call **Star Rent-a-Car** (☎ 242/352-5953) at the airport on Grand Bahama Island (Freeport/Lucaya). On New Providence Island (Nassau/Cable Beach), call **McCartney** (☎ 242/328-0486) or **Teglo** (☎ 809/362-4361).

GASOLINE "Petrol" is easily available in Nassau and Freeport. In the Out Islands, where the cost of gasoline is likely to vary from island to island, you should plan your itinerary based on where you'll be able to get fuel. The major towns of the islands have service stations. You should have no problems on New Providence or Grand Bahama Island unless you start out with a nearly empty tank.

DRIVING REQUIREMENTS A visitor may drive on his or her home driver's license for up to 3 months. Longer stays require a Bahamian driver's license. Insurance against injury or death liability is compulsory.

A word of warning: British tradition lives on in The Bahamas. You must drive on the left!

ROAD MAPS As you emerge at one of the major airports, including those of Nassau (New Providence) and Freeport (Grand Bahama Island), you can pick up island maps that are quite sufficient for routine touring around those islands. However, if you plan to do extensive touring in the Out Islands, you should go first to a bookstore ineither Nassau or Freeport and ask for a copy of *Atlas of The Bahamas,* sponsored by the Ministry of Education in Nassau. It provides touring routes (outlined in red) through all the major Out Islands. Once you arrive on these remote islands, it may be hard to obtain maps.

BREAKDOWNS/ASSISTANCE There are no emergency numbers to call. Before setting out in a rented car, ask the rental company what number you should call in case of a breakdown. Usually it's the car-rental firm itself, which will send someone to help you.

HITCHHIKING

Though technically illegal, this is a commonplace method of travel, particularly in the Out Islands, where there is a scarcity of vehicles. It's a less desirable practice in Nassau, Cable Beach, and Freeport/Lucaya, and it's unheard of on Paradise Island. Please know in advance that *Frommer's Bahamas* does not endorse hitchhiking, not only in the islands but anywhere else in the world. It's too risky these days.

12 Tips on Accommodations

The Bahamas offer a wide selection of accommodations, ranging from small private guest houses to large luxury resorts. Hotels vary in size and facilities, from deluxe (offering room service, sports, swimming pools, entertainment, etc.) to fairly simple hostelries.

There are package deals galore, and though they have many disadvantages, they are always cheaper than "rack rates." (A rack rate is what an individual pays who literally walks in from the street.) Therefore, it's always good to go to a reliable travel agent to find out what, if anything, is available in the way of a land-and-air package before booking into a particular accommodation.

There is no rigid classification of hotel properties in the islands. The word *deluxe* is often used—or misused—when *first class* might have been a more appropriate term. First class itself often isn't. For that and other reasons, we've presented fairly detailed descriptions of the properties, so that you'll get an idea of what to expect once you're here. However, even in the deluxe and first-class resorts and hotels, don't expect top-rate service and efficiency. "Things," as they are called in the islands, don't seem to work as well here as they do in certain fancy resorts of California, Florida, or Europe. Life here has its disadvantages. When you go to turn on the shower, sometimes you get water and sometimes you don't. You may even experience power failures.

Facilities often determine the choice of a hotel, and regardless of your particular interest, there is probably a hotel for you. All the big first-class resort hotels have swimming pools. Usually a beach is nearby if not directly in front of the hotel property. If you want to save money, you can book into one of the more moderate accommodations less desirably located. Then, often for only a small fee, you can use the facilities of the larger and more expensive resorts. However, don't try to "crash" a resort. It's better to be a paying customer. Often if you have lunch or patronize the bar, you can stick around and enjoy the afternoon. Policies vary from resort to resort: Some are stricter than others.

The **winter season** in The Bahamas runs roughly from the middle of December to the middle of April, and hotels charge their highest prices during this peak period. Winter is generally the dry season in the islands, but there can be heavy rainfall regardless of the time of year.

What the Symbols Mean

AP (American Plan): Includes three meals a day (sometimes called full board or full pension).

EP (European Plan): This rate is always cheapest, as it offers only the room—no meals.

MAP (Modified American Plan): Sometimes called half board or half pension, this room rate includes breakfast and dinner (or lunch if you prefer).

Getting Married in The Bahamas

You might prefer a wedding beneath a palm tree instead of a snowbound setting in your hometown. If that's the case, a bevy of islanders can assist you with the legalities. Any large resort in The Bahamas, as well as the Ministry of Tourism's People-to-People program, will help you arrange the details. Contact the Ministry of Tourism at P.O. Box N-3701, Nassau, The Bahamas.

Here's what's required: Both of you must be in The Bahamas at the moment you apply for your wedding license, the price of which is $40. If both of you are single and U.S. citizens, you must obtain an affidavit to that effect from the U.S. embassy in Nassau. The price of this is $10 and will require presentation of proof of identity, such as a passport. If it's applicable, you'll also need to show proof of divorce. Request a waiver of the 15-day residency requirement from the Registrar General, P.O. Box N-532, Nassau, The Bahamas. This waiver will almost always be granted. If all of the above-mentioned requirements are met, you can be married anytime after the third day of your arrival in The Bahamas. No blood test is necessary.

Once you're hitched, a wide array of hotels will present themselves as suitable settings for your honeymoon. The most alluring of these will offer an array of honeymoon packages with various types of money-saving options. For a list of the best honeymoon resorts in The Bahamas, refer to chapter 1.

During the winter months, make reservations 2 months in advance if you can, and if you rely on writing directly to the hotels, know that the mail service is unreliable and takes a long time. At certain hotels it's almost impossible to secure accommodations at Christmas or in February. Again, instead of writing or faxing to reserve your own room, it's better to book through a stateside representative.

The **off-season** in The Bahamas—roughly from mid-April to mid-December (although this varies from hotel to hotel)—amounts to a sale. In most cases, hotel rates are slashed a startling *20%* to *60%*. It's a bonanza for cost-conscious travelers, especially for families who can travel in the summer. Perhaps people think that The Bahamas is a caldron. This is not the case. The fabled Bahamian weather is balmy all year. The mid-80s prevail throughout most of the region, and trade winds make for comfortable days and nights, even in cheaper places that don't have air-conditioning. Truth is, you're better off in The Bahamas than suffering through a roaring August heat wave in Chicago or New York.

THE BAHAMIAN GUEST HOUSE

The guest house is where many Bahamians themselves stay when they're traveling in their own islands. In The Bahamas, however, and to a very limited extent in the Turks and Caicos Islands, the term "guest house" can mean anything. Sometimes so-called guest houses are really like simple motels built around swimming pools. Others are small individual cottages, with their own kitchenettes, constructed around a main building in which you'll often find a bar and restaurant serving local food.

In the Out Islands of The Bahamas, the guest houses are not as luxurious for the most part as those of Bermuda. Although bereft of frills in general, the Bahamian guest houses we've recommended are clean, decent, and safe for families or single women. Many of these guest houses are very basic. Salt spray on metal or fabric takes a serious toll, and chipped paint is commonplace. Bathrooms can fall into the vintage category, and sometimes the water isn't heated—but when it's 85° to 92°F outside, you don't need hot water.

On the other hand, some of these establishments are quite comfortable. Some are almost luxurious; and in addition to giving you the opportunity to live with a local family, they boast swimming pools, private baths in all rooms, and air-conditioning.

ALL-INCLUSIVE PROPERTIES

Increasingly popular in such islands as Jamaica, the all-inclusive resort hotel concept has not yet fully invaded The Bahamas, although there are some. Many people like this concept since they generally know what their final bill will be. At most resorts, everything is included, even drinks in many cases. You get your room and all meals, and many water sports, although some cost extra. Entertainment is also free. Some people find the cost of this all-inclusive holiday cheaper than if they'd paid individually for each item.

The first all-inclusive concept in The Bahamas was launched by **Club Med** (☎ **800/258-2633**) at its property on Paradise Island. This is not a swinging singles kind of place; it's popular with everybody from honeymooners to families with kids along. There's another mammoth Club Med at Governor's Harbour on Eleuthera. Families with kids like it a lot here, and the resort also attracts scuba divers.

The biggest all-inclusive of them all, **Sandals** (☎ **800/SANDALS**), came to The Bahamas in 1995, taking over the once rather exclusive Le Meridien Royal Bahamian on Cable Beach. This Jamaican company is now walking its sandals across the Caribbean, having established firm beachheads in Ocho Rios, Montego Bay, and Negril. The most famous of the all-inclusives (but not necessarily the best), it caters only to male-female couples, having long ago rescinded its initial policy of "Any two people in love."

RENTAL VILLAS & VACATION HOMES

You might rent a big villa, a good-sized apartment in someone's condo, or even a small beach cottage (more accurately called a *cabana*).

Private apartments are also available, with or without maid service. This is more of a no-frills option than the villas and condos. The apartments may not be in buildings with swimming pools, and they may not have a front desk to help you.

Cottages, or cabanas, offer the most freewheeling lifestyle available in these categories of vacation homes. Many ideally open onto a beach, although others may be clustered around a communal swimming pool. Most of them are fairly simple, containing no more than a plain bedroom plus a small kitchen and bath. In the peak winter season, reservations should be made at least 5 or 6 months in advance.

VHR, Worldwide, 235 Kensington Ave., Norwood, NJ 07648 (☎ **800/ 633-3284** or 201/767-9393), offers the most comprehensive portfolio of luxury villas, condominiums, resort suites, and apartments for rent not only in The Bahamas, but also in the Caribbean, Mexico, the United States, and Europe.

Hideaways International, 767 Islington St., Portsmouth, NH 03801 (☎ **800/ 843-4433** in the U.S., or 603/430-4433), publishes *Hideaways Guide,* a 148-page pictorial directory of home rentals throughout the world, with full descriptions so you know what you're renting. Rentals range from cottages to staffed villas to whole islands! On most rentals you deal directly with owners. At condos and small resorts, Hideaways offers member discounts. Other services include specialty cruises, yacht charters, airline ticketing, car rentals, and hotel reservations. Annual membership is $99; a 4-month trial membership is $39.

Rent-a-Home International, 7200 34th Ave. NW, Seattle, WA 98117 (☎ **206/ 789-9377**), specializes in condos and villas. It arranges weekly or longer bookings.

Sometimes local tourist offices will also advise you on vacation-home rentals if you write or call them directly.

FAST FACTS: The Bahamas

American Express   Representing American Express in The Bahamas are Playtours, Shirley Street, between Charlotte and Parliament streets, Nassau (☎ **242/ 322-2931**), and Mundytours, Building 4 Regent Centre, Suite 20, Freeport (☎ **242/352-6641**). At either of these offices you can receive customer service and travel and tour arrangements. Hours are 9am to 5pm Monday through Friday. Traveler's checks are issued upon presentation of a personal check and an American Express card.

Business Hours   In Nassau, Cable Beach, and Freeport/Lucaya, commercial banking hours are 9:30am to 3pm Monday through Thursday, 9:30am to 5pm on Friday. Hours are likely to vary widely in the Out Islands. Ask at your hotel. Most government offices are open Monday through Friday from 9am to 5pm. Most shops are open Monday through Saturday from 9am to 5pm.

Camera & Film   Purchasing film in Nassau/Paradise Island or Freeport/Lucaya is relatively easy. But stock up if you're going to some of the remote Out Islands and need a special kind of film.

Car Rentals   See "Getting Around" in this chapter.

Climate   See "When to Go" in this chapter.

Crime   See "Safety," below.

Currency   See "Money" in this chapter.

Customs   To go through Bahamian Customs, you only need to make an oral baggage declaration, unless you're bringing in something on which duty must be paid. However, your baggage is subject to Customs inspection. Each adult visitor coming into The Bahamas is allowed 50 cigars, 200 cigarettes, or 1 pound of tobacco; 1 quart of spirits; and personal effects, articles that have been in the possession of the visitor before arrival.

The Bahamian government has enacted strict laws regarding possession of dangerous drugs or firearms. Penalties for infractions are severe. Special authorization is necessary to bring firearms into The Bahamas, and licenses are required.

For more information on Customs once you return home, refer to "Visitor Information & Entry Requirements" in this chapter.

Documents Required   See "Visitor Information & Entry Requirements" in this chapter.

Driving Rules   See "Getting Around" in this chapter.

Drug Laws   Importation of, possession of, or dealing in unlawful drugs, including marijuana, is a serious offense in The Bahamas, with heavy penalties. Customs officers, at their discretion, may conduct body searches for drugs or other contraband goods.

Drugstores   Nassau and Freeport are amply supplied with pharmacies (see individual island listings). However, if you're traveling in the Out Islands, it is always best to carry your prescribed medication with you.

Electricity   Electricity is normally 120 volts, 60 cycles, AC. American appliances are fully compatible; British or European appliances will need both converters and adapters.

Embassies & Consulates   The U.S. embassy is on Queen Street, P.O. Box N-8197, Nassau (☎ **242/322-4753**), and the Canadian consulate is on Shirley Street, Nassau (☎ **242/393-2123**). The British High Commission is in the BITCO Building (third floor), East Street, Nassau (☎ **242/325-7471**).

Emergencies   Throughout The Bahamas, the number to call for a medical, dental, or hospital emergency is ☎ **919.** To report a fire, however, call ☎ **411.**

Gambling   Casino gambling is legal in The Bahamas for visitors. Bahamians and Bahamas residents are prohibited from gambling, although they can enter the casinos in the company of friends from elsewhere. Games offered are dice, roulette, blackjack, baccarat, wheel of fortune, and slot machines. There is a casino at Cable Beach on New Providence, one on Paradise Island, and two at Freeport/Lucaya on Grand Bahama Island.

Gasoline   See "Getting Around" in this chapter.

Hitchhiking   See "Getting Around" in this chapter.

Holidays   See "When to Go" in this chapter.

Hospitals   See "Health and Insurance" in this chapter.

Information   For tourist information before you go, see "Visitor Information & Entry Requirements" in this chapter. For information while you're in The Bahamas, see the individual island listings.

Language   In The Bahamas locals speak English, but sometimes with a marked accent that often provides the clue to their ancestry—African, Irish, Scottish, or whatever.

Legal Aid   Most foreign arrests in The Bahamas involve drug offenses, either possession or dealing. If arrested, there is no legal aid service to refer to. You can apply for help at your consulate or embassy (see above), but don't expect much sympathy there. They will give you the name of a local attorney and notify your family—and that's about all. If you're involved in a serious driving offense, you can also contact your consulate, which will provide the name of an attorney to represent you. After that, you're on your own so far as public assistance is concerned.

Liquor Laws   Persons must be at least 17 years of age to order alcoholic drinks in The Bahamas.

Mail & Postage Rates   Only Bahamian postage stamps are acceptable. Beginning in the fall of 1997, to send a postcard to the United States, Canada, or the United Kingdom will cost 40¢. Airmail letters cost 55¢ per half ounce to the United States or Canada, but 60¢ to the United Kingdom.

From the United States, mail to the Out Islands is sometimes slow. Airmail may go by air to Nassau and by boat to its final destination. If a resort has a U.S. or Nassau address, it is preferable to use it.

Maps   In Nassau and Freeport, ask at local tourist offices for maps to both the islands of New Providence and Grand Bahama Island. In Nassau, if available, ask also for a detailed street map of downtown Nassau. Check out the free color map in the back of this guide!

Newspapers & Magazines Three newspapers are circulated in Nassau and Freeport: the *Nassau Guardian,* the *Tribune,* and the *Freeport News.* Circulation in the Out Islands is limited and likely to be slow.

You can find the *New York Times, Wall Street Journal, USA Today, Miami Herald, Times of London,* and *Daily Telegraph* at newsstands in your hotel and elsewhere in Nassau, usually the day after they are published but sometimes later. Such U.S. magazines as *Time* and *Newsweek* are flown in from the mainland.

Passports See "Visitor Information & Entry Requirements" in this chapter.

Pets A valid import permit is required to import any animal into The Bahamas. Application for such a permit must be made in writing, accompanied by a $10 processing fee, to the Director of Agriculture, Department of Agriculture, P.O. Box N-3028, Nassau, The Bahamas (☎ 242/325-7502), a minimum of 3 weeks in advance.

Police In Nassau, call the police at ☎ 919; in Freeport/Lucaya, dial ☎ 911.

Radio & TV Government-owned Radio Bahamas is run by the Broadcasting Corporation of The Bahamas and supported by advertising. ZNS-1, the most powerful of the three, is located in Nassau but can be heard throughout the country. ZNS-2 also operates out of Nassau, and ZNS-3 is based in Freeport.

ZNS TV transmits on Channel 13 in full color, for 6 hours a day Monday through Friday. On Saturday it transmits for 16 hours, on Sunday for 12. Most large hotels have cable television and can receive U.S. telecasts via Miami from all major networks. Islands nearest the United States receive TV without cable.

Rest Rooms Toilet facilities can be found at hotels, restaurants, and air terminals in The Bahamas that are frequented by the public, although they may turn out to be in short supply at some of the points of interest you go to see. On some of the more remote Out Islands not well supplied with public places, you may have difficulty finding a toilet.

Safety When going to Nassau (New Providence), Cable Beach, Paradise Island, or Freeport/Lucaya, exercise the kind of caution you would if visiting Miami. Whatever you do, if you're approached by people peddling drugs, view them as if they had the bubonic plague. Americans and other foreigners have gotten into much trouble in The Bahamas by purchasing illegal drugs.

Women, especially, should take caution if walking alone on the streets of Nassau after dark, particularly if those streets appear to be deserted. Pickpockets (often foreigners) work the crowded casino floors of both Paradise Beach and Cable Beach. See that your wallet or money, or whatever, is secured.

If you're driving a rented car, always make sure your car door is locked, and never leave possessions in view in an automobile. Don't leave valuables, such as cameras and purses, lying unattended on the beach while you go for a swim. If you have valuables with you, don't leave them unguarded in hotel rooms—especially jewelry. Many of the bigger hotels will provide safes. Keep your hotel room doors locked. Bahamian tourist officials often warn visitors, "If you've got it, don't flaunt it." This will minimize the possibility of your becoming a victim of crime.

You're less likely to get mugged in the Out Islands, where life is generally more peaceful. There are some resort hotels that, even today, don't have locks on the doors (never a good policy, in our opinion).

However, drug dealers frequent many of the Out Islands, especially Bimini, because of their proximity to Miami. Take special care if you plan to vacation here. Transporting illegal drugs between Bimini and the Florida coastline is so commonplace that every day the boating set sees bales of marijuana floating on the water as they make the crossing. The marijuana is dumped when vessels are spotted by the coast guard as they approach American territorial waters.

Taxes   Departure tax is $15. International airline and steamship tickets issued in The Bahamas are subject to a nominal tax, which is written into the cost of the ticket. A 9% tax is imposed on hotel tariffs. There is no sales tax in this country.

Telephone, Telex & Fax   Communications by telephone and cable to resorts in The Bahamas have improved recently, although some of the Out Islands are difficult to reach because of distance and equipment. In recent years, virtually every hotel in The Bahamas seems to have installed a fax machine. Direct distance dialing between North America and Nassau, Grand Bahama, the Abacos, Andros, the Berry Islands, Bimini, Eleuthera, Harbour Island, Spanish Wells, the Exumas, and Stella Maris on Long Island is available. Note that the old coin-operated phones are still prevalent, and still swallow coins. Each local call costs 25¢. Those old phones, however, are gradually being replaced by phones that use calling cards (debit cards), similar in appearance to a credit card, that come in denominations of $5, $10, $20, and $50. They can be bought from any office of **BATELCO** (Bahamas Telephone Co.), although in some cases (such as at the British Colonial Hotel), a hotel will sell one to a client without a price markup as a guest service.

BATELCO's main branch is on Kennedy Drive, Nassau (☎ **242/323-4911**), although a popular local branch lies in the commercial heart of Nassau, on East Street off Bay Street.

To get directory assistance within The Bahamas, dial ☎ **916.** To reach an international or a domestic operator within The Bahamas, dial ☎ **0.** There is no difference made in The Bahamas between the two types of operators. To reach the major international services of AT&T, dial ☎ **800/872-2881** from any phone, or head for any phone with AT&T or USA DIRECT written on the side of the booth. Picking up the handset will contact you straightaway with an AT&T operator. These phones are often positioned beside cruise ship docks to help passengers disembarking on shore leave for the day. Cables to The Bahamas are usually delivered by phone or by citizens band radio. Urgent telegrams are charged at double the full rate, although no urgent-rate messages to the U.S. mainland are accepted.

Time   Eastern standard time is used throughout The Bahamas. In recent years, eastern daylight time has been adopted during the summer to avoid confusion in scheduling transportation to and from the United States. April to October, EDT; October to April, EST.

Tipping   Many establishments add a service charge, but it's customary to leave something extra if service has been especially fine. If you're not sure whether service has been included in your bill, ask.

Bellboys and porters, at least in the upper-bracket hotels, expect a tip of $1 per bag. It's also customary to tip your chambermaid at least $2 per day—more if she or he has performed special services such as getting a shirt or blouse laundered. Most service personnel, including taxi drivers, waiters, and the like, expect 15% (20% in deluxe restaurants).

Tourist Offices   See "Visitor Information & Entry Requirements" in this chapter and also specific island chapters.

Water   Technically, tap water is drinkable throughout The Bahamas, and most local residents are accustomed to its slightly brackish taste. We opt for bottled because it tastes better, and because your holiday isn't worth being shortchanged by a queasy stomach. In some outlying places, water might be in short supply. Such populous islands as New Providence, Grand Bahama, and Marsh Harbour have ample pure water, filtered and chlorinated. Resorts tend to filter and chlorinate their water more aggressively than most other establishments on any particular island, and bottled water is available at all tourist facilities, stores, and supermarkets.

On many of the Out Islands rainfall is a main source of water for drinking and other household uses. This is caught and kept in the cisterns that most houses have.

Yellow Pages   All Bahamian telephone numbers appear in one phone book, revised annually, with a helpful yellow pages in the back.

New Providence (Nassau/Cable Beach)

4

One million visitors a year have cast their vote: They want to visit Nassau and adjoining Cable Beach and Paradise Island (see chapter 5). Freeport/Lucaya (see chapter 6) is the runner-up, but Nassau, on New Providence Island, is it if you want to be at the center of it all: the best shopping, the best entertainment, the most historic attractions—plus some of the best beaches in The Bahamas. The Out Islands, which we'll explore in the chapters ahead, are more for people who want peace and quiet or those who'd like to pursue certain sports, such as sailing in the Abacos or fishing in Bimini.

The capital of The Bahamas, the historic city of Nassau is a 35-minute flight from Miami. A tropical indolence still hangs over the city, despite the development and the modern hotels. The commercial and banking hub of The Bahamas, Nassau lies on the north side of New Providence, which is 21 miles long and 7 miles wide at its greatest point.

Cable Beach, a stretch of sand just west of the city, is lined with luxury resorts—in fact, the Nassau/Cable Beach area has the largest tourist infrastructure in The Bahamas, though there's another concentration of luxury hotels on Paradise Island. (Except for Graycliff and the British Colonial Beach Resort, the accommodations within the heart of Nassau itself are lackluster.) When you're based in Nassau/Cable Beach, you have an array of water sports, golf, tennis, and plenty of duty-free shopping nearby—and that's not to mention those powder-soft beaches. In addition, the resorts, restaurants, and beaches of Paradise Island, discussed in the next chapter, are just a short distance away. (Paradise Island, which lies just opposite Nassau, is connected to New Providence Island by a toll bridge—$2 for cars, 25¢ for pedestrians; there's also frequent ferry and water taxi service between Nassau and Paradise Island.)

As the sun goes down, Cable Beach and Paradise Island heat up, with fine dining, glitzy casinos, cabaret shows, moonlight cruises, dance clubs, or romantic evening strolls. (We'd confine that evening stroll to Cable Beach or Paradise Island, not the streets of downtown Nassau, which can be dangerous at night.)

After they've hit the beach, shoppers head for the Straw Market, filled with vendors hawking straw goods and other handicrafts, and for Bay Street. Bay Street is a legend in the islands for its duty-free items, especially china, perfume, crystal, linens, jewelry, watches, leather goods, liquor, and more.

The shops might draw a lot more business than the museums, but no city in The Bahamas is as rich in history as Nassau. The sights aren't to be ignored either. You can take a "royal climb" up the Queen's Staircase to Fort Fincastle. These 66 steps lead to a fort said to have been cut in the sandstone cliffs by slaves in the 1790s.

Other Nassau attractions include Ardastra Gardens, which features 5 acres of landscaping and more than 300 exotic birds, mammals, and reptiles. Most popular among the wildlife are the trained pink flamingos, which march for audiences daily to their trainer's commands.

And visitors love Coral Island, an educational and entertainment theme park located between Nassau and Paradise Island on Silver Cay. The facility has 24 aquariums, including shark and turtle tanks, numerous landscaped parks, and an underwater observation tower allowing visitors to see marine life 20 feet below the surface in a natural sea environment.

One final aspect of Nassau that deserves mention is its remaining overlay of British colonial charm. It's surprising that Nassau has retained this flavor in spite of its location so close to the Florida mainland. It hasn't become Americanized, in other words; it's a long way from becoming another Miami. Stately old homes and public buildings still stand, even though they exist side by side with eyesores such as modern high-rise buildings and government edifices. Tropical foliage lines the streets, where horse-drawn surreys still trot by, taking visitors for leisurely town tours. There is no more romantic way to see Nassau than this. Police officers in immaculate white starched jackets and colorful pith helmets still direct traffic on principal streets.

And what lies beyond the high-rises? Even though 60% of all Bahamians live on New Providence, a great deal of the island remains undeveloped. You can still take trail rides on horseback or perhaps find a secluded beach. You can even go exploring by car or scooter. But don't expect to see lush Jamaican terrain. New Providence Island has mostly pines and palmettos, not the junglelike tropical splendor of islands to the south, including Dominica or even parts of Puerto Rico. If you arm yourself with a good map, you'll find getting around relatively easy.

Even with all that Nassau and Cable Beach, plus Paradise Island, have to offer, we still recommend that you plan at least a long weekend on one of the Out Islands. On many of them the 1950s—or even the 1940s—live on. The contrast between the cosmopolitan aura of Nassau and Cable Beach and the laid-back character of the Out Islands can be startling.

1 Orientation

ARRIVING

BY PLANE   Planes land at **Nassau International Airport** (☎ 242/377-7281), which is a bad introduction to the island. The airport is badly run, with inadequate facilities, extremely poor catering, and uncomfortable waiting rooms. It lies 8 miles west of Nassau by Lake Killarney. You won't want to spend much time here and will want to rush through to your ultimate destination.

Regrettably, the taxi union doesn't allow buses to pick up passengers here and transport them to Cable Beach, Nassau, or Paradise Island. If arrangements are made in advance, special vans from hotels pick up guests. There are any number of car-rental offices here if you plan to have a car while on New Providence Island. For better rates, you should make arrangements in advance in the U.S. You can also take a taxi to your hotel. See "Getting Around," below, for rates. Drivers expect to be tipped 15%, and some will remind you should you "forget."

BY CRUISE SHIP   Nassau is one of the busiest cruise-ship ports in the world. For details on cruise-ship travel, see "Cruises" in chapter 3. In recent years, Nassau has spent millions of dollars increasing its facilities so that now 11 cruise ships can pull into dock at one time! Facilities in Nassau, Cable Beach, and Paradise Island become extremely overcrowded when major cruise ships dock. You'll have to stake out your space on the beach, and you will find shops and attractions overrun with visitors.

Cruise ships dock near Rawson Square, which is the best place to begin a tour of Nassau, as the square is the very center of the city and the shopping area. Unless you want to go to one of the beach strips along Cable Beach or Paradise Island, you don't need a taxi but can go on a shopping expedition near where you dock. The Straw Market is nearby, at Market Plaza; Bay Street (the main shopping artery) is also close; and the Nassau International Bazaar is at the intersection of Woodes Rogers Walk and Charlotte Street.

VISITOR INFORMATION

The Bahamas Ministry of Tourism maintains three **tourist information booths** at the Nassau International Airport. In Arrivals (☎ **242/377-6833** and 242/377-6806), hours are from 8:30am to 11:30pm daily. In Departures (☎ **242/377-1735**) and in the Charter section (☎ **242/377-6782**), hours are daily from 10am to 6pm.

Information can also be obtained from the Information Desk at the Ministry of Tourism's Office, Bay Street (☎ **242/356-7591**). Hours are Monday through Friday from 9am to 5pm.

CITY LAYOUT
MAIN STREETS & ARTERIES

Rawson Square is the heart of Nassau, lying just a short walk from **Prince George Wharf,** where the big cruise ships, usually from Florida, berth. Here you'll see the Churchill Building, which contains the offices of the Bahamian prime minister along with other government ministries.

Busy **Bay Street,** the main shopping artery, begins on the south side of Rawson Square. This was the street of the infamous "Bay Street Boys," a group of rich, white Bahamians who once controlled all political and economic activity on New Providence.

On the opposite side of Rawson Square is **Parliament Square,** with a statue of a youthful Queen Victoria. Here are more government houses and the House of Assembly. These are Georgian and Neo-Georgian buildings, some dating from the late 1700s.

The courthouse is separated by a little square from the **Nassau Public Library and Museum,** which opens onto Bank Lane. It was the former Nassau Gaol (jail). South of the library, across Shirley Street, are the remains of the **Royal Victoria Hotel,** which opened the year the American Civil War was launched (1861) and once hosted blockade runners and Confederate spies.

A walk down Parliament Street leads to the post office, and philatelists may want to stop in, since some Bahamian stamps are collector's items.

Going south, moving farther away from the water, Elizabeth Avenue takes you to the **Queen's Staircase,** one of the major landmarks of Nassau. This leads to Bennet's Hill and Fort Fincastle.

If you return to Bay Street, you'll discover the **Straw Market,** where you can buy all sorts of souvenirs and certainly almost any item made of straw. At the intersection of Charlotte Street is another major shopping emporium, the **Nassau International Bazaar.**

⭐ **Frommer's Favorite New Providence Experiences**

Listening to the Sounds of Goombay. At some local joint, you can enjoy an intoxicating beat and such island favorites as "Goin' Down Burma Road," "Get Involved," and "John B. Sail."

A Ride in a Horse-Drawn Surrey. If you'd like to see Nassau as the Duke of Windsor did when he was governor, consider this unique form of transport. It's elegant, romantic, and nostalgic. Surreys await passengers at Rawson Square, in the exact center of Nassau.

A Glass-Bottom Boat Ride. Right in the middle of Nassau's harbor, numerous craft wait to take you on enchanting rides through the colorful sea gardens off New Providence Island. In the teeming reefs offshore, you'll meet all sorts of sea creatures while an underwater wonderland unfolds before your eyes.

An Idyllic Day on Blue Lagoon Island. It's like an old Hollywood fantasy of a tropical island. Located off the eastern end of Paradise Island, this Blue Lagoon has seven sandy beaches. Boats from Nassau Harbour take you there and back.

If you continue east along Bay Street, you'll reach **Paradise Bridge,** which leads to Paradise Island. If you go west on Bay Street, you'll come to West Bay Street, the road that will take you to Cable Beach and the airport.

FINDING AN ADDRESS   In Nassau, and especially in the rest of The Bahamas, you will seldom if ever find street numbers on hotels or other businesses. Sometimes in the more remote places, you won't even find street names. Get directions before heading somewhere in particular. You can always ask along the way, as Bahamians tend to be very helpful.

2 Getting Around

BY CAR   Three of the biggest U.S.–based car-rental companies maintain branches at the Nassau International Airport, across the street from the main terminal. These include **Avis** (☎ **800/331-2112,** or 242/326-6380 locally), **Budget Rent-a-Car** (☎ **800/472-3325,** or 242/377-7405 locally), and **Hertz** (☎ **800/654-3131,** or 809/393-0871 locally). Avis also maintains branches at the cruise-ship docks and in downtown Nassau on Marlborough Street. Budget has a branch at Chalk's Airline Terminal for anyone arriving at Paradise Island Airport (☎ **242/363-3095**). In addition, Budget will send a driver anywhere on Paradise Island to pick you up and deliver you to its headquarters.

Rates among the various companies are approximately (but not exactly) the same, and insurance regulations are stricter at some than others. Weekly prices are usually calculated at six times the daily rate, so keeping a car for the seventh day usually works out free, although that gives you a price break only if you declare your intention to rent for a full week when you sign your rental contract.

Currently, among the major rental firms, Budget offers the least expensive rate, $282 a week, and some of the most lenient restrictions for their cheapest, non–air-conditioned car. An equivalent car at Hertz rents for $359 a week, whereas Avis charges $419. Drivers at Budget need to be 25 or older. A Budget car with automatic transmission and air-conditioning costs $352 a week.

Each of the companies offers additional insurance for $11.95 to $16.95 per day. The best local companies to rent from include **McCartney Rent-a-Car,**

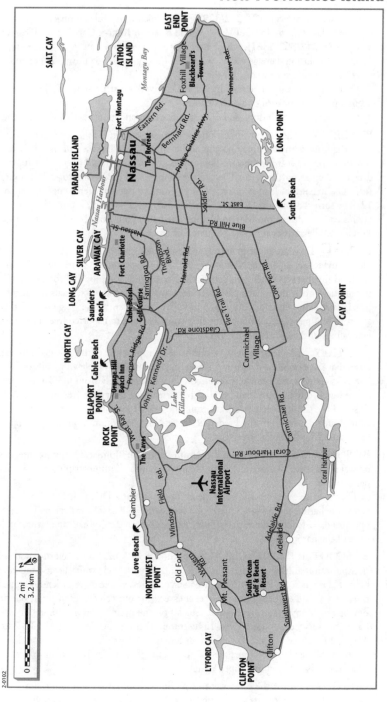

7th Terrace, Centreville (☎ **242/328-0486**), which rents only compact cars, costing $55 a day, plus $8 for CDW. Also good is **Teglo Rent-a-Car,** Mount Pleasant Village (☎ **242/362-4361**), whose fleet of cars range from $59 to $95 daily, plus $13.95 for collision damage waiver (CDW). However, they require a $500 cash deposit before you can drive one off the lot.

There's no tax on car rentals in Nassau. Drivers must present a valid driver's license, plus a credit card or a cash deposit.

Drive on the left, don't drink and drive, and pay extra attention when driving at night.

BY SURREY   The elegant, traditional way to see Nassau is in a horse-drawn surrey—the kind with the fringe on top and a wilted hibiscus stuck in the straw hat shielding the horse from the sun. Before you get in, you should negotiate with the driver and agree on the price. The average charge is $5 per person for a 25-minute ride. The maximum load is three adults plus one or two children under the age of 12. The surreys are available 7 days a week from 9am to 4:30pm, except when horses are rested, 1 to 3pm from May to October, and 1 to 2pm from November to April. You'll find the surreys at Rawson Square, off Bay Street.

BY TAXI   Taxis are more practical, at least for longer island trips, as the rates for New Providence, including Nassau, are set by the government. Working meters are required in all taxis. When you get in, the fixed rate is $2, plus 30¢ for each additional quarter of a mile. Each passenger over two pays an extra $2. Taxis can also be hired at the hourly rate of $20 to $23 for a five-passenger cab. Luggage is carried at a cost of 50¢ per piece, although the first two pieces are transported free. The radio taxi call number is ☎ **242/323-5111.**

BY JITNEY   The least-expensive means of transport is by jitney—medium-size buses that leave from the downtown Nassau area to outposts on New Providence. The fare is 75¢, and exact change is required. They operate daily from 6:30am to 7pm. Some hotels on Paradise Island and Cable Beach run their own free jitney service. Buses to the Cable Beach area leave from the Navy Lion Road depot. Buses to the eastern area depart from the Frederick Street North depot, and buses to the malls leave from Marlborough Street East.

BY BOAT   Water taxis operate daily from 9am to 5:30pm at 20-minute intervals between Paradise Island and Prince George Wharf at a round-trip cost of $2 per person.

There is also ferry service from the end of Casuarina Drive on Paradise Island across the harbor to Rawson Square for a round-trip fare of $2 per person. The ferry operates daily from 9:30am to 4:15pm, with departures every half hour from both sides of the harbor.

BY SCOOTER OR BICYCLE   Motor scooters have become a favorite mode of transportation among tourists. The little mopeds with their white license tags and helmeted riders scoot all over New Providence. Unless you're an experienced moped rider, stay on quiet roads until you feel at ease with your vehicle. Don't start out on Bay Street. Many hotels have rental vehicles on the premises. If your hotel doesn't have this service, contact **Ursa Investment,** Prince George Wharf (☎ **242/326-8329**). Mopeds cost $20 per hour or $30 for 2 hours. For a half day, the charge is $40; a full day is $50. Hours are Monday through Saturday from 8am to 6pm. A $10 deposit is required on moped rentals.

ON FOOT   This is the only way to see Old Nassau, unless you rent a horse and carriage. All the major attractions and the principal stores are close enough to walk to. You can even walk to Cable Beach or Paradise Island, although many prefer a taxi or bus to reach those destinations. Confine your walking to the daytime, and beware of pickpockets and purse snatchers. In the evening, avoid walking the streets of downtown Nassau, where, as mentioned, muggings occur.

FAST FACTS: New Providence

American Express   The local representative is Playtours, 303 Shirley St., between Charlotte and Parliament streets, Nassau (☎ 242/322-2931). Hours are Monday through Friday from 9am to 5pm.

Business Hours   See "Fast Facts" in chapter 3.

Car Rentals   See "Getting Around" in this chapter.

Climate   See "When to Go" in chapter 3.

Currency Exchange   Americans need not bother to exchange their dollars into Bahamian dollars, because the currencies are on par. However, Canadians will need to convert their dollars, and Britishers their pounds, which can be done at local banks or sometimes at your hotel. Hotels, however, offer the least favorable rates.

Dentist   There are numerous dentists in Nassau, all of whom speak English, but for the best treatment go to the dental department of the Princess Margaret Hospital on Sands Road (☎ 242/322-2861).

Doctor   For the best service, use a staff member of the Princess Margaret Hospital on Sands Road (☎ 242/322-2861).

Drugs   The strict drug law of The Bahamas was cited under "Fast Facts" in the preceding chapter, but the warning bears repeating. The authorities do not smile on visitors possessing or selling marijuana or other narcotics, and offenders are speedily and severely punished. A normal lapse of 3 days between arrest and sentencing can be expected. Penalties are harsh.

Drugstores   Try Lowes Pharmacy, Palm Dale (☎ 242/322-7430), which is open Monday through Saturday from 8am to 6:30pm. They also have two branches: East Bay Shopping Center (☎ 242/393-4813), open Monday through Saturday 8am to 8:30pm and Sunday from 9am to 5pm; and Town Center Mall (☎ 242/325-6482), open Monday through Saturday 10am to 9pm and Sunday from 10am to 6pm. Nassau has no late-night pharmacies.

Embassies & Consulates   See "Fast Facts" in chapter 3.

Emergencies   For any major emergency—medical, dental, or even police—call ☎ 919. To report a fire, call ☎ 411.

Eyeglass Repair   The Optique Shoppe, 22 Parliament St. at the corner of Shirley Street (☎ 242/322-3910), is both large and convenient to the center of Nassau. Hours are Monday through Friday from 9am to 5pm and on Saturday from 9am to noon. One-hour service is granted. Contact lenses, glass repairs, and the largest selection of shades and frames in The Bahamas are also offered here.

Holidays   See "When to Go" in chapter 3.

Hospitals   The government-operated Princess Margaret Hospital on Sands Road (☎ 242/322-2861) is one of the major hospitals in The Bahamas. Its bed capacity is 455. The privately owned Doctors Hospital, with 72 beds, is at 1 Collins Ave. (☎ 242/322-8411). This hospital is the most modern private health care facility in the region.

Hotlines   For the Drugs Action Service, dial ☎ **242/322-2308.**

Information   See "Visitor Information," above.

Laundry & Dry Cleaning   The Laundromat Superwash (☎ **242/323-4018**), at the corner of Nassau Street and Boyd Road, offers coin-operated laundry facilities. It is open 24 hours a day, 7 days a week. In the same building is the New Oriental Dry Cleaner (☎ **242/323-7249**). It is open Monday through Thursday 7:30am to 7pm, Friday and Saturday 7:30am to 8pm. Another dry cleaner a short drive north of the center of town is the Jiffy Quality Cleaner (☎ **242/323-6771**) at the corner of Blue Hill Road and Cordeaux Avenue. It is open Monday through Saturday from 7:30am to 7pm.

Newspapers & Magazines   See "Fast Facts" in chapter 3.

Photographic Needs   The largest camera store in Nassau is John Bull, Bay Street (☎ **242/322-3328**), one block east of Rawson Square. It sells top-brand cameras, film, and other accessories. Camera experts are available for advice. It is open Monday and Thursday from 9am to 5pm; Tuesday, Wednesday, and Friday from 9am to 5:30pm; and Saturday from 8:30am to 5:30pm.

Police   Dial ☎ **919.**

Post Office   The Nassau General Post Office, at the top of Parliament Street on East Hill Street (☎ **242/322-3344**), is open Monday through Friday from 9am to 5pm, on Saturday from 9am to 1pm.

Rest Rooms   These are generally inadequate. Visitors often have to rely on the facilities available at airports, hotels, restaurants, and other commercial establishments.

Safety   Women should avoid walking along the often nearly deserted streets of Nassau at night. Cable Beach and Paradise Island are much safer places to be in the evening. For more details, see "Safety" under "Fast Facts" in chapter 3.

Taxes   There is no sales tax, as mentioned. All visitors leaving The Bahamas pay a $15 departure tax.

Telephone, Telex & Fax   Direct long-distance telephone dialing is available. Nearly all major hotels send telexes and faxes; if your hotel is too small to offer such services, go to the main post office (see above). To send a telegram, you can either call from your hotel (paying over the phone with a valid credit card) or visit in person The Bahamas Telecommunications Corp., John F. Kennedy Drive (☎ **242/323-4911**), located beside the main seafront road leading to the resort hotels of Cable Beach.

Transit Information   To summon a taxi, call ☎ **242/323-5111.** There is no central information number for the Nassau International Airport. If you want flight information, you must call individual airlines directly.

Weather   New Providence, which is fairly centrally located in The Bahamas, has temperatures in winter that vary from about 60° to 75°F daily. Summer variations are 78° to the high 80s.

3 Where to Stay

In the hotel descriptions that follow we've listed regular room prices or "rack rates." When you book, however, always inquire about honeymoon specials, golf packages, summer weeks, and other discounts. In many cases, too, a travel agent can get you a package deal that would be cheaper than these official rates.

Hotels add a 4% room tax and a 4% to 6% "resort levy" to your rate. Sometimes this is quoted as part of the tariff, and at other times it is added when your final bill is presented. Always ask if the tax is included when you are quoted a rate. Many hotels also add a 15% service charge to your bill. Check these charges in advance so you won't be shocked when the final tab is presented.

Taxes and service are not included in the rates listed below unless otherwise noted. *Note:* For an explanation of our symbols for rates with meals included, see "Tips on Accommodations" in chapter 3.

In general, we consider hotels that charge from $245 to $280 a night for a double room very expensive. Those rated expensive are in the general range of $160 to $245 a night. Moderately priced hotels ask from $95 to $160 a night for a double; inexpensive places charge under $95 per night for a double. Some hotels, depending on their size and room configurations, can have both moderate and expensive rooms.

We'll lead off with a selection of hotels within the heart of Nassau, followed by Cable Beach. Frankly, most visitors prefer to stay at Cable Beach since the resorts here are right on the sand. However, other visitors have heard of the British Colonial and the Graycliff, and they choose to stay in Nassau at either of these and commute to the beaches at Cable Beach or Paradise Island. Those electing to stay within the town prefer the ambience of Old Nassau's historic district and also want to be near the best shops. And your wallet might be another powerful reason to stay in the historic area; many of the hotels recommended below are far cheaper than the Cable Beach or Paradise Island resorts.

NASSAU
VERY EXPENSIVE

✪ Graycliff. West Hill St., P.O. Box N-10246, Nassau, The Bahamas. ☎ **800/688-0076** in the U.S., 242/322-2796. Fax 809/326-6110. 14 rms. A/C MINIBAR TV TEL. Winter, $255–$280 double; $290–$365 poolside cottage for two. Off-season, $165–$210 double; $210–$290 poolside cottage for two. Rates include continental breakfast. MC, V. Free parking. Bus: 10, 17.

Even though the hotel isn't right on the beach, people who can afford to stay anywhere often choose Graycliff, because it epitomizes Nassau's old-world style and grace. Churchill, of course, can no longer be seen paddling around in the swimming pool with a cigar in his mouth, and the Beatles are long gone, but the three-story Graycliff remains a favorite with whatever movie star happens to be visiting Nassau. Across the street from Government House, it is a well-preserved example of Georgian colonial architecture. The main house was built by Capt. John Howard Graysmith, a pirate noted for his exploits against Spanish shipping boats and commander of the notorious *Graywolf,* which was scuttled off New Providence in 1726. By 1844, Graycliff was a hotel for "gentlefolk and invalids."

Many clients opt for the historic garden rooms in the main house, which are large and individually decorated with antiques. However, the better units are the more modern garden rooms. Yellow Bird, Hibiscus, and Pool Cottage are terrific choices, but the most luxurious accommodation of all is the Mandarino Suite, with an Oriental decor, king-size bed, oversize bathroom, and a private balcony overlooking the swimming pool. The private beach at the British Colonial Beach Resort is about a 5-minute walk from the hotel, and costs $5 per person.

All rooms have such extras as bottles of Perrier and plush robes. Well-heeled travelers with a sense of history like to stay here, as do business travelers who need to be near the center of town. There's nothing on the island to compare with

Nassau Accommodations

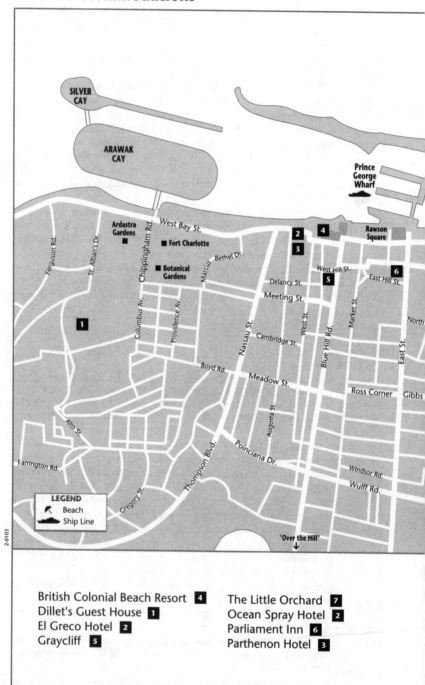

SILVER CAY

ARAWAK CAY

Prince George Wharf

Rawson Square

Ferguson Rd.
St. Alban's Dr.
Ardastra Gardens
Chippingham Rd.
West Bay St.
■ Fort Charlotte
Bethel Dr.
Marcus
■ Botanical Gardens
Columbus Av.
Providence Av.
Nassau St.
West St.
Delancy St.
West Hill St.
East Hill St.
Meeting St.
Cambridge St.
Blue Hill Rd.
Market St.
East St.
North
Boyd Rd.
Meadow St.
Ross Corner
Gibbs
Alto St.
Augusta St.
Poinciana Dr.
Windsor Rd.
Farrington Rd.
Thompson Blvd.
Wulff Rd.
Gregory St.

LEGEND
🏖 Beach
🚢 Ship Line

2-0103

"Over the Hill"
↓

British Colonial Beach Resort **4**   The Little Orchard **7**
Dillet's Guest House **1**   Ocean Spray Hotel **2**
El Greco Hotel **2**   Parliament Inn **6**
Graycliff **5**   Parthenon Hotel **3**

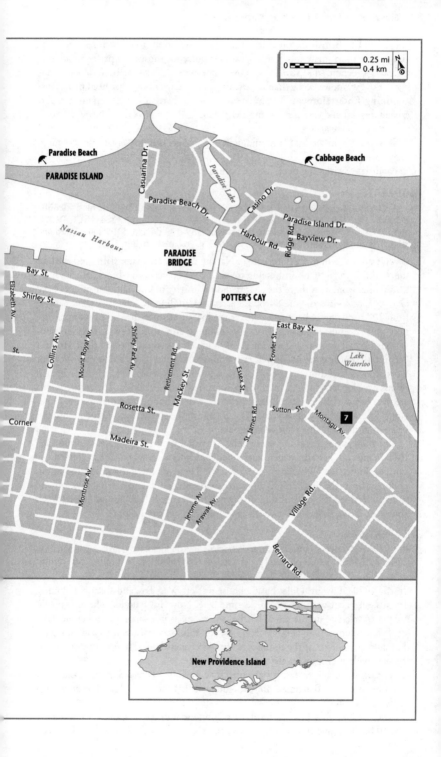

0.25 mi
0.4 km

Paradise Beach
PARADISE ISLAND
Casuarina Dr.
Paradise Lake
Cabbage Beach
Casino Dr.
Paradise Beach Dr.
Paradise Island Dr.
Ridge Rd.
Bayview Dr.
Harbour Rd.

Nassau Harbour
PARADISE BRIDGE
POTTER'S CAY

Bay St.
Shirley St.
Elizabeth Av.
East Bay St.
Fowler St.
Lake Waterloo

St.
Collins Av.
Mount Royal Av.
Shirley Park Av.
Retirement Rd.
Mackey St.
Essex St.
St. James Rd.
Sutton St.
Montagu Av.
7

Corner
Rosetta St.
Madeira St.
Montrose Av.
Jerome Av.
Arawak Av.
Village Rd.
Bernard Rd.

New Providence Island

Graycliff. The British Colonial has history and tradition, too, but it's mammoth. Graycliff is an intimate inn and the leading choice for those who prefer an address with an aristocratic air so strong it can overcome even the tacky air-conditioners hanging out the windows, some shabby carpeting, and a few ceilings that need paint jobs.

Dining/Entertainment: The hotel boasts one of Nassau's finest restaurants, also called Graycliff and certainly the most elegant (see "Where to Dine," below). Always reserve well in advance.

Services: Room service (7am–midnight), concierge, laundry service, dry cleaning, baby-sitting, massage.

Facilities: Swimming pool, Jacuzzi, sauna, health club.

MODERATE

British Colonial Beach Resort. 1 Bay St., P.O. Box N-7148, Nassau, The Bahamas. ☎ **800/ 528-1234** in the U.S., or 242/323-8248. Fax 242/322-2286. 219 rms, 7 suites. A/C TV TEL. Winter, $129–$189 double; $229 suite. Off-season, $89–139 double; $199 suite. Third and fourth persons sharing room $25 each. AE, DC, MC, V. Free parking. Bus: 10, 17.

If you want to be in the historic core of Nassau, near all the major sights and the best shops, this is the only resort hotel in town. It even opens onto a beach, albeit an artificial one. It may not have the charm and exclusivity of Graycliff, but it does have its own appeal—mainly the 8 tropical acres surrounding it. A massive pink bastion from 1922, this hotel has presided over the bay front since the day of its construction, and lies only a few steps from the shopping area of Bay Street. Regular renovations have kept it up to date, the latest of which has introduced a bright, tropical decor to the entire complex, as well as new furnishings and fixtures. The pier out front was used as a backdrop for the James Bond thriller *Never Say Never Again.* The best rooms have lots of windows and French doors leading to balconies. The corner rooms are the most desirable, not only because of their views but because they are more spacious. Room sizes vary greatly, so if you get one of the smaller accommodations your opinion of the hotel may not be as high.

The food is not a reason to stay here. There's the relatively modest Caribe Café Restaurant and Terrace, which serves standard international cuisine at low cost—nothing more (see "Where to Dine," below). There are three championship tennis courts lit for night play, an Olympic-size swimming pool, and a private white-sand beach. Deep-sea fishing and skin diving can be arranged. Free nonmotorized water sports are available including sailing, windsurfing, and snorkeling.

INEXPENSIVE

Dillet's Guest House. Dunmore Ave. and Strachan St., Chippingham, Nassau, The Bahamas. ☎ 242/325-1133. Fax 242/325-7183. 7 suites. A/C MINIBAR TV. Year-round, $60 double. $15 extra third and fourth person. Rates include continental breakfast. AE, MC, V.

In the 1920s, Edward Dillet built a house just off West Bay and welcomed family, friends, and acquaintances to spend time here. Now, his granddaughter, Danielle, invites travelers to do the same. Each of the rooms is non-smoking and comes with cable television, ceiling fans, clock radios, and minibars stocked with soda (no alcohol) and chips. Five of the rooms have full kitchenettes. The house is informal and homey, with afternoon tea the highlight of the day.

The continental breakfast is Bahamian style, with freshly baked pastries, and if you want an authentic Bahamian dinner, request it that morning. They'll even arrange a picnic for you.

The nearest public beaches are about a 7-minute walk away, and you can catch the no. 10 bus to Cable Beach for 75¢. You can also rent a bike at Dillet's and tour the area.

El Greco Hotel. W. Bay St., P.O. Box N-4187, Nassau, The Bahamas. ☎ **242/325-1121.** Fax 242/325-1124. 25 rms, 1 suite. A/C TV TEL. Winter, $90 double; from $150 suite. Off-season, $70 double; from $110 suite. AE, DC, MC, V. Free parking. Bus: 10.

Across the street from Lighthouse Beach, within a 5-minute walk of the shops and restaurants of Bay Street, El Greco is a hotel for those with limited budgets. The Greek owners and staff seem to care about the well-being of their guests—in fact, the two-story hotel seems more like a small European B&B than your typical Bahamian hostelry. It attracts a great deal of European business. The rooms aren't that exciting, but they're clean and comfortable. Rooms are built around a courtyard in the center with a medium-size rectangular pool. Many of the accommodations have a separate sitting room. You can walk to many places nearby for breakfast.

The Little Orchard. Village Rd., P.O. Box N-1514, Nassau, The Bahamas. ☎ **242/393-1297.** Fax 242/394-3526. 16 efficiencies, 12 cottages. A/C TV. Winter, $65–$75 double efficiency; $90–$105 double cottage. Off-season, $60–$70 double efficiency; $75–$90 double cottage. MC, V. Free parking. Bus: 17.

A 5-minute walk from Montagu Beach, this complex offers individual cottage facilities grouped around a central swimming pool in a 2-acre semitropical garden. The cottages are in a residential part of Nassau, close to a large supermarket and a 5-minute drive from tennis and squash courts and several island restaurants. All units have fully equipped kitchens, baths, and daily maid service. Some rooms have balconies.

There's no in-house restaurant, although the Tamarind Hill Restaurant (under different management) is next door (see "Where to Dine," below). Guests can take bus no. 17, which stops near the hotel, to go shopping in downtown Nassau (the bus service also runs to the foot of the bridge leading to Paradise Island). Later, economy-minded vacationers share stories at the convivial Tree Frog Bar, on the premises.

Ocean Spray Hotel. W. Bay St., P.O. Box N-3035, Nassau, The Bahamas. ☎ **242/322-8032.** Fax 242/325-5731. 28 rms. A/C TV TEL. Winter, $75 double. Off-season, $65 double. AE, MC, V. Free parking. Bus: 10.

This modest five-story corner hotel is a short stroll from the shopping district and across the street from the beach. Economy is the main reason to stay here. Bedrooms have twin beds and carpeting and your basic Miami-motel decor. They are clean and reasonably comfortable, however (although furnishings have outlived their usefulness). Students on spring break would be happy here. The hotel has an informal atmosphere and is best known for its restaurant-bar, Europe, which serves good imported wines and excellent international specialties. Ocean Spray offers guests both beach and town, a winning combination in Nassau. You can order breakfast at several places nearby.

Parthenon Hotel. 17 West St., P.O. Box N-4930, Nassau, The Bahamas. ☎ **242/322-2643.** Fax 242/322-2644. 18 rms. A/C TV TEL. Winter, $59 double; $68 triple. Off-season, $62 double; $70 triple. AE, MC, V. Free parking. Bus: 10.

The Parthenon, a small hotel located about 2 minutes from Bay Street and the beaches, is a haven for guests seeking peace and quiet and who don't expect a full-service hotel. That you won't get. Although modern, it's styled in the old Bahamian way, with continuous covered balconies overlooking a well-tended garden. The rooms are clean, plain, and simple, with basic, restrained decor and private baths. Fishing, golf, tennis, and water sports can be arranged. There is no restaurant or bar. Consider this place as a budget alternative only if you like to spend most of your time outdoors instead of lounging around a hotel room.

Parliament Inn. 18 Parliament, P.O. Box 4138, Nassau, The Bahamas. ☎ **242/322-2836.** Fax 242/326-7196. 6 rms. A/C. Year-round, $60 double; $70 triple. AE, DISC, MC, V. Bus: 10.

The yellow and white two-story house is in the middle of the downtown area and is about a 10-minute walk to the nearest beach. The inn is late British style, dating from the 1950s. It's run in a very laid-back fashion by the Wassitch family. Bedrooms are very simply furnished, a real down-home style. The place is really back to basics, but some visitors appreciate its family-like setting, far removed from the megaresorts of Cable Beach. The small inn is the site of the Pick-A-Dilly at 18 Parliament restaurant, which serves a Bahamian cuisine (see "Where to Dine," below).

CABLE BEACH

The glittering shoreline of Cable Beach, located west of Nassau, is topped only by Paradise Island (see chapter 5). It has loyal fans, many of whom think Paradise Island is too snobbish. Cable Beach for years has attracted visitors with its broad stretches of beachfront, a wide array of sports facilities, and lots of entertainment, including casino action. Deluxe or first-class resorts, two of which are all inclusive, line the shoreline. The area was named for the telegraph cable laid in 1892 from Jupiter, Florida, to The Bahamas.

VERY EXPENSIVE

Breezes. P.O. Box N-CBI-3049, Cable Beach, Nassau, The Bahamas. ☎ **800/859-SUPER** or 242/327-5356. Fax 242/327-5155. 386 rms, 5 suites. A/C TV TEL. Winter, $378 double; $538 suite for two. Off-season, $278 double; $458 suite for two. $70 extra person. Rates all inclusive (including drinks). AE, DISC, MC, V. Free parking. Bus: 10.

SuperClubs, which competes successfully with Sandals (see below) in Jamaica, spent $125 million transforming a tired old relic, the Ambassador Beach Hotel, into this all-inclusive resort. Although not as imposing as Sandals, Breezes is located on a prime 900-foot beachfront along Cable Beach. Both couples and single travelers over 16 are accepted here (unlike at Sandals).

The refurbished hotel rooms are newly decorated, with an air-conditioning system that works instead of rattles. Rooms, however, are not as luxurious as they are at Sandals. Everything is included—the room, meals, snacks, unlimited wine (not the finest) with lunch and dinner, even premium brand liquor at the bars, plus activities and airport transfers. Tipping is not allowed.

Dining/Entertainment: Guests at Breezes enjoy fine dining, although not as good as that of some of SuperClub's Jamaican properties, such as San Souci Lido in Ocho Rios or Grand Lido in Negril. Diners can sample routine international fare at the food court, although the Italian restaurant serves a better dinner. A beach-side grill and food and snacks are available throughout the day. Entertainment includes a high-energy disco, a piano bar, and a nightclub. Karaoke is inevitably performed, but the professional "Junkanoo" live shows are better.

Facilities: Beach; swimming pool and Jacuzzis; fully equipped fitness center; aerobics classes; two tennis courts (lit for night play); nonmotorized water sports; volleyball, basketball, and miniature golf.

EXPENSIVE

Nassau Beach Hotel. P.O. Box N-7756, Cable Beach, Nassau, The Bahamas. ☎ **800/ 225-5843** in the U.S., or 242/327-7711. Fax 242/327-7615. 401 rms, 9 suites. A/C MINIBAR TV TEL. Winter, $160–$240 double; $375–$400 one-bedroom suite; $500–$550 two-bedroom suite. Off-season, $150–$205 double; $300 one-bedroom suite; $425 two-bedroom suite. Year-round, $750 penthouse. AE, DC, MC, V. Free parking. Bus: 10.

This place has been somewhat overshadowed by the glitzy resorts a short walk away, but a crowd of loyal fans remains devoted to this hotel. Guests here shun the carnival-like atmosphere at such megaresorts as Marriott. "I don't like to stay at a place that looks like a box of Crayolas in a nuclear meltdown," wrote one visitor. The hotel, though, has a lively atmosphere, with a white-sand beach, lots of land and water sports, plus entertainment in the evening. The large children's activities program makes it a good choice for families, as well.

The hotel was built in the 1940s, with three separate wings in a gray-and-white twin-towered design, and features modified Georgian detailing and tile- and marble-covered floors. In the early 1990s, it was restored by new owners. Today, the place has been enhanced by landscaping and Bahamian touches that include ceiling fans and upholstered wicker furniture. Each of the accommodations contains Queen Anne reproductions and a marble bath with hair dryer and other accessories. However, the hotel is in the process of being sold again as this edition goes to press, so check with the hotel for any changes that might occur.

Dining/Entertainment: The hotel offers seven restaurants, one of which, the Beef Cellar, is reviewed under "Where to Dine," below. Nightlife possibilities include nostalgic rock-and-roll at the waterside Nassau Beach Rock and Roll Café (see "Where to Dine," below), as well as the island's highest-rated native show, "The King and Knights."

Services: Concierge, laundry, baby-sitting.

Facilities: 3,000-foot white-sand beach; six all-weather tennis courts lit for night play, with a resident pro for lessons; health club with weight and exercise machines; water sports; children's program.

Nassau Marriott Resort & Crystal Palace Casino. W. Bay St., P.O. Box N-8306, Cable Beach, Nassau, The Bahamas. ☎ **800/222-7466** in the U.S., or 242/327-6200. Fax 242/327-6459. 767 rms, 109 suites. A/C TV TEL. Winter, $129–$239 double; $200–$305 suite. Off-season, $119–$199 double; $200–$255 suite. MAP rates $40–$60 per person daily. AE, DC, MC, V. Free parking. Bus: 10.

This is the biggest (but not the best) megaresort on Cable Beach, and it's undergone a lot of changes since Marriott took over from Carnival Cruise Lines. When Carnival ran it, it was shamelessly glitzy and was nicknamed "The Purple Palace." Marriott has already toned down the interior colors and is making it a more prestigious address. Its major competitor, which is bigger and (we think) better, is the Atlantis Paradise Island Resort & Casino on Paradise Island. The Nassau Marriott is so self-contained it seems like management doesn't want you to leave the premises during your entire stay. You wouldn't have to, either: Everything is here.

The complex incorporates five high-rise towers, a futuristic central core, and a cluster of gardens and beachfront gazebos—all interconnected with arcades, underground passages, and minipavilions. Bedrooms are modern, spacious, and comfortable, but nowhere near as opulent as the public rooms.

Dining/Entertainment: The complex contains nine restaurants, three bars, a cabaret theater (the Palace Theater, recommended under "New Providence After Dark," below), plus the largest casino in The Bahamas. The restaurants run a wide culinary gamut. The best and most expensive—also the most formal—is the Sole Mare, serving Italian food (see "Where to Dine," below). The Black Angus Grille has some of the best steaks (all imported, of course) on Cable Beach, outclassed only by the Beef Cellar at Nassau Beach. The other restaurants are a varied assortment, everything from a pizza restaurant to a poolside grill. A lackluster Chinese restaurant is another choice, along with a scattering of standard seafood restaurants.

Services: Room service, laundry/valet.

🏨 Family-Friendly Hotels

British Colonial Beach Resort *(see p. 82)* Families who want to anchor right in the center of Nassau will find this hotel their best and safest bet. Since the hotel was built in the 1920s, many of its rooms are among the most spacious on the island, making it roomier and more comfortable for families. A host of dining and sporting choices are further enticement, as is the private white-sand beach right in the heart of the city.

Nassau Beach Hotel *(see p. 84)* Management actively seeks the family trade, offering a large children's activities program, including a play center with slides and swings, a video-game room, and a supervised recreation room.

Radisson Cable Beach Hotel *(see p. 87)* A massive hotel on Cable Beach, dating from the 1980s, this has become a family favorite—largely because of its Camp Junkanoo, which offers daily supervised play for children 3 to 12.

   Facilities: A swimming pool; complete array of water-sports facilities; 10 tennis courts; an 18-hole golf course; health club with sauna, massage facilities, and exercise machines. The artificial sandy "beach," however, is not adequate for such a mammoth hotel.

Radisson Cable Beach Hotel. W. Bay St., P.O. Box N-4914, Cable Beach, Nassau, The Bahamas. ☎ **800/333-3333** or 242/327-6000. Fax 242/327-6987. 669 rms, 31 suites. A/C MINIBAR TV TEL. Winter, $160–$195 double. Off-season, $115–$130 double. Year-round $330–$1,250 suites. AE, DC, MC, V. Free parking. Bus: 10.

   The construction of this massive hotel in the early 1980s was a much-noted event that challenged the near monopoly of Paradise Island and gave to Cable Beach the razzmatazz that later became an indelible part of its image. Owned by the Bahamian government, but managed by a Florida-based hotel conglomerate (the Myers Group) with input from Radisson Hotels, the hotel lies a short walk from the larger and glitzier facilities of the Nassau Marriott Resort & Crystal Palace Casino. The facility has been much improved by a recent $15 million renovation. Designed in a horseshoe-shaped curve around a landscaped beachfront garden, the nine-story building has an Aztec-inspired facade of sharp angles and strong horizontal lines. You'll think Vegas when you see its rows of fountains in front, acres of marble sheathing inside, and four-story lobby with huge windows. Big enough to get lost in, but with plenty of intimate retreats, the hotel offers an almost endless array of things to do, including Camp Junkanoo, supervised play for children 3 to 12.

   Each of the bedrooms is modern, comfortable, and standardized, with private balconies and big-windowed views of the garden or the beach.

   Dining/Entertainment: The hotel contains six restaurants, the most glamorous of which is the Restaurante D'Italia. Enchiladas and such fare are offered at Tequila Pepe's, and the Avocado has Mediterranean cuisine. The Mini-Market Grill serves Caribbean/continental breakfast and lunch buffets. There's also a wide selection of bars. Beach parties and native reviews are often staged.

   Services: 24-hour room service; baby-sitting at Camp Junkanoo, where supervised play is available for children 3 to 12; laundry; dry cleaning; beauty salon; concierge. Readers constantly complain of staff attitude and slow service at this sprawling resort.

   Facilities: 18 tennis courts, 3 racquetball and 3 squash courts, boutiques, adjacent Crystal Palace Casino.

Cable Beach Accommodations

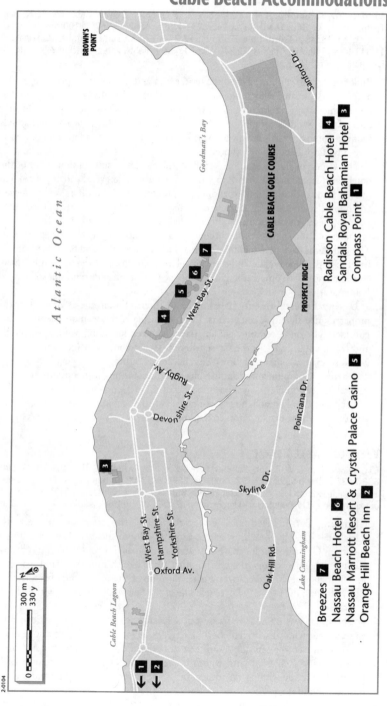

Radisson Cable Beach Hotel **4**
Sandals Royal Bahamian Hotel **3**
Compass Point **1**

Nassau Marriott Resort & Crystal Palace Casino **5**
Orange Hill Beach Inn **2**

Breezes **7**
Nassau Beach Hotel **6**

Sandals Royal Bahamian Hotel. W. Bay St., P.O. Box N-10422, Cable Beach, Nassau, The Bahamas. ☎ **800/SANDALS** or 242/327-6400. Fax 242/327-6961. 100 rms, 96 suites. Winter, $1,885–$2,220 double 7 nights; $2,270–$2,710 suite 7 nights. Off-season, $1,840–$2,195 double 7 nights; $2,340–$2,670 suite 7 nights. Rates all inclusive. AE, MC, V. Free parking. Bus: 10.

Built as a private club in 1946 to shelter the rich and famous from prying eyes, the property first became a hotel, the Balmoral Beach, in 1967. In December 1995, the hotel, which most recently had been the prestigious Le Meridian Royal Bahamian, opened as a Sandals couples-only (male/female) resort. It's now part of Sandals founder Butch Stewart's rapidly growing empire, which began in Jamaica but is now spreading throughout the Caribbean.

This is one of the most upmarket of all the Sandals resorts, although all of the hotel's aristocratic pretensions of the late 1940s are gone forever. Sandals poured $20 million into renovating and expanding the property. Today it offers well-furnished and often elegant rooms in six different categories. The bedrooms are in the Manor House, whereas the suites are in outlying villas. Some of these suites have Jacuzzis and private pools, and some of the bathrooms are as spacious as many big-city apartments. The bedrooms have cove moldings, formal English furniture, and baths loaded with bathrobes, perfumed soaps, and cosmetics. The rooms that face the ocean offer small, curved terraces with ornate iron railings and views of an offshore sand spit still named Balmoral Island.

Dining/Entertainment: Bahamian and international fare is offered in the property's five signature restaurants. Sandals cuisine is always more plentiful than gourmet, but you've certainly got an array of choices, including white-glove service and continental dishes in the Crystal Room. Other choices include southwestern grilled specialties, plus lavish breakfasts and dinner buffets.

Services: Complimentary shuttle bus to casino and nightlife options at nearby Crystal Palace complex, concierge, room service.

Facilities: Sandy beach, hourglass-shaped swimming pool, complete state-of-the-art exercise center, two lit tennis courts, complete array of water sports, access to golf facilities.

WEST OF CABLE BEACH

✪ **Compass Point.** W. Bay St., Gambier, Love Beach, New Providence, The Bahamas. ☎ **800/ 688-7678** in the U.S., or 242/327-7309. Fax 809/327-FAXX. 18 bungalows. TV TEL. Winter, $175 double without kitchenette; $260 double with kitchenette. Off-season, $135 double without kitchenette; $175 double with kitchenette. AE, DC, MC, V. Free parking.

Charming, personalized, and "casually upscale," this is an alternative to the megahotels of Cable Beach, which lie about 6 miles to the east. The place isn't as snobby as Graycliff, but for those who want an intimate inn and don't mind the too vibrant Bahamian colors, there is no other place like this on the island—or even in The Bahamas. Scattered over 2 acres of some of the most expensive terrain in The Bahamas, the property lies beside one of the few sandy coves along the island's northwest.

The hotel was named by its owner, Christopher Blackwell (Jamaican-born entrepreneur who "discovered" Bob Marley), in 1994. It lies adjacent to one of the best-known recording businesses in the Caribbean, Compass Point Studios (a division of Island Records), with whom it shares some of its staff and some of its profitable and, depending on your point of view, very appealing attitudes about business and life.

Each accommodation is a private, fully detached "hut" or cottage painted in multicolored hues. About nine contain kitchenettes; each has exposed rafters, high ceilings, a half dozen windows facing the ocean breezes, and all the privacy afforded by the verdant banana trees that ring each unit. Some units are raised on stilts, others hug close to the ground. On the premises are a tennis court, a swimming pool, a bar, and whatever Caribbean musician happens to be on the island at the time.

The establishment's restaurant (Compass Point), is recommended separately in "Where to Dine," below.

Orange Hill Beach Inn. W. Bay St. just west of Blake Rd., Box N-8583, Nassau, The Bahamas. ☎ **242/327-7157.** Fax 242/327-5186. 32 units. A/C TV. Winter, $90–$95 double; $105 triple; $115 quad; $120 double apt; $130 triple apt; $140 quad apt. Off-season, $80–$85 double; $95 triple; $105 quad; $100 double apt; $110 triple apt; $120 quad apt. AE, MC, V. Free parking.

This hotel, set on 3¹/₂ landscaped, hillside acres, lies about 8 miles west of the congestion of Nassau and 1 mile east of Love Beach. It's for those who want to escape the crowds and stay in a less inhabited part of New Providence Island. The inn is a 9-minute walk from a beach known for its snorkeling. The owners, Judy and Danny Lowe, an Irish-Bahamian partnership, have welcomed more than 500 couples who have selected Orange Hill as the setting for their weddings.

The establishment was built as a private home in the 1920s and became a hotel in 1979 after the Lowes added more rooms and a swimming pool. Rooms and apartments come in a variety of sizes, although most of them are small. Each has a balcony or patio, and a few apartments are equipped with kitchenettes. Much of the clientele here is European, especially during the summer months. On site is a bar serving sandwiches and salads throughout the day, and a restaurant that offers simple but good set-price dinners. Diving excursions to the rich marine fauna of New Providence's southwestern coast are among the most popular activities here, and sea kayaks can be rented on site.

SOUTHWESTERN NEW PROVIDENCE

South Ocean Golf & Beach Resort. SW Ocean Rd., P.O. Box N-8191, Nassau, The Bahamas. ☎ **800/223-6510** or 242/362-4391. Fax 242/362-4728. 249 rms. A/C TV TEL. Winter, $165–$195 double. Off-season, $110–$140 double. Third person $35 extra per day winter; $25 extra per day off-season. AE, DC, MC, V. "The Bahamas Experience Bus," charging $5 one-way into Cable Beach, Nassau, or Paradise Island.

This remote resort, which occupies 18 acres on the less populated pine-covered southwestern shore of New Providence, is about a 45-minute drive southwest of Nassau. With its ornate balconies and white columns, it reminds guests of a colonial plantation house in Georgia or the Carolinas. There is the feel of an American country club here. The hotel offers the best golf and the best diving on the island, and its seclusion also attracts a lot of honeymooners. Many guests purposefully shun the casino glitz of Paradise Island and Cable Beach for the tranquil setting here and for the beaches, which are far less crowded than those along resort-studded Cable Beach.

The guest rooms are equally divided between older but still very comfortable units set inland in a garden around a swimming pool, and newer, more plush units on the beach, the latter decorated in plantation-era style. Go for one of the beach units if you can get it because they have more light and are breezier and more appealing, with two-poster beds, Queen Anne–reproduction chairs, and tile floors.

Dining/Entertainment: The hotel's restaurant, Papagayo, has never been noted for its cuisine, but it does offer good wholesome fare that appeals to most of its mid-America clientele. There's fairly routine nightly entertainment and dancing in the Flamingo Room, but no casino. Many guests retire early here.

Services: Guest-relations staff.

Facilities: Beach, 18-hole golf course, two freshwater swimming pools, array of water-sports activities including top-notch scuba diving, four tennis courts (two lit at night), volleyball on the beach.

4 Where to Dine

In restaurants rated very expensive, expect to spend from $50 to $75 for a meal; in expensive, $25 to $30. In moderate restaurants, dinner goes for $15 to $20. Anything under $12 is considered inexpensive. Drinks and a 15% service charge are extra.

NASSAU
VERY EXPENSIVE

✪ **Graycliff.** W. Hill St. ☎ **242/322-2796.** Reservations required. Jacket advised for men. Dinner main courses $32.75–$42.75; lunch main courses $17.75–$22.75. AE, DC, MC, V. Mon–Fri noon–3pm; daily 7–10pm. Bus: 10, 17. CONTINENTAL.

Graycliff is the only restaurant in The Bahamas that deserves a five-star rating. Part of the previously recommended hotel, an antique-filled colonial mansion located opposite Government House, this restaurant is the domain of connoisseur and bon vivant Enrico Garzaroli. The chefs use local Bahamian products and delicacies whenever available and fashion them into a spicy and hearty cuisine. The chefs are not regional, nor unduly influenced by France. Rather, they apply their original standards and measures to the innovative dishes served, exemplified by grouper soup in puff pastry. They also take plump, juicy pheasant and cook it with pineapple grown on Eleuthera in an award-winning combination. Lobster is another specialty, and they rarely overcook it, covering one side with *beurre blanc* (white butter) and the other side with a sauce prepared with the head of the lobster. The Grand Marnier soufflé is worth the trip across town to sample. The wine list is the finest in the country, with more than 175,000 bottles. The collection of Cuban cigars here—almost 90 types—is said to be the most varied in the world. Before dinner, the ideal spot for a drink is the balcony bar.

EXPENSIVE

Buena Vista. Delancy and Meeting sts. ☎ **242/322-2811.** Reservations recommended. Main courses $28.50–$35; fixed-price dinner $31. AE, DC, MC, V. Daily 7–10pm. Closed Sun, Apr 15–Christmas. Bus: 10, 17. CONTINENTAL.

Although its not quite up there with Graycliff or Sun And . . . , this is definitely third runner-up in the culinary sweepstakes of Nassau. It's 1 block west of Government House. (Delancy Street is opposite the cathedral close off St. Francis Xavier, only a short distance from Bay Street.) It opened back in the 1940s in a colonial mansion set on 5 acres of tropical foliage. Traditional elegance and fine eating have always characterized this place.

You're likely to be shown to the main dining room, unless you request the cozy and intimate Victoria Room, or, even better, the Garden Patio, which has a greenhouse setting and a ceiling skylight. The chef seems to travel the length and breadth of Nassau markets to collect the freshest and finest ingredients, which he puts together in menus bursting with flavor and full of originality. Look for the impromptu daily specials. There is not only nouvelle cuisine here but also a respect for tradition. The rack of lamb Provençale is a classic, but you might want to try instead some of his lighter veal dishes. His cream of garlic soup has plenty of flavor but never overpowers. Instead of wildly fanciful desserts, he makes you appreciate the classics—say, cherries jubilee or his baked Alaska flambé au cognac. Service is deft and efficient, and also polite. Calypso coffee finishes the meal off nicely as you listen to soft piano music.

✪ **Sun And** . . . . Lake View Rd., off Shirley St. ☎ **242/393-1205.** Reservations required. Jacket preferred for men. Main courses $29–$37. AE, MC, V. Tues–Sun 6:30–9:30pm. Closed Aug–Sept. Bus: 10, 17. FRENCH/SEAFOOD.

Near Fort Montagu, this place seems to have been here forever and can name-drop better than anyplace but Graycliff. The fact that a restaurant has endured doesn't necessarily mean it's good—but in this case, it does. Only Graycliff sets a finer table. Sun And . . . is the classic Nassau restaurant, a citadel of top-notch cuisine and service. More than any other venue, it evokes Nassau during the heyday of British colonial charm. To get to this hard-to-find place, you pass over a drawbridge between two pools and then enter a Spanish-style courtyard, complete with fountains. In this fine old Bahamian home, you can order drinks in the patio bar and then dine either inside in cozy quarters or alfresco around the rock pool.

Start with the spicy conch chowder. It gets no better in Nassau. The chef shines with ingeniously prepared dishes such as braised duckling with raspberry sauce. True, this dish is something of a cliché, but it's prepared ever so fine here. The grilled veal chop with portobello mushrooms is one of the more admirably executed dishes, as is the classic roast spring lamb, almost melt-in-your mouth tender and perfectly seasoned without being overpowered with herbs and garlic.

Savvy Nassau foodies always praise Ronne Derckere's incomparable soufflés (even better than the Grand Marnier soufflé at Graycliff). Our favorite is prepared with rum raisins and Black Label Bacardi. More than 100 wines complement the well-thought-out menu.

MODERATE

Caribe Café Restaurant and Terrace. In the British Colonial Beach Resort, 1 Bay St. ☎ **242/322-3301.** Reservations recommended. Main courses $14–$24; lunch $6–$9. Daily 7:30–11am, 11:30am–4pm and 5–11pm. Bus: 10, 17. STEAKS/SEAFOOD.

Renovated in 1995, this down-home eatery was once the dank Blackbeard's Forge, recalling the days when Nassau was a haven for buccaneers. But the place has been considerably lightened up, both in its decor and in its food. Because it's near the cruise-ship docks, it is likely to be overrun on the days when a heavy armada is in port. You may want to retreat elsewhere (see below) if all the tables look full, since service tends to be bad then.

Otherwise, at lunch you can get the food your kid has been crying for, including beef burgers or freshly made salads. At night the offerings are more varied, although it's never exactly gourmet fare. The seafood platter is dull, but the sautéed shrimp and chicken breast on a bed of spinach with Dijonaise sauce is filled with flavor. And if you don't like the chef's cookery, you can always cook the meal yourself. Grills are placed on the tables where you can prepare a New York sirloin or a lamb cutlet grilled with mint. Each of the wood-and-chrome tables has a box-shaped vent for the smoke to escape.

East Villa Restaurant and Lounge. E. Bay St. ☎ **242/393-3377.** Reservations required. Main courses $17.95–$31. AE, MC, V. Daily 5:30–10:30pm. MANDARIN/SZECHUAN/CANTON.

Next door to the Nassau Yacht Club, this Chinese eatery is rather upscale, often attracting rich Florida yachties to its dimly lit precincts. Exotic fish aquariums and elegant Chinese statuettes set the mood for the fine viands served here. One savvy local woman, who dines here at least once a week, called it "a delight of the heart." Perhaps she'd had too much to drink, but many of the dishes are a pleasure to taste.

Nassau Dining

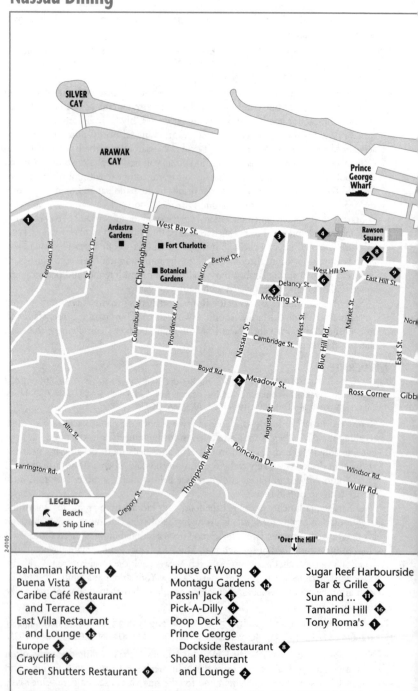

SILVER CAY

ARAWAK CAY

Prince George Wharf

❶

Ardastra Gardens ■

Chippingham Rd.

West Bay St.

❸

❹

Rawson Square

Ferguson Rd.

St. Alban's Dr.

■ Fort Charlotte

Bethel Dr.

❽

❼

■ Botanical Gardens

Marcus

West Hill St.

East Hill St.

❾

❻

Delancy St.

❺

Meeting St.

Columbus Av.

Providence Av.

Nassau St.

Cambridge St.

West St.

Blue Hill Rd.

Market St.

East St.

Nor

Boyd Rd.

❷ Meadow St.

Ross Corner

Gibb

Alto St.

Augusta St.

Poinciana Dr.

Windsor Rd.

Farrington Rd.

Thompson Blvd.

Wulff Rd.

Gregory St.

LEGEND

Beach

Ship Line

"Over the Hill"
↓

Bahamian Kitchen ❼
Buena Vista ❺
Caribe Café Restaurant
   and Terrace ❹
East Villa Restaurant
   and Lounge ⓯
Europe ❸
Graycliff ❻
Green Shutters Restaurant ❾

House of Wong ❾
Montagu Gardens ⓮
Passin' Jack ⓭
Pick-A-Dilly ❾
Poop Deck ⓬
Prince George
   Dockside Restaurant ❽
Shoal Restaurant
   and Lounge ❷

Sugar Reef Harbourside
   Bar & Grille ❿
Sun and ... ⓫
Tamarind Hill ⓰
Tony Roma's ❶

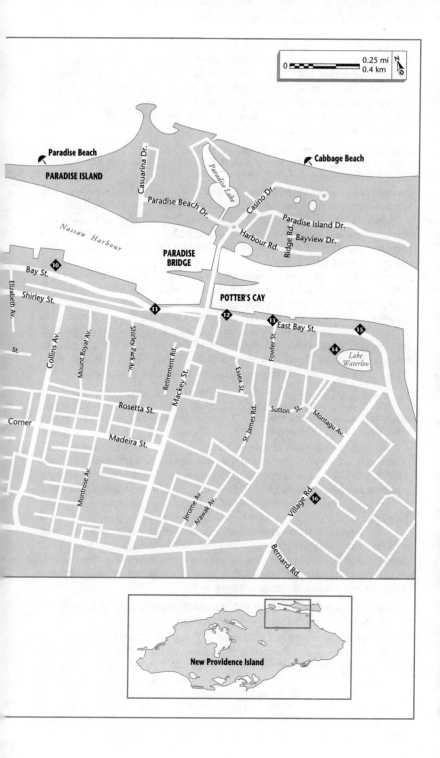

Paradise Beach

PARADISE ISLAND

Casuarina Dr.

Paradise Beach Dr.

Paradise Lake

Casino Dr.

Cabbage Beach

Paradise Island Dr.

Ridge Rd.

Bayview Dr.

Nassau Harbour

Harbour Rd.

PARADISE
BRIDGE

POTTER'S CAY

10 Bay St.

Shirley St.

Elizabeth Av.

St.

Collins Av.

Mount Royal Av.

Shirley Park Av.

Retirement Rd.

Mackey St.

Essex St.

Fowler St.

East Bay St.

15

14 Lake
Waterloo

Rosetta St.

Corner

Madeira St.

Montrose Av.

Jerome Av.

Arawak Av.

St. James Rd.

Sutton St.

Montagu Av.

Village Rd.

16

Bernard Rd.

11

12

13

New Providence Island

0   0.25 mi
     0.4 km

N

93

We especially like how the chefs feel at home in various kitchens of the provinces of China, each one different. Zesty Szechuan flavors appear on the menu, but there are less-spicy alternatives from the Cantonese culinary repertoire, including sweet and sour chicken and steamed vegetables with cashews and water chestnuts. *Hung shew* or walnut chicken is one of our favorite dishes. Lamb chops, a disappointment in most Bahamian restaurants, are a favorite dish here. Waiters are adept at guessing your gastric threshold: mild, medium, or zesty hot.

Europe. In the Ocean Spray Hotel, W. Bay St. ☎ **242/322-8032.** Lunch main courses $8–$14; set lunch $12; dinner main courses $8–$24. AE, MC, V. Mon–Fri 8am–midnight, Sat 4:30pm–midnight. Bus: 10. GERMAN/CONTINENTAL.

Attached to an inexpensive hotel (see "Where to Stay," above), Europe offers the best German specialties in Nassau. Admittedly, this may not be the kind of food you came to Nassau for, and it's a little heavy for the tropics, but the dishes are properly rendered and politely served. Admirers are drawn to Europe's low prices and to its change-of-pace fare—this is where you go when you think you can't stare another grouper or conch in the face.

Robust flavors have traveled across the ocean rather well. At least the horde of German visitors on our last visit agreed. When the waiter suggests hearty soups to begin, he means it—perhaps lima bean and sausage. Naturally, there is bratwurst and quite good sauerbraten (the island's best, although admittedly there's not much competition). If you don't opt for the Wiener schnitzel, you might settle for a perfectly done pepper steak cognac. The chef will also prepare two kinds of fondue: bourguignonne and cheese. Everybody's favorite dessert is the meltingly moist German chocolate cake. All right, we said it was heavy. Diet tomorrow.

Green Shutters Restaurant. 48 Parliament St. ☎ **242/325-5702.** Lunch main courses $6.95–$21.50; dinner main courses $10.50–$27; fixed-price lunch $6.95. AE, MC, V. Daily 11:30am–4pm and 6–11pm. Bar open daily 11am–midnight. Restaurant closes 8pm Sun Sept–Jan. Bus: 10, 17. ENGLISH/BAHAMIAN.

Located just 2 blocks south of Rawson Square, this place is like a transplanted English pub in the tropics. A favorite with British expatriates, it offers three imported English beers along with some pub grub favorites such as steak-and-kidney pie, bangers and mash, shepherd's pie, and fish-and-chips. These dishes taste like what mother used to make (providing you had an English mother from the Midlands). Bahamian specialties are also served, including the inevitable grouper and conch chowder. Some of these aren't bad and are an improvement over the pub grub. Sandwiches at lunch are particularly good and well stuffed, including the triple-decker club. Courage beer is on tap, but the bartender will also make you a frozen daiquiri.

This place is macho and sporty, with a giant TV screen and secondary monitors airing live sporting events throughout the year.

House of Wong. Marlborough St. ☎ **242/326-0045.** Reservations recommended. Main courses $8.50–$22. AE, MC, V. Daily 11am–11pm. ASIAN.

In the heart of downtown Nassau, House of Wong is the latest incarnation of the famed Mai Tai Chinese-Polynesian Restaurant, which used to stand near Fort Montagu. Peter Wong and his family brought all their recipes for Polynesian, Szechuan, and Cantonese dishes, even some Hawaiian ones, to their new kitchen. This place is still the leading Asian restaurant in Nassau, although the kitchen staff may be stretching itself a bit far with all these culinary influences. Before your meal, try one of the exotic drinks that complement the Asian theme: a Volcanic Flame (served with flaming rum), a Lover's Paradise, or perhaps a Fog Cutter.

🙂 Family-Friendly Restaurants

Green Shutters Restaurant *(see p. 94)* This restaurant in downtown Nassau is noted for its well-stuffed sandwiches, potato skins, and wide selection of burgers. Kids also like its simple fare, including fried chicken and seafood kabobs, and especially the chocolate cake for dessert.

Caribe Café Restaurant and Terrace *(see p. 91)* in Nassau's British Colonial Beach Resort, is one of the best places to take children for food they know and love, especially steak and jumbo shrimp kabobs. Few of them ever say no to the coconut cream layer cake either.

In the Polynesian mood? You might choose chow samsee, deviled Bahamian lobster, Mandarin orange duck, or sizzling steak. Szechuan dishes include hot shredded spiced beef, kung pao chicken ding, and lemon chicken. Among the Cantonese selections are chicken almond ding, moo goo gai pan, and sweet-and-sour chicken or pork. The restaurant also has take-out service. You get a lot of good food and polite service for the price.

Montagu Gardens. E. Bay St. ☎ **242/394-6347.** Reservations required. Main dishes $19–$28.50. AE, MC, V. Mon–Sat 6–10pm. STEAK/SEAFOOD.

At the edge of Lake Waterloo, this restaurant is installed in an old mansion at the eastern end of Bay Street. Because of its relative isolation, it seems little known and is especially ignored by most guidebooks. However, the food merits a trip here. The dining room is in a courtyard garden. The chefs get some of the best seafood and beef on the island. They are especially noted for their Angus beef, which they carve into T-bones, filet mignons, and ribeye. These succulent dishes can be prepared as you wish them. In addition, they also offer baby back ribs and, on most occasions, a perfectly seasoned and cooked rack of lamb. If you're wandering around Nassau at night (not a good idea) and looking for some good seafood, head to this safe oasis. The stuffed lobster tail is a might ordinary, but they do wonders with that old Bahamian standby, grouper, and also serve some moist and well-seasoned dolphin. If you eat too much here you can dance the night away (and the calories) at Club Waterloo adjoining.

Passin' Jack. In the Nassau Harbour Club Hotel, E. Bay St. ☎ **242/394-3245.** Main courses $13–$20. AE, MC, V. Daily 7–11am, noon–3pm, and 6–10pm. Bus: 17. BAHAMIAN/AMERICAN.

Located on the lobby level of an unpretentious modern hotel on Bay Street, a half mile east of the Paradise Island Bridge, this likable restaurant was established in 1993. It's named after the schools of passin' jack (a cousin of the amberjack) that Bahamian fishers have traditionally caught by the hundreds every September. In addition to well-flavored food, the restaurant offers a panoramic view over the Paradise Island Channel to one of the country's most mysterious houses, an enormous villa built by a reclusive Saudi sheik in the late 1980s. Passin' Jack's doesn't pretend to be what it's not: It's a local favorite where people come to drink and to chow down. The staff will be just as nice to you if you come in for a sandwich or for a soul food favorite such as cracked conch or grouper fingers. Baby back ribs (not as good as Tony Roma's) fill many a plate, and for those who desire it the chef will throw a strip steak or even a filet mignon on the grill. The special drink of the house, the Passin' Jack, combines the best parts of a frozen rum runner with a frozen piña colada for one heady libation.

Poop Deck. Nassau Yacht Haven Marina, E. Bay St. ☎ **242/393-8175.** Main courses $12.95–$34; lunch $9.95–$14.95. AE, MC, V. Daily noon–5pm and 5:30–10:30pm. Bus: 10, 17. BAHAMIAN.

This is a favorite with the yachties and others who find a perch on the second-floor, open-air terrace, which overlooks the harbor and Paradise Island. If you like your dining with a view, there is no better place in the heart of Nassau. At lunch, you can order such standard fare as conch chowder (perfectly seasoned) or else some juicy beef burgers. The waiters are friendly, the crowd convivial, and the festivities continue into the evening with lots of drinking and good cheer. Native grouper fingers served with peas 'n' rice is the Bahamian soul food dish on the menu. The owners also like to serve spicy native dishes, which they fancifully call Rosie's special chicken or Bahama Mama's grouper. Two of the best seafood selections are the fresh lobster and the stuffed deviled crab. The creamy homemade lasagne with crisp garlic bread is another fine choice.

Sugar Reef Harbourside Bar & Grill. Bay St. ☎ **242/356-3065.** Reservations recommended. Main courses $17–$26.95. AE, MC, V. Daily 11am–3pm and 6–10:30pm. CARIBBEAN.

Sometimes you like to dine with a view. In Nassau, one of the best options is this restaurant, which has dining both inside and out. We especially like it at night with its view of the harbor and the glittering lights of Paradise Island. Fortunately, the food is worthy, too. The owner and his band of merry waiters like to show off their cookery, especially in their use of sauces, many of which are made with tropical fruits. It might take some getting used to, but they dazzle you with sauces made from papaya, guava, and banana. Their grilled chicken breast in mango sauce is a delight. Dishes seem to be lighthearted in texture and taste. The chef always shops for fresh seafood—none better than the catch of the day. Cracked conch is invariably featured, as it is to Nassau what Wiener schnitzel is to Vienna. You can also order some zesty crab cakes and on most nights the Bahamian lobster (ask that it not be overcooked to be on the safe side).

INEXPENSIVE

Bahamian Kitchen. Trinity Place, off Market St. ☎ **242/325-0702.** Reservations not accepted. Main courses $8.95–$24; lunches $6–$18. AE, DC, MC, V. Mon–Sat 11:30am–10pm. Bus: 10, 17. BAHAMIAN.

Next to Trinity Church, this is one of the best places for good, down-home Bahamian food at modest prices. Specialties include lobster Bahamian style, fried red snapper, conch salad, stewed fish, curried chicken, okra soup, and pea soup and dumplings. Most dishes are served with peas 'n' rice. You can order such old-fashioned Bahamian fare as stewed fish and corned beef and grits, all served with johnnycake. This is the type of food the Bahamians have loved and survived on for decades. There is a take-out service if you're planning a picnic. The place is honest, decent, and upright.

Pick-A-Dilly at 18 Parliament. 18 Parliament St. ☎ **242/322-2836.** Lunch main courses $6–$14; dinner main courses $9–$15. AE, MC, V. Mon–Sat 11am–4pm and 5–10pm. Bus: 10. BAHAMIAN/AMERICAN.

This downtown restaurant lies within the palm-studded tropical garden of Nassau's oldest continually operating hotel, the Parliament. Casually dressed diners come here for Bahamian seafood in a verdant setting. Appetizers include conch salad and chowder. The fish is well prepared, especially the house special, grilled or blackened grouper. You might also try the cracked conch. Grouper and conch remain the strong suit because that's what many of the regulars grew up on and continue to order (even though a lot more food options are available today than in the good old days). Desserts include key lime pie, mud pie, or "bananas à la Dilly." There's a large tropical drink menu featuring the best frozen fruit daiquiris in Nassau. Ever had a soursop daiquiri?

Prince George Dockside Restaurant. Bay St. (just west of Rawston Sq.). ☎ **242/ 322-5854.** Reservations recommended. Main courses $11–$23.40. MC, V. Daily 5:30–10pm. GREEK/INTERNATIONAL.

Originally from Greece, owner George Papageorge put this wharfside place on the culinary dining maps of Nassau. A native of Athens, Papageorge, who has lived in Nassau for some 50 years, seems to be everybody's favorite bistro owner. With grace and Greek charm, he runs his restaurant with a professional yet unpretentious air. The food is good, too, which is why both locals and visitors patronize the place in almost equal numbers. You can dine indoors or outside on a patio with a view of the wharf. The atmosphere is relaxed and friendly. Even the so-called American dishes seem to have a certain European flair. A typical dinner begins with a bowl of conch salad, but you'd please George more if you ordered his native Greek salad. On our last visit, the broiled shrimp stuffed with crabmeat was a delight, as were the fettuccine Alfredo and the tender osso bucco perfectly cooked as in Milan. Of course, George will also prepare a T-bone steak if you don't want to muck about with all these European dishes.

Shoal Restaurant and Lounge. Nassau St. ☎ **242/323-4400.** Main courses $9.50–$13.95. AE, MC, V. Daily 7:30–10am, 11:30am–2:30pm, and 5:30–10pm. BAHAMIAN.

Many of our good friends in Nassau maintain this is the best dive for local food, real Bahama Mama style. We're not entirely convinced this is true, but we rank it near the top for authentic flavor. The place is at its most beehive active on Saturday morning when half of Nassau seemingly shows up for the chef's specialty, boiled fish and johnnycake. This may or may not be your fantasy, but if you're a Bahamian it is like pot liquor and turnip greens with cornbread to a Southerner. Far removed from the well-trodden tourist path, this restaurant is steadfastly a local favorite. After all, where can you get a good bowl of okra soup these days? Naturally, conch chowder is the favorite opener. Many diners follow that chowder with more conch—"cracked" this time. But you can also order more unusual dishes such as Bahamian-style mutton using native spices and herbs. The seafood platter with such delights as lobster, shrimp, and fried grouper is more international in appeal. Peas 'n' rice accompany all dishes. As one habitué informed us, "It's just like my mama would have cooked if she'd known how."

Tamarind Hill. Village Rd. ☎ **242/393-1306.** Reservations recommended. Lunch main courses $8.25–$14.75; lunch buffet $9; dinner main courses $11.75–$27.50. MC, V. Daily 11am–4pm and 6–11pm. Bus: 17 (Soldier Rd. Bus). CARIBBEAN.

This is a favorite neighborhood restaurant for scores of Nassau residents who appreciate its charms and conviviality. It was named after the huge tamarind tree that grows in the front yard of the restaurant, a brightly painted building that was originally a private home in the 1960s. Set about a mile east of the Paradise Island Bridge in a residential neighborhood uphill from Mont Ague Beach, it's outfitted with primitive paintings, potted plants, and brightly painted metal sculptures. At least a half dozen types of burgers are offered, as well as sandwiches and salads. More substantial fare includes grouper in a nut crust, jerk pork tenderloin, fresh catch of the day prepared in any of about four different ways, cracked conch, conch fritters, and crepes with lobster and shrimp. The lunch buffet includes traditional Bahamian dishes, such as steamed conch and curried mutton, as well as the usual baby back ribs and fried fish. The food is quite innovative at times and always filled with zesty, spicy flavors. The best drinks at the bar? A Tamarind Hill Cooler or a Tamarind Hill Smoothie.

Tony Roma's. Saunders Beach, W. Bay St. ☎ **242/325-6502.** Main courses $7–$22. AE, MC, V. Daily noon–11pm. Bus: 10. RIBS.

Okay, it's a chain, but this place on the main road between Nassau and Cable Beach offers rib-sticking portions and good value. The stone-trimmed building affords views of Saunders Beach from its open-air veranda. Inside, the decor includes exposed paneling, captain's chairs, and ceiling fans.

Stick to the ribs. Barbecued in a special sauce, they come in small (lunchtime) or large orders and can be accompanied by barbecued chicken as part of the same platter. The best hamburgers on the island, a zesty Bahamian conch chowder, chef's or green salad, and panfried grouper are also offered. For an appetizer, we always order the onion rings, which are served in a steaming loaf with a spicy sauce. This chain restaurant has the formula down pat.

CABLE BEACH
EXPENSIVE

The Beef Cellar. In the Nassau Beach Hotel. ☎ **242/327-7711.** Reservations recommended. Main courses $11–$29. AE, DC, MC, V. Daily 6–10pm. STEAK/SEAFOOD.

If you like steak, this is the best place to go on Cable Beach. Their steaks are hardly the rival of the Palm in New York, but they are juicy, succulent, and tender—and cooked just as you like. Located downstairs from the hotel's lobby, within a short walk of the glittering casino at the neighboring Nassau Marriott Resort, the Beef Cellar features a warmly masculine decor of exposed stone and leather, two-fisted drinks, and tables that have individual charcoal grills for diners who prefer to grill their own steaks.

A limited but well-chosen selection of U.S.–bred beef is featured, including beef kabobs, New York sirloin, filet mignon, grilled veal loin chops, and the inevitable surf and turf.

The Black Angus Grille. In the Nassau Marriott Resort and Crystal Palace Casino, W. Bay St. ☎ **242/327-6200.** Reservations recommended. Main courses $17.50–$35. AE, DC, MC, V. Mon–Sat 6–11pm. Bus: 10. INTERNATIONAL/STEAK/SEAFOOD.

This is your best bet for dining if you're testing your luck at the Crystal Palace Casino nearby. It's the favorite of hundreds of casino goers within this mammoth hotel as it serves some of the best beef and steaks along Cable Beach. The Beef Cellar (see above) has the edge, but this is a close runner-up. The elegantly decorated restaurant lies one floor above the gambling tables.

Although steaks are frozen and flown in from the mainland, they are well pre-pared—succulent and juicy—and cooked to your specifications. The filet mignon is especially delectable, although the T-bone always seems to have more flavor. Prime rib is a nightly feature. The kitchen also prepares a number of sumptuous seafood platters. Bahamian lobster tails here are fresh and flavorful. Two other good bets for the non-steak crowd are the chicken carbonara and the fish-studded pasta.

✪ **Sole Mare.** In the Nassau Marriott Resort & Crystal Palace Casino, W. Bay St. ☎ **242/327-6200.** Reservations required. Main courses $19–$35. AE, DC, MC, V. Tues–Sun 6–11pm. Bus: 10. NORTHERN ITALIAN.

This is the premier choice for elegant dining along Cable Beach, and it also serves the best Northern Italian cuisine along the beach strip. The chefs are well trained and inventive in their cuisine. A filet of whatever fresh fish is available that day appears on the menu and is the keynote of many a delectable meal here. Many of their other ingredients have to be imported from the mainland, but the chefs still work their magic with them. Their spinach salad tastes market fresh, or else you might begin with an apple-scented lobster bisque laced with cream and cognac that is so velvety smooth it's worth the calorie overload. Veal sautéed with endive is something usually encountered in a little upmarket tavern in northern Italy, but appears here perfectly prepared and given extra flavor with white wine and capers. The grilled tuna was moist inside but had a crisp flavor on the outside during our most recent sampling. The dessert soufflés are hardly the equal of those served at Sun And . . . , but are a delight in every way, especially when served with a vanilla sauce.

MODERATE

Margaritaville. In the Radisson Cable Beach Hotel, W. Bay St. ☎ **242/327-6000.** Main courses $15–$24. Thurs–Tues 11:30am–2:30pm and 5–11pm. MEXICAN.

Jimmy Buffett to our knowledge has never appeared here, but we are certain that if he were in Cable Beach he'd show up . . . margarita in hand. Although stateside visitors are used to finding a Margaritaville in every town they hit, a real Mexican restaurant is a bit of an oddity in The Bahamas. The place has a real irreverent style, as exemplified by waitresses toting shot glasses on their hips. They believe in keeping that Tequila pouring. Avoiding a faux cactus, you can peruse the menu. It's all familiar fare to Tex-Mex fans. The restaurant serves buffet style, with appetizers like black bean soup and tortilla chips with queso or salsa. For a main course, what would you expect but fajitas, tacos, burritos, tamales, and chimichangas? But is it any good? We've found that after enough margaritas, you, like Rhett, might truly not give a damn. On Sunday, they have a live band and salsa contest.

Rock and Roll Café. Adjacent to Nassau Beach Hotel. ☎ **242/327-7711.** Sandwiches and salads $7.50–$13; platters $9–$22. AE, MC, V. Daily noon–2am. INTERNATIONAL/BAHAMIAN.

Set in an open-sided building midway between two of Cable Beach's resort hotels, this restaurant, a Hard Rock Cafe clone, combines tropical weather, rock-and-roll music, and enough music-related paraphernalia to thrill any groupie. The decor includes a model of a World War II fighter plane suspended over the bar, framed publicity shots of bands, and lots of memorabilia from the golden age of rock-and-roll. There's a view of the sea, an option of dining either indoors or on a beachfront terrace, and an array of drinks (the strawberry daiquiri is the most popular). Food includes the usual selection of sandwiches (both vegetarian and meat-stuffed), barbecued pork, stuffed potato skins, and ribs. This is an amusing place; the cuisine is secondary to the fun people have here. On the opposite side of the French windows that illuminate the dining room, you'll find an outdoor terrace for sunlit (or starlit) meals. The weekly high point? Every Friday night, a miniature version of the Bahamian carnival parade (Junkanoo, starring a stylized representation of the mythical character of Johnny Canoe) promenades through the dining room. Kids love it.

INEXPENSIVE

Café Johnny Canoe. In the Nassau Beach Hotel, W. Bay St. ☎ **242/327-3373.** Breakfast $5–$7; main courses $6.75–$22. AE, MC, V. Daily 7:30am–midnight. INTERNATIONAL.

Although it's set on the less desirable side of the Nassau Beach Hotel (the one facing West Bay Street), that doesn't seem to detract from this place. Within a yellow-painted interior accented with framed antique photographs of Old Nassau, you can order a wide range of the kind of dishes that everybody (especially families) seems to like: burgers, all kinds of steaks, seafood, and chicken dishes. The best items on the menu are blackened grouper and barbecued fish.

The outdoor terrace (site of volleyball games and other tournaments) is often mobbed by college students, especially during spring break. Live rock-and-roll concerts and karaoke are frequently part of the agenda at this very popular restaurant. In addition, diners receive free entrance to The Zoo, a separately recommended disco (see the "New Providence After Dark" section of this chapter), which is owned by the same management.

WEST OF CABLE BEACH

✪ The Restaurant at Compass Point. W. Bay St., Gambier, Love Beach. ☎ **242/ 327-4500.** Reservations necessary. Lunch platters $5–$15; dinner main courses $17–$30. AE, MC, V. Daily 7am–9:30pm. CALIFORNIAN/CARIBBEAN.

Located in the previously recommended hotel at Compass Point, a former private home, this is one of the best restaurants on New Providence Island. It is the only restaurant to join the stellar ranks of Graycliff and Sun And . . . in years. It's not as elegant as either of those, but it ranks up there near the top.

Its cuisine is a combination of California and Caribbean, with many innovative dishes—some influenced by Thailand. It attracts not only visitors, but savvy local foodies. Lunch offerings include pizzas and pastas, but also tandoori fried calamari and jerk chicken salad. At night, many of the chef's dishes have a touch of whimsy, including grilled fresh fish with a tropical fruit and sweet pepper salsa.

Rack of lamb appears here with a guava-roasted garlic glaze, adding a new dimension to this classic dish. The risotto with a variety of mushrooms and fresh herbs is the best we've ever sampled on the island. The grilled and blackened fish served here tops that prepared by any chef on Cable Beach. The agnolotti filled with conch is a masterful, original dish. To really pique your taste buds, ask for the Bahamian makki roll with conch, mango, and cucumber served with wasabi and pickled ginger.

✪ Traveller's Rest. W. Bay St., near Gambier (9 miles west of the center of Nassau). ☎ **242/ 327-7633.** Lunch main courses $8.50–$20.50; dinner main courses $19–$22.50. AE, MC, V. Daily 11am–11pm. Closed last 2 weeks in Sept. Western Transportation bus to and from Nassau, $1.75 each way. BAHAMIAN/SEAFOOD.

A Bahamian culinary tradition, this is the best bet for dining on local fare. Set in a grove of sea-grape and palm trees facing the ocean, Traveller's Rest serves typical Bahamian fare and seafood. You can dine outside under a portico or on the terrace. If it's rainy (highly unlikely), you can go inside the tavern with its small bar and decor of local paintings. Many diners bring their swimsuits and use the white-sand beach across from the restaurant; others arrive in their own boats. In this laid-back atmosphere, you can feast on grouper fingers, barbecue ribs, curried chicken, steamed or cracked conch, or minced crawfish, and finish perhaps with guava cake, the best on the island. The conch salad served on the weekends is said to increase virility in men.

PICNIC FARE & WHERE TO EAT IT

You can find many places to buy picnic fare on New Providence. A longtime favorite for selling "the fixins" is **Roscoe's at the Red Roof,** West Bay Street (☎ **242/ 322-2810**). Located next to the water, a mile west of the Paradise Island Bridge, the shop offers more than 150 kinds of cheeses, smoked salmon cutlets, and the fixings for dozens of kinds of sandwiches. Among the best is the crabmeat. You'll also find smoked meats from Germany, exotic rye breads from Canada, and daily take-out specials of such foods as quiche and lasagna. There's a small cluster of tiny tables if you prefer to eat in. Roscoe's is open Monday through Friday 7:30am to 5pm and Saturday 9am to 5pm.

If you have a kitchenette, you might head for one of the fishing boats that moor beneath the Paradise Island Bridge and buy fresh lobster or conch to take home and transform into salad. You could also buy portions of johnnycake-to-go from the previously recommended **Bahamian Kitchen,** or stock up on cold cuts and soda at any of Nassau's supermarkets.

An ideal spot for a picnic is **Fort Charlotte,** off West Bay Street on Chippingham Road (see below). After touring its dank dungeons, find a sunny spot on the grounds for your picnic.

Others might prefer to enjoy their picnic while taking in the tropical foliage of the Botanical Gardens (see below). Children especially find the spot delightful.

5 Beaches, Water Sports & Other Outdoor Activities

One of the great sports centers of the world, Nassau (and the islands that surround it) is a marvelous place for swimming, sunning, snorkeling, scuba diving, boating, waterskiing, and deep-sea fishing, as well as tennis and golf.

At last count, there were 32 different sports being actively pursued in The Bahamas. You can learn more about any of them by calling **The Bahamas Sports and Aviation Information Center** (☎ **800/32-SPORT** or 305/932-0051) from anywhere in the continental United States. Call Monday through Friday from 9am to 5pm, EST. Or write the center at 19495 Biscayne Blvd., Suite 809, Aventura, FL 33180.

BEACHES

The most popular beach on New Providence Island is **Cable Beach,** which offers all sorts of water sports as well as easy access to shops, casino action, bars, and restaurants. The area was named for the telegraph cable laid in 1892 from Jupiter, Florida, to The Bahamas. Cable Beach runs for some 4 miles and is incredibly varied. You'll need to hunt for a spot on the strip that's suitable for you. Waters can be rough and reefy, but then calm and clear.

Cable Beach is far superior to the meager beach of Nassau, the **Western Esplanade,** which sweeps westward from the British Colonial. But if you're staying in a Nassau hotel and don't want to make the trip to Cable Beach, you might use the local beach instead; it has rest rooms, changing facilities, and a snack bar.

At some point in a visit, even Cable Beach beach buffs like to desert the sands here in favor of **Paradise Beach** on Paradise Island (see chapter 5). Paradise Beach is even more convenient to residents of Nassau hotels, because all they have to do is walk, drive, or take a boat to nearby Paradise Island. Paradise Beach can be reached by boat from the Prince George Wharf. Round-trip tickets cost $3 per person. You must pay an additional $3 for admission to the beach, but this fee includes the use of a shower and locker. An extra $10 deposit is required for the safe return of towels. If you're traveling with children under 12, you pay $1 admission for each of them. It's also possible to drive to the beach across the Paradise Island Bridge for a toll of $2; and you can walk across for only 25¢.

To reach **Saunders Beach,** where many of the local people go on weekends, take West Bay Street toward Coral Island. This beach lies across from Fort Charlotte. The main reason to go to this beach is to escape the crowds descending on Cable Beach or Paradise Beach.

On the north shore, past the Cable Beach Hotel properties, is **Caves Beach,** some 7 miles west of Nassau. It stands near Rock Point, right before the turnoff along Blake Road that leads to the airport. Since visitors often don't know of this place, it's another good spot to escape the hordes. It's also a good beach with soft sands.

Continuing west along West Bay Street you reach **Love Beach,** across from Sea Gardens, a good stretch of sand lying east of Northwest Point. Love Beach, although not big, is a special favorite of beach buffs. Mostly local islanders know of its charm, but they don't necessarily like to spread the word, fearing it might be overrun like Cable Beach.

BOAT CRUISES

Cruises from the harbors around New Providence Island are offered by a number of operators, with trips ranging from daytime voyages for diving, picnicking, sunning, and swimming to sunset and moonlight cruises.

Flying Cloud. Paradise Island West Dock. ☎ **242/393-1957.**

This outfit features catamaran cruises carrying 50 people on day and sunset trips, or a maximum of 30 for dinner. It's a good bet for people who want a more intimate cruise and shy away from the heavy volume carried aboard Majestic Tours catamarans (see below). Snorkeling equipment is provided free. A half-day charter costs $35 per person, a $2^{1}/_{2}$-hour sunset cruise goes for $30. The $3^{1}/_{2}$-hour dinner cruise is $50 per person (half price for children). The 57-foot catamaran was designed and built by Gold Coast Yachts. Sailings are daily, with departure times depending on the type of cruise. Round-trip transportation to the dock from your hotel is included.

Majestic Tours Ltd. Hillside Manor. ☎ **242/322-2606.**

Majestic Tours will book 3-hour cruises on two of the biggest catamarans in the Atlantic, offering views of the water, sun, sand, and outlying reefs. This is the biggest and most professionally run of the cruise boats. Its major drawback—at least to some passengers—is that there are too many other passengers aboard. *Yellow Bird* is suitable for up to 250 passengers, and *Tropic Bird* carries up to 170. They depart from Prince George's Dock. Ask for the departure point when you make your reservation. The cruises include a 1-hour stop on a relatively isolated portion of Paradise Island's Cabbage Beach. The cost is $15 per adult, with children under 12 paying $7.50. Snorkeling equipment is $10 extra. Departures are Tuesday, Wednesday, Friday, and Saturday at 1:15pm.

Nassau Cruises Ltd. Paradise Island Bridge. ☎ **242/363-3577.**

This company maintains a trio of motorized yachts, the *Calypso I, Calypso IV,* and the *Islander.* These are the most luxurious cruises offered. Their trip to uninhabited Blue Lagoon Island (see "Easy Side Trips to Nearby Islands," below) is reason enough to sail with them. Equipped with bars, their yachts depart from a point just west of the toll booth on the Paradise Island Bridge. Daytime trips depart every day for the secluded beaches of Blue Lagoon Island, a 4-mile sail east of Paradise Island. The day sails leave at 10am and 11:30am and come back from the island at 1:30pm, 3pm, and 4:30pm. The Day Pass is $20 for adults and $10 for children and pays for the boat ride only. The all-inclusive day pass is $45 for adults and $10 for children and covers transportation, the boat ride, lunch, two daiquiris, and all non-motorized water sports.

Topsail Yacht Charters. British Colonial Beach Resort Dock. ☎ **242/393-0820.**

Wind Dance and *Liberty Call* leave for all-day cruises from this dock, offering many sailing and snorkeling possibilities. This is your best bet if you're seeking a more romantic cruise and don't want 100 people aboard. The cruises usually stop at Rose Island, which is a charming, picture-perfect spot, with an uncrowded white sandy beach and palm trees. Topsail has added a third ketch to its fleet, the 54-foot *Riding High,* which is bigger than the 41-foot *Wind Dance* or the 36-foot *Liberty Call.* Cruise options are plentiful, including a half day of sailing, snorkeling, and exploring, costing $34. A full day goes for $49. Champagne-and-cocktail cruises in the evening are also popular, going for $35 per person. A private dinner cruise is a favorite for honeymooners—the 3-hour moonlit sail costs $35. All vessels are available for private charter.

FISHING

Many travelers come to Nassau just to fish. May through September are the best months for the oceanic bonito and the black-fin tuna; June and July for blue marlin; and November through May for the amberjack found in reefy areas. The list seems endless.

This is, of course, a costly sport. Arrangements can be made at big hotels. Prices are usually $300 for a half-day boat rental for parties of two to six or $600 for a full day's fishing.

The best charter operator is at **Nassau Yacht Haven** (☎ **242/393-8173**), which has both a 35-foot boat and a 42-foot boat. Fishing is mainly close to shore. It takes 15 to 20 minutes to reach a drop-off where wahoo and barracuda abound. This charter is recommended not only for its quality fishing, but for its convenience since you don't have far to travel before you start fishing. Another reliable operator is the **Charter Boat Association** (☎ **242/363-2335**), offering 8 to 10 boats in their fleet. This company features both half-day and full-day rentals for vessels that can seat six comfortably. The half-day charter is $300 and the full-day is $600. Each additional person is charged from $40 to $50 depending on boat size. Fishing choices are plentiful: You can choose from trolling for wahoo, tuna, and marlin in the deep sea to casting in the shallows for snapper, amberjack, grouper, and yellowtail. Anchoring and bottom fishing offer calmer options. We recommend this charter since you are given a lot of leeway in deciding where you want to fish and how much time you want to spend at it. Another attractive feature is the different types of fishing they offer.

FITNESS CLUBS

The Palace Spa, in the **Crystal Palace Complex,** West Bay Street (☎ **242/ 327-6200**), adjoins the Radisson Cable Beach and is the best gym on the island. It offers a Stairmaster, cardiovascular exercise equipment, a whirlpool, a steam room, saunas, and free weights. Radisson residents pay a $5 deposit for lockers and towels. Nassau Marriott Resort guests pay $8 per day or $30 per week, and nonguests are charged $10 per day or $30 per week. Sneakers and shorts are required in the fitness area, and children under 14 are not admitted. Hours are Monday through Friday from 6am to 9pm and Saturday and Sunday from 10am to 6pm.

GOLF

Some of the best golfing in The Bahamas is found in Nassau. The following courses are open to the public, not just to guests of the hotels who operate the properties.

Cable Beach Golf Course. W. Bay Rd., Cable Beach. ☎ **242/327-6000.**

This is a spectacular 18-hole, 7,040-yard, par-72 championship golf course, but it's not as challenging as the one at the South Ocean Golf Course (see below). The Cable Beach course is under the management of the Radisson Cable Beach Hotel, but it's often used by guests of the other hotels nearby. Greens fees are $55 for residents of Radisson, $65 for all other players. Carts can be rented for $60.

South Ocean Golf Course. SW Bay Rd. ☎ **242/362-4391.**

The best course on New Providence Island and one of the best in The Bahamas is a 30-minute drive from Nassau on the southwest edge of the island. The course has palm-fringed greens and fairways. Overlooking the ocean, the 6,706-yard beauty has some first-rate holes with a backdrop of trees, shrubs, ravines, and undulating hills. The 18-hole, USPGA-sanctioned course has a par of 72. The lofty elevation of this course offers panoramic water views, including an area of the Atlantic called "Tongue of the Ocean." Golf architect Joe Lee designed the course with four challenging water holes and made very effective use of the rolling terrain. Greens fees are $45, plus $35 for a golf cart. It's best to phone ahead in case there's a golf tournament scheduled for the day you had planned to play.

HORSEBACK RIDING

On the southwest shore, **Happy Trails Stables,** Coral Harbour (☎ **242/362-1820**), offers a 1-hour and 20-minute horseback trail ride for $45 per person. This includes free transportation to and from your hotel. The weight limit for riders is 200 pounds. The stables are signposted from the Nassau International Airport, which is 2 miles away. Children must be 8 or older. Reservations are required, especially during the holiday season.

JOGGING

Most joggers on New Providence Island prefer to run along Cable Beach, either the beach itself or West Bay Street. If you head west toward Delaport Point and eventually Rock Point, you'll encounter less traffic than if you go east toward Nassau. If you have a car, you might drive west of Cable Beach to Gambier or Love Beach nearby, and then jog along West Bay Street in the Old Fort area. There's not much traffic in this part of the island.

SNORKELING, SCUBA DIVING & UNDERWATER WALKS

Your hotel will probably have snorkeling equipment, but if you want a more organized outing, or if you want scuba diving, the following outfitters cater to all ability levels.

Bahama Divers. E. Bay St. ☎ **242/393-5644.**

Packages available here include a half day of snorkeling to offshore reefs, costing $20 per person, and a half-day scuba trip with preliminary pool instruction for beginners, going for $60. Half-day excursions for experienced divers to offshore coral reefs with a depth of 25 feet go for $35, and half-day scuba trips for certified divers to deeper outlying reefs, drop-offs, and blue holes cost $60. Participants receive free transportation from their hotel to the boats. Children must be 12 or older. Reservations are required, especially during the holiday season.

Hartley's Undersea Walk. E. Bay St. ☎ **242/393-8234.**

The Hartleys offer an exciting and educational experience. They take you out from Nassau Harbour aboard the yacht *Pied Piper*. On the 3½-hour cruise, you're submerged for about 20 minutes, making a shallow-water descent to a point where you walk along the ocean bottom through a "garden" of tropical fish, sponges, and other undersea life. You'll be guided through the underwater world wearing a helmet that allows you to breathe with ease and to see. Entire families can make this walk, which costs $45 per person in groups of five. You don't even have to be able to swim to make this safe adventure. Two trips are operated at 9:30am and 1:30pm, Tuesday through Saturday. Arrive 30 minutes before departures.

Stuart Cove's Dive South Ocean. SW Bay St., South Ocean. ☎ **800/879-9832** in the U.S., or 242/362-4171.

Stuart Cove's is about 10 minutes from top dive sites, including the coral reefs, wrecks, and underwater airplane structure used in filming James Bond thrillers. The Porpoise Pen Reefs, named for Flipper, and steep sea walls are also on the diving agenda. An introductory scuba program costs $99, with morning two-tank dives priced at $70. All prices for boat dives include tanks, weights, and belts. An open-water certification course starts at $660. Bring along two friends and the price drops to $360 per person. Escorted boat snorkeling trips cost $30. A special feature is a series of shark-dive experiences priced from $115. In one outing, Caribbean reef sharks swim among the guests. In one dive, called "Shark Arena," divers kneel down while a dive master feeds the sharks off a long pole. Another experience, a "Shark Buoy" in 6,000 feet of ocean, involves a dive among silky sharks at about 30 feet. They swim among the divers while the dive master feeds them.

OTHER WATER SPORTS

Your best bet is **Sea Sports,** Nassau Marriott Resort and Crystal Palace Casino, West Bay Street (☎ 242/327-6200), which has a full program, renting both non-motorized and motorized equipment. It is the oldest and the best water-sports company in The Bahamas. You can rent Hobie Cats, Sunfish, Windsurfers, or even a kayak. Prices range from $5 for a kayak for 30 minutes up to $40 for a Hobie Cat for 1 hour. Parasailing is possible, costing $40 for 5 to 6 minutes, as is waterskiing, costing $70 for 1 hour. A snorkel trip, including gear, costs $25. Many additional activities, such as scuba diving or deep-sea fishing, can also be arranged here.

TENNIS

Courts are available at only some hotels. Guests usually play free or for a nominal fee, whereas visitors are charged.

Most of the courts at Cable Beach are under the auspices of the **Radisson Cable Beach Hotel,** West Bay Street (☎ 242/327-6000), which offers 18 courts. Residents of Radisson play for free until 4pm. After that, illumination costs $15 per hour. The night rate applies to all players. During the day, non-Radisson guests pay $10 per person.

Other hotels offering tennis courts include the **Nassau Beach Hotel,** West Bay Street, Cable Beach (☎ 242/327-7711), with six Flexipave night-lit courts; and the **British Colonial Beach Resort,** 1 Bay St., Nassau (☎ 242/322-3301), with three hard-surface courts, one of which is lit.

6 Seeing the Sights: From a Parade of Pink Flamingos to a Spectacular Coral Reef

Most of Nassau can be covered on foot, beginning at Rawson Square in the center, where the stalls of the Straw Market are found. We also enjoy the native market

Special Moments & Little-Known Gems

Over-the-Hill. Few visitors take this trip any more, but it used to be a tradition to go "Over-the-Hill," a reference to Nassau's most colorful area. "Over-the-Hill" is the actual name of this poor residential district, where the descendants of former slaves built compact, rainbow-hued houses, leaving the most desirable lands around the harbor to the rich folks. This, not the historic core of Nassau around Rawson Square, is truly the heart of Bahamian-African culture.

The thump of the Junkanoo-Goombay drum can be heard here almost any time of the day or night. The area never sleeps, or so it is said. Certainly not on Sunday morning, when you can drive by the churches and hear hell and damnation promised to all sinners and backsliders.

This fascinating part of Nassau begins a quarter of a mile south of Blue Hill Road, which starts at the exclusive Relais & Châteaux property, Graycliff. But once you're Over-the-Hill, you're a long way from the vintage wine and expensive Cuban cigars of Graycliff. Some people—usually savvy store owners from abroad—come here to buy local handicrafts from individual vendors. The area can be explored on foot (during the day only), but many visitors prefer to drive.

The Retreat (Village Road; ☎ **242/393-1317**). The Retreat consists of 11 acres of the most unspoiled gardens on New Providence, even more intriguing than the Botanical Gardens. They are home to about 200 species of exotic palm trees. You'll think you've wandered into *Arabian Nights*. Half-hour tours of the grounds are given Tuesday through Thursday at noon. This is the home of The Bahamas National Trust, and the grounds (without the tours) can be visited Monday through Friday from 9am to 5pm for a $2 admission. Not a lot of people know about The Retreat. It is the true oasis of Nassau.

Arawak Cay. This small artificial island lies right in the heart of Nassau, across West Bay Street (from the Botanical Gardens, walk back along Chippingham Road). The cay was created by the Bahamanian government to store large tanks of fresh water from Andros Island. You don't go here to look at the storage tanks, however. This is where locals go to sample their favorite food, conch. The mollusk is cracked before your eyes (not everybody's favorite attraction), and you're given some hot

on the waterfront, a short walk through the Straw Market. Here is where Bahamian fishers unload a variety of produce and fish—crates of mangoes, oranges, tomatoes, and limes, plus lots of crimson-lipped conch. To experience this slice of Bahamian life, go any morning Monday through Saturday before noon.

The best way to see some of the major public buildings of Nassau is to take our walking tour (see below), which will give you not only an overview of the historical monuments, but also a feel for the city and its history. Then you can concentrate on specific sights you'd like to take in, notably Ardastra Gardens and Coral Island Bahamas.

✪ Ardastra Gardens. Chippingham Rd. ☎ **242/323-5806.** Admission $10 adults, $5 children. Daily 9am–5pm. Bus: 10.

The main attraction of the Ardastra Gardens, almost 5 acres of lush tropical planting located about a mile west of downtown Nassau near Fort Charlotte, is the parading flock of pink flamingos. The Caribbean flamingo, national bird of The Bahamas, had almost disappeared by the early 1940s but was brought back to

sauce and told to chow down. With it you can sample a favorite drink of the islands, coconut milk laced with gin (an acquired taste, to say the least). However, if
you participate in this ritual, you'll feel like a real Bahamian.

Junkanoo Expo (Prince George Wharf; ☎ 242/356-2731). It's highly likely you'll
miss the real thing (a parade beginning at 2am on Boxing Day, December 26), but
you can relive the Bahamian Junkanoo carnival at this expo. One of the city's newer
museums, it lies in an old Customs warehouse. All the glitter and glory of Mardi
Gras come alive in this museum, with its display of fantasy costumes used for the
holiday bacchanal. The museum recreates the Junkanoo festivities with costumes,
masks, and other paraphernalia. You can even watch a videotape of the last Junkanoo
Day. Admission is $1 adults or 50¢ for children. It is open Monday through Satur-
day from 9am to 5pm and Sunday from 3 to 5pm.

Hairbraider's Centre (Prince George Dock). If you've ever wanted to get your hair
braided but were hesitant, a visit here will persuade you. The government sponsors
this open-air pavilion. Female cruise-ship passengers—even men if their hair is long
enough—are especially fond of getting their hair braided. All sorts of braiding experts are on hand at this center to test their expertise on you. By the time you get
back on ship (or land if you're at one of the resorts), you'll definitely have a new
look. However long you want to keep that look is nobody's business but your own.

Potter's Cay. Although Potter's Cay is right in the heart of Nassau, lying under
the bridge leading to Paradise Island, it offers a unique opportunity to observe local life. Sloops from the Out Islands pull in here, bringing their fresh catch along
with plenty of conch. You are likely to see the chef who will be preparing your fresh
fish that night, buying it off the boat from one of these fishers (unless he's using
frozen fish from Miami). Freshly grown herbs and vegetables are also sold here,
along with plenty of limes (the preferred seasoning for fish in The Bahamas). Tropical fruits such as paw-paw (papaya), pineapple (usually from Eleuthera), and bananas are also sold. For many foreign visitors, this will be their first time to taste
conch. Little stalls sell raw conch marinated in lime juice, conch salad, conch soup,
and spicy conch fritters just made in the deep fat.

significant numbers through the efforts of the National Trust. They now flourish in
the rookery on Great Inagua. A flock of these exotic feathered creatures has been
trained to march in drill formation, responding to the drillmaster's oral orders with
long-legged precision and discipline. The Marching Flamingos perform daily at
11am, 2pm, and 4pm.

Other exotic wildlife at the gardens include boa constrictors (very tame), kinka-
jous (honey bears) from Central and South America, green-winged macaws, peacocks
and peahens, blue-and-gold macaws, capuchin monkeys, iguanas, hutias (a ratlike
animal indigenous to the islands), ring-tailed lemurs, red-ruff lemurs, margays,
brown-headed tamarins (monkeys), and a crocodile. There are also numerous
waterfowl to be seen in Swan Lake, including black swans from Australia and
several species of wild ducks.

You can get a good look at the flora of the gardens by walking along the sign-
posted paths. Many of the more interesting and exotic trees bear plaques with their
names.

Atlantis Submarine. Clifton Pier, Lyford Cay (18 miles west of Nassau). ☎ **242/327-3740.**

If you'd like another view of New Providence—the way the fish see it—you can take a tour in an air-conditioned submarine. About seven to eight trips per day, starting at 7:30am, are offered. The 2¹/₂-hour trip introduces you to the whole cast of The Bahamas "water world." The cost is $74 for adults (half price for children). If you board the 7:30am special, you get an early-bird discount: $59 per adult (half price for children). When you make a reservation, you can arrange to have the company van pick you up at your hotel.

✪ **Crystal Cay.** On Silver Cay just off W. Bay St. ☎ **809/328-1036.** Admission $16 adults, $11 children 5–12. Children under 5 free. Daily 9am–6pm. It's directly off the main harbor entrance to Nassau on Silver Cay between downtown Nassau and Cable Beach. Bus: 10.

Crystal Cay is a marine park with a network of 24 saltwater aquariums, landscaped park areas, nature trails, lounges, shops, and a restaurant. By far the most outstanding feature is the Underwater Observation Tower. You descend a spiral staircase to a depth of 20 feet below the surface of the water, where you can view tropical fish in their natural habitat, coral reefs, and abundant sea life, seen through 24 large, clear windows. The tower rises 100 feet above the water, with two viewing decks plus a bar where you can have a drink while enjoying a panoramic view of Nassau, Cable Beach, and Paradise Island.

Crystal Cay is the home of the world's largest man-made living reef. The Reef Tank gives visitors a 360° view of colorful coral, sponges, tropical fish, and varied forms of sea life. Unlike other exhibits of this type in the western hemisphere, where models are used and backgrounds are merely painted, everything in this reef is alive and real. Everything exists as it would in the ocean by way of an "open system" that provides more than 48,000 gallons of unfiltered sea water every hour to Crystal Cay's tank and ponds.

Sharks native to the Caribbean can be seen in the Shark Tank from either the overhead viewing deck or the underwater viewing area. There are also pools of graceful stingrays and majestic sea turtles. Feeding time at the marine exhibits is a favorite of visitors and park employees alike.

The park also includes nature trails, with lush tropical foliage, waterfalls, and exotic trees and wildlife, and a cluster of small seaside souvenir shops. There's even a Pearl Bar where oysters containing pearls can be selected and purchased right on the spot.

Botanical Gardens. Chippingham Rd. ☎ **242/323-5975.** Admission $1 adults, 50¢ children. Mon–Fri 8am–4pm. Bus: 10, 17.

More than 600 species of tropical flora are found in the 18-acre park, located near Fort Charlotte. Don't expect tightly manicured landscaping, though. These gardens are badly maintained. Two freshwater ponds, with lilies, water plants, and tropical fish, and a small cactus garden are highlights of the gardens. After viewing them, you can take a leisurely walk along one of the trails that cut through the terrain. In other words, hiking made easy. The curator will answer your questions.

Fort Fincastle. Elizabeth Ave. ☎ **242/322-2442.** Admission 50¢ adults and children. Mon–Sat 9am–4pm. Bus: 10, 17.

Reached by climbing the Queen's Staircase, this fort was constructed in 1793 by Lord Dunmore, the royal governor. You can take an elevator ride to the top and walk on the observation floor (a 126-foot-high water tower and lighthouse) for a nice view of the harbor. The tower is the highest point on New Providence.

Although the ruins of the fort can hardly compete with the view, you can walk around on your own or be guided. Don't worry about finding a guide; they will find you. Very assertive young men wait to show you around, although there isn't that much to see, except some old cannons. The so-called bow of this fort is patterned like a paddle-wheel steamer, the kind used on the Mississippi. Although built to defend Nassau against a possible invasion, no shot was ever fired.

Fort Charlotte. Off W. Bay St. on Chippingham Rd. ☎ **242/322-7500.** Free admission. Mon–Sat 8:30am–4pm. Bus: 10, 17.

Begun in 1787 and built with plenty of dungeons, Fort Charlotte is the largest of Nassau's three major defenses. It used to command the western harbor. Named after King George III's consort, it was built by Gov. Lord Dunmore, who was also the last royal governor of New York and Virginia. Its 42 cannons never fired a shot, at least not at an invader. Within the complex are underground passages and a waxworks, which can be viewed on free tours.

Fort Montagu. Eastern Rd. Free admission. No regular hours. Bus: 10, 17.

Fort Montagu was built in 1741 and stands guard at the eastern entrance to the harbor of Nassau. It's the oldest fort on the island. The Americans captured it in 1776 during the War of Independence. Less interesting than Fort Charlotte and Fort Fincastle, the ruins of this place are mainly for fort buffs. Many visitors find the nearby park, with well-maintained lawns and plenty of shade, more interesting than the fort. Many vendors peddle local handicrafts in the park, so you can combine a look at a ruined fort with a shopping expedition if you're interested.

Blackbeard's Tower. Yamacraw Hill Rd. Free admission. Open all day.

This historic mossy ruin stands 5 miles east of Fort Montagu and can be reached by jitney (bus). These crumbling remains of a watchtower are said to have been used by the infamous pirate Edward Teach in the 17th century. The ruins are only mildly interesting—there isn't much left of the place's buccaneering past. What's interesting is the view. With a little imagination you can see Blackbeard peering out from here at an unsuspecting ship about to enter the harbor. Blackbeard is also said to have lived here, but this is hardly well documented.

Pompey Museum. At Vendue House, Bay St. at George St. ☎ **242/326-2566.** Admission $1 adults, 50¢ children. Mon–Fri 10am–4:30pm, Sat 10am–1pm. Closed for lunch 1–2pm Mon, Wed, Fri. Bus: 10, 17.

Vendue House was built of cut limestone blocks around 1769. It served as the island's slave market until 1834, when the practice was outlawed throughout the British Empire by an act of Parliament. Named after the leader of a 19th-century slave revolt in the Exumas that almost toppled the ruling patriarchs, the museum houses an exhibition on Bahamian life, as well as the work of one of the country's most prolific artists, Amos Ferguson, called "the father of Bahamian art."

This is the best place in all of The Bahamas to see the work of this remarkable artist, now in his 70s, who expresses a deep spirituality in his whimsical folk paintings. His work is uniquely Bahamian, with echoes of Africa. Many of the paintings depict scenes from Bahamian folklore and even old Junkanoo characters. Most of his work is about the history of The Bahamas, religion, or "ole story," a term used by the islanders to refer to their body of folklore.

WALKING TOUR
Historic Nassau

Start: Rawson Square.
Finish: Prince George Wharf.
Time: 2 hours.
Best Times: Monday through Saturday between 10am and 4pm.
Worst Times: Sunday when many places are closed; and any day lots of cruise ships are in port.

Begin your tour at:

1. Rawson Square, the center of Nassau, lies directly inland from Prince George Wharf, where many of the big cruise ships dock. It is the crossroads of the city. It seems that everyone passes through here, from the prime minister of The Bahamas to bankers and local attorneys, to cruise-ship passengers, to visitors from Paradise Island on shopping trips, to Junkanoo bands. On the square is the Churchill Building, where the controversial Lynden Pindling conducted his affairs as prime minister for 25 years before his ouster in 1992. The present prime minister and some other government ministries use the building today. Look for the statue of Sir Milo Butler, a former shopkeeper who became the first governor of The Bahamas when independence from Britain was granted in 1973.

Across Rawson Square is:

2. Parliament Square, dominated by a statue of a youthful Queen Victoria. To the right of the statue stand more Bahamian government office buildings, and to the left is the House of Assembly, the oldest governing body in continuous session in the New World. In the building in back of the statue, the Senate meets; this is a less influential body than the House of Assembly. Some of these Georgian-style buildings date from the late 1700s and early 1800s.

The Supreme Court building stands next to the:

3. Nassau Public Library and Museum (actually opening onto Bank Lane), a building from 1797 that once was the Nassau Gaol (jail). If you want to pop in here for a look you can do so Monday through Thursday from 10am to 8pm, Friday from 10am to 5pm, and Saturday from 10am to 4pm. Chances are you will have seen greater libraries in your day. What's amusing is that the small prison cells are now lined with books. Other than what's inside the books, the only other item of interest is the library's collection of old documents dating from colonial days and its many historic prints. In 1873, it became the public library.

Just across Shirley Street from the library is:

4. the former site of the **Royal Victoria Hotel.** In its day, the hotel was the haunt of Confederate spies, royalty, smugglers of all sorts, and ladies and gentlemen. Horace Greeley pronounced it "the largest and most commodious hotel ever built in the tropics," and many agreed with this American journalist. The hotel experienced its heyday during the American Civil War. It is said that at the Blockade Runners' Ball, some 300 guests consumed 350 magnums of champagne. Former guests have included two British prime ministers, Neville Chamberlain and the man who replaced him, Winston Churchill. Prince Albert, consort of Queen Victoria, also stayed here at one time. The hotel closed in 1971. After being destroyed by fire, it was demolished and razed to the ground. Today, on its former site sits one of Nassau's showcase parking lots. Ironically, the parking lot seems to be such a source of pride to the city, that it is unlikely that the Royal Victoria will ever be rebuilt, at least in that spot.

After imagining its former splendor, head south along Parliament Street.

☕ **TAKE A BREAK**   If you'd like some time out, try the **Green Shutters Restaurant,** 48 Parliament St. (☎ **242/325-5702**). This popular restaurant and English-style pub occupies a colonial house nearly two centuries old. People come here for their favorite pick-me-up or to enjoy a typical English lunch, perhaps shepherd's pie or other pub grub. It is lively both day and night, one of the few places where locals mingle happily with visitors.

At the end of Parliament Street stands:

5. **The Nassau General Post Office,** where you may want to purchase Bahamian stamps if you're a collector. You can also mail letters and packages.

   Armed with your purchases of colorful Bahamian stamps, walk east on East Hill Street and turn left onto East Street, then right onto Shirley Street, and head straight on Elizabeth Avenue. This will take you to the landmark:

6. **Queen's Staircase,** leading to Bennet's Hill. In 1793, slaves cut these 66 steps out of sandstone cliffs. Upon their completion, they provided access from the center of Old Nassau to:

7. **Fort Fincastle,** built in 1793 by Lord Dunmore, who had a talent for constructing unnecessary forts at great expense. Designed in the shape of a paddle-wheel steamer, the fort kept looking out for marauders who never came. It was eventually converted into a lighthouse, as it occupied the highest point on the island. The tower is more than 200 feet above the sea, providing a panoramic view of Nassau and its harbor.

   A small footpath leads down from the fort to Sands Road. Once you reach it, head west (left) until you approach East Street again, then bear right. When you come to East Hill Street (again), go left, as you will have returned to the post office. Continue your westward trek along East Hill Street, which is the foothill of:

8. **Prospect Ridge.** This was the old dividing line between Nassau's rich and poor. The rich people (nearly always white) lived along the waterfront, often in beautiful mansions, one once occupied by Lord Beaverbrook, the British newspaper magnate. The African Bahamians went "over the hill" to work in these rich homes during the day, but returned to Prospect Ridge to their own homes (most often shanties) at night. They lived in such places as seedy Grant's Town, originally settled in the 1820s by freed slaves. Near the end of East Hill Street, you come to:

9. **Gregory Arch.** This tunnel was cut through the hill in 1850; after its opening, working class African Bahamians didn't have to go "over the hill"—and steep it was—but could go through the arch to return to their villages.

   At the intersection with Market Street, go right. On your right rises:

10. **St. Andrew's Kirk** (Presbyterian). Called simply the "Kirk," the church dates from 1810 but has seen many changes over the years. In 1864 it was enlarged, with the addition of a bell tower, among other architectural features. This church had the first non-Anglican parishioners in The Bahamas.

    On a steep hill, rising to the west of Market Street, you see:

11. **Government House,** on your left, the official residence of the governor-general of the archipelago. This is the queen's representative to The Bahamas. The post today is largely ceremonial, as the actual governing of the nation is in the hands of an elected prime minister. This pink-and-white neoclassical mansion dates from the dawn of the 19th century. Poised on its front steps is a rather jaunty statue of

Christopher Columbus, which was presented to the then colony of The Bahamas by its ruling governor, Sir James Carmichael Smyth, who'd assumed the post in 1829. Visitors can't just walk in and call on the governor-general, but they can sign a guest book in a tiny guardhouse near the exit gate.

Opposite the road from Government House on West Hill Street rises:

12. Graycliff. A Georgian building from the 1720s, this deluxe hotel and restaurant— a stamping ground of the rich and famous—was constructed by Capt. John Howard Graysmith in the 1720s. In the 1920s, it achieved fame—or perhaps notoriety—when it was run by Polly Leach, a pal of gangster Al Capone. Later it was purchased by Lord and Lady Dudley, who erased the old memories and furnished it with grand flair and taste. It attracted such famous guests as the Duke and Duchess of Windsor and Winston Churchill.

Upon leaving Graycliff, you will see a plaque embedded in a hill. The plaque claims that this site is the spot where the oldest church in Nassau once stood.

On the corner of West Hill Street and West Street is Villa Doyle, former home of William Henry Doyle, chief justice of the Bahamian Supreme Court in the 1860s and 1870s.

Opposite it stands:

13. St. Francis Roman Catholic Church, constructed between 1885 and 1886. It was the first Catholic church in The Bahamas, and funds to construct it were raised from the Archdiocese of New York.

Continue along West Street until you reach Marlborough. Walk a short block that leads to Queen Street, and go right, passing the front of the American embassy. At the corner of Queen Street and Marlborough rises:

14. The British Colonial Beach Resort, dating from 1923. It was for a time run by Sir Harry Oakes, once the most powerful man in The Bahamas and a friend of the Duke of Windsor. Oakes' still unsolved murder in 1943 was called "the crime of the century." Constructed on the site of Fort Nassau, an old hotel on this spot was called simply Hotel Colonial—but it burned in 1922. The site has been used in films, including James Bond thrillers. One part of the hotel fronts George Street where you'll find:

15. Vendue House, one of the oldest buildings in Nassau. It was once called the Bourse (Stock Exchange) and was the site of many slave auctions. It is now a museum.

16. Christ Church Cathedral is not far from Vendue House on George Street. Dating from 1837, this is a Gothic Episcopal cathedral, and is often the venue of important state ceremonies, including the opening of the Supreme Court, with its procession of bewigged, robed judges followed by barristers—all accompanied by music from the police band.

If you turn left onto Duke Street, and proceed along Market Street, you reach:

17. The Straw Market, opening onto Bay Street. A favorite of cruise-ship passengers, this market offers not only straw products, but all sorts of souvenirs and gifts. Bahamian women will not only weave you a basket, but braid your hair with beads if you want.

Next, take the narrow little Market Range, leading to:

18. Woodes Rogers Walk, named for a former governor of the colony, who fell on bad days and eventually ended in a debtors' prison in London before coming back as royal governor to Nassau. Head east along this walk for a panoramic view of the harbor, with its colorful mail and sponge boats. Here markets sell vegetables and fish and lots and lots of conch. The walk leads to:

Walking Tour—Historic Nassau

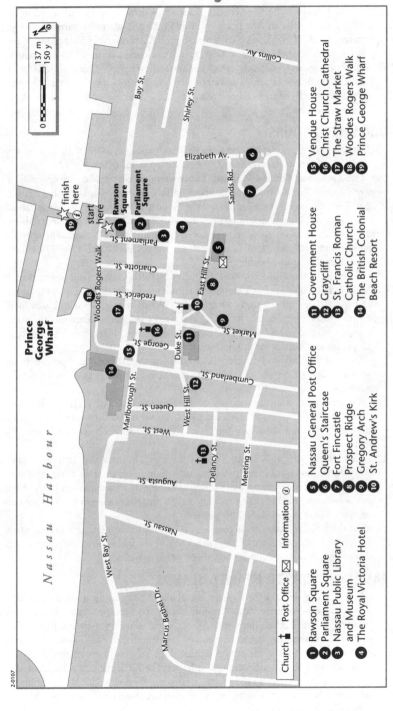

Church †   Post Office ⊠   Information ⓘ

1. Rawson Square
2. Parliament Square
3. Nassau Public Library and Museum
4. The Royal Victoria Hotel
5. Nassau General Post Office
6. Queen's Staircase
7. Fort Fincastle
8. Prospect Ridge
9. Gregory Arch
10. St. Andrew's Kirk
11. Government House
12. Graycliff
13. St. Francis Roman Catholic Church
14. The British Colonial Beach Resort
15. Vendue House
16. Christ Church Cathedral
17. The Straw Market
18. Woodes Rogers Walk
19. Prince George Wharf

Nassau Harbour

Prince George Wharf

Bay St.
Shirley St.
Collins Av.
Elizabeth Av.
Sands Rd.
Parliament St.
Charlotte St.
Frederick St.
East Hill St.
Market St.
George St.
Duke St.
Cumberland St.
West Hill St.
Queen St.
Marlborough St.
West St.
Augusta St.
Delancy St.
Meeting St.
Nassau St.
West Bay St.
Marcus Bethel Dr.
Woodes Rogers Walk

Rawson Square
Parliament Square
finish here
start here

137 m
150 y
0

2-0107

113

19. Prince George Wharf, where the cruise ships dock. It was constructed in the 1920s, the heyday of American Prohibition, to provide more harbor space for the hundreds of bootlegging craft running the American blockade against liquor. It was named for the Duke of Kent (Prince George) in honor of his visit here in 1928. Its most aristocratic vessel is always the yacht of Queen Elizabeth II, the HMS *Britannia,* which has been a frequent visitor, notably in 1985 when the queen arrived as the honored guest at a meeting of the leaders of the Commonwealth.

ORGANIZED TOURS

There's a lot to see in Nassau, and tours have been arranged to suit your taste for seeing the colorful historic city, as well as the outlying sights of interest.

Free Goombay Guided Walking Tours, arranged by the Ministry of Tourism, leave from the Tourist Information Booth on Rawson Square at 10am and again at 2pm; there are no tours on Thursday or on Sunday afternoon. Tours last for about 45 minutes and include descriptions of some of the city's most venerable buildings, with commentaries on the history, customs, and traditions of Nassau. The tours do require an advance reservation as schedules may vary. Call ☎ **242/326-9772** to confirm that tours are on schedule.

Majestic Tours, Hillside Manor, P.O. Box N-1401, Cumberland Street, Nassau (☎ **242/322-2606**), offers a number of trips, both night and day, to many points of interest. A 2-hour city-and-country tour leaves daily at 2:30pm and goes to all points of interest in Nassau, including the forts, the Queen's Staircase, the water tower, the Straw Market (passing but not entering it), and other sights. The tour costs $18 per person, but ask for summer specials.

An extended city-and-country tour, also leaving daily at 2:30pm, includes the Ardastra Gardens on its route. The charge is $28 per person, half price for children.

A combination tour, departing Tuesday, Wednesday, and Thursday at 10am, is just that—a combination of all the sights you see on the first tour listed above, plus the Botanical Gardens and lunch, at a cost of $36 per person, half price for children.

Majestic has a nightclub tour Tuesday through Thursday and Saturday nights. They take you to one of Nassau's leading nightclubs to see an exotic floor show consisting of limbo, fire dancing, and other entertainment. Transportation to and from your hotel is included in the prices. The tour without dinner goes for $28 per person; with dinner included, $60 per person.

For information about these tours, as well as for reservations and tickets, many hotels have a Majestic Tours Hospitality Desk in the lobby, and others can supply you with brochures and information about where to sign up.

EASY SIDE TRIPS TO NEARBY ISLANDS

A short boat trip will take you to several small islands lying off the north coast of New Providence. One of these, **Blue Lagoon Island,** has become very popular, to the point where several cruise ships offer day trips here to their passengers. Just 3 miles north of the Narrows at the eastern end of Paradise Island, Blue Lagoon has seven beaches. Although the name evokes images of a barely clad Brooke Shields cavorting on a desert isle, the reality is quite different. There's dancing to a live band, diving with sea creatures at Stingray City, parasailing, snorkeling, kayaking, shopping, and a lunch buffet, among many other things. They also have hammocks to relax in and a children's play area with toys.

Blue Lagoon Island has had several owners, including the British Navy, cartoonist John McCutcheon, and author William Styron (*Sophie's Choice*). McCutcheon built a watchtower in the 1940s to replace one destroyed by an earlier hurricane, adding his own special touch to the structure. He covered the walls of the first floor with his collection of rocks from famous places around the world, such as a brick taken from the Great Wall of China.

Now Ludwig Meister owns the island, and Nassau Cruises Ltd. (See "Boat Cruises" under "Beaches, Water Sports & Other Outdoor Activities," above) leases it and provides the transportation. Nassau Cruises' all-inclusive day pass gets you to and from the island, buys your lunch and two tropical drinks, and pays for nonmotorized water-sports and snorkeling equipment.

Discovery Island, renamed in honor of the 1992 quincentennial of Columbus's landing in The Bahamas, used to be known as Balmoral Island, for it was the private stamping ground of the now defunct Balmoral Club. But all that changed long ago on this island, which is visible offshore from the hotels strung along Cable Beach. A haven for picnickers and sun worshipers, it is ringed by a superb beach, with a network of paths connected to the dock. There's even a lookout for "sundowners," as well as a bar and barbecue along with toilets and changing rooms. Recreational facilities include windsurfing, parasailing, snorkeling, waterskiing, and volleyball. The small sandy cay can be reached by a 5- to 10-minute boat ride. A round-trip ticket costs $10 for adults and children. Boats depart daily from the water-sports kiosk at Nassau Marriott Resort & Crystal Palace Casino every half hour from 9:30am to 4pm. For more information, call ☎ **242/327-6200.**

Athol Island and **Rose Island** are slivers of land poking up out of the sea northeast of the Prince George waterfront docks of Nassau. Shelling is one of the lures of these little islands. Do-it-yourself skippers can make the trip in motorboats.

7 Shopping

You can find a variety of bargains in Nassau—Swiss watches, Japanese cameras, French perfumes, Irish crystal and linens, and British china, usually, but not always, at prices below those charged in stores in the United States.

In 1992, The Bahamas abolished import duties on 11 categories of luxury goods, including china, crystal, fine linens, jewelry, leather goods, photographic equipment, watches, fragrances, and other merchandise. Antiques, of course, are exempt from import duty worldwide. Even though prices are "duty free," you can still end up spending more on an item in The Bahamas than you would back in your hometown. It's a tricky situation.

If you're contemplating a major purchase, such as a good Swiss watch or some expensive perfume, it's best to do some investigation in your hometown—especially your hometown discount outlets—before making a serious purchase in The Bahamas. While the alleged 30% to 50% discount off stateside prices might be true in some cases, it's not true in most cases, because American discount centers are aggressively marketing and selling as never before. In fact, some items, when everything is factored in, are often cheaper in the States.

Certain cameras and electronic equipment, we have discovered, are listed in The Bahamas as being sold, say, 20% or more below the manufacturer's "suggested retail price." That sounds good, except the manufacturer's suggested price might be a lot higher than you'd pay back in your hometown. Therefore, you aren't getting the discount you think you are. Some shoppers even take along department store catalogs from the States to determine if they are indeed getting a bargain.

Of course, while exercising all caution, you'll never know for sure if you're getting the best price. You invariably run into somebody somewhere who paid less for the same merchandise.

There seems to be a lot of price-fixing going on in Nassau. For example, a bottle of Chanel is likely to sell for pretty much the same price regardless of the store.

How much you can take back home depends on your country of origin. Americans, for example, can bring back $600 worth of merchandise tax free, plus one liter of alcohol (wine, liquor, or liqueur) and 200 cigarettes or 100 non-Cuban cigars if they've been away for 48 hours and have not claimed a similar exemption in the past 30 days. For more details, plus Customs requirements for some other countries, refer to "Customs" in chapter 3.

The principal shopping areas are Bay Street and its side streets downtown, as well as the shops in the arcades of hotels.

Don't try to bargain with the salespeople in Nassau stores as you would with merchants at the Straw Market (see "Markets," below). The price asked in the shops is the price you must pay, but you won't be pressed to make a purchase. The salespeople here are courteous and helpful in most cases.

Stores in Nassau are generally open from 9am to 5 or 5:30pm Monday through Saturday. Most stores are closed on Sunday. Stores that are open on Sunday are noted below. The Straw Market does business 7 days a week.

In lieu of street numbers along Bay Street (true in most cases), look for signs advertising the various stores.

ANTIQUES

Marlborough Antiques. Corner of Queen and Marlborough sts. ☎ **242/328-0502.**

This store carries the type of antiques you'd expect to find in a shop in London: antique books, antique maps and engravings, English silver (both sterling and plate), and the kinds of unusual table settings (fish knives, etc.) that might have been better appreciated by older, more formal generations. Among the most appealing objects for nostalgia buffs are the store's collection of antique photographs of Old Bahamas, any of which might be treasured by an island historian. Also displayed are works by Bahamian artists Brent Malone and Maxwell Taylor.

ART

Charlotte's Gallery. Charlotte St. ☎ **242/322-6310.**

This nonprofit organization sells only Bahamian-produced art. Some of it isn't to everybody's taste, but much of the collection is interesting. Some large-size original oil paintings are sold, but many pieces are small, ideal for the souvenir collector.

The Green Lizard. W. Bay St. ☎ **242/356-3439.**

This store specializes in Haitian art, but also offers some Bahamian handcrafts. Some of its merchandise is made locally, and other items are imported. Its handmade wood chimes are collector's items. The store also carries one of The Bahamas most celebrated creations: the hammock.

Kennedy Gallery. Parliament St. ☎ **242/325-7662.**

Although many locals come here for custom framing, the gallery also sells original art work by well-known Bahamian artists, along with pottery and sculpture.

In case you want to see the world.

At American Express, we're here to make your journey a smooth one. So we have over 1,700 travel service locations in over 120 countries ready to help. What else would you expect from the world's largest travel agency?

do more®

 Travel

http://www.americanexpress.com/travel

In case you want to be welcomed there.

We're here to see that you're always welcomed at establishments everywhere. That's why millions of people carry the American Express® Card – for peace of mind, confidence, and security, around the world or just around the corner.

do more

Cards

In case you're running low.

We're here to help with more than 118,000 Express Cash

locations around the world. In order to enroll, just call

American Express before you start your vacation.

do more

Express Cash

And just in case.

We're here with American Express® Travelers Cheques and Cheques *for Two.*® They're the safest way to carry money on your vacation and the surest way to get a refund, practically anywhere, anytime.

Another way we help you…

do more

**Travelers
Cheques**

BRASS & COPPER

Brass and Leather Shop. 12 Charlotte St. ☎ **242/322-3806**.

With two branches on Charlotte Street, between Bay and Shirley streets in Nassau, this shop offers English brass, handbags, luggage, briefcases, attachés, and personal accessories. Shop no. 2 has handbags, belts, scarves, ties, and small leather goods from such famous designers as Furla, Bottega Veneta, Pierre Balmain, and others. If you look and select carefully, you can find some good buys here.

CIGARS

Pipe of Peace. Bay St., between Charlotte and Parliament sts. ☎ **242/325-2022**.

The Pipe of Peace is called the "world's most complete tobacconist," and here you can buy Cuban and Jamaican cigars; however, the Cuban cigars can't be brought back to the United States. For the smoker, the collection is amazing. The shop also sells such name-brand watches as Casio, Guess, and Anne Klein. Even if you don't smoke, you might slip in here looking for some souvenirs or perhaps some locally made handcrafts. They even sell chocolates and pecans. Open Sunday from 10am to 3pm.

CLOCKS

Tick-Tock. Bay and Market sts. ☎ **242/325-7136**.

This outfit offers a selection of wooden clocks handcrafted in the Black Forest region of Germany. It also carries a selection of Bahamian stamp watches and Bahamian coin watches.

COINS & STAMPS

Bahamas Post Office Philatelic Bureau. In the General Post Office, at the top of Parliament St. on E. Hill St. ☎ **242/322-3344**.

Here you'll find beautiful Bahamian stamps slated to become collector's items. One of the most sought-after stamps uses sea shells as a motif.

Coin of the Realm. Charlotte St., just off Bay St. ☎ **242/322-4497**.

This family-run shop lies in a lovely building, more than two centuries old, that was hewn out of solid limestone. The shop offers not only fine jewelry, but also mint and used Bahamian and British postage stamps, as well as rare and not-so-rare Bahamian silver and gold coins. It also sells old and modern paper currency of The Bahamas. Bahama pennies, the ones minted in 1806 and 1807, are now rare and expensive items.

CRYSTAL & CHINA

Treasure Traders. Bay St. ☎ **242/322-8521**.

This offers the biggest selection of gifts made of crystal and china in The Bahamas. All the big names in china are here, including Rosenthal and Royal Copenhagen. The crystal selection includes Waterford, Lalique, and Orrefors. There are a multitude of designs, and the store sells not only traditional designs but also modern sculpted glass.

EMERALDS

Greenfire Emeralds. Bay St. and Fifth S. Terrace, Centerville. ☎ **242/322-2841**.

These are the emerald specialists of Nassau, selling hand-picked Colombian emeralds in 18-karat gold settings. Exotic gemstones include tanzanite, rhodolite, atatite, and tourmaline. You can pick up some discounted designer leather bags here, including those of Paloma Picasso. Swiss watches are also sold, including Omega and Ebel. A complete Lalique crystal studio is on site, with vases, decanters, figurines, and more. Ask to see their special collection of pre-Columbian jewelry.

FASHION

Barry's Limited. Bay and George sts. ☎ **242/322-3118.**

One of Nassau's more formal and elegant clothing stores, this shop sells garments made from lamb's wool, English cashmere, and the kinds of upscale garments you might wear to a meeting of your local bankers. Elegant sportswear (including Korean-made Guayabera shirts) as well as suits are also sold here. Most of the clothes are for men, but women often stop in for a look at the fancy handmade Irish linen handkerchiefs and the stylish cuff links, studs, and other accessories.

The Bay. Bay St. ☎ **242/356-3918.**

This Manhattan-style boutique carries a wide selection of designer clothing for both genders, but we didn't find any great bargains. The selection is elegant in a casual way. If you pick and choose carefully, you'll probably come up with something you can't find back home.

Bonneville Bones. Bay St. ☎ **242/328-0804.**

The name alone will intrigue, but it hardly describes what's inside. This is the best men's store we've found in Nassau. You can find everything here, from the usual T-shirts and designer jeans to elegantly casual clothing, including suits. You will look especially good in a lightweight Perry Ellis suit at the casino later in the evening.

Cole's of Nassau. Parliament St. ☎ **242/322-8393.**

This boutique offers the most extensive selection of designer fashions in Nassau. Women can be outfitted from top to bottom in everything from swimwear to formal gowns, from sportswear to lingerie and hosiery. Gift items are also sold. Cole's also sells sterling-silver and costume jewelry. Open on Sunday from 10am to 6pm.

A second shop is at the Mall at Marathon, Marathon and Robinson roads (☎ **242/393-3542**). Open Sunday from noon to 5pm.

Fendi. Charlotte St. at Bay St. ☎ **242/322-6300.**

This is Nassau's only outlet for the well-crafted Italian-inspired accessories (handbags, luggage, shoes, watches, cologne, wallets, and portfolios) endorsed by the famous leather-goods company. Its choice of gift items might solve some of your gift-giving quandaries.

The Girls from Brazil. Bay St. ☎ **242/323-5966.**

This is the best outlet for swimwear in Nassau. The walls alone are intriguing, featuring wooden cutouts of well-endowed Brazilians in bikinis. Prices are reasonable when compared to similar outlets in the Caribbean and Florida. The store on the upper floor also sells a collection of casual clothing for children and women, plus craft and gift items from Central America. There's also a branch on the lower floor of an outlet at Charlotte and Bay streets.

Mademoiselle, Ltd. Bay St. at Frederick St. ☎ **242/322-5130.**

The store specializes in the kinds of resort wear that looks appropriate at either a tennis club or a cocktail party. It features locally made batik garments by Androsia.

Swimwear, sarongs, jeans, and halter tops are also the rage here, as well as all the wonderfully scented soaps, lotions, and paraphernalia (through their on-site "Body Shop" boutique) you need for herbal massages and beauty treatments. Open Sunday from 10am to 5pm.

HANDICRAFTS

Bahamas Plait Market. Wulff Rd. ☎ **242/326-4192.**

Located right in the heart of Nassau, this is another good outlet for 100% Bahamian-made products and is far superior to the Straw Market, where some of the items are imported from Asia. It's got a fine collection of place mats, jewelry boxes, hats, and bags. This process of turning palm fronds into plait takes 4 weeks, so it's a labor-intensive product, which explains the relatively high prices.

The Plait Lady. The Regarno Building, Victoria and Bay sts. ☎ **242/356-5584.**

Bahamians are proud of their handmade straw items, which are woven from fronds of the pond-top or silver-top palms, harvested only during a new moon. If you look carefully at some of the items sold at the famous Straw Market, you'll see the label Made in Taiwan (unless the vendor removed the tag already). However, if you're looking for the real thing—100% Bahamian—head to this outlet near The Sugar Reef Restaurant. The handmade straw wares are the finest in Nassau. Conch shell mats, trays, and baskets, and many other handcrafts are also sold here. Especially intriguing are the coiled baskets from Red Bays on Andros. Sometimes these are woven with fabric from the famed Androsia Batik, also made on Andros.

Seagrape. W. Bay St. ☎ **242/327-1308.**

The main focus of the shop is Bahamian arts and crafts, some of which are made by persons with disabilities. They also have gift items, costume jewelry, and casual wear, including Androsia batik made on the island of Andros. They have a second shop in the Radisson Mall (☎ **242/327-5113**), which is on West Bay Street, as well.

JEWELRY

John Bull. Corner of Bay and East sts. ☎ **242/322-4253.**

The jewelry department here offers classic selections from Tiffany & Co.; cultured pearls from Mikimoto; the creations of David Yurman, Stephen Lagos, Carrera y Carrera, and Sea Life by Kanbana; and Greek and Roman coin jewelry, as well as Spanish gold and silver pieces. It's the best name in the business. The store also features a wide selection of watches, cameras, perfumes (including Estee Lauder, Chanel, and Calvin Klein offered at 25% or more off stateside prices), cosmetics, leather goods, and accessories. It is one of the best places in The Bahamas to buy a Gucci or a Cartier watch. The outlet has been the authorized agent for Rolex in The Bahamas for 30 years, and the store itself has been doing business since 1929.

Little Switzerland. Bay St. ☎ **242/322-1493.**

Little Switzerland features a wide variety of jewelry, watches (including Ebel, Rado, Omega, and Tag-Heuer), china, perfume (Oscar de la Renta, Dior, and Chloe), crystal, and leather in top brands. With various branches in The Bahamas and throughout the Caribbean, this store has long stood for quality. You'll never have to worry that you're getting ripped off here. Figurines from Royal Doulton and Lladró, as well as crystal by Schott Zwiesel and, of course, Waterford are also sold.

LEATHER

In addition to the stores mentioned below, another good store for leather goods is the Brass and Leather Shop, described under "Brass and Copper," above.

Gucci. Saffrey Sq., Bay St., corner of Bank Lane. ☎ **242/325-0561.**

This shop, opposite Rawson Square, is the best for leather goods in Nassau. The shop offers a wide selection of designer handbags, wallets, luggage, briefcases, gift items, scarves, ties, designer casual wear and evening wear for men and women, umbrellas, shoes, and sandals, all by Gucci of Italy. Also featured are Gucci watches and perfume.

Leather Masters. Parliament St. ☎ **242/322-7597.**

This well-known retail outlet carries an internationally known collection of leather bags, luggage, and accessories by Ted Lapidus, Lanvin, and Lancel of Paris; Etienne Aigner of Germany; and "i Santi" of Italy. Leather Masters also carries luggage by Piel and Marroquinera of Colombia, leather wallets by Bosca, and pens, cigarette lighters, and watches by Colibri. Silk scarves and neckties, as well as sunglasses by designers Ted Lapidus and Giorgio Armani are also featured.

LINENS

The Linen Shop. Ironmongery Bldg., Bay St., near Charlotte St. ☎ **242/322-4266.**

This is the best outlet for linens in Nassau. It sells beautifully embroidered bed linens, Irish handkerchiefs, hand-embroidered women's blouses, and tablecloths. Look also for the most exquisite children's clothing and christening gowns in town.

MAPS

Balmain Antiques. Mason's Bldg., Bay St., near Charlotte St. ☎ **242/323-7421.**

A wide and varied assortment of 19th-century etchings, engravings, and maps, many of them antique and all reasonably priced. Other outlets have minor displays of these collectibles, but this outlet has the finest. Some items go back 400 years. It's usually best to discuss your interests with Mr. Ramsey, the owner, so he can direct you to the proper drawers. His specialties include The Bahamas, America at the time of the Civil War, and black history. He also has a collection of military historical items. You'll find the shop on the second floor, three doors east of Charlotte Street.

MARKETS

The **Nassau International Bazaar** consists of some 30 shops selling international goods in a new arcade. A pleasant place for browsing, the $1.8-million complex sells goods from around the globe. The bazaar runs from Bay Street down to the waterfront (near the Prince George Wharf). With cobbled alleyways and garreted storefronts, the area looks like a European village.

   Prince George Plaza, Bay Street (☎ 242/322-5854 for information), is popular with cruise-ship passengers. Many fine shops (Gucci, for example) are found here. When you get tired of shopping, you can dine at the open-air rooftop restaurant that overlooks Bay Street.

   The **Straw Market** in Straw Market Plaza on Bay Street seems to be on every shopper's itinerary. Even those who don't buy anything come here to look around. Bahamian craftspeople weave and pleat straw hats, handbags, dolls, place mats, and other items—including straw shopping bags for you to carry your purchases in. You can buy items ready-made—often in Taiwan—or order special articles, perhaps bearing your initials. You can also have fun bargaining for the lowest price.

MUSIC

Cody's Music and Video Center. E. Bay St., corner of Armstrong St. ☎ **242/325-8834.**

The finest record store in The Bahamas, Cody's specializes in the contemporary music of The Bahamas and the Caribbean. The father of owner Cody Carter was mentor to many of the country's first Goombay and Junkanoo artists. The store also sells videos, compact discs, and tapes.

PERFUMES & COSMETICS

The Beauty Spot. Bay and Frederick sts. ☎ **242/322-5930.**

The largest cosmetic shop in The Bahamas, this outlet sells duty-free cosmetics, including Lancôme, Chanel, YSL, Elizabeth Arden, Estee Lauder, Clinique, Prescriptives, and Biotherm, among others. It also operates facial salons.

Lightbourn's. Bay and George sts. ☎ **242/322-2095.**

A pharmacy 100 years ago, Lightbourn's is a family-owned and operated business that today carries a wide selection of duty-free fragrances and cosmetics. It is known for the quality of its goods and its service.

The Perfume Bar. Bay St. ☎ **242/322-3785.**

Nassau has several good perfume outlets, notably John Bull and Little Switzerland, which also stock a lot of nonperfume merchandise. But this little gem has exclusive rights to market Boucheron and Sublime in The Bahamas. It also stocks the Clarins line (but not exclusively).

The Perfume Shop. Corner of Bay and Frederick sts. ☎ **242/322-2375.**

In the heart of Nassau, within walking distance of the cruise ships, the Perfume Shop offers duty-free savings on world-famous perfumes. Treat yourself to a flacon of Eternity, Giorgio, Poison, Lalique, Shalimar, or Chanel. Those are just a few of the scents for women. For men, the selection includes Drakkar Noir, Polo, and Obsession.

SHOES

Alexis. Corner of Rosetta and Montgomery sts. ☎ **242/328-7464.**

Need a pair of leather pumps for an impromptu, spur-of-the-moment rendezvous with the prime minister and his wife? When it's shoes you want, this outlet has one of the best selections, including women's footwear by Evan Picone, Timothy Hitsman, and Bandolino.

STEEL DRUMS

Pyfroms. Bay St. ☎ **242/322-2603.**

If you've fallen under the Junkanoo spell and want to take home some steel drums, you've come to the right place. Admittedly, they're not for everybody, but they'll always be useful if island fever overtakes you after you return home.

8 New Providence After Dark

Gone are the days when tuxedo-clad gentlemen and elegantly gowned ladies drank and danced the night away at such famous native nightclubs as the Yellow Bird and the Big Bamboo. You still get dancing now, along with limbo and calypso, but for most visitors, the major attraction is gambling.

Cultural entertainment in Nassau is limited. The chief center for this is the **Dundas Center for the Performing Arts,** which sometimes stages ballets, plays, or musicals. Call ☎ 242/393-3728 to see if a production is planned at the time of your visit.

A CASINO

Crystal Palace Casino. W. Bay St., Cable Beach. ☎ **242/327-6200.** No cover.

This dazzling casino—the only one on New Providence Island—is now run by Nassau Marriott Resort, having taken over from Carnival. Its major competitor is the casino at Paradise Island (see chapter 5). Although some experienced gamblers claim you get better odds in Vegas, this casino nevertheless stacks up well against all the major casinos of the Caribbean. Decorated in hues of purple, pink, and mauve, the 35,000-square-foot casino is filled with flashing lights. The gaming room features 750 slot machines in true Las Vegas style, along with 51 blackjack tables, 9 roulette wheels, 7 craps tables, a baccarat table, and 1 big six. An oval-shaped casino bar extends onto the gambling floor, and the Casino Lounge, with its bar and bandstand (offering live entertainment), overlooks the gaming floor. Open daily Sunday through Thursday from 10am to 4am, and Friday and Saturday 24 hours.

THE CLUB & MUSIC SCENE

BahaMen Culture Club. Nassau and W. Bay sts. (behind the Dolphin Hotel). ☎ **242/356-6266.** Cover Wed, Fri, Sat $20; Sun $15.

Some locals compare this place to a warehouse, but they crowd in anyway to hear the Junkanoo music of the BahaMen, a six-member band that's one of the most famous in Nassau. It's one of the only places where Junkanoo festivities continue year-round. BahaMen music—which is produced with an electric keyboard and guitars, and lots of percussion—alternates with recorded DJ music here. The club, which has two bars, a stage, and a checkerboard dance floor, is open Wednesday through Friday from 8pm to 4am, Saturday from 6pm to 4am. There's no cover charge for women on Wednesday nights, and entrance is free for everyone every Saturday between 6 and 8pm.

Club Waterloo. E. Bay St. ☎ **242/393-7324.** Cover $5.

This very popular disco is right on Lake Waterloo. With dance floors both inside and out, it is one of the most popular clubs on the island. For Nassau at least, the club is fairly sophisticated, offering both European and American dance music. Live bands play on every night except Monday. The club is closed Sunday, but otherwise offers dancing until 4am. Thirsty? There are five bars.

Rock and Roll Café. In the Nassau Beach Hotel, Cable Beach. ☎ **242/327-7711.** No cover.

Set on the beachfront of one of Cable Beach's more staid hotels, this loud and iconoclastic nightclub attracts the under-30 crowd. Patterned after the Hard Rock Cafe in London, it features loud music, a wide selection of beer and tropical drinks, and a noteworthy collection of rock-and-roll memorabilia. There's also a big-screen TV showing sporting events. See "Where to Dine," above, for more information. Open daily from noon to 2am.

The Zoo. West Bay St. at Saunders Beach. ☎ **242/322-7195.** Cover Sun–Thurs $20; Fri–Sat $40.

Opened in 1994, and set midway between Cable Beach and the western periphery of Nassau, this is the largest and best-known nightspot of its kind on New Providence.

It's housed on two floors of what was once a warehouse, although the architects who designed the place originally would never recognize it today. It contains five bars, an indoor/outdoor restaurant (Zooley's), and a sometimes crowded dance floor that attracts mainly an under-30 crowd. Each of the five bars has a different theme, including an underwater theme, a jungle theme, and a *Gilligan's Island* theme. The sports bar is complete with pool tables, wide-screen broadcasts of sporting events, and lots of macho paraphernalia. The most raucous area of the complex is on the street level, where young people tend to drink and dance more enthusiastically than upstairs. If you're looking for a respite from the brouhaha below, climb a flight of stairs to the "VIP Lounge" (open to anyone, not just VIPs), which offers stiff drinks and the chance for dialogue. Most of the complex is open nightly from 8pm to 4am, although the restaurant (Zooley's) serves salads, sandwiches, and platters every night from 6pm until dawn.

STAGE SHOWS

Palace Theater. In the Crystal Palace Casino, W. Bay St., Cable Beach. ☎ **242/327-6200.** Admission for show and dinner, $45; show and two drinks, $30.

This 800-seat theater is one of the major nightlife attractions of The Bahamas. With fake palm trees on each side and lots of glitz, it's an appropriate setting for the Las Vegas–style extravaganzas that are presented on its stage.

Dinner in the theater is a fixed-price affair with an international menu. Many guests, however, prefer to dine in one of the resort's eight other restaurants and arrive either before or after their meal to see the glittery shows. Advance reservations are recommended, especially on Tuesday and Saturday nights, when many of the seats might be filled with cruise-ship passengers. On Sunday and Thursday, no dinner is offered, and the show is presented at 9pm only. On Tuesday and Saturday, dinner is at 6pm, with shows at 7:30, 9:30, and 11:30pm. On Wednesday and Friday, dinner is at 7pm, followed by shows at 9 and 11pm. The theater is closed Monday.

THE BAR SCENE

Banana Boat Bar. In the Nassau Beach Hotel. ☎ **242/327-7711.**

This lobby bar is used primarily by guests of this previously described hotel, but it's open to all and attracts everybody from newlyweds to those who married when Eisenhower was in office. It's one of the best places on Cable Beach for a drink and some light entertainment. On Thursday, Friday, and Saturday, live entertainment performs from 10pm to 2:30am. On Friday night, the bar stages dance contests and selects the best-dressed couple. Drinks are half price at happy hour, from 5 to 7pm. There's a two-drink minimum. The bar is open daily from 5pm to 2:30am.

Cudabay Bar. In the Nassau Harbour Club Hotel, E. Bay St. ☎ **242/393-0771.**

This bar is next to Passin' Jack, a previously recommended dining choice. The bar attracts a 25- to 45-year-old crowd. Many patrons stop in for a drink without ever moving on to a meal at Passin' Jack. Outfitted in a Bahamian-American sports theme, with banners, prominent TV screens, and the kind of dart boards you expect to find in a British pub, it functions as a regular drinking bar throughout the afternoon and early evening, and becomes something between a karaoke club and a disco later in the evening. It's open daily from 3pm to around 2am, or whenever the last reveler leaves.

Palm Patio Bar. In the British Colonial Beach Resort, 1 Bay St. ☎ **242/322-3301.**

The Palm Patio Bar is a good rendezvous, usually attracting a relatively mature crowd who find it a safe haven for a drink and some small-scale entertainment if they're staying in Nassau. Many scenes from the James Bond flick *Never Say Never Again* were shot here. There is live music every Thursday, Friday, Saturday, and Sunday from 8:30pm to 1am. Open daily from 5:30pm to midnight. Happy hour is Thursday and Friday from 5:30 to 7:30pm.

Paradise Island 5

ocated just 600 feet off the north shore of Nassau, Paradise Island, celebrated for its white-sand Paradise Beach, is a favorite vacation spot for East Coast Americans. Now the priciest real estate in The Bahamas, the island once served as a farm for Nassau and was known as Hog Island. Purchased for $294 by William Sayle in the 17th century, it cost A&P grocery chain heir Huntington Hartford $11 million in 1960. He decided to rename the 4-mile-long sliver of land Paradise. He eventually sold out his interests.

In addition to its beaches, the island boasts beautiful foliage, including brilliant red hibiscus and a grove of casuarina trees sweeping down to form a tropical arcade.

Long a retreat for millionaires, the island experienced a massive building boom in the 1980s. Its old Bahamian charm is now gone forever as high-rises, condos, the second homes of the wintering wealthy, and a gambling casino have taken over.

For those who want top hotels, casino action, Vegas-type revues, some of the best beaches in The Bahamas, and a posh address, Paradise Island is it. It outclasses both Cable Beach, its closest rival, and Freeport/Lucaya. True, Paradise Island is overbuilt and overly commercialized, but it's a choice vacation spot nonetheless. It's perfect for a quick 3- or 4-day vacation.

The centerpiece of Paradise Island is the Atlantis Paradise Island Resort & Casino, which is comprised of two towers, the Paradise Club and the Paradise Island Casino (see "Where to Stay," below). It's the world's most complete island resort and casino. There's nothing in Europe, not even on the Riviera, and certainly nothing in the Caribbean to match it.

The megadevelopers haven't completely ruined the island's natural beauty. In spite of its original name, it never resembled a pigsty.

1 Orientation

Although Paradise Island is treated as a separate entity in this guide, it is actually part of New Providence, to which it is connected by a bridge. Therefore, view this section as a companion to chapter 4 on New Providence. For "fast facts" information, such as how to find a hospital, and for transportation details, such as how to get to Paradise Island from the Nassau International Airport, refer to the previous chapter. Except for the glittering casino at Paradise Island and a few minor attractions, you'll need to refer to the New Providence chapter for the major sightseeing attractions, as well as for a wider array of sports and recreation choices.

ARRIVING   Airlines that fly directly to Paradise Island include **Paradise Island Airlines** (☎ **800/786-7202**), with flights from Palm Beach, Fort Lauderdale, Fort Myers, and Miami, and **Pan Am Air Bridges** (☎ **800/424-2557**), with daily service from Miami.

Paradise Island International Airport, which was inaugurated in 1989 and has a 3,000-foot runway, allows passengers to land directly on the island. Landing here eliminates the Customs delays at Nassau International Airport, as well as the expensive 30-minute taxi ride. The airport itself doesn't have a number. For information, you can call **Paradise Island Airways** (see above). A U.S. Customs office (☎ **242/363-3383**) at Paradise Island clears passengers disembarking from international connections, mainly from Florida.

If you arrive at the **Nassau International Airport** (see chapter 4 for information on flying into Nassau), there is no airline bus waiting to take you to Paradise Island unless you're on a package deal that includes transfers. If you're not renting a car, you'll need to take a taxi. Taxis in Nassau are metered. It will usually cost you $22 to go by cab from the airport to your hotel. The driver will also ask you to pay the $2 bridge toll.

VISITOR INFORMATION   Paradise Island does not maintain a tourist office of its own, so refer to the tourist facilities in downtown Nassau (see "Orientation," at the beginning of chapter 4). The concierge or the guest services staff at your hotel can also give you information about the local attractions.

ISLAND LAYOUT   Paradise Island's finest beaches lie on the Atlantic (northern) coastline, whereas the docks, wharves, and marinas are located on the southern side. Most of the island's largest and glossiest hotels and restaurants, as well as the famous casino and a lagoon with carefully landscaped borders, lie west and north of the roundabout. The area east of the roundabout is less congested, with only a handful of smaller hotels, a golf course, the Versailles Gardens, the Cloister, the airport, and many of the island's privately owned villas.

2 Getting Around

Rather than renting a car, most visitors to Paradise Island prefer instead to walk around the island's most densely developed sections and hire a taxi or take the Casino Express (see below) for the occasional longer haul. At least two of the island's more far-flung hotels, including the Holiday Inn and the Ocean Club, maintain minivans to carry their guests to and from the casino. For information on renting a car, refer to "Getting Around" at the beginning of chapter 4.

The most popular way to reach nearby Nassau is to walk across the $2 million toll bridge. Pedestrians pay 25¢.

BY TAXI   If you want to tour Paradise Island or New Providence by taxi, you can make arrangements. Taxis wait at the entrances to all the major hotels. The going hourly rate is about $20 to $23 in cars or small vans, depending on the size of the vehicle.

BY BOAT   If you're without a car and don't want to take a taxi or walk, you can take a **ferry** to Nassau. The ferry to Nassau leaves from behind the Café Martinique on Casino Drive. It runs every half hour, and the 10-minute ride costs $2 round-trip. Quicker and easier than a taxi, the ferry deposits you right at Bay Street. Daily service is from 9:30am to 4:15pm.

Water taxis also operate between Paradise Island and Prince George Wharf in Nassau. They depart daily from 8:30am to 6pm at 20-minute intervals. Round-trip fare is $3 per person.

TRANSPORTATION FOR ATLANTIS PARADISE ISLAND   If you are a guest at one of the properties of Atlantis Paradise Island Resort & Casino, you can take a complimentary tour of the island, leaving Monday through Friday at 2pm. There is no tour on Tuesday.

BY BUS   No public buses are allowed on Paradise Island, unlike New Providence. However, a bus marked **Casino Express Shuttle** runs frequently throughout the day and for most of the night. The fare is $1. Despite its name, it will take you practically anywhere you want to go on Paradise Island, not just to the casino.

3 Where to Stay

At hotels rated very expensive, expect to spend from $400 to $695 a night for a double room. Most hotels on Paradise Island are in the expensive category, charging from $175 to around $300 for a double room. Moderate hotels charge from $95 to $175 a night for a double room. In the off-season (mid-April to mid-December), prices are slashed by at least 20%—and perhaps a lot more. But because Paradise Island's summer business has increased dramatically in the 1990s, you'll never see some of the 60% reductions that you might find at a cheaper property in the Greater Nassau area. Paradise Island doesn't have to lower its rates to attract summer business. For inexpensive accommodations, refer to the recommendations on New Providence Island (see chapter 4). Paradise Island is not a budget destination!

VERY EXPENSIVE

✪ **Ocean Club.** Ocean Club Dr., P.O. Box N-4777, Paradise Island, The Bahamas. ☎ **800/ 321-3000** in the U.S., or 242/363-3000. Fax 242/363-2424. 58 rms, 4 suites, 5 private villas. A/C MINIBAR TV TEL. Winter, $400–$695 double; $1,050–$1,150 suite; $1,100–$1,200 villa. Off-season, $335–$395 double; $595–$645 suite; $695 villa. AE, DC, MC, V.

Sun International's Ocean Club is the most prestigious address on Paradise Island. It's a far more exclusive retreat than the megahotel Atlantis, a fun-in-the-sun family resort. Guests can revel in the casino and nightlife activities of Atlantis nearby, but then retire to this more tranquil, secluded, and small-scale retreat. The white-sand beach that lies adjacent to the hotel is arguably the best in the Nassau/Paradise Island area. This is also one of the best-developed tennis resorts in The Bahamas. The tasteful rooms are plushly comfortable and have minibars and spacious tile baths.

The real heart and soul of the resort lies in the surrounding gardens, which were designed by the island's former owner, Huntington Hartford. This resort, in fact, was once his private home. Formal gardens surround a French cloister set on 35 acres of manicured lawns. The 12th-century carvings of the Cloister are visible at the crest of a hill, across a stretch of terraced waterfalls, fountains, a stone gazebo, and rose gardens. Bigger-than-life statues dot the vine-covered niches on either side of the gardens. Begin your tour of the gardens at the large swimming pool, whose waters feed the series of reflecting pools that stretch out toward the cloister.

The walkways to the accommodations run down the verandas, which ring one of the garden courtyards.

Dining/Entertainment: At night the Courtyard Terrace (see "Where to Dine," below) is illuminated by a pair of fountains.

Services: Concierge, baby-sitting, complimentary shuttle to casino and golf course.

Facilities: Beach, nine well-maintained tennis courts (the best on the island) with a full-time tennis pro.

EXPENSIVE

Atlantis Paradise Island Resort & Casino. Casino Dr., P.O. Box N-4777, Paradise Island, The Bahamas. ☎ **800/321-3000** in the U.S., or 242/363-3000. Fax 242/363-3957. 1,147 rms, 62 suites. A/C MINIBAR TV TEL. Winter, $215–$415 double; $595 suite. Off-season, $130–$325 double; from $370 suite. Extra person $55. AE, DC, MC, V.

Atlantis is the world's most complete island resort and casino. This is *the* megaresort in The Bahamas, a self-contained "water world." It hardly has the private-club aura of the previously recommended Ocean Club, but it outranks every other property on the island. Once owned by Merv Griffin, the property was getting stale and a bit run-down until Sun International acquired it in 1994, pouring millions into the resort, giving it a new lease on life and a lot more.

The name Atlantis is taken seriously. Sun built the world's largest outdoor open-water aquarium (it will remind you of Sea World). Even nonguests come here to view this attraction, which has underground grottoes; coral reefs; long, white-sand beaches; a lagoon for water sports; water slides; a predator lagoon alive with sharks, barracuda, and stingrays; an underwater viewing tunnel; 800 running feet of cascading water-falls; and a quarter-mile-long Lazy River ride for tubing. In all, it's a 14-acre water-scape, with six exhibition lagoons housing some 100 species of tropical fish.

This resort is filled with so many entertainment and dining facilities that many visitors never leave the compound.

Set atop a sandy, pine-dotted strip of land between 3 miles of beachfront and the calm waters of a saltwater lagoon, the resort consists of three structures interconnected by a series of passageways, arcades, and gardens. The focal point is the Paradise Is-land Casino (see "Paradise Island After Dark," below), on either side of which rise the two towers.

Accommodations in both towers are very comfortable and conservatively stylish, although rooms in the Reef Club are slightly larger, more recently renovated, and more expensive. The most expensive rooms are on the concierge floor of the Reef Club, which has a special reception area and provides enhanced service and ameni-ties. Regardless of its location, each room contains a refrigerator, a balcony with water view, plus dozens of amenities.

Dining/Entertainment: There are 12 gourmet and specialty restaurants, a dozen bars and lounges, and a full array of discos and nightlife possibilities. The best of these will be previewed later.

Services: Hair and beauty salon, travel desk, room service, 24-hour medical ser-vice, concierge desk, baby-sitting, valet parking, in-house laundry, supervised children's program at Camp Paradise.

Facilities: Beach, fitness club and sauna, jogging path, two theaters, all water sports, Paradise Island Golf Club with an 18-hole course located nearby, 14-acre waterscape.

Bay View Village. Harbour Rd., P.O. Box SS-6308, Paradise Island, The Bahamas. ☎ **800/757-1357** in the U.S. and Canada, or 242/363-2555. Fax 242/363-2370. 30 units. A/C TV. Win-ter, $160 one-bedroom suite for two; $230 penthouse for two; $270 townhouse for four; $290–$320 villa for four; $420 villa for six. Off-season, $120 one-bedroom suite for two; $170 penthouse for two; $195 townhouse for four; $205–$220 villa for four; $295 villa for six. AE, MC, V.

More than 20 kinds of hibiscus and many varieties of bougainvillea beautify this 4-acre condominium complex. If you get the right nest here, you'll find the accommodations superior to Club Land'Or, its major competitor (see below). Although it is near the geographic center of Paradise Island, it's only a short walk to either the sands of Cabbage Beach or the harbor. It has no beach of its own. Each accommodation has its own kitchen, patio or balcony, and daily maid service. The rooms aren't equipped with phones, but one can be installed upon request. The villas and town houses have dishwashers, and some have views of the harbor. A full-time personal cook can be arranged on request. The units come in a wide variety of sizes. The largest can hold up to six occupants. Rates are slightly less for weekly rentals. Penthouse suites contain roof gardens opening onto views of the harbor.

Dining/Entertainment: The restaurants, nightlife, and casino of Atlantis are only a few minutes away. Bay View has a poolside cafe, the Hibiscus, that serves a full breakfast and lunch daily and dinner twice a week.

Services: Baby-sitting.

Facilities: Three swimming pools, tennis court, two coin-operated laundry rooms, minimarket.

Club Land'Or. Paradise Dr., P.O. Box SS-6429, Paradise Island, The Bahamas. ☎ **242/363-2400.** Fax 242/363-3403. (For reservations and information, contact the club's executive offices: 7814 Carousel Lane, Suite 200, Richmond, VA 23294. ☎ 800/446-3850 in the U.S., except 800/552-2839 or 804/346-8200 in Virginia). 70 apts. A/C. Winter, $215 apt for two. Off-season, $155 apt for two. AE, DC, MC, V.

Across the saltwater canal from Atlantis, these self-sufficient time-share apartments are in three-story buildings set in a landscaped garden dotted with shrubs and reflecting pools. Although the club isn't located on the bay, the beach is a short drive away. There's a small freshwater swimming pool, as well as a promenade beside the canal for guests interested in sniffing the salt air. If you wish to try your luck at the casino, you must drive there. Facilities include the Oasis lounge and the Blue Lagoon Restaurant. The management hosts an energetic activities program. Each of the accommodations includes a separate bedroom, a patio or balcony, a fully equipped kitchenette, and a living room. Baths are utilitarian, showers but no tubs. Some apartments are said to be suitable for four, but we think that would call for a very friendly quartet who wouldn't mind the cramped conditions. The rates depend on the view (garden or water).

Club Méditerranée. Casuarina Dr., P.O. Box N-7137, Paradise Island, The Bahamas. ☎ **800/CLUB-MED** in the U.S., or 242/363-2640. Fax 242/365-3496. 352 rms. A/C. Winter (all inclusive), $1,245 per person weekly; Christmas and New Year's, $1,365–$1,540 per person weekly. Off-season (all inclusive), from $800 per person weekly. AE, MC, V. Free parking.

Club Med opened in 1977, but the original grounds for the club were formed by joining the former Porcupine Club, a yachting club famous in the 1930s, with the estate of Lady Baillie, a British millionaire, and the estate of Mrs. Killiam, a Canadian heiress. It is the Killiam estate that supplies the hotel with its Olympic-size swimming pool and lush garden. Club Med occupies 21 acres and is made up of two wings of three-story pastel bungalows curving along a 3-mile beach. It appeals to visitors who like lots of activities as opposed to the more tranquil Ocean Club, or places where people more or less have to fend for themselves as they do at Bay View Village. In 1996, Club Med began a $15 million renovation project that will continue through March 1998, for the purpose of turning the hotel into a Finest Village, the most deluxe version of the club. They are enlarging and remodeling all the rooms and public areas, including the restaurants, the bar, and the theater. They will also be adding 41 single-occupancy rooms with queen-sized beds. The room plans call for a mix of furniture and art from the Orient and the Caribbean, and the bathrooms will be redone in white marble.

Accommodations are twin-bedded rooms, small but comfortably furnished with white-cane furniture and not a lot else. In the middle of the complex stands a Georgian-style mansion housing public rooms and restaurant facilities. A walk through the landscaped garden brings members harborside and to the main restaurant. The resort accepts children under 12, but there are no special facilities for them. Mostly the place is for people without children. It attracts lots of honeymooners and single people in their 30s. The biggest draw is the tennis facilities, which are among the best in The Bahamas.

Dining/Entertainment: Facilities include an intimate restaurant (offering both indoor and outdoor dining), a disco, a beach bar, and an open-air theater/dance floor/ bar complex. As in most Club Meds, the cuisine relies more on quantity than quality.

Facilities: Beach; swimming pool; 18 tennis courts, with 6 lit at night; fitness center; aerobics classes.

Pirate's Cove Beach Resort. Casuarina Dr., P.O. Box SS-6214, Paradise Island, The Bahamas. ☎ **242/363-2101.** Fax 242/363-2206. 479 rms, 87 suites. A/C TV TEL. Winter, $220–$250 double. Off-season, $145–$170 double. Year-round, $165–$200 suite. AE, DC, DISC, MC, V.

This 18-story resort lying on a crescent-shaped private beach and rising above a forest of pine trees is the tallest in The Bahamas. That may or may not be what you had in mind for a beachside vacation. Pirate's Cove doesn't pretend to be a chic address like Ocean Club. The hotel is especially popular with families because of its Captain Kids day camp with supervised activities for children 4 to 12. When not occupied there, kids can have fun at the Pirate's Den game room and the video arcade. Special activities for children are sometimes staged in the evening so parents can dine alone. A 90-foot-long replica of *Bonny Anne,* a pirate ship that once terrorized the waters around Nassau, stands as the centerpiece of the swimming pool area. Rooms are bright and cheery, but nothing better than you would find in a good, moderately priced Miami motel.

Dining/Entertainment: Restaurants include Matilda's poolside snack bar for hamburgers, cold beer, and tropical drinks, and the garden-style Calico Jack's for breakfast or lunch. The Paradise Grill offers the regular seafood and beef specialties. A musical group provides dance tunes every night until 1am. Buffets and poolside parties are held weekly.

Services: Laundry, baby-sitting, room service (7am to 11pm).

Facilities: Three tennis courts and a full-time pro, crab races and other organized games and contests, two Jacuzzis, exercise/fitness room, water-sports center.

✪ **Radisson Grand Resort.** Casino Dr., P.O. Box SS-6307, Paradise Island, The Bahamas. ☎ **800/333-3333** in the U.S., or 242/363-2011. Fax 242/363-3193. 327 rms, 33 suites. A/C MINIBAR TV TEL. Winter, $175–$265 double; $420–$500 one-bedroom suite; $520–$650 two-bedroom suite. Off-season, $165–$215 double; $400 one-bedroom suite; $500 two-bedroom suite. AE, DC, MC, V.

The Radisson has a dramatic 14-story exterior with spacious balconies that afford sweeping water views from each of the plushly furnished bedrooms. It is more elegant and understated than the Atlantis, although not as prestigious as the Ocean Club. The hotel has been vastly improved recently, as it had grown a bit stale. The architects chose to build this palace on an uncluttered 3-mile stretch of beach so that guests leaving the shelter of the poolside terrace could settle almost immediately onto one of the waterside chaise lounges. The Radisson is within walking distance of the casino, restaurants, and nightlife facilities of the Atlantis Paradise Island Resort & Casino properties.

Paradise Island Accommodations

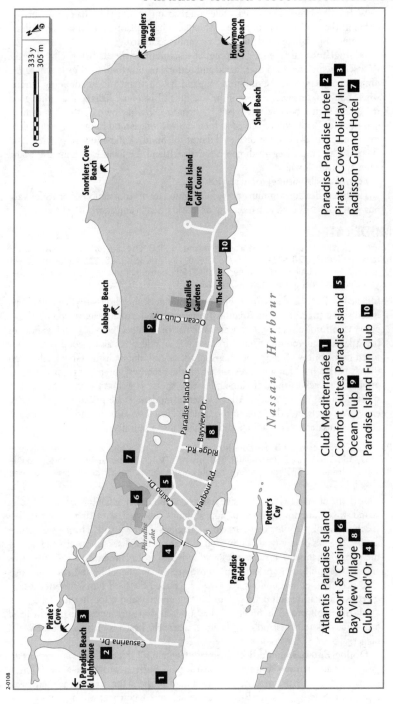

Atlantis Paradise Island
Resort & Casino **6**

Bay View Village **8**

Club Land'Or **4**

Club Méditerranée **1**

Comfort Suites Paradise Island **5**

Ocean Club **9**

Paradise Island Fun Club **10**

Paradise Paradise Hotel **2**

Pirate's Cove Holiday Inn **3**

Radisson Grand Hotel **7**

2-0108

Welcoming drinks are served while you relax on comfortable chairs near the waterfall in the soaring reception area, which also has a plant-rimmed lagoon. All the accommodations here are deluxe and tastefully decorated.

Dining/Entertainment: The premier restaurant of the Radisson Grand is the Rôtisserie, which serves lobster, steak, and seafood nightly from 6:30 to 11pm. Other dining choices include the multilevel Verandah Restaurant and its adjoining terrace, where you can dine with a view of the sea. Julie's Ristorante Italiano is another good restaurant with moderate prices (see "Where to Dine," below). Sunbathers in need of a poolside drink will be served at their chaise lounges, and burgers as well as lobster or chicken salads are available all day at the Sundeck Bar and Grille. After dark, check out the most elegant disco on Paradise Island, Le Paon (see "Paradise Island After Dark," below).

Services: Baby-sitting, room service, valet.

Facilities: Beach, swimming pool, four lighted tennis courts, fleet of boats for various water pursuits such as parasailing or jet-skis. Scuba and snorkeling lessons.

MODERATE

Comfort Suites Paradise Island. Paradise Island Dr., P.O. Box SS-6202, Paradise Island, The Bahamas. ☎ **800/228-5150** or 242/363-3680. Fax 242/363-2588. 220 junior suites with kitchens. A/C MINIBAR TV TEL. Winter, $159–$199 double. Off-season, $130–$180 double. Rates include continental breakfast. AE, DC, MC, V.

Opened in 1991, and a favorite with honeymooners, this three-story, all-suite hotel is across the street from the Atlantis. If the mammoth Atlantis seems too overpowering, Comfort Suites might be a nice alternative. You get the splash and wonder of the Atlantis, but you don't have to stay there all night. It's also a good value compared to the pricey Ocean Club and Atlantis, or even the Radisson Grand. Although there's both a pool bar and a restaurant on the premises, guests are granted signing privileges at each of the drinking-and-dining spots, as well as the pool, beach, and sports facilities of the nearby Atlantis. Accommodations are priced by their views, either over the island, the pool, or the garden. They have such amenities as a minibar, an in-room safe, a clock radio, a coffeemaker, and a hair dryer.

Paradise Island Fun Club. Harbour Rd., P.O. Box SS-6249, Paradise Island, The Bahamas. ☎ **242/363-2561.** Fax 242/363-3803. 250 rms. A/C TV TEL. Winter, $699 per person double, 3 nights. Off-season, $389 per person, 3 nights. Rates include meals, drinks, tips, and taxes. AE, DC, MC, V.

This is one of only two all-inclusive resorts (the other being Club Med) on Paradise Island. It is more downscale in its appeal than Club Med, attracting more families. It offers one of the most cost-conscious vacations on the island. The 12-story hotel lies on 21 acres of low-lying sandy ground near the island's southeastern end, facing the narrow channel that separates Paradise Island from Nassau. In 1996, the owners spent $6 million on renovations, mostly to update the lobby and check-in areas with new fixtures and upholstery. They also added the Golf Fun Park, an 18-hole executive miniature golf course, with putting greens, sand traps, driving cages, and a full-time golf pro. The hotel also has a beach, but surf lovers usually opt for a 5-minute walk to the island's north shore, where the beach is broader and the waves bigger.

Dining/Entertainment: Both the plain Captain's Table and the Terrace Restaurant serve an ongoing series of run-of-the-mill buffets, with once-a-week limbo parties and nightly performances of Bahamian music. More exciting is the newest restaurant, Salerno's Italian Ristorante, which offers gourmet dining on a garden terrace. There are also three bars and a karaoke disco.

> ## 🏨 Family-Friendly Hotels
>
> **Radisson Grand Resort** *(see p. 130)*   A high-rise hotel with a panoramic view of the beach, the Radisson offers family packages that reduce its regular rates substantially. In summer and during Easter and Christmas, activities for children from 5 through 13 are organized at Camp Caribbean.
>
> **Pirate's Cove Beach Resort** *(see p. 130)*   Many repeat visitors are drawn to this family favorite, which opens onto Pirate's Cove Beach. This is the most family-oriented hotel on the island. It's an activity-packed resort, with much fun planned for children ages 4 through 12.
>
> **Atlantis Paradise Island Resort & Casino** *(see p. 128)*   This water world extravaganza offers fun for all ages. Families are delighted with its activity-oriented Camp Paradise (ages 4 to 12), which operates year-round.

Services: Complimentary snorkeling trip, sunset cruise, and beach excursion three times a week; organized games; aerobics classes.

Facilities: Minigym with exercise bicycles, table tennis, toys for children, L-shaped swimming pool.

Paradise Paradise Hotel. Casuarina Dr., P.O. Box SS-6259, Paradise Island, The Bahamas. ☎ **800/321-3000** in the U.S., or 242/363-3000. Fax 242/363-2540. 100 rms. A/C MINIBAR TV TEL. Winter, $90–$100 double; off-season, $85–$95 double. Extra person $55. AE, MC, V.

Sun International acquired this property from Merv Griffin and turned it into a less expensive annex of the Atlantis compound. When Merv ran the show, the rooms were getting grungy, but before he left he ordered new carpets, draperies, and paint jobs. So things aren't as tatty as they once were, but this place is not the equal of the Atlantis by any means. However, many guests prefer the Paradise for its relative tranquillity and lower prices. It draws a mostly young crowd.

The property lies on the western tip of the island in a rambling veranda-lined building. Half the accommodations offer direct access to the beach, which lies on the far side of a cluster of trees. Living here is a bit like being in a forest. The hotel restaurant is a short distance away in a teepee-shaped building directly on the beach. Guests are not locked into any meal plan, although many of them opt to arrange for one of the resort's dine-around plans. The hotel also offers free transportation by shuttle bus to the casino and its adjacent bars and restaurants. Included free are a variety of water sports: sailing, snorkeling, windsurfing, waterskiing, and bicycles.

4 Where to Dine

Paradise Island offers an array of the most dazzling, and the most expensive, restaurants in The Bahamas. If you're on a strict budget, cross over the bridge into downtown Nassau, which has far more reasonably priced places to eat. Although meals on Paradise Island may be expensive, they're often unimaginative.

Surf and turf appears on many a menu. The greatest collection of restaurants is owned by Sun International. They are all near the casino. There are other good places outside this complex, however, including the Courtyard Terrace at the Ocean Club (the most prestigious) and the Rôtisserie at the Radisson Grand Resort, which is that hotel's showcase restaurant.

EXPENSIVE

✪ **Café Martinique.** In the Atlantis, Casino Dr. ☎ **242/363-3000.** Reservations required. Jackets required for men. Main courses $31–$38. AE, DC, MC, V. Daily 7–11pm. FRENCH/CONTINENTAL.

This is one of the best restaurants in The Bahamas, serving everything from beef Wellington to cherries jubilee. James Bond, that gourmet himself, dined here in *Thunderball.* The best French and continental food on Paradise Island is served here, and it is backed up by a well-stocked cellar. Patrons can dine either inside or outdoors. The *fin de siècle* decor suggests the Moulin Rouge of Paris.

When you first sit down, you are presented with a list of dessert soufflés. The chef is justifiably proud of these delicacies, but because of the time and preparation involved, many people order the dessert first. Especially popular are the soufflé Grand Marnier and the soufflé au chocolat. These soufflés are the equal of (not better than) the famous ones served at Sun And… in Nassau.

Then it's on to a dazzling menu, with an appealing list of hors d'oeuvres likely to include everything from escargots bourguignon to a sublime foie gras with truffles. Fish dishes are limited, but select, including fresh Bahamian grouper, that eternal favorite. For a main course, you might like the grenadine de veau au Calvados, which is prepared perfectly here, or chateaubriand with béarnaise sauce, or perhaps a perfectly roasted rack of lamb Provençale. Café Bahamian is a nice finish. Diners once glided here by boat, but nowadays they cross the bridge.

Courtyard Terrace. In the Ocean Club, Ocean Club Dr. ☎ **242/363-3000.** Reservations required. Jacket and tie required for men. Main courses $35–$45. AE, MC, V. Dinner daily 7 and 9pm seatings. CONTINENTAL/BAHAMIAN.

Although the cuisine is not the island's finest, when the moon is right, an evening meal here can be the closest thing to paradise on the island. You dine amid palms, flowering shrubs, and a fountain in a flagstone courtyard surrounded by colonial verandas. Live music wafts from one of the upper verandas to the patio below. This isn't the most glittering dining room on the island, but it's the most sophisticated. Women should bring some kind of evening wrap in case it becomes chilly.

The menu includes a strong showing of the classics. You get beefsteak tartare, prime sirloin, lobster quiche, and chateaubriand. Naturally, such a menu also calls for rack of lamb. The shrimp Provençale or the calves' liver lyonnaise, if featured, might have more zest. Nassau grouper is invariably served, but practically every restaurant offers that. But when the candles flicker in the breeze, the music floats down, and the table setting includes Wedgwood china and crisp linen, there are few complaints, except for the slow service. (Remember that James Bond chose Café Martinique instead of here.)

Mama Loo's. In the Coral Tower, Atlantis, Casino Dr. ☎ **242/363-3000.** Reservations recommended. Main courses $17.50–$31.50. AE, DC, MC, V. Tues–Sun 6:30–10pm. CHINESE/CARIBBEAN.

Many people come here just to hang out in the bar, but if you're in the mood for a Chinese meal worthy of the best Chinese restaurants in New York City, you'll be ushered to a table in a dining room complete with high-back wicker chairs, spinning ceiling fans, flaming torches from an overhead chandelier, and lots of potted palms. The menu includes dishes from the Szechuan, Cantonese, Polynesian, and Caribbean repertoire. The best dish on the menu is Mama Loo's stir-fried lobster, beef, and broccoli with ginger. There's also curried conch, an array of Chinese soups, curried salads, twice-barbecued pork, deboned duckling Imperial, spicy Paradise chicken, and Szechuan shrimp. Meals can be accompanied by tea or by any of several deceptively potent tropical drinks.

The Rôtisserie. In the Radisson Grand Hotel, Casino Dr. ☎ **242/363-2011.** Reservations recommended. Main courses $15–$29.95. AE, DC, MC, V. Daily 6–11pm. STEAK/SEAFOOD/INTERNATIONAL.

The premier restaurant of this deluxe hotel is deliberately understated, with oversize rattan chairs and exposed stone. Here you will enjoy the thickest cuts of steak and prime rib on Paradise Island. From behind a glass window, a team of uniformed chefs prepares the beef to your specifications.

After a bit of a slump, the restaurant is up and running again with its fairly conservative cuisine. If you want Jamaican jerk spicing, go elsewhere. The mozzarella cheese sticks and conch fritters might best be left to a Nassau tavern's repertoire instead of this place, but the escargot (baked with herb garlic butter and Boursin herb cheese) or the smoked salmon are more on target.

The chef prepares a fresh soup every day, although other choices rarely rise above onion soup or conch chowder. It is in the treatment of the meats that the chef's true glory is revealed. The New York sirloin steak is flambé grilled to order, as is the porterhouse. Both are worthy choices and reason to go here in the first place. The meat may be shipped in frozen, but it rises to its full flavor again on the grill, especially when served with the parsley garlic butter.

✪ Villa d' Este. Bird Cage Walk, Coral Tower, Casino Dr. ☎ **242/363-3000.** Reservations required. Main courses $18.50–$33. AE, DC, MC, V. Thurs–Tues 6:30–11pm. ITALIAN.

Nassau's most elegant Italian restaurant offers classic dishes prepared with skill and served with flair. Italian murals decorate the walls. The restaurant takes its name from the world-famed hotel on Lake Como, although the cuisine doesn't begin to equal that gathering place of the world's elite. The freshly made fettuccine Alfredo is almost perfect. It can be served as a first course or as a main dish. A good-tasting Florentine version of minestrone is also served. Main dishes include several chicken and veal dishes, including our favorites, deviled chicken and scaloppini alla parmigiana. The *carte* does not concentrate solely on predictably expensive dishes. Desserts feature a selection of pastries from the trolley. Many guests finish their meal with an espresso, after sampling one of the delectable pastries made fresh every day.

The Water's Edge. At the Atlantis, Casino Dr. ☎ **242/363-3000.** Reservations recommended. Main courses $19.50–$35. AE, DC, MC, V. Daily, 7:30am–noon and 6:30–10pm. EURO/MEDITERRANEAN.

This is one of the first restaurants conceived by Atlantis after they committed themselves to a total refurbishment of the old Merv Griffin resort. One of the most upscale of the many dining spots within the resort, it was designed with three 15-foot waterfalls that splash into an artificial lagoon just outside the dining room's windows. Huge chandeliers illuminate the room, which has views of an open kitchen, where a battalion of chefs work to create such dishes as paella Valencia or grilled salmon with French beans, potatoes, olives, and artichokes. The oak-smoked and spit-roasted duckling with figs and braised cabbage won our hearts. Many guests come here just to sample the pizza and pasta specialties. The pizzas are standard fare, but some of the pastas have a bit of zest, including penne *à l'arrabbiata* with a spicy tomato sauce. The chef pays special attention to the antipasti, which evokes the tangy flavors of the Mediterranean, especially the soup *au pistou* (vegetables with basil and roasted garlic). Depending on the night, some of these dishes are better than others. Mainly, the problem here is that the food has a hard time competing with the ambience.

MODERATE

Blue Lagoon. In the Club Land'Or, Paradise Dr. ☎ **242/363-2400.** Reservations required. Main courses $17–$53. AE, DC, MC, V. Daily 5–10pm. SEAFOOD.

Lying across the lagoon from Atlantis, this restaurant is located two floors above the reception area of the Club Land'Or. Go here to escape the glitter and glitz of the Sun International properties, especially the restaurants along Bird Cage Walk, site of the casino. A view of the harbor and Paradise Lake, as well as music from an island combo, will complement your candlelight meal. The nautical decor includes polished railings and lots of full-grain hardwood. The restaurant is basically a good, moderately priced choice. Many of the fish dishes, however, are excellent, including stone crab claws or the Nassau conch chowder. The chef even whips up a good Caesar salad for two. If broiled grouper amandine is not your idea of a good time (after all, there is just so much grouper one can consume), try some of the other dishes such as steak au poivre with a brandy sauce or duck à l'orange, or even chicken chasseur. Yes, you will probably have had better versions of these dishes elsewhere, but they are competently prepared and served here, even though the meats are shipped in frozen. Desserts include such old reliables as Tía Maria parfait or crêpes suzette.

Boat House. In Atlantis, Casino Dr. ☎ **242/363-3000.** Reservations required. Three-course fixed-price menus $34.50–$42.75. AE, DC, MC, V. Daily, 6:30, 7, 9, and 10pm seatings. STEAKS.

The Boat House is located next to the Paradise Lagoon near the superior Café Martinique. Behind its nautical facade, the richly polished leather and hardwood contribute to a fun, clubhouse ambience. You cook your own dinner on the charcoal grill that's the focal point of each group of diners. If the weather's hot, the charcoals are likely to heat you up, as well. Top-quality meats, imported from the mainland, are the house specialties.

The menu offers nine main courses, each of which is priced as part of a full meal. Choices include "King of the Sea," a Bahamian lobster tail; a 12-oz. T-bone steak; grilled swordfish; and tender prime filet mignon. Each main course is accompanied by Bahamian conch chowder, to which a generous splash of sherry is added at your table. Also offered are a crisp Boat House salad and a baked potato or rice. Cheesecake, chocolate cake, and coffee are included in the meal.

Columbus Tavern. Paradise Island Dr. ☎ **242/363-2534.** Reservations required for dinner. Main courses $16–$24.95. MC, V. Daily 7am–midnight. CONTINENTAL/BAHAMIAN.

Far removed from the glitz and glamour of the casinos, the tavern seems relatively little known, even though Erika and Peter Kugler opened it some 6 years ago. It deserves to be sought out, as it serves good food at affordable (not cheap) prices. The tavern has the typical nautical decor (don't come here for that), with tables placed both inside or, far more desirably, outside overlooking the harbor. The bar is worth a visit in itself, with its long list of drinks, many of them in the tropical Bahama Mama style. What would a local restaurant be without launching you into your repast with conch chowder? But you can also dine more elegantly on such appetizers as cheese-stuffed mushrooms and foie gras. Even though imported frozen, both the chateaubriand and rack of lamb were flawless. You can also order a decent veal cutlet and a quite good filet of grouper with a tantalizing lobster sauce.

Julie's Ristorante Italiano. In the Radisson Grand Resort, Casino Dr. ☎ **242/363-2011.** Main courses $11.95–$23.95. AE, DC, MC, V. Daily 6–11pm. ITALIAN.

If you want first-rate Italian cookery, head for the Villa d'Este, previously recommended. But if you'd like something more moderately priced, and more of the

Paradise Island Dining

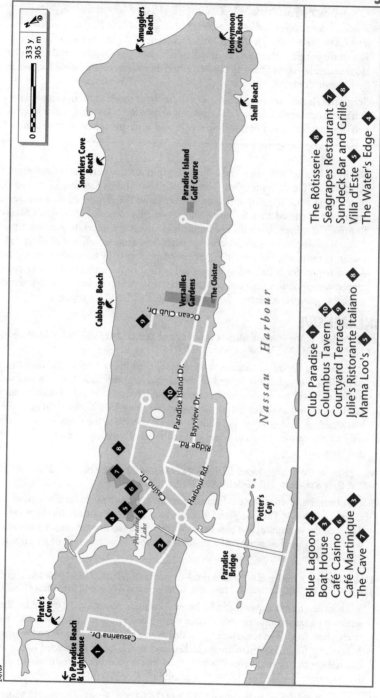

Club Paradise ①
Columbus Tavern ⑩
Courtyard Terrace ⑨
Julie's Ristorante Italiano ⑧
Mama Loo's ⑤

The Rôtisserie ⑥
Seagrapes Restaurant ⑦
Sundeck Bar and Grille ⑧
Villa d'Este ⑤
The Water's Edge ④

Blue Lagoon ②
Boat House ③
Café Casino ⑥
Café Martinique ③
The Cave ⑦

137

> ### 👪 Family-Friendly Restaurants
>
> **The Cave** *(see p. 138)*   At the Atlantis, this is one of the most popular lunchtime venues for burgers, salads, and sandwiches. Kids love entering the simulated rock-sided tunnel lined with flaming torches. Later, they might return before it closes at 5pm for an ice cream.
>
> **Seagrapes Restaurant** *(see p. 138)*   Off the lobby of the Atlantis, this tropical restaurant serves three meals a day. It's especially known for its low-price buffet lunches and dinners. Barbecued ribs, shrimp créole, and apple pie appear on the menu.

Mamma Mia school, then come here. In spite of the cute names for some of the dishes—"Don't Squeeza My Tomato Salad" or "Julie's Caesar's Salad"—much of the food is quite good and robust. Curiously, the dinner salad, a medley of vegetables, is named after Il Duce—and comes in a choice of Mussolini's Mama's flavors. The gimmick of this restaurant is that you get to create your own pasta dish, choosing from a wide selection of pastas and sauces. Veal and chicken dishes dominate the menu, and most are quite acceptable, especially the chicken parmigiana. A house specialty is Bahamian lobster tail with shrimp, scallops, and mushrooms topped with Alfredo sauce. You can also order fish, various shrimp dishes, or else the inevitable grouper, appearing this time decorated with tricolor peppers.

INEXPENSIVE

Café Casino. In the Paradise Island Casino, Casino Dr. ☎ **242/363-3000.** Main courses $7.50–$18. AE, DC, MC, V. Daily 11–4am. AMERICAN.

If you want a late-night snack or a break from the gaming tables, head over to this coffee shop located at the far end of the casino. Its menu includes pizza and well-stuffed sandwiches—corned beef, pastrami, and Reubens—as well as many kinds of salad. The cafe also serves full-course meals, including New York sirloin or broiled, blackened, or fried grouper, but your best bet is to stick to the sandwiches. Go here only for the convenience and when you get bored of winning all that money at the gaming tables.

The Cave. At the Atlantis, Paradise Dr. ☎ **242/363-3000.** Lunch platters $5–$12. AE, DC, MC, V. Daily 8am–6pm. BURGERS/SALADS/SANDWICHES.

This burger and salad joint is located near the beach of the most lavish hotel and casino complex on Paradise island. It caters to the bathing suit and flip-flops crowd. To reach the restaurant, you pass beneath a simulated rock-sided tunnel illuminated with flaming torches worthy of a pirate rendezvous. The selection of ice creams is suitable for mid-afternoon cool-offs.

Club Paradise. In the Paradise Paradise Hotel, Casuarina Dr. ☎ **242/363-3000.** Main courses $19–$32. AE, DC, MC, V. Daily 8–11am, noon–4:30pm, and 6–9:45pm. STEAKS/SEAFOOD.

With its beachfront location and barbecue specialties, this is a good choice for those who want a casual ambience with ocean views, good value, and good, although relatively plain, food. The restaurant is in a thatch-roofed pavilion directly on the beach. Everything from Bahamian fried chicken and veal T-bone to seafood paella and cracked conch is served here. The basic food mix is good but far from outstanding. It's essentially the kind of cuisine you'd find in a good tavern.

Seagrapes Restaurant. In the Atlantis. ☎ **242/363-3000.** Breakfast buffet $15.95 lunch buffet $15.95 weekend brunch $21.95 dinner buffet $26.95. AE, DC, MC, V. Daily 7–11am, noon–3pm, and 5:30–10pm. INTERNATIONAL.

Buffet lunches and dinners are the specialty of this pleasantly decorated tropical restaurant. This is one of the mass-market eateries of the Atlantis, catering mainly to those, including families, who want an alternative to the more pricey options reviewed above. Tropical foods from around the world are featured, including Cuban, Caribbean, and Cajun dishes. These dishes are more bountiful than haute cuisine, but most people don't come here expecting the best food on Paradise Island. Instead they want a lot of food for not a lot of money, and that's what they get. The restaurant, which can seat 200 to 300 diners at a time, overlooks the lagoon and has a marketplace look, with little stalls and different stations making up the buffet offerings.

5 Beaches, Water Sports & Other Outdoor Activities

Visitors interested in something more than lazing on the beaches have only to ask hotel personnel to make the necessary arrangements. Guests at Atlantis (☎ 242/363-3000), for example, can have access to a surprising catalog of diversions without so much as leaving the hotel property. They can splash in private pools (one with a swim-up bar); play tennis, Ping-Pong, and shuffleboard; ride the waves; snorkel; or rent Sunfish, Sailfish, jet skis, banana boats, and catamarans from contractors located in kiosks in the hotel's lobby.

BEACHES

For comments about **Paradise Beach,** refer to "Beaches, Water Sports & Other Outdoor Activities" in chapter 4. Paradise Island has a number of smaller beaches, as well, including **Pirate's Cove Beach** and **Cabbage Beach,** both of which are on the north shore of the island. Cabbage Beach is a particular favorite with broad sands that stretch for at least 2 miles. Casuarinas, palms, and sea grapes border it. It's likely to be crowded with patrons of the megaresorts, such as Atlantis. Escapists find something approaching solitude on the northwestern stretch of the beach where the only access is by boat or foot.

FISHING

Sports anglers can fish close to shore for grouper, dolphin, red snapper, crabs, even lobster. Farther out, in first-class fishing boats fitted with outriggers and fighting chairs, they troll for billfish or the giant marlin that Hemingway used to pursue regularly in The Bahamas.

The best way to hook up with this pastime is to go to the activities desk of your hotel. All hotels have contacts with local fishers who take their clients out for a half- or full-day's fishing. For other possibilities, refer to "Beaches, Water Sports & Other Outdoor Activities" in chapter 4.

FITNESS CENTER

Paradise Island Fitness Center, at the Atlantis, Casino Dr. (☎ 242/363-3000), is the best. Here you will find state-of-the-art equipment, including treadmills, exercise bikes, rowing machines, and weights. Aerobics are also offered. Massages are available, as well. The club is free, but it's open only to guests of one of the Sun International properties, such as the Atlantis. Hours are daily from 7am to 7pm.

GOLF

Paradise Island Golf Club. Paradise Island Dr. ☎ **242/363-3925.**

Located at the east end of the island, this superb club, owned by Sun International, has an 18-hole championship course, designed by Dick Wilson, and a fully stocked

---

⭐ **Frommer's Favorite Paradise Island Experiences**

Dazzling Stage Shows. In the Las Vegas tradition, some of the world's greatest showbiz extravaganzas are staged at the Atlantis showroom of the Paradise Island Casino.

Watching the Sunset at the Cloister. Here amid the reassembled remains of a 14th-century French stone monastery, once owned by William Randolph Hearst, you can enjoy one of the most beautiful pink and mauve sunsets in all The Bahamas.

A Day at Paradise Beach. It's not only one of the best beaches in The Bahamas, but also in the Caribbean, as well. The beach is dotted with *chikees* (thatched huts) for when you've had too much of the sun.

A Night at the Casino. The Paradise Island Casino has been called one giant "pleasure palace." Many visitors arrive on the island just to test their luck in this 30,000-square-foot casino. The nearby Bird Cage Walk is home to some of the finest restaurants in The Bahamas.

---

pro shop. It is the only golf course on Paradise Island. From May through November, greens fees are $45 for 18 holes; in winter, the rate is $100. Fees include golf cart. Golfers, who have included Jack Nicklaus, Gary Player, and other stars, face the challenge of hitting a ball through the twirling blades of a small windmill, through a waterpipe, over or around a lion's den, among other obstacles. The 14th hole of the 6,771-yard, par-72 course has the world's largest sand trap: The entire left side over the hole is white-sand beach. Golfers who want more variety will find two other courses on New Providence Island (see "Beaches, Water Sports & Other Outdoor Activities" in chapter 4).

JOGGING

Paradise Island is more congested than New Providence Island, especially on the main traffic artery, Paradise Island Drive. However, if you run south along Harbour Road leading to Harbour Cove, you'll find less traffic. You might also want to jog, as many do, along either Cabbage Beach or Paradise Beach on the north shores.

SNORKELING, SCUBA DIVING & PARASAILING

Sea & Ski Ocean Sports, Radisson Grand Resort, Casino Drive (☎ 242/363-3370), is the best all-around center for water sports on the island, specializing in scuba diving and snorkeling. A one-tank dive, all equipment included, costs $35; a two-tank dive goes for $60. Snorkeling reef trips depart daily at 10am and 2pm, costing $25 with all equipment included. Parasailing is offered, as well, costing about $40, depending on the ride. Windsurfers rent for $20 per hour. If you'd like to go out in a Sunfish, the fee is $20 per hour, or else $35 for a Hobie Cat.

TENNIS

If you're a true tennis buff, you'll head for the previously recommended **Club Meditérranée** (☎ 242/363-2640), which has the largest court complex on the island, a total of 18 clay composition courts. Six of these courts are lit for night games. There are ball machines, plus a full staff of instructors who offer expert advice. There's also instant-replay TV.

The second major venue for tennis is in the **Ocean Club,** Ocean Club Drive (☎ **242/363-3000**). Many visitors come to Paradise Island just for tennis, which can be played day or night on the nine Har-Tru courts near the Ocean Club. Guests booked into the cabanas and villas of the club can practically roll out of bed onto the courts. Although beginners and intermediate players are welcome, the courts are often filled with first-class competitors. Two major tennis championships a year are played at the Ocean Club courts, drawing players from the world's top 20.

Other hotels with courts include: **Atlantis** (☎ 242/363-3000), with nine hard-surface courts; **Pirate's Cove Beach Resort** (☎ 242/326-2101), with three night-lit asphalt courts; and the **Radisson Grand Resort** (☎ 242/363-2011), with four night-lit Har-Tru courts and lessons available.

6 Seeing the Sights: From a Dazzling Casino to a Secluded Cloister

To prevent guests from getting bored with "just going to the beach," most of the big hotels here have activity-packed calendars, especially for that occasional windy, rainy day that comes in winter. Hordes of Americans can be seen taking group lessons in such activities as backgammon, whist, tennis, and cooking and dancing Bahamian style. They are even taught how to mix tropical drinks, such as a Goombay Smash or a Yellow Bird.

✪ **Atlantis Paradise Island Resort & Casino.** Casino Dr. ☎ **242/363-3000.** No cover. Open 24 hours.

Regardless of where you're staying—even if it's at the remotest hotel on New Providence (see chapter 4)—you'll want to visit this lavish hotel, restaurant complex, casino, and entertainment center. It is *the* big attraction of Paradise Island. Of course, the rich and famous have visited before you. Donald Trump tried his luck at running the place before he finally passed it along to former talk-show host and TV producer Merv Griffin, who sold it in 1994. The new owner is Sol Kerzner, who built the fabled Sun City complex in South Africa.

You could spend all day here—and all night, too—wandering through the glitzy shopping malls; sampling the international cuisine of the varied restaurants; gambling in the casino at roulette wheels, slot machines, and blackjack tables; or seeing Vegas-style revues. During the day you can dress casually, but at night you should dress up a bit, especially if you want to patronize one of the better restaurants. (See individual restaurant listings in "Where to Dine," above.)

The most crowded time to visit is between 8 and 11pm any night of the week. There is no cover to enter: You pay just for what you gamble away (and that could be considerable), eat, drink, or watch in the case of a show, although some entertainment in the bars is free, except for the price of the liquor.

The Cloister. Ocean Club, Ocean Club Dr. ☎ **242/363-3000.** Free admission. Open anytime.

Located in the Versailles Gardens of the Ocean Club, this 12th-century cloister, originally built by Augustinian monks in France, was reassembled here stone by stone. Huntington Hartford, the A&P heir, purchased the cloister from the estate of William Randolph Hearst at San Simeon in California. Regrettably, when the newspaper czar originally bought the cloister, it had been dismantled in France for shipment to America, but the parts had not been numbered. Arriving unlabeled on Paradise Island, the cloister baffled the experts until artist and

Special Moments & Little-Known Gems

The Versailles Gardens at the Ocean Club. If you head up Paradise Island Drive, you will reach Ocean Club Drive and this garden of tranquillity. It was a "folly" ordered landscaped by the A&P heir, Huntington Hartford, and it's the loveliest spot on Paradise Island, far removed from the glitz and faux-glamour of the casinos. Its seven terraces are a frequent venue today for Bahamian or foreign weddings. Statues of some of Hartford's favorite people are found in the gardens, including Mephistopheles, Franklin D. Roosevelt, and even Napoleon. The gardens are open anytime you want to visit them—day or night—and there's no admission.

The House of Mystery. Before you reach the Cloister at the Ocean Club on Ocean Club Drive, turn right onto Bayview Drive. This will take you to the most luxurious and opulent private mansion in all The Bahamas. You can't go in, but you can drive past. The house is owned by a mysterious sheik who created a bit of Arabian Nights fantasy on Paradise Island, far away from his home (wherever that is). The mansion has been the subject of much local speculation since it was first built. The house runs the length of the drive. A total of 16 four-light lampposts illuminate the way at night. The house is surrounded by a wall. A statue of Neptune (along with who knows what else) guards the main gate. Occasionally, a dark limousine will emerge from this gate. Otherwise, there is little sign of life. To get an invitation here is almost unthinkable, regardless of your credentials. In the tradition of Huntington Hartford, statues dot the grounds. At the end of the property is a total of eight garages.

Sampling a Conch Salad. Just once in your life if you've never had it before—or even if you have—you've got to sample a Nassau conch salad. The best we could find on the island is at the **Sundeck Bar and Grille,** at the Radisson Grand Resort on Casino Drive (☎ **242/363-3500**). There is no more local dish than this, unless it's conch chowder, which is also served, or even a conch burger, which has been known to appear on the menu, or the ever-popular conch fritter. Bahamians eat conch the way Americans devour the Big Mac. This mollusk—called "the snail of the sea"—reminds Pacific Coast residents of abalone. The uncooked conch is marinated in Old Sour, a hot pepper sauce, to break down its tissue and to add an extra tangy flavor. It's served with diced small red or green peppers along with chopped onions. You'll soon acquire a taste for it. Sundeck chefs make it fresh daily but only on a limited basis. They warn, "When it's gone, it's gone." You'd better go early. Hours are daily from 11am to 5:30pm. Main courses range from $6 to $11.95.

sculptor Jean Castre-Manne set about to reassemble it piece by piece. It took him 2 years, and what you see today, presumably, bears some similarity to the original. The gardens, which extend over the rise to Nassau Harbour, are filled with tropical flowers and classic statues.

7 Shopping

For serious shopping, you'll want to cross over the Paradise Island Bridge into Nassau (see chapter 4). However, many of Nassau's major stores also have shopping outlets on Paradise Island.

Greenfire Emeralds Ltd. In the Atlantis, Casino Dr. ☎ **242/363-4188.**

For a rich collection of emeralds and jewelry from Colombia, as well as other precious and semiprecious stones and pearls from around the world, you can't go wrong by shopping at Greenfire Emeralds Ltd., also agents for Seiko watches.

Jewels of the Sea. In the Pirate's Cove Beach Resort. ☎ **242/363-3420.**

Original designs in coral and natural pearls are spread out before you, including earrings, necklaces, and bracelets crafted from Bahamian conch shells.

John Bull. In Atlantis, Casino Dr. ☎ **242/363-3956.**

Known for its Bay Street store (see "Shopping," chapter 4) and as a pioneer seller of watches throughout The Bahamas, John Bull sells watches, jewelry, and designer accessories.

Mademoiselle. In the Atlantis, Casino Dr. ☎ **242/363-3000.**

For chic women's clothing by European and American designers, this is an excellent place to shop. Mademoiselle specializes in sophisticated apparel for women up to size 14. They also offer a range of accessories, such as belts and jewelry. For this type of clothing, it's a good choice.

8 Paradise Island After Dark

Among all the islands of The Bahamas, nightlife reaches its zenith on Paradise Island. There is no other spot with the diversity of attractions, especially after dark, that this self-contained playground can offer. The best choices are covered below.

A CASINO

✪ **Paradise Island Casino.** In the Atlantis, Casino Dr. No cover. ☎ **242/363-3000.** Open 24 hours.

All roads on the island eventually lead to the focal point of the nightlife: the extravagantly decorated casino run by Sun International. It's the only casino on the island, and it's superior to the one at Cable Beach (see "New Providence After Dark," in chapter 4). It's a pleasure palace in the truest sense of the term. No visit to Nassau would be complete without a promenade through the Bird Cage Walk, where assorted restaurants, bars, and cabaret facilities make this one of the single most-visited attractions anywhere outside the United States. For sheer gloss, glitter, and showbiz extravagance, this mammoth 30,000-square-foot casino, with adjacent attractions, is the place to go.

The gaming tables, open daily from 10am to 4am, provide the main attraction in the enormous room, where Doric columns, a battery of lights, and a mirrored ceiling vie with the British colonial decor. Some 1,000 whirring and clanging slot machines operate 24 hours a day.

From mid-morning until early the following morning, the 38 blackjack tables, the 9 roulette wheels, and the 8 tables for craps, 3 for baccarat, and 1 for big six are seriously busy with the exchange of large sums of money.

A REVUE

Atlantis Showroom. In the Atlantis, Casino Dr. ☎ **242/363-3000.** Dinner show, $55; "cocktail show" (including two drinks), $40.

You can count on this place to offer the most spectacular shows in The Bahamas, outshining anything that the theater at Cable Beach or the showrooms of Freeport put on. Visitors usually purchase tickets in advance at the booth adjacent to the casino. The most recent revue is called *Sunsation!* It features dances based on Baha-mian Junkanoo and is suitable entertainment for the whole family. Hot island rhythms are the backdrop for rather brilliant dancers in colorful island costumes. Along with this, you get state-of-the-art lighting and audio and laser effects.

Dinner is offered nightly Tuesday through Saturday, beginning at 7pm, with the show going on promptly at 8:30pm. A cocktail show is offered nightly Tuesday through Saturday, beginning at 10:30pm, unless preempted by some other entertain-ment. Call for reservations and ticket information, or even to see what's showing at the time of your visit.

A COMEDY CLUB

Joker's Wild. In the Atlantis. ☎ **242/363-3000.** Admission $12.50.

This is the only comedy club in The Bahamas, with a company of funny people who work hard to make their casino-loving clients laugh. It is located on the casino floor in the Pastiche Lounge. Performances begin Tuesday to Sunday at 9:30pm and last for about an hour and 30 minutes. At least three different comedians will appear on any given night, hailing from The Bahamas as well as ports as far away as London and New York. Scotch and soda costs $5.

A DISCO

Le Paon (The Peacock). In the Radisson Grand Resort, Casino Dr. ☎ **242/363-2011.** No cover, but the two-drink minimum costs $15.

This spacious, multilevel disco is in the back of the hotel's main lobby. If you're with a group of friends, you may want to establish your headquarters at the circular ban-quette in the middle of the floor, close to the dancing area. The bar is long and pro-vides views of the ocean. Open Thursday through Sunday from 9pm to 2am.

THE BAR SCENE

There are so many different nightspots at the Atlantis, Casino Dr. (☎ **242/363-3000**), that a visit to each of them could occupy an entire evening for anyone who wanted to "discover" the perfect tropical libation. Drinks in each of these places cost from $4 each.

One of the best vantage points for a view of both the entrance of the casino and Bird Cage Walk is the cozy **Gallery Bar** in the Atlantis. It offers seating in low-slung, comfortable chairs and an English-club atmosphere. Hours are from 11am to 4pm daily.

If you're looking for a taste of Polynesia, head for the bar in **Mama Loo's restau-rant** (see "Where to Dine," above), off the casino's arcade, where fruited cocktails exude a hint of the Pacific.

Grand Bahama (Freeport/Lucaya)

6

Big, bold, and brassy best describes Grand Bahama Island, site of Freeport/Lucaya. It doesn't have the class of Bermuda, the chic of Paradise Island, or the tranquillity of Harbour Island (off the coast of Eleuthera). But it's a major tourist destination, nevertheless, attracting the types who prefer Atlantic City over Palm Beach.

The second most popular tourist destination in The Bahamas (Nassau is first), Grand Bahama lies just 50 miles and less than 30 minutes by air off the Florida coast. That puts it just 76 miles east of Palm Beach, Florida. Grand Bahama is known for its water sports and pristine white sandy beaches. It's also got cosmopolitan glitz and glamour, too much so for some visitors.

The heartbeat of Grand Bahama Island is the resort of Freeport/Lucaya, center of major sightseeing, shopping, gambling, water sports, and nightlife. The dining's not gourmet here, but there's excellent golf and tennis, and enough sun and surf to appeal to most visitors.

Grand Bahama is more than an Atlantic City clone, however. Because the island is so big, most of it remains relatively unsettled. There are plenty of quiet places to get close to nature, including the Rand Memorial Nature Center and the Garden of the Groves (see below). The Lucayan National Park, with its underwater caves, forest trails, and a secluded beach, is another favorite attraction.

If you're not interested in gambling at one of the island's two casinos, or if you're not interested in Vegas-style cabaret revues, there are alternatives here.

Just miles from Freeport/Lucaya are serene places where you can wander in a world of casuarina, palmetto, and pine trees. During the day you can enjoy long stretches of open beach, broken by inlets and little fishing villages. The island's most interesting destination is the fishing village of West End, the westernmost settlement on the island, located 28 miles from Freeport. Here locals and visitors enjoy Bahamian cuisine and learn about Grand Bahama's buccaneering and rum-running days.

The reviews of Grand Bahama Island are definitely mixed. Some discriminating travelers who could live anywhere have built homes here; whereas others vow never to set foot on the island again, finding it "tacky" or "uninspired." Judge for yourself.

Freeport/Lucaya was once just a dream, a low-lying pinewood forest that almost overnight turned into one of the world's major resorts. The resort was the dream of Wallace Groves, a Virginia-born financier who saw the prospect of developing the island into a miniature Miami Beach. Today, with El Casino, the International Bazaar, high-rise hotels, golf courses, marinas, and a bevy of continental restaurants, that dream has been realized.

Originally, Freeport was developed as an industrial-free zone in 1956. Groves wanted to attract international financiers who could appreciate the fact that Grand Bahama was only 3 hours by air from New York.

The Lucaya district was developed 8 years later, as a resort center along the coast. It has evolved into a blend of residential and tourist facilities. As the two communities grew, their identities became almost indistinguishable. But elements of their original purposes still exist today. Freeport is the downtown and attracts visitors with its commerce, industry, and own resorts, whereas Lucaya is called the garden city and pleases residents and vacationers alike with its fine sandy beaches.

A major sports center, Freeport/Lucaya has six championship golf courses, plus a nine-hole executive layout. Water sports—skiing, skin diving, swimming, fishing, sailing—abound. With some 40 tennis courts on the island, there's plenty of opportunity to hit the ball. There are also riding stables and jogging tracks.

Grand Bahama Island is the northernmost and fourth-largest landmass in The Bahamas. It is 73 miles long and 4 to 8 miles wide. Nearly everything here is new, including the people. Before the development boom, the population numbered only 4,000, but now it stands at 41,000. Historically, not much happened here since Ponce de León landed searching for the Fountain of Youth—that is, until the bulldozers moved in.

1   Orientation

For a general discussion on traveling to The Bahamas, refer to chapter 3.

ARRIVING

BY PLANE   A number of airlines fly to Freeport from points within the continental United States. Since Nassau provides the country's most important air link to the rest of the world, many visitors arrive in Nassau, then change to one of the five daily flights operating between Nassau and Freeport on **Bahamasair** (☎ 800/222-4262). Planes can hold up to 50 passengers each, take 40 minutes en route, and charge $128 round-trip. For a same-day return, it costs $96.

BY CRUISE SHIP   Because of its proximity to the Florida coastline, Freeport is popular with cruise ships that depart and return from the U.S. mainland on the same day. (For a review of major cruise lines sailing to Freeport, see "Cruises" in chapter 3.) Some of the most popular short-term cruises are run by **Palm Beach Cruise Line,** 2790 N. Federal Hwy., Boca Raton, FL 33431 (☎ 800/841-7447 or 561/394-7450), which offers them every Monday, Tuesday, Thursday, and Saturday, departing from the port of West Palm Beach at 8am and returning there by midnight the same day.

Passengers can stay on Grand Bahama for a few days or make the most of 3 hours ashore in Freeport (just enough time for some shopping, a margarita, and a visit to the casino) before cruising back to Florida. The cost for this cruise ranges from $79 to $89 per person, plus $36 in port taxes for each visitor. The cost includes three meals, a shipboard cabaret show and video movies, an onboard swimming pool, and live calypso entertainment. If you want to rent a cabin for the course of the day (for midafternoon naps or whatever), you can arrange for one for an additional charge ranging between $25 and $125, depending on size and location. Other onboard facilities include a casino, bingo games, and skeet shooting.

The ship used by Palm Beach Cruise Line is the *Viking Princess,* built in Helsinki in 1964 and fully refurbished in 1992. For those passengers wishing to use the *Princess* as a relaxed means of starting and ending a short vacation on Grand Bahama, Palm Beach Cruise Line can arrange discounted hotel accommodations in Freeport.

SeaEscape, 140 S. Federal Hwy., Dania, FL (☎ **800/432-0900** in the U.S., 800/327-7400 in Canada, or 954/925-9700), sails from Fort Lauderdale to Freeport. Cruises carry 1,200 passengers and depart from the Port Everglades Terminal in Fort Lauderdale and land at Freeport Harbour. Sailing time is about 5 hours each way, and the cost is $118 per person, including port charges and three buffet meals. Cruises depart on Monday, Wednesday, Friday, and Sunday between 7 and 8am, depending on the day of the week. The ship contains a full casino, three restaurants, a disco, two bars, and a limbo bar beside the swimming pool.

VISITOR INFORMATION

Assistance and information are available at the **Grand Bahama Tourism Board,** International Bazaar in Freeport (☎ **242/352-6909**). Another information booth is at Port Lucaya (☎ **242/373-8988**), and yet another is at the Freeport International Airport (☎ **242/352-2052**). Hours are 9am to 5:30pm Monday through Saturday.

ISLAND LAYOUT

Getting around Freeport/Lucaya is fairly easy because of its flat terrain. Although Freeport and Lucaya are frequently mentioned in the same breath, newcomers should note that whereas Freeport is a landlocked collection of hotels and shops rising from the island's center, Lucaya is a waterfront section of hotels, shops, and restaurants clustered next to a saltwater pond on the island's southern shoreline. Both were conceived as separate developments during their inception, but over the years, expansion has somewhat blurred their borders.

Freeport lies midway between the northern and southern shores of Grand Bahama Island. Bisected by some of the island's largest roads, it contains the biggest hotels, as well as two of the most-visited attractions in the country: The Bahamas Princess Resort and Casino, and the International Bazaar shopping complex. The local straw market, where inexpensive souvenirs of your visit to The Bahamas can be bought, lies just to the right of the entrance to the International Bazaar.

In addition to its hotels, Freeport contains many banks, small local businesses, and government offices, most of which lie along East Mall Drive, a short walk from the bazaar. Most of these businesses and organizations are centered around Churchill Square. West of the International Bazaar, flanking both sides of West Sunrise Highway, are two of the island's four golf courses, the Emerald and the Ruby (see "Beaches, Water Sports & Other Outdoor Activities," below).

To reach **Port Lucaya** from Freeport, head east from the International Bazaar along East Sunrise Highway, then turn south at the intersection with Seahorse Road. Within about 2^1/$_2$ miles, it will lead to the heart of the Lucaya complex, Port Lucaya.

Set between the beach and a saltwater pond, Port Lucaya's architectural centerpiece is Count Basie Square. It's named for the great entertainer, who used to have a home on the island. Within a short walk to the east and west, along the narrow strip of sand between the sea and the saltwater pond, rise most of the hotels of Lucaya Beach, as well as the headquarters of the famed Underwater Explorers Society (see "Beaches, Water Sports & Other Outdoor Activities," below).

Heading west of Freeport and Lucaya, the West Sunrise Highway passes industrial complexes such as The Bahamas Oil Refining Company. At the junction with Queen's Highway, you can take the road northwest all the way to the **West End,** a distance of some 28 miles from the center of Freeport. Along the way you pass Freeport Harbour, where cruise ships dock. Just to the east lies Hawksbill Creek, a village known for its fish market. After passing this, you go through quaint villages with names like Eight Mile Rock and Bootleg Bay Village. West End used to be a haven for bootleggers running liquor to the United States during the Prohibition era.

Much less explored is the **East End** of Grand Bahama. It's located some 45 miles from the center of Freeport and is reached via the Grand Bahama Highway, which, despite its name, is rather rough in parts. Allow about 2 hours of driving time to reach the East End. The **Rand Memorial Nature Centre** lies about 3 miles east of Freeport. About 7 miles on is **Lucaya National Park.** Beyond the park is Gold Rock, a U.S. missile-tracking station. About 5 miles further along the highway lies the hamlet of Free Town. East of Free Town is the village of High Rock, known for its Emmanuel Baptist Church. From here, the road gets considerably rough, finally ending in MacLean's Town, which celebrates Columbus Day every year with a conch-cracking contest. From here, it's possible to take a water-taxi ride across Runners Creek to an exclusive club, Deep Water Cay, which is patronized mainly by fishers, although it's open to the public.

FINDING AN ADDRESS   In Freeport/Lucaya, but especially on the rest of Grand Bahama Island, you will almost never find a street number on a hotel or a store. Sometimes in the more remote places, you won't even find a street name. In lieu of numbers, locate places by prominent landmarks or hotels.

2 Getting Around

BY TAXI   The government sets the taxi rates, and the cabs are metered (or should be). A trip from the airport to one of the hotels in Freeport or Lucaya costs about $10. No buses connect the airport with the hotels. The cost is $2 for the first quarter mile, plus 30¢ for each additional quarter mile. You can call for a taxi, although most of them wait at the major hotels or the cruise-ship dock to pick up passengers. One major taxi company is **Freeport Taxi Company,** Old Airport Road (☎ 242/ 352-6666), open 24 hours. Another is **Grand Bahama Taxi Union** (☎ 242/ 352-7101), also open 24 hours.

BY BUS   There is public bus service from the International Bazaar to downtown Freeport and from the Pub on the Mall to the Lucaya area. The typical fare is $1. A private company, **Franco's People Express,** runs a twice-daily service from the International Bazaar and Lucaya Beach to West End; the trip costs $8 round-trip. Check with the tourist office (see "Visitor Information," above) for bus schedules. There is no number to call for information.

BY LOCAL AIR SERVICE   You can charter a plane for sightseeing tours above Grand Bahama from **Major's Airline,** Freeport International Airport (☎ 242/ 352-5778). Airborne excursions over the lagoons, golf courses, and outlying reefs of the island, suitable for one to three passengers, cost around $100 per hour. The airline has regular flights to Bimini, for $90 round-trip, and to Walker's Cay, $82 round-trip.

A competitor is **Taíno Air Service,** Freeport International Airport (☎ 242/ 352-8885). Flying nine-passenger propeller planes, they offer trips from Freeport to

---

⭐ Frommer's Favorite Grand Bahama Experiences

Frolicking with Dolphins. Swimmers and snorkelers interact with bottle-nosed dolphins as part of a "familiarization program." Your session is videotaped, and for most visitors, the video provides a lifetime souvenir of an unforgettable experience.

Cycling Freeport/Lucaya. Good roads and a pancake-flat terrain make cycling around these two resorts easy on the body. After your explorations, bike to Fortune Beach, one of the best beaches on the island.

Discovering Rand Memorial Nature Centre. Walk along the nature trails of this 100-acre site with a knowledgeable guide who describes the exotic flora and fauna of his homeland. Keep your eyes peeled for the rich bird life, ranging from olive-capped warblers to the West Indian flamingo.

Eleuthera (Governor's Harbour and North Eleuthera) for $80 each way. Flights are on Thursday, Friday, Saturday, and Sunday. On Friday and Saturday, there are flights to South Andros for $85 each way, to Central Andros for $77 each way, and to North Andros for $77 each way. From Freeport to Great Abaco (Marsh Harbour), the cost is $60 each way.

BY CAR   Your need for a car will be less pressing on Grand Bahama than in Nassau because of the self-contained nature of many of the island's major hotels. Still, if you want to explore, and drive yourself, you can try **Avis** (☎ **800/331-2112,** or 242/352-7666 locally), or **Hertz** (☎ **800/654-3001,** or 242/352-9250 locally). Both these companies maintain offices in small bungalows outside the exit of the Freeport International Airport.

Note: Regarding Budget Rent-a-Car, know in advance that for many years a Bahamas-based car-rental company, without authorization, copied Budget's name and logo and plastered them on billboards around Grand Bahama, despite much confusion from prospective renters, many lawsuits, and much consternation from Budget in Chicago. Although their advertising is less visible in recent years than in the past, know that if you decide to rent from the company calling itself Budget in Freeport, your rental will not be subject to the insurance-policy safeguards or the maintenance standards of the reputable and well-respected U.S.–based Budget Rent-a-Car.

Avis and Hertz each charge a daily or weekly rate, with unlimited mileage included. The arithmetic usually works out that the per-day rate is reduced for rentals of a week or more. You usually get the cheapest tariff by reserving a car several days in advance.

Although conditions are subject to change, Hertz offers the least expensive rates—an air-conditioned car with automatic transmission for $323 per week, with unlimited mileage included. On Grand Bahama Island, the Hertz affiliate is known as Red Kap Car Rentals.

The cheapest car at Avis also features air-conditioning and automatic transmission, but rents for $389.70 per week, with unlimited mileage.

Each of the three companies offers an optional collision damage waiver (CDW), priced at between $11.95 and $13.95 a day. Most major credit card companies cover the CDW if you pay for the rental using their card; check with your credit card company for details and to determine if this coverage extends to The Bahamas.

One of the best local companies is **Star Rent-a-Car,** Old Airport Road (☎ **242/352-5953**), which rents everything from a Suzuki Swift to a Jeep Wrangler. Rates range from $35 to $60 per day with unlimited mileage, plus another $10.95 per day for a CDW.

ON FOOT   You can explore the center of Freeport or Lucaya on foot, but if you want to make excursions into the East End or the West End, you'll either need a car or public transportation (highly erratic) because the distances are too far.

BY BICYCLE OR MOTORSCOOTER   Bicycles and motorscooters are good means of transport here. Try **Honda Cycle Shop,** Queen's Highway (☎ 242/352-7035). A two-seater scooter requires a $100 deposit, unless you pay with a credit card, and rents from $50 per full day. Gas is provided, and there's no charge for mileage. The rental agency also supplies helmets, which are required by law, for drivers and passengers. The operator of the vehicle must also have a valid driver's license. Bicycles require a $50 deposit and cost $20 for a full day and $12 for a half day (4 hours). The establishment is open daily from 9am to 5pm.

FAST FACTS: Grand Bahama

American Express   The local representative is Mundytours, Block 4 Regent Centre, Suite 20, Freeport (☎ 242/352-4444). Hours are 9am to 6pm Monday through Friday.

Business Hours   See "Fast Facts" in chapter 3.

Car Rentals   See "Getting Around" earlier in this chapter.

Climate   See "When to Go" in chapter 3.

Currency Exchange   Americans need not bother to exchange their dollars into Bahamian dollars, as the currencies are on par. However, Canadians will need to convert their dollars or Britons their pounds, which can be done at local banks or sometimes at a hotel. Hotels, however, offer the least-favorable rates.

Dentists   A reliable dentist is Dr. Larry Bain, Sun Alliance Building, Pioneer's Way, Freeport (☎ 242/352-8492). Hours are Monday through Wednesday from 8:30am to 4pm and Thursday and Friday from 8:30am to noon.

Doctors   For the fastest and best service, use a member of the staff at the Rand Memorial Hospital (see "Hospitals," below).

Drugs   The strict drug laws of The Bahamas were cited under "Fast Facts" in chapter 3, but the warning bears repeating. Offenders are speedily and severely punished.

Drugstores   For prescriptions and other pharmaceutical needs, go to Mini Mall, 1 West Mall, Explorer's Way, where you'll find L.M.R. Prescription Drugs (☎ 242/352-7327), next door to Burger King. Hours are Monday through Saturday from 8am to 9pm and Sunday 8am to 3pm.

Embassies & Consulates   See "Fast Facts" in chapter 3.

Emergencies   For all emergencies call ☎ 911, or dial ☎ 0 for the operator.

Eyeglass Repair   The biggest specialist in eyeglasses and contact lenses is the Optique Shoppe, 7 Regent Centre, downtown Freeport (☎ 242/352-9073). Hours are Monday through Friday from 9am to 5pm and Saturday from 9am to noon.

Holidays   See "When to Go" in chapter 3.

Hospitals   If you have a medical emergency, contact the Rand Memorial Hospital, East Atlantic Drive (☎ 242/352-6735; ambulance emergency, ☎ 242/352-2689). This is a government-operated, 90-bed hospital.

Information   See "Tourist Information," above.

Laundry & Dry Cleaning   Freeport's hotels almost universally provide both laundry and dry-cleaning services. You can also take your dry cleaning or laundry to Jiffy Cleaners and Laundry, West Mall at Pioneer's Way (☎ **242/352-7079**). This outlet is open Monday through Saturday from 8am to 6pm.

Newspapers & Magazines   The *Freeport News* is an afternoon newspaper published Monday through Saturday except holidays. The two dailies published in Nassau, the *Tribune* and the *Nassau Guardian,* are also available here, as are some New York and Miami papers, especially the *Miami Herald,* usually on the date of publication. American news magazines, such as *Time* and *Newsweek,* are flown in on the day of publication.

Photographic Needs   Virtually every major hotel in Grand Bahama offers kiosks for the sale and processing of film. If your hotel doesn't have such a service, head for the shopping arcade in The Bahamas Princess Resort and Casino. Otherwise, there are several within the International Bazaar.

Police   In an emergency, dial ☎ **911.**

Post Office   The main post office is on Explorers Way in Freeport (☎ **242/352-9371**). Airmail is delivered daily; surface mail, weekly. Open Monday through Friday from 8:30am to 5:30pm.

Radio & TV   See "Fast Facts" in chapter 3.

Rest Rooms   These are generally inadequate. Visitors often have to rely on the facilities available at hotels, restaurants, cafes, and other commercial establishments.

Safety   Naturally, you should safeguard your valuables and take all the precautions on Grand Bahama you would when traveling anywhere. Avoid walking—or jogging—along lonely roads. There are no particular "danger zones," but stay alert since Grand Bahama is a center for drugs and crime.

Taxes   There is no city tax other than the 4% national tax already mentioned, which is imposed on hotel rates. There is also a 4% to 6% "resort levy." All visitors leaving The Bahamas also pay a $15 departure tax.

Taxis   See "Getting Around" earlier in this chapter.

Telephone, Telexes & Faxes   Direct long distance telephone dialing is available. Nearly all major hotels send telexes and faxes, but if yours is too small to offer such services, go to the main post office (see above). To send a telegram, head for or call the Freeport branch of The Bahamas Telecommunications Company, West Mall at Pioneer's Way (☎ **242/352-6220**). It's open 24 hours a day.

Transit Information   To call for airport information, dial ☎ **242/352-6020;** to summon a taxi, call ☎ **242/352-6666;** for bus schedules, call the tourist office at ☎ **242/352-8044.**

Weather   Grand Bahama, in the north of The Bahamas, has temperatures in winter that vary from about 60° to 75°F daily. Summer variations range from 78° to the high 80s. In Freeport/Lucaya, phone ☎ **242/352-6675** for weather information.

3 Where to Stay

Your choice is between hotels in the Freeport area, near the Princess Casino and the International Bazaar, or at Lucaya, closer to the beach.

Remember: In most cases, a 4% room tax, a resort levy of 4% to 6%, and a 15% service charge will be added to your final bill. Be prepared.

Hotels rated expensive usually charge from $130 to $200 for a double room. Those viewed as moderate ask anywhere from $100 to $130 for a double room. Inexpensive establishments charge $100 or under for a double. These are high-season (December through April) tariffs.

FREEPORT

EXPENSIVE

✪ **Bahamas Princess Resort and Casino.** The Mall at W. Sunrise Hwy., P.O. Box F-42623, Freeport, Grand Bahama, The Bahamas. ☎ **800/223-1818** in the U.S., 242/352-6721 for the Princess Country Club, or 242/352-9661 for the Princess Tower. Fax 242/352-4485. 942 rms, 23 suites. A/C TV TEL. Winter, $95–$125 Country Club double; $180–$240 suite; $150–$180 Tower double; from $290 suite. Off-season, $80–$105 Country Club double; $160–$220 suite; $125–$140 Tower double; from $240 suite. MAP $42 extra per person daily. Up to two children under 12 stay free in parents' room. AE, DC, MC, V.

All glitz and glitter, the star of Freeport's resort hotels is a multimillion-dollar resort/golf/convention complex that's set on 2,500 acres of tropical grounds, but not on the beach. There are in fact two "Princesses": the Princess Country Club and the Princess Tower. Together they form the most sophisticated and largest resort on Grand Bahama Island. Located 10 minutes from the airport, near the International Bazaar, the resort also has one of the largest casinos in the country.

The **Princess Country Club** attracts families, honeymooners, golfing buffs, and others. The hotel's design is not unlike an enormous low-rise wagon wheel, with a Disneyland type of minimountain at its core, surrounded by a swimming pool with cascading waterfalls. The hotel is so spread out that guests often complain that they need ground transport to reach their bedrooms, which number 561, plus 4 suites. Nine wings, sheltering buildings that are only two or three stories high, radiate from the pool. Some of the rooms have kitchenettes and are sold as time-share units. Wings 1, 3, and 8 are the least desirable. Accommodations come in several classifications; however, even the standard rooms are well equipped, with two comfortable double beds, dressing areas, and tile baths. Both the Country Club and the Tower also rent out a number of lavishly furnished suites.

The **Princess Tower,** lying across the Mall from its larger sibling, is smaller and more tranquil, containing 19 suites and 381 luxuriously furnished, large units. The Tower adjoins the Princess Casino and the International Bazaar. It rises 10 floors and stands on 7¹/₂ acres of grounds. The Arabic motif, set by the Moorish-style tower, with turrets, arches, and a white dome, is continued through the octagon-shaped lobby. Guest rooms are designed in both "tropical and traditional," as they say here. Each contains two double beds and individual climate control.

Dining/Entertainment: Premier dinner choices at the Princess Country Club include the Rib Room, the most deluxe establishment at the Country Club, and Guanahani's, which offers smoked ribs and other dishes in a setting overlooking the waterfall (see "Where to Dine," below). Guests can order three meals a day at the rather standard Patio, which also has a view overlooking the pool. The tropical John B offers rather ordinary lunch, dinner, and late-night snacks, such as hamburgers and quiche.

At the Princess Tower, two of the best restaurants are Morgan's Bluff and La Trattoria (see "Where to Dine," below). Other dining options include the Lemon Peel and the outdoor La Terraza, which in season has a breakfast buffet. Also noteworthy is the Crown Room, set adjacent to the casino, where a fair continental cuisine is served amid an elegant decor. In the Palm Pavilion, a buffet dinner and show, *Goombaya!* (in which tribal dances depict the heritage of the Bahamian people), is presented at 6:30pm on Wednesday and Saturday.

Services: Baby-sitting, massage, room service (7am to 10pm), concierge, and guest relations desk.

Facilities: Two 18-hole championship golf courses nearby; 12 tennis courts (8 lit at night); two swimming pools (one Olympic size); Jacuzzi; nearby private beach with white sand and shuttle-bus service to hotel; full program of water sports, including deep-sea fishing.

Xanadu Beach Resort & Marina. Sunken Treasure Dr., P.O. Box F-42438, Freeport, Grand Bahama, The Bahamas. ☎ **242/352-6782.** Fax 242/352-5799. 139 rms, 47 one-bedroom suites. A/C TV TEL. Winter, $89–$145 double; $195 suite. Off-season, $89–$99 double; $145 suite. AE, MC, V. Free parking.

Originally built as condominiums and once a refuge for the reclusive millionaire Howard Hughes, this symmetrical 12-story tower has never recaptured its heady high of the 1980s. Although now a bit in decline, it is nevertheless a viable choice for those who want to escape that behemoth, the Bahama Princess Resort and Casino. It sits amid a complicated series of marinas and peninsulas, a few steps from a wide sandy beach. The hotel, just 10 minutes from the international airport, was inspired by a line from Coleridge: "In Xanadu did Kubla Khan a stately pleasure dome decree." In 1969, when it opened, it was an exclusive private club whose members included "rat packers" Sammy Davis Jr. and Frank Sinatra. Those famous names are long gone and aren't coming back. Today Mr. and Mrs. mid-America are checking in.

Carefully balanced with evenly spaced rows of carved balconies, the hotel boasts the kind of pyramid-shaped roof you'd expect on a Tibetan monastery. Rooms are attractively and comfortably furnished, among the finest in Freeport.

Dining/Entertainment: The premier restaurant and one of the best on Grand Bahama is Escoffier, serving dinner only (continental cuisine). The hotel also offers the rather standard Casuarina Café and Bar and the Ocean Front Bar and Grill.

Services: Baby-sitting, room service.

Facilities: Tennis courts, swimming pool, and easily booked water sports on premises; golf course nearby.

MODERATE

Castaways Resort. International Bazaar, P.O. Box F-42629, Freeport, Grand Bahama, The Bahamas. ☎ **242/352-6682.** Fax 242/352-5087. 130 rms. A/C TV TEL. Winter, $72–$92 double. Off-season, $60–$82 double. AE, MC, V.

Castaways is a modest and unassuming hotel despite its platinum location adjacent to the International Bazaar and the Princess Casino. You stay here because of its location and the low price; it's hardly a challenger to its Princess neighbor. It's not on the beach, but a free shuttle will take you to Xanadu Beach, the best sandy strip nearby. The four-story hotel has pagoda roofing and an indoor and outdoor Caribbean garden lobby and is surrounded by gardens. Accommodations are only average and are decorated in a style that evokes a typical roadside motel. The best rooms are on the ground floor near the swimming pool. These are the rooms that give this hotel a moderately priced rating; other accommodations fall into the inexpensive category. In the lobby you'll find a gift shop, a clothing shop, a game room, and tour desks. The Flamingo Restaurant features lackluster Bahamian and American dishes. There is a swimming-pool area with a wide terrace and a pool bar that offers sandwiches and cool drinks. The Yellow Bird Night Club stays open until 3am and features limbo dancers, fire-eaters, and all that jazz Monday through Saturday. The manager's cocktail party, a complimentary feature, is held on Monday. Services include a laundry room, baby-sitting, and continuous free transportation to Xanadu Beach, 5 minutes away.

Freeport/Lucaya Accommodations

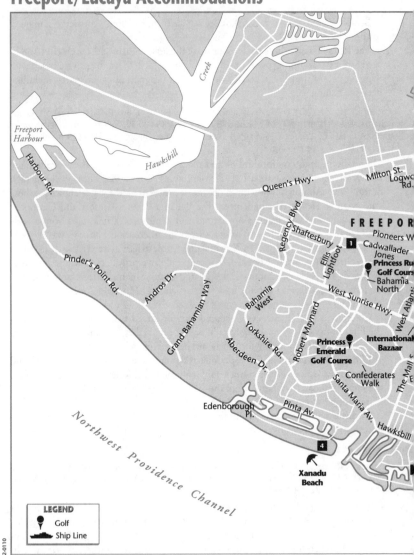

Bahamas Princess
  Resort and Casino **3**
Castaways Resort **2**
Clarion Atlantik Beach Lucaya Golf
  and Country Club **10**
Club Fortuna Beach **13**
Coral Beach **7**
Grand Bahama Beach Resort **9**

Lakeview Manor Club **1**
Lucayan Beach Resort & Casino **12**
Pelican Bay at Lucaya **11**
Port Lucaya Resort & Yacht Club **8**
Running Mon Marina & Resort **5**
Silver Sands Sea Lodge **6**
Xanadu Beach Resort and Marina **4**

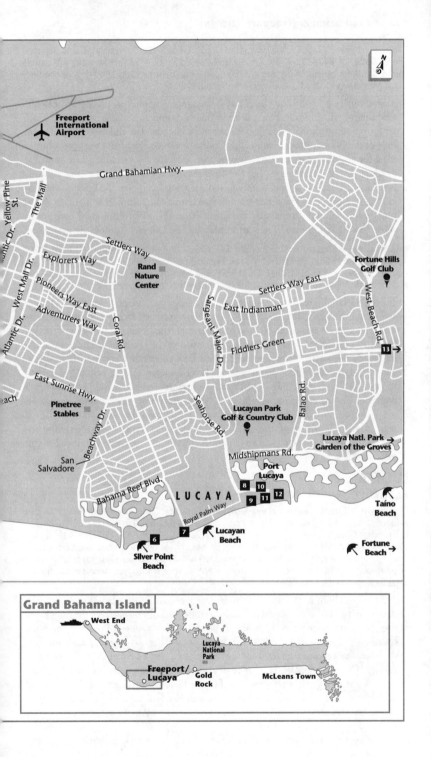

Freeport
International
Airport

Grand Bahamian Hwy.

Settlers Way

Explorers Way

Rand
Nature
Center

Pioneers Way East

Adventurers Way

Coral Rd.

Settlers Way East

East Indianman

Fiddlers Green

Sargeant Major Dr.

Fortune Hills
Golf Club

West Beach Rd.

13 →

East Sunrise Hwy.

Atlantic Dr. Yellow Pine St.

The Mall

West Mall Dr.

Atlantic Dr.

Beach

Pinetree
Stables

Seahorse Rd.

Beachway Dr.

San
Salvadore

Lucayan Park
Golf & Country Club

Balao Rd.

Lucaya Natl. Park
Garden of the Groves →

Midshipmans Rd.

Port
Lucaya

Bahama Reef Blvd.

L U C A Y A

Royal Palm Way

8   10
9 11 12

Taíno
Beach

6

7

Silver Point
Beach

Lucayan
Beach

Fortune
Beach →

Grand Bahama Island

West End

Lucaya
National
Park

Freeport/
Lucaya

Gold
Rock

McLeans Town

155

Lakeview Manor Club. Cadwallader Jones Dr., P.O. Box F-42699, Freeport, Grand Bahama, The Bahamas. ☎ **242/352-9789.** Fax 242/352-2283. 52 apts. A/C TV. Year-round, $75 double studio, $450 double studio per week; $100 double one-bedroom apt, $600 double one bedroom apt per week. AE, MC, V. Closed one week in Nov.

Today this resort is a time-share, but it was originally built as private apartments. Catering to self-sufficient types, it offers one-bedroom and studio apartments, each with tropical furniture, a private balcony, and a kitchen. The club overlooks the fifth hole of the PGA-approved Ruby Golf Course. It stands away from the beach, but is ideal for golfers or for anyone to whom a sea view isn't important. There is no bar or restaurant on the premises, but the hotel maintains a daily complimentary shuttle bus that travels to the dining, drinking, and shopping facilities of the International Bazaar and beach areas. The resort features two tennis courts (not lit at night), a swimming pool, reduced greens fees, and other extras. This place is a good bargain for those seeking tranquillity. The staff seems a bit lax. Laundry facilities are available.

Running Mon Marina & Resort. Box F-42663, 208 Kelly Ct., Freeport, The Bahamas. ☎ **800/315-6054** or 242/352-6834. Fax 242/352-6835. 31 rms. A/C TV TEL. Winter, $75 double; off-season, $62 double. AE, DC, MC, V. The hotel maintains free shuttle-bus service to and from the International Bazaar and the beach near the Xanadu Hotel.

This 1991 hotel—really, a pastel-pink motel—is a great value. It caters to yachties and those who like to live at marinas as opposed to on the beach. It also attracts those who prefer peace and quiet. Ringed by waterways, the L-shaped, two-story property has as its centerpiece a 66-slip marina developed in the late 1960s. The hotel and a nautically decorated restaurant were added later to enhance the marine facilities, which had, by that time, become extremely well known. All the well-planned bedrooms face the marina, and each is simply but comfortably outfitted with flowered draperies, an unstocked refrigerator, and wicker furniture. The complex lies within a 5-minute drive east of the Xanadu Beach Hotel on a flat and sandy landscape pierced with a labyrinth of man-made saltwater lagoons. There's a diving facility on-site and a full-service octagonal restaurant (the Mainsail) that serves sandwiches and platters at lunch.

LUCAYA
EXPENSIVE

✪ **Clarion Atlantik Beach Lucaya Golf and Country Club.** Royal Palm Way, P.O. Box F-42500, Lucaya, Grand Bahama, The Bahamas. ☎ **800/622-6770** in the U.S., 800/848-3315 in Canada, or 242/373-1444. Fax 242/373-7481. 123 rms, 52 apts. A/C TV TEL. Winter, $140–$180 double; $200 junior suite; $220 one-bedroom apt for two; $320 two-bedroom apt for four; $400 three-bedroom apt for six. Off-season, $120–$155 double; $170 junior suite; $190 one-bedroom apt for two; $270 two-bedroom apt for four; $330 three-bedroom apt for six. Rates include American breakfast. AE, DC, MC, V.

After a $5-million renovation, this Swiss International Hotel is better than ever, the island's most luxurious property. Located 6 miles east of Freeport, it's the only highrise (16 floors) in the area. Combining European flair with tropical style, the hotel opens onto a palm-shaded beach—its best asset. In a family-oriented environment, the hotel rents rooms that are well furnished with a view of either the ocean or yacht harbor. The best standard hotel rooms, as opposed to suites, are on the fifth floor. Many European guests prefer this hotel to the Princess, as they are more interested in the beach strip than the casino and International Bazaar. It's a major competitor of the Xanadu, which appeals to a similar market. The suites are actually apartments, each equipped with a kitchenette.

Dining/Entertainment: Special features include a shopping arcade, a lounge, and an espresso bar. There are several places to dine, including the Butterfly Brasserie

> ### 🏨 Family-Friendly Hotels
>
> **Bahamas Princess Resort and Casino** *(see p. 152)*   This massive hotel doesn't just attract Atlantic City types headed for the casino. It also does a large, family-oriented business year-round. Two children's playgrounds with supervised activities are available.
>
> **Castaways Resort** *(see p. 153)*   Located right at the International Bazaar, this family favorite lets children under 12 stay free in rooms with their parents. There's a large swimming pool plus a free shuttle to Xanadu Beach.

coffee shop and Alfredo's Restaurant, for Italian cuisine. The Arawak Dining Room overlooks the "balancing boulders of Lucaya," a 110-foot-wide, 20-foot-high waterfall surrounded by tropical colors.

   Services: Shuttle bus to nearby golf course, laundry, baby-sitting, room service, beauty salon, massages.

   Facilities: 18-hole golf course, health and fitness spa, the only windsurfing school on the island, complete water-sports facility, boating, deep-sea fishing, tennis, large pool.

Grand Bahama Beach Resort. Royal Palm Way (Lucaya Beach), P.O. Box F-42496, Lucaya, Grand Bahama, The Bahamas. ☎ **800/813/8426** or 242/373-1333. Fax 242/373-8662. 500 rms. A/C TV TEL. Winter, $130–$160 double; off-season, $110–$140 double. AE, DISC, MC, V.

Even as we speak, this is a beach resort in the making. Although the hotel remained open in 1996, it underwent a $20 million facelift with renovations continuing deep into 1997. Sun and Sea Estates, a Swiss-based company that has been involved in resort properties in the islands for 30 years, purchased both this property and the Lucayan Beach Resort from the Hotel Corporation of The Bahamas. The cost was $20 million, the largest investment ever in the history of Grand Bahama.

   The company owns Clarion Atlantik Beach, as well, which makes it the largest employer on the island. Sun and Sea also purchased a 7-acre tract of land between the Grand Bahama Beach and the Clarion on which it plans to build a 250-room, five-star resort.

   All 500 rooms have been upgraded considerably, as have the pool and beach areas. Jogging and in-line skating tracks have been installed. The hotel lies across from the Port Lucaya Marketplace, another reason to book here. Most of the bedrooms have private balconies with a view of the ocean.

   Dining/Entertainment: Currently, the hotel serves breakfast only, although guests can dine at Alfredo's Italian Restaurant next door at the Clarion Atlantik Beach or in the Arawak Dining Room at the Lucaya Golf & Country Club. At the Tiki Beach Bar on-site, guests can enjoy drinks and snacks. By the time of your visit, full dining facilities might be an option.

   Services: Room service, laundry, baby-sitting.

   Facilities: Beach, tennis courts, freshwater swimming pool, kiddie pool, children's playground, beauty salon, sailing, and deep-sea fishing (charters can be arranged).

Lucayan Beach Resort & Casino. Royal Palm Way, P.O. Box F-40336, Lucaya, Grand Bahama, The Bahamas. ☎ **800/772-1227** in the U.S., or 242/373-7777. Fax 242/373-6916, or 305/471-5658 in Miami. 243 rms. A/C TV TEL. Winter, $155–$200 double. Off-season, $130–$180 double. Special package rates available. MAP $35 extra per person daily. AE, MC, V.

Set on a 16-acre spit of land midway between the open sea and a protected inlet, this low-rise hotel is often heavily booked in winter by clients drawn to its location opening onto 2 miles of white sandy beaches. It also attracts those who like their casinos on the beach, as opposed to the Princess, which isn't on the water. In 1996 the hotel underwent a $24 million massive renovation that included the casino and all the guest rooms. The casino added more slots and games, and the rooms were redecorated in neutral and pastel color schemes. The property is owned by Sun and Sea Estates, a Swiss-based company that also runs the Clarion and the Grand Bahama Beach Resort.

The hotel contains one of the island's two casinos and lies within walking distance of the Port Lucaya Marketplace. The accommodations are in two wings that stretch toward a garden filled with tropical trees and shrubs. Each room has a veranda and all the comforts you'd expect from a major international hotel. The best accommodations are in the Lanai Wing fronting the ocean; they have extra large balconies or patios with beach access.

Dining/Entertainment: The hotel has a casino, a collection of popular but rather standard restaurants, and a cabaret act. The best restaurant, Monte Carlo, and the cabaret are reviewed separately (see "Where to Dine" and "Grand Bahama After Dark," below).

Services: Room service (weekends only), laundry, baby-sitting, daily activities program for children.

Facilities: Sweeping expanse of pristine beachfront, pool, host of water-related activities (sailing, snorkeling, and waterskiing), four tennis courts, nearby golf course.

MODERATE

Pelican Bay at Lucaya. P.O. Box F-42654, Royal Palm Way, Lucaya, Grand Bahama Island, The Bahamas. ☎ 242/373-9550. Fax 242/373-9551. 48 rms. A/C TV TEL. Winter, $120 double; $145 triple. Off-season, $110 double; $135 triple. AE, MC, V.

Pelican Bay opened in the fall of 1996, a creation of Bahamian-based New Hope Holding Company, Ltd. The company has bought several tracts of land in the Lucaya area, some of which are to be used for a luxury residential development. The hotel itself is being presented as accommodations for travelers with sophisticated tastes who don't have a budget to match. The rooms have Italian tile floors and white-washed furniture, with neutral drapes and linens. Each unit comes with a wet bar, satellite TV, and a safe, as well as a balcony with a view of the nearby waterway and marina.

The hotel has one main restaurant, the Ferry House, which specializes in Danish food and serves breakfast, lunch, and dinner daily. The Pool Bar offers a light breakfast every morning and drinks and snacks all day. They are right by the Port Lucaya Marketplace, where restaurants and entertainment spots abound, and within easy reach of the Lucayan Beach Casino.

The beach is across the street, and UNEXSO, the best dive facilities in The Bahamas, is next door. If you want to stick a little closer to home base, Pelican Bay has a swimming pool and a hot tub at the center of the grounds.

✪ **Port Lucaya Resort & Yacht Club.** P.O. Box F-42452, Bell Channel Bay Rd., Lucaya, Grand Bahama, The Bahamas. ☎ 800/323-5655 or 242/373-6618. Fax 242/373-6652. 160 rms, 3 suites. A/C TV TEL. Winter, $100–$135 double; $175 one-bedroom suite; $250 two-bedroom suite. Off-season, $80–$110 double; $150 one-bedroom suite; $200 two-bedroom suite. AE, MC, V.

With its own 50-slip marina, lying next to the Port Lucaya Marketplace, this is an even better choice than the Running Mon Marina & Resort, its major competitor. Opening in 1993, the resort consists of a series of pastel-colored structures that guests reach via golf cart after checking in. A cluster of 10 two-story buildings encase a pool area with a Jacuzzi.

Cruise-ship passengers often wind down here after 3 or 4 days at sea. The medium-size rooms have tile floors and are attractively and comfortably furnished with rattan pieces and big wall mirrors. The rooms are divided into various categories, ranging from standard to deluxe, and open either onto the marina (preferred by yachtie guests), the Olympic-size swimming pool, or the well-landscaped garden. The hotel's restaurant offers standard Bahamian and international dishes. Local music is offered at daily breakfast and dinner buffets.

If you don't want to hear the sounds coming from the lively marketplace, request units 1 through 6, which are more tranquil and away from the noise. Nonsmokers can reserve a room in units 5 or 6. The accommodation also has two bars plus a laundry service.

INEXPENSIVE

Coral Beach. Royal Palm Way, P.O. Box F-42468, Lucaya, Grand Bahama, The Bahamas. ☎ **242/373-2468.** Fax 242/373-5140. 10 units. A/C MINIBAR TV. Winter, $98.80 double; $113.10 triple. Off-season, $61.10 double; $69.90 triple. AE, MC, V.

Built in 1965 as an upscale collection of privately owned condominiums, this peacefully isolated property sits amid gardens and groves of casuarinas in a residential neighborhood. If you're seeking this type of accommodation, the Silver Sands Sea Lodge (see below) is better, with comparable prices. However, if that establishment is fully booked, consider this as an alternative. Some of the apartments and rooms contain verandahs, and all have kitchens. More suitable for older travelers, the complex rents large but rather severely furnished units. A recently opened restaurant, the Garden Café, provides international food at reasonable prices and is open daily for breakfast and dinner. You're also within walking distance of more glamorous facilities, including the Port Lucaya Marketplace and the Lucayan Beach Resort & Casino. On the premises is a sandy beach, as well as a swimming pool.

☺ **Silver Sands Sea Lodge.** Royal Palm Way, P.O. Box F-402385, Lucaya, Grand Bahama, The Bahamas. ☎ **242/373-5700.** Fax 242/373-1039. 85 apts, 11 suites. A/C TV TEL. Winter, $95 double; $105 one-bedroom suite. Off-season, $75 double; $95 one-bedroom suite. MC, V.

This modest lodge, 7 miles east of the Freeport International Airport, consists of three buildings clustered around two swimming pools. It appeals roughly to the same type of economy-minded families who would stay at the Castaways Resort (see above), which is similar in price and appeal. The choice between the two comes down to location—Castaways is for those who want to be near Freeport and the International Bazaar, whereas Silver Sands is for those seeking more of a beach holiday. A condominium complex, about three-quarters of the lodge's accommodations are available for rent. Set 100 yards from a white-sand beach are modern studio apartments, plus one-bedroom first-class suites, all with a view of the pool area, the marina, or the garden. All the spacious units have balconies and fully equipped kitchens. There is babysitting and laundry service. Although swimming and snorkeling are possible from the nearby beach, most serious water-sports enthusiasts head for the facilities at Lucaya Beach, which is three-quarters of a mile to the east. The lodge, however, has two lighted hard-surface tennis courts, two paddleball courts, two shuffleboard courts, and a poolside snack bar. The main restaurant, La Phoenix (see "Where to Dine," below), is one of the best in the Freeport/Lucaya area.

SOUTHEASTERN GRAND BAHAMA

Club Fortuna Beach. 1 Dubloon Rd., P.O. Box F-42398, Freeport, Grand Bahama, The Bahamas. ☎ **242/373-4000.** Fax 242/373-5555. 204 rms. A/C. Winter, $165–$185 double; $143–$163 triple; $132–$152 quad. Off-season, $135–$155 double; $117–$137 triple; $108–$128 quad. Children 5 and under free. Children 6–12 50% off per day in parents' room (maximum of two). Rates include meals, and land and water sports. AE, MC, V.

Of the many resorts on Grand Bahama Island, this is the most finely tuned to the Italian aesthetic. It is, in fact, sort of an Italian clone of a Club Med, attracting a relatively young clientele. Some of the women like to go topless, which is not common in The Bahamas. The property does not easily compare with any other on the island: It's unique. It attracts more and more Americans every year who like the concept of an all-inclusive vacation. That concept, incidentally, although prevalent on Paradise Island, has not invaded Grand Bahama Island yet except for Club Fortuna. Established in 1993, it lies 6 miles east of the International Bazaar in the southeastern part of the island, amid an isolated landscape of casuarinas and scrubland. Vaguely modeled on lines similar to those of Club Med, it caters to a mostly European clientele (usually Italian) who appreciate the 35 secluded acres of beachfront and the barrage of organized sports activities that are included in the price.

Bedrooms lie within a series of two-story, sherbet-colored outbuildings. About three-quarters of the bedrooms have ocean views, the others overlook the garden. Each has a private balcony, a private safe, and two queen-size beds. Singles can book one of these rooms, but they are charged 40% more than the per-person double-occupancy rate.

Dining/Entertainment: All meals are served buffet style in a pavilion near the beach. Actually, some of the best Italian dishes on Grand Bahama Island are served here, although not the equal of a first-class trattoria in Rome. Nightly entertainment is provided by Bahamian and Italian performers. There is a disco and a few bars.

Services: Italian language lessons, baby-sitting, laundry, massage.

Facilities: Sailing, windsurfing, weight training, volleyball, tennis, daily aerobics classes, outings to a nearby golf course, exercise room, children's playground, beauty salon.

4 Where to Dine

In restaurants classified as expensive, expect to spend from $35 per person for dinner, excluding drinks, tip, and the 15% service charge. Moderate means $25 to $30 dinners, and a place charging under $20 for dinner is inexpensive.

FREEPORT
EXPENSIVE

Crown Room. In the Princess Casino, the Mall at W. Sunrise Hwy. ☎ **242/352-6721.** Reservations required. Jackets for men required. Main courses $19.95–$54. AE, DC, MC, V. Tues–Sat 6:30–11pm. INTERNATIONAL.

The Crown Room is for those who prefer casino dining. It looks like a chic dining room on an art deco ocean liner, with pink-marble accents, brass-trimmed walls, and rose-colored mirrors. As you peruse the menu, light jazz is played in the background. Whatever you whisper to your dining partner is likely to be overheard, as tables are a little bit too crowded. Prices are high for Freeport, but this Crown Room tries to be regal. The service and the costly ingredients seem to justify the high tabs.

It's quite easy to fill up on the selection of hot and cold appetizers, ranging from shrimp deJonge to liver pâté. The best of the main dishes, in our view, is the perfectly roasted rack of lamb, with the medallions of veal coming in a close second. If the supply is available, the chef will also serve you quite a presentable lobster dinner. Pasta dishes are also quite succulent. Sometimes the chef will have a surprise on the menu, but for the most part it's elegant country club fare from a standard international repertoire.

✪ **Guanahani's Restaurant.** In the Princess Country Club, the Mall at W. Sunrise Hwy. ☎ **242/352-6721.** Reservations recommended. Main courses $17.95–$27.95; 3-course early-bird dinner $14.95. AE, DC, MC, V. Sun–Thurs 5:30–10:30pm. BARBECUE/SEAFOOD.

Guanahani is the Lucayan Indian word for the island of San Salvador in The Bahamas, which is a meaningless name for a place serving some of the best barbecue on the island. The chef prepares island roasts and barbecues by marinating top-quality meats and then roasting them for hours in specially constructed ovens. You're not confined to barbecue, as many other dishes are offered, including chicken, fish, or shrimp, which can be grilled or blackened. The hickory-smoked ribs are the best item on the menu, although Bahamian lobster makes a savory alternative. Other dishes include a tender beef brisket, and the chef will always grill you a sirloin steak if you want. If conch chowder is on the menu for a starter, we suggest you order it. The chefs probably ran out of enthusiasm here a long time ago, but they've prepared the same dishes for so long they've perfected them. The restaurant lies within the poolside arcade of this previously recommended hotel. To enter, you cross over a small drawbridge. The decor is country-style tropical, with massive brass chandeliers and lots of exposed wood. Guanahani closes on Friday and Saturday nights when most other Grand Bahama restaurants do their peak business.

✪ **The Rib Room.** In the Princess Country Club, the Mall at W. Sunrise Hwy. ☎ **242/352-6721.** Reservations required. Jackets required for men. Main courses $18.75–$28; early-bird fixed-price meal $23.50 (6–7pm only). AE, DC, MC, V. Thurs–Mon 6–11pm. SEAFOOD/STEAK.

Go here for the island's best steaks. Although not as good as the fabled Palm Restaurant, this place isn't bad for Grand Bahama Island. Portions are hugely generous. Everything is served in the atmosphere of a British hunting lodge. If you don't want one of the steaks, although the steak au poivre (pepper steak) is quite good, opt instead for the blue-ribbon prime rib of beef with a passable Yorkshire pudding. Special praise goes to the broiled Bahamian lobster, but not even a weak clap to the native grouper. Shrimp can be succulent when it's not overcooked, and steak Diane, although rather fully flavored, is meltingly textured. The wine list is reasonably priced.

Ruby Swiss Restaurant. W. Sunrise Hwy. at W. Atlantic Ave. ☎ **242/352-8507.** Reservations required for dinner. Main courses $4.25–$14.75 at lunch; $13.50–$28.50 at dinner; late-night main courses $4.75–$27.75. AE, DC, MC, V. Mon–Fri 11am–4pm and 6–10:30pm; Sat–Sun 6pm–5am. INTERNATIONAL.

Airy and imaginative, this restaurant, which opened in 1986, contains two bars (one, rescued from a Victorian building, is an antique), an inviting dining room, and a less formal eating area. The restaurant, which has a Swiss owner, is popular with the increasing number of Europeans winging in to Grand Bahama Island. Although Bahamian dishes are served, most diners visit for a taste of the continent. The establishment is known for its large servings, fine service, and music at dinner. The spacious restaurant is adjacent to the Bahamas Princess Tower. It doesn't, however, have the cozy ambience of the Escoffier Grill Room (see below), which would be better for a romantic evening.

Lunch might feature such standard fare as Reuben or club sandwiches, seafood or Caesar salads, or burgers. A pâté maison, however, has the most flavor. For dinner, you can opt for the catch of the day, which is often grouper (rarely overcooked), or the zesty Créole-style shrimp. Although an odd choice for The Bahamas, the filet Stroganoff is also quite good. Finish off with a Viennese strudel, the dessert specialty. The late-night snacks, served until 5am, include omelets, sandwiches, and burgers.

Freeport/Lucaya Dining

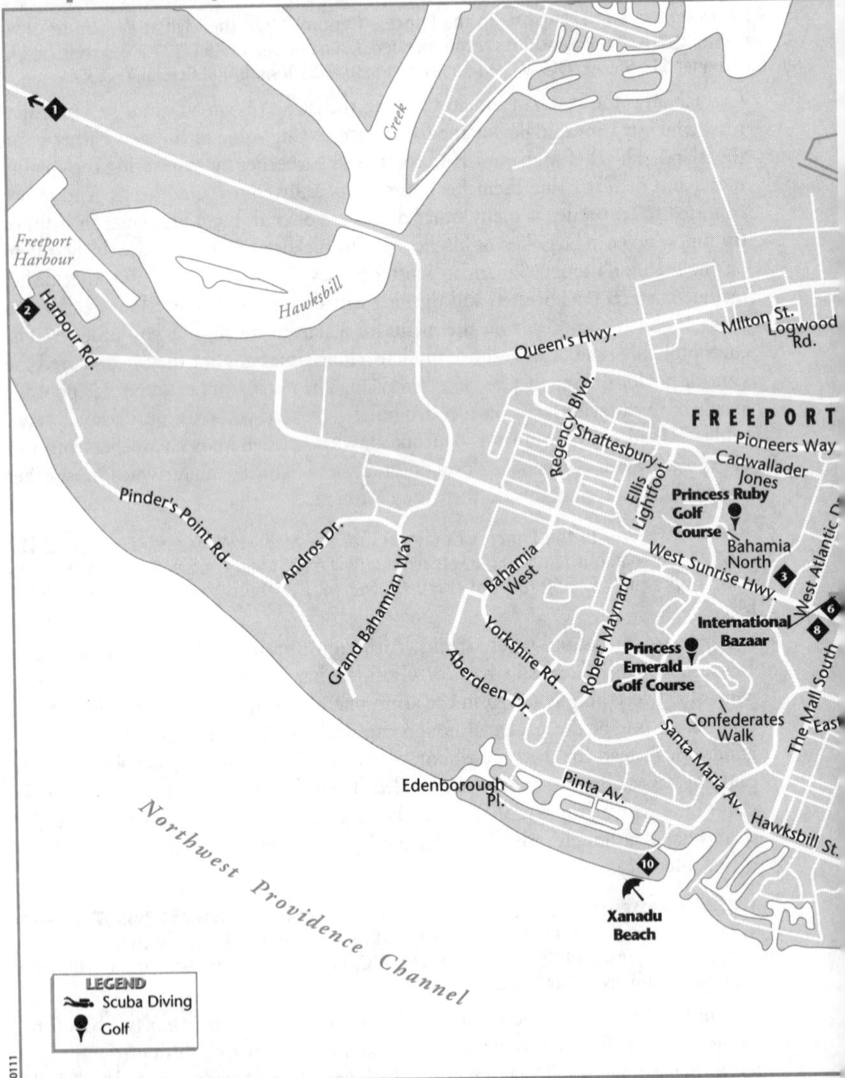

LEGEND
- Scuba Diving
- Golf

Bavarian Beer Garden 8
Becky's Restaurant 8
Britannia Pub 12
Buccaneer Club 1
Café Michel 8
Captain's Charthouse
   Restaurant 9
China Temple 8

Crown Room 8
Escoffier Grill
   Room/Café Casuarina 10
Fatman's Nephew 14
Geneva's 4
Guanahani's Restaurant 8
Japanese Steak House 8
Kaptain Kenny's 8

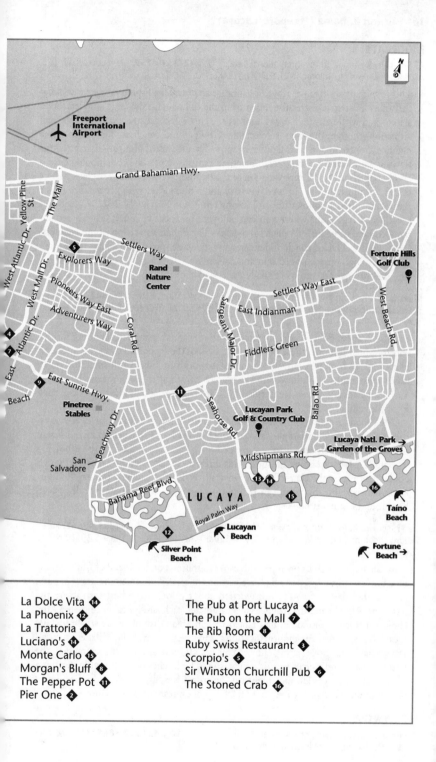

La Dolce Vita ⑭
La Phoenix ⑫
La Trattoria ⑧
Luciano's ⑭
Monte Carlo ⑮
Morgan's Bluff ⑧
The Pepper Pot ⑪
Pier One ❷

The Pub at Port Lucaya ⑭
The Pub on the Mall ❼
The Rib Room ❽
Ruby Swiss Restaurant ❸
Scorpio's ❺
Sir Winston Churchill Pub ❻
The Stoned Crab ⑯

MODERATE

✪ **Kaptain Kenny's.** In the International Bazaar, ☎ **242/351-4759.** Main courses $7–$25. AE, MC, V. Daily 4pm–midnight. SEAFOOD/STEAKS.

This restaurant is a treasure trove of nautical paraphernalia; fishing nets are cast along the walls, lobster traps are suspended from the ceiling, and the large wooden tables are covered with treasure maps. Don't let the corny decor distract you from the real attraction, though; the food is delectable. Grouper and conch are highlights of the menu, each prepared in several different ways. Try the stuffed grouper—filled to overflowing with lobster, shrimp, crab meat, and mushrooms. The conch bolognaise is also a good choice and a nice variation of the traditional pasta with meat sauce. There is also live music Friday through Tuesday and a disc jockey who plays dance music until 2am. There's another Kaptain Kenny's at Taíno Beach (☎ **242/373-8689**), a great beach restaurant where you can enjoy an inexpensive lunch. Highly recommended here is the grilled conch sandwich—The Bahama's version of the New Orleans "Po Boy." Diced conch, tomatoes, and onions are mixed with a tangy lime juice, then piled high on a seasoned bun and cooked on an open grill. For a smaller appetite, the shrimp and crab meat salads are a good choice.

Morgan's Bluff. In the Princess Tower, the Mall at W. Sunrise Hwy. ☎ **242/352-9661.** Reservations recommended. Main courses $17.95–$25.50. AE, DC, MC, V. Wed–Sun 6–9pm. SEAFOOD.

Families searching for a good moderately priced seafood restaurant often opt for this choice, which is located near the reception desk of the Princess Tower. It looks a bit like a high-tech pirate's lair, which means it appeals to kids. All this nautical decor leaves most adults blasé, however. The place is named after the notorious buccaneer Sir Henry Morgan, who once terrified the Caribbean using sails like those suspended from the ceiling.

The captain's platter of mixed seafood is more filling than innovative. However, this is a good place to sample cracked conch (fried like a Wiener schnitzel) if you haven't tried it before. Lobster is treated with care and respect here, appearing Thermidor style or else in a bisque. Kids often go for the seafood crepes, although adults may prefer the clams Benedict instead. When the catch of the day (local or imported) is right, this place can be right on target, although some fish dishes can be pale and uninteresting.

La Trattoria. In the Princess Tower, the Mall at W. Sunrise Hwy. ☎ **242/352-9661.** Reservations recommended. Main courses $9.95–$26.50. AE, DC, MC, V. Daily 5:30–10:45pm. ITALIAN.

This cafe terrace with its open parasols evokes a trattoria on the island of Capri. Come here for your pizza and pasta fix. Five versions of pizza and some nine kinds of pasta are featured daily. If you're not worried about calories, the best tasting are the fettuccine Alfredo and the spaghetti alla carbonara, each a full meal unto itself. Other choices include saltimbocca, that fabled veal and ham dish of Rome which literally means "jump-into-your-mouth." It didn't. However, the veal alla Milanese is an always reliable but not exciting choice. You can also mix and match, rearranging the pastas, meats, and sauces to suit your tastes. The kitchen will also whip you up a Caesar salad. On certain nice nights, if the crowd is right, the place can be a lot of fun, with diners lingering over their final cup of espresso or cappuccino.

INEXPENSIVE

Geneva's. Kipling Lane, the Mall at W. Sunrise Hwy. ☎ **242/352-5085.** Main courses $8–$15.95. No credit cards. Daily 7am–11pm. BAHAMIAN.

If you want to eat where the Grand Bahama locals eat, head for Geneva's, where the food is the way it was before the hordes of tourists invaded. The namesake is Geneva Monroe, who's aided by her sons, Francis and Robert. This restaurant sticks to the mainstay of the local diet—conch—which has fed and nourished Bahamians for centuries. In fact, Geneva's is one of the best places to sample this treat of the sea. The Monroe family will prepare it for you stewed, cracked, or fried, or in a savory conch chowder that makes an excellent starter. Grouper (there's no escaping grouper in The Bahamas) also appears, prepared in every imaginable way. To get you into the mood of things, the rum-laced Bahama Mama is the specialty drink of the bartender.

The Pepper Pot. E. Sunrise Hwy. at Coral Rd. ☎ **242/373-7655.** Reservations not accepted. Breakfast $3.75–$5.25; main courses $7.50–$12.50; vegetarian plates $2.50–$6.50. No credit cards. 24 hours. BAHAMIAN.

This might be the only establishment on Grand Bahama that specializes in Bahamian take-out food. You'll find it after about a 5-minute drive east of the International Bazaar, in a tiny shopping mall. You can order take-out portions of the best carrot cake on the island, as well as a savory conch chowder, the standard fish and pork chops, chicken souse (an acquired taste), cracked conch, sandwiches and hamburgers, and an array of daily specials. The owner is Ethiopian-born Wolansa Fountain.

The Pub on the Mall. Ranfurley Circus, Sunrise Hwy. ☎ **242/352-5110.** Reservations recommended. Lunch main courses $6–$15; daily special one-course platter lunch $5.95; dinner main courses $10–$25. AE, MC, V. Prince of Wales Lounge, daily noon–2am. Islander's Roost, Mon–Sat 5pm–1am. Silvano's Italian Restaurant, Tues–Sun 5:30–11pm. INTERNATIONAL.

Contained on the same floor of the same building and administered by the same management, you'll find three distinctive eating areas, each with a separate theme. This place is more interesting than its competitor, Sir Winston Churchill Pub. All three of the restaurants lie opposite the International Bazaar and attract many locals. The Prince of Wales Lounge evokes medieval Britain and serves a lunchtime menu of shepherd's pie, fish-and-chips, platters of roast beef or fish, and real English ale. The ale wins out as the best item on the menu of pub grub. The Islander's Roast has a faux-medieval setting with coats of arms and a tapestry of Richard the Lionhearted. The food is good—but not *that* good. The thrifty can order only a main platter and find it very filling and satisfying. All those fabled dishes that visitors seek when they go to London appear here on the menu, as well, including certified Angus beef, fish, fowl, and prime rib. Silvano's brings a continental touch with its copious portions of pasta and veal along with some imported beefsteaks. The homemade fettuccine wins over the cannelloni.

Scorpio's. W. Mall Drive at Explorer's Way. ☎ **242/352-6969.** Breakfast from $3.75; lunch platters $6–$19.50; dinner main courses $8.75–$19.75. AE, MC, V. Daily 7am–1am. Bar, Mon–Wed 7am–1am; Thurs–Sun 7am–3am. BAHAMIAN.

Named after the astrological sign of its Bahamas-born owner, this restaurant offers a welcome respite from the burgers and pizza that seem to prevail in downtown Freeport. It lies at a busy traffic junction, within a cement-sided building painted both inside and out in a medley of earth-toned colors. There's a bar inside, where tropical drinks (especially rum punch) are the popular libations, and a respectable dining room where the staff wears black-and-white uniforms. There's a branch of this restaurant at Port Lucaya, but we find the food here better. Here you get the full repertoire of some Bahama Mama who knows how to rattle those pots and pans, turning out delectable lobster salads, perfectly done steaks, and steamed chicken. Naturally, the kitchen knows how to prepare conch in about every way one would want it. Peas 'n' rice, that Bahamian staple, goes with everything.

Sir Winston Churchill Pub. East Mall, next to the Straw Market and the International Bazaar. ☎ **242/352-8866.** Pizzas $8–$22.75; salads and sandwiches $3.25–$5.50; pastas $6–$13.75. AE, MC, V. Daily noon–2am. INTERNATIONAL.

In spite of its name, this has become mainly a pizzeria. In an upstairs location, it is often visited by the casino crowd when they grow bored with the slot machines. Don't expect much here in the way of cuisine, although it remains an enduring watering hole with many repeat visitors. Try one of about a dozen different pizzas, or choose from a selection of pastas, salads, and sandwiches.

THE INTERNATIONAL BAZAAR
MODERATE

Becky's Restaurant. International Bazaar. ☎ **242/352-8717.** Bahamian or American breakfasts $2.50–$5.95; lunch main courses $2.75–$13.95; dinner main courses $7.95–$22. No credit cards. Daily 7am–10pm. BAHAMIAN/AMERICAN.

This pink-and-white restaurant offers authentic Bahamian cuisine prepared in the time-tested style of the Out Islands. Go here to tank up before a day of serious shopping at the bazaar. Owned by Becky Tucker and Berkeley Smith, the place offers a welcome respite from the relentless glitter of the nearby casino.

Breakfasts are either all-American or Bahamian and are available all day. Also popular are such dishes as minced lobster, curried mutton, fish platters, baked or curried chicken, and conch salads. Stick to the Bahama Mama specialties. The array of American dishes is lackluster. Soup is included with the purchase of steak or lobster.

Café Michel. International Bazaar. ☎ **242/352-2191.** Reservations recommended for dinner. Lunch main courses $5–$11; dinner main courses $10–$27. AE, MC, V. Mon–Sat 7am–10:30pm. BAHAMIAN/AMERICAN.

At first you think this might be a French bistro set amid the bustle of the International Bazaar. But, alas, it turns out to be a mere coffee shop. However, it's a good place for refueling when you're shopping the bazaar. There are about 20 tables outside, placed under red umbrellas and bistro-style tablecloths. Inside are about a dozen more. Local shoppers know to come here not only for coffee, but for platters, salads, and sandwiches throughout the day. In the evening, the aura grows slightly more formal (but not much). Both American and Bahamian dishes are served, including seafood platters, steaks, and, of course, grouper.

Japanese Steak House. International Bazaar. ☎ **242/352-9521.** Main courses $19.95–$49.95; early-bird special (5–8:30pm) $15.95. AE, MC, V. Daily 5–10:30pm. JAPANESE.

You've seen it all before and perhaps in better formats, but this touch of Asia in the tropics does provide a welcome relief from all that Bahamian grouper. The restaurant does not compare favorably to top Japanese restaurants in New York, but it serves its customers admirably nevertheless. Kimono-clad waitresses are the height of graciousness as they serve sukiyaki steak. The incredibly tender kobe steak, however, is the main attraction. The chefs put on a spectacular show for you as they serve you their hibachi-grilled New York strip steak and a lobster tail. All of the meals include soup, salad, and five different vegetables, as well as rice. The Japanese pepper steak is full of flavor, as is the spicy teriyaki pork loin. Long tables for groups are at the front. You can also request a table in the rear if you'd like to dine Japanese style. The early bird here gets the bargain.

INEXPENSIVE

Bavarian Beer Garden. International Bazaar. ☎ **242/352-5050.** Pizza, hamburgers, and sausages $2.50–$10, beer from $3. No credit cards. Daily 10:30am–9pm. GERMAN/BAHAMIAN.

Its tables are reassuringly battered, and its owners may or may not have ever been to Germany, but the Teutonic aura of a Bavarian beer garden thrives here. Set beneath the Moorish-style arches of the International Bazaar, the place features at least a dozen kinds of imported beer, recorded versions of oom-pah-pah music, such German fare as knockwurst, bockwurst, and sauerkraut, and a selection of pizzas. On a hot day, all this wurst and sauerkraut may not be what you had in mind. If so, you might opt for fried chicken instead. The chef also prepares cracked conch, but you'll get better versions of that in any of the little Bahamian eateries recommended.

China Temple. International Bazaar. ☎ **242/352-5610.** Main courses $8.75–$32; lunch from $6.50. AE, MC, V. Mon–Sat 10:30am–10:30pm. CHINESE.

This is a Chinese eatery—not a lot more—that also does take-out. Its food is about the same as you'd get in a similar place in New York. It has outdoor cafe tables, or you can retreat inside. It's recommendable because over the years it's consistently turned out to be the dining bargain of the bazaar. The menu is strictly chop suey or chow mein; this place doesn't attract the serious gourmet of the Orient. Everything's familiar and standard on the menu, including sweet-and-sour fish. The best thing about this restaurant is its prices.

LUCAYA
EXPENSIVE

Escoffier Grill Room/Café Casuarina. In the Xanadu Beach Resort, Sunken Treasure Dr., Lucaya. ☎ **242/352-6782.** Reservations recommended for dinner. Lunch platters (Café Casuarina) $8.50–$12.50; dinner main courses $13.50–$40, dinner all-you-can-eat buffet $18.20. AE, MC, V. Café Casuarina daily noon–5pm; Escoffier Grill daily 6–10:30pm, dinner buffet (in Escoffier Grill) 6:30–8:30pm. INTERNATIONAL.

The food here is competently prepared and served with a flourish, but many diners are attracted because of the legend of reclusive billionaire Howard Hughes, owner and sometime resident during the 1970s of this hotel. His tastes affected the decor of the more formal of the two restaurants, the Escoffier Grill, whose walls are sheathed in burnished mahogany and brass. If you drop in for lunch, you'll dine within the airy Café Casuarina set behind big windows with a view of the resort's swimming pool. Dinners (served in the Escoffier Grill) feature an all-you-can-eat buffet whose culinary theme (Italian, Bahamian, international) changes every night. Dishes are competently prepared in the international style—guaranteed not to excite, but not to displease either. The minced lobster on a recent visit played a second billing to the grilled or blackened swordfish. Grouper reared its head again, as well, this time with an amandine coating. All those international favorites such as smoked salmon and chateaubriand appear on the menu, or else you can go for a taste of The Bahamas instead: batter-fried cracked conch. There's a rumor that the ghost of Howard Hughes sometimes enters the restaurant and consumes a simple meal after wandering through the upper corridors of the hotel.

✪ **Monte Carlo.** In the Lucayan Beach Resort & Casino, Royal Palm Way. ☎ **242/373-7777.** Reservations recommended. Main courses $12–$26.50. AE, MC, V. Tues–Sun 6pm–midnight. Closed Tues in summer. CONTINENTAL.

Located a few steps from the entrance to the busy Lucayan Casino, this is the most elegant—and most expensive—restaurant in the previously recommended hotel. Its minimalist decor includes a collection of gray-and-white tables and framed silk scarves. A uniformed staff offers the best service in the area. One reason to go here is for the seafood, which is some of the freshest available from the banks of The Bahamas. If you like to dine on big-game fish, in the tradition of Hemingway, order the Bimini wahoo steak, which is quite delicate and is served with a zesty Provençale sauce. Mahi mahi also comes from the shores of Bimini, and chefs here like to fry it Bahamian style. From Andros comes a yellowtail filet, a specialty perfectly suited for charbroiling with garlic butter. Red snapper is also a local favorite. Ask for it to be charbroiled, too, if that's your preference. The meat and poultry dishes, on the other hand, are your standard roast chicken, filet mignon, or rack of lamb. A Caribbean seafood gumbo made from fresh local seafood is a hearty opening.

⭐ **The Stoned Crab.** At Taíno Beach, Lucaya. ☎ **242/373-1442.** Reservations recommended. Main courses $18–$34.50. AE, MC, V. Daily 5–10:30pm. SEAFOOD.

This restaurant, with its 14-story pyramid roof, opens onto Taíno Beach and is the favorite of well-heeled local residents. It's the place likely to be recommended by a hotel reception desk when you ask, "Where do you go to get the best food on the island?" We like the seafood here even more than that served at Monte Carlo (see above). Guests can dine inside or on the beach patio. This place fills up at night, not only with visitors, but also with local residents who know about the large portions and the fine seafood.

To get you going, try the conch chowder. The snow crab claws are sweet and delicate. The restaurant specializes in a number of other crab dishes, including crab Andrew and a crab and avocado cocktail. Dolphin (the fish, not the mammal) is regularly featured, as is the game fish wahoo. Fresh, not frozen, fish are used whenever possible. Accompaniments include a salad, as well as home-baked raisin bread. You can finish your meal with Irish coffee. You might also order a carafe of the house wine; the restaurant has a very nice burgundy bottled under its own label in France. The bartender's special is a "Stoned Crab," a drink based on various liqueurs, fruit juices, and rum. At night, taxis are usually lined up outside to drive you off to the Princess Casino.

MODERATE

Britannia Pub. King's Rd. on Bell Channel. ☎ **242/373-5919.** Main courses $6–$27.50. DC, MC, V. Daily 4pm–4am. BAHAMIAN/GREEK.

This faux-Tudor structure houses one of Grand Bahama's most convivial bars. Patrons gather at the bar to watch sports on TV, while drinking English beer on draft. The pub is also a restaurant, which does a good job of filling you up if you're not too discriminating in your tastes. Although you expect typical English pub grub, you are surprised to encounter moussaka (not a bad version at that) and shish kebabs on the menu. That's when the bartender informs you that one of the owners, Takis Telecano, is Greek. Other and more typically Bahamian meals are served, as well, including cracked conch and grouper meunière—those old standbys. They also prepare lobster tails (warn them not to overcook them) and some barbecued ribs, as well. It's been pleasing its steady customers since 1968, and so far we've gotten no complaints from readers.

Captain's Charthouse Restaurant. E. Sunrise Hwy. and Beach Dr. ☎ **242/373-3900.** Main courses $13.95–$24.95; early-bird dinner $8.95 (5–6:30pm). AE, DC, MC, V. Daily 5–9:30pm (last seating). INTERNATIONAL.

In a casual, treetop-level dining room, guests here can select from a menu of 1950s favorites, such as prime rib of beef, teriyaki steak, chateaubriand for two, lobster Thermidor, and grouper filet, along with some good seafood dishes. You don't come here for new wave cookery; this is the place for the old standards mom and pop enjoyed. The chunky lobster Thermidor, baked in its shell, is actually better than that

🏃 Family-Friendly Restaurants

Morgan's Bluff *(see p. 164)* This family restaurant, named after the 17th-century pirate Sir Henry Morgan, has a nautical decor and red neon "portholes." Located in the Princess Tower, it offers seafood specialties that appeal to most members of the family. Casual dress is the rule.

Pier One *(see p. 183)* In the West End, children and their families "walk the plank" to reach this dining room resting on stilts above the water. A nearby shark pool thrills kiddies and grown-ups alike.

Japanese Steak House *(see p. 166)* In a setting of umbrellas, lanterns, and rice-paper doors, kids get a kick out of sitting Japanese style on the floor. Kimono-clad waitresses serve Hibachi meals. Families on a budget can opt for the early-bird specials.

at Monte Carlo. Even the grouper filet tasted delicate, reminding us that it is one of the finest of all Bahamian fish. (We are not antigrouper, as some of our reviews might indicate. It's just that we don't like to dine on it every night of the week, as sometimes can happen in the Out Islands.) Meals are served with tasty homemade bread and a do-it-yourself salad bar. Portions are large, but if you still have an appetite, the homemade desserts include key lime pie. A happy hour is held in the Mates Lounge from 5 to 7pm, with complimentary hors d'oeuvres. Entertainment is also presented nightly, with a Bahamian revue on Tuesday, Friday, and Sunday at 9pm. Courtesy transportation to and from your hotel is offered.

PORT LUCAYA
EXPENSIVE

La Dolce Vita. Port Lucaya Marina. ☎ **242/373-8652.** Reservations required. Main courses $15–$25. AE, MC, V. Daily 11am–2:30pm and 5–11pm. Closed Sept. ITALIAN.

Next to the Pub at Port Lucaya (see below) is a small, upscale Italian restaurant with modern decor and traditional food. They serve freshly made pastas and Italian-style pizzas on a patio overlooking the marina or in the 44-seat dining room. Start with the homemade mozzarella or the arugula and baby artichoke salad, which are both quite good and much more interesting than the grilled vegetables. The main dishes from the Chef Paul Prudhomme school of cooking include veal scallopini, ravioli stuffed with lobster, linguini with clams, and angel hair pasta with fresh tomatoes and arugula. They also offer a wide range of pizzas, made to order (as are the pastas) with whatever ingredients are in season and available. For dessert, try the tiramisu or the chocolate flan, followed by an espresso.

✪ Luciano's. Market Place, Port Lucaya. ☎ **242/373-9100.** Reservations required. Main courses $14.50–$32. AE, DISC, MC, V. Daily 5:30–9:45pm (last seating). CONTINENTAL.

Luciano's is one of the most upscale Continental restaurants on Grand Bahama. Although it is found upstairs from a Pizza Hut, you'll quickly abandon all thoughts of fast food when you enter this place. You can go early and enjoy an apéritif in the little bar inside or on the wooden deck overlooking the marina. Food is freshly prepared and beautifully served. The atmosphere here is generally more sophisticated than at most Grand Bahama eateries. Smoked salmon is a good opening, and the seafood crepes, filled with lobster, grouper, shrimp, and scallops, are even better. Fish and shellfish—fresh when available—are regularly featured and delicately prepared without their natural good tastes being submerged or completely disguised in sauces. Steak

Diane is one of Luciano's classics. But a specialty that elicits far more praise is the veal Luciano—milk-fed veal sautéed with shrimp and plump pieces of lobster and served in a spicy but not overpowering cream sauce.

MODERATE

The Pub at Port Lucaya. Market Place, Port Lucaya Marina. ☎ **242/373-8450.** Main courses $6.95–$22.50. AE, MC, V. Daily 11am–midnight. INTERNATIONAL.

Your hunger pangs can be satisfied at this twin restaurant whose premises is divided between a nautical and woodsy-looking pub and a slightly more formal, big-windowed restaurant (La Dolce Vita, see separate review above) serving mostly Italian food. Regardless of which dining area you select, everything seems to taste better if it's preceded with a beer or a rum-based Painkiller in the pub. You can dine indoors or out, the latter offering views of the port. Menu items include cracked conch, fish strips, Caesar salads, lamb chops, and such traditional English pies as steak-and-ale or shepherd's.

INEXPENSIVE

✪ **Fatman's Nephew.** Market Place, Port Lucaya. ☎ **242/373-8520.** Main courses $6.50–$26. AE, MC, V. Mon and Wed–Sat noon–11pm, Tues and Sun 5–11pm. BAHAMIAN.

In another location, "Fatman" became a legend on Grand Bahama Island. Although he's no longer with us, the Fatman must have left his recipes and cooking skills to another generation of cooks. Today the place, which used to cater mainly to locals, has gone touristy, but much of the same Bahamian fare is still served. The restaurant overlooks the marina at Port Lucaya. Guests can enjoy drinks or meals inside a well-decorated main dining room; but most diners prefer to eat on a large deck where they can survey the action below. As you climb the steps, check out "today's catch" posted on the blackboard menus. Dishes are likely to include about a dozen kinds of game fish, such as wahoo and Cajun blackened kingfish. If you don't want fish, try the zesty curried chicken. For the complete experience, begin your meal with either a freshly made conch salad or conch chowder.

La Phoenix. In the Silver Sands Sea Lodge, Royal Palm Way. ☎ **242/373-5700.** Reservations recommended. Main courses $15–$22. MC, V. Daily 5:30–10:30pm. BAHAMIAN/INDIAN/AMERICAN.

Amusing, witty, and nautically inspired, this highly recommendable restaurant sits above the reception area of a previously endorsed hotel. An eclectic decor of driftwood paneling, Bahamian paintings, plants, and intimate table groupings provides for fun evenings. You'll definitely escape the crowds at this offbeat and little-known place. The chef is likely to whip you up a savory kettle of seafood stew and does pretty well with the kabobs, too, either lobster or sirloin steak. It's best, however, to postpone that chicken Kiev until the Russian Tea Room reopens. Top off your meal with either Nassau or Irish coffee, both generously spiked.

5 Beaches, Water Sports & Other Outdoor Activities

BEACHES

Grand Bahama has some 60 miles of white-sand beaches rimming the blue-green waters of the Atlantic. The heaviest concentration of beaches is in the Lucaya area, site of the major resort hotels. Most of these resorts have their own beaches and offer fairly active water-sports programs. The mile-long **Xanadu Beach,** at the Xanadu

Beach Resort in the Freeport area, is one of the premier beaches. The resort beaches are the most crowded in winter.

Other island beaches include **Taíno Beach,** site of The Stoned Crab restaurant, lying to the east of Freeport, plus **Smith's Point** and **Fortune Beach,** the latter one of the finest beaches on Grand Bahama. Another good beach, about a 20-minute ride east of Lucaya, is **Gold Rock Beach,** a favorite picnic spot with the locals, especially on weekends.

The **Lucaya National Park,** which is about 12 miles from Lucaya, contains one of the most secluded beaches on Grand Bahama. (See below.)

BOAT CRUISES

Mermaid Kitty. Port Lucaya Dock. ☎ **242/373-5880.**

Any tour agent can arrange for you to go out on this vessel, supposedly the world's largest twin-diesel-engine glass-bottom boat. You'll get a panoramic view of the beautiful underwater life that lives off the coast of Grand Bahama. Cruises depart from Port Lucaya behind the Straw Market on the bay side at 9:30, 11:15am, 1:15, and 3:15pm, except Monday and Friday when only two tours leave at 9:30 and 11am. The tour lasts 1½ hours, costs $15 for adults and $8 for children 6 to 12, and is free for children 5 and under.

Paradise Watersports. Sunken Treasure Dr., Xanadu Beach. ☎ **242/352-2887.**

Their sunset cruise, at $25 per person, which includes dance music, unlimited Bahama Mamas (the drink, that is), wine, cheese, and crackers, is the best sunset cruise on Grand Bahama Island. The 1½-hour glass-bottom-boat ride costs $15 for adults and $8 for children under 12.

Superior Watersports. P.O. Box F-40837, Freeport. ☎ **242/373-7863.**

This tour company offers some of the most fun cruises in the waters around Grand Bahama on its *Bahama Mama,* a two-deck 72-foot catamaran. Best is its Robinson Crusoe Beach Party, daily from 11am to 4:30pm. It costs $49 per person. There's also a sunset booze cruise, daily from 5:30 to 7:30pm, that goes for $25. For an underwater cruise, try the company's semi-submarine, the *Seaworld Explorer.* The sub itself does not descend; instead, you walk down into the hull of the boat and watch the sealife glide by. The sub departs daily at 10, 11:30am, 1:30, and 3pm, and costs $29 for adults and $19 for children 12 and under.

THE DOLPHIN EXPERIENCE

✪ **Underwater Explorers Society (UNEXSO).** Next to Port Lucaya, opposite Lucayan Beach Casino. ☎ **242/373-1250.**

A group of bottle-nosed dolphins are involved in a unique dolphin/human familiarization program at Dolphin Experience, located at UNEXSO. This "close encounter" program allows participants to observe these intelligent and friendly animals close up and to hear an interesting talk by a member of the animal-care staff. This is not a swim-with-the-dolphins type of program, but you can step onto a shallow wading platform and interact with the dolphins. The experience is an educational adventure for all ages. The animals are released daily to swim with scuba divers in the open ocean. The program, which includes a close-up observation of the dolphins, costs $29. Diving with the dolphins in the open ocean goes for $105. Most Dolphin Experience sessions are videotaped with copies made available to participants for $19.95. Because of the popularity of the program, advance reservations are essential. In the United States, call ☎ **800/992-DIVE** or 305/351-9889.

FISHING

In the waters off Grand Bahama you can fish for barracuda, snapper, grouper, yellowtail, wahoo, and kingfish, along with other denizens of the deep.

Reef Tours, Ltd. Port Lucaya Dock. ☎ **242/373-5880.**

Reef Tours offers the least expensive way to go deep-sea fishing around Grand Bahama Island. Adults pay $60 if they fish, $40 if they only go along to watch. Four to six fishers can charter the entire craft for $275 to $425 per half day or $550 to $800 per whole day. Departures for the half-day excursion are at 8:30am and 1pm 7 days a week. Included in the cost are bait, tackle, and ice.

Running Mon Marina. 208 Kelly Ct., Bahama Terrace. ☎ **242/352-6833.**

A half-day's deep-sea fishing costs $60 per person, and a full day goes for $120 per person. Up to six people can charter an entire boat for $360 for trips that last from 8am to noon or else from 1 to 5pm daily.

FITNESS CLUBS

For complete fitness services, try the **Princess Fitness Centre** in the Princess Country Club, Bahamas Princess Resort and Casino, the Mall at West Sunrise Highway (☎ **242/352-6721,** ext. 4606).

It's open to both guests and nonguests and offers a sauna, facials, massages, and use of an exercise room with body-building equipment. It is open Monday through Friday from 10am to 6pm and on Saturday and Sunday from 10am to 4pm.

Another good place to try is the **Olympic Fitness Center,** Clarion Atlantik Beach, Royal Palm Way (☎ **242/373-1444**), open daily from 7am to 6:30pm. Two aerobics classes a day are given. Equipment includes weights and Universal gym machines. The facility is free but available only to hotel guests.

The **YMCA Scandinavian Fitness Centre,** East Atlantic Drive and Settler's Way (☎ **242/352-7074**), is open to the general public Monday through Friday from 5am to 9pm and Saturday from 6am to 1pm. It costs $5 a day to work out here. Two aerobics classes are given Monday through Friday (only one on Saturday). They have the regular weights and machines, although their equipment isn't as state of the art as that of the Bahamas Princess or the Clarion Atlantik.

GOLF

This island boasts more golf links than any other island in The Bahamas. The courses are within 7 miles of one another, and you usually won't have to wait to play. All courses are open to the public year-round, and clubs can be rented from all pro shops on the island.

Fortune Hills Golf & Country Club. Richmond Park, Lucaya (5 miles east of Freeport). ☎ **242/373-4500.**

Designed as an 18-hole course, the back 9 were never completed. You can replay the front 9 for 18 holes and a total of 6,916 yards from the blue tees. Par is 72. Greens fees are $18 for 9 holes, $28 for 18. Electric carts cost $24 and $32 for 9 and 18 holes, respectively. The nearest hotels are the Atlantik Beach and the Lucayan Beach Resort & Casino.

Lucayan Park Golf & Country Club. Lucaya Beach. ☎ **242/373-1066.**

This is the best-kept and most-manicured course on Grand Bahama. The course was recently made over and is quite beautiful. It's known for a hanging boulder sculpture at its entrance. Greens are fast, and there are a couple of par 5s more than 500 yards long. It totals 6,824 yards from the blue tees and 6,488 from the whites. Par is 72. Greens fees are $50 for 9 holes or $70 for the day. This includes a mandatory shared golf cart. We'll let you in on a secret: Even if you're not a golfer, sample the food at the club restaurant—everything from lavish champagne brunches to first-rate seafood dishes.

Princess Emerald Golf Course. The Mall South. ☎ **242/352-6721.**

This is one of two courses owned and operated by The Bahamas Princess Resort and Casino (see below for the Princess Ruby Course). The Emerald Course was the site of The Bahamas National Open some years back. The course has plenty of trees along the fairways, as well as an abundance of water hazards and bunkers. The toughest hole is the ninth, a par 5 with 545 yards from the blue tees to the hole. Greens fees are $51 for 9 holes or $75 for 18 holes. Discounts are granted to hotel guests.

Princess Ruby Golf Course. W. Sunrise Hwy. ☎ **242/352-6721.**

This championship course was designed by Joe Lee in 1968 and was the recent site of the Michelin Long Drive competition. Greens fees are $51 for 9 holes, $75 for 18 holes, including electric carts. It's a total of 6,750 yards if played from the championship blue tees.

HORSEBACK RIDING

Pinetree Stables. N. Beachway Dr., Freeport. ☎ **242/373-3600.**

These are the best riding stables in The Bahamas, superior to rivals on New Providence Island (Nassau). Pinetree offers trail rides to the beach Tuesday through Sunday at 9, 10, 11am, noon, and 2pm. The cost is $35 per person for a ride lasting $1^{1}/_{2}$ hours. Lessons in dressage and jumping are available at $35 for 45 minutes of instruction.

JOGGING

On Grand Bahama Island, the traffic is light once you leave Freeport. The best routes for early morning jogs are the West Sunrise Highway and the East Sunrise Highway, which spread out in either direction from the International Bazaar in Freeport.

If you're staying at a hotel in Lucaya, it's best to get up early in the morning and run around Royal Palm Way heading in the direction of the Taíno, where you can plunge in and cool off after your jog.

PARASAILING

Clarion Atlantik Beach Lucaya Golf and Country Club. Royal Palm Way. ☎ **242/373-1444.**

This is the best center on the island for this increasingly popular sport. The cost is $25 for from 5 to 7 minutes.

SEA KAYAKING

If you'd like to explore the waters off the island's north shore, you can do so by calling **Kayak Nature Tours, Ltd.** (☎ **242/373-2485**), which arranges trips through the mangroves where you can see wildlife as you paddle. The trips go for $75 per person and are offered daily from 8:30am to 5pm. A picnic lunch is included. Both single and double kayaks are used on these jaunts. Children must be at least 10 years of age.

SNORKELING & SCUBA DIVING

Paradise Watersports. Sunken Treasure Dr., Xanadu Beach. ☎ **242/352-2887.**

Located at the Xanadu Beach Resort and Marina, this outfit offers a variety of activities. On the snorkeling trips, you cruise to a coral reef on a 48-foot catamaran. The cost is $18 per person. Paddleboats rent for $7 for a half hour, $10 per hour. Waterskiing is priced at $15 for a 1½-mile ride. Parasailing costs $30 for a 4-minute ride. See "Boat Cruises," above, for their offerings.

✪ **Underwater Explorers Society (UNEXSO).** Lucaya Beach. ☎ **242/373-1244.**

UNEXSO is one of the premier facilities for diving and snorkeling throughout The Bahamas and Caribbean. There are 12 dive trips daily, including reef trips, shark dives, wreck dives, and night dives. Also, this is the only facility in the world where divers can dive with dolphins in the open ocean (see "The Dolphin Experience," above). A popular 3-hour learn-to-dive course is offered daily. Over UNEXSO's 30-year history, more than 50,000 people have completed this course. For $89, students learn the basics in UNEXSO's training pools. Then, the same day, they dive the beautiful shallow reef with their instructor. For experienced divers, a guided reef dive is $35, a three-dive package is $89, and a 20-dive card is $299. A snorkeling trip to the reef costs $18, all equipment included. A half-hour snorkeling lesson is $10.

TENNIS

The **Bahamas Princess Resort and Casino,** The Mall at West Sunrise Highway, has a near monopoly on tennis courts on Grand Bahama. The Princess Country Club (☎ 242/352-6721) has six hard-surface courts, and the Princess Tower (☎ 242/352-9661) has three. Guests and nonguests are charged $7 per hour. Lessons are also available. The courts are open daily from 8:30am to dusk. If you want to play at night, you have to call and reserve a special time. It costs $12 for the courts to be lighted.

Another option is the **Flamingo Beach Resort** (Royal Palm Way; ☎ 242/373-1333), which has four hard-surface courts. The cost is $5 per hour for guests and nonguests alike. There is no night play. The **Lucayan Beach Resort** (Royal Palm Way; ☎ 242/373-6545) also has four hard courts (not illuminated). Guests of the resort play free; nonguests are charged $5 per hour. Courts are available daily from 8am to dusk.

Xanadu Beach Resort and Marina (Sunken Treasure Drive; ☎ 242/352-6782) offers three clay courts (not lit for night play). The courts are free to both registered guests and nonguests and are open to play at any time. Lessons run from $5 per group or from $15 to $25 for individuals. Racquets and balls can be rented for $5.

WINDSURFING

Paradise Watersports (see "Boat Cruises," above) at Xanadu Beach rents sailboards for $15 an hour, plus a $25 deposit.

6 Exploring the Island: Getting Close to Nature

Except for the coral, rock, and pines, there isn't much on Grand Bahama that's very old, unless you count some of the native Lucayan artifacts. However, efforts to beautify the island have paid off in interesting botanical gardens and parks where you can see tropical plants in all their glory (in the right seasons).

Special Moments & Little-Known Gems

The Music at Count Basie Square. Located in the center of the Port Lucaya waterfront restaurant and shopping complex, Count Basie Square contains a vine-covered bandstand where the best live music to be heard on the island is performed nightly. And it's free. The square honors the "Count," who used to have a grand home on Grand Bahama. Steel bands, small Junkanoo groups, even gospel singers from a local church are likely to be heard performing here, their voices or music wafting across the 50-slip marina.

The Star Club. If you'd like to see what's left of The Bahamas "the way it was," head for The Star Club, Bayshore Road (☎ 242/346-6207), in the West End. When it was built in the 1940s, it was the first hotel on Grand Bahama, and many famous guests stayed here over the years. It's no longer a hotel, but the place is still going strong and is open daily from 10am to 1am. Sometimes people leaving the casino late at night motor over here to eat grouper fingers, play pool, or listen to the taped music. The club is still run by the family of the late Austin Henry Grant Jr., a former Bahamian senator and a local legend in the West End. A full range of drinks is available, as well as Bahamian chicken in the bag, burgers, fish-and-chips, and "fresh sexy" conch prepared as chowder, fritters, or salads. But you don't really go here for the food. You can also drop in next door at Austin's Calypso Bar, a real Grand Bahama dive if there ever was one. Anne Grant, the owner, will tell you about the good ol' days.

LUCAYA NATIONAL PARK: FEATURING THE MOST SECLUDED BEACH ON GRAND BAHAMA

This 40-acre park, filled with mangrove, pine, and palm trees, contains one of the loveliest, most secluded beaches on Grand Bahama. The long, wide, dune-covered stretch of sandy beach is found by following a wooden path winding through the trees. As you wander through the park, you'll cross Gold Rock Creek, fed by a spring from what is said to be the world's largest underground freshwater cavern system. Two of the caves can be seen. They were exposed when a portion of ground collapsed. The pools in the caves are composed of six feet of freshwater atop a heavier layer of saltwater. Spiral wooden steps have been built down to the pools. There are 36,000 passages in the cavern system.

The freshwater springs once lured native Lucayans, those Arawak-connected tribes who lived on the island and depended on fishing for their livelihood. They would come inland to get fresh water for their habitats on the beach. Lucayan bones and artifacts, such as pottery, have been found in the caves, as well as on the beaches.

For more information about the park, contact the Rand Nature Centre (☎ 242/352-5438). To reach the park, which is about 12 miles from Lucaya, drive east along Midshipman Road, passing Sharp Rock Point and Gold Rock.

OTHER PLACES TO EXPERIENCE NATURE

Garden of the Groves. Intersection of Midshipman Rd. and Magellan Dr. ☎ 242/352-4045. Admission $5 for adults, $2.50 for children. Garden, Mon–Fri 9am–4pm, Sat–Sun and holidays 10am–4pm. Palmetto Café, Mon–Fri 9am–4pm, Sat 9am–noon.

The prime attraction of Grand Bahama is this 11-acre garden, which honors its founder, Wallace Groves, and his wife, Georgette. Seven miles east of the

International Bazaar, this scenic preserve of waterfalls and flowering shrubs has some 10,000 trees.

Tropical birds flock here, making this a lure for bird-watchers and ornithologists. There are free-form lakes, footbridges, ornamental borders, lawns, and flowers. A small nondenominational chapel, open to visitors, looks down on the garden from a hill. The Palmetto Café (☎ 242/373-5668) serves snacks and drinks, and a Bahamian straw market is located at the entrance gate.

Hydroflora Garden. On East Beach at Sunrise Hwy. ☎ **242/352-6052.** Admission $3 adults, $1.50 children. Mon–Fri 9–5pm, Sat 9am–4pm.

At this artificially created botanical wonder, you can see 154 specimens of plants that grow in The Bahamas. A special section is devoted to bush medicine, which is widely practiced by Bahamians (who have been using herbs and other plants to cure everything from sunburn to insomnia since the native Lucayans were here centuries ago). Guided tours cost $5 per person. Call for a reservation.

Rand Nature Centre. E. Settlers Way. ☎ **242/352-5438.** Admission $5 adults, $3 children (5–12), free 4 and under. Mon–Fri 9am–4pm, Sat 9am–1pm; guided tours at 10am and 2pm Mon–Fri.

This 100-acre pineland sanctuary, located 2 miles east of the center of Freeport, is the regional headquarters of The Bahamas National Trust, a nonprofit conservation organization. Forest nature trails highlight native flora and "bush medicine" and provide opportunities for bird-watching. Wild birds abound at the park, and a freshwater pond is home to a flock of West Indian flamingos, the national bird of The Bahamas. On the first Saturday of every month at 8am, a bird-watching tour is given. They also offer a wildflower walk on the last Saturday of the month, starting at 8am. Other features of the nature center include native animal displays, a replica of a Lucayan Indian village, an education center, and a gift shop selling nature books and souvenirs.

ORGANIZED TOURS

Several informative tours of Grand Bahama Island are offered. One reliable company is **H. Forbes Charter Co.,** the Mall at West Sunrise Highway, Freeport (☎ **242/352-9311**). From its headquarters in the lobby of the Bahamas Princess Country Club, it offers half- and full-day bus tours. The most popular option is the half-day Super Combination Tour, priced at $16 per adult and $12 per child under 12. It includes guided visits to the botanical gardens, drive-through tours of residential areas and the island's commercial center, and stops at the island's deep-water harbor. Shopping and a visit to a wholesale liquor store are also included on the tour. Tours depart Monday through Saturday at 9am and 1pm and last 3¹/₂ hours.

7 Shopping

There's no place in The Bahamas for shopping quite like the International Bazaar, where goods from around the world come together. True, its architectural heyday was in the early 1960s, and some cite it as a commercially viable example of Bahamian kitsch in poured concrete and plastic. But the place seems perfectly suited for its role as a shoppers' theme park, a sort of born-to-shop Disney World. In the nearly 100 shops, you're bound to find something that is both unique and a bargain. Here you'll find African handcrafts, Chinese jade, British china, Swiss watches, Irish linens, and Colombian emeralds—and that's just for starters.

The **Straw Market,** beside the International Bazaar, contains items with a special Bahamian touch—colorful baskets, hats, handbags, and place mats—all of which make good gifts and souvenirs of your trip. (As in the Straw Market in Nassau, some items sold here are actually made in Asia.)

Shopping hours in Freeport/Lucaya are 9:30am to 3pm Monday through Thursday, 9:30am to 5pm on Friday. Many shops are closed on Saturday and Sunday. However, in the International Bazaar, hours vary widely. Most places there are open Monday through Saturday. Some begin business daily at 9:30am; others don't open until 10am. Closing time ranges from 5:30 to 6pm.

SHOPPING THE INTERNATIONAL BAZAAR

One of the world's most unusual shopping marts, the International Bazaar, at East Mall Drive and East Sunrise Highway, covers 10 acres in the heart of Freeport. There is a major bus stop at the entrance of the complex. Unfortunately, buses aren't numbered, but those marked "International Bazaar" will take you right to the gateway. Visitors walk through the much-photographed Toril Gate, a Japanese symbol of welcome, into a miniature world's fair setting. Continental cafes and dozens of shops loaded with merchandise await visitors. The bazaar blends architecture and cultures from some 25 countries. The place was re-created with cobblestones, narrow alleys, and authentically reproduced architecture.

On a street patterned after the Ginza in Tokyo, just inside the entrance to the bazaar, is the Asian section. A rich collection of merchandise from the Far East can be found here, including cameras, handmade teak furniture, fine silken goods, and even places where you can have clothing custom-made. If browsing among the jade figurines and kimonos makes you think of Japanese food, drop in at the Japanese Steak House (see "Where to Dine," above), for sushi or other food.

To the left you'll find the Left Bank of Paris, or a reasonable facsimile, with sidewalk cafes where you can enjoy a café au lait and perhaps a pastry under shade trees. In the Continental Pavilion, there are leather goods, jewelry, lingerie, and gifts at shops with names such as Love Boutique.

A narrow alley leads you from the French section to East India, where shops sell such exotic goods as taxi horns and silk saris. Moving on from the India House, past Kon Tiki, you arrive in Africa, where you can purchase carvings or a colorful dashiki.

For a taste of Latin America and Iberia, make your way to the Spanish section, where serapes and piñatas hang from the railings. Imports are displayed along the cobblestoned walks.

Many items sold in the shops here are said to cost 40% less than if you bought them in the United States, but don't count on that. You can have purchases sent anywhere you wish.

Here's a description of the various shops in the bazaar.

ART

Flovin Gallery. Arcade. ☎ **242/352-7564.**

This gallery sells original Bahamian and international art, frames, lithographs, posters, and Bahamian-made Christmas ornaments and decorated coral. It also offers handmade Bahamian dolls, coral jewelry, and other gift items. Another branch is at Port Lucaya (see below).

CRYSTAL & CHINA

Island Galleria. Arcade. ☎ **242/352-8194.**

China by Wedgwood, Lenox, and Aynsley, and crystal by Waterford, are the major lure of this store. It has the island's most extensive collection. The store is also located in the Port Lucaya Marketplace.

FASHIONS

London Pacesetter Boutique. Arcade. ☎ **242/352-2929.**

Here you'll find stylish sportswear, cashmere sweaters, Spanish-made resort wear, and assorted European fashions.

HANDCRAFTS

Bahamian Souvenir Outlet. In the International Bazaar. ☎ **242/352-2947.**

If you're seeking just routine souvenirs of your visit to The Bahamas, along with Bahamian gift items, this outlet offers many inexpensive items. You'll find the usual array of T-shirts, key rings, mugs, and all that stuff here. The location is below the Ministry of Tourism.

JEWELRY

Colombian Emeralds International. South American Section. ☎ **242/352-5464.**

This is a branch of the world's foremost emerald jeweler, offering a wide array of precious gemstone jewelry and one of the island's best watch collections. Careful shoppers will find significant savings over U.S. prices. The outlet offers certified appraisals and free 90-day insurance. There are two branches at the Port Lucaya Marketplace (☎ **242/373-8400**).

Jeweler's Warehouse. Spanish Section. ☎ **242/352-6425.**

This shop sells 14-karat gold, silver, and gemstone jewelry. Discounts can range to as much as 40%, but that calls for some careful shopping. Semiprecious beads and coral items are made in The Bahamas. There is also a large selection of famous name watches, including Fossil and Reebok that are discounted up to 60%.

John Bull. Far East Section. ☎ **242/352-7515.**

Formerly known as Ginza, this outlet, a cousin of the better known main branch on Bay Street in Nassau, is renowned for its fine selection of quality watches, jewelry, perfumes, leather goods, cameras, and gifts. Its watch selection is particularly choice, including all the big names such as Rolex and Raymond Weil. Some of its best jewelry is Mikimoto cultured pearls and Kabana Sea Life. The leather collection is also among the island's finest, with classic names such as Dooney & Bourke and Moschino.

Sea Treasures. Spanish Section. ☎ **242/352-2911.**

Sea Treasures sells 14- and 18-karat gold and silver jewelry inspired by the sea and handcrafted on the island. Prices go from $5 to $3,000. The staff will show you gold necklaces and bracelets, along with diamonds, topazes, pearls, and both pink and black coral.

LEATHER GOODS

Fendi. In the International Bazaar. ☎ **242/352-7908.**

This is the best outlet for quality leather products. They carry the major Fendi line of leather goods, including suitcases, purses, coats, watches, and even perfume.

The Leather Shop. In the International Bazaar. ☎ **242/352-5491.**

This is another good outlet, carrying a much more limited Fendi line, but also many other designers including Land and HCL. Additional leather goods include shoes and gift items.

Unusual Centre. In the International Bazaar. ☎ **242/352-3994.**

This store is different from the competition in that it carries a wide array of items made of eel skin, as well as some goods made from exotic feathers such as peacock.

LLADRÓ FIGURINES

Lladró Gallery. In the International Bazaar. ☎ **242/352-2660.**

Lovers of Lladró figurines welcome the chance to add to their collections by visiting the best-stocked emporium of Lladró on Grand Bahama Island. If you appreciate the elongated limbs and wistful mannerisms of characters in the 17th-century paintings of El Greco, you'll appreciate Lladró. The gallery also stocks a less extensive collection of figures by Swarovski and a limited collection of Waterford crystal.

MISCELLANY

The Old Curiosity Shop. Arcade. ☎ **242/352-8008.**

This shop specializes in antique English bric-a-brac, including original and reproduction items: Victorian dinner rings and cameos, antique engagement rings, lithographs, old and new silver and porcelain, and brass candlesticks and trivets.

Far East Traders. In the International Bazaar. ☎ **242/352-9280.**

This outlet offers a collection of Oriental goods such as linens, hand-embroidered dresses and blouses, silk robes, lace parasols, smoking jackets, and kimonos.

MUSIC

Intercity Music. In the International Bazaar. ☎ **242/352-8820.**

This is the best music store on the island. You get not only Bahamian music, but soca, reggae, and all the music of the islands. CDs, records, and tapes are sold. You can also purchase Bahamian posters and flags, portable radios, Walkmans, and blank audio tapes, along with accessories for camcorders.

PERFUMES & FRAGRANCES

Les Parisiennes. French Section. ☎ **242/352-5380.**

This outlet offers a wide range of perfumes, including the latest from Paris. It also sells Lancôme cosmetics and skin-care products.

The Perfume Factory Fragrance of The Bahamas, Ltd. At the rear of the International Bazaar. ☎ **242/352-9391.**

This is the top fragrance producer in The Bahamas. The shop is housed in a model of an 1800s mansion, in which visitors are invited to hear a 5-minute commentary and to see the mixing of fragrant oils. There's even a "mixology" department where you can create your own fragrance from a selection of oils. The shop's well-known products include Island Promises, Goombay, Paradise, and Pink Pearl (which has conch pearls in the bottle). The shop also sells Guanahani, a new fragrance created to commemorate the 500th anniversary of Columbus' first landfall in the New World. (Guanahani was the Indian name for the southern Bahamian island of San Salvador, traditional site of Columbus' landing.) Other perfumes and colognes include Sand, the number-one Bahamian-made men's fragrance in the country. Sand is also the top-selling men's fragrance in the Caribbean section of Walt Disney World.

Parfum de Paris. French Section. ☎ **242/352-8164.**

Here you'll find practically all major French perfumes and colognes. Discounts are sometimes granted with prices up to 40% less than in the United States. There's another branch at Port Lucaya Marketplace (☎ **242/373-8404**).

SHOES

Gemini. In the International Bazaar. ☎ **242/352-4809.**

Although most of its inventory consists of stylish (usually Italian-made) shoes for women, this store is also well stocked with accessories, including handbags, wallets, belts, T-shirts, and a wide collection of jewelry (some of it gold-plated) inspired by the aesthetic of Coco Chanel.

STAMPS & COINS

Bahamas Coin and Stamp Ltd. Arcade. ☎ **242/352-8989.**

This is not only the original but also the major coin dealer on the island. It specializes in Bahamian coin jewelry, ancient Roman coins, and relics from sunken Spanish galleons. It also carries a vast selection of antique U.S. and English coins and paper money.

SHOPPING PORT LUCAYA MARKETPLACE

The first of its kind in The Bahamas, Port Lucaya on Seahorse Road was named after the original settlers of Grand Bahama. This is a shopping and dining complex set on 6 acres near the Lucayan Beach Resort & Casino, the Grand Bahama Beach Hotel, and the Clarion Atlantik Beach. Free entertainment, such as steel-drum bands and strolling musicians, adds to a festival atmosphere.

The complex rose on the site of a former Bahamian straw market, but the craftspeople and their straw products are back in full force after having been temporarily dislodged.

Full advantage is taken of the waterfront location. Many of the restaurants and shops overlook a 50-slip marina, home of a "fantasy" pirate ship featuring lunch and dinner/dancing cruises. A variety of charter vessels are also based at the Port Lucaya Marina. Dockage at the marina is available to visitors coming by boat to shop or dine.

A boardwalk along the water makes it easy to watch the frolicking dolphins and join in other activities at the Underwater Explorers Society (UNEXSO). (For more information, see "Beaches, Water Sports & Other Outdoor Activities," above)

Merchandise in the shops of Port Lucaya ranges from leather to lingerie to wind chimes. Traditional and contemporary fashions are featured for men, women, and children.

Coconits by Androsia. Port Lucaya. ☎ **242/373-8387.**

This is the Port Lucaya outlet of the famous batik house of Andros Island. Its designs and colors capture the spirit of The Bahamas. Fabrics are handmade on the island of Andros, and the store sells quality, 100% cotton resort wear, including simple skirts, tops, jackets, and shorts for women. It also offers a colorful line of children's wear.

Flovin Gallery II. Port Lucaya. ☎ **242/373-8388.**

This branch of the art gallery located in the International Bazaar sells a collection of oil paintings (both Bahamian and international), along with lithographs and posters. In its limited field, it's the best in the business. It also features a number of gift items, such as handmade Bahamian dolls, decorated corals, and Christmas ornaments.

Jeweler's Warehouse. Port Lucaya. ☎ **242/373-8400.**

This is a place for bargain hunters looking for good buys on discounted, close-out 14-karat gold and gemstone jewelry. Discounts range up to 50%. The quality of many of these items, however, remains high. Guarantees and certified appraisals are possible.

Photo Specialist. Port Lucaya. ☎ **242/373-1244.**

This is the best place on the island to purchase video and photo equipment. It carries an extensive range of merchandise, including tapes and batteries. It has Sea &

I love 0-800-99-0011
in the springtime.

**All you need for the
fastest, clearest connections home.**

Every country has its own AT&T Access Number which makes calling from France and other countries really easy. Just dial the AT&T Access Number for the country you're calling from and we'll take it from there. And be sure to charge your calls on your AT&T Calling Card. It'll help you avoid outrageous phone charges on your hotel bill and save you up to 60%.* 0-800-99-0011 is a great place to visit any time of year, especially if you've got these two cards. So please take the attached wallet card of worldwide AT&T Access Numbers.

ttp://www.att.com/traveler

a complete list of AT&T Access Numbers and other helpful services, call 1-800-446-8399.
est and clearest connections from countries with voice prompts, compared to major U.S. carriers on calls to
U.S. Clearest based on customer preference testing. * Compared to certain hotel telephone charges based on
a to the U.S. in October 1995. Actual savings may be higher or lower depending upon your billing method,
e of day, length of call, fees charged by hotel and the country from which you are calling. "I Love Paris"
e Porter) © 1952 Chappel & Co. (ASCAP). © 1997 AT&T

Sea 35mm underwater cameras for rent starting at $10 a day. The outlet will also repair cameras.

UNEXSO Dive Shop. Port Lucaya. ☎ **242/373-1244.**

This is the premier dive shop of The Bahamas. It sells everything related to the water—swimsuits, wetsuits, underwater cameras, shades, hats, souvenirs, state-of-the-art diver's equipment, and computers.

8 Grand Bahama After Dark

Grand Bahama has Las Vegas–type revues, casino action, dance clubs, and native entertainment such as steel bands. Many resort hotels stage their own entertainment at night, and these shows are open to the general public.

LOCAL CULTURAL ENTERTAINMENT

A nonprofit repertory company, the **Freeport Players' Guild,** Regency Theatre (☎ 242/352-5533), offers about four plays during its September-to-June season. The average ticket price is $10. The **Grand Bahama Players** (☎ 242/373-2299), is a local amateur group that also uses the Regency Theatre for its productions. Works by Bahamian, West Indian, and North American playwrights are presented. Sometimes performances are staged at the International Bazaar. Call for information. Performances of both of the above groups are advertised in local papers.

CASINOS

Lucayan Beach Casino. In the Lucayan Beach Resort, Royal Palm Way. ☎ **242/373-7777.**

The center of casino action at Lucaya Beach, this casino is as large as its competitor (see below). With 20,000 square feet, it offers 550 super slots. Happy hour lasts daily from 4 to 7pm. Novices can take free gaming lessons daily at 11am or 7pm. The casino is open daily from 9am to 3am. Entrance is free.

Princess Casino. The Mall at W. Sunrise Hwy. ☎ **242/352-7811.**

Most of the nightlife in Freeport/Lucaya centers around this glittering, giant, Moroccan-style palace, one of the largest casinos in The Bahamas and the Caribbean. Under this Moorish-domed structure, visitors play games of chance and attend Las Vegas–type floor shows. They can also dine in a first-class restaurant, the Crown Room (see "Where to Dine"). The casino is open daily from 9am to 3am. Entrance is free.

CABARET

Casino Royale Showroom. In The Bahamas Princess Resort and Casino, the Mall at W. Sunrise Hwy. ☎ **242/352-6721.** Cover (including two drinks) $25.

The shows here come and go, but there are usually Las Vegas–type revues. Expect more than a dozen performers who cavort in Goombay-inspired colors with lots of glitter and a smattering of toplessness. Advance reservations are a good idea. Two shows a night are presented from Tuesday to Sunday, with the first at 8:30 and the second at 10:45pm. Usually closed for 2 weeks during the month of September.

Flamingo Showcase Theatre. In the Lucayan Beach Resort, Royal Palm Way. ☎ **242/373-7777.** Cover (including two drinks) $29.95.

If you're staying at Lucaya, you'll want to attend the Flamingo Showcase Theatre. The Bahamian-style revues here are among the best in The Bahamas. Performances are Wednesday and Saturday at 8 and 10pm. Reservations are required. A dinner-and-show package (buffet dinner) costs $39.95 per person.

THE CLUB & MUSIC SCENE

Yellow Bird Show Club. In the Castaways Resort, International Bazaar. ☎ **242/373-7368.** Cover (including two drinks and tip) $20.

Located in the rear of the Castaways Resort, this spot offers an evening of Bahamian entertainment, with steel drums, the limbo, conga drums telling stories, fire dancing, and glass eating. The show even presents a highly stylized version of the Caribbean Queen of Calypso. From Monday through Saturday, doors open at 8:15pm, with show time at 9pm. You can disco here after the show.

9 A Side Trip to West End

If you're looking for a refreshing escape from the plush hotels and casinos of Freeport/Lucaya, head to West End, 28 miles from Freeport. At this old fishing village you'll get glimpses of how things used to be before package-tour groups began descending on Grand Bahama.

To reach West End, you head north along Queen's Highway, going through Eight Mile Rock, to the northernmost point of the island. West End has several good restaurants, so you can plan to make a day (or a night) of it.

A lot of the old buildings of the village are now dilapidated, but a nostalgic air prevails. Many old-timers remember when rum boats were busy and the docks buzzed with activity day and night. This was from about 1920 to 1933, when Prohibition reigned in the United States—but not with great success. West End was so close to the U.S. mainland that rum-running became a lucrative business, with booze flowing out of West End into Florida at night. Al Capone is reputed to have been a frequent visitor.

Villages along the way to West End have colorful names, such as Hawksbill Creek. For a preview of some local life, try to visit the fish market along the harbor here. You'll pass some thriving harbor areas, too, but the vessels you'll see will be oil tankers, not rumrunners.

Eight Mile Rock is a hamlet of mostly ramshackle houses that stretch along both sides of the road for—you guessed it—8 miles. At West End, you come to an abrupt stop. Then it's time to visit the weathered old Star Club (see above). If you stick around till nighttime, you're likely to hear some calypso music nearby. You can also enjoy a meal at the Buccaneer Club before heading back to Freeport/Lucaya to catch the last show at the casino.

WHERE TO DINE

Buccaneer Club. Deadman's Reef. ☎ **242/349-3794.** Reservations required. Main courses $16–$30. AE, MC, V. Tues–Sun 5–11pm. CONTINENTAL/BAHAMIAN.

The Buccaneer Club is a tropical version of a German beer garden and is the best place to eat in the West End. The whimsical decor was created by Heinz Fischbacher and his Bahamian wife, Kitty. The compound is ringed with stone walls, within which palm-dotted terraces and foot-stomping alpine music provide lots of fun for the yachting crowd you'll see here. The collection of inner rooms contains mismatched crystal chandeliers, pine trim, and a beer-hall ambience that's unique in The Bahamas. Many of the dishes would be familiar to denizens of Middle Europe, including a not bad Wiener schnitzel and an excellent veal Oskar, the latter perhaps a bit heavy on a tropic night. Fresh fish and breaded shrimp are also served if you don't want to order meat. Twice a week, the Fischbachers host beach parties, which cost $45 per person. The price includes transportation from hotels, an hour-long open bar, a buffet, a beer-drinking contest, crab races, limbo dancing, and lively games of musical chairs.

Pier One. Freeport Harbour. ☎ **242/352-6674.** Reservations recommended for dinner. Lunch main courses $2–$32; dinner main courses $17.95–$40. AE, MC, V. Mon–Sat 11am–4pm; daily 5–10pm, Sun 3–10pm. BAHAMIAN/INTERNATIONAL.

Many people head to this restaurant-on-stilts because it's close to the cruise-ship dock—this is the first Bahamian restaurant many visitors see. It's also an ideal venue at which to sample some fresh Bahamian seafood, whether you're off a cruise ship or driving west from Freeport. It rises on stilts a few steps from the water's edge. A footbridge leads to an interior loaded with nautical artifacts. Don't overlook the high-ceilinged bar as a rendezvous for a round of drinks before your meal. There are several dining rooms, the most desirable of which overlooks schools of fish. The lunch fare includes a delectable version of a cream-based clam chowder. Fresh oysters are also available. The house specialty is actually baby shark, prepared in a number of different ways. (There's a shark pool on site.) We prefer ours sautéed with garlic, or else you can have it stuffed with cheese and crabmeat, which tends to overpower its natural flavor. A fresh fish of the day is also featured, and this wouldn't be a Bahamian restaurant if it didn't feature pan-fried grouper. As for the shrimp curry or the roast prime rib, you're likely to have had better versions of these dishes elsewhere. For dessert, you might try Italian rum cake or key lime pie.

7

Bimini, the Berry Islands & Andros

In this chapter we begin a journey through the Out Islands—a very different world from that found in the major tourist meccas of Nassau, Cable Beach, Paradise Island, and Freeport/Lucaya.

Bimini, the Berry Islands, and Andros are each quite different. Bimini is famous and overrun with tourists, particularly in summer, but visitors will have the Berry Islands practically to themselves. These two islands are to the north and west of Nassau and might be called the "westerly islands," as they, along with Grand Bahama, lie at the northwestern fringe of The Bahamas. They are the closest islands to the Florida coastline.

In contrast, much larger Andros is located southwest of Nassau. In many ways Andros is the most fascinating. It is actually a series of islands and is laced with creeks and dense forests, once said to have been inhabited by mysterious creatures.

Each of the three island chains attracts a different type of visitor. **Bimini,** just 50 miles off the east coast of Florida—and the setting for Hemingway's *Islands in the Stream*—lures the big-game fisher, the yachtie from Miami, and even the drug dealer from South Florida (smuggling drugs so close to the Florida mainland is big business, of course).

The Biminis are home to world-famous sports fishing, excellent yachting and cruising, and some good scuba diving. Bimini offers the angler seas swarming with tuna, dolphinfish, amberjack, white and blue marlin, swordfish, barracuda, and shark, along with many other varieties. Bonefish are also plentiful around the flats off the coast of Alice Town, the capital. But the blue marlin is the prize. Bahamians think so highly of this fish that they even put it on their 100-dollar bill. Scuba divers can see black coral trees over The Bimini Wall and reefs off Victory Cay. Bimini Undersea Adventures (see below) provides a comprehensive diving program.

The **Berry Islands** is the kind of place a William Buckley type, or even a Steve Forbes, would retreat to. The resort also attracts fishers, but this string of islands, which has only 700 residents, is mainly for escapists—that is, rich escapists. The islands' very limited accommodations (some of which used to be private clubs) lie near the Tongue of the Ocean, home of the big-game fish.

The actor Douglas Fairbanks Jr., a former chairman of the Chub Cay Club's development board, was once used to attract jet-setters and film people to this laid-back pocket of posh.

Andros, the largest island in The Bahamas, is still mainly uninhabited. If the island nation still has an unexplored wilderness, this is it. Its barrier reef, the third largest in the world, makes Andros a diver's dream. The reef plunges 6,000 feet to a narrow drop-off known as the Tongue of the Ocean. Water also creates Andros's mysterious blue holes, which are formed when subterranean caves fill with seawater, causing the ceiling to collapse and expose clear, deep pools. These also are a diver's delight.

Few come here any more looking for Sir Henry Morgan's pirate treasure, said to have been buried in one of the caves off Morgan's Bluff on the north tip of the island. But Andros does attract fishers, as it is known for its world-class fishing for marlin and the bluefin tuna. Its bonefishing is perhaps the best in the world.

Andros also attracts the naturalist, drawn to its forest and mangrove swamps, home to a wide variety of birds and animals, including the nonpoisonous Bahamian boa constrictor and the 6-foot-long iguana. The Bahamian national bird, the West Indian flamingo, can also be spotted during migration in late spring and summer.

1 Bimini

Bimini is known as the big-game fishing capital of the world, and fishing is excellent throughout the year in flats, on the reefs, and in the streams. Ernest Hemingway came to write and fish, and here he wrote much of *To Have and Have Not.* He also publicized Bimini around the world with his novel *Islands in the Stream.*

Located 50 miles east of Miami, Bimini consists of a number of islands, islets, and cays, including North and South Bimini, the targets of most visitors. You'll most often encounter the word *Bimini,* but it might be more proper to say *The Biminis* since North Bimini and South Bimini are two distinct islands, separated by a narrow ocean passage. There is ferry service between the two. Tourist facilities are on North Bimini, mostly in Alice Town, its major settlement.

Guided by native fishers, visitors can go bonefishing or deep-sea fishing. Divers find the reefs laced with conch, lobster, coral, and many tropical fish. Sightseers are allowed to visit the **Lerner Marine Laboratory for Marine Research** on North Bimini.

Off North Bimini, in 30 feet of water, are some large, hewn-stone formations that some people claim to be from the lost continent of Atlantis.

Bimini's location off the Florida coastline is at a point where the Gulf Stream meets the Bahama Banks. This fact has made Bimini a favorite cruising ground for America's yachting set, who follow the channel between North and South Bimini into a spacious, sheltered harbor where they can stock up on food, drink, fuel, and supplies at well-equipped marinas.

Hook-shaped North Bimini is 7½ miles long. Combined with South Bimini, it makes up a landmass of only 9 square miles. That's why Alice Town looks so crowded. Another reason is that a large part of Bimini is privately owned, and despite pressure from the Bahamian government, the landholders have not sold their acreage. Bimini can't "spread out" until they do.

At Alice Town, the land is so narrow that you can walk "from sea to shining sea" in just a short time. Most of Bimini's population of some 1,600 people live in Alice Town. Other hamlets include Bailey Town and Porgy Bay.

South Florida visitors flock to Bimini in the summer months; winter, especially from mid-December to mid-March, is quieter. Fishers and divers, as mentioned, have been attracted to Bimini for years. But more recently Bimini has attracted increasing numbers of visitors who don't care about sports at all. If you're not a fisher or scuba diver, one of the most interesting experiences in Bimini is to cruise the cays that begin south of South Bimini. Each has its own special appeal, beginning with Turtle Rocks and stretching to South Cat Cay (the latter of which is uninhabited). Along the way you'll pass Holm Cay, Gun Cay, and North Cat Cay.

If you go to Bimini, you'll hear a lot of people mention Cat Cay, and you may want to go here. You can stay overnight at the marina, which lies 8 miles off South Bimini. Transient slips are available to mariners. The island is the domain of **Cat Cay Yacht Club,** with headquarters at 1100 Lee Wagener Blvd., Suite 101, Fort Lauderdale, FL 33315 (☎ **954/359-8272**). The initiation fee is $10,000. This is a privately owned island, attracting titans of industry and famous families. It is for the exclusive use of Cat Cay Club members and their guests, who enjoy a golf course, tennis, a large marina, white-sand beaches, and club facilities such as restaurants and bars. Many wealthy Americans maintain homes on the island, which has a private airstrip.

Don't confuse Cat Cay with Cat Island, far to the south (see chapter 11).

GETTING THERE   *Note:* A passport or a birth certificate with picture ID is required for entry to Bimini. An outbound (return) ticket also must be presented to Bahamian Customs before you will be allowed entry. Passengers returning from Bimini to the United States must pay a $15 departure tax.

By Plane   Although it lies closer to the Florida coastline than any of the other Bahamian islands, many Americans fly to Bimini, often by chartering a small aircraft or by flying their own plane. The island's only airstrip is at the southern tip of South Bimini, a time-consuming transfer and ferryboat ride away from Alice Town on North Bimini, site of most of the archipelago's hotels and yacht facilities.

The best way to avoid this transfer is to fly the small **Pan Am Air Bridge** (formerly Chalk's International Airlines) located at 1000 MacArthur Causeway, Miami, FL 33132 (☎ **800/424-2557**). Pan Am has a fleet of 17-passenger amphibious aircraft that land in the waters near Alice Town. Pan Am offers flights daily from Miami; an additional flight is also offered Saturdays and Sundays. The 20- to 30-minute flights depart from the calm waters at Watson Island Terminal, near downtown Miami. A round-trip ticket costs $161. There is a baggage allowance of only 30 pounds per passenger. If you're carrying heavy travel or fishing gear, you'll be hit with overweight charges. In addition, Pan Am doesn't allow any hand luggage on board. Every piece of your luggage must be weighed and checked in.

By Boat   In the olden days, the traditional way of going from Nassau to Bimini was by a slow-moving boat. That sea trip still exists. You can go by sea on the MV *Bimini Mack,* which leaves from Potter's Cay Dock in Nassau and stops at Cat Cay and Bimini. The vessel leaves Nassau weekly but with no set schedule. For details about departure, call the dockmaster at Potter's Cay Dock in Nassau (☎ **242/393-1064**).

GETTING AROUND   If you've taken our advice and traveled lightly to Bimini, you can walk to your hotel from the point where the seaplanes land in Alice Town. If not, then a small minibus will transport you for $3 per person. If you arrive at the small airport on South Bimini, it is a $5 taxi and ferry ride to Alice Town.

Very few visitors need a car on Bimini—in fact, there are no car-rental agencies. Most people walk to where they want to go. The walk is up and down King's Highway, which has no sidewalks. It's so narrow that two automobiles have a tough time squeezing by.

This highway, lined with low-rise buildings, splits Alice Town on North Bimini. If you're a beachcombing type, stick to the side bordering the Gulf Stream. It's here you'll find the best beaches. The harborside contains a handful of inns (most of which

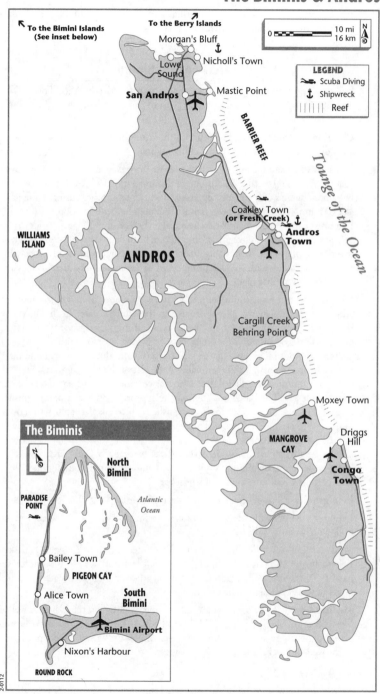

The Biminis & Andros

To the Bimini Islands
(See inset below)

To the Berry Islands

Morgan's Bluff

Nicholl's Town

Lowe
Sound

San Andros

Mastic Point

0 _____ 10 mi
16 km

N

LEGEND
- Scuba Diving
- Shipwreck
- Reef

BARRIER REEF

Tongue of the Ocean

WILLIAMS
ISLAND

ANDROS

Coakley Town
(or Fresh Creek)

Andros
Town

Cargill Creek
Behring Point

Moxey Town

Driggs
Hill

MANGROVE
CAY

Congo
Town

The Biminis

N

North
Bimini

PARADISE
POINT

Atlantic
Ocean

Bailey Town

PIGEON CAY

Alice Town

South
Bimini

Bimini Airport

Nixon's Harbour

ROUND ROCK

2-0112

187

are reviewed below), along with marinas and docks where supplies are unloaded. You'll see many Floridians arriving on yachts.

FAST FACTS: Bimini

Banks   The Royal Bank of Canada has a branch office in Alice Town (☎ 242/ 347-3031), open Monday and Friday 9am to 3pm and Tuesday, Wednesday, and Thursday from 9am to 1pm.

Clothing   If you're going to Bimini in the winter months, you'd better take along a windbreaker for those occasional chilly nights.

Customs & Immigration   The Pan Am Air Bridges' plane from Miami stops right near the Alice Town office of Customs and Immigration (☎ 242/368-2030) for The Bahamas. There's only one immigration officer, plus another customs official.

In Miami you will have been handed a Bahamian Immigration Card to fill out. You must carry proof of your citizenship. For U.S. visitors, that most ideally would be a passport, but a voter-registration card or a birth certificate will also do. The latter two require photo ID. Regrettably, many passengers cross over from Miami with only a driver's license, which will not be accepted by immigration. Customs may or may not examine your baggage.

Drugs   The rumrunners of the Prohibition era have now given way to a more deadly criminal: the smuggler of illegal drugs into the United States from The Bahamas. Because of its proximity to the U.S. mainland, Bimini, as is no secret to anyone, is now a major drop-off point for drugs, many of which have found their way here from Colombia. If not intercepted by the U.S. Coast Guard, these drugs will find their way to the Florida mainland and eventually to the rest of the United States.

Buying and/or selling illegal drugs, such as cocaine and marijuana, is an extremely risky business in The Bahamas. You may be approached several times by pushers on Bimini, but make sure you don't get "pushed" into jail. If caught with any illegal drugs on Bimini, or elsewhere in The Bahamas, you will be apprehended and will face immediate imprisonment.

Incidentally, all sorts of undercover agents, particularly U.S. narcotics agents, are likely to be found on Bimini, often bearded and sometimes looking like 1967 hippies, blending well into the social landscape.

Emergencies   To call the police or report a fire, dial ☎ 919.

Laundry   Most of the housekeeping staffs of the major hotels, for a fee, will be glad to do your laundry for you.

Mail   If you're sending mail back to the United States, we suggest you skip the Bahamian postal service entirely and drop your letter off at Pan Am airlines' special basket. You can use U.S. postage stamps, and your mail will reach its mainland target far quicker than by the usual route.

Medical Care   There are a doctor, nurses, and a dentist on the island, as well as the North Bimini Medical Clinic (☎ 242/347-3210). However, for a medical emergency, patients are usually airlifted to either Miami or Nassau. Helicopters can land in the well-lit baseball field on North Bimini.

WHERE TO STAY

Accommodations in Bimini are extremely limited, and it's almost impossible to get a room during one of the big fishing tournaments unless you've reserved way in advance. Inns are cozy and simple; many are family owned and operated (chances are, your innkeeper's name will be Brown). Furnishings are often time worn, the paint chipped. No one puts on airs here; the dress code, even in the evening, is very simple and relaxed. From wherever you're staying in Alice Town, it's usually easy to walk to another hotel for dinner or drinks.

MODERATE

✪ **Bimini Big Game Fishing Club & Hotel.** King's Hwy., P.O. Box 609, Alice Town, Bimini, The Bahamas, or P.O. Box 523238, Miami, FL 33152. ☎ **800/737-1007** in the U.S., or 242/347-3391. Fax 242/347-3392. 35 rms. 12 cottages. 4 penthouse apts. A/C TV TEL. Year-round, $149–$162 double; $180 cottage for two; $298 penthouse. Extra person $22. AE, MC, V.

Run by the Bacardi Rum people, this is the premier place for accommodations in Bimini. Filled with anglers and yachties, the hotel is the largest place to stay on the island. It's a self-contained world with well-furnished guest rooms in the main building, surrounded by cottages and first-rate penthouse apartments, the latter often housing VIPs. The general manager, Curtis Carroll, is the most experienced hotelier on the island, and he will see to your requests and help ease your adjustment to Bimini, especially if you want to know about fishing in all its many forms.

Established in 1946, most of the hotel's accommodations are in its central structure, where each unit is large and equipped with two beds. Everything is clean and comfortable, and the rooms have patios or porches opening onto a marina and the club's swimming pool. The ground-floor cottages are even more spacious than the standard bedrooms and have tiny kitchenettes with refrigerators—but cooking is strictly forbidden. If you want to charcoal-broil your catch of the day, you will have to use one of the outdoor grills.

A freshwater swimming pool is set aside for guests so that it won't be overrun with day-trippers. Guests can also play tennis.

The hotel is also the best place to go for food on the island, plus it's an entertainment hub (see "Where to Dine" and "Bimini After Dark," below). Usually the best anglers at the big-game fishing tournaments stay here, and during the tournaments it's next to impossible to get a room without reservations long in advance.

Bimini Blue Water Resort Ltd. King's Hwy., P.O. Box 601, Alice Town, Bimini, The Bahamas. ☎ **242/347-3166.** Fax 242/347-3293. 10 rms, 2 suites. A/C TV. Year-round, $90 double; $190 suite; $285 Marlin Cottage. AE, MC, V.

Blue Water is essentially a resort complex for sportfishers, with complete dockside services, containing 32 modern slips. It's one of the finest places of its kind in The Bahamas. The main building is a white, frame waterfront Bahamian guest house, the Anchorage, where Michael Lerner, the noted fisherman, used to live. It's at the top of the hill, with a dining room and bar from which you can look out onto the ocean. The regular bedrooms contain double beds, wood-paneled walls, and white furniture. Picture-window doors lead to private balconies. The swimming pool is set amid a tropical garden and has an adjoining refreshment bar.

The Marlin Cottage, although much altered, was one of Hemingway's retreats in the 1930s. He used it as a main setting in *Islands in the Stream*. It has three bedrooms, three baths, a large living room, and two porches. In honor of his memory, the hotel sponsors the Hemingway Billfish Tournament every March.

Sea Crest Hotel & Marina. P.O. Box 654, Kings Hwy., Alice Town, Bimini, The Bahamas. ☎ **242/347-3071.** Fax 242/347-3495. 11 rms, 1 suite. A/C TV. Year-round, $83.20 double; $185 suite. MC, V.

Built in 1981 and upgraded every year since, this hotel lies right on the main highway, the first hotel to give the Bimini Big Game Fishing Club and Hotel some real competition, although it's still not as good as that traditional leader. Rooms in this three-story hotel, which looks like a motel, are at their best on the third floor, because they have better ocean or bay views. Rooms don't have phones, and many are small, but they're comfortably furnished in a simple, traditional way. Accommodations open onto small balconies. Since the location is right in the heart of Alice Town, you can generally walk where you want to go. The Sea Crest is a family favorite, and dining is possible on-site at Captain Bob's, which is independently operated and serves good seafood. The hotel is also a favorite of the boating crowd, as it offers a small 18-berth marina.

INEXPENSIVE

Compleat Angler Hotel. King's Hwy., P.O. Box 601, Alice Town, Bimini, The Bahamas. ☎ **242/347-3122.** Fax 242/347-3293. 12 rms. A/C. Year-round, $65–$80 double. AE, MC, V.

Right on the main street, and affiliated with Bimini Blue Water Resort, this small and time-worn hotel was built in the 1930s, when big-game fishing was at its peak. The building is designed like an old country house, with Bahamian timber. The wood on the face of the building is from rum barrels used during the Prohibition era. Ernest Hemingway made the hotel his headquarters on and off from 1935 to 1937 while he was stalking marlin, and the room in which he stayed is still available to guests. He penned parts of *To Have and Have Not* here. At the bar, you'll find Ossie Brown, your helpful bartender, host, and manager. You can swim, dine, shop, or fish right at your doorstep, and fishing charters can be booked at the hotel. *Note:* Because of the famous, noisy bar on the premises, this hotel is only suitable for night owls.

WHERE TO DINE
EXPENSIVE

Gulfstream Restaurant. In the Bimini Big Game Fishing Club & Hotel, King's Hwy., Alice Town. ☎ **242/347-3394.** Reservations recommended for dinner. Main courses $16–$28. AE, MC, V. Daily 7:30–10:30am and 7–10pm. Closed Jan to mid-Feb. AMERICAN/CONTINENTAL.

This place consistently serves the finest food on the island in its curved dining room opening onto the pool. Murals by Phil Brinkman depict scenes relating to the legend and lore of Bimini. A good wine list complements the many dishes served. Dinner includes many island specialties, such as crisp homemade Bimini bread and freshly caught kingfish, along with broiled local lobster and grouper meunière. Instead of french fries, why not go Bahamian and order peas 'n' rice with your meal? If you're tired of fish, the kitchen will serve you a good steak, roast prime rib of beef, or lamb chops. In all, it's good, plain cooking—nothing too fancy.

MODERATE

Big Game Sports Bar. In the Bimini Big Game Fishing Club & Hotel, King's Hwy., Alice Town. ☎ **242/347-3391.** Main courses $6.50–$19. AE, MC, V. Daily noon–11pm. SEAFOOD.

This sports bar, which attracts some of the best fishers from South Florida, is upstairs overlooking the marina. Menu items are displayed near the cash register. During lunch the popular bar serves conch in many ways, including conch fritters, conch salad, conch chowder, and cracked conch, which is breaded like veal cutlet alla Milanese. But conch pizza is the specialty and is well worth the visit here. You can also order grouper fingers, barbecued back ribs, hamburgers, sandwiches, or a daily special. Tables overlook not only the marina but the flats beyond. Although standard fare, the food is always reliable as is the view.

Red Lion Pub. King's Hwy., Alice Town. ☎ **242/347-3259.** Main courses $10–$18. No credit cards. Tues–Sun 6–10pm; pub Tues–Sun 11am–2pm and 6–10pm. BAHAMIAN.

This centrally located restaurant is far larger than its simple facade would imply. In a relaxed, friendly atmosphere, it's one of the best places on the island to retreat to after a day of fishing and sailing. The dining room is in a large extension of the original pub and overlooks the marina in back. Above the cash register hangs a bit of nostalgia: a photograph of Stephanie Saunders, daughter of owner Dolores Saunders, who won the title of Miss Bimini in 1977. The well-prepared meals include the local fish of the day, cracked conch, barbecued ribs, baked grouper in foil, followed by either key lime pie or banana cream pie. It's the kind of meal you might be served if you visited the home of a typical family on Bimini.

Anchorage Dining Room. In the Blue Hole Water Resort, King's Hwy., Alice Town. ☎ **242/347-3166.** Main courses $12–$24; lunches $3–$10. AE, MC, V. Daily noon–4pm and 6–10pm. SEAFOOD/BAHAMIAN.

This dining room overlooks the harbor of Alice Town. At night, if you're seeking atmosphere "at the top of the hill," it has the jump on every other establishment. You can see the ocean through picture windows. Have a before-dinner drink in the bar. The modern, paneled room is filled with captain's chairs and Formica tables. You might begin your dinner with conch chowder, then follow with one of the tempting seafood dishes, including spiny broiled lobster or perhaps a chewy cracked conch. They also do fried Bahamian chicken and a New York sirloin. The cookery is straightforward and reliable, never pretending to be more than it is.

WATER SPORTS & OTHER OUTDOOR ACTIVITIES
✪ FISHING

Bimini is called the "Big Game Fishing Capital of the World," and Ernest Hemingway, above all others, made famous the sport practiced here. But Zane Grey came this way, too, as did Howard Hughes. Richard Nixon used to fish here aboard the posh cruiser of his friend Bebe Rebozo. In the trail of Hemingway, fishers today still flock to cast lines in the Gulf Stream and the Bahama Banks. The annual Bacardi Rum Billfish Tournament and the Hemingway Billfish Tournament bring world anglers to Bimini in March.

Of course, everyone's after the "big one," and a lot of world records have been set in this area: marlin, sailfish, swordfish, wahoo, grouper, and tuna. Fishing folk can spin cast for panfish and boat snapper, yellowtail, and kingfish. Many experts consider stalking bonefish, long a pursuit of baseball great Ted Williams, to be the toughest challenge in the sport.

Five charter boats are available in Bimini for big-game and little-game fishing, with some center-console boats rented for both bottom and reef angling. At least eight bonefishing guides are available, and experienced fishers who have made repeated visits to Bimini know the particular skills of each of these men who will take you for a half or full day of "fishing in the flats," as bonefishing is termed. Most skiffs hold two anglers, and part of the fun in hiring a local guide is to hear his fish stories and other island lore. If a guide tells you that 16-pound bonefish have turned up, don't think he's making it up. Such catches have been documented.

Reef and bottom fishing on Bimini are easier than bonefishing and can be more productive. There are numerous species of snapper and grouper to be found, as well as amberjack. This is the simplest and least expensive boat fishing, as you need only a local guide, a little boat, tackle, and a lot of bait. Sometimes you can negotiate to go out bottom fishing with a Bahamian, but chances are he'll ask you to pay for the

Island in the Stream

Nevil Norton Stuart, a Bahamian, came to Bimini in the late 1920s and purchased the Fountain of Youth, a Prohibition-era bar. He renamed it the Bimini Big Game Fishing Club. In 1940 Stuart reclaimed land in Bimini harbor, constructed a marina, and added several cottages along with a desalination plant. Thus began the legend of one of the most highly publicized sportfishing meccas in the world.

Film stars, including Judy Garland and Sir Anthony Hopkins, among others, have lodged at the club. Martin Luther King Jr. visited twice. Of course, no one immortalized the island as much as Hemingway, who called it "My Island in the Stream."

Today the complex has grown to more than 50 rooms, including cottages and penthouses, and it's owned by the rum makers Bacardi International. In the 100-slip marina can be found enormous sportfishing boats, costing more than several million dollars, proudly standing alongside simple outboard-powered runabouts.

Today the club hosts many fishing tournaments throughout the year, including the Bacardi Rum Billfish Tournament in March. This week-long world-class event attracts the biggest names in sportfishing and is regarded by many fishers as the event of the year to win.

boat fuel for his trouble. That night, back at your Bimini inn, the cook will serve you the red snapper or grouper you caught that day. Most hotel owners will tell you to bring your own fishing gear to Bimini. A couple of small shops sell some items, but you'd better bring major equipment with you. Bait, of course, can be purchased locally.

Bimini Big Game Fishing Club & Hotel. King's Hwy., Alice Town. ☎ **242/339-3391.**

Here you can charter a 41-foot Hatteras at $900 for a full day of fishing, or $500 for a half day. A Bertram, either 31 or 28 feet, will cost $600 for a full day, $400 for a half.

Bimini Blue Water Marina. King's Hwy., Alice Town. ☎ **242/347-3166.**

This place can give you a list of people whose boats are available for charter. The going rate is around $550 for a half day and $700 for a full day.

SNORKELING & SCUBA DIVING

This has become an increasingly popular sport in the last 20 years. Visitors can snorkel above a wonderland of black coral gardens and reefs, or go scuba diving and explore wrecks and blue holes, plus a mysterious formation on the bottom of the sea that some people claim is part of the lost continent of Atlantis. Bimini waters are known for a breathtaking drop-off at the rim of the continental shelf, a cliff extending 2,000 feet down, a veritable underwater mountain. Another major attraction for snorkelers and divers, not to mention fish, is the *Sapona,* lying hard aground in 15 feet of water ever since it was blown here by a hurricane in 1929. In the heyday of the Roaring Twenties, the ship served as a private club and speakeasy.

✪ **Bimini Undersea.** King's Hwy., Alice Town. ☎ **242/347-3089.**

The people to see here are Bill and Nowdla Keefe. Full-day snorkeling trips cost $25. Scuba rates are $39 for a one-tank dive, $69 for a two-tank dive, and $89 for a three-tank dive. Night dives go for $40. All-inclusive dive packages are also available. For further information or reservations, the Keefes can be reached by mail at P.O. Box 693515, Miami, FL 33269 (☎ **800/348-4644** or 305/653-5572).

TENNIS

You'll find hard-surface courts at the Bimini Big Game Fishing Club & Hotel (☎ 242/347-3391), King's Highway, which are complimentary and reserved for hotel guests and members. The courts are lit for night play, and you can purchase balls at the club.

EXPLORING THE WRECKAGE OF THE *SAPONA*

One of the chief points of interest off the coast of Bimini can be reached only by boat. It's the *Sapona,* which was built by Henry Ford during World War I. This huge concrete ship lies between South Bimini and Cat Cay. It was once a private club and a rumrunner's storehouse in the Roaring Twenties. The 1929 hurricane blew it ashore, and in World War II, U.S. Navy pilots used it as a practice bomb range. Now spearfishers are attracted to the ruins, looking for the giant grouper. The dive operators on Bimini include it in their repertoire.

EXPLORING THE ISLANDS: FOLLOWING IN THE FOOTSTEPS OF PONCE DE LEÓN AND PAPA HEMINGWAY

At the southern tip of North Bimini, **Alice Town** is all that many visitors ever see of the islands. The hotel center of Bimini, it can be thoroughly explored in an hour or two.

Nothing is spick-and-span in Alice Town. First-timers are warned not to judge The Bahamas by Bimini. A yachting guide poses a question: "Would you judge the rest of America if you visited only Miami?"

If you're traversing the island, you may want to stop off at the **Bimini Straw Market,** speak with some of the Bahamians, and perhaps pick up a souvenir.

King's Highway runs through the town and continues north. It's lined with houses painted gold, lime, buttercup yellow, and pink that gleam in the bright sunshine.

At some point you may notice the ruins of Bimini's first hotel, the Bimini Bay Rod and Gun Club. Built in the early 1920s, it did a flourishing business until a hurricane wiped it out later in that decade. It was never rebuilt.

If you're on the trail of Papa Hemingway, you'll want to visit the **Compleat Angler,** King's Highway (☎ 242/347-3122), where there is a museum of Hemingway memorabilia. The collection of prints and writings describes the times he spent in Bimini, mainly from 1935 to 1937. The prints are posted in the sitting room downstairs. Much of this memorabilia makes interesting browsing. There are a number of books by Hemingway in the library collection. If you haven't read it, you might want to pick up his novel *Islands in the Stream,* which is partly devoted to Bimini.

If you want to cross over to **South Bimini,** like Ponce de León did looking for the Fountain of Youth, you can take a ferry, costing $3 and leaving every 20 minutes, from Government Dock. The ferry ride takes about 10 minutes or so.

Once you land on South Bimini, you can rent a taxi to see the island's limited attractions for about $15. There's not a lot to see, but you are likely to hear some "tall tales" worth the cab fare.

In terms of **shopping** in Bimini, the Bimini Big Game Fishing Club & Hotel, King's Highway, has some of the best duty-free liquor buys in town. If you're a souvenir collector, ask at the front office for T-shirts, sunglasses, coffee mugs, and Big Game Club hats.

BIMINI AFTER DARK

You can dance to a Goombay beat or try to find some disco music. Most people have a leisurely dinner, drink a lot in one of the local taverns, and go back to their hotel

Myths of Bimini

Bimini has long been shrouded in myths, none greater than the one claiming that the lost continent of Atlantis lies off the shores of North Bimini. This legend grew because of the weirdly shaped rock formations that lie submerged in about 30 feet of water near the shoreline. Pilots flying over North Bimini have reported what they envision as a "lost highway" under the sea. This myth continues, and many scuba divers are attracted to North Bimini to explore these rocks.

Ponce de León came to South Bimini looking for that legendary Fountain of Youth. He never found it, but people still come to South Bimini in search of it. Near the turn of the century it was reported that a religious sect came here to "take the waters." Supposedly, there was a bubbling fountain, or at least a spring, in those days. If you arrive on South Bimini and seem interested enough, a local guide (for a fee) will be only too happy to show you "the exact spot" where the Fountain of Youth once bubbled.

rooms by midnight so they can get up early to continue pursuing the elusive "big one" the next morning. Every bar in Alice Town is likely to claim that it was Hemingway's favorite. He did hit quite a few of them, in fact. There's rarely a cover charge anywhere unless some special entertainment is being offered.

The Compleat Angler Hotel. King's Hwy., Alice Town. ☎ **242/347-3122.**

Constructed of Prohibition-era rum kegs, the bar is host to an unconventional clientele who come to dance to the nightly calypso band and drink Goombay Smashes. This is the favorite watering hole for every visiting Hemingway buff. Ossie Brown, the bartender (he's also the manager), makes the best planter's punch in The Bahamas, and he challenges anyone to make a better one. The place, as mentioned, is filled with Hemingway memorabilia, and it's open daily from 11am "until...."

Bimini Big Game Fishing Club & Hotel. King's Hwy., Alice Town. ☎ **242/347-3391.**

Beginning at midmorning and lasting until midnight at least, the bars of this previously recommended hotel are the most frequented places in town. Tall tales of the big one that got away fill the air. The Big Game Sports Bar (see "Where to Dine," above) starts serving its famed conch pizza at noon. No less than four TV sets are positioned for your favorite sports program, or you may want to enjoy a hand of cards. It's the best room in which to entertain yourself during those lazy days in Bimini. The poolside Barefoot Bar, open from midmorning to late afternoon, serves favorite island drinks and ice-cold beer. Off the main dining room of the Gulfstream Restaurant is the Gulfstream Bar, featuring Ratti, the island's best known calypsonian, singing the songs of the island and strumming them on his guitar. Naturally, since Bacardi owns the place, all the rum punches are made with Bacardi rums.

TIPPING A GLASS AT THE END OF THE WORLD

One of the almost mandatory requirements of any trip to Bimini is to have a drink at the **End of the World Bar** on King's Highway in Alice Town. When you get here, you may think you're in the wrong place—it's just a waterfront shack with sawdust on the floor. It was the late New York congressman, Adam Clayton Powell, who put this bar on the map in the 1960s. Between stints in Washington battling Congress and preaching at the Abyssinian Baptist Church in Harlem, the controversial congressman could be found sitting at a table here. Regardless of what Powell's fellow lawmakers thought of him, he was a hero locally, and many people of Bimini still remember him. While the bar doesn't attract the media attention it did in Powell's heyday, it's still going strong as a local favorite, and everybody takes a felt marker and signs his or her name. It's open daily from 9am to 3am.

2 The Berry Islands

A dangling chain of cays and islets on the eastern edge of the Great Bahama Bank, the unspoiled and serene Berry Islands begin 35 miles northwest of New Providence (Nassau), 150 miles east of Miami. This 30-island archipelago is known to sailors, fishers, yachtspeople, Jack Nicklaus, and a Rockefeller or two, as well as to the beach-combers who explore its uninhabited reaches.

As a center of fishing, the Berry Islands are second only to Bimini. At the tip of the Tongue of the Ocean, called TOTO, world-record-setting big-game fish are found, along with endless flats (the shallow bodies of water near the shore where bonefish congregate). In the "Berries" you can find your own tropical paradise islet, enjoying—totally isolated and sans wardrobe—the white-sand beaches and palm-fringed shores. Some of the best shell collecting in The Bahamas is found on the beaches of the Berry Islands and in their shallow-water flats.

The main islands are, beginning in the north, Great Stirrup Cay, Cistern Cay, Great Harbour Cay, Anderson Cay, Haines Cay, Hoffmans Cay, Bond's Cay, Sandy Cay, Whale Cay, and Chub Cay.

The largest island within the Berry Islands is Great Harbour Cay, which sprawls over 3,800 acres of sand, rock, and scrub. Development here received a great deal of publicity when Douglas Fairbanks Jr. was connected with its investors. It became a multimillion-dollar resort for jet-setters who occupied waterfront town houses and villas overlooking the golf course or marina. There are 7 1/2 miles of almost solitary beachfront. Once Cary Grant, Brigitte Bardot, and other stars romped on this beach.

Bond's Cay, a bird sanctuary in the south, and tiny Frazer's Hog Cay (stock is still raised here) are both privately owned. An English company used to operate a coco-nut and sisal plantation on Whale Cay, also near the southern tip.

Sponge fishers and their families inhabit some of the islands. One of the very small cays, lying north of Frazer's Hog Cay and Whale Cay, has, in our opinion, the most unappetizing name in the Bahamian archipelago: Cockroach Cay.

GETTING THERE Great Harbour Cay is an official point of entry for The Bahamas if you're flying from a foreign territory such as the United States. You can fly to the Great Harbour Cay airstrip.

Charter flights are arranged from South Florida. These include **Tropical Diversions** (☎ **954/921-9084**), flying from Fort Lauderdale to Great Harbour Cay, usu-ally in a five-passenger, twin-engine Piper Seneca and **Island Express** (☎ **954/359-0380**), which also operates charters from Fort Lauderdale, winging in to Chub Cay Airport.

If you're contemplating the mail-boat sea-voyage route, the MV *Champion II* leaves Potter's Cay Dock in Nassau weekly on Tuesday at 7pm, heading for the Berry Is-lands. Inquire at the Potter's Cay Dock for an up-to-the-minute report (contact the dockmaster at ☎ **242/393-1064**).

ESSENTIALS The Great Harbour Cay Medical Clinic is at Bullock's Harbour on Great Harbour Cay (☎ 242/367-8400). The police station is also at Bullock's Harbour (☎ 242/367-8373).

GREAT HARBOUR CAY

An estimated 700 residents live on Great Harbour Cay, making it the most populated island of the Berry chain. Its main settlement is Bullock's Harbour, which might be called the "capital of the Berry Islands." The cay is about 1 1/2 miles wide and some 8 miles long. There isn't much in town: a grocery store and some restaurants. Most visitors arrive to stay at the Great Harbour Cay Yacht Club & Marina (see "Where to Stay & Dine," below), outside of town. Fishers are especially fond of the place.

Great Harbour Cay lies between Grand Bahama Island and New Providence (Nassau). It's 60 miles northwest of Nassau and 150 miles east of Miami, about an hour away from Miami by plane or half a day by powerboat. Unlike most islands in The Bahamas, the island isn't flat but contains rolling hills.

Deep-sea fishing possibilities abound here, including billfish, dolphinfish, king mackerel, and wahoo. Light-tackle bottom fishing is also good, netting yellowtail, snapper, barracuda, and triggerfish, as well as plenty of grouper. Bonefishing here is among the best in the world.

The Great Harbour Cay marina is called "world class," with some 80 slips and all the amenities. Some of Florida's fanciest yachts pull in here. When you tire of fishing, there are 8 miles of white-sand beaches. There is also a nine-hole golf course, designed by Joe Lee, plus four clay tennis courts.

WHERE TO STAY & DINE

Great Harbour Cay Yacht Club & Marina. Great Harbour Cay, Berry Island, The Bahamas (mailing address: P.O. Box N-918, Nassau, or 3512 N. Ocean Dr., Hollywood, FL 33019). ☎ **800/343-7256** or 242/367-8838. Fax 242/367-8115. 18 units. A/C TV. Year-round, $90–$350 double. AE, MC, V.

The two-level waterfront town houses here overlook the marina. Each has its own private dock, topped off with a garage and patio. Other units are on the beach. Although privately owned, these accommodations are rented on a daily or weekly basis by the resort. Of course, each unit is individually furnished by the owner, whose taste may not necessarily be yours. The town houses have a light, airy feeling, with some 1,600 square feet of living space. Each has 2 bedrooms and 2 1/2 baths and is suitable for up to 6 people. Fully equipped kitchens are featured. Beach villas, covered in cedar shakes, have tile floors and a Mediterranean-type decor. They can be rented in various configurations—from studio apartments to two-bedroom units. Daily maid service is included.

Dining facilities include the Wharf, serving breakfast and lunch; Basil's Bar and Restaurant at the end of the marina, serving three meals a day; and the Tamboo Club, at the west end of the marina—open Wednesday through Monday for drinks and dinner only.

CHUB CAY

Named after a species of fish that thrives in nearby waters, Chub Cay is well-known to sportfishing enthusiasts. A self-contained hideaway with a devoted clientele, it's the southernmost of the Berry Islands, separating the mainland of South Florida from the commercial frenzy of Nassau.

Chub Cay's development began in the late 1950s as the strictly private (and rather Spartan) enclave of a group of Texas-based anglers and investors. It was originally uninhabited, but over the years a staff was imported, dormitory-style housing was built for them, and the island's most famous man-made feature (its state-of-the-art, 90-slip marina) was constructed within the 979-acre island's most prominent natural feature, a sheltered lagoon.

After recovering from severe damage inflicted in 1992 by Hurricane Andrew, Chub Cay is little more than a tranquil, scrub-covered sand spit with awesome amounts of marine hardware, a dozen well-accessorized private homes, the above-mentioned marina, and a complex of buildings devoted to the Chub Cay Club (see below). Today, membership in the club begins at around $2,000 a year and grants reduced rates for marina slip rental, boat repairs, and hotel room and villa rental. Non-members, however, are welcome to use the facilities and rent rooms at the rates listed below.

There's a liquor store and a yachties' commissary on the island, an outlet for the sale of marine supplies, and a concrete runway for landing anything up to and including a 737. Most visitors reach Chub Cay by private yacht from the Florida mainland, but if you prefer to charter your fishing craft on Chub Cay, you'll find a mini-armada of suitable craft at your disposal. Island Express Airlines (☎ 954/359-0380) flies to Chub Cay from Fort Lauderdale Thursday through Sunday at 8am and 1:30pm. Charter flights can be arranged with the help of the Chub Cay Club's desk staff. If you opt to fly here, travel light; there's a baggage allowance of no more than 50 pounds per passenger.

The water temperature around Chub Cay averages a tepid 80° to 85°F year-round, even at relatively deep depths. There's only a small tidal change, and under normal conditions, there is no swell or noticeable currents in offshore waters.

Many divers have waxed enthusiastic over the dive spots of Chub Cay, including Chub Wall and Mamma Rhoda Rock. Despite the dozens of examples of rare coral that ring the island, remember that it's forbidden by Bahamian authorities to bring back coral as souvenirs. In fact, it violates local ecological laws to take anything from the sea for purposes other than obtaining food.

It is said that one reason that fishing is so good near Chub Cay is because bait fish and lures are scented by hungry pursuers swimming in from TOTO (Tongue of the Ocean). They include dolphinfish, mako sharks, barracudas, wahoos, and the 300-pound blue marlins described by Hemingway in *Islands in the Stream*. Unknown to these big fish, yet another hunter of the human kind is waiting.

WHERE TO STAY & DINE

Chub Cay Club. Chub Cay, Berry Islands, The Bahamas. ☎ **800/662-8555** or 242/325-1490. Fax 242/322-5199. (For expedition of all forms of mail, write Chub Cay Club, P.O. Box 661067, Miami Springs, FL 33266. ☎ **305/445-7830**.) 24 rms, 8 villas, 2 town houses. A/C MINIBAR TV. Year-round, $110–$150 double; $300 one-bedroom villa for two with kitchen; $400 two-bedroom villa for four with kitchen; $450 duplex town house for four with kitchen; $500 three-bedroom villa for up to six with kitchen. Discounts available for stays of a week or more. AE, MC, V.

Simple, breezy, uncluttered, and comfortable, these air-conditioned accommodations are the only available option on all of Chub Cay. It prides itself on its marina, its freshwater swimming pools, and the many sandy beaches nearby. Throughout the resort, there's a nautical, laid-back kind of feeling, and a clublike atmosphere. Don't expect inspired architecture. Buildings throughout the islands are functional, weatherproof, and not particularly stylish. None of the rooms has a phone, although there are phone facilities available at the reception desk. Their absence enhances the feeling of isolation, a welcome relief to many of the clients.

Dining/Entertainment: There's a restaurant (the Harbour House), with its own bar, as well as the Cay Bar set beside the pool, and the Hilltop Bar on the island's highest elevation. The latter contains a TV for sports broadcasts, pool tables, and occasional bouts of live music.

Services: Fishing guides, diving guides, laundry, baby-sitting.

Facilities: Scuba diving, snorkeling, Laundromat, two tennis courts, two swimming pools, shopping boutique.

3 Andros

The largest island in The Bahamas, Andros is also one of the biggest unexplored tracts of land in the Western Hemisphere. Mostly flat, its 2,300 square miles are riddled with lakes and creeks, and most of the local residents, who still indulge in fire dances and go on wild boar hunts on occasion, live along the shore.

The most mysterious island in The Bahamas, Andros is 100 miles long and 40 miles wide. Its interior consists of a dense, tropical forest, really rugged bush, and mangrove country. The marshy and relatively uninhabited west coast is called the "Mud," and the east coast is paralleled for 120 miles by the second-largest underwater barrier reef in the world. The reef drops to more than a mile into the Tongue of the Ocean, or TOTO. On the eastern shore, this "tongue" is 142 miles long and 1,000 fathoms deep.

Lying 170 miles southeast of Miami and 30 miles west of Nassau, Andros, although spoken as if it were one island, is actually three major land areas: **North Andros, Middle Andros,** and **South Andros.** Ferries, operated free by the Bahamian government, ply back and forth over the waters separating Mangrove Cay from South Andros. At the end of the road in North Andros, private arrangements can be made to have a boat take you over to Mangrove Cay. In spite of its size, Andros is very thinly populated, its residents numbering around 5,000, although the tourist population swells it a bit. The temperature range here averages from 72° to 81°F.

The Spaniards, who came this way in the 16th century looking for slaves, called the island La Isla del Espíritu Santo or the "Island of the Holy Spirit." The name didn't catch on, although it came from the belief that the Holy Spirit dwells over water, with which Andros is abundantly supplied—Andros constantly ships the precious liquid to water-scarce New Providence (Nassau) in barges.

The name used for the island today is believed by some experts to have come from Sir Edmund Andros, a British commander.

You won't find the western side of Andros much written about in yachting guides, as it is almost unapproachable by boat due to the tricky shoals. The east coast, however, has miles of unspoiled beaches and is studded with little villages. Hotels have been built here that range from simple guest cottages to dive resorts to fishing camps. "Creeks" (we'd call them rivers) intersect the island at its midpoint. Also called "bights," they range in width from 5 to 25 miles, and they are dotted with tiny cays and islets.

Few people draw comparisons between overly developed Paradise Island and underdeveloped Andros. However, their tourism industries have a common ancestor, Dr. Axel Wenner-Gren, a Swedish industrialist who invested in what was then Hog Island (renamed Paradise Island). Dr. Wenner-Gren also built the Andros Yacht Club, to the south of Fresh Creek on Andros. That now defunct club began to attract the island's first tourists in the years following World War II.

The fishing at Andros is famous, establishing records for blue marlin caught offshore. Skindivers report that the coral reefs are among the most beautiful in the world.

A word of warning: Be sure to bring along plenty of mosquito repellent.

GETTING THERE   By Plane   Reaching Andros is not that difficult. **Bahamasair** (☎ **800/222-4262** in the U.S.) has flights to the airports at Andros Town and San

The Three-Toed Bahamian Elf

One of the legends of Andros island is that aborigines live in the interior. These were thought to be a lost tribe of native Arawaks—remnants of the archipelago's original inhabitants, who were exterminated by the Spanish centuries ago. However, low-flying planes, looking for evidence of human settlements, have not turned up any indication to support this far-fetched assertion. But who can dispute that chickcharnies (red-eyed Bahamian elves with three toes, feathers, and beards) live on the island? Even the demise of Neville Chamberlain's ill-fated sisal plantation was blamed on these mischievous devils.

The chickcharnie once struck terror into the hearts of superstitious islanders. They were supposed to live in the depths of the Androsian wilderness, making their nests in the tops of two intertwined palm trees. Tales are told of how many a woodsman in the old days endured hardship and misery because he thoughtlessly felled the trees that served as stilts for a chickcharnie nest. Like the leprechauns of Ireland, the chickcharnies belong solely to Andros. They are the Bahamian version of the elves, goblins, fairies, and duppies of other lands. Children may be threatened with them if they fail to behave, and business or domestic calamity is immediately attributed to their malevolent activities.

The origin of the legend is shrouded in mystery. One story has it that the tales began in the late 19th century when a Nassau hunting enthusiast who wanted to protect his duck-hunting grounds in Andros invented the malicious elves to frighten off unwanted interlopers. Another has it that the myth was brought to The Bahamas by bands of Seminoles fleeing Florida in the early 1840s to escape the depredations of white settlers. Some of the Seminoles settled on the northern tip of Andros. But the most probable explanation is one that traces the chickcharnie to a once-living creature—an extinct 3-foot-high flightless barn owl (*Tyto pollens*)—that used to inhabit The Bahamas and West Indies.

According to The Bahamas National Trust, the local conservation authority, such a bird, "screeching, hissing and clacking its bills in characteristic barn owl fashion, hopping onto its victims or pouncing on them from low tree limbs, would have been a memorable sight. And a frightening one."

The species may have survived here into historical times, and Andros, being the largest Bahamian landmass, was probably able to sustain *Tyto pollens* longer than the smaller islands. It is probable that the early settlers on Andros encountered such beasts, and it's possible that *Tyto pollens* was the inspiration for the chickcharnie. In any event, chickcharnie tales are still told in Andros, and there is no doubt that they will live on as a fascinating part of The Bahamas' cultural legacy.

Andros twice daily. Four weekly flights land at Congo Town on South Andros. It is only a 15-minute flight from Nassau to, say, Andros Town. There is also a small airstrip on Mangrove Cay. Flight schedules are subject to change.

If you're going to Small Hope Bay Lodge, there is a 1-hour flight service from Miami International to Andros Town.

Warning: Make sure you know where you're going in Andros. For example, if you land on South Andros and you've been booked in a hotel at Nicholl's Town, you'll find connections nearly impossible at times (both ferryboats and a rough haul across a bad highway).

Taxi drivers—what few there are—know when the planes from Nassau are going to land, and they drive out to the airports, hoping to drum up some business. Taxis are most often shared. A typical fare from Andros Town Airport to Small Hope Bay Lodge is about $20.

By Boat   Many locals, along with a few adventurous visitors, use the mail boats as a means of reaching Andros; the trip takes 5 to 7 hours across some beautiful waters.

North Andros is serviced by the MV *Lisa J. II,* a mail boat that departs Potter's Cay Dock in Nassau heading for Morgan's Bluff, Mastic Point, and Nicholl's Town. It departs Nassau on Wednesday, returning to Nassau on Tuesday.

The MV *Moxey* departs Nassau on Monday, calling at Long Bay Cays, Kemps Bay, and the Bluff on South Andros. It heads back to Nassau on Wednesday.

For details about sailing and costs, contact the dockmaster at Potter's Cay Dock in Nassau (☎ **242/393-1064**).

GETTING AROUND   Transportation can be a big problem on Andros. If you have to go somewhere, it's best to use one of the local taxi drivers.

By Car   What cars there are to rent are in North Andros. These are few and far between, owing to the high costs of shipping cars to Andros. The weather also takes a great toll on the cars that are brought in (the salt in the air erodes metal), so no U.S. car-rental agencies are represented. Your best bet is to ask at your hotel to see what's available. It's not really recommended that you drive on Andros because roads are mainly unpaved and in bad condition, and gasoline stations are scarce. Outlets for car rentals come and go faster here than anybody can keep up. Currently **AMKLCO Car Rental** at Fresh Creek (☎ **242/368-2056**) rents a few cars, costing from $75 to $80 daily, with a $200 deposit required. Mileage is unlimited "unless you go too much."

FAST FACTS: Andros

Banks   These are rare on Andros. There is one, the Canadian Imperial Bank of Commerce (☎ **242/329-2382**), in San Andros. It is open Wednesday from 10am to 2pm.

Clothing   Dress is casual, and don't come to Andros expecting to catch up on your dry cleaning. If you need shirts and blouses washed and ironed, ask at your hotel. Even if they don't have a service themselves, they usually know someone in the community who "takes in wash."

Mail   The island has no big post office as such, although there is a post-handling office in the Commissioner's Office in Nicholl's Town on North Andros (☎ **242/ 329-2034**). Hours are Monday through Friday from 9am to 5:30pm. Hotel desks will sell you Bahamian stamps. Make sure you mark cards and letters airmail; otherwise, you'll return home before they do. Each little hamlet in Andros has a store that serves as the post office.

Medical Care   Government-run clinics are at North Andros (☎ **242/329-2055**) and at Central Andros (☎ **242/368-2038**). Bring along whatever drugs (legal ones) or medicines you'll need while visiting Andros. Local supplies are very limited.

Police   Call the police on North Andros at ☎ **919**; on Central Andros at ☎ **242/ 368-2626**; and on South Andros at ☎ **242/369-0083.**

Telephone   Service is available only at the front desks of hotels.

Traveler's Checks   Your hotel probably will be able to cash traveler's checks for you, but if not, there is one bank on Andros (see "Banks," above).

WHERE TO STAY

Chances are your hotel will be in North Andros, in either Andros Town or Nicholl's Town.

North Andros is the most developed of the three major Andros islands. **Nicholl's Town** is a colorful old settlement with some 600 people and several places serving local foods. Most visitors come to Nicholl's Town to buy supplies at a shopping complex.

Directly to the south is **Mastic Point,** which was founded in 1781. If you ask around, you'll be shown to a couple of concrete-sided dives that offer spareribs and Goombay music. To the north of Nicholl's Town is **Morgan's Bluff,** namesake of Sir Henry Morgan (a pirate later knighted by the British monarch).

Andros Town, with its abandoned docks, is another hamlet, lying about a 29-mile drive south of Nicholl's Town. The major reason most visitors come to Andros Town is either to stay at the Small Hope Bay Lodge (see below) or to avail themselves of its facilities. The biggest retail industry, Androsia batik, is in the area, too. The scuba diving—minutes away on the barrier reef—is what lures the world to this tiny place. Many people come here just for the shelling, as well.

On the opposite side of the water is **Coakley Town.** If you're driving, before you get to Andros Town you may want to stop and spend some restful hours on the beach at the hamlet of Staniard Creek, another old settlement on Andros. There's a South Seas aura here.

Now moving south to the second major landmass, **Central Andros** is smaller than either North or South Andros. It's also the least built-up. The island is studded with hundreds upon hundreds of palm trees. Queen's Highway runs along the eastern coastline, but the only thing about this road that's regal is its name. In some $4^{1}/_{2}$ miles you can practically travel the whole island. Talk about sleepy—this place drowses, and for that very reason many people come here to get away from it all. They don't find much in the way of accommodations. There are a few guest houses a half mile from the Mangrove Cay Airport. Boating, fishing, scuba diving, and snorkeling are the popular sports practiced here.

Another hamlet (don't blink as you pass through or you'll miss it) is **Moxey Town,** where you'll see conch being unloaded from the fishing boats.

The third and last major land area, **South Andros** is the home of the wonderfully named Congo Town. The pace here is that of an escargot on a marathon. The Queen's Highway, lined in part with pink-and-white conch shells, runs for about 25 miles or so. The island, as yet undiscovered, has some of the best beaches in The Bahamas, and you can enjoy them almost by yourself.

NORTH ANDROS
Cargill Creek

Cargill Creek Fishing Lodge. Cargill Creek, Andros, The Bahamas. ☎ **242/368-5129.** Fax 242/368-5046. 11 rms, 3 cottages. A/C TV. Year-round (AP), $50 double, per person. AE, MC, V. Closed July–Aug.

One of the best accessorized hotels in the Andros, this 1990 fishing lodge opened on a 7-acre tract containing many fruit trees. At times there are so many fly fishers and spin fishers staying at the lodge that it looks like one of those famed Ernest Hemingway look-alike contests staged every year in Key West, Florida. The hotel complex consists of white stucco buildings with marine blue trim set directly on the waterfront. Accommodations are furnished with Florida tropical pieces. Cottages contain two full bedrooms, two baths, and a sitting room.

Meals are served in a pleasantly airy restaurant, trimmed with Andros cedar and set close to the waterfront pier and pool with patio. A sample dinner menu of simple Bahamian dining might include conch fritters, broiled grouper with a green salad, and rice and pigeon peas, followed by pineapple upside-down cake.

The resort specializes in guided bonefishing on the flats in and around the bights of Andros. Trips can be arranged on-site for about $300 per person. For reservations call the lodge Monday through Saturday from 9am to 5pm or Sunday from 10am to 3pm.

Andros Town

Landmark Hotel & Restaurant. Andros Town, Andros, The Bahamas. ☎ and fax **242/ 368-2082.** 15 rms. A/C TV. Winter, $60 double. Off-season, $50 double. No credit cards.

This unpretentious place is a candidate for one of the most laid-back hotels on Andros, where the competition is really stiff for that title. Check in only if you're the self-sufficient type who doesn't demand a lot of service. Rooms are sheathed in planks of pinewood and feature modern windows, big closets, private bath, and balcony. Calabash Bay Beach is within a 5-minute walk of the hotel, and guests rarely lack for companionship because of the lively bar and restaurant (Carmetta's) on the premises. The house drink, the Andros Special, is memorable. Full and low-cost meals are served throughout the day. This is one of the most popular nightlife spots on the island. Some of its patrons are nightclubbing students from Andros Island's branch of the Marine Biology Studies Center.

○ **Lighthouse Yacht Club & Marina.** Andros Town, Andros, The Bahamas. ☎ **800/ 835-1019** or 242/368-2308. Fax 242/368-2300. 20 rms. A/C TV. Year-round, $150 double. MAP $42 per person extra. AE, DC, DISC, MC, V.

Infinitely superior to the Landmark Hotel, this complex lies at the mouth of Fresh Creek and features an 18-slip marina. A favorite of the yachting crowd, who desperately needed such a place in Andros, the hotel rents comfortably furnished bedrooms, each with air-conditioning and a private bath. Scuba divers, snorkelers, and fishers make ample use of the beach and the offshore waters, as the hotel lies near one of the world's largest barrier reefs and the deep Tongue of the Ocean. Fishing charters are readily available, and scuba diving and snorkeling can easily be arranged. The package rates offered by the hotel, in addition to room and meals, include airport pick-up. The hotel also has a swimming pool and a good restaurant serving Bahamian and American dishes. In addition to the marina, the hotel also offers two clay tennis courts lit at night.

Fresh Creek

Chickcharnie Hotel. Fresh Creek, Andros Town, Andros, The Bahamas. ☎ **242/368-2025.** 16 rms (10 with bath). A/C TV. Year-round, $40 double without bath, $60–$75 double with bath. MC, V.

Charmingly named after those mischievous Bahamian elves, this hotel is 3 miles east of the Andros Town Airport on the waterfront. A simple two-story concrete structure, the no-frills hotel attracts fishers and an occasional business traveler. Eight of the rooms have air-conditioning, private baths, and TVs with satellite hookups. The other rooms have sinks with hot and cold running water, access to a bathroom off the hallway, and ceiling fans. Island-born Charles Gay, the owner, runs a grocery store on the ground floor of the building. In the hotel's spartan dining room, three meals are served daily: fish, chicken, lobster, or conch.

If you'd like to go fishing, the best person to contact is Bill Braynen (the hotel will make the arrangements). He owns 10 boats, charging from $120 for a half day or

$240 for a full day in a medium-size bonefishing craft. The cost is $300 for a full day of fishing above the reefs in a 25-foot boat.

✪ **Small Hope Bay Lodge.** P.O. Box 21667, Fort Lauderdale, FL 33335. ☎ **800/223-6961** in the U.S. and Canada, or 242/368-2014. Fax 242/368-2015. 20 cabins. Winter (AP), $330 double. Off-season (AP), $300 double. AE, MC, V.

At Fresh Creek, this is the premier diving and fishing resort of Andros, and one of the best in the entire Bahamas. It's an intimate and cozy beachside cottage colony, engulfed by tall coconut palms. The resort is now the oldest dive operation in the country. Its name comes from a prediction (so far, accurate) from pirate Henry Morgan, who claimed there was "small hope" of anyone finding the treasure he'd buried on Andros. There is a spacious living and dining room where guests congregate for conversations and meals. Andros Town Airport is a 10-minute taxi ride from the lodge. The beach is at the doorstep. Cabins are made of coral rock and Andros pine and are decorated with Androsia batik fabrics. Honeymooners like to order breakfast served on their water bed.

For groups of three or more, the resort has a limited number of family cottages, featuring two separate rooms connected by a single bath. Single travelers have a choice of staying in a family cottage with private accommodations (which is the same as per-person double occupancy) or staying in a regular cottage with private bath, to which $45 per person is added nightly.

The bar is an old boat, dubbed *Panacea*. The food is wholesome, plentiful, and good—conch chowder, lobster, hot johnnycake. The chef will even cook your catch for you. Lunch is a buffet; dinner, a choice of seafood and meat every night. Children under 12 dine in the game room. A picnic lunch can be prepared for those who request it. Drinks are offered on a rambling patio built out over the sea. Nightlife is spontaneous—dancing in the lounge or on the patio, watching underwater movies and slides. Definitely don't wear a tie at dinner.

When you're making a reservation, inquire about special dive packages. This is the lodge's specialty (see "Water Sports & Other Outdoor Activities," below). The owners have been diving for more than 3 decades, and they have sufficient equipment, divers, boats, and flexibility to give guests any diving they want, whether it be shallow or deep. If you'd rather fish, the lodge can hook you up with an expert guide, especially for bonefishing.

Nicholl's Town

Conch Sound Resort Inn. P.O. Box 23029, Nicholl's Town, Andros, The Bahamas. ☎ **242/329-2060** or 242/329-2341. 7 rms, 6 cottages with kitchens. A/C TV. Year-round $80 double; $190–$200 double occupancy of a cottage with kitchen. No credit cards.

This is a basic motel and cottage complex set within a pine forest on the northern outskirts of Nicholl's Town, a 5-minute walk to the beach. Built in 1988, the establishment consists of a compound of coral-colored cement-block buildings that include a half dozen motel rooms and a half dozen cottages with kitchens. Furnishings are for the most part Formica-covered pieces. Each room has its own satellite TV reception. Maid service and complimentary shuttle-bus service to and from the local airport are included in the price. There's a restaurant and bar on the premises open daily from 9am to midnight.

Green Windows Inn. Box 23076, Nicholl's Town, Andros. ☎ **242/329-2194.** Fax 242/329-2016. 11 rms. TV. Year-round, $65 double without bath; $81 double with bath. AE.

Kenny Robinson and her husband, Patrick, run this hotel set in a lush landscape of fruit trees and palms, where guests like to take their after-meal walks. The rooms are on the second floor of the two-story inn, and two of them have private baths and air-conditioning. All the accommodations come with satellite TV, and the rooms without private baths have ceiling fans. The restaurant caters only to hotel guests, with mainly seafood and local food cooked to order. Dinner runs anywhere from $14. The beach is only a 5-minute walk from the inn, and the Robinsons can arrange bonefishing and snorkeling trips. There's a small grocery store and a car-rental agency on site.

Behring Point

Charlie's Haven. Behring Pt., Andros, The Bahamas. ☎ **242/368-4087.** 10 rms. A/C. Year-round (AP), from $130 double. No credit cards.

Located about 25 miles from Andros Town Airport and near some of the best bone-fishing banks in the world, this is a remote outpost for fishers who like rustic hospitality. Many anglers have tried other fishing spots in The Bahamas, but once they find this place they return here again and again. Its main appeal for many patrons, most of whom are men (although families sometimes come, too), is its isolation and rather rawboned qualities. Many tall tales of fish that got away are swapped over the informal meals served here. There's occasionally live entertainment, as well as a separate bar. The concrete building sits on the edge of the sound separating North Andros from Mangrove Cay. The air-conditioned bedrooms have ceiling fans, simple, white walls, and a minimum of furniture.

Fishing can be arranged with Charles Smith, patriarch of the family that owns the hotel and one of the region's most respected bonefishing guides. Mr. Smith's sons, some or all of whom you're likely to meet here, include Henry, Andy, and Prescott.

SOUTH ANDROS

Emerald Palms By-the-Sea. Driggs Hill, P.O. Box 800, South Andros, The Bahamas. ☎ **800/ 742-4276** or 242/369-2661. Fax 242/369-2667. 20 rms. A/C MINIBAR TV. Winter, $110 double; $190 suites. Off-season, $100 double; $160 suites. MAP $40 per person extra. AE, MC, V.

Staying at this laid-back place is a lot like staying at a beachside ranch. The accommodations are set on 5 miles of beachfront on an island containing 10,000 palm trees. The hotel is informally casual—a place to get away from urban life for a sojourn on a white-sand beach. Guests are treated like members of the family.

Scattered over the palm-studded property are hammocks, a freshwater swimming pool, a tennis court, and shuffleboard. The dining room features Bahamian seafood. Outdoor steak barbecues and seafood buffets are sometimes held. The rooms are large and comfortable. This resort has some of the fanciest decorations in Andros, and some of the most special amenities, including VCRs, lanai-style rooms, four-poster beds with plantation house mosquito netting—all in all, a relaxed, tropical ambience. South Bight marina is $1^1/_2$ miles away, serving as a yacht anchorage for anyone who wants to arrive by boat. The hotel is 2 miles from the Congo Town Airport, and you can rent a car or bicycle if you wish.

WHERE TO DINE

Andros follows the rest of The Bahamas in its cuisine (see chapter 2). Conch, in all its many variations, is the staple of most diets, along with heaping peas 'n' rice and johnnycake, and pig or chicken souse.

The best places to dine are at the major hotels, including those previously recommended: the **Chickcharnie Hotel,** Fresh Creek, near Andros Town (☎ **242/ 368-2025**); and if you're in South Andros, **Emerald Palms By-the-Sea,** outside Congo Town (☎ **242/369-2661**). Most guests book into these hotels on the

Modified American Plan, which frees them to shop around for lunch. At any of these hotels a dinner will run around $25 to $30 per person.

If you're touring the island during the day, you'll find some local spots that serve food. If business has been slow at some of these little places, however, you might find nothing on the stove. You take your chances.

NORTH ANDROS
Cargill Creek
Dig-Dig's Restaurant. Cargill Creek. ☎ **242/368-5097.** Reservations required for dinner. Main courses $15–$26. No credit cards. Lunch or dinner by prearrangement only. AMERICAN/ BAHAMIAN.

If you're heading south, you might want to know about one of the most charming restaurants in the region. Set in a pleasant and cozy pink house, ringed with a garden beside the main highway, this establishment is inextricably tied to the personalities of its owners, Elizabeth (Liz) and Alton Bain. The cuisine reflects the national origins (Canada and The Bahamas, respectively) of the two and includes cracked conch, grouper cutlets, crayfish, and chicken. An appetizer is included with the main course. Your menu will be prearranged, and your arrival will probably be celebrated with a jug of the house special drink (a mixture of gin, sweetened condensed milk, and fresh coconut water) set beside your waiting table. Because they get so little business in these parts—especially from drop-in clients searching for a luncheon or dining spot—the owners ask you to call them if you'd like to have them prepare a lunch or dinner for you.

Nicholl's Town
Big Josh Seafood Restaurant and Lounge. Lowe Sound. ☎ **242/329-7517.** Main courses $7–$15. AE, MC, V. Daily 7–11am, 1–4pm, and 5–11pm. SEAFOOD.

Like the bonefishers who hang out at Lowe Sound, you'll find good local dishes at this place. The restaurant was established years ago by the late Joshua Bootle, a legendary bonefishing guide. The restaurant is managed today by his widow, Malvese, who still does most of the cooking herself. She turns out her own versions of chicken, pork, steak, crayfish, and conch—but mostly the catch of the day. The simple cookery is the same as she's always served her family.

BEACHES, WATER SPORTS & OTHER OUTDOOR ACTIVITIES
Golf and tennis fans should go elsewhere, but those who want some of the best bonefishing and scuba diving in The Bahamas should flock to Andros.

BEACHES
The eastern shore of Andros, stretching for some 100 miles, is an almost uninterrupted palm grove opening onto beaches of white or beige sand.

FISHING
As mentioned previously, Andros is called the "Bonefish Capital of the World." The actual capital is Lowe Sound Settlement, a tiny hamlet with only one road. It lies 4 miles north of Nicholl's Town. Fishers come here to hire bonefish guides.

Regardless of what area you're staying in—North, Central, or South Andros— someone at your hotel can arrange a fishing expedition.

Charlie's Haven. Behring Pt., North Andros. ☎ **242/368-4087.**

Already recommended as a rustic hotel, Charlie's Haven is one of the best places for fishing. Bonefishing trips are arranged for $130 for a half day, $240 for a full day.

Small Hope Bay Lodge. Andros Town, North Andros. ☎ **242/368-2014.**

This lodge also arranges fishing. A guide will take you where there is superb bonefishing. They also offer fly, reef, and deep-sea fishing. Tackle and bait are provided.

SNORKELING & SCUBA DIVING

As mentioned before, scuba divers and snorkelers are attracted to Andros because of the barrier reef, which lies on the eastern shore along the Tongue of the Ocean. Blue holes, coral gardens, drop-offs, wall-and-reef diving, and wrecks make it even more enticing. The best dive operations are previewed below.

❂ **Small Hope Bay Lodge.** Fresh Creek, Andros Town, Central Andros. ☎ **800/223-6961** in the U.S. and Canada, or 242/368-2014.

This lodge lies a short distance from the barrier reef, with its still-unexplored caves and ledges. A staff of trained dive instructors at the lodge caters to levels of expertise from beginners to experienced divers. (The staff members have various credentials, including certification from some of the world's professional diving organizations.) Snorkeling expeditions can be arranged, as well as scuba outings, and the staff claims to be able to teach novices to dive even if they can't swim. Visibility underwater exceeds 100 feet on most days, with water temperatures ranging from 72° to 84°F.

Without hotel accommodations, half-day excursions to the reef, with snorkeling gear included, cost $15; with scuba gear, $45. Scuba instruction is free. Night dives cost $50 per person and require a minimum of six participants. To stay at the hotel here for 5 nights and 6 days, all-inclusive (meals, tips, taxes, airport transfers, and three dives a day), costs $1,045 per person. All guests are allowed access to the beachside hot tub whirlpool, as well as to all facilities, such as free use of sailboats, Windsurfers, and bicycles.

Diving the Blue Holes

Among other claims to fame, Andros is known for its "blue holes," which rise from the briny. Scattered at various points along the coast, they can be reached either in rented boats or else as part of guided trips. The most celebrated blue hole is Uncle Charlie Blue Hole, which is mysterious and fathomless. It was publicized by Jacques Cousteau. The other blue holes are almost as incredible. Essentially, these are narrow circular pits that plunge straight down as much as 200 feet through rock and coral into murky, difficult-to-explore depths. Most of them begin under the level of the sea, although others appear unexpectedly (and dangerously) in the center of the island, usually with warning signs placed around the perimeter.

One of these blue holes, called Benjamin's Blue Hole, is named after its discoverer, George Benjamin. In 1967 he found stalactites and stalagmites 1,200 feet below sea level. What was remarkable about this discovery is that stalactites and stalagmites are not created underwater. This has led to much speculation that The Bahamas are actually mountaintops, all that remains of a mysterious continent (Atlantis?) that sank beneath the sea. Although Cousteau came this way to make a film, making the Blue Holes of Andros internationally famous, most of them, like most of the surface of the island itself, remain unexplored. Tour boats leaving from Small Hope Bay Lodge will take you to these holes.

EXPLORING THE ISLAND: FEATURING THE WORLD'S SECOND-LARGEST BARRIER REEF

Andros is vastly unexplored—and with good reason. Getting around takes some doing. Roads—what roads there are—are badly maintained and potholed, except for the main arteries. Sometimes you're a long way between villages or settlements, and if your car breaks down, all you can do is stop and wait, hoping someone will come along and give you a ride to the next settlement, where (you pray) there will be a skilled mechanic. If you're striking out on an exploration, make sure you have a full tank, as service stations are not plentiful.

All of Andros certainly can't be explored by car, although there is a dream that as Andros develops, it will be linked by a road and causeways stretching some 100 miles or more. Most of the driving and exploring is confined to North Andros, and there only along the eastern sector, going by Nicholl's Town, Morgan's Bluff, and San Andros.

If you're driving on Central or South Andros, you must stay on the rough Queen's Highway. The road in the south is paved and better than the one in Central Andros, which should be traveled only in an emergency or by a local.

Drivers from all over the world come to explore the **Andros barrier reef,** which runs parallel to the eastern shore of the island. After Australia's Great Barrier Reef, this is the largest in the world, but unlike the one in Australia, which is some 200 miles off the coast, the barrier reef of Andros is easily accessible, beginning a few hundred yards offshore.

One side of the reef is a peaceful haven for snorkelers and scuba divers, who report that the fish are tame (often a grouper will eat from your hand, but don't try it with a moray eel). The water here is from 9 to 15 feet deep. On the other side of the reef it's a different story. The water plunges to a depth of a full mile into the awesome TOTO (Tongue of the Ocean). One diver reported that, as an adventure, diving in the ocean's "tongue" was tantamount to a flight to the moon.

Much marine life thrives on the reef, and it attracts nature lovers from all over the world. The weirdly shaped coral formations alone are worth the trip. This is a living, breathing garden of the sea, and its caves are often called "cathedral-like."

For many years the U.S. Navy has conducted research at a station on the edge of TOTO. The research center is at Andros Town. It is devoted to oceanographic, underwater weapons, and antisubmarine research. Called AUTEC (Atlantic Undersea Testing and Evaluation Centre), this is a joint U.S. and British undertaking.

When the station first opened, Androsians predicted that the naval researchers would turn up "Lusca." Like the Loch Ness monster, Lusca had been reported as having been sighted by dozens of locals. The sea serpent was accused of sucking both sailors and their vessels into the dangerous blue holes around the island's coastline. No one has captured Lusca yet, but the blue holes do exist.

Near Small Hope Bay at Andros Town you can visit the workshop where **Androsia batik** is made (the same Androsia batik sold in the shops of Nassau and other towns). Androsia's artisans create their designs using hot wax on fine cotton and silk fabrics. The fabrics are then made into island-style wear, including blouses, skirts, caftans, shirts, and accessories. All hand painted and hand signed, the resort wear comes in dazzling red, blue, purple, green, and earth tones. You can visit the factory in Andros Town (☎ 242/368-2080) Monday through Friday from 7:30am to 4pm.

Morgan's Bluff, at the tip of North Andros, lures men and women hoping to strike it rich. The pirate Sir Henry Morgan is supposed to have buried a vast treasure here, but it has eluded discovery to this day. Many have searched for it in vain.

Bird-watchers are attracted to Andros for its varied **bird population.** In the dense forests, in trees such as lignum vitae, mahogany, madeira, "horseflesh," and pine, lives a huge feathered population: many parrots, doves, and marsh hens. (Ever hear a whistling duck?)

Botanists are lured here by the **wildflowers** of Andros. It is said that some 40 to 50 species of wild orchids thrive here, some found nowhere else. New discoveries are always being made, as more and more botanists study the rich vegetation of Andros.

One custom in Andros is reminiscent of the Tennessee Williams drama *Suddenly Last Summer*. This is the catching of land crabs, which leave their burrows and march relentlessly to the sea to lay their eggs. The annual ritual occurs between May and September. However, many of the hapless crabs will never have offspring; both visitors and Androsians walk along the beach with baskets and catch the crustaceans before they reach the sea. Later, they clean them, stuff them, and bake them for dinner.

DISCOVERING RED BAY VILLAGE

Typical of discoveries that continue to make Andros mysterious is Red Bay Village, where inhabitants were found living as a tribe as recently as a quarter of a century ago. Their leader was a chief, and old rituals were religiously followed. The passage of time had made little difference to these people. Now the world comes to their door, and changes are inevitable, although the people still follow their longtime customs. The village, it is believed, was settled sometime in the 1840s by Seminoles and blacks fleeing slavery in Florida.

The village is located off the northwestern coast of Andros. A causeway now connects the village to the mainland, and tourists can visit. Red Bay Village can be reached by road from Nicholl's Town and San Andros. You should be polite and ask permission before indiscriminately photographing these people.

The Abaco Islands   8

Called the "top of The Bahamas," the Abaco Islands comprise the northernmost portion of The Bahamas. The boomerang-shaped miniarchipelago is 130 miles long and consists of both Great Abaco and Little Abaco, as well as a sprinkling of cays (pronounced "keys"). The islands are about 200 miles east of Miami and 75 miles north of Nassau.

People come here mainly to explore the outdoor life, especially if they like spectacular sailing and plentiful fishing. The diving is excellent, too. If you're not a sailor, a diver, or a fisher, you can enjoy the place as a retreat far removed from the worldly pleasures of Freeport/Lucaya, Nassau, or Paradise Island.

Many residents of the Abacos are descendants of Loyalists who left New England after the American Revolution. Against a backdrop of sugar-white beaches and turquoise water, pastel-colored clapboard houses and white-picket fences retain the Cape Cod architectural style of their ancestors. The best settlements to visit for old-world charm are Green Turtle Cay (New Plymouth), Elbow Cay (Hope Town), and Man-O-War Cay. One brightly painted sign in Hope Town says it all: "Slow Down, You're in Hope Town." The same could be said for all the Abacos.

Ponce de León landed here in 1513 looking for the Fountain of Youth. Visitors, many of them retired Americans, still arrive searching, if not for eternal youth, at least for a pleasant way of life that has disappeared from much of the world.

Fishers find some of the finest offshore fishing in The Bahamas, and yachters call this the "world's most beautiful cruising grounds" (a title also bestowed upon the Exumas). In the interior are wild boar, and, we are told, wild ponies, although we've never seen the latter.

After Nassau, Paradise Island, and Freeport/Lucaya, the Abacos, with many first-rate resorts, are the most visited attraction in The Bahamas. The weather is about 10°F warmer than in southern Florida, but if you visit in January or February, don't expect every day will be beach weather. Remember, Miami and Fort Lauderdale, even Key West, can get chilly at times. When winter squalls hit, temperatures can drop to the high 40s in severe cases. Spring in the Abacos, however, is one of the most glorious and balmy seasons in all the islands. In summer it gets very hot around noon, but if you act as the islanders do and find a shady spot, the trade winds will cool you off.

Fishing, swimming, and especially boating are the top sports on the Abacos. There are also diving, golf, and tennis. If you're the boating type, the favorite pastime is to rent a small boat, pack a picnic (or have it done for you), and head for one of the uninhabited cays just big enough for two.

Excellent marine facilities, with guides, charter parties, and boat rentals are available on Great Guana Cay, Green Turtle Cay, Hope Town, Marsh Harbour, Treasure Cay, and Walker's Cay. Sunfish, Sailfish, Hobie Cats, and Morgan bareboats are available. In fact, Marsh Harbour is the bareboat-charter center of the northern Bahamas (renting a boat with everything but the crew).

Anglers from all over the world come to test their skill against the blue marlin, kingfish, dolphin (the fish, not the mammal), yellowfin tuna, sailfish, wahoo, amberjack, and grouper. Fishing tournaments abound at Walker's Cay. There are plenty of Boston Whalers for bottom fishing and Makos for reef fishing and trolling. Many cruisers for deep-sea fishing can be rented.

Scuba divers can dive the depths with UNEXSO (Underwater Explorers Society) and discover the Abacos' caverns, inland "blue holes," coral reefs, and gardens, along with marine preserves and wrecks. Night dives are featured. Top-rated dive centers can be found at Marsh Harbour, Hope Town, Treasure Cay, and Walker's Cay, all offering NAUI/PADI instructors and a full line of equipment sales, rentals, and air fills.

A LITTLE HISTORY

Once the waters around the Abacos swarmed with Robert Louis Stevenson–type pirates and treasure ships. It is estimated that 500 to 600 Spanish galleons—many treasure laden—went to their watery graves in and around the Abaco reefs. To this day, an occasional old silver coin or a doubloon is found along the beaches, particularly after a storm.

As mentioned, many of the Bahamians who live in the Abacos are descendants of Loyalists who left New England or the Carolinas during the American Revolution. An Elizabethan accent still exists in their speech. They founded towns like New Plymouth and Hope Town, which are reminiscent of New England fishing villages. Many of these early settlers were shipbuilders, and to this day many Abaconians claim that the finest island boats are those built with Abaco pine by the Man-O-War Cay artisans. This is still the boatbuilding center of The Bahamas, and it is also rather grandly acclaimed as "the finest sailing capital" in the world.

Other early settlers were farmers who, when they found that they could not make a living in that line—the soil wasn't fertile enough—turned to *wrecking* (the business of salvaging ships that were wrecked or foundered on the reefs). Since there wasn't a lighthouse in the Abacos until 1836, many vessels crashed on the shoals and rocks, and salvagers legally claimed the cargoes, at the same time saving the lives of crews and passengers when possible. However, this enterprise became so profitable that some unscrupulous wreckers deliberately misled ships to their doom and became rich from the spoils.

Most of the "Tories"—descendants of the British Loyalists—still live on Elbow Cay, Green Turtle Cay, and Man-O-War Cay. From a sightseeing point of view, these are the principal islands of the Abacos to visit, as they are, in our opinion, more interesting than the Abaco "mainland." The first-timer will likely head for Treasure Cay, Marsh Harbour, Walker's Cay, or Green Turtle Cay, but repeat visitors gravitate to more esoteric destinations.

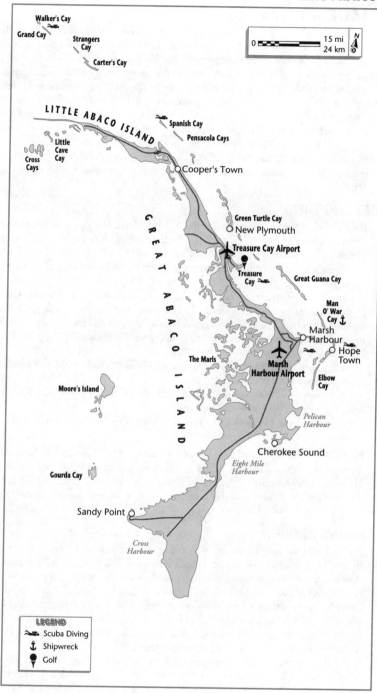

Walker's Cay

Grand Cay

Strangers Cay

Carter's Cay

0   15 mi
      24 km
N

LITTLE ABACO ISLAND

Spanish Cay

Pensacola Cays

Little Cave Cay

Cross Cays

Cooper's Town

GREAT ABACO ISLAND

Green Turtle Cay

New Plymouth

Treasure Cay Airport

Treasure Cay

Great Guana Cay

Man O' War Cay

Marsh Harbour

Hope Town

Marsh Harbour Airport

The Maris

Moore's Island

Elbow Cay

Pelican Harbour

Cherokee Sound

Eight Mile Harbour

Gourda Cay

Sandy Point

Cross Harbour

LEGEND
Scuba Diving
Shipwreck
Golf

2-0113

A TASTE OF THE ABACOS

For a "taste of the Abacos," skip some of the hotel restaurants and seek out the places where the local tends to go. In Marsh Harbour, conch salad is sold right on the docks. "It'll make a man out of you," one local vendor tells everybody, even if the person is a woman. If you stick around long enough, you'll see Billy Thompson coming by in his little truck. He is said to make the world's best homemade soursop and mango ice cream. The best baker on the island is Terell Russell, and you can sample his rolls, muffins, cakes (superb), and nearly 10 kinds of bread at the **Flour House Bakery,** next to Sharkee's Pizza along the waterfront. The best pizzas are sold at **Sapodilly** (☎ 242/367-3498). If you're around on Thursday night, drop in to Sapodilly for the all-you-can-eat Bahama buffet, costing $17.50. Bahamian fried chicken, curried grouper, cracked conch, and all that good stuff will weigh down your plate.

GETTING THERE

BY PLANE   Three airports service the Abacos: Marsh Harbour (the major one), Treasure Cay, and Walker's Cay. The official points of entry are Marsh Harbour, Treasure Cay, Walker's Cay, and Green Turtle Cay (New Plymouth). Green Turtle Cay doesn't have an airstrip, but many people of the yachting set clear Customs and Immigration there.

Many visitors arrive from Nassau or Miami on **Bahamasair** (☎ 800/222-4262). Flight schedules change frequently in The Bahamas, but you can usually get a daily flight out of Nassau, going first to Marsh Harbour, then on to Treasure Cay. If you're in West Palm Beach or Miami, you can usually get a direct morning flight to Marsh Harbour and Treasure Cay.

Gulfstream International (☎ 800/992-8532) flies daily from Miami and Fort Lauderdale to Marsh Harbour.

US Airways (☎ 800/428-4322) flies daily from Orlando to Treasure Cay and from West Palm Beach to Marsh Harbour.

American Eagle (☎ 800/433-7300) flies daily from Miami nonstop to Marsh Harbour.

BY BOAT   The MV *Champion II* heads out from Potter's Cay Dock in Nassau on Tuesday at 10am, calling first at Sandy Point, then Moore's Island and Bullock's Harbour, before returning to Nassau on Thursday at 10am (trip time: 11 hours). For details of sailings (subject to change) and costs, contact the dockmaster at Potter's Cay Dock in Nassau (☎ 242/393-1064).

GETTING AROUND

BY TAXI   Unmetered taxis, often shared with other passengers, meet all arriving flights. They will take you to your hotel if it's on the Abaco "mainland"; otherwise, they will deposit you at a dock where you can hop aboard a water taxi to one of the neighboring offshore islands such as Green Turtle Cay or Elbow Cay. The majority of visitors use a combination taxi and water taxi ride to reach the most popular hotels. From Marsh Harbour Airport to Hope Town on Elbow Cay costs about $11 for the transfer. From the Treasure Cay Airport to Green Turtle Cay, the cost is about $13. Elbow Cay costs about $10 for the transfer.

It's also possible to make arrangements for a taxi tour of Great or Little Abaco. These, however, are expensive. You don't really see that much either. It's better to go sightseeing in one of the Loyalist settlements, such as New Plymouth. That you can do on foot.

BY CAR If you wish to explore Abaco on your own, you can rent a car, usually for $70 a day or $350 per week. Try **H and L Car Rentals,** Don MacKay Boulevard, Marsh Harbour (☎ **242/367-2840**), which is open Monday through Saturday from 7am to 6pm. Economy to full-size American cars are rented.

Another local outlet renting cars is **Agatha Archer Car Rental** at Archers Hill, Marsh Harbour, P.O. Box AB20463 (☎ **242/367-2148**). Rates begin at $75 per day. Types of vehicles include Ford Thunderbirds.

BY FERRY Mostly, you'll use **Albury's Ferry Service** (☎ **242/367-3147**). Its departures from Marsh Harbour coincide with incoming and outgoing flights. It provides ferry connections to Elbow Cay (Hope Town) and Man-O-War Cay, a 20-minute trip to either destination. The one-way fare is $8. The boats run from Hope Town and from Man-O-War Cay to Marsh Harbour at 8am and 1:30pm daily, making the run from Marsh Harbour to the two island ports at 10:30am and 4pm. On Monday, Thursday, and Saturday there is also a departure from Marsh Harbour at 12:15am. For car-ferry service to Green Turtle Cay, see "Green Turtle Cay," below.

BY SCOOTER If you'd like to take this more adventurous way to see Abaco, contact **H & L Rentals,** the car-rental people, located downtown in Marsh Harbour. (See "By Car," above.) They rent 100cc motorbikes for two people for $35 per day or $175 per week. Hours are Monday through Saturday from 7am to 6pm.

1 Spanish Cay

Set 12 miles northwest of Green Turtle Cay, this island was named after the pair of Spanish galleons that sank offshore during the 17th century. Originally owned by Queen Elizabeth II, the island was purchased in the 1960s by Texas-based investor (and former owner of the Dallas Cowboys) Clint Murchinson. After his death in the early 1980s, two successive Florida conglomerates poured time, money, and landscaping efforts into developing the island as a site for upscale private homes.

Although its vegetation began with little more than stunted shrubs and sea grapes, today, the narrow, 3-mile-long, 185-acre island is forested with 6,000 palms, descendants of the original 800 specimens brought in by Murchinson in the 1970s. Unusual among the coral-and-sand islands of the northern Bahamas, Spanish Cay is relatively vertiginous, rising to a panoramic altitude of 65 feet above sea level. The little island has 5 beaches and about 7 miles of shoreline. Most residents of the inn (see below) and the island's private homes maneuver their way along the island's paved roads by electric-powered golf carts.

The island contains a 70-slip, state-of-the-art marina, 4 private homes, and a collection of 13 garden suites available to overnight guests. The island also has a pair of restaurants (each with its own bar), the more upscale of which (the Wrecker's Raw Bar) is built on stilts above the tidal flats of the island's Atlantic shore. Among other amenities are a 5,000-foot airstrip, a complete PADI-certified dive shop, a handful of sailing vessels for excursions above the coral reefs of the Sea of Abaco, and a congenial staff, which for the most part is ferried in every day from the nearby community of Cooper's Town. Most visitors arrive by private boat, chartered aircraft, or by the occasional flights from Fort Lauderdale on Island Express Airlines. Other options include flying to Treasure Cay on Bahamasair, then arranging water transport from there through the hotel.

WHERE TO STAY & DINE

The Inn at Spanish Cay. P.O. Box 882, Cooper's Town, Abaco, The Bahamas. ☎ **800/ 688-4752** or 242/365-0083, or 201/539-6450 in New Jersey. Fax 242/365-0083. 13 garden suites (most with kitchen), 4 apts. A/C MINIBAR. Year-round, $200 garden suite, $250 one-bedroom apt, $300 two-bedroom apt. MC, V.

Pending an eventual purchase of a home or building site, these accommodations offer some of the most secluded, off-the-beaten-track lodgings in the northern Bahamas. Furnishings in the suites include tropical fabrics and lots of rattan and wicker. Decoration in the private homes includes whatever struck the fancy of the individual (absentee) homeowner, but tends to include summery, easy-to-care-for, Florida-inspired decors.

Dining options include more formal meals in the Wrecker's Raw Bar. Less-expensive casual fare (sandwiches, salads, and platters) are served near the marina in the Point House, which overlooks the Sea of Abaco.

2 Walker's Cay

This is the northernmost and outermost of the Abaco chain of islands, and one of the smallest, lying at the edge of the Bahama Bank. The cay produces its own fresh water and electricity. Coral reefs surrounding this island drop off to depths of some 1,000 feet. It's known around the world as one of the best deep-sea fishing resorts and has been featured on ABC-TV's *American Sportsman* on several occasions. It is usually mentioned as being the "Top of The Bahamas."

Ponce de León is said to have stopped here in 1513 looking for fresh water. That was just 6 days before he "discovered" Florida. From the 17th century, this was a place known to pirates, who stored their booty here. It became a bastion for blockade-runners during the American Civil War, and later it was a hideout for rumrunners in the days of U.S. Prohibition.

To service those who want to reach the island, Walker's Cay Hotel and Marina operates its own plane service, Walker's International (☎ **954/359-1400**). The airline makes the 45-minute flight from Fort Lauderdale to Walker's Cay every day except Tuesday.

WHERE TO STAY & DINE

Walker's Cay Hotel and Marina. Walker's Cay, Abaco, The Bahamas. ☎ **800/432-2092** in the U.S. and Canada, or 954/359-1400 in Fort Lauderdale. Fax 954/359-1414. 62 rms, 3 villas. A/C. Sept 11–Feb, $120–$140 double; from $200 villa. Mar–Sept 10, $140–$160 double; from $250 villa. MAP $37.50 per person extra. AE, DC, MC, V.

This self-contained, 100-acre resort has the largest full-service, privately owned marina in the Abacos, and each year it runs what has become the largest deep-sea fishing tournament in The Bahamas. Come here for the fishing and the marina—not for the rather standard motel-like units where maintenance is generally poor. In this remote outpost, furnishings are generally tired and worn.

If you're planning a winter visit, ask a travel agent (or call directly) to see if the resort will still be offering its "Discover Us Package." Its most recent one included 3 days and 2 nights, with round-trip airfare from Fort Lauderdale or West Palm Beach, for $339 per person. A similar summer package costs $419 per person.

Dining/Entertainment: The cuisine is not reason to stay here. Meals are generally adequate, consisting of both Bahamian and American dishes, but readers have complained of the salad bars and the breakfast buffets. The Lobster Trap Lounge evokes the early Bahamas of Hemingway. The Conch Pearl and the dining terrace overlook the sea.

Services: Laundry, baby-sitting.

Facilities: Two all-weather tennis courts; every kind of water sport from scuba diving to skiing; freshwater and saltwater swimming (although the meager beach is not reason enough to visit); some of the finest offshore fishing in The Bahamas, just 5 minutes from the 75-slip marina (many world records have been set here).

3 Green Turtle Cay (New Plymouth)

Three miles off the east coast of Great Abaco, Green Turtle Cay is the jewel of the archipelago, a little island with an uneven coastline, deep bays, sounds, and good beaches, one of the best stretching for 3,600 feet. There are green forests, gentle hills, and secluded inlets. The island is 3½ miles long and half a mile across, and lies some 170 miles due east of Palm Beach, Florida.

Water depths seldom exceed 15 to 20 feet inside the string of cays that trace the outer edge of the Bahama Bank. It is the reefs outside the cays that provide the abundance of underwater flora and fauna that delights snorkelers and anglers. The coral gardens that make up an inner and an outer reef teem with colorful sea life, and shelling on the beaches and offshore sandbars is among the finest in The Bahamas.

If you have a boat, you can explore such deserted islands as Fiddle Cay to the north and No Name Cay and Pelican Cay to the south of Green Turtle Cay.

New Plymouth, at the southern tip of the cay, is an 18th-century settlement that has the flavor of a New England sailing port back in the days when such towns were filled with boatbuilders and fishers. Much of the masonry of the original town was made from lime produced from conch shells, broken up, burned, and sifted for cement. Records say that the alkali content was so high that it would burn the hands of the masons who used it.

Clapboard houses with gingerbread trim line the narrow streets of the little town, which once had a population of 1,800 people, now shrunk to 400. Green Turtle Cay became known for the skill of its shipbuilders, although the industry, like many others in the area, failed when total emancipation of the slaves came to The Bahamas in 1838.

Parliament is the village's main street, and you can walk its entire length in only 10 minutes, acknowledged only by a few clucking hens. Many of the houses have front porches, which are occupied in the evening by people enjoying the breezes.

GETTING THERE   Most guests fly to Treasure Cay Airport, where a taxi will take them to the ferry dock for departures to Green Turtle Cay (New Plymouth).

At the dock, you may have to wait a while for the ferry. It's about a 10-minute ride to Green Turtle Cay from the dock. The ferry will take you directly to the Green Turtle Club, if you're staying there, or to New Plymouth. This land-and-sea transfer costs $13 per person.

ESSENTIALS   Banks   Service is limited. Barclay's Bank PLC operates a branch (☎ 809/365-4144) open only from 10am to 1pm on Tuesday and Thursday.

Crime   There's no crime in New Plymouth, unless you import it yourself. There is a little jail made of stone, which makes visitors chuckle: The doors have fallen off. No one can remember when, if ever, it held a prisoner.

Medical Care   If you need medical attention on Green Turtle Cay, there is a clinic (☎ 242/365-4028) run by a nurse.

Post Office   Green Turtle Cay's post office (☎ 242/365-4242) is entered through a pink door. It has a public telephone. Hours are Monday through Friday from 9am to noon and from 1 to 4:30pm.

Shopping   In New Plymouth, there are several hole-in-the-wall gift shops, and otherwise meagerly stocked grocery stores offer freshly baked Bahamian bread.

WHERE TO STAY
EXPENSIVE

✪ **Green Turtle Club.** Green Turtle Cay, Abaco, The Bahamas. ☎ **242/365-4271.** Fax 242/365-4272. 28 rms, 3 suites. A/C. Winter, from $155 double; $186 poolside suite for two; $276 villa for up to four. Off-season, $125 double; $165 poolside suite for two; $215 villa for up to four. Prices higher at Christmas. Children under 12 stay free in parents' room. Extra person $20. MAP $36 per adult extra, $24 per child extra. AE, MC, V. Closed end of Aug to mid-Nov. Most guests arrive at Treasure Cay Airport, then take a taxi (there are usually plenty there) to the ferry dock, where a water taxi will take you to the club.

The only four-star hotel in the Abacos, this club attracts those who like to fish, snorkel, and explore reefs, but is mainly a premier attraction for yachties and divers. Spread across 80 acres, the resort was built on a half-moon–shaped beach off which yachts of all sizes ride at anchor. The flag-festooned bar is the social center of the resort. Today its ambience is very much that of a clubhouse, lodge, and country club, capped with heavy rafters and flanked on one side by a panoramic verandah and on the other by a pine-covered dining room.

The Green Turtle Yacht Club has its base here. It's associated with the Birdham Yacht Club, one of the oldest in England, and with the Palm Beach Yacht Club. Members have their own villas right on the water, often with private docks, although temporary guests will be lodged in spacious bungalows set on the side of the hill. Rooms have benefited from a tasteful restoration which has turned them into the most upscale in the Abacos. French draperies, oak floors, terra-cotta–tiled patios, and colonial styling add grace notes to the accommodations. There are no locked doors on this tree-dotted estate. Also, the only telephone is the one in the main office, where the staff can organize an array of sporting as well as sightseeing excursions.

Some guests choose to walk the several miles into New Plymouth, or you can take a boat. The waters around the resort are shallow enough that landlubbers can spot schools of fish and sometimes even a green turtle paddling along above the sandbanks.

There's an unmistakably British note here—both in the evening meals which begin with before-dinner cocktails beside a roaring fire in the bar (in chilly weather only, of course), and in the courteous staff, who offer assistance yet don't intrude on anyone's tranquillity. Arrangements can be made for a boat trip into New Plymouth, and laundry service is available. There's a swimming pool dug into one of the flower-dotted hillsides in case swimmers don't want to bathe in the waters off the hotel's beach.

MODERATE

Bluff House Club & Marina. Green Turtle Cay, Abaco, The Bahamas. ☎ **242/365-4247.** Fax 242/365-4248. 9 rms, 18 suites, 3 villas. A/C. Year-round, $90–$100 double; $105–$120 suite for two; $130–$150 deluxe upper suites; $175–$195 one-bedroom villa for two; $265–$295 two-bedroom villa for four; $330–$380 three-bedroom villa for six. MAP $35 per person extra. AE, DISC, MC, V.

Far more informal and laid-back than Green Turtle Cay, Bluff House has 12 acres fronting the Sea of Abaco on one side and the harbor of White Sound on the other. The house sits atop an 80-foot-high peninsula that rises from its own private pink-powder sandy beach set against a backdrop of palm, oak, and pine-forested jogging

Far from the Madding Crowd

The settlers of New Plymouth were Loyalists who found their way here from other parts of the Abacos shortly before the end of the 18th century, with some "new" blood thrown in when émigrés from Eleuthera moved to Marsh Harbour and other Abaconian settlements. The people today are mostly named Curry, Lowe, Russell, Roberts, and especially Sawyer. Because they all came from the same rootstock—English, Welsh, and Scottish—and because of a long history of intermarriage, many of the faces are amazingly similar: deeply tanned, often freckled skin, blue eyes, and red or blond hair. The people here are friendly but not outgoing, having lived for generations far from the madding crowd.

One morning we spent an hour with a lifelong resident. The next morning, encountering what we took to be the same man on the ferryboat, we resumed our conversation, only to learn we were talking to a different man entirely. "No relation," he said, until chided by a woman passenger, which elicited from him, "Well, I think my mother's cousin did marry . . . ."

The insularity of these people has also caused their speech patterns to retain many facets of those their forebears brought from the mother country, with even a smattering of cockney to flavor it. Many drop their initial letter *h,* using it instead at the beginning of words that start with vowels. You may hear someone ordering "'am" and with it some "heggs." Also, the letter *v* is often pronounced "w", and vice versa.

Many of the inhabitants of New Plymouth today are engaged in turtling, lobstering, shark fishing, and sponging. New Plymouth is a so-called "sister city" to Key West, Florida, and if you have ever visited there, you'll see startling similarities between the American people of "conch" descent and the Abaconians, even to their wrecking history, fishing industries, and appearance.

A big event in the day-to-day life of the people of New Plymouth is the arrival at the Government Dock of the mail boat from Nassau. People gather there also whenever the ferryboat is arriving or leaving, just to keep tabs on what's going on.

There is no auto traffic in New Plymouth except for a few service vehicles—but who needs a car? You can walk all the way around the village in a fairly brief stroll.

trails. It is a 5-minute boat ride from the village of New Plymouth, and a boat takes guests to the village three mornings a week for sightseeing and shopping and also for a Saturday-night dance.

The main building has paneled and glass walls, slow-whirling tropical fans, wicker furnishings, and polished wooden floors. A wide, wooden deck surrounds the swimming pool, sheltered by palms and offering a panoramic view of the surrounding waters and the sunsets.

The hotel offers beach or hillside villas and split-level suites, as well as hotel rooms. For complete seclusion and views, the hotel also offers so-called "tree houses," which have private porches and balconies. The best accommodations are the spacious colonial-style suites, with balconies opening onto views of the Sea of Abaco. Inside, the decor includes floral bedcovers and tropical furniture. The resort is open year-round, attracting a "same time next year" clientele.

Dining/Entertainment: Breakfast and dinner (including complimentary wine) are served in the main Club House, where drinks and fresh hors d'oeuvres are offered before a candlelit dinner that features local conch, grouper, snapper, and lobster, as well as roast duck à l'orange. The Beach Club, open daily, serves luncheons featuring Bahamian cracked conch and fresh grouper, as well as hamburgers and other American favorites.

Services: Baby-sitting, laundry.

Facilities: Full-service, 15-slip marina with boats for rent; swimming pool; tennis court; free use of rackets, balls, and snorkeling equipment; gift shop/boutique; arrangements made for reef fishing, deep-sea fishing, bonefishing, and a snorkeling/fishing picnic during which your guide will take you diving for seafood to be cooked at lunch.

✪ **New Plymouth Inn.** New Plymouth, Green Turtle Cay, Abaco, The Bahamas. ☎ **242/365-4161,** or 305/665-5309 in Florida. Fax 242/365-4138. 9 rms. A/C. Year-round (MAP), $110–$120 double. MC, V. Closed Sept.

This restored two-story New England–Bahamian–style inn stands next door to the former home of Neville Chamberlain, the prime minister of Great Britain on the eve of World War II. It's more like a guest house or a big B&B than either the Green Turtle Club or Bluff House. Richard Nixon was once a guest, whereas Jimmy Carter stayed at the Green Turtle Club. The inn has colonial charm, a Loyalist history, cloistered gardens, and a patio pool, and it's in the heart of New Plymouth village. It was one of the few buildings in town to survive the 1932 hurricane. The inn is run by Wally Davies, an expert diver and swimmer. He has turned the New Plymouth Inn into a charming oasis, refurbishing the 150-year-old building with taste and care.

The inn has wide, open verandahs, intricate cutout wooden trim, and an indoor A-frame dining room. The comfortable hammock on the front porch is constantly fought over. The light and airy rooms are kept spotlessly clean, and each has a private bath and shower. Some units are air-conditioned. Many of the same guests have come back every year since the inn opened in 1974.

Dining/Entertainment: Out on the verandah, you can smell night-blooming jasmine mixing with fresh-baked island bread. Island candlelit dinners of fresh native lobster, snapper, conch, and vintage wines are served. Roasts, steaks, chops, and imported beer in frosty steins are also part of the menu. The bar and lounge, which overlook the garden's small freshwater swimming pool, are the social center of the establishment. The Sunday brunch is the most popular on the island.

Facilities: Swimming pool; nearby tennis; fishing and snorkeling can be arranged.

COTTAGE RENTALS

Coco Bay Cottages. P.O. Box AB22795, Green Turtle Cay, Abaco, The Bahamas. ☎ **800/752-0166** or 242/365-5464. Fax 242/365-5465. 4 cottages. TEL. Year-round, $150–$230 daily; $800–$1,400 weekly. MC, V. Free docking.

On the north end of Green Turtle Cay, at a point where 500 feet of land separate the Atlantic from the Sea of Abaco, this cottage complex is ideal for those who'd like to anchor in for a while. It enjoys a 70% repeat clientele. Furnished in a refreshing style of Caribbean furnishings and pastel colors, the oceanfront property occupies 5 acres, dotted with some 50 tropical fruit trees. Each of the cottages has two bedrooms and a living and dining room with a fully equipped kitchen and microwave. Rebuilt in 1988 and renovated in 1996, the cottages have been much improved over the years. Linens and kitchen utensils are provided. Cooling is by ceiling fans and trade winds. Guests come directly to the property by water taxi from the airport dock. They have a selection of two different beaches, and three stores can be found in New Plymouth for guests who want to cook their own meals.

Deck House. White Sound, Green Turtle Cay, Abaco, The Bahamas. ☎ **513/821-9471** in Cincinnati, Ohio (for information, write to Dorothy Lang, 535 Hickory Hill Lane, Cincinnati, OH 45215). 2 units. Year-round, $825 per week for four; $1,070 per week for six. No credit cards.

Deck House lies on the leeward side of the island at the entrance to White Sound. Rented weekly as a complex, it can house up to six people. It consists of two bedrooms and two baths, plus a small guest house for two with bath—in other words, it houses three couples "with privacy." There is a living room, plus a kitchen. Linens and all utensils are provided. Out back is a sundeck. Owners A. V. and Dorothy Lang prefer bookings from Saturday noon to Saturday noon, and only one group at a time can rent the site. Incidentally, a maid comes in Saturday to put things in order. As an added bonus, the Langs include a 30-horsepower Malibu, a Butterfly, and the use of a Sunfish at no additional charge.

WHERE TO DINE

The hotels previously recommended have the best food on the island. But if you'd like a change of pace for either lunch or dinner, we recommend the following small dining rooms in New Plymouth.

Laura's Kitchen. Parliament St. ☎ **242/365-4287.** Reservations recommended for dinner. Lunch $4.50–$8.75; dinner $10–$15. No credit cards. Daily 11am–3pm and 5:30–9pm. Closed Sept. BAHAMIAN.

On the main street of town, across from the Albert Lowe Museum, this family-owned eatery occupies a well-converted white Bahamian cottage. Owner Laura Sawyer serves lunch and dinner in a simple, homey decor. The food she serves is what her family has eaten for generations: fried grouper, fried chicken, and a tasty cracked conch.

Rooster's Rest Pub and Restaurant. Gilliam's Bay Rd. ☎ **242/365-4066.** Reservations recommended for dinner. Main courses $9.50–$14; lunch burgers and snacks $3.75–$6.50. No credit cards. Mon–Sat 11:30am–9:30pm. BAHAMIAN.

Rooster's, the local dive, serves good Bahamian food, including lobster, conch, and fresh fish in an atmosphere that is decidedly casual, the way The Bahamas "used to be." The cook also prepares some tasty ribs. The establishment lies just beyond the edge of town. All main courses in the evening are served with peas 'n' rice, coleslaw, and potato salad. Nouvelle cuisine hasn't washed up on these shores yet.

TAKING IN THE SCENE AT MISS EMILY'S BLUE BEE BAR

The most famous bar in the Out Islands is **Miss Emily's Blue Bee Bar,** Victoria Street at New Plymouth on Green Turtle Cay in the Abacos (☎ 242/365-4181). This bar is likely to be the scene of the liveliest party in the Out Islands at any time of day. Despite its simplicity, the family-run bar is one of the most famous places east of Miami. When we were last here, an energetic party was developing just before lunch, as a yachtswoman from West Virginia was demonstrating the frug she'd learned long ago in college, to enthusiastic applause. This and more are likely to be happening at this hallowed bar, where the walls near the bar area are covered with the business cards of past clients, including Glen Campbell, Jimmy Buffett, and the late Lillian Carter. The Goombay Smash, the specialty here, has been called "Abaco's answer to atomic fission." Its recipe includes secret proportions of coconut rum, "dirty" rum, apricot brandy, and pineapple juice. The owner (she's really Mrs. Emily Cooper) is filled with humor and anecdotes. Failing health makes it impossible for her to always be on duty at the bar, but she has taught her daughter, Violet Smith, how to make the secret recipe. Tips at the bar go to St. Peter's Anglican Church. No food is served here. The bar is open Monday to Saturday from 10am until late.

WATER SPORTS & OTHER OUTDOOR ACTIVITIES

Some critics have hailed the yearly **Regatta Week** at Marsh Harbour as the "premier annual yachting event in the Abacos." Every year, it's held sometime between

The Lost Settlement

Carleton was the first settlement in the Abacos, but it no longer exists. It was situated to the north and a little east of Treasure Cay (then called Lovel's Island) and separated from the cay by Carleton Creek, a rivulet that flowed to join the sea. The little town was abandoned some 200 years ago and largely forgotten until 1979, when the site of the settlement was discovered and artifacts were found by archaeological excavation. In a bicentennial ceremony in 1983, a point of land near the site was designated Carleton Point, and a bronze plaque was placed there describing Carleton's brief history.

Loyalist refugees had fled the United States in 1783 following the formation of the new country and the withdrawal of British troops from the former colonies. They migrated to The Bahamas, some settling in the Abacos, which were uninhabited at the time. Their aim was grandiose—they thought they could establish a colony that would become a new agricultural/mercantile empire under the protection of the British Crown.

Carleton, named for Sir Guy Carleton, who had been British commander in chief in New York, did not fulfill the dreams of the colonists. They staked out claims to land, but they learned, as had other settlers in other parts of The Bahamas, that this was not farming country. They built ships, but could not produce cargoes for them. The town initially had a population of 600 people, but civil strife and a devastating hurricane added to their woes, and soon some two-thirds of the settlers moved 18 miles to the southeast to found Marsh Harbour. Others moved to Cocoa Plum Creek and elsewhere, and some left The Bahamas. By 1800 Carleton had ceased to exist.

The Loyalists remaining in the Abacos were joined by migrants from Harbour Island on Eleuthera, who taught them to fish and even how to farm the rough acreage. This union formed the nucleus from which today's Abaconians descend.

Independence Day in the United States and Independence Day in The Bahamas (July 4 and July 10). The events include sailboat races in many categories, with crews from around the world competing. A great number of the yachties participating in this event stay at the Green Turtle Club (see above).

Another event that draws visitors is the **Green Turtle Club Fishing Tournament,** held sometime in May. In 1984, the winner hooked a 500-pound blue marlin that was so heavy the competing participants from other boats generously came aboard the winning craft to bring the fish in.

For **tennis,** the choice is very limited. There's a court at Bluff House (☎ 242/365-4247), where guests play for free and nonresidents are charged $10 per hour.

The previously recommended Bluff House Club & Marina (☎ 242/365-4247) is the place to go for **scuba** facilities. It also offers **snorkeling** and **"diving with the dolphins."** The hotel also has access to a 29-foot sportsfish boat, with all equipment included. **Bonefishing** is on a smaller boat. Each trip takes about four hours, and the schedule depends completely on the tide. Bonefish, pound for pound, are the strongest, most "fighting" fish in The Bahamas.

If you want to go **deep-sea fishing,** the people to see are the Sawyer family, two brothers and a father. Referrals are usually made through the Green Turtle Club (☎ 242/365-4271), or you can call directly at ☎ 242/365-4173. Prices are negotiated.

EXPLORING THE ISLAND: A JOURNEY TO THE 18TH CENTURY

New Plymouth celebrated its bicentennial in 1984 by opening a **Memorial Sculpture Garden** in the center of town across from the New Plymouth Inn. A monument honors American Loyalists and also some of their notable descendants, including Albert Lowe, a pioneer boatbuilder and historian. The garden is designed in the pattern of the Union Jack.

Albert Lowe Museum. Parliament St. ☎ **242/365-4094.** Admission $3 adults, $1.50 children. Mon–Sat 9–11:45am and 1–4:15pm.

More than anything else we've seen in The Bahamas, this museum gives a view of the rawboned and sometimes difficult history of the Out Islands. You could easily spend a couple of hours reading the fine print of the dozens of photographs that show the hardship and the valor of citizens who changed industries as often as the economic circumstances of their era dictated.

There's a garden in the back of the beautifully restored Loyalist home where the caretaker will give you a guided tour of the stone kitchen, which occupants of the house used as a shelter when a hurricane devastated much of New Plymouth in 1932. Inside the house a narrow stairway leads to a trio of bedrooms that reveal the simplicity of 18th-century life on Green Turtle Cay. Amid antique settees, irreplaceable photographs, and island artifacts, you'll see a number of handsome ship models, the work of Albert Lowe, for whom the museum was named.

Also displayed are paintings by Alton Lowe, son of the former boatbuilder and founder of the museum. Cherub-faced and red-haired, Alton, who now resides in Miami most of the time, has for some time been one of the best-known painters in The Bahamas. His works hang in collections all over the world. Many of Alton Lowe's paintings have been used as the background for Bahamian postage stamps, blowups of which are displayed in the museum. Whoever guides you on your tour might open the basement of the house for you, as well, where you'll see some of Alton Lowe's work, and that of other local painters, for sale.

GREEN TURTLE CAY AFTER DARK

Rooster's Rest Pub and Restaurant. Gilliam's Bay Rd. $2 cover. ☎ **242/365-4066.**

An out-of-the-way nightspot, and recommended separately as a restaurant, Rooster's attracts a crowd, including both yachting people and locals, who gather here every Friday and Saturday night. Beer costs $3.50 per bottle. Not visible from most of Parliament Street, the pub/restaurant is at the far side of a hill beyond the edge of town. Open Monday through Saturday from 11:30am to 10pm.

4 Treasure Cay

Treasure Cay, called Lovel's Island in records as far back as the 1780s, was once separated from the Abaco mainland by Carleton Creek. Over the years, however, landfill operations have joined the two, although Treasure Cay retains the name. It now contains one of the most popular and elaborate resorts in the Out Islands. On the east coast of Great Abaco, it boasts not only 3½ miles of private sandy beach, widely recognized as one of the top-10 beaches in the world, but also one of the finest marinas in the Commonwealth, with complete docking and charter facilities.

Before the opening of the tourist complex, the cay was virtually unsettled. So the resort has become the "city," providing its thousands of visitors with all the supplies they need, including medical goods, grocery-store items (liquor, naturally), and even bank services. The real-estate office peddles the condos, and the builders predict that they will one day reach a capacity of 5,000 guests. What is hoped is that many visitors will like Treasure Cay so much that they'll buy into it.

Treasure Cay also is the host of two of the most popular tournaments in The Bahamas: the Treasure Cay Billfish Championship in April and the Treasure Cay Invitational in May.

WHERE TO STAY & DINE

Treasure Cay Hotel-Resort & Marina. Treasure Cay, Abaco, The Bahamas. ☎ **800/ 327-1584** or 242/365-8535. Fax 954/525-1699. For reservations, Treasure Cay Services, Inc., 2301 S. Federal Hwy., Fort Lauderdale, FL 33316 (☎ 954/525-7711). 64 rms, 36 suites and villas. A/C TV TEL. Winter, $130 double; $180 suite for two; $350 villa for up to four. Off-season, $80 double; $110 suite for two; $195–$285 villa for up to four. MAP $34 per person extra. AE, DC, MC, V.

One of the biggest and best of the Out Island resorts, this property attracts boaters, golfers, fishers, and divers, as well as yachties and the escapists seeking a remote yet rather luxurious retreat. The foundation for this resort was laid in 1962, when the potential of its position near one of the finest beaches in the world was recognized by groups of international investors. One of the most popular in the Out Islands, the resort has attracted celebrities, including George C. Scott, who filmed *Day of the Dolphin* here.

The vast majority of the peninsula (1,200 acres), as well as the marina facility, all of the villas, 80 privately owned condominiums, the tennis courts, and several blocks of other housing, remains under the ownership of the original investors. Guests sometimes rent electric golf carts (priced at around $35 a day) or bicycles, which enable them to more easily visit the far-flung palm and casuarina groves of this sprawling compound.

Guests of the resort appreciate the *House and Garden* look of the architecture, the tropical plantings, the beachfront, an excellent golf course, and the marina facilities. Most accommodations overlook the dozens of sailing craft moored in the marina and are simply furnished in conservatively modern tropical motifs. Villas usually contain private kitchens and two bedrooms.

Dining/Entertainment: The restaurant, the Spinnaker, serves a good international cuisine, and two bars are in operation. Occasional evening musical entertainment is offered.

Services: Small-boat rentals, fishing guides for sportfishing and bonefishing, all-day or all-afternoon snorkeling excursions by boat.

Facilities: 150-slip marina, 18-hole golf course, scuba charters, golf-cart rentals, full array of water sports, bicycle rental, six tennis courts, and ferryboat running to Green Turtle Cay three times a day.

WATER SPORTS & OTHER OUTDOOR ACTIVITIES

The **Treasure Cay Golf Club** (☎ 242/365-8045), Treasure Cay, offers 6,985 yards of fairways and was designed by Dick Wilson, although it's hardly the best course this famed golf architect ever designed. Greens fees are $40 for 18 holes. This is the only golf course in the Abacos, and it lies half a mile from the center of the resort.

Full-service facilities for a variety of **water sports** are offered at the **Treasure Cay Marina** (☎ 242/365-8250). Fishing boats with experienced skippers will guide anglers to tuna, marlin, wahoo, dolphin, barracuda, grouper, yellowtail, and snapper. Treasure Cay's own bonefish flats are just a short cruise from the marina. A full day of bonefishing costs $225, a half day $150; a sportfishing boat goes for $285 for a half day, $395 for a full day.

In addition, sailboat, Hobie Cat, and windsurfing board rentals can be arranged, as well as rental of snorkeling gear and **bicycles.** The marina has showers, fish cleaning facilities, 24-hour weekday laundry service, and water and electricity hookups.

5 Marsh Harbour

The largest town in the Abacos, Marsh Harbour on Great Abaco is the third largest in The Bahamas. The first settlers were a group of Loyalists who were among those who tried to start a town called Carleton near Treasure Cay. The Abaconians who live here are usually shy but gracious.

Marsh Harbour is also a shipbuilding center, but tourism accounts for most of its revenues. The town, however, is absolutely devoid of the quaint New England charm of either New Plymouth or Hope Town. Marsh Harbour has a shopping center and various other facilities not found in many Out Island settlements. You'll even spot the green turrets of a "castle" here, which was designed and constructed by Evans Cottrell, who wrote *Out Island Doctor.*

The shoreline provides one of the finest anchorages in the Out Islands, which is what lured the first settlers here 200 years ago. There are good water-taxi connections, making this a center for exploring some of the offshore cays, including Man-O-War and Elbow cays. Its international airport serves not only the resorts at Marsh Harbour but those at Elbow Cay (Hope Town).

We prefer to treat Marsh Harbour more as a refueling and transportation depot than as a sightseeing attraction. However, because of its location—roughly in the center of the island—you may want to use it as a base, since it has a number of good inns. Several hotels will rent you a bike if you want to pedal around the town.

In July, Marsh Harbour hosts **Regatta Week,** the premier yachting event in the Abacos, attracting sailboats and their crews from around the world.

ESSENTIALS   Banks   If you're going to be in the Abacos for an extended vacation, Marsh Harbour can serve your banking needs in an emergency. Some cays have banks that operate only 3 hours a week. In Marsh Harbour, go to Barclays Bank, on Don MacKay Boulevard (☎ **242/367-2152**). Hours are Monday through Thursday from 9:30am to 3pm and Friday from 9:30am to 5pm.

Car Rentals   See "Getting Around" at the beginning of this chapter.

Drugstore   For your pharmaceutical needs, go to the Chemist Shop Pharmacy, Don MacKay Boulevard (☎ **242/367-3106**). Hours are Monday through Friday from 8:30am to 5:30pm and Saturday from 8:30am to 1pm.

Medical Care   The best medical clinic in the Abacos is in Marsh Harbour, the Great Abaco Clinic, Queen Elizabeth Road (☎ **242/367-2510**). Hours are Monday through Saturday from 9am to 4pm.

Police   Dial ☎ **242/367-2560.**

Post Office   Marsh Harbour's post office (☎ **242/367-2571**) is on Don MacKay Boulevard. Hours are Monday through Friday from 9am to 5:30pm.

Shopping   There isn't much, but a good address to know is the **Loyalist Shoppe,** Don MacKay Boulevard (☎ **242/367-2701**), where you can stock up on books, stationery, magazines, and office supplies. You can also pick up some routine Bahamian gift items and souvenirs of your visit. Open Monday through Friday from 9am to 5pm, and Saturday 9am to noon.

WHERE TO STAY
EXPENSIVE

Abaco Towns by the Sea. P.O. Box 20486, E. Bay St., Marsh Harbour, Abaco, The Bahamas. ☎ **800/322-7757** in the U.S., or 242/367-2227. Fax 215/938-0656 in the U.S. 65 units. A/C. Year-round, $135–$185 unit for one to six. AE, MC, V.

If you like this resort complex, you can purchase time shares. This is about as good as Marsh Harbour gets, except for the superior Great Abaco Beach Resort (see below). Set on sandy soil on a hilly terrain, it offers lagoon-type beaches looking out over the Sea of Abaco. A cluster of white stucco villas are grouped in a flowering landscape that includes bougainvillea, coconut palms, hibiscus, and banana trees scattered over a property that's deluxe for the area. Since any unit can accommodate up to six, this could be an economical choice, depending on the size of your party. Each accommodation offers two bedrooms, a combined living and dining area, a modern kitchen (with microwave and dishwasher), and ceiling fans. Each unit is also equipped with its own outdoor grill. Linens, bath, and beach towels are provided, and maid service is available for another $15 per day.

Dining/Entertainment: A poolside bar and grill is only routine, but you can walk to several restaurants nearby for more elaborate dinner fare. Live entertainment and dancing are featured 3 nights a week.

Services: Daily activities program, including visits to islands offshore, snorkeling, scuba, fishing, and golf.

Facilities: Swimming pool; lit tennis courts; boutique; bicycle, scooter, and car rentals; nearby sailing and powerboat rentals; jet skis, Sunfish, and sailboards.

Great Abaco Beach Hotel. P.O. Box AB25011, Marsh Harbour, Abaco, The Bahamas. ☎ **242/367-2158,** or 800/468-4799 in the U.S.; 305/359-2720 in Florida. Fax 242/367-2819. 80 rms, 6 villas. A/C TV TEL. Winter, $195 double; $335–$375 villa for four. Off-season, $135 double; $265–$325 villa for four. AE, DISC, MC, V.

Created by a former pilot who served with Canadian forces in World War II, this resort—the best at Marsh Harbour—attracts guests interested in diving and fishing. The two-wing, three-story resort is in two parts: the hotel with handsomely furnished rooms with views opening onto the Sea of Abaco and the Boat Harbour Marina, which has slips for 180 boats and full docking facilities. Each room is furnished in a simple tropical decor—comfortable but far from luxurious. However, rooms with four-poster beds draped in mosquito netting add a nostalgic, plantation-era tone. There are also six villas, each with two bedrooms, two baths, a kitchen and living room area, and private decks. To reach the place, you can take a taxi from Marsh Harbour Airport, a distance of 4 miles.

Dining/Entertainment: The Anglers Restaurant is one of Marsh Harbour's best (see separate recommendation below). You can swim up to the Sand Bar for light snacks and grog.

Services: Laundry.

Facilities: Two swimming pools, 150-slip marina, two tennis courts, fitness center, fishing charters, diving trips, boat rentals, car and bicycle rentals, sightseeing tours.

MODERATE

Nettie's Different of Abaco. Casuarina Pt., P.O. Box AB20092, Abaco, The Bahamas. ☎ **242/366-2150.** Fax 242/327-8152. 8 rms. A/C. $225 double. Rates include all meals. No credit cards.

Set within the hamlet of Casuarina Point, 18 miles south of Marsh Harbour, this is a small, family-managed bonefishing club built at the edge of a saltwater marsh favored by birds, wild hogs, and iguana. Opened in 1993, it's surrounded by a wide deck and a garden and contains a bar and restaurant where the only food available is the Bahamian fare that the staff will recite to you before you sit down for your meal. (The dining room's theme revolves around the primitive household implements that the owner, Nettie Symonette, has hung on her walls. Nonresidents are welcome to drop in for two-course meals priced from $10 to $18 each.) Each of the bedrooms contains a screened-in porch, a ceiling fan, and simple furnishings. If you opt for a stay at this hotel, you'll be exposed to the inner workings of a closely knit, isolated community of residents firmly committed to preserving their environment. Nettie has created a living museum that takes you back through 100 years of the island's history. The place is not luxurious, and it probably won't be to everyone's liking, but its allure is most obvious to bonefishing enthusiasts. Those who appreciate ocean reefs and virgin beaches will also appreciate the place. The hotel is closely associated with several bonefishing guides in the neighborhood, any of whom can arrange full-day fishing excursions for around $250 per couple. (Not all equipment is included in this fee. Be sure you understand all aspects of the arrangements before you commit yourself to a full-fledged fishing expedition here.)

More than any other tourist complex in the Abacos, this one shows the most optimism about a rapid expansion during 1997 and 1998. At this writing, Ms. Symonette had acquired access to three other clusters of lodging, each of which lies within walking distance of the mini-empire's original core (the 8-room bonefishing club referred to as "Nettie Different of Abaco"). If all goes as planned, as many as 42 additional units, some of which are configured as suites, may be available by the time of your visit. Most will be rented by the week, at prices that range from $225 to $700, double occupancy, with meals included.

INEXPENSIVE

Conch Inn Resort & Marina. P.O. Box AB20469, Marsh Harbour, Abaco, The Bahamas. ☎ 242/367-4000. Fax 242/367-4004. 9 rms. A/C TV. Year-round, $85 double. Extra person $10. MC, V.

Set at the junction of Bay Street and the southeastern edge of the harbor, this is a low-slung, one-story hotel whose premises are leased on a long-term basis by one of the world's largest yacht-chartering companies, the Moorings. It doesn't have the ambience of Great Abaco Beach Hotel or Abaco Towns by the Sea, but it's less expensive. Its exterior is painted in white, with pink and blue trim, and its bedrooms are earth-toned hideaways that contain both a queen-size and a double bed, a table, and two chairs. Roll-aways are available for extra occupants. All rooms overlook the yachts bobbing at any of 75 slips in the nearby marina.

Clients at this casual hotel include scuba aficionados and repeat visitors sailing Florida-based yachts who appreciate the opportunity to tie in for fuel, ice, fresh water, and use of the Laundromat, hotel rooms, restaurant, and bar. On the premises are an open-air swimming pool, fringed with palm trees, and a nearby branch of the Dive Abaco scuba facility. The on-site restaurant and bar (Conch Inn Café and Conch Out Bar) are under independent management and are recommended separately in "Where to Dine," below.

BUNGALOW RENTALS

The Lofty Fig Villas. P.O. Box AB20437, Marsh Harbour, Abaco, The Bahamas. ☎ and fax **242/367-2681.** 6 villas. A/C. Dec 15–Sept 15, $108 per day or $702 per week for two. Extra person $15. Sept 16–Dec 14, $90 per day or $585 per week for two. Extra person $10. MC, V.

This family-owned bungalow colony across from the Conch Inn overlooks the harbor. It doesn't have the services and comforts of the places recommended previously, but attracts more self-sufficient types likely to include divers, fishers, snorkelers, and just plain beachcombers. It is superior, however, to Pelican Beach Villas, its major competitor, recommended below. Built in 1970, it stands in a tropical landscape with a freshwater pool. All units are air-conditioned and equipped for housekeeping. Rooms have one queen-size bed and a queen-size hide-a-bed sofa, a fully tiled bathroom, a dining area, a kitchen, and a private screened-in porch. Maid service is provided Monday through Saturday. There is a gazebo with a barbecue at poolside. The location is about a 10-minute walk to a supermarket and shops, and restaurants and bars lie just across the street. Marinas, a dive shop, and boat rentals are also close at hand.

Pelican Beach Villas. Pelican Shores, P.O. Box AB20304, Marsh Harbour, Abaco, The Bahamas. ☎ **800/642-7268** or 242/367-3600. Fax 242/367-3603. 5 cottages. A/C TV TEL. Year-round, $155 daily or $975 weekly for two. Extra person $10 daily, $50 weekly. Children under 12 stay free. MC, V.

In a double waterfront location—a beach in front and a lagoon in back—this cottage colony offers five pink two-bedroom, two-bath accommodations, all fronting on the sea. Every unit has a fully equipped kitchen and sleeps up to six with sleeper sofas. An 87-foot-long dock on the lagoon side of the property accommodates rental boats and is ideal for snorkeling or diving. Nestled in a grove of casuarina trees with its own small cove, the cottages are well furnished in a comfortable Bahamian style, with cathedral ceilings. Shaded picnic tables and beachfront hammocks are outside, and it's only a walk to bakeries and liquor and grocery stores. There's an on-site caretaker.

WHERE TO DINE

Conch Inn Café/Conch Out Bar. At the Conch Inn (The Moorings), Bay St. ☎ **242/367-2319.** Lunch salads, sandwiches, and platters $4–$8.75; main courses $9.50–$22. MC, V. Daily 8am–4pm; Wed–Sun 6–9pm (last order). BAHAMIAN/INTERNATIONAL.

This is the most amusing, sophisticated, and international restaurant in Marsh Harbour. Set adjacent to the Conch Inn and the upscale marina facilities of the Moorings, it attracts whatever yachtie happens to be on-island at the time, and counts among its roster of visitors a surprising array of professional sports players, as well as boaters from as far away as Newport, Bristol (England), and the Azores. The menu is appropriately laden with fish dishes. These include shrimp and crabmeat salad, lobster salad, seafood platters, at least four different preparations of grouper and snapper, and just about everything a chef could conceivably concoct from a conch. The regulars don't even have to consult the menu. All they need to do is ask, "What's good?" on any given night. Stick with the daily specials and skip the tired desserts. And if you're frittering away a few hours before your plane ride out of Marsh Harbour and want to drop in for a drink, consider a Conch Killer, whose yellow color derives from a potent mixture of rums and fruit juices.

Anglers Restaurant. In the Great Abaco Beach Hotel, Marsh Harbour. ☎ **242/367-2158.** Reservations recommended for dinner. Main courses $17–$28. AE, MC, V. Daily 7:30–10:30am, 11:30am–2:30pm, and 6:30–10pm. BAHAMIAN/INTERNATIONAL.

At the Boat Harbour, overlooking the Sea of Abaco, this establishment is the main restaurant in the previously recommended hotel. It has a nautical theme and a Bahamian decor. Dock pilings rise from the water, and the place is open and airy. The menu changes daily, but fresh seafood—your best bet—is always featured, along with a well-chosen selection of meat and poultry dishes. Begin with chilled papaya soup or perhaps the lobster-and-crab pâté. For a main course, try such typical dishes as hogfish and shrimp with a broccoli and basil cream sauce. Desserts are homemade. On Thursday, a buffet is presented, with such dishes as curried conch, fried chicken, and barbecued ribs. The food isn't lavish, but it's good and dependable, particularly if you focus on the fish dishes.

The Jib Room. Marsh Harbour Marina, Pelican Shores. ☎ **242/367-2700.** Main courses $10–$15. MC, V. Daily 10am–3pm; Wed–Thurs and Sun 6:30–10pm. BAHAMIAN/AMERICAN.

This restaurant is the drinking arena of local residents and boat owners who like its welcoming spirit. The Jib Room Restaurant is downstairs, and the canopied Jib Room Bar is upstairs. The canopy is called "the yellow glow," since at night the roof acts as a yellow beacon to boaters in the harbor. Some nights are theme nights—for example, the place to be on Sunday is at the Jib's steak barbecue, which features a live band. About 300 steaks are served that day. Wednesday is another favorite night, with baby back ribs and live music on the agenda. Thursday nights are also special, with slightly more refined fare. Dishes include a seafood platter, New York strip steak, and broiled lobster. Yes, you've had it all before and in better versions, but dishes are well prepared. It's the convivial spirit among the boaters that forms the amusement here, more than the food.

Mangoes Restaurant. Front St., Marsh Harbour. ☎ **242/367-2366.** Reservations recommended. Main courses $16.50–$21.50; lunch $7.50–$12.50. AE, MC, V. Daily 11:30am–2:30pm and 6:30–9pm. Bar, daily 11:30am–midnight. BAHAMIAN/AMERICAN.

Mangoes is the best restaurant, and certainly the most popular, on the island, attracting both yachties and residents. Set near the harborfront, it is also one of the town's most distinctive buildings. It boasts a cedar-topped bar and a cathedral ceiling that soars above a deck jutting out over the water. Somehow the chefs seem to try a little harder here, offering that typical grilled chicken breast but enlivening it with garlic and ginger. Pork tenderloin gets into the island spirit with its coating of mango sauce, and the veal piccata in white wine and lemon juice shows continental flair. Our faithful friend, grilled grouper, is dressed up a bit with black olives, tomatoes, and onions in the style of Provence. Of course, a lot of standard, regular fare is on the menu, as well, including barbecue baby back ribs and cracked conch. Your best bet, as in nearly all Bahamian restaurants, might be the fresh catch of the day. At lunch you can sample their famous "conch burger."

Wally's. E. Bay St., Marsh Harbour. ☎ **242/367-2074.** Reservations recommended for dinner. Main courses $18–$24; lunch $6–$12. AE, MC, V. Tues–Sat 11:30am–3pm and 6–9pm. Closed 6 weeks during Sept and Oct. BAHAMIAN/INTERNATIONAL.

Wally's competes with Mangoes as one of the island's most popular eateries. It occupies a well-maintained pink colonial villa on a lawn dotted with begonias across the street from the water. There's an outdoor terrace, a boutique, and an indoor bar and dining area filled with Haitian paintings. The special drinks are daiquiris, Bahama Mamas, and Goombay Smashes. Instead of the standard conch fritters, opt for the conch cakes in a mango cream sauce as an appetizer. The chef prepares the best Bahamian cracked conch at Marsh Harbour, and even the endangered turtle steak appears on the menu. Perhaps you'll be more politically correct and order the grilled dolphin (the fish, not the mammal) instead. Meat-eaters will also find the typical filet mignon and grilled lamb chops (of course, these are imported). Main dishes come with a generous house salad and vegetables. The kitchen also prepares one of the best lunches in town, everything from conch or dolphin burgers to chicken platters along with some well-stuffed sandwiches.

WATER SPORTS & OTHER OUTDOOR ACTIVITIES

All the hotel keepers at Marsh Harbour can help fix you up with the right people to take care of your sporting requirements. For variety, you can also take the ferry over to Hope Town and avail yourself of the facilities offered there.

BOAT CHARTERS

Abaco Bahamas Charters. 10905 Cowgill Place, Louisville, KY 40243. ☎ **800/626-5690.**

If you'd like to try bareboating in The Bahamas—that is, without captain or crew—one of your best deals is to contact Abaco Bahamas Charters, where weekly charters of a 44-foot boat begin at $2,300. A $500 deposit is required. Only experienced sailors can rent.

The Moorings. P.O. Box AB20469, Marsh Harbour. ☎ **800/535-7289** or 242/367-4000.

This is one of the leading charter-boat outfitters in The Bahamas. It operates out of the Conch Inn Resort and Marina. The outlet is particularly well suited for first-time charters. With one of its vessels you can enjoy short sails between the islands, stopping at white sandy beaches and snug anchorages. The Moorings operates out of a 75-berth marina, with all fuel and equipment supplied. Daily rates generally range from $260 to $590, with a skipper costing another $120 per day.

Sea Horse Boat Rentals. P.O. Box AB20013, Great Abaco Beach Resort, Marsh Harbour. ☎ **242/367-2513.**

For the casual boater, this outfit offers some of the best rentals. An 18-foot Boston whaler rents for $94 per day, and you can also book a 22-foot Privateer for $105 per day. Other vessels are also for rent, and all boats are equipped with a Bimini top, coolers, compass, and swimming platform, along with life jackets, paddle, docking lines, and other equipment. You can also rent bicycles at this outlet for $9 per day. The outfitter is open daily from 8am to 5pm. It's located at the Boat Harbour Marina.

Sunsail. Annapolis Landing Marina, 980 Awald Rd., Ste. 302, Annapolis, MD 21403. ☎ **800/327-2276** in the U.S. and Canada, or 410/280-2553 outside the U.S. and Canada.

If you've got a good track record as a sailor, even of small boats, you can charter a yacht here big enough for the entire family, with just yourself as skipper, to sail to all those remote cays you've heard about. Sunsail, based in Marsh Harbour but with bookings arranged at Annapolis, is the operator of the largest charter fleet in The Bahamas. A bareboat charter is likely to cost you less than a comparable land-based vacation in the Out Islands or in Florida. Of course, you can cook your own meals in the fully equipped galley, complete with icebox (on larger boats, refrigerator and freezer). You can barbecue your steak and fish on a hibachi fixed to the stern rail. You can go where you like, subject to instructions to keep out of shoal waters and stay, with one exception, within the line of the outer cays. Most of the time you cruise in waters 6 to 18 feet deep with the bottom clearly visible.

When you board your boat, you'll find it cleaned, fueled, watered, provisioned, inspected, and ready to sail. Sunsail will give you and your crew a complete familiarization briefing on everything on board from bow to stern—anchors, rigging, sails, engine, radio, lights, navigational aids, cooking equipment, and the outboard dinghy towed astern of every boat. Before you actually sail, they'll give you a chart briefing, warning you of the few dangerous areas, how to "read" the water, and how best to make the Whale Cay ocean passage that takes you to the northern section of Abaco Sound.

Bareboat charters are usually in the range of $1,045 to $4,975 per week, depending on the vessel and the season. For more information, or reservations, write to Sunsail at the above address.

TENNIS

Great Abaco Beach Hotel. Marsh Harbour. ☎ **242/367-2158.**

Two lit hard-surface courts are available at this hotel. Nonguests pay $10 for a game.

SNORKELING & SCUBA DIVING

Dive Abaco. Marsh Harbour. ☎ **800/247-5338** in the U.S., or 242/367-2787.

Dive Abaco offers personally guided tours for scuba divers and snorkelers alike. You can explore tunnels and caverns in the world's third-longest barrier reef. Resort courses for uncertified divers are all inclusive for $100. Scuba trips, including tanks and weights for certified divers, are $70. Snorkeling trips are $35. Both dive and snorkel trips depart daily at 9:30am, and afternoon trips are as demand dictates. Shop hours are daily from 8:30am to 5pm. Ask for owner-operator Keith Rogers.

6 Great Guana Cay

Longest of the Abaco cays, Great Guana, on the east side of the chain, stretches 7 miles from tip to tip and lies between Green Turtle Cay and Man-O-War Cay. The cay has a 7-mile-long beach, which is unsurpassed in The Bahamas. The reef fishing is superb, and bonefish are plentiful in the shallow bays.

The settlement stretches along the beach at the head of the palm-fringed Kidd's Cove, named after the pirate; and the ruins of an old sisal mill near the western end of the island make for an interesting detour. The island has about 150 residents, most of them descendants of Loyalists who left Virginia and the Carolinas to settle in this remote place, often called the "last spot of land before Africa."

As in similar settlements in New Plymouth and Man-O-War Cay, their houses resemble old New England. Over the years the traditional pursuits of the islanders have been boatbuilding and carpentry. They are also farmers and fishers. It won't take you long to explore the village, because it has only two small stores, a one-room schoolhouse, and an Anglican church—and that's about it.

Instead of automobiles, small boats are used for getting around the island. On the cay, boats are available to charter for a half day or a full day (or a month, for that matter). For example, a 23-foot sailboat, fully equipped for living and cruising, is available for charter, and deep-sea fishing trips can be arranged.

Albury's Ferry Service, Marsh Harbour (☎ 242/365-6020), runs a charter service to Great Guana Cay, a one-way ride costing $95 for one to six passengers.

WHERE TO STAY & DINE

Guana Beach Resort. P.O. Box AB20474, Great Guana Cay. (Mailing address: 140 S. University Blvd., Fort Lauderdale, FL 33324.) ☎ **242/367-3590.** Fax 954/423-9786. 8 rms, 7 suites. A/C. Winter, $99–$130 double; $150–$210 suite. Off-season, $79–$115 double; $115–$175 suite. MAP $35 per person extra. MC, V.

This is a "no shoes" type of place. You can't get more remote or more laid-back than this. Yet you do so with a relative degree of comfort. The only hotel on the island, this remotely located resort of comfortably furnished units is ideal for boat owners and escapists who like its barefoot policy. Gordon and Mary Sadler, from Stamford, Connecticut, liked the resort when they first saw it, with its 7 miles of white sandy beaches and coconut palm trees. They purchased it and renovated it, adding such touches as a freshwater pool. Accommodations have their own kitchens. Rooms are furnished in a casual, relaxed, Bahamian style. If you're over for just the day, you can use the resort as a convenient base with marina, dining, and bar facilities. Conch burgers with cold beer are often served for lunch. Informal local entertainment is often arranged. Baby-sitting can also be arranged, and laundry facilities are available. Bicycles can be rented for island tours.

7 Man-O-War Cay

Visiting here is like going back in time. The island has some lovely beaches, and many visitors come here to enjoy them—but it's best to leave your more daring swimwear for other shores.

Some find the people here puritanical in outlook. They are deeply religious, and there is no crime—unless you bring it with you. Alcoholic beverages aren't sold, although you can bring your own supply.

Like New Plymouth, Man-O-War is a Loyalist village, with indications of a New England background. The pastel clapboard houses, built by ships' carpenters and trimmed in gingerbread, are set off by freshly painted white-picket fences intertwined with bougainvillea.

The people here are basically shy, but they do welcome outsiders to their remote, isolated island. They are proud of their heritage, and many, especially the old-timers, have known plenty of hard times. They are similar to (and related to many of) the "conchs" of Key West, a tough, insular people who have exhibited a proud independence of spirit for many years.

If you look through the tiny listing for this cay in the phone book, you'll see that the name Albury predominates. In this famed boatbuilding capital of The Bahamas, Albury long ago became synonymous with that business. You can still see descendants of the early Alburys at work at a boatyard on the harbor. Albury shipbuilders still make Man-O-War runabouts, so often seen sailing in the waters of the Abacos.

Tourism has really only just begun on Man-O-War Cay. Because of the relative lack of hotels and restaurants, many visitors come over just for the day, often in groups from Marsh Harbour.

To reach Man-O-War Cay, you must cross the water from Marsh Harbour. **Albury's Ferry Service** (☎ **242/367-3147** in Marsh Harbour, or 242/365-6010 in Man-O-War) leaves from a dock near the Great Abaco Beach Resort there. The round-trip fare is $12 for adults and $6 for children, and the ride takes about 45 minutes. Except for a few service vehicles, the island is free of cars. But if you want to explore—and don't want to walk—ask around and see if one of the locals will rent you a golf cart.

WHERE TO STAY

Schooner's Landing. Man-O-War Cay, Abaco, The Bahamas. ☎ **242/365-6072.** Fax 242/365-6285. 4 two-bedroom townhouse condos. A/C TV. Oct–May, $850 per week or $150 per day. June–Sept, $995 per week or $175 per day. 3-day minimum stay required. AE, MC, V.

Set within an isolated position on Man-O-War Cay's northeastern edge, this four-unit apartment complex is the only officially designated place to stay on the island. At the time of its construction (1985), its architects wisely added a seawall between its lawns and hibiscus shrubs and the crashing surf, requiring a detour for swimmers and snorkelers who meander a short distance down to the sands of a nearby beach. Each two-story unit contains a kitchen, ceiling fans, two private bathrooms, a TV whose only reception comes from an adjacent VCR machine, and a summery decor of wicker and rattan furniture. There's no bar or restaurant on-site, but either of two grocery stores on the island will deliver, and most visitors opt to cook in, anyway. Facilities include a private dock for anyone who arrives by private boat, and barbecue facilities lie within a gazebolike structure on the grounds.

EXPLORING THE ISLAND: FROM SCULPTURES TO SAILS

Joe's Studio (☎ 242/365-6082), on the harborfront, sells an inventory of island-related odds and ends that make this an appealing stopover. Favorite items for sale here are the models of local sailing dinghies crafted from mahogany and mounted in half profile on a board. They're a substantial and durable souvenir of your visit. Other items include original watercolors, handcrafted woodwork from native woods, and nautical souvenirs and gifts. Hours are Monday through Saturday from 9am to 5pm.

The most unusual store and studio on the island, **Albury's Sail Shop** (☎ 242/365-6014), occupies a house at the eastern end, overlooking the water. Part of the floor space is devoted to the manufacture (and the other half to the display) of an inventory of brightly colored canvas garments and accessories. The cloth that is universally used—8-ounce cotton duck—once served as sailcloth for the community's boats. When synthetic sails came into vogue, four generations of Albury women put the cloth and their talents to use. Don't stop without chatting with the Albury women. Hours are Monday through Saturday from 7:30am to 5pm.

8 Elbow Cay (Hope Town)

Elbow Cay, noted for the many white sandy beaches that attract hundreds of visitors to its shores, is connected by a regular 40-minute, $8 round-trip **ferry** or **water-taxi** service to Great Abaco at Marsh Harbour. Call Albury's Ferry Service at ☎ 242/367-3147 for more information. The cay's largest settlement is **Hope Town**, a little village with a candy-striped, 120-foot lighthouse, the most photographed attraction in the Out Islands. The kerosene-powered light is still in service.

You can climb to the top of the lighthouse for a sweeping view of the surrounding land and water. From the time construction on this beacon first began in 1838, it came under a great deal of harassment from the Abaco wreckers, who lived on salvaged cargo from wrecked and foundered ships. Seeing an end to their means of livelihood, they did much to sabotage the light in the early days.

Hope Town, often called a "time-warp" hamlet, like other offshore cays of the Abacos, was settled by Loyalists who left the new United States and came to The Bahamas to remain subjects of the British Crown. It has clapboard, saltbox cottages weathered to a silver gray or painted in pastel colors, with white picket fences setting them off. The buildings may remind you of New England, but this palm-fringed island has a definite South Seas flavor.

Over the years Hope Town has attracted many famous visitors, some of whom, such as Dr. George Gallup, the pollster, liked it so much that they built "homes away from home" here.

The island is almost free of vehicular traffic. In exploring Hope Town, you can take one of two roads: "Up Along" or "Down Along," the latter running along the water.

Malone seems to be the most popular name here. The founding mother of the town circa 1783 (perhaps 1775) was Wyannie Malone, who came here as a widow with four children. Her descendants are still a big part of the population of 500 full-time residents. A **museum** on Queen's Highway (no phone) is dedicated to

Wyannie's memory and contains exhibits tracing the rich history of the cay. It's generally open from 10am to noon, but you can't be sure. Donations are welcome.

ESSENTIALS   Drugstore   Try the Clear View Drug Store, Gilliam Road (☎ 242/366-0026), which is open Monday through Friday from 8am to noon and from 12:30 to 5pm.

Post Office   There is a local post office (☎ **242/366-0098**), but expect mail sent from here to take a long time. The location is at the head of the upper public dock. Hours are Monday through Friday from 9am to 1:30pm and from 2:30 to 5pm.

WHERE TO STAY
MODERATE

Abaco Inn. Hope Town, Elbow Cay, Abaco, The Bahamas. ☎ **800/468-8799** in the U.S., or 242/366-0133. Fax 242/366-0113. 12 rms, 2 suites. A/C. Winter, $120–135 double. Off-season, $90–$100 double. Year-round, $175 one-bedroom suite. MAP $35 per person extra. AE, MC, V.

This is the area's most sophisticated and desirable resort, although it no longer enjoys the chic reputation it had in its heyday of the 1980s. It nestles on a ridge of sandy soil on the narrowest section of Elbow Cay, about 1¹/₂ miles south of Hope Town. As you stand on the ridge, you'll find yourself on a strategically important land bridge between the crashing surf of the jagged eastern coast and the sheltered waters of White Sound and the Sea of Abaco to the west. An informal "barefoot elegance" and welcoming enthusiasm prevail. The resort's social center is in a modern and rambling clubhouse with a fireplace and the most appealing bar on the island.

Each of the accommodations, which are scattered between the palms and sea grapes of the sandy terrain, has a hammock placed conveniently nearby for quiet afternoons of reading or sleeping, a ceiling fan, private bath, and a comfortable decor of white wooden walls and conservative furniture. The new suites have been outfitted with kitchenettes. When you tire of your cabin with its carefully maintained privacy, you can dream of faraway places from a perch in the cedar-capped gazebo, which sits between the saltwater pool and the rocky tidal flats of the Atlantic.

Club Soleil Resort. Western Harbourfront, Hope Town, Elbow Cay, The Bahamas. ☎ **242/366-0003.** Fax 242/366-0254. 6 rms. A/C MINIBAR TV. Winter, $115 double; $125 triple; $135 quad. Off-season, $110 double; $120 triple; $130 quad. MAP $32 per person extra. MC, V.

Because of its isolated position near the lighthouse on the mostly uninhabited western edge of Hope Town's harbor, you'll have to arrive at this Spanish-style resort by boat. If you bring your own, you can moor it at this establishment's marina, but if you happen not to have one, a phone call to the owners can quickly arrange a free waterborne transfer from any nearby coastline you designate. Rooms are contained in a two-story, motel-like annex, whose windows overlook a swimming pool, as well as the boats that moor at the wooden pier. Each room contains two double beds, a coffeemaker, and a small refrigerator. The restaurant is covered separately in "Where to Dine," below.

Hope Town Harbour Lodge. Hope Town, Abaco. ☎ **800/316-7844** or 242/366-0095. Fax 242/366-0286. 20 rms. A/C. Year-round, $110–$145 double; $120–$155 triple; $135–$165 quad. MC, V. Restaurant closed Sept–Oct.

Set on a hilltop overlooking 1¹/₂ miles of beach and the hamlet of Hope Town, the core of this much-renovated, two-story inn began its life as an English brigadier's private home in 1948. Today, it's the domain of the Gale and Kenyon families, whose yacht rental service (Island Marine) is the oldest and largest in The Bahamas. Accommodations consist of 14 modest rooms in the main house (whose windows overlook

Hope Town's harbor) and 6 ocean-view rooms (without kitchens) scattered around the swimming pool, within a garden. Each of these overlooks the Atlantic and lies across the road from the main building. Accommodations are comfortable but simple. Each room was renovated in 1993, and each has a ceiling fan. Restaurants on-site include an upper-floor room within the main building, whose view includes both the harbor and the Atlantic, and a less formal eatery beside the hotel's swimming pool that serves only breakfast and lunch. Facilities include a marina and a staff who can arrange most water sports.

VILLA RENTALS

Hope Town Hideaways. Hope Town, Elbow Cay, Abaco, The Bahamas. ☎ **242/366-0224.** Fax 242/366-0434. 5 units. A/C TEL. Dec 16–Sept 15, $175 double; $250 triple or quad; off-season, $140 double; $190 triple or quad. MC, V.

These complete island homes let guests feel like "locals," or at least like second-home owners. These gingerbread-trimmed villas attract families, couples, and fishing buddies. Each unit has a large kitchen. The villas lie on 11 acres bordering the water, and each has a large deck, a dining room, a living area with two single daybeds, and two bedrooms with queen-size beds and deck entrances. Each of the master bedrooms includes custom built-in beds, dressers, makeup vanities, as well as reading lamps, a large bath with shower, and a private entrance deck. Each unit sleeps one or two couples (the limit is six guests per villa). Furnishings are elegant and attractive. The most recent addition is a honeymoon cottage with a gazebo shower and tub and an outside garden. The villa cluster lies in the shadow of the lighthouse, overlooking boats moored in the harbor and the clapboard houses of Hope Town. Owners Chris and Peggy Thompson do everything from overseeing housekeeping to arranging rental boats, guided fishing trips, picnics, island-hopping excursions, and scuba-and-snorkeling trips.

Sea Spray Resort & Marina. White Sound, Elbow Cay, Abaco, The Bahamas. ☎ **242/366-0065.** Fax 242/366-0383. 6 villas. A/C. Year-round, $700–$1,125 per week for one to four persons. AE, MC, V.

On 6 acres of landscaped grounds, these one- and two-bedroom villas are owned and operated by Monty and Ruth Albury, who run them in a welcoming, personal way. They recently renovated and expanded the resort, refurbishing the rooms and the restaurant, adding another restaurant, and constructing an additional 35 slips in the marina. The Alburys share their vast experience of what to see and do on Elbow Cay and in the Abaco area. You can bicycle, sail, go deep-sea fishing, snorkel, bonefish, or explore nearby deserted islands.

All of the villas have comfortable Bahamian tropical furnishings, with full kitchens and decks overlooking the water. Sea Spray also operates an informal clubhouse restaurant, serving Bahamian and American dishes. Its newer restaurant, the Boat House, overlooking the marina dockside, serves a Bahamian cuisine with European flair. Some of the extras the resort offers include daily maid service, unlimited Sunfish use, a private barbecue pit, and free boat dockage up to 23 feet, as well as a freshwater swimming pool. The location is 3¹/₂ miles south of Hope Town along the coastal road.

WHERE TO DINE

Abaco Inn. Hope Town. ☎ **242/366-0133.** Reservations required. Main courses $16–$26; lunch $4–$10. AE, MC, V. Daily 7am–11:30pm. BAHAMIAN/AMERICAN.

The best food on the island is served in the clubhouse of the previously recommended hotel, within view of the crashing surf and a weathered gazebo. The chef prepares such lunch dishes as conch chowder, lobster salad, pasta primavera, and salads with delectable homemade dressings laced with tarragon and other herbs. There is a changing dinner menu of seafood and meats, each expertly seasoned and well prepared. Typical meals are likely to begin with seafood bisque or vichyssoise, followed by broiled lobster, grilled tuna with béarnaise sauce, or, our favorite, broiled red snapper with a light salsa. The key lime pie or coconut pie is delectable. The inn will send a minivan to collect you from other parts of the island if you phone in advance.

Club Soleil Resort. Western Harbourfront, Hope Town. ☎ 242/366-0003. Reservations recommended for dinner. Lunch main courses $5.50–$11; dinner main courses (including appetizers, salad, soup) $16–$26.50. MC, V. Daily 8–10am, noon–2pm, and 6–9pm. BAHAMIAN/ SEAFOOD.

This pleasant restaurant, on the premises of a marina, lies within a sunny building set on piers, on the western side of Hope Town's harbor. To reach it, you'll arrive either by private yacht or by phoning the owners in advance. (They'll send a boat to meet you wherever you specify.) Lunch might include conch burgers, cheeseburgers, and an array of such salads as Niçoise and lobster.

In the evening there's a vast improvement over this standard luncheon fare. Snapper, grouper, or kingfish are likely to be featured, and these dishes can be heart-warming if cooked just right and served with butter and garlic sauce. The broiled seafood platter is a another good choice, served with lemon and garlic. For those who don't want fish that night, the typical rack of lamb Provençale or a good steak will provide diversions, although these ingredients are shipped in frozen from the mainland.

Harbour's Edge. Hope Town. ☎ **242/366-0087.** Reservations not accepted. Main courses $18–$24; lunch $6–$10. MC, V. Wed–Mon 11:30am–3pm and 5–9pm. Closed mid-Sept to mid-Oct. BAHAMIAN.

One of the town's most popular and best restaurants is set on piers above the water, in a clapboard house next to the post office. A bar is found near the entrance, with an adjacent waterside deck for watching the passage of boats. There's also a tile-floored dining room, where the crackle of VHF radio is always audible. Boat owners and local residents reserve tables on the short-wave radio, channel 16. Lunch includes conch fritters, conch chowder, hamburgers, sandwiches, and conch platters. All this is typical, but flavorful nonetheless. In the evening the dinners are also plain but well prepared, the type of food boaters like to eat in The Bahamas and elsewhere. Generous portions of panfried pork chops, char-grilled grouper, New York strip steak, and fried chicken take care of anybody's hunger pangs.

Hope Town Harbour Lodge, Upper Terrace/Main Dining Room and Reef Bar & Grille. Hope Town. ☎ **242/366-0095.** Breakfast $6.50–$9.75; lunch $4–$11.50; dinner $7–$22. MC, V. Daily 8–10am, 11:30am–2:30pm, and Tues–Sat 6:30–9pm. BAHAMIAN/ AMERICAN.

The Reef Bar & Grille only serves lunch, and is next to the pool. The Main Dining Room offers breakfast and dinner with a choice of seating either inside or outside on a terrace overlooking the harbor. For lunch it's nothing fancy—only the regular conch fritters, freshly made salads, and burgers. But there is something special: a lobster burger. Try it: you'll become addicted. Dinners tend to be light, the main offerings usually being pastas and salads, along with Bahamian food. Start with the coconut-battered lobster bites or else the steamed conch, then move on to the stewed fish, which is a favorite of the regulars, or the deep-dish vegetable lasagna. The menu changes nightly, so check ahead to see what is being offered that evening.

Rudy's Place. Center Line Rd., Elbow Cay. ☎ **242/366-0062.** Reservations required. Three-course fixed-price dinners $20–$25, plus drinks. MC, V. Mon–Sat 6:30–8:45pm (last order). Closed Sept–Oct. BAHAMIAN.

Because of its isolated position in a wooden house in a valley in the center of the island, this restaurant provides free transportation before and after dinner. It's owned by Rudy Moree, who prepares recipes handed down from his Bahamian grandmother. These, adapted to the tastes of his international clientele, might include crayfish tails baked with Parmesan and butter, a delectable broiled shrimp in a white wine and garlic sauce, or even a passable roasted duck in an orange sauce. You'll dine in a modern dining room sheathed with knotty pine.

EXPLORING THE ABACOS BY BOAT

On your own in a rented boat is an ideal way to explore the Abacos. **Island Marine,** Parrot Cay in Hope Town (☎ 242/366-0282), will set you up. With one of its rental boats, you can cruise to the boatbuilding settlement of Man-of-War Cay, to artist Pete Johnson's bronze foundry-gallery in Little Harbour, and to many uninhabited cays and deserted beaches where you can go shelling, beachcombing, exploring, and picnicking.

Small-boat rentals range from a 17-foot Boston Whaler to 20-foot Man-O-War boats, even 22-foot Aquasports. Prices run from $80 to $105 per day or $400 to $595 per week. Island Marine is open daily from 8am to 5pm. Resident Bahamian guides will also take you out in a rental boat or their own craft to enjoy bone, reef, or deep-sea fishing. Abundant in local waters are grouper, snapper, wahoo, yellowtail, dolphinfish, and kingfish.

SHOPPING

Of course, no one comes to Hope Town just to shop, but once you're here you might want to buy a souvenir or gift. At Kemp's Straw Market, Hope Town, you can find some gift items made by local residents.

Ebb Tide Gift Shop. Hope Town. ☎ **242/366-0088.**

The best-stocked gift shop in town is found in a white clapboard house with yellow trim one block from the harbor. Inside you'll find many treasures, including Androsia batiks made on Andros, along with costume jewelry, T-shirts, original watercolors, and fabrics sold by the yard. Many other souvenirs are displayed. Hours are Monday through Saturday from 9am to 4:30pm. Closed Labor Day to mid-October.

El Mercado. Hope Town. ☎ **242/366-0053.**

Several of the items sold here are handcrafted. The selection includes hand-painted T-shirts, gold and silver jewelry, framed maps, gift items, Latin American handcrafts, and Bahamian carvings. Hours are Monday through Saturday from 9:30am to 4:30pm.

9 Little Harbour

In the Abaco gift and souvenir shops you'll see a remarkable book, *Artist on His Island,* detailing the true-life adventures of Randolph and Margot Johnson, who lived a *Swiss Family Robinson*–type adventure with their three sons. Arriving on this southerly point of the Abacos aboard their old Bahamian schooner, the *Langosta,* they lived in one of the natural caves on the island until they eventually erected a thatched dwelling for themselves.

That was some time ago—in 1951. Now the Johnsons, including son Pete, have achieved international fame as artists and sculptors while still living on their own Little Harbour island, a cay shaped like a circle, with a white-sand beach running along most of it.

If you ask at your hotel in Marsh Harbour, chances are that an arrangement can be made for you to visit the island, which is serviced by Albury's Ferry. This is the southernmost stop of the ferry line. Since the island is private property, you are asked to treat it as if it's someone's home you're visiting—as indeed it is.

On the island is a foundry in which Mr. Johnson, using an old "lost-wax" method, casts his bronze sculptures, many of which are in prestigious galleries today. Mrs. Johnson creates porcelain figurines of island life—birds, fish, boats, and fishers. She also works in glazed metals. They welcome visitors at their studio daily from 10 to 11am and from 2 to 3pm. It's also possible to purchase their art, which comes in a wide price range.

Eleuthera, Harbour Island & Spanish Wells

Founded in 1648, Eleuthera Island was the first permanent settlement in The Bahamas. It is the "birthplace of The Bahamas," a sort of Bahamian Plymouth Rock. In search of religious freedom, the Eleutherian Adventurers came here from Bermuda, finding and colonizing the long, narrow island that still carries their name (Greek for freedom). The locals call it "Cigatoo."

What these adventurers found was an island 100 miles long and a bow shot wide (an average of 2 miles), lying on the eastern flank of The Bahamas. Today Eleuthera is an island of white- and pink-sand beaches edged by casuarina trees, high, rolling green hills, sea-to-sea views, dramatic cliffs, sheltered coves, old villages of pastel-washed cottages, and resorts built around excellent harbors. Eleuthera and its satellite islands, Spanish Wells and Harbour Island, are a water-lover's haven. For superb snorkeling, reef diving, and surfing, simply step into the water. Eleuthera and the Abacos have somewhat the same appeal, although boaters are more drawn to the Abacos. In many ways, if you're seeking that "Cape Cod" in the tropics aura, Harbour Island is even more evocative a site than is New Plymouth or Hope Town in the Abacos.

Eleuthera begins 70 miles east of Nassau and can be reached by a 30-minute air flight. It encompasses about 200 square miles. The island is known for its ocean holes that swirl saltwater into land-locked rock formations.

The population today, estimated at 10,000, is a medley of farmers, shopkeepers, and fishers. Roads run along the coastline, although you'll find that some of them are not adequately paved.

Eleuthera rivals the Abacos in its lure for the foreign visitor. Along with the Abacos, it has the largest concentration of resort hotels outside of Nassau/Paradise Island and Freeport/Lucaya.

Of the 10 destinations recommended in this chapter, **Harbour Island** gets our vote as the number-one choice. Dunmore Town on Harbour Island declared itself the so-called capital of The Bahamas in 1648 when Captain William Sayle and the Eleutherian Adventureres arrived and is the island's oldest and most charming settlement. Many visitors who have traveled all over The Bahamas consider Harbour Island the most beautiful in the archipelago, and we concur.

Spanish Wells is another small island just off the north end of Eleuthera. Spanish galleons put sailors ashore to fill the ships' casks with fresh water after long sea voyages—hence the present-day name of the island.

The fishing and diving in the waters around Eleuthera are top-notch. The islands offer a wide choice of coral gardens, reefs, drop-offs, wrecks, and drift dives. Fishers come to Eleuthera for bottom, bone-, and deep-sea fishing, testing their skill against the dolphinfish, the wahoo, the blue or white marlin, the Allison tuna, and the amberjack. Charter boats are available at Powell Point, Rock Sound, Spanish Wells, and Harbour Island. Sunfish, sailboats, and Boston Whalers for reef fishing can also be rented.

GETTING THERE

BY PLANE   Eleuthera has three main airports. North Eleuthera Airport, obviously, serves the north along with two major offshore cays, Harbour Island and Spanish Wells. Governor's Harbour Airport serves the center of the island, and Rock Sound International Airport handles traffic to South Eleuthera. Make sure, when making your reservations, that your flight will arrive at the right airport; one visitor flew into Rock Sound Airport, only to face a $100 taxi ride and a water-taxi trip before reaching his final destination of Harbour Island in the north.

Bahamasair (☎ 800/222-4262) offers daily flights between Nassau and the three airports, North Eleuthera, Governor's Harbour, and Rock Sound. Bahamasair also has direct flights from Miami to each of the airports twice weekly.

In addition, several commuter airlines, with regularly scheduled service, fly from the Florida mainland with either nonstop or one-stop service. Many private flights use the North Eleuthera Airport, with its 4,500-foot paved runway. It is an official Bahamian port of entry, and a Customs and Immigration official is on hand.

USAir Express (☎ 800/428-4322) operates what might be the most popular way of reaching two of Eleuthera's airports directly from the mainland of Florida. Flights depart once a day from Fort Lauderdale flying nonstop to North Eleuthera, then continuing on after a brief unloading of passengers and baggage to Governor's Harbour. **American Eagle** (☎ 800/433-7300) offers twice-daily flights from Miami to Governor's Harbour with three flights on Saturday and Sunday.

BY MAIL BOAT   Several mail boats from Nassau, leaving from Potter's Cay Dock, visit Eleuthera, but their schedules are subject to change because of weather conditions. For more details of sailings, consult the dockmaster at Potter's Cay Dock in Nassau (☎ 242/393-1064).

The MV *Current Pride* goes from Nassau to Current Island, serving lower and upper Bogue. It departs Nassau at 7am Thursday, returning on Tuesday.

The MV *Bahamas Daybreak II* leaves Nassau, heading for North Eleuthera, Spanish Wells, and Harbour Island; it also makes a stopover at the port in North Eleuthera. Departures are on Thursday at 7am from Nassau, with a return on Sunday.

The *Bahamas Daybreak III* departs on Monday for South Eleuthera, stopping at Rock Sound.

1 Rock Sound

Located in South Eleuthera, Rock Sound is a small, tree-shaded village, the principal center of the island and once its most exclusive enclave. The closing of the famous Cotton Club and the equally famous Windermere Club has, temporarily at least, halted the flow of famous visitors, who have included everybody from Princess Di

Eleuthera, Harbour Island & Spanish Wells

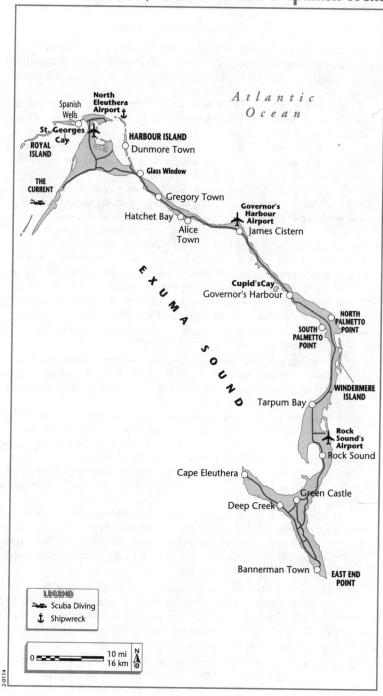

Spanish Wells

North Eleuthera Airport

St. Georges Cay

ROYAL ISLAND

THE CURRENT

HARBOUR ISLAND
Dunmore Town

Glass Window

Gregory Town

Hatchet Bay

Alice Town

Governor's Harbour Airport
James Cistern

Atlantic Ocean

EXUMA SOUND

Cupid'sCay
Governor's Harbour

NORTH PALMETTO POINT

SOUTH PALMETTO POINT

WINDERMERE ISLAND

Tarpum Bay

Rock Sound's Airport
Rock Sound

Cape Eleuthera

Green Castle

Deep Creek

Bannerman Town

EAST END POINT

LEGEND
🐌 Scuba Diving
⚓ Shipwreck

0 ___ 10 mi
___ 16 km

N

2-0114

The Eleutherian Adventurers

Long before the first English colonists arrived, Eleuthera was inhabited by native Lucayans. However, around the mid-16th century, Spaniards came this way, capturing the peaceable people and shipping them out to the Caribbean as slaves.

Pirates plied the waters off Eleuthera and its adjacent islands, but after the removal of the Lucayans there were no inhabitants here for a century, until Capt. William Sayle led the Eleutherian Adventurers here from Bermuda to start a new life. The founding party consisted of about 70 people. They had a rough time of it. Dangerous reefs on the north coast of the island caused their ship and cargo to be lost. Trapped, they had to live off the land as best they could, initially inhabiting a cave (for a description, see "The Current," below). Many of them nearly starved, but they nevertheless drew up their own constitution, promising justice for all. Help came from Virginia colonists who sent food to the little band of adventurers.

Life on Eleuthera proved too much for many of the founding party, however. Many, including Captain Sayle, later returned to Bermuda. But reinforcements were on the way, both from Bermuda and from England, some bringing slaves with them. A permanent settlement had been founded. Freed slaves also came to this island and established settlements. The next wave of settlers were fleeing Loyalists leaving the new United States to continue living under the British Crown. These settled principally in two offshore cays, Harbour Island and Spanish Wells.

to titans of industry. Both of these hotels at press time remain closed, and each was reason enough to go to Rock Sound in the first place. Now you can have many of South Eleuthera's best beaches to yourself until one or both of these properties recover under some new incarnation.

Rock Sound opens onto Exuma Sound and is located to the south of Tarpum Bay. The town is at least two centuries old, and it has many old-fashioned homes with picket fences out front. Once it was notorious for the wreckers who lured ships ashore with false beacons. In those days it was known as "Wreck Sound."

Besides having an airport, Rock Sound also boasts a shopping center, but not a lot else. Many residents who live in South Eleuthera come here to stock up on supplies.

The Ocean Hole, which is about 1¼ miles east of the heart of the town, is a saltwater lake that eventually links to the sea. You can walk right down to the edge of the water. This is one of the most attractive spots on Eleuthera. The "hole" is said to be bottomless. Many tropical fish can be seen here; they seem to like to be photographed—but only if you feed them first.

ESSENTIALS   Car Rentals   Ask at your hotel for what's available. No national car-rental agencies operate here. Dingle Motor Service, King's Street (☎ **242/334-2031,** or 242/334-2231 after 5pm), will rent you a vehicle at $60 a day or $350 per week. This agency will deliver to either Rock Sound or Governor's Harbour if you notify them of the time of your arrival.

Medical Care   A doctor and four resident nurses form the staff of the Rock Sound Medical Clinic (☎ **242/334-2226**). Office hours are daily from 9am to 1pm. After that, the doctor is always available to handle emergency cases.

Police   Telephone ☎ **242/334-2244** to call the police.

WHERE TO STAY

As of this writing, the famous Cotton Bay Club—the reason the glitterati went to Rock Sound in the first place—remains closed, with no announced date for its reopening. What remains to house guests are one or two places so simple they can be recommended only to the most undemanding clients.

Edwina's Place. P.O. Box 30, Rock Sound, Eleuthera, The Bahamas. ☎ **242/334-2094.** 9 rms. A/C. Year-round, $75 double. No credit cards. Closed Sept–Oct.

This Bahamian-owned place is just a mile south of Rock Sound airport. Its utter simplicity is balanced by the enthusiastic hospitality of the aging Mrs. Edwina Burrows, who vows to carry on in spite of the spectacular drop-off in tourism in South Eleuthera. Set directly on the water, her guest rooms are furnished plainly. No one in the area has much money for state-of-the-art maintenance. There is a restaurant on the premises, but it's only open for breakfast and, occasionally, for a requested dinner. This place is not for everyone, but Edwina is a dear old soul.

All village facilities are within walking distance of the motel. Most of the guests live in their swimsuits, so dress is decidedly casual. Tennis, snorkeling, scuba diving, deep-sea fishing, and boating can be arranged by the management.

WHERE TO DINE

Sammy's Place. Albury's Lane, Rock Sound. ☎ **242/334-2121.** Reservations recommended only for special meal requests. Bahamian breakfasts $7; lunch $3–$7; main courses $8–$18. MC, V. Daily 8am–10pm. BAHAMIAN.

Hot gossip and cheap, juicy burgers make this the most popular hangout in Rock Sound. Go here for a slice of the local life. It's on the northeastern approach to the settlement, in a neighborhood that even the owner refers to as "the back side of town." Opened in 1987 by entrepreneur Sammy Culmer (who's assisted by Margarita, his daughter), it's contained within a two-story, white-sided building constructed of cement blocks. Inside, within a peach-colored decor whose only view overlooks the street outside, you can order drinks (which include Bahama Mamas and rum punches), conch fritters, conch chowder, marinated conch salads, Creole-style grouper, breaded scallops, pork chops, and lobster. If you happen to drop in before 11am, you might be tempted by a Bahamian breakfast of stewed fish with johnnycakes, or a selection of egg dishes or omelets. Everything is very simple here, but many visitors prefer it for its almost complete lack of pretension.

A quartet of simple, bare-boned bedrooms lie upstairs. Each costs $60 per night, single or double occupancy. Breakfast is extra.

A SIDE TRIP TO CAPE ELEUTHERA

After leaving Rock Sound you can head south bypassing the currently closed Cotton Bay Club and continuing through the hamlets of Green Castle and Deep Creek as you cut northwest along the only road leading to Cape Eleuthera. If you continue directly south, you'll reach the end of the island chain, Bannerman Town.

Now relatively deserted, Cape Eleuthera was once a chic address when it was the site of a resort and yacht club that drew some of the movers and shakers from the East Coast of America. Right now the Cape Eleuthera Hotel caters exclusively to visitors from Northern Italy. But once upon a time the yacht club drew some of the biggest names in America, including Richard Nixon and his pal Bebe Rebozo. They are gone now and not coming back. Once some of the top golfers in America played its Bruce Devlin–Bob van Haage 18-hole course, which winds its way along the water. The splendid white sandy beaches—a trio of them—are still here, and locals claim the deep-sea fishing is as fine as it ever was. Go here for the natural beauty of the area—and the memories.

2 Windermere Island

Windermere is a very tiny island, connected by a bridge to "mainland" Eleuthera. It is midway between the settlements of Governor's Harbour and Rock Sound.

This island couldn't be more discreet. "We like to keep it quiet around here," one of the staff at the presently closed Windermere Island Club once told us. But, regrettably for this once deluxe and snobbish citadel, that wasn't always possible. When Prince Charles first took Princess Di here in the 1980s, she was photographed in her swimsuit, even though pregnant, and the picture gained wide notoriety, much to the horror of the club.

Prince Charles himself had first heard of the club long ago, through his great-uncle, Earl Mountbatten of Burma, who was assassinated in 1979 while sailing off Ireland. He was one of the island's more frequent visitors and one of its major enthusiasts.

The well-heeled on both sides of the Atlantic, not only the Mountbattens but also the Astors and the Biddles, have flocked to this club, along with an occasional visiting head of state and tycoons of industry.

At press time, the Windermere Club is closed, but check with a travel agent about its status, as properties in South Eleuthera have a long history of suddenly closing and just as suddenly reopening.

Even without its chief attraction, Windermere Island is worth a day trip all on its own, especially Savannah Sound, which has lovely sheltered beaches and facilities for waterskiing, sailboating, snorkeling, and skin diving. There are also excellent beaches for shelling. Frequent picnics are arranged at West Beach on Savannah Sound, and there is good bonefishing, with some catches more than 10 pounds.

BEACHES, WATER SPORTS & OTHER OUTDOOR ACTIVITIES

Visitors can enjoy a number of activities, from **bonefishing** to **windsurfing.** The dockmaster at West Beach is well qualified to guide and advise about bonefishing, or perhaps you'd like to go **deep-sea fishing** for white marlin, dolphinfish, grouper, wahoo, Allison tuna, and amberjack, just a few of the big fish found in these waters.

West Beach, a good place for sunning and swimming (great for children), is about a 10-minute walk from the shut-down Windermere Club. The beach is on Savannah Sound, the body of calm, protected water separating Windermere from the main island of Eleuthera.

3 Tarpum Bay

If you're looking for an inexpensive holiday on high-priced Eleuthera, head here. A waterfront village, some 9 miles north of Rock Sound, it has a number of guest houses that take in economy-minded tourists who aren't too demanding—in fact, who aren't demanding at all. This tiny settlement with its many pastel-washed houses is a favorite of artists who have established a small colony here.

The area flourished as a pineapple-export center from the 1870s until the 1940s, when the industry was felled by competition from Hawaii and Cuba. That's when many of the present clapboard homes with their gingerbread trim were constructed. Nowadays an air of nostalgia pervades this old community. It's also good for fishing.

The community's artistic patriarch is a Scottish-Irish sculptor and painter who since 1957 has occupied an oceanfront house on the northern edge of the hamlet.

Bearded, psychic, and gracious, Peter MacMillan-Hughes, at his **MacMillan-Hughes Gallery and Castle** (☎ 242/334-4091), has sold paintings to an impressive array of patrons, including Lord Mountbatten. His pen-and-ink tinted maps, drawings of birds, and hand-lettered poems and histories are displayed in many prominent homes. He built the tower of the limestone castle that rises from the center of town, a short walk from his studio. More recently, he added a second tower with stained-glass windows and a new art gallery to the castle. Soft-spoken and accessible, Mr. MacMillan-Hughes is the single most interesting tourist attraction at Tarpum Bay. Visitors are welcome to show up at his door during daylight hours.

WHERE TO STAY

Cartwright's Ocean Front Cottages. Bay St., Tarpum Bay, Eleuthera, The Bahamas. ☎ **242/334-4215.** 4 cottages. Year-round, $90 one-bedroom cottage double; $110 two-bedroom cottage triple or quad; $150 three-bedroom cottage (up to six persons). No credit cards.

Cartwright's is a cluster of simple cottages right by the sea, with fishing, snorkeling, and swimming at your door. This is one of the few places where you can sit on your patio and watch the sunset. The cottages, most recently renovated in 1996, are fully furnished, with utensils, stove, refrigerator, and pots and pans. Maid service is also provided. The establishment is within walking distance of local stores and restaurants. The owners are helpful. Hervis Jr. operates an informal taxi business and will meet you at Rock Sound airport, 7 miles away.

Hilton's Haven Motel and Restaurant. Tarpum Bay, Eleuthera, The Bahamas. ☎ **242/334-4231.** 10 rms, 1 apt. Year-round, $55 double; $65 triple; $65 apt for four. MAP $17 per person. No credit cards.

This is a Bahamian two-story structure with covered verandahs. It's modest, unassuming, and completely unpretentious, if that's what you're seeking. The prices are decent, too. Comfortably furnished apartments, each with a private sun patio and bath, are rented. The units come with either air-conditioning or ceiling fans. What makes this place special is Mary Hilton herself, everybody's "Bahama Mama." In fact, as a professional nurse, she has delivered some 2,000 of Eleuthera's finest citizens.

If you arrive hot and thirsty, she'll get a fresh lime off a tree and make you a drink. To provide a retirement income for herself, she started Hilton's Haven. "Hilton is my God-given name," she says. "I never met Conrad."

The main tavern-style dining room, with a library in the corner, provides well-cooked food; the cuisine puts its emphasis on freshly caught fish. You can order grouper cutlets with peas 'n' rice, steamed conch, and an occasional lobster. There is also a well-stocked bar. Lunches, costing from $8 each, are served from 12:30 to 2:30pm, and dinners, from $12 to $18 each, are offered from 6:30 to 8pm.

4 Governor's Harbour

After passing through Tarpum Bay, the next destination is Governor's Harbour, which, at some 300 years old, is the island's oldest settlement. This is believed to have been the landing place of the Eleutherian Adventurers. The largest settlement in Eleuthera after Rock Sound, it lies about midway along the 100-mile-long island. It has an airport where Bahamasair comes in on both morning and evening flights from Nassau.

The town today has a population of about 750, with some bloodlines going back to the original settlers, the Eleutherian Adventurers, and to the Loyalists who followed some 135 years later. Many old homes—waiting for "discovery"—can still be seen. A quiet nostalgia prevails amid the bougainvillea and casuarina trees.

Leaving Queen's Highway, you can take a small bridge to Cupid's Cay. The bridge to the cay is thought to be about a century and a half old. As you're exploring, you'll come upon one of the most interesting buildings in the area, an old Anglican church with its tombstone-studded graveyard.

The long-ago opening of the Club Med brought renewed vitality to the sleepy village. Tourism has unquestionably altered Governor's Harbour.

ESSENTIALS If you're staying outside the town in one of the housekeeping colonies, you may find much-needed services and supplies in Governor's Harbour or at nearby Palmetto Point.

Bank Governor's Harbour has a branch of Barclays Bank International, Queen's Highway, P.O. Box 22 (☎ 242/332-2300). It is open Monday through Thursday from 9:30am to 3pm and Friday from 9:30am to 5pm.

Medical Care On Queen's Highway is the Governor Harbour's Medical Clinic (☎ 242/332-2001). Hours are Monday through Friday from 9am to 5:30pm. The clinic is also the site of a dentist's office. The dentist is here at 9:30am Monday through Wednesday and Friday only. Call for an appointment before going there.

Police To telephone the police, call ☎ 242/332-2111.

Post Office Governor's Harbour has a post office on Haynes Avenue (☎ 242/332-2060). Hours are Monday through Friday from 9am to 4:30pm.

Shopping For gifts or souvenirs, try Norma's Gift Shop, Queen's Highway (☎ 242/332-2002), which sells batik dresses, blouses, skirts, beachwear, swimwear, and men's shirts, as well as jewelry, French perfume, and T-shirts. There is also a selection of Bahamian gifts and souvenirs. Hours are Monday through Friday from 9am to 5:30pm, Saturday from 9am to 6pm.

Nearby is another place to shop, Brenda's Boutique, Haynes Avenue (☎ 242/332-2089). This two-room store occupies a clapboard-sided building a few steps away from the only traffic light in Eleuthera. Inside is a large inventory of T-shirts, sundresses, bathing suits, and such Bahamian souvenirs as conch jewelry. Hours are Monday through Saturday from 9am to 5:30pm.

WHERE TO STAY

Club Med. French Leaves, P.O. Box EL20080, Governor's Harbour, Eleuthera, The Bahamas. ☎ **800/CLUB-MED,** or 212/750-1687 in New York City. Fax 242/332-2855. 288 rms. A/C. Winter, $910–$1,540 per person double; $590–$1,000 per child aged 2–11 sharing parents' room. Off-season, $870 per person double; $590 per child aged 2–11. Rates are all-inclusive and per week. AE, MC, V.

This is one of the most child-oriented Club Meds in the chain, and if you're not crazy about little ones—laughing, playing, and screaming all day—you may want to seek more tranquil pastures. Lying 8 miles from Governor's Harbour airport, the club fronts on an unspoiled beach of fine sand and hardy vegetation. You'll find a cluster of peach-colored twin-bedded bungalows constructed in two- and three-story colonies. Built on the Atlantic side, the club replaced the first hotel on Eleuthera, French Leave, which once stood on this site. There's heavy emphasis here on social life for families with children. Activities include daylong picnics, nightly entertainment, disco, organized games in the resort's centerpiece free-form swimming pool (set in a garden), and taped classical music concerts after sunset.

Each room contains bright colors, furniture crafted from bamboo, and a private bathroom. Three full meals a day, including free unlimited beer and wine at lunch and dinner, plus most water sports and evening entertainment, are included in the rates. Tariffs are all-inclusive, except for drinks consumed at hours other than mealtimes; there are several bars scattered throughout the property. The club is heavily booked by French groups in midsummer, with more North Americans in wintertime.

The club's scuba program costs extra and is not geared to experienced divers—only to beginners. Those just taking up the sport go through a series of four lessons before their first deep dive in the nearby harbor. All equipment and instruction are provided. Waterskiing, snorkeling, sailing, tennis (eight courts, two lit for night play), picnics, aerobics, and jogging on the pale pink sands of the beach are ways most members spend their days. Children enjoy the club's Circus School, where a team of instructors teach fundamentals of tightrope walking, low-level trapeze work, trampolining, greasepaint makeup, and costuming. At the end of their stay, children perform in the club's weekly circus performance.

Laughing Bird Apartments. Haynes Ave./Birdie St., P.O. Box EL25076, Governor's Harbour, Eleuthera, The Bahamas. ☎ **800/688-4752** or 242/332-2012. Fax 242/332-2358. 4 apts. A/C. $65–$90 double; $100 triple; $110 quad. DISC, MC, V.

These very plain apartments lie near the Cupid's Cay section in the center of Eleuthera. These units are best for people who want to settle in for a week or so rather than those seeking an overnight stopover. The location is within walking distance of many shops, and sports facilities lie nearby. Arrangements can be made for waterskiing, surfing, fishing, sailing, tennis, golf, and snorkeling.

Efficiency apartments come with a living/dining/sleeping area, with a separate kitchen and a separate bath. Apartments, which front the beach, sit on an acre of landscaped property. Facilities include a beach and garden, plus tables and chairs for outdoor eating, along with a garden barbecue. Hammocks and a thatched beach cabana make for the easy life.

A GOOD PLACE TO EAT

The Blue Room (☎ **242/332-2736**) is an ugly fluorescent place at Governor's Harbour, but many Club Med guests like to slip away here even though their meals are already paid for at the hotel. In spite of the surroundings, The Blue Room serves a rollicking souse, and its baked Eleuthera chicken is second to none.

5 Palmetto Point

On the east side of Queen's Highway, south of Governor's Harbour, North Palmetto Point is a little hamlet where visitors rarely venture (although you can get a meal there). Far from the much-traveled tourist routes, this laid-back town will suit visitors seeking an escapist retreat.

Also south of Governor's Harbour, on the western coast of Eleuthera, the beach-fronting South Palmetto Point has some inexpensive housekeeping units.

WHERE TO STAY

Palmetto Shores Vacation Villas. P.O. Box EL25131, Governor's Harbour, Eleuthera, The Bahamas. ☎ **242/332-1305.** Fax 242/332-1305. 10 villas. A/C TV. Winter, $90–110 one-, two-, and three-bedroom villas for two. Off-season, $80–$100 one-, two-, and three-bedroom villas for two. Year-round, $180 two-bedroom villa for four. Extra person $20 summer, $30 winter. MC, V.

The creation of a local builder, this resort is a good choice for a simple housekeeping holiday. There are no luxuries of any kind, and you certainly can't come here expecting full hotel service. Asa Bethel rents villas suitable for two to four guests. Units are built in a plain Bahamian style, with wraparound balconies, and they open directly onto your own private beach. Furnishings are simple but reasonably comfortable, VCRs are included, and the villas lie within walking distance of local shops and tennis courts. All villas have living rooms and kitchens. Deep-sea fishing and waterskiing are available. Free Sunflower sailboats are also provided. You can rent a flipper, mask, and snorkel, and car rentals can be arranged.

Unique Village. North Palmetto Pt., The Bahamas (send mail to P.O. Box EL25187, Governor's Harbour, Eleuthera, The Bahamas). ☎ **800/688-4752** or 242/332-1830. Fax 242/332-1838. 10 rms, 2 one-bedroom apts with kitchenettes, 2 two-bedroom villas with kitchens. A/C TV. Winter, $110–$130 double; $150 one-bedroom apt for two; $180 two-bedroom apt for up to four. Extra person $25 extra per day. Off-season, $90–$110 double; $130 one-bedroom apt; $160 two-bedroom apt for up to four. MAP $35 per person per day. MC, V.

This hotel is the creative statement of a Palmetto Point businessman whose most visible ventures included the local hardware store (Unique Hardware). Built in 1992, the hotel prides itself on offering a wider range of different types of accommodations (everything from conventional single or double rooms to two-bedroom self-catering villas) than virtually any other hotel on the "mainland" of Eleuthera.

The hotel consists of a cluster of buildings whose roofs, exterior and interior walls, tiled floors, and amenities are mostly white. There's a bar and restaurant (the Unique) on-site, but few other sporting amenities. (Although there are no sailing, scuba, or tennis courts on-site, the staff can direct enthusiasts to other facilities that lie within a reasonable drive. Access to them will almost certainly require a car.) Part of the appeal of this place is affected by its position on a steep rise above the Atlantic coast of Eleuthera. The beach is accessible after a 2-minute descent via a flight of wooden steps. A sandy cove prefaces an oceanfront dotted with coral reefs whose bulk breaks up much of the Atlantic surf.

WHERE TO DINE

Mate & Jenny's Pizza Restaurant & Bar. South Palmetto Pt., right off Queen's Hwy. ☎ **242/332-1504.** Pizza $7–$22; main dishes $5–$23. MC, V. Hours daily 11am–3pm and 5:30–10pm. BAHAMIAN/AMERICAN.

This popular restaurant (known for its conch pizza) has a jukebox, video games, a pool table, and a dartboard. It's the most popular local dive and eatery, completely modest and unassuming in every way. The Bethel family will also prepare panfried grouper, cracked conch, or light meals, including snacks and sandwiches. Many patrons come here just to drink. Try their Goombay Smash, rumrunner, or piña colada. Ever had Bahamian Kalik beer?

Muriel's Home Made Bread and Restaurant. North Palmetto Pt. ☎ 242/332-1583. Reservations required for dinner. Main courses $5.50–$10. No credit cards. Mon–Sat noon–2pm and 6–8pm. BAHAMIAN.

If you're an adventurer, a good place to go is Muriel Cooper's operation. She runs a bakery and a take-out food emporium. Her rich and moist pineapple and coconut cakes are some of the best you'll find in the Out Islands. A limited menu includes full dinners, such as chicken with chips, cracked conch, conch chowder, and conch fritters. A dining room, decorated with family memorabilia, is available for clients who want to eat indoors. If you want a more elaborate meal, you'll have to stop by in the morning to announce your arrival time and menu preference. This is true Bahama Mama cookery—nothing else.

Unique Village Restaurant & Lounge. In the Unique Village, North Palmetto Pt. ☎ **242/332-1830.** Main courses $14.95–$26.95. MC, V. Daily 7:30–11:30am, noon–5pm, and 6–10pm. BAHAMIAN/AMERICAN.

This is the best place for food in the area, offering the widest menu. In this previously recommended hotel, you can drop in for a Bahamian breakfast, and we're talking boiled or stewed fish served with johnnycakes or else steamed corned beef and grits. You can also order a regular breakfast, as well, including hearty omelets. Lunch offerings include zesty conch chowder and an array of salads. Burgers are also served along with what the kitchen calls "Bahamian belly pleasers," including the steamed catch of the day. At night the choice grows, including the best New York sirloin available in mid-Eleuthera, coming in sizes ranging from 8 to 16 ounces. Platters from the sea are usually quite good, including everything from a tasty lobster Thermidor to grouper amandine. Cracked conch fried in a light beer batter was one of the better renderings of this dish we've sampled on the island.

6 Hatchet Bay

Twenty-five miles north of Governor's Harbour, Hatchet Bay was once known for its plantation that raised prize Angus cattle. But that operation now produces poultry and dairy products. The unused chicken parts are thrown to devouring fish at "Shark Hole."

Hatchet Bay Harbour is one of the finest in The Bahamas, a favorite port of call for hundreds of private yachts and charter boats. Full docking facilities and moorings are available. The area is known for its high, rolling green hills, sea-to-sea views, pink- and white-sand beaches, and excellent fishing on both shores. You may want to veer off Queen's Highway and take one of the side roads, such as Lazy Road or Smile Lane.

WHERE TO STAY

Rainbow Inn. P.O. Box EL25053, Governor's Harbour, Eleuthera, The Bahamas. ☎ **800/ 688-0047** in the U.S., or 242/335-0294. Fax 242/335-0294. 9 units. A/C. Year-round, $105 for one or two in a studio; $165 one-bedroom apt for four; $175 two- or three-bedroom villas for four to six. MAP $30 extra. MC, V. Closed Sept 15–Nov 15.

Two miles south of Alice Town, the Rainbow Inn is an isolated collection of cedar-sided bungalows, each designed in the shape of an octagon. The accommodations are simple but comfortable. Each has a private bath, lots of exposed wood, and a ceiling fan. All of the units also contain kitchenettes. There's a sandy beach a few steps away, a swimming pool, and a tennis court. Free tennis balls and rackets are provided, along with snorkeling gear and bikes. Free guided tours of the Hatchet Bay Caves are offered, and rental cars are available at the inn.

The bar/restaurant has a high beamed ceiling and a thick-topped bar where guests down daiquiris and piña coladas. The popular restaurant features live Bahamian music and one of the most extensive menus on Eleuthera. Local Bahamian food includes fish, conch chowder, fried conch, fresh fish, and Bahamian lobster, and international dishes feature French onion soup, escargots, and steaks, followed by key lime pie for dessert. Dinner costs $14 to $25 per person.

7 Gregory Town

Gregory Town stands in the center of Eleuthera against a backdrop of hills, which break the usual flat monotony of the landscape. A village of clapboard cottages, it was once famed for growing pineapples. It still grows them, but not as it used to. However, the local people make a good rum out of the fruit, and you can visit the **Gregory Town Plantation and Distillery,** where pineapple rum is still produced. You're allowed to sample it, and surely you'll want to take a bottle home with you.

WHERE TO STAY

The Cove Eleuthera. Queen's Hwy., P.O. Box GT1548, Gregory Town, Eleuthera, The Bahamas. ☎ 800/552-5960 in the U.S. and Canada, or 242/335-5142. Fax 242/335-5338. 24 units. A/C. Winter, $109–$129 double; $119 triple. Off-season, $89–$109 double; $99 triple. Children under 12 stay free in parents' room. MAP $33 per person extra. MC, V.

On a private sandy cove, this year-round resort is set on 28 acres partially planted with pineapples. The resort consists of a main clubhouse and seven tropical-style buildings nestled on the oceanside. The comfortable rooms with tile floors are furnished in pastel fabrics and rattan furniture. Each has a private bath and a porch. The restaurant (see below) serves three meals a day, and the lounge and the poolside Pineapple Patio are open daily for drinks and informal meals. Kayaks, bicycles, and a minuscule freshwater pool compete with hammocks for your time. No TV or phones are there to distract you. The Cove lies 1 1/2 miles northwest of Gregory Town and 3 miles southeast of the Glass Window.

WHERE TO DINE

The Cove. Queen's Hwy. ☎ **242/335-5142.** Breakfast $4.50–$9; main courses $10–$32; lunch $5–$12. AE, MC, V. Daily 8–10:30am, noon–2:30pm, and 6:30–8:30pm. BAHAMIAN/AMERICAN.

In the previously recommended hotel, lying 1 1/2 miles north of Gregory Town, this spacious dining room is your best bet for food in the area. The restaurant is spacious and decorated in a light, tropical style. Lunch, which begins with the inevitable conch chowder, is usually a sandwich or a burger. Here's your chance to try a conchburger, a generous patty of ground conch blended with green pepper, onion, and spices. All the food is homemade. Conch also appears several times in the evening, including the best cracked conch in town, which has been tenderized and dipped in a special batter and fried to a golden perfection. Eleuthera is also known for its chicken. The kitchen serves the best fried chicken in the area. It too appears a golden brown. This is not haute cuisine, but good native fare. They also offer a vegetarian menu. The Mermaid Lounge features an underwater theme complete with an 8-foot gilded grouper suspended from the ceiling and a mermaid mural. The owners invite you to come early to enjoy the sunset from the patio, which surrounds a freshwater pool and overlooks the serene coves.

Monica's Restaurant. Shirley St. ☎ **242/335-5053.** Reservations required. Main courses $10–$20. No credit cards. Mon–Sat 7–9pm. BAHAMIAN/AMERICAN.

While in Gregory Town, follow your nose: A tantalizing aroma of freshly cooked food will draw you here. Not only do the locals come to Monica's for their conch fritters and hot patties, but visitors flock here, as well. You might begin with conch chowder, then follow with stuffed spiny lobster, pigeon peas 'n' rice, grouper fingers, or barbecued chicken. Dishes are often accompanied by scalloped potatoes or tossed salad. For dessert, try a coconut cream pie, or better yet, the acclaimed pineapple pie. Always call first before heading here since Monica's has been known to close for long periods of time when business is slow.

EXPLORING THE AREA: THE GLASS WINDOW & BEYOND

Dedicated surfers have come here from as far away as California and even Australia to test their skills on the "second-best wave in the world." (The best is in Hawaiian waters.)

An increasingly popular activity here is spelunking (exploring and studying caves). South of the town on the way to Hatchet Bay are several caverns worth visiting, the largest of which is called simply the **Cave.** It has a big fig tree out front, which the people of Gregory Town claim was planted long ago by area pirates who wanted to conceal the cave because they had hidden treasure in it.

Local guides (you have to ask around in Gregory Town or Hatchet Bay) will take explorers through this cave. The bats living inside are harmless, even though they must resent the intrusion of tourists with flashlights. At one point the drop is so steep—about 12 feet—that you have to use a ladder to climb down. Eventually you reach a cavern studded with stalactites and stalagmites. At this point, you're faced with a maze of passageways leading off through the rocky underground recesses. The cave comes to an abrupt end at the edge of a cliff, where the thundering sea is some 90 feet below.

After leaving Gregory Town and driving north, you come to the famed **Glass Window,** the chief sight of Eleuthera. This is the narrowest point of Eleuthera. Once a natural rock arch bridged the land, but it is gone, replaced by an artificially constructed bridge. As you drive across it, you can see the contrast between the deep blue of the ocean and the emerald green of the shoal waters of the sound. The rocks rise to a height of 70 feet. Often, as ships in the Atlantic are being tossed about, the crew has looked across the narrow point to see a ship resting quietly on the other side. Hence the name Glass Window.

8 The Current

The inhabitants of the Current, a settlement in North Eleuthera, are believed to have descended from a tribe of Native Americans. A narrow strait separates the village from Current Island, where most of the locals make their living from the sea or from plaiting straw goods.

This is a small community where the people often welcome visitors. There are no crowds and no artificial attractions. Everything focuses on the sea, which is a source of pleasure for the visiting tourists but a way to sustain life for the local people.

From the Current, you can explore some interesting sights in North Eleuthera, including **Preacher's Cave.** This is where the Eleutherian Adventurers found shelter in the mid-17th century when they were shipwrecked with no provisions. However, if you want to be driven there, know that your taxi driver may balk. The road is treacherous on his expensive tires. If you do reach it, you'll find a cave that has been compared to an amphitheater. The very devout Eleutherian Adventurers held religious services inside the cave, which is pierced by holes in the roof, allowing light to intrude. The cave is not far from the airport, in a northeasterly direction.

Another sight is **Boiling Hole,** which is in a shallow bank that boils at changing tides.

WHERE TO STAY

Sandcastle Apartments. The Current, Eleuthera, The Bahamas. ☎ **242/359-7377.** Fax 242/393-0440. 1 duplex apt (with bath and kitchenette). A/C. Year-round, $70 for one or two; extra persons $5 each. No credit cards.

Even the most embittered victim of Hurricane Andrew agrees that some benefits eventually derived from that destructive storm. What had been a pair of hastily built cottages catering to the tourist trade was so badly damaged that a complete rebuilding rendered it substantially better than before. For escapists looking for a location far removed from the usual tourist circuit, this utterly plain but airy accommodation might be a good bet. The on-site kitchen, the easy access to a simple grocery store within a 5-minute walk, and the self-contained nature of this extremely modest accommodation often appeal to families. There's a double bed in the bedroom, a queen-sized pullout bed in the living room, and a view over shallow offshore waters where children can wade safely for a surprisingly long distance offshore. The unit lies just across the road from the sea, and if you want to explore, bicycles are available for rent at $10 a day.

9 Harbour Island

One of the oldest settlements in The Bahamas, founded before the United States was a nation, Harbour Island lies off the northern end of Eleuthera, some 200 miles from Miami. It is 3 miles long and half a mile wide.

Affectionately called "Briland," Harbour Island is studded with good resorts and is famous for its spectacular pink-sand beach, which runs the whole length of the island on its eastern side. The beach is protected from the ocean breakers by an outlying coral reef, which makes for some of the safest bathing in The Bahamas. Except for unseasonably cold days, you can swim and enjoy water sports year-round. The climate averages 72°F in winter, 77° in spring and fall, and 82° in summer. Occasionally they have cool evenings with a low of around 65° from November to February.

For years, inhabitants of Harbour Island were engaged in farming and boatbuilding, along with fishing and sponge diving. Farms are still worked today on the main body of Eleuthera on land given to the Brilanders by Andrew Devereaux, a colonel in the British army back in 1783. The Civil War in the United States brought an economic boom to the area, as the Brilanders prospered by running the blockade that the Union had placed on shipping to and from the Confederate States.

By 1880 Dunmore Town had become the second most important town of The Bahamas. It not only was a port of entry, but also had a major shipyard (turning out vessels as large as four-masted schooners), as well as a trio of sugar mills. It also produced rum. Eventually the town fell on bad times, but Prohibition in the United States brought another economic boom as rum-running became a major source of income.

The Brilanders suffered a great financial setback with the repeal of Prohibition, followed by the Great Depression and World War II. In recent years, tourism has brought some prosperity.

GETTING THERE & GETTING AROUND By plane, Harbour Island is only $1^1/_2$ hours from Fort Lauderdale or Miami and a 30-minute flight from Nassau. To get here, you take a flight to the North Eleuthera airstrip, from which it's a 1-mile taxi ride to the ferry dock. The taxi costs $3 per person. The final lap is a 2-mile direct ferry ride to Harbour Island, at a cost of $4 per person. Most people don't need transportation on the island. They walk to where they're going or take a golf cart. Some hotels have these for rent.

If you want to go some distance on the island, call **Reggie's Taxi** at ☎ **242/ 333-2116** or **Big M Taxi Service** at ☎ **242/333-2043.**

Michael's Cycles on Colebrooke Street (☎ **242/333-2384**) is the best place to go if you want some mobility other than your own feet. The shop is open daily from 8am to 8pm. Bikes rent for $10 per day, and you can also rent two-seater motorbikes for $30 a day, or even a two-seater golf cart for $40 a day.

ESSENTIALS **Bank** The Royal Bank of Canada, just up the hill from the city dock (☎ **242/333-2250**), is open Monday through Thursday from 9:30am to 3pm and Friday from 9:30am to 5pm.

Hospital   The Harbour Island Medical Clinic, at Dunmore Town (☎ 242/333-2227), handles routine medical problems. Hours are Monday through Friday from 9am to 1pm.

Pharmacy   Harbour Pharmacy Health Care and Prescription Service can be found on the waterfront 4 blocks north of the fig tree (☎ 242/333-2174). In addition to health-and-beauty aids, it fills prescriptions and offers over-the-counter drugs. Hours are daily from 9am to 5pm.

Police   The police can be called at ☎ 242/333-2111.

WHERE TO STAY
EXPENSIVE
✪ **Dunmore Beach Club.** Colebrook Ln., P.O. Box EL27122, Harbour Island, The Bahamas. ☎ 242/333-2200. Fax 242/333-2429. 12 units. A/C. Nov–May (AP), $340 double. June–Aug (AP), $290 double. MC, V. Closed Sept–Oct.

This colony of cottages is an elegant oasis placed in a tropical setting of trees and shrubbery on well-manicured grounds along the 3-mile pink-sand beach. It's not as elaborate but is cozier than its nearest rival, Pink Sands. The Bahamian-style bungalows are an attractive combination of traditional furnishings and tropical accessories. Excellent Bahamian and international meals are served in a dining room with a beamed ceiling, shutter doors, and windows with views. Breakfast is offered on a garden terrace under pine trees with a clear view of the beach. Dinner is served at one sitting at 8pm. Men are required to wear jackets at dinner in winter (ties optional). Nonresidents can dine here (call for reservations) for $45 per person. A clubhouse is the focal point for socializing, and a living room with a library and a fireplace is another cozy nook, as is the bar-lounge with rattan furniture.

✪ **Pink Sands.** Chapel St., Harbour Island, The Bahamas. ☎ 800/OUTPOST or 242/333-2030. Fax 242/333-2060. 23 one-bedroom cottages, 3 two-bedroom cottages. A/C TV TEL. Winter (MAP), $460–$525 one-bedroom cottage; $550–$595 two-bedroom cottage. Off-season (MAP), $305–$330 one-bedroom cottage; $360–$400 two-bedroom cottage. AE, MC, V.

Long acclaimed as the finest accommodation in the Out Islands, this is a sophisticated hideaway, just the place to sneak away with that special someone. It's an elite retreat on a 28-acre beachfront estate that functions a bit like a private club, although it's less snobbish than Dunmore Beach Club. Its owner is Chris Blackwell, the founder of Island Records who is increasingly known as a hotel entrepreneur. Rebuilt after Hurricane Andrew of 1992, it's now better than ever. The resort's greatest asset is its 3-mile stretch of private pink-sand beach, which is sheltered by a barrier reef.

Well-furnished and fully restored bedrooms have either an ocean or a garden view. All rooms have central air-conditioning, pressurized water systems, walk-in closets, satellite TVs, CD players, wet bars with beverages, private outside patios with teak furnishings, and a full bathroom with imported tile. Interior designs feature marble floors with area rugs, oversize Adirondack furnishings, local artwork, and batik fabrics from the Island Trading Company. Rooms are also equipped with telephones and data jacks, along with fax machines and cellular phones if needed.

Dining/Entertainment: Hotel guests booked in here get the best meals on the island. Dinner features a four-course meal nightly that's the best and the freshest around.

Services: Room service, personal laundry services.

Facilities: Private beach, freshwater pool, three tennis courts (one lit for night games), gym, clubhouse, beach palapa/tiki bar. There's also a library with state-of-the art visual equipment for think-tank sessions.

Ocean View. P.O. Box 134, Harbour Island, The Bahamas. ☎ **242/333-2276.** Fax 242/333-2459. 9 rms. Year-round, $295–$325 double; $325 cottage next door. Rates include breakfast and dinner. AE, MC, V.

This is one of the most ambivalent places on Harbour Island, loved by its devotees, shunned by clients who don't happen to agree with Canadian-born owner Pip Simmon's vision of what she wants her ongoing house party to be. The setting is a 30-year-old house midway between Runaway and Dunmore Beach Club. It's an airy dwelling, evocative of a private home, with antiques, original artwork, and pleasantly decorated compact bedrooms. Breakfast and dinner are included in the price. Be alert to Ms. Simmon's idiosyncratic and sometimes jarring vision. In her own words, "I own the joint," which basically gives her license to reject whomever she pleases. Take your chances.

MODERATE

Coral Sands. Chapel St., Harbour Island, The Bahamas. ☎ **800/468-2799** in the U.S. and Canada, or 242/333-2350. Fax 242/333-2368. 25 rms, 8 suites. A/C. Winter, $165 double; $210 suite for two. Off-season, $120 double; $155 suite for two. Extra person in suite $15. MAP $40 per person extra. AE, DC, MC, V. Closed U.S. Labor Day to Nov 14.

Coral Sands is the beachfront lair of two remarkable people, Brett and Sharon King. Theirs is a self-contained, all-purpose resort built on 14 hilly and tree-covered acres overlooking a beach of pink sand and lying within walking distance of the center of Dunmore Town.

Brett King had an adventurous life before coming to Harbour Island. A wartime flyer and veteran of 134 combat missions in Europe and Africa, and winner of many medals for his bravery and daring, he later became an actor. He worked with Bette Davis, John Wayne, and Robert Mitchum and dated, among others, Elizabeth Taylor. He came to Harbour Island to complete plans for the resort, which had been envisioned by his father before his death. Brett stayed, and the rest of the story is now part of Harbour Island lore.

Since their opening in 1968, the world has come to their door. Sharon, a gracious hostess, runs between answering phone calls and welcoming guests as if to her own private party, which at times it becomes. California born and bred, Sharon is known for her style and vivacity.

Each of the rooms has been refurbished in a Caribbean motif. The main building contains singles and doubles. The suites, which have ocean-view patios, sleep four persons and are ideal for families.

Dining/Entertainment: The food is one of the reasons for staying here. It's like good home cooking, with a selection of American, Bahamian, and international dishes. For example, if you take lunch at the Beach Bar Sun Deck, order a bowl (not a cup) of some of the best-tasting conch chowder in the islands, served with a slice of freshly made coconut bread. You might follow with a toasted lobster sandwich, which other hotels have tried to imitate. Dinner at the Mediterranean Café might be preceded by one of the potent rum drinks in the Yellow Bird Bar. Your appetizer might be conch fritters, and your main course might be a fresh Bahamian fish, such as grouper, prepared in a number of ways. Outsiders who call for a reservation can order dinner from 7 to 8pm. Entertainment is often provided in the nightclub in the park, where you can dance under the stars.

Services: Beach umbrellas and chaise lounges provided; picnic lunches available should you desire to explore some uninhabited islands nearby. Laundry.

Facilities: Tennis court lit at night; sailboats, rowboats, surf riders, and snorkeling equipment; all water sports, including boats and gear, can be arranged.

Romora Bay Club. Colebrook St., Harbour Island, The Bahamas. ☎ **800/327-8286** in the U.S., or 242/333-2325. Fax 242/333-2500. 29 rms, 9 suites and villas. A/C TEL. Winter, $160–$180 double; $195 suite for two; $195 villa for two. Off-season, $120–$140 double; $155 suite for two; $170 villa for two. Children under 10 say free in parents' room. Rates include breakfast and lunch. AE, MC, V.

The hotel has recently undergone a change of ownership. Lionel Rotcage has not only taken over—he has completely rebuilt the hotel with the intent of making it more appealing to families. Romora Bay was a favorite stop for divers, so he has also renovated the club's dive shop (see "Water Sports & Other Outdoor Activities," below).

Fronting both the beach and the harbor, the hotel stands in a decades-old semitropical garden with tall coconut palms, filmy pine trees, and beds of flowering shrubbery. The accommodations assure more privacy than most, and only yards away is a harbor where you can swim in clear waters. Each unit has a private patio, ceiling fan, CD player, and in-room movies. Room service is available 24 hours a day. Each of the villas come with a full kitchen.

Dining/Entertainment: Buffet luncheons are served at the waterfront patio and bar. Home cooking is a feature, with continental, Bahamian, and American cuisine served. The homemade breads and pastries are superb, and an extensive wine list has been added.

Services: All flights are met at the airport by taxis for the 1-mile drive to the ferry dock. There's a 2-mile ferry ride direct to the club's private dock.

Facilities: Fitness center, tennis courts, Sunfish rentals, deep-sea fishing.

Runaway Hill Club. Colebrook St., P.O. Box EL27031, Harbour Island, The Bahamas. ☎ **800/728-9803** in the U.S., or 242/333-2150. Fax 242/333-2420. 10 rms. A/C. Winter, $200–$235 double. Off-season, $160–$200 double. MAP $50 per person extra. No children under 16. AE, MC, V. Closed Sept 5–Nov 14.

Small and intimate, the hotel overlooks the pink sands of Briland's beach. This club is far superior to nearby rivals, the Romora Bay Club or Valentine's. The resort, built in 1947 as a private home, was later sold to two sisters from New Zealand who ran it as a small inn. After they sold the property, the hotel remained closed for several years. In 1983 a group of Brilanders renovated the property and opened it to the public. The hotel has 7 acres of beachfront and a huge lawn, separated from Colebrook Street by a wall. The mansion's original English colonial dormers are still prominent, as are the four stately palms set into the circular area in the center of the driveway. In winter, a crackling fire is sometimes built in the hearth near the entrance. Each bedroom is different, giving the impression of lodging in a private home, as this used to be.

Dining/Entertainment: Dinners are served on the breeze-filled rear porch overlooking the swimming pool. Nonresidents are welcome.

Facilities: Freshwater swimming pool set into a steep hillside and surrounded by plants; pink sandy beach; bicycle rental; fishing trips and water sports can be arranged.

Valentine's Yacht Club & Inn. Harbourfront, Harbour Island, The Bahamas. ☎ **242/333-2142.** Fax 242/333-2135. 21 rms. A/C. Winter, $120–$130 double. Off-season, $95–$120 double. MAP $35 per person extra. AE, MC, V. Closed Sept 4–Nov 17.

Valentine's is a low-slung, rustic-modern, comfortable place near the sea, and is more motel in style than the more intimate properties we've visited so far. Regardless, it remains the favorite of visiting yachties. Because of its dive center, it also competes with Ramora for the diver trade. It's also a 47-slip marina complex, totally rebuilt after Hurricane Andrew. You register in the wood-paneled main building. In back, in view of the dining room, there's a swimming pool where first-time divers may have just finished their introductory lessons. Simple accommodations sit bungalow style, each with its own private verandah, in a somewhat hilly flowering garden.

Dining/Entertainment: The Bahamian cuisine served in the restaurant is usually preceded by drinks in the comfortably intimate wood- and brass-trimmed bar. Dinner is served by candlelight at tables where artificial gold coins sparkle beneath laminated surfaces and hanging ship's lanterns—each an antique—cast an intimate glow. Either before or after dinner, you might enjoy one or two of the bartender's almost hallucinogenic Goombay Smashes. The bar area often provides live entertainment, becoming one of the social centers of town.

Services: Full-service 47-slip marina with everything you could need for your yacht, including a "yacht-sitting" service, which makes this dock one of the focal points of the marine activities on Harbour Island. Laundry service.

Facilities: Swimming pool, a tennis court, hot tub/Jacuzzi. For information on the Dive Shop, which offers everything a scuba or snorkeling aficionado could want, see "Water Sports & Other Outdoor Activities," below.

INEXPENSIVE

Tingum Village. Harbour Island, Eleuthera, The Bahamas. ☎ **242/333-2161.** Fax 242/333-2161. 12 rms, 1 cottage. A/C. Year-round, $75–$85 double, $85 triple, $175 cottage for 10. MAP $35 extra. AE, MC, V.

The hotel is just off the main street, and a 3-minute walk to the beach. Set in a tropical garden, Tingum Village offers basic but comfortable accommodations at low prices. Each of the rooms has air-conditioning, ceiling fans, and a patio with wicker furniture. The cottage is meant for 6 to 8 people, though it can hold up to 10 (but that would be very cramped). The hotel's restaurant, Ma Ruby's, overlooks the garden and offers standard Bahamian and American food. It is well known for its cheeseburgers, which the manager says were ranked as one of the 10 best in the world by "Mr. Cheeseburger in Paradise" himself, Jimmy Buffett. The prices range from $6 to $18 for the à la carte menu; a four-course fixed price dinner is $25. The restaurant is open daily from 8am to midnight.

WHERE TO DINE

If you'd like to sample some real local fare, often in shacks so ramshackle you might not want to venture inside, you can. It calls only for a spirit of adventure. Take **Ma Ruby's** (☎ **242/333-2161**) on Harbour Island. Some islanders claim you can get your best meal in Eleuthera if Ma Ruby (the cook and owner) prepares it. Her conchburger is worthy of an award. She's been stewing chicken or baking grouper and serving them in a trellised courtyard for a long while, and she's got a lot of devoted fans.

If you don't want to dress up for lunch, you can head for a shack, **Seaview Takeaway** (☎ **242/333-2542**), at the foot of the ferry dock. Here you can feast on all that good stuff: pig's feet, sheep tongue souse, and most definitely cracked conch. Everything tastes better with fungi or rice 'n' peas. Dress as you would to clean out your garage on a hot August day.

MODERATE

Runaway Hill Club. Colebrook St. ☎ **242/333-2150.** Reservations required. Fixed-price dinner from $50. AE, MC, V. Mon–Sat at 8pm. Closed Sept 5–Nov 12. BAHAMIAN/AMERICAN.

Known for its well-prepared food, this dining room enjoys a sweeping view over a sandy slope stretching down the beach. Inside, the decor is pastel, with wicker and rattan furniture and a fine collection of watercolors the owner has spent years collecting. The restaurant is contained in a hotel (see "Where to Stay," above), but outside guests are welcome for the single-service meal. The kitchen prepares suprême of chicken piccata, conch marinara, crabmeat soup with scotch, spicy lobster bisque, and many versions of local fish. The food is always solid and reliable and sometimes delightful. Dessert might be French chocolate pie with a meringue crust and walnuts.

Valentine's Yacht Club & Inn. Harbourfront. ☎ **242/333-2142.** Main courses $18–$30; fixed-price dinner $25; lunch $10; breakfast from $8. AE, MC, V. Daily 7:30–10:30am, 11:30am– 2:30pm, and 7:30–10pm. Closed Sept 4–Nov 17. BAHAMIAN/AMERICAN.

Don't even think of a meal here without stopping for a drink in the Reach Bar beforehand. Surrounded by nautical accessories and burnished paneling, you can while away the predinner hours with denizens of the island's boating crowd. This place has none of the formality of the Runaway Hill Club (see above) but attracts divers, boaters, and other visitors who like its informality. It's sporty and macho. The fare in the dining room is often more filling than gourmet, including steamed pork chops, steak or grouper cutlets, baked stuffed grouper, and an occasional roast leg of lamb.

INEXPENSIVE

Angela's Starfish Restaurant. Dunmore and Grant sts. ☎ **242/333-2253.** Reservations recommended. Main courses $12–$22; lunch $7–$11; breakfast $4–$7. No credit cards. Daily 8–10:30am and 11am–8:30pm. BAHAMIAN.

This is the local eatery where many of the islanders go themselves, and it serves the most authentic Eleutheran cuisine. Residents as well as visitors literally plan their Sunday around an evening meal here, although it's equally crowded on other nights. Run by Bahamians Angela and Vincent Johnson, the house sits on a hill above the channel in a residential section somewhat removed from the center of town. Angela can often be seen in the kitchen baking.

Cracked conch and an array of seafood are specialties, and chicken potpie and pork chops are frequently ordered. It's the type of food a Bahama mama would serve her family. You can dine on the palm-dotted lawn with its simple tables and folding chairs, although for chilly weather there's an unpretentious dining room inside near the cramped kitchen. Some of the best local food is offered here. It can get quite festive at night, after the candles are lit and the crowd becomes jovial.

WATER SPORTS & OTHER OUTDOOR ACTIVITIES

The diving in this part of The Bahamas is among the most diversified in the region, with visibility in midsummer reaching as much as 200 feet on good days. A 197-foot steel freighter, the **Carnarvon** (also spelled *Caernarvon* and pronounced in endlessly different variations by the locals), sank in 1917 and is today one of the highlights of the region. Nearby are the badly rusted chassis of a half dozen railway boxcars reportedly captured by Confederate soldiers from the Union army during the Civil War and sold to the owner of a sugar plantation in Cuba. Hit by a hurricane during their southbound transit, the barge containing them sank, scattering the boxcars along the sea bottom. Today, only the wheelbases remain visible above the reef fish and kelp that have made the site their home.

The most spectacular dive site of all, however, judged among the 10 top dive sites in the world and visited by scuba enthusiasts from as far away as Europe, is the **Current Cut Dive.** One of the fastest (nine knots) drift dives in the world, it involves the descent of a diver into the fast-moving current racing between the rock walls that define the underwater chasm between Eleuthera and Current Island. Swept up in the underwater currents with schools of stingrays, mako sharks, and reef fish, divers are propelled along a half mile of underwater distance in less than 10 minutes. The dive is defined as one of the highlights of a diver's career.

Romora Bay Club Dive Shop. Colebrook St. ☎ **242/333-2323.**

This club is fully geared for a wide array of water sports. The sandy bottom of the sheltered bathing precincts off the hotel (see "Where to Stay," above) serves as the learning area for the introductory scuba lessons. An introductory lesson followed by a half-day dive trip costs $45, with equipment included; those who prefer snorkeling can join a half-day expedition for $18 per person. Guided scuba trips cost $30 per tank in daytime, $45 for night dives. Call to agree on departure time.

The dive shop changed hands in 1996 and was upgraded. The new owner, Jeff Fox, is assisted by four PADI instructors. Experienced divers can rent any piece of scuba equipment they need here, and the dive packages offered by Romora Bay Club are some of lowest priced in the islands.

Valentine's Dive Center. Harbourfront. ☎ **800/383-6480** or 242/333-2309.

Valentine's has a full range of dive activities. The dive center is in a wooden building near the entrance to Valentine's Marina. Lessons in snorkeling and scuba diving for beginners are given daily at 9:30am. Snorkeling from a boat costs $20 for a half-day tour. A full certification course for scuba is taught for $425. Single-tank dives, daily at 9:30am and 1:30pm, cost $30; two-tank dives go for $55; and night dives (four divers minimum) are $45 per person. Underwater cameras, with film included, rent for $15 for a half day, $25 for a full day. The guides at Valentine's are proud to point out the wreck of the *Carnarvon* (mentioned above). Cave and cavern dives are also conducted.

10 Spanish Wells

Called a "quiet corner of The Bahamas," Spanish Wells is a colorful cluster of houses on St. George's Cay, half a mile off the coast of northwest Eleuthera. It is characterized by its sparkling bays and white beaches, sleepy lagoons, and a fine fishing and skin-diving colony.

The Eleutherian Adventurers were the first people to inhabit St. George's Cay after the Spanish had exterminated the original residents, the Arawaks (Lucayans). However, it was prominent on the charts of Spanish navigators as the final landfall for galleons heading home from the New World laden with plunder. The Spaniards early on sank a well here from which to replenish their potable water before setting off across the Atlantic. Hence the name "Spanish Wells." Ponce de León noted this stopover, where he was able to get water, if not the youth-giving liquid for which he was searching.

After the American Revolution, Loyalists joined the descendants of the Eleutherian Adventurers at Spanish Wells. Some of these, particularly those from southern plantations in America, did not stay long on St. George's Cay, however, as the Spanish Wellsians were adamantly opposed to slavery. Since slaves had been brought by the new wave of immigrants hoping to start island plantations, they were forced to move on to other parts of The Bahamas with their African bondsmen. The people of Spanish Wells still have strong religious beliefs, and there's a bounty of churches on the island.

The towheaded, blue-eyed people of this little town number fewer than 1,500 souls. More than half the people on the island are named Pinder. As the saying goes, "We was Pinders before we married, and we're Pinders now." The names Albury, Higgs, Sawyer, and Sweeting are also prominent. The islanders' patois blends 17th-century English with the accents of others who have settled on the island over the centuries. For years they have been known as good seamen and spongers, and some of them are farmers. Because of the infertile soil on St. George's Cay, however, they have to do their planting on "mainland" Eleuthera.

Over the centuries, the Spanish Wellsians have tried their hand at many economic ventures, from growing cotton and pineapples for export to shipbuilding, lumbering, and fishing. Of these, fishing and some agriculture have been lasting moneymakers, joined today by tourism. Many have grown rich on harvesting spiny lobster.

You can walk or bicycle through the village, looking at the houses, some more than 200 years old, which have New England saltbox styling but bright tropical coloring. You can see handmade quilts in many colors, following patterns handed down from generations of English ancestors. No one locks doors here or removes ignition keys from cars.

There are those who suggest that the island doesn't offer much to do, but this is disputed by those who just want to snorkel, scuba dive, fish, sunbathe, read, or watch the sun set. You'll also have a choice of tennis, sailing, volleyball, shuffleboard, or windsurfing.

GETTING THERE   To reach the island, you can fly to the airstrip on North Eleuthera, from which taxis will deliver you to the ferry dock. Regardless of the time of day you arrive, a ferryboat will either be waiting for passengers or about to arrive with a load of them. A memorable skipper of one of them is Caleb Sawyer, who runs a well-maintained speedboat, the *Moldie Crab* (☎ 242/333-4254). The boat runs between Gene's Bay in North Eleuthera to the main pier at Spanish Wells. The ferries depart whenever passengers show up. The cost is $10 per person round-trip.

WHERE TO STAY

Spanish Wells Yacht Haven. Harbourfront, P.O. Box SW-27427, Spanish Wells, The Bahamas. ☎ 242/333-4255. Fax 242/333-4649. 3 rms, 2 apts. A/C. Winter, $78 double; $95 apt for up to four. Off-season, $75 double; $95 apt for up to four. AE, MC, V.

One of the most modern marinas in the islands is now owned by Nassau Yacht Haven, which also rents basic apartments and rooms for the boating crowd or any other visitors to Spanish Wells. As for the marina facilities, they include a self-service laundry, hot and cold showers, an ice machine, a saltwater swimming pool, and a lounge and restaurant. You can also get Exxon marine fuels and lubricants. Should you not happen to have a yacht to service, you'll find a quintet of rentable rooms. Each of them has serviceable furniture and a private bath. Two of them contain small kitchenettes.

WHERE TO DINE

Jack's Outback. Harbourfront. ☎ 242/333-4219. Main courses $11–$20. AE, MC, V. Daily 9am–10pm. BAHAMIAN.

This little place stands along the waterfront on the way to Spanish Wells Yacht Haven. It's known for its home cooking and Bahamian foods. Many hungry boaters come here just to sample the fish fingers. Painted in pink and white with red lettering, it is a simple but welcoming little place. It offers the usual array of sandwiches and hamburgers. But you can also order some good local dishes. Cracked conch is invariably offered, as is conch chowder. However, everything depends on what is available locally on any particular day.

10 The Exuma Islands

The Exuma island chain is one of the prettiest in The Bahamas. Some liken its beauty to that of Polynesia. Shades of jade, aquamarine, and amethyst in deeper waters turn to transparent opal near sandy shores: The water and the land appear almost inseparable. Sailors and their crews like to stake out their own private beaches and tropical hideaways, and several vacation retreats have been built by wealthy Europeans, Canadians, and Americans.

Most of our resort recommendations are in and around George Town, the pretty, pink capital of the Exumas, on Great Exuma. A community of some 900 residents, it was once considered a possible site for the capital of The Bahamas because of its excellent Elizabeth Harbour (see below).

The cruising grounds around the Exumas, which are scattered over an ocean area of 90 square miles, are among the finest to be found in the western hemisphere, if not in the world, for both sail- and powerboats. They rival both those of the Grenadines in the Caribbean and the Abacos in The Bahamas. Which one yachties prefer depends on personal taste. Each is Valhalla, if you're a boater. If you don't come in your own craft, you can rent one here, from a simple little Daysailer to a fishing runabout, with or without a guide. The annual regatta in April in Elizabeth Harbour has attracted such notables as Prince Philip and the ex-king of Greece, Constantine. The Exumas are often referred to by yachting people as "where you go when you die if you've been good."

Snorkeling and scuba-diving opportunities draw aficionados from around the world to the Exuma National Land and Sea Park, a vast underwater preserve, and to the exotic limestone and coral reefs, blue holes, drop-offs, caves, and night dives. Dive centers in George Town and Staniel Cay provide air fills and diving equipment.

Fishing is top grade here, and the "flats" on the west side of Great Exuma are famous for bonefishing. You can find (if you're lucky) blue marlin on both sides of Exuma Sound, as well as sailfish, wahoo, and white marlin, plus numerous others. Other popular activities include playing tennis, windsurfing, and waterskiing.

The Exumas are among the friendliest islands in The Bahamas, the people warmhearted and not (yet) spoiled by tourism. They seem genuinely delighted to receive and welcome visitors to their shores. They grow a lot of their own food, including cassava, onions, cabbages, and pigeon peas on the acres their ancestors worked as slaves.

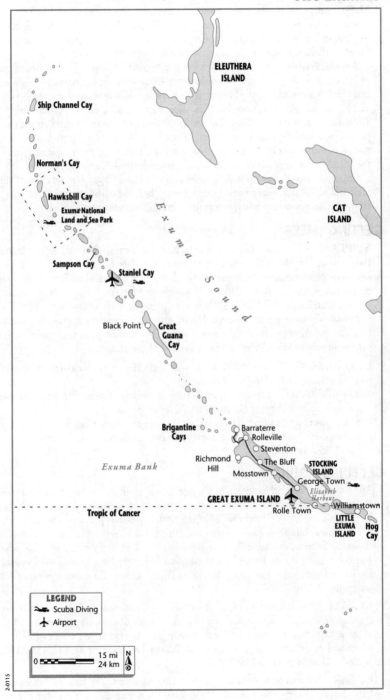

The Exumas

ELEUTHERA ISLAND

Ship Channel Cay

Norman's Cay

Hawksbill Cay

Exuma National Land and Sea Park

CAT ISLAND

Exuma Sound

Sampson Cay

Staniel Cay

Black Point

Great Guana Cay

Brigantine Cays

Exuma Bank

Barraterre

Rolleville

Steventon

Richmond Hill

The Bluff

Mosstown

STOCKING ISLAND

George Town

Elizabeth Harbour

GREAT EXUMA ISLAND

Rolle Town

Williamstown

Tropic of Cancer

LITTLE EXUMA ISLAND

Hog Cay

LEGEND

Scuba Diving

Airport

0   15 mi
           24 km

N

2-0115

Many fruits grow on the cays, including guavas, mangoes, and avocados. You can watch these fruits being loaded at Government Wharf in George Town for shipment to Nassau. The sponge industry is being revived locally, as the product of the sea is found in shallow waters and creeks to the south side of the Exumas.

A spiny, sandy chain of islands, the Exumas, which begin just 35 miles southeast of Nassau, stretch more than 100 miles from Beacon Cay in the north to Hog Cay and Sandy Cay in the south. These islands have not been developed like the Abacos and Eleuthera, but they have much to offer, with crystal-clear waters on the west around the Great Bahama Bank and the 5,000-foot-deep Exuma Sound on the east, plus uninhabited cays ideal for picnics, rolling hills, ruins of once-great plantations, and coral formations of great beauty. Although it's crossed by the Tropic of Cancer, the island has average temperatures ranging from the mid-70s to the mid-80s.

On most maps this chain is designated as the "Exuma Cays," but only two of the main islands—Great Exuma and Little Exuma—bear the name. A single-lane bridge connects those two cays, where the major communities are concentrated.

GETTING THERE

BY PLANE   The most popular way to visit the Exumas is to fly there aboard **Bahamasair** (☎ **800/222-4262**), which has daily service from Nassau. A flight usually leaves Nassau in the morning some time between 8:45am and 9:15am, depending on the day. There are also midafternoon flights on Monday, Friday, and Saturday.

American Eagle (☎ **800/433-7300**) serves Exuma from Miami daily.

Exuma has some private airstrips, but its major commercial airport—the Exuma International Airport—is 10 miles from George Town, the capital. (For flights to the private airstrip at Staniel Cay, refer to section 4 of this chapter.)

BY MAIL BOAT   Several mail boats leave from Potter's Cay Dock in Nassau, stopping at various points along the Exumas.

The MV *Grand Master* goes from Nassau to George Town. Departures are on Tuesday at 2pm. It returns to Nassau on Friday morning.

Since hours and sailing schedules are subject to change because of weather conditions, it's best to check with the dockmaster at Potter's Cay Dock in Nassau (☎ **242/393-1064**).

GETTING AROUND

After your arrival at the airport in George Town, chances are you'll meet Kermit Rolle. He's known to everybody. You can stop in at **Kermit's Airport Lounge,** Exuma International Airport (☎ **242/345-0002**), which is just across from the airport terminal building. Kermit, who runs things up in Rolleville, knows as much about the Exumas as anyone else (maybe more). You'll be lucky if Kermit is free, and you can negotiate a deal with him to take you in his car for a tour of the Exumas. He's filled with local lore (see "Where to Dine," below, for a description of his lounge).

BY TAXI   If your hotel is in George Town, it will cost about $24 to get there in a taxi from the airport. Rides often are shared. The island has only a few taxis. Most of them wait at the airport. Hotels can usually get you a taxi if you need to go somewhere and don't have a car. For a taxi, call **Exuma Transport** at ☎ **242/336-2101,** or **Leslie Dames** at ☎ **242/357-0015.**

BY CAR   It's also possible to rent a car during your stay. Try **Exuma Transport,** Main Street, George Town (☎ **242/336-2101**). They have cars to rent for $60 per day and up, or $300 per week. A $200 deposit is required.

In Search of the Red-Legged Thrush

Under the protection of The Bahamas National Trust, **Exuma National Land and Sea Park** begins at Conch Cut in the south and extends northward to Wax Cay Cut, encompassing Halls Pond Cay, Warderick Wells, Shroud Cay, Hawksbill Cay, Cistern Cay, and Bell Island, as well as numerous other small, uninhabited islands. It lies to the northwest of Staniel Cay.

The park is some 22 miles long, and much of it is a sea garden with reefs, some only 3 to 10 feet beneath the water's surface. The park is reached only by chartered boat and is very expensive to visit.

This is an area of natural beauty that can be enjoyed by skin divers and yachties, but it's unlawful to remove any plant, marine, or bird life. Before 1986, visitors were allowed to fish for spiny lobster, hog fish, conch, and such, but the park is now designated a marine replenishment nursery.

Many bird-watchers visit the park, looking for the red-legged thrush, the night-hawk, even the long-tailed "Tropic Bird," plus many, many more winged creatures.

This was once the home of the Bahamian iguana, which is now found only on Allan's Cays, a tiny island group just north of Highborne Cay. The government is taking belated steps to protect this creature, which is found nowhere else in the world. If a person kills or captures an iguana, the penalty on conviction is a fine of as much as $300 and/or imprisonment for up to 6 months.

FAST FACTS: The Exumas

Banks   In George Town, a branch of the Bank of Nova Scotia, Queen's Highway (☎ **242/336-2651**), is open Monday through Thursday from 9:30am to 3pm, on Friday from 9:30am to 5pm.

Customs   The Bahamian Customs office (☎ **242/345-0071**) is at the Exuma International Airport.

Docking   If you come to the Exumas aboard your own boat, Exuma Docking Services, Main Street, George Town (☎ **242/336-2578**), has slips for 52 boats, with water and electricity hookups. There's a restaurant on the premises, and you can replenish your liquor stock from the store here. They also have a Laundromat, fuel dock, land-based fuel pumps, and a store selling supplies for boats and people.

Dry Cleaning   To get dry cleaning done, go to Exuma Cleaners, Queen's Highway, George Town (☎ **242/336-2038**), open Monday through Saturday from 9am to 5pm.

Medical Care   The government-operated medical clinic in George Town can be reached by phone at ☎ **242/336-2088.**

Police   To call the police in George Town, dial ☎ **242/336-2666,** but only for an emergency or special services.

1 George Town

The Tropic of Cancer runs directly through George Town, the capital and principal settlement of the Exumas, located on the island of Great Exuma. Some 900 people live in this tranquil seaport village, which opens onto a 15-mile-long harbor. George Town, part in the tropics and part in the temperate zone, is a favorite port of call for the yachting crowd. Its one road runs parallel to the shoreline of the harbor. Flights from Nassau, Miami, and Fort Lauderdale come into nearby Exuma International Airport.

Sometimes the streets of George Town are nearly deserted, except when the mail boat from Nassau arrives at Government Wharf, bringing everybody out. If you've rented a housekeeping unit on the Exumas, you can come here to buy fresh fish when the fishers come in with their catches.

If you need to stock up on supplies, George Town is the place, as it has more stores and services than any other place in the Exumas. There are dive centers, marinas, and markets, as well as a doctor and a clinic.

George Town often doesn't bother with street names, but it is so small that everything is easy to find.

WHERE TO STAY
MODERATE

✪ **Club Peace and Plenty.** Queen's Hwy., P.O. Box EX29055, George Town, Great Exuma, The Bahamas. ☎ **800/525-2210** in the U.S. and Canada, or 242/336-2551. Fax 242/336-2093. 35 units. A/C TV. Winter, $140–$175 double. Off-season, $110–$150 double. AE, DISC, MC, V.

In the heart of George Town is this attractive and historic waterside inn, the classic island hostelry. In spite of its credentials, however, it isn't as luxurious as Coconut Cove Hotel. Once it was a sponge warehouse and later it was the home of a prominent family before it was converted into a hotel in the late 1940s, making it the oldest in the Exumas. It was named for a vessel that brought Loyalists from the Carolinas to the Exumas. The two-story pink-and-white hotel has dormers and balconies opening onto a water view. The units are all tastefully furnished.

The grounds are planted with palms, crotons, and bougainvillea. Peace and Plenty fronts on Elizabeth Harbour, which makes it a favorite of the visiting yachting set, including Prince Philip. The hotel faces Stocking Island and maintains a private beach club there, offering food and bar service, as well as miles of sandy dunes. A free boat makes the run to Stocking Island for hotel guests. There is a small free-form freshwater pool on the patio of the hotel; drinks are served here. There are also two cocktail lounges. One of these lounges, converted from an old slave kitchen, is filled with nautical gear, including lanterns, rudders, and anchors. Food consists of continental, Bahamian, and American specialties.

The hotel recently started a dine-around program, which costs $42 per person extra. Guests can have dinner at one of three hotels, and transportation is included. Dining at the hotel is both indoor and outdoor. Calypso music is played on the terrace. Naturally, the sporting life holds forth here, and Sunfish sailing, fishing, diving, and boating are all the rage. The resort will rent you snorkeling gear and Windsurfers, and even arrange snorkeling trips to nearby reefs. Fishing packages can also be arranged for bonefishers. The staff here can also arrange bookings in their Peace and Plenty Beach Inn, also in George Town. All-inclusive packages are sold to bonefishers who book in here on 4- or 5-day blocks.

✪ **Coconut Cove Hotel.** Queen's Hwy., P.O. Box EX29299, George Town, Great Exuma, The Bahamas. ☎ **242/336-2659.** Fax 242/336-2658. 10 rms, 1 suite. A/C TV. Winter, $128–$153 double; $206–$226 suite. Off-season, $100–$125 double; $178–$198 suite. MC, V.

Set on an acre of palm-dotted sandy soil, 1 mile west of George Town, in a neighborhood known as the Jolly Hall District, this 10-unit hotel began its saga as the private home of Thomas Chimento and his wife, Pamela Predmore. Built as a home in the mid-1980s, its main building is a long (96-foot), single-story rectangular bungalow whose ocean-facing side is composed almost entirely of sliding glass doors. Inside, mahogany doors and panels glow. Many were constructed by Tom himself, a former New York–based manufacturer of doors and panels. It is the most luxurious accommodation in the Exumas, but not the traditional favorite, an honor bestowed upon Club Peace and Plenty.

Upscale accommodations include beachfront rooms with private terraces, plus other rooms overlooking an aquatic pond and tropical gardens. These also have private terraces. All accommodations have a view of the ocean and are equipped with private baths. The Paradise Suite, a favorite with honeymooners, is the special place to stay, furnished with a Jacuzzi, an oversize bath, and a private hot tub on the terrace. All the accommodations have queen-size beds, refrigerators, bathrobes, toiletries, and both air-conditioning and ceiling fans. The club also has a modest beachfront freshwater pool, plus a "Sandbar" for poolside drinks. Stocking Island, a sand spit, lies within a 5-minute boat ride offshore and shelters the hotel from the direct action of the surf. Good snorkeling lies all around.

The Palms at Three Sisters. Mount Thompson, P.O. Box EX29215, Georgetown, Great Exuma, The Bahamas. ☎ **800/688-4752** or 242/358-4040. Fax 242/358-4043. 12 rms, 2 villas. A/C TV. Winter, $105 double; $125 triple; $125 villa. Off-season, $75 double; $90 triple, $100 villa. Extra person $20 each. MC, V.

In December of 1994, this resort opened on an isolated spot 7 miles from its nearest neighbor, adjacent to a 1,200-foot stretch of one of the best beaches in the Exumas. Set on 6^1/$_2$ acres of windswept oceanfront about 9 miles northwest of George Town, the property benefited from thousands of dollars' worth of improvements to what had, until then, been a somewhat rundown resort. Its manager is Welsh-born Treffor Davies, former manager of George Town's Peace and Plenty resort, who directs his 15-member staff in the day-to-day details of one of the most interesting resorts in the Exumas. Rooms lie within a two-story, motel-like building and have English colonial details and simple, summery furniture. Meals and drinks are served in a low-slung annex, with views stretching out over the Atlantic. There's a flowering patio where live music is presented every Friday, a tennis court that is lit for night play, an on-site swimming pool, and plenty of opportunity for calm, low-key seclusion and privacy. A dozen bicycles are available for the use of guests.

The resort, incidentally, is named after a trio of rocks (the Three Sisters) whose composition is radically different from the coral that comprises the rest of the Exumas. They jut about 15 feet above sea level just offshore from this resort's beach and serve as a beacon for picnic excursions by motor launch that the hotel arranges to a sandy cay offshore. Snorkeling is excellent in the shallow waters offshore, and rental of fishing boats and fishing equipment is easily arranged.

Peace and Plenty Beach Inn. Harbourfront, P.O. Box EX29055, George Town, Great Exuma, The Bahamas. ☎ **800/525-2210** in the U.S. and Canada, or 242/336-2250. Fax 242/336-2253. 16 rms. A/C. Winter (all inclusive), $174–$199 per person double; $150–$175 per person triple; $138–$163 per person quad. Off-season (all inclusive), $154–$179 per person double;$137–$162 triple; $128–$153 quad. Up to two children 12 and under free in parents' room. AE, MC, V.

You can also stay at the previously mentioned Club Peace and Plenty's two-story annex, located a mile west of George Town. It opened in 1991, and immediately became the most world-class bonefishing resort in The Bahamas (or the Caribbean for that matter). It's also a favorite resort for snorkelers, offering a special Jean-Michel Cousteau snorkeling program. This hotel is the tranquil choice. For some "action," you can go over to the Club Peace and Plenty. It contains first-class and well-furnished double rooms that open onto 300 feet of white-sand beach. The bedrooms have Italian tile floors as well as balconies overlooking Bonefish Bay and Elizabeth Harbour.

In late 1996, the inn became all inclusive. The rates cover all meals, tax and service charges, the shuttle bus to George Town, the ferry to Stocking Island, house wine with dinner, and transfers. An adjacent structure housing the bar and restaurant was designed to reflect the colonial flavor of George Town. A freshwater pool offers an alternative to ocean bathing, and Whaler Skiff rentals are available if you'd like to explore Elizabeth Harbour. Scuba diving, snorkeling, and fishing excursions can be arranged.

INEXPENSIVE

Regatta Point. Regatta Point, Kidd Cove, P.O. Box EX29006, George Town, Great Exuma, The Bahamas. ☎ **800/688-4752** in the U.S., or 242/336-2206. Fax 242/336-2046. 6 units. Winter, $122–$142 double; $178 two-bedroom apt for up to four. Off-season, $104–$120 double; $158 two-bedroom apt for up to four. Extra person $20. MC, V.

Regatta Point lies on a small cay just across the causeway from George Town. The cay used to be known as Kidd Cay, named after the notorious pirate. Overlooking Elizabeth Harbour, the present complex consists of six efficiency apartments, which are not air-conditioned, although the cross ventilation is good. Ceiling fans help, too. This little colony hums with action in April during the Family Island Regatta. Your hostess, American Nancy Bottomley, does much to ease your adjustment into the slow-paced life of the Exumas. She discovered this palm-grove cay—really bush country—in 1963 and opened the little colony of efficiencies in 1965. She even had to build the causeway herself. Each of the pleasantly furnished, summery units has its own kitchen. Maid service is provided for all these housekeeping units.

There is a little beach for the use of guests, and Mrs. Bottomley will help with arrangements for water sports and outings. Sunfish boats and bicycles are available at no extra charge. One guest liked the place so much he stayed for 7 years. Those guests who don't want to cook for themselves can take dinner out in George Town. They have a choice of the already-recommended hotels in town or one of the local restaurants. Grocery stores are fairly well stocked if you want to do it yourself, however. The hotel staff will direct you to their whereabouts.

Two Turtles Inn. Main St., P.O. Box EX29051, George Town, Great Exuma, The Bahamas. ☎ **242/336-2545.** Fax 242/336-2528. 14 rms. A/C TV. Winter, $88 double; $98 triple; $108 quad. Off-season, $68 double; $78 triple; $88 quad. Children under 12 stay free in parents' room. AE, MC, V.

Set opposite the village green, midway between the town's harborfront and a saltwater estuary known as Victoria Pond, this two-story hotel is as popular for its drinking and dining facilities as for its plain accommodations. It doesn't have the style and character of the properties previously recommended, but its prices are more alluring for those on a budget. Originally built of stone and stained planking in the early 1960s, the hotel is arranged around a courtyard, the centerpiece of which is the enormous Norfolk pine that is the envy of gardeners throughout the island. Each room has a ceiling fan and a private bath. Beach enthusiasts and watersports aficionados head for the facilities of Peace and Plenty, a short walk away. Tennis, sailing, boating, snorkeling, and scuba diving can be arranged through other nearby hotels.

WHERE TO DINE

In general, the best places to take meals in George Town are the main hotels, reviewed above, although there are exceptions.

MODERATE

Club Peace and Plenty Restaurant. In the Club Peace and Plenty, Queen's Hwy. ☎ **242/ 336-2551.** Reservations recommended. Main courses $12.50–$35; lunch $10; breakfast $7. AE, MC, V. Daily 7:30–10:30am, noon–2:30pm, and 6:30–10pm. FRENCH/ITALIAN/BAHAMIAN/ AMERICAN.

Club Peace and Plenty has the finest island dining rooms, where there is good home cooking and enough of it so that no one leaves unsatisfied. Who knows who might be seated at the next table? In days of yore, it might have been an ex-king, Constantine of Greece, or maybe Jack Nicklaus. The frequently arriving yachties "from anywhere" provide conversation and amusement. You might begin with conch salad or one of the salads made with hearts of palm or hearts of artichoke, then follow with local lobster. Bahamian steamed grouper regularly appears on the menu (of course), and it's simmered with onions, sweet pepper, tomatoes, and thyme. But you can also order such special dishes as an herb-flavored Cornish game hen, recently sampled, that was juicy and perfectly roasted and flavored. For the traditionalist, grilled T-bone steak flambé appears, as does a duckling in orange sauce that's not bad at all. You sit under ceiling fans, looking out over the harbor, at a table right off the hotel's Yellow Bird Lounge. Windows on three sides and candlelight make it particularly nice in the evening.

But you can also visit for lunch, when the selection includes homemade soups, followed by, perhaps, a conch burger, a chef's salad, or deep-fried grouper. Breakfast offerings include french toast or scrambled eggs and sausage. But if you want to go truly Bahamian, you'll order the breakfast of boiled fish and grits.

The Palm. At the Palms at Three Sisters Hotel. ☎ **242/358-4043.** Breakfast $4.25–$9; lunch platters and sandwiches $5–$10; dinner main courses $14–$26.50; sunset specials $12–$14. MC, V. Daily 7:15am–9pm. INTERNATIONAL.

Set beside a sandy, isolated beach, 9 miles northwest of the Exuma capital, this airy, ocean-facing restaurant is associated with one of the island's newest resorts. Breakfasts are the kind of hearty steak-and-egg fare appreciated by serious mariners, although such dishes as Bahamian coconut pancakes, Exuma-style stewed fish with grits or johnnycakes, and omelets with grilled tomatoes are also featured. Lunches include lobster salads, conch chowder, grouper fingers, burgers, and sandwiches. Dinners are more formal. Although the fare is familiar and international, it is well prepared. Flame-broiled grouper might be your best and freshest choice.

INEXPENSIVE

Eddie's Edgewater. George Town. ☎242/336-2050. Main courses $7–$16. AE, MC, V. Mon–Sat 7:30am–midnight. BAHAMIAN.

Overlooking Lake Victoria, this popular restaurant is run by Victor and Andrea Brown, who provide diners with good, traditional Bahamian food, nothing more. The place is unpretentious and unfussy. Among the choices are conch chowder, okra soup, grouper, and the endangered turtle steak. On Monday nights, a local band plays from 7:30 to 11pm. The place is very casual, and it doesn't close until the last person staggers out, which sometimes is as late as 2am.

Kermit's Airport Lounge. Exuma International Airport. ☎ **242/345-0002.** Reservations not accepted. Platters from $4.75; cheeseburgers $4; beer $3. No credit cards. Daily 8am until the last airplane takes off. BAHAMIAN.

Owned by one of the island's most entrepreneurial taxi drivers, Kermit Rolle, this simple but appealing place lies across the road from the entrance to the island's airport. Views from inside encompass the sight of airplanes taking off and landing and help to define this as a semiofficial waiting room for most of the island's flights. This eatery is for convenience, not for a stunning cuisine. The cook will fry you some fish, and there's always beans and rice around. Johnnycake and sandwiches are also available, along with burgers and an array of tropical drinks. Until an airplane flies you to a better restaurant, this place might come in handy.

Sam's Place. Main St. ☎ **242/336-2579.** Main courses $11–$22.50; breakfast from $5; lunch from $4.50. DISC, MC, V. Daily 7am–10pm. BAHAMIAN.

If Bogie were alive today, he'd surely head for this second-floor restaurant and bar overlooking the harbor in George Town. It opened in 1987 and is one of the best restaurants in Great Exuma, popular with the yachting set. The decor has been called "Bahamian laid-back." Sam Gray, the owner, offers breakfasts to catch the early boating crowd. Lunches could include everything from freshly made fish chowder to spaghetti with meat sauce. You'll also be able to order an array of sandwiches throughout the day. The dinner menu changes daily, but you're likely to find such well-prepared main courses as Exuma lobster tail, roast lamb, Bahamian steamed chicken, and panfried wahoo, a welcome change when you're suffering from grouper overload. Of course, you can always get native conch chowder. At dinner the talk here is of one of everybody's dreams—that of owning a private utopia, one of those uninhabited cays still remaining in the Exuma chain.

WATER SPORTS & OTHER OUTDOOR ACTIVITIES
BOAT TRIPS

If you want to make the Exumas a 1-day excursion, try **The Fantastic Exuma Powerboat Adventure.** The name may sound silly, but the trip provides travelers an excellent overview of the area. The boat departs Nassau Harbour at 9am and arrives in the Exuma Cays about an hour later. There are several stops, with snorkeling and scuba diving at a reef, a visit with the iguanas on Allan's Cay, feeding stingrays along the shore, and a barbecue lunch. A full bar is available all day, and the drinks are free. For more information and prices, contact **Powerboat Adventures,** P.O. Box CB 13315, Nassau, The Bahamas (☎ **242/327-5385**).

FISHING

Many visitors come to the Exumas just to go **bonefishing.** The best arrangements can be made at **Club Peace and Plenty,** Queen's Highway (☎ **242/345-5555**), from which you can go out for a half day. The Exumas offer miles of wadable flats (shallow bodies of water) and trained guides accompany you. Fly instruction and equipment are also offered.

KAYAKING

Ibis Tours, 5798 Sunpoint Circle, Boynton Beach, Florida (☎ **800/525-9411**), experienced guides of the Florida Everglades, also paddle the waters of the Exumas. There is no more adventurous way to see this island chain than by kayak. High-performance fiberglass kayaks are used. They have sails to take advantage of the prevailing south wind. The price includes guides, all meals, the boat, and all paddling equipment, as well as all the camping equipment you need, including tents and mattresses. The expeditions mostly spend time in the Exuma National Land and Sea Park. The 8-day adventure costs $1,020–$1,350 per person.

SCUBA DIVING

The lectures and oral commentary offered by **Exuma FantaSea,** Queen's Highway (☎ **242/336-3483**), are as articulate and scientifically grounded as anything you'll find in The Bahamas. The company is run by Ed Haxby, a Florida-born marine biologist who is assisted by his Inagua-born wife, Madeline. They specialize in taking groups of six or fewer divers into the offshore reefs and mysterious blue holes, explaining before and after the dive what was seen and offering ecologically conscious narratives on underwater life. PADI instruction is available from a resort course, priced at $90 for those interested in sampling the scuba experience for the first time, and from certification courses ranging from basic open-water diving up through advanced courses. They emphasize specialized certification in a wide variety of areas, including underwater naturalist, night diving, and underwater photography. While the specialty courses range in price, certified divers can join one-tank "eco-dives" for $55 and two-tank dives for $85. The company maintains two dive boats, 20 and 25 feet in length, plus a 15-boat fleet of Boston Whaler rental boats you can drive yourself with daily rates of $80 for a 17-footer to $110 for an 18-footer. Weekly rates are also available.

EXPLORING THE ISLAND: FEATURING A STRAW MARKET, THE MYSTERY CAVE & THE WHITE-SAND BEACHES OF STOCKING ISLAND

There isn't much to see here in the way of architecture except the confectionery pink-and-white **Government Building,** which was "inspired" by the Government House architecture in Nassau. Under an old ficus tree in the center of town, there's a straw market where you can talk to the friendly Exumian women and perhaps purchase some of their handcrafts.

George Town has a colorful history, despite the fact that it appears so sleepy today. (There's so little traffic, there is no need for a traffic light.) Pirates used its deep-water harbor in the 17th century. What was called the "plantation aristocracy," mainly from Virginia and the Carolinas, settled here in the 18th century. In the next 100 years **Elizabeth Harbour,** the focal point of the town, became a refitting base for British man-of-war vessels, and the U.S. Navy used the port again during World War II.

The greatest attraction is not George Town but ✪ **Stocking Island,** which lies in Elizabeth Harbour. It faces the town across the bay, less than a mile away. This long, thin barrier island has some of the finest white-sand beaches in The Bahamas. Snorkelers and scuba divers come here to explore the blue holes, and it is also ringed with undersea caves and coral gardens. Boat trips leave daily from Elizabeth Harbour heading for Stocking Island at 10am and 1pm. The cost is $5 per person one-way. However, guests of the Peace and Plenty hotel ride free.

Mystery Cave is a famous dive site, tunneling for more than 400 feet under the hilly, 7-mile-long island with its palm-studded beaches.

If you'd like to go shelling, walk the beach that runs along the Atlantic side. You can order sandwiches and drinks at the beach club on the island, which is run by Club Peace and Plenty (see above). Stocking Island used to be a private enclave for guests at Club Peace and Plenty, but it is now used by all visitors.

Landlocked **Lake Victoria** covers about 2 acres in the heart of George Town. It has a narrow exit to the harbor and functions as a diving-and-boating headquarters.

One of the offshore sights in Elizabeth Harbour is Crab Cay, which can be reached by boat. This is believed to have been a rest camp for British seamen in the 18th century.

In April, the **Family Island Regatta** draws a yachting crowd from all over the world to Elizabeth Harbour. It's a rollicking week of fun, song, and serious racing

Why Everyone Is Named Rolle

The history of the Exumas is not much documented before the latter part of the 18th century. It is assumed that the island chain was inhabited by Lucayans at least until the Spaniards wiped them out. Columbus didn't set foot on this chain of islands. However, from the northern tip of Long Island, he is believed to have seen Little Exuma, naming whatever was in the area "Yumey." At least, that's how the island chain appears on a map of the New World from 1500.

By the late 17th century, Great Exuma had become a major producer of salt, and permanent settlers began to arrive. The sailing vessels of the salt merchants were constantly harassed by pirates, but some families from Nassau must have looked on this as the lesser of two evils. On New Providence they were subjected to the terrorism inflicted by both the pirates and the Spanish, and in the latter part of the 17th century and the first of the 18th, they fled to the relative peace of the Exumas (they still do!).

Some Loyalist families, fleeing the newly established United States of America after British defeat, came to the Exuma Cays in 1783, but nothing like the number that settled in Harbour Island, New Plymouth, and Spanish Wells. In the 18th century, cotton and salt were "king" on the Exumas. English plantation owners brought in many slaves to work the fields, and many of today's Exumians are direct descendants of those early slaves, who were mostly of African origin. The "king" did not stay long on the throne. Insects went for the cotton, and salt lands such as those of the Turks and Caicos Islands proved much too competitive for those of the Exumas, so these pursuits were eventually abandoned.

when the island sloops go all out to win. It's said that some determined skippers bring along extra crewmen to serve as live ballast on windward tacks, then drop them over the side to lighten the ship for the downwind run to the finish. The event, a tradition since 1954, comes at the end of the crawfish season. The George Town regatta is the most popular of all the traditional sloop races held in the archipelago.

SHOPPING

Unless you're one of the islanders who resides permanently in Great Exuma, chances are you won't visit George Town just to shop. However, there are a few places where you can purchase souvenirs and gifts.

Exuma Liquor and Gifts. Queen's Hwy. ☎ **242/336-2101.**

The most popular store in town, this place sells liquor, wine, and beer. Hours are Monday through Saturday from 9am to 5pm.

Peace and Plenty Boutique. Queen's Hwy. ☎ **242/336-2222.**

This boutique stands next to the Sandpiper and across the street from the previously recommended Club Peace and Plenty, which owns it. Its main draw is a selection of Androsia batiks for women. Androsia cloth is sold by the yard. You can also find the usual practical items such as film and suntan oil.

A line of saltwater fly-fishing equipment is available for rent or sale. They also have a large selection of men's and women's sports clothes. Hours are Monday through Saturday from 9am to 2pm and from 3 to 5pm.

Most of the white owners went back to where they came from, but the slaves, having no such option, stayed on, subsisting by working the land abandoned by their former owners and taking the names of those owners as their own. A look through the George Town directory turns up such names as Bethel, Ferguson, and especially Rolle, the same as those of the long-gone whites.

It becomes immediately apparent, however, that every other person is named Rolle. One elderly woman, sitting in front of her little shanty painted in florid tricolors, and wearing a Bahama Mama T-shirt, confided, "You're born a Rolle, all your cousins are called Rolle, you marry a Rolle and have children called Rolle, and you are a Rolle and all the mourners at your funeral, related or not, are called Rolle." She claimed that since everyone in the Exumas keeps track of their blood relatives, the locals know which Rolle is "real family" and which is not related by blood. "That's got to be kept in mind," she said, "when it comes time to get married."

At one time Lord John Rolle held much of the Exumas under a grant from the British Crown, giving him hundreds of acres. He is reported to have owned 325 slaves who worked this acreage, but Lord Rolle never set foot on his potentially rich plantation. Stories vary as to what happened to the slaves—whether they were, as some claim, freed by Lord Rolle and given the land by him, or whether, upon being released from bondage by the United Kingdom Emancipation Act in 1834, they took over the land, with or without Rolle's approval. Whichever, descendants of those same slaves are important Exumians today.

The Sandpiper. Queen's Hwy. ☎ **242/336-2084.**

The Sandpiper stands across from Club Peace and Plenty. Its highlights are the original serigraphs by Diane Minns, but it also offers a good selection of Bahamian arts and crafts, along with such items as Bahamian straw baskets (or other hand-crafted works), sponges, ceramics, watches, and postcards. Diane designs and silk screens T-shirts here in the shop, and she welcomes anyone to watch her at work. It is open Monday through Saturday from 8am to 1pm and from 2 to 5pm.

SIDE TRIPS

Queen's Highway, which is still referred to as the "slave route," runs the length of Great Exuma, and you may want to travel it, in either a taxi or a rented car, to take in the sights in and around George Town.

Rolleville, named after Lord Rolle, is still inhabited by descendants of his freed slaves. It is claimed that his will left them the land. This land is not sold but is passed along from one generation to the next.

Rolleville is 28 miles to the north of George Town. As you travel along the highway, you'll see ruins of plantations. This land is called "generation estates," and the major ones are Steventon, Mount Thompson, and Ramsey. You pass such settlements as Mosstown (which has working farms), Ramsey, the Forest, Farmer's Hill, and Roker's Point. Steventon is the last settlement before you reach Rolleville, which is the largest of the plantation estates. There are several beautiful beaches along the way, especially the one at Tarr Bay and Jimmie Hill.

Some visitors may also want to head south of George Town, passing Flamingo Bay and Pirate's Point. In the 18th century Captain Kidd is said to have anchored at Kidd Cay (here you can stay at the Regatta Point, recommended previously).

Flamingo Bay, the site of a hotel and villa development, begins just half a mile from George Town. It's a favorite rendezvous of the yachting set and bonefishers.

WHERE TO DINE

Iva Bowe's Central Highway Inn Restaurant & Bar. Queen's Hwy. Located a quarter of a mile from the entrance to the International Airport and about 6¹/₂ miles northwest of George Town. ☎ **242/345-7014.** Main courses $8–$15; lunch $7–$10. No credit cards. Mon–Sat 10am–10pm. BAHAMIAN.

This roadside tavern, operated by Mrs. Lorraine Bowe-Lloyd, specializes in very tender cracked conch. The conch is marinated in lime, pounded to make it tender, and then fried with her own special seasonings. It's the best in the Exumas. You might also try her crawfish salad or shrimp scampi. Her food is good Bahamian cookery.

Kermit's Hilltop Tavern. Rolleville. ☎ **242/345-6006.** Reservations required for dinner. Lunch platters $8; 3-course dinners $18–$21. No credit cards. Lunch and snacks daily 8am–9pm; dinner by prior arrangement only. BAHAMIAN.

Originally built in the 1950s by members of the Rolle family, this stone-sided social center sits atop the highest point in Rolleville, with a view over the rest of the town. Today, it's open as a tavern and general meeting place for almost everyone in town, as well as for people passing through. Lunch and drinks are served continuously throughout the day and early evening, but more formal meals of chicken, fish, or lobster should be arranged by phone in advance. Try Kermit's curried mutton, steamed conch, or panfried grouper. It's one of the most authentic places for true Bahamian cuisine. "They cook the way my mama used to," one diner told us, "and that's why we come here." Call it Bahamian soul food. Some of the produce comes fresh from his farm. The place lies about 20 miles north of George Town.

2 Little Exuma

This is a faraway retreat, the southernmost of the Exuma Cays. It has a subtropical climate, despite being actually in the tropics, and beaches of white sand. In some places, sea life is visible more than 60 feet down in the clear waters. The island, about 12 square miles in area, is connected to Great Exuma by a 200-yard-long bridge. It's about a 10-mile trip from the George Town airport.

Less than a mile offshore is **Pigeon Cay,** which is uninhabited. Visitors often come here for the day and are later picked up by a boat that takes them back to Little Exuma. You can go snorkeling and visit the remains of a wreck, some 200 years old, right offshore in about 6 feet of water.

On one of the highest hills of Little Exuma are the remains of an old pirate fort. Several cannons are located near it, but documentation is lacking as to when it was built or by whom. Pirates didn't leave too much data lying around.

Coming from Great Exuma, the first community you reach on Little Exuma is called **Ferry,** so named because the two islands were linked by a ferry service before the bridge was put in. See if you can visit the private chapel of an Irish family, the Fitzgeralds, erected generations ago.

Along the way, you can take in **Pretty Molly Bay,** site of the now-shuttered Sand Dollar Beach Club. Pretty Molly was a slave who committed suicide by walking into the water one night. The natives claim that her ghost can still be seen stalking the beach every night.

Many visitors come to Little Exuma to visit the **Hermitage,** a plantation constructed by Loyalist settlers. It is the last surviving example of the many that once stood in the Exumas. It was originally built by the Kendall family, who came to Little Exuma in 1784. They established their plantation at **Williamstown** and, with their slaves, set about growing cotton. But they encountered so many difficulties having the cotton shipped to Nassau that in 1806 they advertised the plantation for sale. The ad promised "970 acres more or less," along with "160 hands" (referring to the slaves). Chances are you'll be approached by a local guide who, for a fee, will show you around. Ask to be shown several old tombs in the area.

Also at Williamstown (look for the marker on the seaside), you can visit the remains of the **Great Salt Pond.**

Finally, the explorer who has to "see everything" can sometimes get a local to take him or her over to **Hog Cay,** the end of the line for the Exumas. This is really just a spit of land, and there are no glorious beaches here. As such, it's visited mainly by those who like to add obscure islets to their list of explorations.

Hog Cay is privately owned, and it is farmed. The owner seems friendly to visitors. His house lies in the center of the island. There is also an old lookout tower with a 5-foot cannon at its base. At one time it stood guard for ships coming and going into Elizabeth Harbour.

SPECIAL MOMENTS ON LITTLE EXUMA

Dropping in on the Shark Woman   When you go to Little Exuma, you might ask a local to direct you to the cottage of Gloria Patience, the "most unforgettable character of the Exumas." Her house, called Tara, lies on the left side of the road after you come over the bridge. She is famous and much publicized as the Shark Woman. Now in her 70s, she earns her living collecting sharks' teeth, which she sells to jewelers. Called the "Annie Oakley of the Out Islands," this barefoot septuagenarian has some tall fish stories to tell, and she's told them to such people as Peter Benchley, author of *Jaws.* She's also appeared on television with Jacques Cousteau. She discounts some modern theories that sharks are kindly souls with a bad press. Take it from the woman who's bagged at least 1,800 of them single-handedly: "They're vicious." The biggest deadly choppers, she claims, are found in the jaws of the female hammerhead. She sells the flesh of her prey to restaurants, although she says she doesn't eat shark meat herself. Her home, a house split by the Tropic of Cancer, is like a museum, and you can come here on a shopping expedition, not only for shark teeth, but for all the flea-market stuff and more valuable pieces she's collected over the years. She's a remarkable woman.

Rolling Through Rolle Town   On the road to Little Exuma, you come to the hamlet of Rolle Town, which is another of the generation estates that was once, like Rolleville in the north, owned by Lord Rolle and is populated today with the descendants of his former slaves. This sleepy town has some houses about a century old. In an abandoned field, where goats frolic, you can visit the Rolle Town Tombs, burial ground of the McKay family, who all died young. Capt. Alexander McKay, a Scot, came to Great Exuma in 1789 after he was granted 400 acres for a plantation. His wife joined him in 1791, and soon after, they had a child. However, tragedy struck in 1792, when Anne McKay and her child died. She was only 26. Perhaps grief stricken, her husband died the following year. Their story is one of the romantic legends of the island. The village claims a famous daughter, Esther Rolle, the actress. Her parents were born here, but they came to the United States before she was born.

3 Barraterre

For years linked to the world only by boat, Barraterre during the 1980s became connected to "mainland" Great Exuma by a road. The area is now open for development, but no one here expects that to happen soon. The place is no more than a sleepy hamlet, and everybody seems to be named McKenzie. As you're heading north on Queen's Highway, instead of continuing to "end of the line" Rolleville, turn left in the direction of Stuart Manor. You pass through Alexander and keep going until you reach the end of another road, and there lies little Barraterre, asleep in the sun. For the boating crowd, it is the gateway to the Brigantine Cays, which stretch like a necklace to the northwest.

Here you'll see how the "life of the cays" is lived, with the biggest event being the arrival of the mail boat, which is a vital link to the outside world. No one, not even any of the McKenzies, is absolutely certain how the place got its name. Perhaps it came from the French, *bar terre,* or "land obstruction."

The Barraterrians live in a hilly community, with vividly painted houses (many in decay).

4 Staniel Cay

Staniel Cay lies 80 miles southeast of Nassau at the southern end of the little Pipe Creek archipelago, which is part of the Exuma Cays. It's an 8-mile chain of mostly uninhabited islets, sandy beaches, coral reefs, and bonefish flats. There are many places for snug anchorages, making this a favorite yachting stopover in the mid-Exumas. Staniel Cay, known for years as "Stanyard," has no golf course or tennis courts, but it's the perfect island for "the great escape." It was described by one yachting visitor as lying "in a sea of virtual wilderness."

Staniel Cay has also been featured in several films, including the James Bond thrillers *Thunderball* and *Never Say Never Again,* and the movie *Splash.*

GETTING THERE   Before the coming of the airplane, it took days to reach the island from Miami or Nassau, but now it has a 3,000-foot paved airstrip. Some of the vacation homes on Staniel Cay today are owned by pilots. A telecommunications center links the island with both The Bahamas and the United States.

Air service from Fort Lauderdale can be arranged by calling **Island Express** at ☎ **954/359-0380.**

WHERE TO STAY

Happy People Marina. Staniel Cay, the Exumas, The Bahamas. ☎ **242/355-2008.** 8 rms. Year-round, $70 double. No credit cards.

This marina is operated by an Exumian, Kenneth Rolle. His mother was the famous Ma Blanche, who had a mail boat named for her. He offers motel-like rooms on the water, as well as a restaurant and bar, a swimming pool, and a private beach. There are dockage facilities, but no ability to fuel or service the majority of the island'svisiting yachts. The prevailing atmosphere is casual, and all of the rooms face the waterfront.

Meals and drinks are served in a separate building closer to the center of town, within a minute of the marina. Known as the Royal Entertainer Lounge, it sometimes welcomes local bands and serves meals according to a flexible schedule. Lunches cost from around $5 to $8 per person, dinners around $16 to $24.

EXPLORING THE ISLAND

An annual **bonefishing festival** is sponsored here on August 5, during the celebration of Bahamian Independence Day.

The Happy People Marina (☎ **242/355-2008**) arranges sportsfishing trips with local guides, as well as snorkeling trips.

There are about 100 Bahamians living on this island, and there's a local **straw market** where you can buy handcrafts, hats, and handbags. The little cay was settled in the mid-18th century. Its oldest building is a 200-year-old shell.

Just off Staniel Cay is the **Thunderball grotto,** one of the most beautiful diving and snorkeling sights in The Bahamas. Some scenes from the James Bond movie *Thunderball* were filmed here. Divers can explore the grotto, but removal of anything but yourself is forbidden, as it is under the protection of The Bahamas National Trust. At low water, it's possible to swim here; a blowhole in the roof illuminates the cave. Tropical fish can be seen in their natural habitat. Another James Bond flick, *Never Say Never Again,* was also partially filmed at this grotto, as was the comedy *Splash.*

5 Sampson Cay

In the heart of what has been called the "most beautiful cruising waters in the world," tiny Sampson Cay has a certain charm. It lies directly northwest of Staniel Cay and just to the southeast of the Exuma National Land and Sea Park. It has a full-service marina and some accommodations (see below), as well as a small dive operation. Along with Staniel Cay, Sampson Cay has the only marina in the Central Exumas. To fly into Sampson Cay, you must first go to Staniel Cay. However, most visitors arrive in their own boats. Local guides take out sportfishers for the day; this can be arranged at the club. Sampson Cay lies 67 nautical miles southeast of Nassau and is one of the safest anchorages in the Exumas and a natural "hurricane hole." The cay lies near the end of Pipe Creek, which has been called a "tropical Shangri-la."

WHERE TO STAY

Sampson's Cay Colony. Sampson Cay, the Exumas, The Bahamas. ☎ **242/355-2034.** Fax 242/355-2034. 2 units. A/C. Year-round, $115–$150 double. No credit cards.

Your host here is Mrs. Rosie Mitchell, whose husband, Marcus, is well known in these parts for his marine salvage company, which rescues yachts foundering on nearby rocks and reefs.

Each of the establishment's units has a tiny kitchenette (with a hot plate, sink, and refrigerator, but no oven).

Community life revolves around the grocery store and commissary, the fuel and dockage facilities of the marina, and the bar and restaurant favored by visiting yachtspeople. The nautically decorated clubhouse serves drinks and sandwiches anytime of the day to anyone who shows up, but reservations are required before 4pm for the single-seating dinner, which is served nightly between 7 and 8pm. A fixed-price meal costs $22 to $24 per person. (Reservations can be made via ship-to-shore radio on Channel 16 VHF.)

On the premises, a pair of 13-foot Boston Whalers can be rented for $45 per half day, or $60 for a full day.

6 Norman's Cay

Throughout the Exumas, you'll see islands with NO TRESPASSING signs posted. In some cases this is meant with a vengeance. In the early 1980s, at least on one island, you could have been killed if you had gone ashore!

On a summer day long ago, the boat containing our party sailed by Cistern Cay. Back then, we were told that Robert Vesco owned part of that island. "He likes to keep it *very, very private* here," our guide cautioned, heading for friendlier shores. (Vesco, of course, is the financier much wanted by the U.S. government.) Even though the fugitive is long gone (under arrest in Cuba), people around here still like to keep it quiet.

Perhaps the most bizarre Out Islands episode in all The Bahamas was centered around Norman's Cay, one of the northernmost islands in the Exumas, 44 nautical miles southeast of New Providence Island. At one time when we stayed at the former hotel here, Norman's Cay Club, this was a South Seas island–type outpost. Reportedly it was once the retirement home of the pirate Norman.

This was always a very special cay. It isn't flat, since parts rise to 50 feet above sea level. It is heavily wooded with lignum vitae, royal poinciana, palmetto, tamarind, and casuarina, and it is a bird-watcher's paradise. Snorkeling and scuba diving on the coral heads are among the best in the Exumas, with vertical drop-offs, black-coral forests, spectacular cuts, and wrecks. The location is adjacent to the Exuma National Land and Sea Park.

In the old days you might have run into Ted Kennedy, Walter Cronkite, or William F. Buckley Jr. enjoying the pleasures of Norman's Cay. The remote outpost enjoyed great popularity with a Harvard/Boston clique.

However, in the 1980s the situation changed drastically when a German-Colombian, Carlos Lehder (pronounced *Leader*) Rivas (his mother's name), purchased most of the island. The story of his purchase of Norman's Cay was mentioned in the 1985 *Newsweek* article "Empire of Evil," documenting the horrors of cocaine smuggling. A short time after Lehder purchased the property, the Colombian flag was flying over Norman's Cay, and many of the wintering wealthy fled in horror from the island when they returned to find their homes broken into and trashed.

Norman's Cay, experts have stated, became the major distribution point for drug export to the United States. Millions of dollars worth of cocaine was flown from Colombia and deposited in hangars at Norman's Cay before being smuggled into the United States. It is estimated that some 30 pilots crashed attempting to fly in their illegal cargoes. You can still see the wreckage of a C-46 that went down in the bay.

When an undersecretary of state arrived from Washington and landed on the island, he was ordered off at gunpoint by a Colombian commando. He left, but when he returned to the U.S. capital, he launched a major protest. Apparently, strong pressure was applied by the U.S. government on the Bahamian government to clean up the act at Norman's Cay.

Lehder fled Norman's Cay for further adventures in Colombia, where he was captured and extradited to the United States (he was later tried, convicted, and imprisoned).

Norman's Cay may one day realize its tourist potential again, but for the moment it remains relatively abandoned, visited only by a stray yachting party or perhaps one of the American Canadian Caribbean Cruise line's vessels, who visit the backwaters of The Bahamas and call here because of the good beaches and snorkeling possibilities.

The Southern Bahamas

This cluster of islands on the southern fringe of The Bahamas is one of the last frontier outposts that can be reached in a relatively short time from the U.S. mainland. Their remote location is one of the most compelling reasons to visit them. That is, to see life the way it used to be. Some of the islands are proud to proclaim that "we are as we were when Columbus first landed here."

But their history hasn't been that uneventful. In the 18th century, Loyalists from the Carolinas and Virginia came here with slave labor and settled many of the islands. For about 20 years they had thriving cotton plantations until a blight struck and killed the industry. In 1834, the United Kingdom Emancipation Act freed slaves throughout the British Empire. The Loyalists moved on to more fertile ground, in many cases leaving behind the emancipated blacks, who were left with nothing. Many people in the Southern Bahamas have had to eke out a living as best they can farming and fishing.

With some notable exceptions, such as on Long Island, tourism developers have stayed clear of these islands, although they have enormous potential, since most of them have excellent beaches, good fishing, and fine dive sites.

If you consider visiting any of these islands, be forewarned that transportation will be a major problem. Also, except for two or three resorts, accommodations are severely limited. For these and other reasons, "yachties" have been the primary visitors up to now.

Many changes are in the wind for the Southern Bahamas. But right now there's almost no traffic, no banks, no lawyers.

1 Cat Island

Untainted by tourism, Cat Island is the sixth-largest island in The Bahamas and the location of the highest point, at 206 feet, in the country. The fishhook-shaped island—some 48 miles long and 1 to 4 miles wide—comprises about 150 square miles of land area about 130 miles southeast of Nassau and 325 miles southeast of Miami. Cat Island is not to be confused with Cat Cay. The cay is a little private island near Bimini. Cat Island—named after the pirate Arthur Catt—is located near the Tropic of Cancer, between Eleuthera and Long Island. It has one of the best climates in The Bahamas, with temperatures in the high 60s during the short winters, rising to the mid-80s in summer, with trade winds making the place even more comfortable. Some 2,000 residents call it home.

With its virgin beaches, Cat Island is one of the most beautiful islands in The Bahamas, and it is visited by so few people it could be called "undiscovered." However, many local historians claim that Cat Island residents were the first to see Columbus. The great explorer himself was believed by some to have been first welcomed here by the peaceful Arawaks.

Cat Island remains mysterious to some even now. It's known as a stronghold of such strange practices as *obeah* (West Indian witchcraft) and of miraculously healing bush medicines. Its history has been colorful. Regardless of whether or not Columbus stopped off here, the island has seen a parade of adventurers, slaves, buccaneers, farmers, and visionaries of many nationalities.

A straight asphalt road (in terrible shape) leads from the north to the south of the island. Along the way you can select your own beach, and chances are you'll have complete privacy. These beaches offer an array of water sports, and visitors can go swimming or snorkeling at several places. Fernandez Bay is a picture-postcard, white-sand beach set against a turquoise blue sea and lined with casuarina trees. The island's north side is wild, untamed shoreline. Boating and diving are among the main reasons to go to Cat Island. Diving lessons are available for novices.

Arthurs Town, in the north, is the major town and the boyhood home of actor Sidney Poitier. (He has many relatives still living on the island, including one or two amazing look-alikes we recently spotted.) Poitier shared memories of his childhood home in his book *This Life*.

GETTING THERE   By Plane   A commercial flight on Bahamasair (☎ **800/ 222-4262** in the U.S.) leaves Nassau for Arthurs Town on Sunday and Thursday at 6:45am. There is also an airport near the Bight, the most scenic village on the island.

By Mail Boat   Cat Island is also serviced by mail boat. The MV *North Cat Island Special* (☎ **242/393-1064**) departs Potter's Cay Dock in Nassau weekly, heading for Bennett's Harbour and Arthurs Town. It leaves on Tuesday at 2pm and returns to Nassau on Thursday. Another vessel, MV *Sea Hauler* (☎ **242/393-1064**), departs Potter's Cay in Nassau on Tuesday at 2pm, going to Old and New Bight, with a return on Saturday.

GETTING AROUND   There is no taxi service available on Cat Island. Hotel owners, if notified of your arrival time, will have someone drive to the airport to pick you up. You can, however, rent a car from **Russell Brothers,** Bridge Inn, New Bight (☎ **242/342-3014**), to go exploring on your own. Prices begin at $75 daily, with unlimited mileage. Hours are Monday through Saturday from 7:30am to 6pm in the summer, and 8am to 6:30pm in the winter.

WHERE TO STAY & DINE

Bridge Inn. New Bight, Cat Island, The Bahamas, ☎ **800/688-4752** or 242/342-3013. Fax 242/342-3041. 12 rms. A/C MINIBAR TV. Winter, $80 double; $95 triple. Off-season, $70 double; $85 triple. Package rates available. No credit cards.

Lying 300 yards from a beach, the Bridge Inn is owned by Cat Islander Allan Russell, who is ably assisted by a group of family members. This is not the premier place to stay on the island, however. That honor goes to Fernandez Bay Village. The inn offers baby-sitting services so that parents can play tennis or go diving, windsurfing, jogging, bicycling, fishing, or just sightseeing with the knowledge that their youngsters are being carefully tended and are having fun, too. Bedrooms are modest. Each unit can house three to four guests. Located on the premises are a full bar and a restaurant that serves a rather simple Bahamian and international cuisine. Room service is also available. Local jam sessions ("rake and scrape") are easily arranged for your

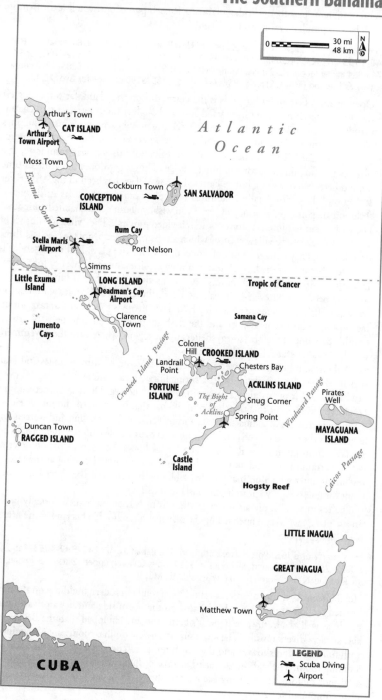

The Southern Bahamas

0   30 mi
    48 km
N

Atlantic Ocean

Arthur's Town
CAT ISLAND
Arthur's Town Airport
Moss Town

Exuma Sound

Cockburn Town
CONCEPTION ISLAND
SAN SALVADOR

Rum Cay
Stella Maris Airport
Port Nelson

Simms

Little Exuma Island
LONG ISLAND
Deadman's Cay Airport

Tropic of Cancer

Jumento Cays

Clarence Town

Samana Cay

Crooked Island Passage

Colonel Hill
CROOKED ISLAND
Landrail Point
Chesters Bay

FORTUNE ISLAND
ACKLINS ISLAND

The Bight of Acklins
Snug Corner

Pirates Well

Duncan Town
RAGGED ISLAND

Spring Point

MAYAGUANA ISLAND

Windward Passage

Castle Island

Hogsty Reef

Caicos Passage

LITTLE INAGUA

GREAT INAGUA

Matthew Town

CUBA

LEGEND
Scuba Diving
Airport

2-0116

entertainment, usually on Friday night. As Russell points out, you'll learn that life can be "no problem, mon, on Cat Island."

Fernandez Bay Village. Three miles north of New Bight, Cat Island, The Bahamas. ☎ **800/940-1905** or 242/354-3043; 954/474-4821 in Plantation, FL. Fax 242/342-3051, or 954/474-4864 in Plantation, FL. 9 units. Winter (MAP), $185–$215 villa for two; $205–$210 cottage for two. Off-season (MAP), $165–$195 villa for two; $185–$190 cottage for two. AE, MC, V.

Opening onto Fernandez Bay, this is the best resort on the island, far surpassing either the Bridge Inn or the Greenwood Inn. Although rustic it has a certain charm, mainly because of its position on a curvy white sandy beach set against casuarinas blowing in the trade winds. The beach, or anywhere else for that matter, is never crowded on Cat Island. Go here only if you really want to get away from it all; this place is far too laid-back for full hotel service. Things get done, but it takes time around here. No one's in a hurry. Fernandez Bay Village has been in the Armbrister family since it was originally established on a plantation in 1870. Its rusticity and seclusion are part of its charm, and yet, if you wish, you can get acquainted with other guests with similar interests (or even watch video movies). The "village" consists of six full housekeeping villas, each of which sleeps up to six people, as well as three double-occupancy cottages, built of stone, driftwood, and glass. Full maid service is provided. Because of the lack of nearby dining facilities, most clients opt for accommodations with MAP, which in this case means either breakfast or lunch ("because so many people don't even eat breakfast") and dinner. Yachtspeople, who moor in the water offshore (there are no marina facilities), often visit the resort to take advantage of the resort's general store and the fresh supplies to be found here. Nearby is Smith's Bay, one of the best storm shelters in the region, where even the government mail boats take refuge during hurricanes.

Breakfast and lunch are served in a clubhouse decorated with antiques and Haitian art. The clubhouse also features a sitting library area, a stone fireplace, and overhead fans, and it opens onto a view of the beach and sea. Dinners are served on a beach terrace adjacent to a thatched roof tiki bar that is run on the honor system.

There is free use of Zuma sailboats and bicycles, and snorkeling and waterskiing are also on the agenda. Scuba and fly-fishing services are also offered. Rental vans are available from Jason's Car Rental at $85 for 24 hours. You can picnic on deserted beaches around the island and then dine on authentic island cuisine at the resort's restaurant, after which on many nights a blazing bonfire near the water is the focal point for guests who want to listen to island music.

The resort will supply air transportation from Nassau on request (usually in the private plane owned and operated by the manager himself). Flights land at the nearby New Bight Airport.

Hotel Greenwood Inn. Port Howe, Cat Island, The Bahamas. ☎ **242/342-3053.** Fax 242/342-3053. 20 rms. Year-round, $99 double; $119 triple. Children under 12 stay free in parents' room. Free meals for children up to 6 years old. AE, MC, V.

Hotel Greenwood Inn, open year-round, is a group of modern buildings on the most isolated section of the island. It's located on the ocean side and has a private sandy beach, as well as a freshwater pool. It's better run and equipped than the Bridge Inn and attracts divers mostly. The spacious oceanview double rooms are all equipped with full baths and showers and their own terraces. There is an all-purpose bar and a dining room. The staff meets each Bahamasair flight when it arrives. The inn has a 40-foot motorboat for diving excursions, and its Tabaluga Diving Base has complete equipment for 20 divers at a time.

EXPLORING THE ISLAND: PLANTATIONS, PEAKS & A HERMITAGE

There's an interesting Arawak cave at Columbus Point on the southern tip of the island. In addition, you can see the ruins of many once-flourishing plantations. Some old stone mounds are nearly 200 years old. Early planters, many of them Loyalists, marked their plantation boundaries with these mounds. These include the **Deveaux Mansion,** built by Col. Andrew Deveaux of the fledgling U.S. Navy, who recaptured Nassau from the Spanish in 1783. The plantation's heyday was during the island's short-lived cotton boom. Yet another mansion, **Armbrister Plantation,** lies in ruins near Port Howe.

You can hike along the natural paths through native villages and past exotic plants. Finally, you reach the peak of **Mount Alvernia,** the highest point in The Bahamas, at 206 feet above sea level. Here you will be rewarded with a spectacular view. The mount is capped by the **Hermitage,** a religious retreat built entirely by hand by the late Father Jerome, the former "father confessor" of the island, who was once a mule skinner in Canada. Curiously, the building was scaled to fit his short stature (he was a very, very short man). Formerly an Anglican, this Roman Catholic hermit priest became a legend on Cat Island. He died in 1956 at the age of 80, but his memory is kept very much alive here.

The island's **Annual Three-Day Regatta** takes place every summer, usually at the end of July. It attracts the largest collection of visitors to Cat Island; the inns prove inadequate to receive them.

2 San Salvador/Rum Cay

This may be where the New World began. For some years it has been believed that Christopher Columbus made his first footprints in the western hemisphere here, although some scholars strongly dispute this. The easternmost island in the Bahamian archipelago, San Salvador lies 200 miles southeast of Nassau. It is some 63 square miles in area, much of which is occupied by water. There are 28 landlocked lakes on the island, the largest of which is 12 miles long and serves as the principal route of transportation for most of the island's population of 1,200. A badly maintained 40-mile road circles the perimeter of San Salvador.

The tiny island keeps a lonely vigil in the Atlantic. The Dixon Hill Lighthouse at South West Point, about 165 feet tall, can be seen from 90 miles away. The light is a hand-operated beacon fueled by kerosene. Built in the 1850s, it is the last lighthouse of its type in The Bahamas. The highest point on the island is Mount Kerr at 138 feet.

Except for an odd historian or two, very few people ever visited San Salvador. Then Club Med–Columbus Isle opened, and the joint's been jumping ever since. At least at the Club Med property. Away from here, San Salvador is as sleepy as it ever was, although it's been known for years as one of the best dive sites in The Bahamas. The snorkeling and fishing are equally as good, as are the white sandy beaches.

Whether or not it was actually on this island, Columbus and his men did make landfall at around 2am on the moonlit night of October 12, 1492. The native population, probably awakened from a sound sleep, called these strange creatures "men from Heaven." Perhaps "men from Hell" would have been a better description. The Spanish discovery of this island and others led to a holocaust, as the Spanish wiped out the native populations.

The Columbus Question

In 1492 a small group of peaceful Lucayan natives (Arawaks) went about their business of living on a little island they called Guanahani, where they and their forebears had lived for at least 500 years. Little did they know how profoundly their lives would change when they greeted the arrival of three small, strange looking ships bearing Columbus and his crew of pale, bearded, oddly costumed men. It is said that when he came ashore, Columbus knelt and prayed—and claimed the land for Spain.

Unfortunately, the event was not so propitious for the reportedly handsome natives. Columbus later wrote to Queen Isabella that they would make ideal captives—perfect servants, in other words. It wasn't long before the Spanish conquistadores cleared the island—as well as most of The Bahamas—of Lucayans, sending them into slavery and early death in the mines of Hispaniola (Haiti) in order to feed the Spanish lust for gold from the New World.

But is the island now known as San Salvador the actual site of Columbus' landing? No lasting marker was placed by Columbus on the sandy, sun-drenched island he had come to, resulting in much study and discussion during the last century or so as to just where he really did land. Some say that it was on one of the cays of the Turks and Caicos Islands; others claim that it was on Cat Island.

In the 17th century, an English pirate captain, George Watling, took over the island and built a mansion to serve as his safe haven. The island was listed on maps for about 250 years as Watling's (or Watling) Island.

In 1926 the Bahamian legislature formally changed the name of the island to San Salvador, feeling that enough evidence had been brought forth to support the belief that this was the site of the landing of Columbus. Then in 1983, artifacts of European origin (beads, buckles, and metal spikes) were found here together with a shard of Spanish pottery, plus Arawak pottery and beads. It is unlikely that the actual date of these artifacts can be pinned down, although they are probably from about 1490 to 1560. However, the beads and buckles fit the description of goods recorded in Columbus' log.

National Geographic magazine published a meticulously researched article in 1986 written by its senior associate editor, Joseph Judge, with a companion piece by the former chief of the magazine's foreign editorial staff, Luis Marden, setting forth the belief that Samana Cay, some 65 miles to the southeast of the present San Salvador, was Guanahani, the island Columbus named San Salvador when he first landed in the New World. The question may never be absolutely resolved, but there will doubtless be years and years of controversy about it. And nevertheless, history buffs still flock here every year hoping to follow in the footsteps of Columbus.

GETTING THERE

Club Med (see below) solves transportation problems for its guests by flying them in on weekly charter planes from Miami or Eleuthera. Otherwise, Riding Rock Inn (see below) has charter flights every Saturday from Fort Lauderdale. You can also rely on public transportation by land or sea, but if you do, you'll have to wait a long time before getting off the island.

BY PLANE Bahamasair (☎ 800/222-4262) has lots of flights to the island because of the Club Med. Departure times from Nassau are constantly changing, so check with the airline for a schedule. They do, however, have nonstop flights from Miami on Thursday and Sunday at 1:30pm.

BY MAIL BOAT   From Nassau, M/VT *Maxine* leaves Tuesday heading for San Salvador and Rum Cay. The trip takes 18 hours under uncomfortable conditions. For details about sailing, contact the dockmaster at Potter's Cay Dock in Nassau (☎ 242/393-1064).

GETTING AROUND

Taxis meet arriving planes and will take you to Riding Rock Inn (see below), where you can rent a car for $85 a day to explore the island on your own. You can also rent **bicycles** here at $8 a day. The latter are the most popular means of transport for visitors.

ESSENTIALS

Hospital   The San Salvador Medical Clinic (☎ 242/331-2105) services the island's residents, but serious cases are flown to Nassau. The clinic is open 24 hours Monday through Friday. Only emergencies are handled on Saturday and Sunday.

Police   To call the police, dial ☎ 919. (Phones are rare on the island, but the front desk at Riding Rock Inn will place calls for you.)

WHERE TO STAY & DINE

✪ **Club Med–Columbus Isle.** Two miles north of Cockburn Town, San Salvador, The Bahamas. ☎ **800/CLUB-MED** or 242/331-2000. Fax 242/331-2458. 270 rms. A/C MINIBAR TV TEL. Winter, $1,150–$1,700 per person per week. Off-season, $1,050 per person per week. No discounts for children. Children under 12 not recommended. Rates include all meals, drinks during meals, and most sports activities. AE, MC, V.

This is one of the most ecologically conscious, and one of the most luxurious, Club Meds in the western hemisphere. Set at the edge of one of the most pristine beaches in the archipelago (2 miles of white sand), about 2 miles north of Cockburn Town, the resort is the splashiest place in the entire Southern Bahamas. Its promoters estimate that more than 30% of the island's population works within the club.

   Most of the prefabricated buildings were barged to the site beginning in 1991. The resort is built around a large free-form swimming pool whose waters, because of the color of the tile, exactly match the color of the nearby ocean. The public rooms are some of the most lavish and cosmopolitan in the country, with art and art objects imported from Asia, Africa, Oceania, the Americas, and Europe and assembled by a battalion of designers. Bedrooms each contain a private balcony or patio, furniture that was custom-made in Thailand or the Philippines, sliding glass doors, and feathered wall hangings crafted in the Brazilian rain forest by members of the Xingu tribe. Each room is large (among the largest in the entire chain) and decorated in shades of blue and green. Dozens of multilingual GOs (guest relations organizers, or *gentils organizateurs*) are on hand to help initiate newcomers into the resort's many diversions. Unlike many other Club Meds, this one does not encourage children and deliberately offers no particular facilities for their entertainment.

   Dining/Entertainment: The main dining room, where meals are an ongoing series of buffets, lies in the resort's center. Two specialty restaurants offer Italian and grilled food, respectively. Eating en masse is not the only option. Nonfat, low-calorie, and vegetarian dishes are featured. Nightly entertainment is presented in a covered, open-air theater and dance floor behind one of the bars.

   Facilities: 10 tennis courts (3 lit for night play), fitness center, the largest scuba facility in the Club Med chain, windsurfing, kayaking and kayak–scuba diving, and a mini-armada of Hobie Cats and other sailing craft.

Riding Rock Inn. Cockburn Town, San Salvador, The Bahamas. ☎ **800/272-1492** in the U.S., or 954/359-8353 in Florida. Fax 954/359-8254 in Florida. 42 rms. A/C. Year-round, $95–$120 double; $109–$135 triple; $140 quad. Dive packages available. MC, V.

San Salvador's second resort is the motel-style Riding Rock Inn, which is almost exclusively (95%) patronized by divers and underwater enthusiasts. Its simple ambience is a far cry from the extravagant Club Med. Each accommodation faces either a pool or the open sea. The most recent improvement to the inn is an 18-room oceanfront building, where the bedrooms are decorated in a tropical decor, with two double beds, satellite TV, a refrigerator, telephone, and air-conditioning. The resort specializes in weeklong packages that include three dives a day, all meals, and accommodations. Packages begin and end on Saturday and, if a client pays a $265 supplement, can include specially chartered round-trip air transportation from Fort Lauderdale. Although most of this resort's clients are already experienced and certified divers, beginners can arrange a $105 resort course for the first day of their visit and afterward participate in most of the community's daily dives. Full PADI certification can also be arranged for another supplement of $400.

Accommodations contain tropics-inspired furnishings and ceiling fans. An island tour is included in the rates, but after that, most clients find that the best way to navigate is by bicycle (the hotel rents them, plus scooters). On the premises are a restaurant serving routine Bahamian specialties and a bar whose seating area juts above the water on a pier.

BEACHES, WATER SPORTS & OTHER OUTDOOR ACTIVITIES

The **beaches** of San Salvador, miles and miles of sandy shores with rarely a bather in site, are ideal for shelling, swimming, or snorkeling. Try **Bamboo Point, Fernandez Bay, Long Bay,** or **Sandy Point.**

Associated with the Riding Rock Inn (see above), **Guanahani Dive Ltd.** (☎ 242/331-2631) offers dive packages, as well as snorkeling, fishing, and boating trips. One-, two-, and three-dive trips cost from $40, $55, and $75, respectively.

Riding Rock Inn also has a tennis court where guests can play for free.

EXPLORING THE ISLAND: COMMEMORATING COLUMBUS

Among the settlements on San Salvador are Sugar Loaf, Pigeon Creek, Old Place, Holiday Track, and Fortune Hill. United Estates, which has the largest population, is a village in the northwest corner near the Dixon Hill Lighthouse. The U.S. Coast Guard has a station at the northern tip of the island.

Bonefishers are attracted to Pigeon Creek, and some record catches have been chalked up here. Except for the party people at Club Med, San Salvador is mainly visited by the boating set who can live aboard their craft. If you're visiting for the day, you'll find one or two local cafes, serving seafood.

Chicago Herald Monument. Crab Cay.

If a preponderance of monuments is anything to go by, this is, in fact, the San Salvador Columbus visited and named. The *Chicago Herald* installed a monument to the explorer in 1892, but it is highly unlikely—in fact, almost impossible—that any landing was made at this site. It opens onto reefs along the eastern shore, surely a dangerous place for a landing.

Olympic Games Memorial. Long Bay.

This memorial to Columbus, located 3 miles south of Cockburn Town, was erected in 1968 to commemorate the games in Mexico. Runners carrying an Olympic torch circled the island before coming to rest at the monument and lighting the torch there.

The torch was then taken to Mexico on a warship for the games. Another marker is underwater, supposedly where Columbus dropped anchor on his *Santa María*.

Just north of the monument stands the **Columbus Monument,** where on December 25, 1956, Ruth Durlacher Wolper Malvin, a Columbus scholar and widow of Hollywood producer David L. Wolper, established a simple monument commemorating the landfall of Columbus in the New World. Unlike the *Chicago Herald* monument, this spot is actually supposed to be the place where Columbus and his men landed.

Watling's Castle. French Bay.

Watling's Castle, also known as Sandy Point Estate, has substantial ruins that are about 85 feet above sea level. The area is located some 2¹/₂ miles from the "Great Lake," on the southwestern tip of the island. Local "experts" will tell you all about the castle and its history. Only problem is, each "expert" we've listened to—three in all, at different times—has told a different story about the place. Ask around and perhaps you'll get yet another version. One of the most common legends involves a famous pirate who made his living either by salvaging the wreckage from foundered ships or by attacking ships for their spoils.

Farquharson's Plantation. West of Queen's Hwy., near South Victoria Hill. Free admission. Open anytime.

In the early part of the 19th century, some Loyalist families moved from the newly established United States to this island, hoping to get rich from farmland tended by slave labor. That idea ended when the United Kingdom Emancipation Act freed the slaves in 1834. The plantation owners moved on, but the former slaves stayed behind.

A relic of those times, Farquharson's Plantation is the best-known ruin on the island. People locally call it "Blackbeard's Castle," but it's a remnant of slavery days, not of the time of pirates. You can see the foundation of a great house, a kitchen, and what is believed to have been a punishment cell.

COCKBURN TOWN

San Salvador is one of the most unspoiled of the Bahamian Out Islands—not that much has changed since Columbus landed except the opening of the Club Med. It has wooded hills, lakes, and white-sand beaches. Its people are hospitable. Some still practice obeah and bush medicine.

The island's capital, Cockburn (pronounced *Coburn*) Town, is a harbor village that takes its name from George Cockburn, who is said to have been the first royal governor of The Bahamas to visit this remote island. That was back in 1823.

Look for the town's landmark: a giant almond tree. Whatever is happening at San Salvador generally takes place here, especially the Columbus Day parade held every October 12.

New World Museum. North Victoria Hill. No phone. Admission $1. Open anytime during the day.

This museum, located 3¹/₂ miles north of Riding Rock Inn, has relics dating from Indian times, but you'll have to ask until you find someone with a key if you want to go inside. The museum lies just past Bonefish Bay in the little village of North Victoria Hill. It's part of a large estate, called Polaris-by-the-Sea and is owned by Ruth Durlacher Wolper Malvin, widow of Hollywood producer David L. Wolper.

Holy Saviour Roman Catholic Church. Cockburn Town.

The very first Christian worship service to be held in the New World was conducted according to the Catholic rites. It thus seems fitting that the Roman Catholic

Diocese of The Bahamas in 1992 dedicated a new church on San Salvador on the eve of the 500th anniversary of the Columbus landfall.

DISCOVERING RUM CAY & CONCEPTION ISLAND

"Where on earth is Rum Cay?" you ask. (That's pronounced *key*, of course.) Even many Bahamians have never heard of it. Located midway between San Salvador and Long Island, this is another cay, like Fortune Island (see below), that time forgot.

That wasn't always the case, though. The very name conjures up images of swash-bucklers and rumrunners, and it was doubtless at least a port of call for those doughty seafarers, as it was for ships taking on supplies of salt, fresh water, and food before crossing the Atlantic or going south to Latin America. The cay's name is supposed to have derived from the wrecking of a rum-laden sailing ship upon its shores.

Like many other Bahamian islands, this one for a while attracted British Loyalists fleeing the new United States of America. They were drawn here by the hope of es-tablishing themselves as farmers and plantation overlords, but even those brave and homeless immigrants abandoned the island as unproductive. Salt mines were the mainstay of the island's economy before they were wiped out by a hurricane at the turn of the century. After that, most of the inhabitants migrated to Nassau, so that by the 1970s the population of Rum Cay stood at "80 souls."

The well-known underwater cinematographer Stan Waterman once described Rum Cay as the "unspoiled diving jewel of The Bahamas." For that reason, a diving club was opened here in 1983, but it closed, regrettably, in 1990. Port Nelson, the island's capital, is where most of the Rum Cay's present 100 inhabitants live.

Some maintain that Rum Cay was the island where Columbus landed next after finding and naming San Salvador. He dubbed that second island Santa María de la Concepción. However, many students of history and navigation believe that the sec-ond stop was at the island today called Conception, which lies northwest of Rum Cay and about the same distance northeast of Long Island. You'll have to go here in a private boat.

Joseph Judge, a writer whose articles have appeared in *National Geographic,* believes that neither of these islands was Columbus's second stop. He holds that, based on modern computer science and knowledge of the ocean bottom and currents, the is-land the discoverer named Santa María de la Concepción has to be Crooked Island.

The uninhabited Conception Island is under the protection of The Bahamas Na-tional Trust, which preserves it as a sea and land park. It's a sanctuary for migratory birds. The most esoteric divers find excellent dive sites here, and the rapidly dimin-ishing green turtle uses its beaches as egg-laying sites. *Note:* Park rules are strict about littering or removing animal or plant life.

With the demise of the Rum Cay Club, tourist traffic to the island came to a halt except for the odd yachting party or two. But with the increased interest in tourism that followed the 1992 Columbus celebrations, the area is gaining renewed interest. At present, you can make private arrangements with boaters on San Salvador to take you to see these time warp islands.

3 Long Island

Most historians agree that Long Island, which has only recently emerged as a minor tourist resort, was the third island Columbus sailed to during his first voyage of dis-covery. The Lucayans (Arawaks) who lived here at the time (and who had come from South America via Cuba) called their island Yuma, but Columbus renamed it Fernandina, in honor of King Ferdinand, and claimed it for Spain.

Loyalist plantation owners came here in the 18th century from the Carolinas and Virginia, bringing with them their slaves and their allegiance to the British Crown. There was a brief cotton boom, but when the slaves were freed in 1834, the owners abandoned the plantations and left the island. Inhabited by the former slaves, Long Island slumbered for years, until German resort developers began investigating its resources in the 1960s.

The Tropic of Cancer runs through this long, thin sliver of land, located 150 miles southeast of Nassau. The island stretches for some 60 miles, running from north to south, and averages 1¹/₂ miles wide. It's only 3 miles wide at its broadest point.

Long Island is characterized by high cliffs in the north, wide and shallow sand beaches, historic plantation ruins, native caves, and Spanish churches. It is also the site of the saltworks of the Diamond Crystal Company. The island's present population numbers some 3,500 people. Offshore are famed diving sites, such as the Arawak "green" hole, a "bottomless" blue hole of stunning magnitude. The best beach bets include Deal's Beach, Cape Santa Maria Beach, Salt Pond Beach, Turtle Cove Beach, and the South End beaches, the latter offering miles of waterfront with powdery white or pink sands.

In June, the sailors of Long Island participate in the big event of the year, the 4-day **Long Island Regatta.** They've been gathering since 1967 at Salt Pond for this annual event. In addition to the highly competitive sailboat races, Long Island takes on a festive air with calypso music and reggae and lots of drinking and partying. Many expatriate Long Islanders come home at this time, usually from Nassau, New York, or Miami, to enjoy not only the regatta but rake-and-scrape music (accordion playing).

GETTING THERE By Plane There are two airstrips here, which are connected by a bad road. The **Stella Maris** strip is in the north, and the other, called **Deadman's Cay,** is in the south, north of Clarence Town. **Bahamasair** (☎ 800/222-4262 in the U.S.) flies direct from Miami on Thursday and Sunday at 12:45pm.

By Mail Boat From Nassau, the MV *Abilin* sails weekly to Clarence Town on the southern end of Long Island. Departures are on Tuesday, and the trip takes a grueling 18 hours. For information contact the dockmaster at Potter's Cay Dock, Nassau (☎ 242/393-1064).

GETTING AROUND The **Stella Maris Resort Club** (☎ 242/338-2051) can make arrangements to have you picked up at the airport upon arrival and can also arrange for a rental car.

ESSENTIALS Police The **police** can be reached by calling ☎ 242/338-8555 or 242/337-0444.

WHERE TO STAY & DINE

✪ **Cape Santa Maria Beach Resort.** Cape Santa Maria, off Queen's Hwy., Long Island, The Bahamas. ☎ 800/663-7090 or 242/338-5273. Fax 242/357-1006. 6 cottages. A/C. Winter, $245 double; off-season, $195 double. Extra person $50. MAP $65 per person extra. AE, DISC, MC, V.

Since opening, this cozy nest has become the most luxurious resort on the island, taking over the position long held by the Stella Maris Resort Club. Six cottages with two rooms each are centered around a clubhouse, and the entire complex opens onto a 4-mile strip of white sand, which was the reason for the resort's creation in the first place. All units are only 60 feet from the beach. Although the accommodations don't have phones or TVs, each room is air-conditioned and also has ceiling fans. Bedrooms have a light, tropical, and airy feeling, with marble floors and tasteful rattan furniture. There's also a screened-in porch with ceiling fans so you can enjoy the outdoors without the mosquitoes, the curse of the Southern Bahamas. The place is ideal for families, and several accommodations are configured so that children will have a separate room. The on-site Canadian managers, Dan and Dorothy Baker, are the most welcoming innkeepers on the island, and they run a fine operation in a remote location. Their restaurant is also good, serving a tasty Bahamian, North American, and seafood cuisine. Along with free beach equipment come bikes, snorkeling gear, and sailboards.

Stella Maris Resort Club. Ocean View Dr., P.O. Box LI30105, Long Island, The Bahamas. ☎ **800/426-0466,** 242/338-2051, or 954/359-8236 for the Fort Lauderdale booking office. Fax 242/338-2052, or 954/359-8238 in Fort Lauderdale. 21 rms; 11 one-bedroom cottages and apts; 13 two-, three-, or four-bedroom bungalows or villas. Winter, $130 double; $165 triple; $150–$185 one-bedroom cottages and apts; $260–$490 bungalows or villas. Off-season, $115 double; $150 triple; $135–$170 one-bedroom cottages and apts; $250–$445 bungalows or villas. AE, MC, V.

Situated on the Atlantic, the Stella Maris Resort Club stands in a palm grove and overlooks the coastline. It was built on the grounds of the old Adderley's Plantation. Courtesy transportation is provided to a 3-mile beach reserve. Accommodations vary widely—rooms, studios, apartments, and cottages with from one to four bedrooms. All of the buildings, including the cottages and bungalows, are set around the clubhouse and a trio of pools.

Each accommodation has its own walk-in closet and fully equipped bath. Some bungalows are 100 feet from the water, others are directly on its edge. The inn serves Bahamian cuisine, as well as continental specialties. Dress here is informal.

The inn provides rum punch parties, cave parties, barbecue dinners, Saturday dinners, and dancing. There are two hard-surface tennis courts and numerous water sports. Divers and snorkelers can choose between coral head, reef, and drop-off diving, along the protected west coast of the island, at the north, and all along the east coast, around Conception Island and Rum Cay. Waterskiing and bottom and reef fishing are also offered; there are three good bonefish bays close by. Some 12-foot Scorpion and Sunfish sailboats are free to hotel guests.

Thompson Bay Inn. Main Rd., Thompson Bay, P.O. Box LI30123, Stella Maris, Long Island, The Bahamas. 8 rms. Year-round, $65 double. No credit cards.

Located at Salt Pond, 12 miles south of Stella Maris, Thompson Bay Inn is a modest two-story stone inn. You couldn't get much simpler than this place, but some escapists seek it out, finding the two properties recommended above too expensive or too elaborate for their tastes. The inn's combination bar, lounge, dance hall, and restaurant serves plain Bahamian dishes, including conch, grouper, and peas 'n' rice. Dinners cost $15 each. Rooms are simply furnished, and the inn's four baths are shared.

Note: To telephone the inn you must call the Deadman Cay's operator (☎ **242/ 337-0099**). The operator will call the inn on the VHF radio and deliver your message.

EXPLORING THE ISLAND: MORE PLANTATIONS

Most of the inhabitants live at the unattractively named **Deadman's Cay.** Except for Burnt Ground, other settlements have colorful and somewhat more pleasant names: Roses, Newfound Harbour, Indian Head Point, and at the northern tip of the island,

Cape Santa Maria, generally believed to be the place where Columbus landed and from which he looked on the Exumas (islands that he did not visit). Our favorite name, however, is Hard Bargain. No one seems to know how this hamlet got its name. Hard Bargain, now a shrimp-breeding farm, lies 10 miles south of Clarence Town.

Try to visit **Clarence Town,** located 10 miles south of Deadman's Cay, along the eastern coastline. It was here that the stubby little priest, Father Jerome, who became known as the "father confessor" of the islands, built two churches before his death in 1956—St. Paul's, an Anglican house of worship, and St. Peter's, a Roman Catholic church. The "hermit" of Cat Island (you can visit his Hermitage there) was interested in Gothic architecture. He must also have been of a somewhat ecumenical bent, having started his ministry as an Anglican but embracing Roman Catholicism along the way.

The days when local plantation owners figured their wealth in black slaves and white cotton are recalled in some of the ruins you can visit. The remains of **Dunmore's Plantation** at Deadman's Cay stand on a hill with the sea on three sides. There are six gateposts (four outer and two inner ones), as well as a house with two fireplaces and wall drawings of ships. At the base of the ruins is evidence that a mill wheel was once used. It was part of the estate of Lord Dunmore, for whom Dunmore Town on Harbour Island was named.

In the village of Grays stand the ruins of **Gray's Plantation,** where you'll see the remnants of at least three houses, one with two chimneys. One is very large, and another seems to have been a one-story structure with a cellar.

Adderley's Plantation, off Cape Santa Maria, originally occupied all the land now known as Stella Maris. The ruins of this cotton plantation's buildings consist of three structures that are partially intact but roofless.

Two underground sites that can be visited on Deadman's Cay are **Dunmore's Caves** and **Deadman's Cay Cave.** You'll need to hire a local guide if you wish to explore these. Dunmore's Caves are believed to have been inhabited by Lucayans and later to have served as a hideaway for buccaneers. The cave at Deadman's Cay, one of two that lead to the ocean, has never been fully explored. There are two native drawings on the cavern wall.

FISHING ON LONG ISLAND

Savvy fishers come here instead of the more famous places, such as Andros. The secret of the good fishing found here is the presence of a major current stream, called the North Equatorial Current, which originates in the Canary Islands. This stream washes the shores of Long Island. In its wake the current transports huge schools of blue marlin, white marlin, sailfish, rainbow runners, yellowfin tuna, blackfin tuna, wahoo, and dolphin (dorado). Wahoo is best hunted from September through November. Catches weigh from 10 to 90 pounds. Some yellowfin have weighed 150 pounds. The small blackfin tuna (July through December) weigh from 10 to 30 pounds. In addition, there are miles and miles of reef fishing, with hundreds of species, including snapper or grouper that have been known to weigh 100 pounds. A jew fish caught here weighed 500 pounds. Inshore fishing for bonefish is also possible. These fish can be caught from an anchored boat, from the beach, or while wading in water one foot in depth. Local hotels will hook you up with five or six guides who have boats and tackle.

4 Acklins Island & Crooked Island

These little tropical islands approximately 240 miles southeast of Nassau comprise an undiscovered Bahamian frontier outpost. Columbus came this way looking for gold. Much later Acklins Island, Crooked Island, and their surrounding cays were hideouts for pirates who attacked vessels in the Crooked Island Passage, which is the narrow waterway that separates the two islands and through which Columbus sailed. Today a well-known landmark, the Crooked Island Passage Light, built in 1876, guides ships to a safe voyage through the slot. Also known as the Bird Rock lighthouse, it is a popular nesting spot for ospreys, and the light still lures pilots and sailors to the Pittstown Point Landing Resort. A barrier reef begins near the lighthouse, stretching down off Acklins Island for about 25 miles to the southeast.

Although Acklins Island and Crooked Island are separate, they are usually mentioned as a unit because of their proximity to one another. Together the two islands form the shape of a boomerang. Crooked Island, the northern one, is 70 square miles in area, whereas Acklins Island, to the south, occupies 120 square miles. Both islands have good white-sand beaches and offer fishing and scuba-diving possibilities. Both islands are inhabited mainly by fishers and farmers.

In his controversial article in *National Geographic* in 1986, Joseph Judge identified Crooked Island as the site of Columbus's second island landing, the one he named Santa María de la Concepción.

It is estimated that by the end of the 18th century there were more than three dozen working plantations on these islands, begun by Loyalists fleeing mainland North America in the wake of the Revolutionary War. At the peak plantation period, there could have been as many as 1,200 slaves laboring in the 3,000 "doomed" acres of cotton fields (which were later wiped out by a blight). The people who remained on the island survived not only by fishing and farming, but in the mid-18th century, they began stripping the Croton Cascarilla shrub of its bark to produce the flavoring for Campari liquor.

GETTING THERE & GETTING AROUND   There's an airport at Colonel Hill on Crooked Island and another airstrip at Spring Point, Acklins Island.

Bahamasair (☎ **800/222-4262** in the U.S.) has two flights a week from Nassau, on Tuesday at 9am and Saturday at 9am, to Crooked Island and Acklins Island, with returns to Nassau scheduled on the same day.

There is also **mail-boat service** aboard the MV *Lady Mathilda*. It leaves Potter's Cay Dock in Nassau, heading for Acklins Island, Crooked Island, Fortune Island (Long Cay), and Mayaguana Island each week. Check on days of sailing and costs with the dockmaster at Potter's Cay Dock in Nassau (☎ **242/393-1064**).

A government-owned ferry service connects the two islands; it operates daily from 9am to 4pm. It links Lovely Bay on Acklins Island with Browns on Crooked Island. The one-way fare is $4.

Once you arrive at Crooked Island, there is a taxi service available, but because of the lack of telephones, it's wise to advise your hotel of your arrival—they will probably send a van to meet you.

ESSENTIALS   Hospitals   There are two government-operated clinics. Phones are few on the island, but your hotel desk can reach one of these clinics by going through the operator. The clinic on Acklins Island is at Spring Point and Chesters Bay, and the one on Crooked Island is at Landrail Point.

Police   The police station on Crooked Island can be reached by dialing ☎ 242/ 336-2197.

WHERE TO STAY & DINE

Crooked Island Beach Inn. Cabbage Hill, Crooked Island, The Bahamas. ☎ **242/344-2321.** 6 rms. Year-round, $60 double. No credit cards.

Built of cement and cinderblock in the early 1980s, this simple and isolated ocean-view hotel lies directly on the beach. It's about a 5-minute drive north of the island's airport. The place is run by the Rev. Ezekiel Thompson and his daughter, who might be able to rent you a small boat for $40 a day or a car for $60 a day. Bedrooms open directly onto a verandah and are about as basic as you can get, although few visitors who check in here expect luxury. Each contains a ceiling fan, a private bathroom, and a scattering of basic furniture. Although there is no formal restaurant, breakfast can be arranged if you request it the night before, and lunch and dinner can be prepared if you ask for them in advance. The beach at the hotel is often piled high with dead sea grass, which attracts flies. The beaches are better northwest and southeast of the inn, where there is also some good snorkeling.

Pittstown Point Landing. Landrail Point, Crooked Island. ☎ **800/752-2322** or 242/ 344-2507. Fax 704/881-0771. For reservations and information, contact Pittsdown Point Landing, 238A Airport Rd., Statesville, NC 28677. 12 rms. Winter, $110 double; $120 triple; $130 quad. Off-season, $90 double; $100 triple; $110 quad. Full board $55 per person extra. AE, MC, V.

Located at the extreme northwestern tip of Crooked Island, this hotel is so isolated you'll forget all about the world outside. For most of the early years of its life, it was a well-guarded secret shared mostly by the owners of private planes who flew in from the mainland of Florida for off-the-record weekends. Even today, about 80% of the clients arrive by one- or two-engine aircraft that they fly themselves as part of island-hopping jaunts around The Bahamas. The island maintains its own 2,300-foot, hard-surface landing strip, which is completely independent from the one used for the twice-per-week flights from Nassau on Bahamasair.

In 1994, a group of investors upgraded the place, taking great care not to alter its raffish, escapist appeal. Surrounded by scrub-covered landscape at the edge of a turquoise sea, it lies $2^1/_2$ miles north of the hamlet of Landrail Point (population 60), on a sandy peninsula. Within easy access are some of the weirdest historic sites in The Bahamas, including the sunbaked ruins of a salt farm (Marine Farms Fortress) that was sacked by American-based pirates in 1812.

Spartan accommodations lie within three low-slung, cement-sided buildings that are painted white with a turquoise trim. They lie directly on the beach, usually with screened-in porches facing the sea. Because of the constant trade winds blowing in, the bedrooms don't have air-conditioning, only large paddle-shaped ceiling fans. All accommodations have private bathrooms. The entire resort shares only one telephone/fax, which is reserved for emergency calls.

Meals are served in a stone-sided building that was originally erected late in the 1600s as a barracks for the British West Indies Naval Squadron and later served as the region's post office. The restaurant serves seafood and North American and Bahamian specialties. Hotel residents always arrive on the MAP plan, but since this establishment is the most appealing hotel and restaurant on the island, you're likely to find a scattering of yacht owners or aviators who drop in spontaneously for refreshment.

EXPLORING THE ISLANDS: UNCOVERING A PIRATE HIDEOUT & MORE

Crooked Island opens onto the **Windward Passage,** the dividing point between the Caribbean Sea and The Bahamas. Whatever else he may have named it, it is said that when Columbus landed at what is now Pittstown Point, he called it Fragrant Island because of the aroma of its many herbs. One scent was cascarilla bark, used in a native liqueur, called Cascarilla Liqueur, which is exported. For the best view of the island, go to Colonel Hill, if you didn't land at the Crooked Island Airport (also known as the Colonel Hill Airport) when you arrived.

Guarding the north end of this island is the **Marine Farms Fortress,** an abandoned British fortification that saw action in the War of 1812. It looks out over Crooked Island Passage and can be visited (ask your hotel to make arrangements for you).

Also on the island is **Hope Great House,** with orchards and gardens, dating from the time of George V of England.

Other sights include **French Wells Bay,** a swampy delta leading to an extensive mangrove swamp rich in bird life, and the **Bird Rock Lighthouse,** built a century ago.

At the southern end of Acklins Island lies **Castle Island,** a low and sandy bit of land where an 1867 lighthouse stands. Pirates used it as a hideout, sailing forth to attack ships in the nearby passage.

Acklins Island has many interestingly named hamlets—Rocky Point, Binnacle Hill, Salina Point, Delectable Bay, Golden Grove, Goodwill, Hard Hill, Snug Corner, and Lovely Bay. Some Crooked Island sites have more ominous names, such as Gun Point and Cripple Hill.

VISITING FORTUNE ISLAND: A TIME WARP

Lying off the coast of Crooked Island, Fortune Island is truly an island that time forgot. Boaters on Crooked Island will take you here. Your hotel will put you in touch with one. Based on research done for an article in *National Geographic,* experts believe that Fortune Island (sometimes confusingly called Long Cay) is the one Columbus chose to name Isabella, in honor of the queen who funded his expedition. Once it had a thriving salt and sponge industry, now long gone. Its only real settlement is Albert Town, which is classified as a ghost town, but officially isn't. There are some hardy souls still living there. Fortune Hill on Fortune Island is the local landmark, visible from 12 miles away at sea. This small island got its name from the custom of hundreds of Bahamians who went here in the two decades before World War I. They'd wait to be picked up by oceangoing freighters, which would take them as laborers to Central America—hence, they came here to "seek their fortune."

5 Mayaguana Island

"Sleepy Mayaguana" it might be called. It seems to float adrift in the tropical sun, at the remote extremities of the southeastern "edge" of The Bahamas. It occupies 110 square miles and has a population of about 500. It's a long, long way from the powers at Nassau, who rarely visit here.

Standing in the Windward Passage, Mayaguana is just northwest of the Turks and Caicos Islands. It's separated from the British Crown Colony by the Caicos Passage. Around the time of the American Civil War, inhabitants of Turks Island began to settle in Mayaguana, which before then had dozed undisturbed for centuries.

Pink Flamingos: Not Just Lawn Art in The Bahamas

Inagua, the most southerly of The Bahamas, and third-largest in the chain, lies just off the eastern tip of Cuba. Partially because of its isolation, it's home to some of the best-stocked bird colonies in the western hemisphere. In fact, its human population of 1,200 is outnumbered by the island's vast colonies of pink flamingos. When seen as an ensemble, they present a surreal vision. They're so plentiful on Inagua that some of them even roost on the runway of the island's airport, as well as at thousands of other locations throughout the flat, heat-blasted landscape.

Dedicated bird-watchers who are willing to forego comforts usually trek inland to the edges of the many brackish lakes in the island's center. About half the island is devoted to a national park; the island's most viable industry involves distilling salt from the local salt flats. For detailed information on bird-watching on Inagua, ornithologists can contact The Bahamian National Trust (administrators of about 270 square miles of the island's bird-breeding interior) at P.O. Box N-4105, Nassau, The Bahamas (☎ 242/393-1317). Matthew Town, the island's largest hamlet, offers the island's only bona fide hotel rooms. Despite the hardships and inconveniences, a view of the pink flamingos of Inagua is an ornithologist's dream. The most desirable season for viewing them is from November until June.

Acklins Island and Crooked Island lie across the Mayaguana Passage. Mayaguana is only 6 miles across at its widest point, and about 24 miles long. Its beaches are enticing, but you'll rarely see a tourist on them, except an occasional German. A few tourism developers have flown in to check out the island, but so far no activity has come about. Because of its remote location, the United States has opened a missile-tracking station here.

Its southern location makes it ideal in winter. If you come to Mayaguana to escape a harsh winter back home, no one will ever think of looking for you here. Summers are scorchingly hot, however.

GETTING THERE   By Plane   Getting to Mayaguana presents a problem. Bahamasair (☎ 800/222-4262 in the U.S.) flies in here to a little airstrip, but only the most adventurous travelers seek the place out. Flights arrive from Nassau Monday and Friday at 9am.

By Mail Boat   From Nassau, the MV *Lady Mathilda*, going also to Crooked Island, Acklins Island, and Fortune Island (Long Cay), makes a stop at Mayaguana. For information, check with the dockmaster at Potter's Cay Dock in Nassau (☎ 242/393-1064).

WHERE TO STAY & DINE   There are no hotels. However, if you should arrive and aren't staying on a boat, go to Abraham's Bay, the biggest and most populated place on the island, where you might find some locals who will take in guests for the night. They'll feed you some locally caught seafood and give you a bed. Visiting here is truly an offbeat adventure, but some hearty and adventurous souls come for that reason alone.

6 Great Inagua

The most southerly and the third-largest island of The Bahamas, flat Great Inagua, some 40 miles long and 20 miles wide, is home to 1,200 people. It lies 325 miles southeast of Nassau. Henri Christophe, the self-proclaimed Haitian king, is supposed to have had a summer palace built for himself here in the very early part of the 19th century, but no traces of it can be found today. This island is much closer to Haiti than it is to Nassau.

In 1687, long before the coming of Christophe, a Captain Phipps recovered 26 tons of Spanish treasure from sunken galleons off these shores.

This is the site not only of the Morton Salt Crystal Factory, here since 1800, but also of one of the largest nesting grounds for flamingos in the western hemisphere. The National Trust of The Bahamas protects the area around Lake Windsor, where the birds breed and the population is said to number 50,000. Besides the pink flamingo, the Bahamian national bird, you can also see roseate spoonbills and other bird life here.

Flamingos used to inhabit all of The Bahamas, but the bird is nearly extinct in many places. The reserve can only be visited with a guide.

Green turtles are raised here, too, at Union Park. They are then released into the ocean to make their way as best they can; they, too, are an endangered species. The vast windward island, almost within sight of Cuba, is also inhabited by wild hogs, horses, and donkeys.

The settlement of **Matthew Town** is the chief hamlet of the island, but it's not of any great sightseeing interest. Other sites have interesting names, such as Doghead Point, Lantern Head, Conch Shell Point, Mutton Fish Point, and Devil's Point (which makes one wonder what happened there to give rise to the name). There's an 1870 lighthouse at Matthew Town.

Little Inagua has no population. It's just a speck of land off the northeast coast of Great Inagua, about 30 square miles in area. It has much bird life, though, including West Indian tree ducks, and wild goats and donkeys.

GETTING THERE & GETTING AROUND   Bahamasair (☎ 800/222-4262 in the U.S.) flies to Matthew Town Airport from Nassau on Monday and Friday at 9am.

You can also go by mail boat aboard the MV *Lady Mathilda,* which makes weekly trips from Nassau to Matthew Town (schedule varies). The boat leaves Nassau on Wednesday and comes back on Sunday. Call the dockmaster's office (☎ 242/393-1064) at Potter's Cay in Nassau for details.

Taxis (☎ 242/339-1284) meet incoming flights from Nassau. There's a guest house at Matthew Town on the southwest coast, 1 1/2 miles from the airport.

If you need a car, check with **Inagua Trading Ltd.** (☎ 242/339-1390), but don't expect the vehicles to be well maintained. One of the best ways to explore the island is by bike: Call **Pour More Bar** at ☎ 242/339-1232, or **Crystal Beach View** at ☎ 242/339-1550.

ESSENTIALS   Hospital   The Inagua Hospital can be called at ☎ 242/339-1249.

Police   The police can be reached by dialing ☎ 242/339-1263.

WHERE TO STAY

Main House. Matthew Town, Inagua, The Bahamas. ☎ 242/339-1267. 6 rms. A/C. Year-round, $50 double. No credit cards.

Main House is owned by Morton Bahamas Ltd., the salt people. This place is for people who *really* want to get away from it all and for devotees of flamingos, which abound on the island. Only six bedrooms are rented, and the furnishings are extremely modest. All of the rooms have private baths. Life is casual and decidedly informal.

Sunset Apartments. Matthew Town, Inagua, The Bahamas. ☎ **242/339-1362.** 2 apts. TV. Year-round, $150 double. No credit cards.

Currently, these two apartments, although far from luxurious, are your best bets for living on Inagua. One duplex is currently available in this beachfront motel, and two more are in the process of being added. The owner, Ezzard Cartwright, doesn't seem to be in any hurry to get them finished, but the ones he has to offer now are quite pleasantly furnished and comfortable. The apartments have two bedrooms, full kitchens, ceiling fans, and living and dining rooms. The decor and the furniture are Caribbean-style, the floors tiled with terra-cotta. Out back are small patios, and about 60 feet away is the beach. There's also a picnic area with tables and a gas grill for cookouts.

Walkine's Guest House. Gregory St., Matthew Town, Inagua, The Bahamas. ☎ **242/ 339-1612.** 5 rms (3 with bath). A/C TV TEL. $60 double. No credit cards.

Set a half mile south of Matthew Town, this simple guest house took great pains to paint its exterior blue and its bedrooms a rosy tone of shell pink. Your hosts are Eleanor and Kirk Walkine, who built their establishment in 1984 across the road from the beach. There are no dining facilities on-site. Rooms are about as modest as you'd ever want them to be, and racks are used to hang your clothes in lieu of a closet. The two rooms without bath are very small.

WHERE TO DINE

Cozy Corner. William St., Matthew Town. ☎ **242/339-1440.** Platters $9–$14. No credit cards. Daily 9:30am–10:30pm. BAHAMIAN/AMERICAN.

The most consistently reliable restaurant outside any of the guesthouses is this lime green, stone-built house 2 blocks from the sea. Your hosts, Rosemary Ingraham and her daughter, Veronica, maintain a colloquial and friendly bar, where beer, rum punch, and gossip seem to be one of the staples of the town. Menu items include a simple roster of mostly fried foods that are almost always accompanied with french fries. Examples include fried conch, fried chicken, burgers and "whopper burgers," and whatever kind of fried seafood is available from local fishers on the day of your visit.

7 Ragged Island & Jumento Cays

This, the most remote territory recommended in this guidebook, might come under the classification of "faraway places with strange-sounding names." The area is visited by very few tourists, except for stray people who come in on yachts.

The thing that's truly memorable here is the sunset, which, except in the rare times when clouds obscure the sky and the horizon, bursts forth in some of the most spectacular shades of gold, purple, red, and orange—and sometimes with a green flash reflecting in the crystal-clear waters.

This island group, a miniarchipelago, begins with Jumento Cays off the west point of Long Island and runs in a half-moon shape for some 100 miles down to Ragged Island; Little Ragged Island is the southernmost bit of land at the bottom of the crescent. They comprise the southeastern limit of the Great Bahama Bank.

Ragged Island and its string of uninhabited cays are the backwaters of The Bahamas, since most of them are so tiny and so unimportant they don't often appear on maps. However, visitors who return from this area talk of the remarkable beauty of these little pieces of land and coral.

Sailing in this area in bad weather is dangerous because of the unrelenting winds. Otherwise, the cays would be better known among the boating crowd. In summer it's usually a good place to cruise the waters.

Like nearly all the islands in this chapter, Ragged Island knew greater prosperity when hundreds of inhabitants worked its salt flats. Today Duncan Town, the little hamlet still standing on the island, is all that's left of the island's better days. Its people are hardworking and weather-beaten, and many have a difficult time making a living. Nassau seems to have forgotten this outpost of the nation.

Some of the little cays, from Jumento Cay around the semicircle toward Ragged Island, have names such as No Bush Cay, Dead Cay, Sisters Cay, Nurse Cay, Double-Breasted Cay, and Hog Cay. There's a Raccoon Cay, as well as a Raccoon Cut. A light tower stands on Flamingo Cay.

Visitors are so rare that anybody's arrival is treated as an event, and the townspeople are eager to help in any way they can. There's a 3,000-foot paved airstrip here, but it's only accessible to private planes, so it's not used much.

A **mail boat**, MV *Emmipt and Cephas,* leaves Potter's Cay in Nassau on Tuesday at 2pm en route to Ragged Island. It returns on Thursday. For details about costs and sailing, contact the dockmaster at Potter's Cay Dock, Nassau (☎ **242/393-1064**).

Regrettably, there are no hotel facilities for tourists.

Turks & Caicos Islands

The Turks and Caicos Islands (or "Turks and Who?" as they're often called) have long been called the "forgotten islands." They have recently been discovered by sun-seeking vacationers, however, and there's now talk of a "second Bahamas" in the making. Although they are actually a part of the Bahamian archipelago, they are under a separate government and are tucked away to the east of the southernmost islands of The Bahamas. Directly north of Haiti and the Dominican Republic, they lie at the crossroads of the Caribbean and the Americas. Technically, this obscure outpost is not part of the Caribbean but on the fringe of the Atlantic. *Le Figaro* of Paris once quoted a developer, and we concur, that, "These islands will be the only place left where the jet set, tired of Florida and The Bahamas, will be able to take refuge." They already are!

The Turks take their name from a local cactus with a scarlet blossom, which resembles a Turkish fez. The word *caicos* is probably derived from the word *cayos,* Spanish for cays or small islands.

Grand Turk and Salt Cay (which constitute the Turks Islands) and Cockburn Harbour (South Caicos) are ports of entry.

Many of the islanders today work in the salt-raking industry; others are engaged in the export of lobsters (crayfish) and conch, as well as conch shells. But more and more the citizens of this little country feed off the tourist industry.

The mean temperature in these islands is 82°F, dropping to 77° at night, but the cooling breezes of the prevailing trade winds prevent the climate from being oppressive, a fact that vacationers are learning and taking advantage of. The first VIP to recognize the attractions of these islands for a holiday retreat was Haiti's self-proclaimed king, Henri Christophe, who is rumored to have made excursions to South Caicos in the early 19th century.

The Turks and Caicos Islands are a coral-reef paradise, shut off from the world, free of pollution and crowds. Even with the increasing development under way, the beauty and tranquillity of this little island chain are sure to be maintained for the foreseeable future.

The inns of the Turks and Caicos Islands, except those on Providenciales (Provo), are small and personally run and very casual. Entertainment on the island is most often impromptu. The islands have no TV, no daily papers, but there is a radio station. Most visitors are interested in skin diving and scuba diving, fishing, sailing, and boating. Divers still dream of finding that legendary chest of gold hidden in the coral reefs or underwater caverns.

What has made Turks and Caicos a belated tourist destination for those who have already "done" both The Bahamas and the Caribbean is its 225 miles of beaches. Sometimes the beaches of white sand run for miles; others are small and found at secluded coves. Most of the beaches of the little archipelago are made of a white sand of soft coralline. Of course, nude sunbathers and others prefer some of the uninhabited cays for their skinny-dipping.

Note: These islands are recommended only to those readers who dare to venture off the beaten track.

A LOOK AT THE PAST

The Arawaks first settled the Turks and Caicos Islands. Ponce de León sighted the little chain in 1512, although there are those who believe that Columbus landed here, not at San Salvador (Watling Island) or Samana Cay in The Bahamas. It was not far to the south, in the waters off the north coast of Hispaniola (the part that is now Haiti), that the *Santa María,* the flagship of Columbus' discovery fleet, sank on Christmas night, 1492.

The claim that Columbus landed here has been endorsed by eminent Caribbean historians in recent years. Symposia on the subject have presented supporting data. The assertion is that Grand Turk was the site of the first landfall of Columbus, on October 12, 1492, and that he set foot on the island's western shores later that same day. He was supposedly greeted by the native Arawaks, who called the island Guanahani.

Pirates marauding the Spanish Main learned of the hidden coves of the Turks and Caicos Islands and used them as refuges when they ventured out to plunder Spanish galleons sailing out of Cuba and Haiti. This nest of cutthroats was called "Brothers of the Coast." The most famous of them was Rackam the Red, an Englishman.

After the Arawaks were removed from the islands to face their doom in the mines of Hispaniola, the islands had no permanent inhabitants until 1678. In that year the Bermudians, who had built ships and were searching for goods to trade with the American colonies, established the salt-raking industry. The Spanish drove the Bermudians away in 1710, but they soon returned and thereafter repelled attacks by both Spain and France. Their ranks were augmented during and after the American Revolution by Loyalists who fled America, bringing their slaves with them.

Bermuda finally lost out in 1799, when the Bahamian assembly in Nassau gave representation to its little island neighbors to the southeast. This attachment to The Bahamas ended in 1848, when the people of the Turks and Caicos Islands petitioned to withdraw from the assembly. They said the Bahamian government had paid no attention to them except to send salt-tax collectors, and that they saw the mail boat only four times each year.

The islands were allowed to break their ties with their northern relatives and to have their own president and council, supervised as a separate colony by the governor of Jamaica. After a quarter century, however, they were annexed by Jamaica as a dependency. It was not until 1962, when Jamaica became independent, that the little group of islands became a separate British Crown Colony.

The Turks and Caicos Islands are mainly self-governing today. Queen Elizabeth selects a governor to be her representative in island affairs; this governor appoints the chief minister who, in turn, appoints minor ministers.

Generally, dress on these islands is informal. Light cotton clothing is the most comfortable, although beachwear is best left for the beach. Jackets or ties are not required in the evening for men in bars or dining rooms. A light sweater is advisable for breezy evenings. It is customary to greet people you encounter walking along the roads.

The Turks & Caicos Islands

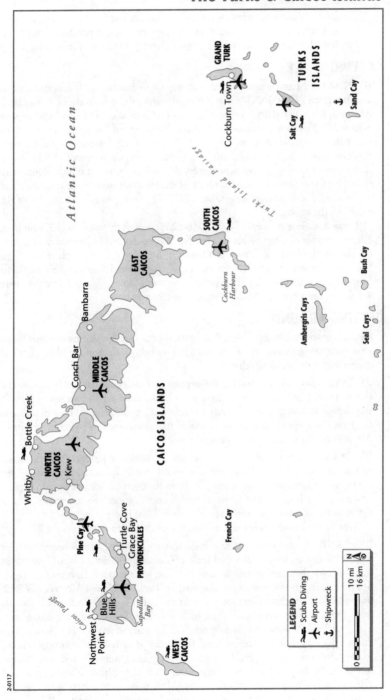

The food specialties are whelk soup, conch chowder and fritters, lobster, and special types of fresh fish. If you're interested in shopping, you can purchase native straw and shell work, sponges, and rare conch pearls here and there on the islands.

GETTING THERE

BY PLANE   Miami is the only U.S. gateway for flights into the Turks and Caicos, and **American** (☎ 800/433-7300) is the only carrier flying from the U.S. mainland. American offers two daily nonstop flights to Providenciales. The first flight departs Miami at 1:20pm and the second at 5:20pm. Flight time is 1 hour 39 minutes. Even the early departure is late enough in the day to permit transfers from any of the hundreds of flights winging into Miami from virtually everywhere every day. The return flights from Provo to Miami depart every day at 7:50am and 4:05pm. Round-trip tickets for passengers who reserve at least 14 days in advance and who remain abroad for between 3 and 30 days range from $217 to $354, depending on the day of the week and the season.

    Turks & Caicos Airways (☎ 800/946-4255) doesn't fly from the U.S. mainland, but it does offer nonstop flights on Monday, Wednesday, Friday, Saturday, and Sunday departing Nassau for Provo at 11am. On Monday and Friday there is a flight from Freeport to Provo at 12:15pm, and on Wednesday and Saturday there are flights from Puerto Plata (Dominican Republic) to Provo. On Sunday and Tuesday there are also air links between Santo Domingo and Provo.

GETTING AROUND

Getting around can be a problem. Car-rental agencies are few and far between (most visitors don't use this means of transport, but see below). Each of the islands has taxi drivers with just-adequate vehicles.

BY TAXI   Taxis can be found at the airports on Providenciales, South Caicos, and Grand Turk. They'll quote you a fixed price to and from the various hotels. They'll also deposit you on an isolated beach and return at a predetermined time to pick you up. Don't be surprised if your ride is shared (the government is trying to save fuel). Ask your hotel to make arrangements for you.

BY CAR   Because the island is so large, and its hotels and restaurants so far-flung, you might find a car on Providenciales useful. See individual island listings for car-rental agencies. Except for Grand Turk, on the other islands you have to depend on taxis or locals to get you about, although hotels or inns can sometimes arrange rentals with residents who might rent you their house buggy.

    Note: In the British tradition, cars throughout the country drive on the left.

BY PLANE   Some visitors opt to visit the country's outlying islands because of their marine life and get-away-from-it-all sense of isolation. The most leisurely way to do this is by boat, but barring your access to a yacht, you can travel on one of the eight- or nine-passenger propeller planes operated by **Turks & Caicos Airways** (☎ 809/946-4255). Most convenient are the airline's "patch flights." Eastbound, they fly from Providenciales to North Caicos, Middle Caicos, South Caicos, and terminate at Grand Turk. Westbound, they fly the same itinerary in reverse. The planes touch down briefly after only a few minutes' flight time at each of the above-mentioned islands, depositing passengers, luggage, and supplies en route. In addition, the airline offers 10 daily flights between the country's most populous islands, Provo and Grand Turk. The price is $50 each way. Most passengers traveling to Salt Cay arrive by boat, but those who prefer to fly opt for one of the Monday, Wednesday, or Friday flights (two round-trip flights on each of those days) between Grand Turk and Salt Cay. Small islands, such as Pine Cay, are serviced only by prearranged charter flights.

FAST FACTS: Turks & Caicos Islands

American Express   American Express is not represented anywhere on the Turks and Caicos Islands.

Banks   For cashing traveler's checks and for other banking services on Provo, head for Barclay's Bank, Butterfield Mall (☎ **809/946-4246**). The Bank of Nova Scotia is also at Butterfield Mall (☎ **809/946-4750**). On Grand Turk, try Barclay's Bank, Front Street (☎ **809/946-2831**) or the Bank of Nova Scotia, also on Front Street (☎ **809/946-2506**). Banking hours are Monday through Thursday from 8:30am to 2:30pm and Friday from 8:30am to 4:30pm.

Business Hours   Most business offices are open Monday through Friday from 8:30am to 4 or 4:30pm.

Climate   The islands receive approximately 21 inches of rainfall annually. The Turks and Caicos mean monthly temperature is 80°F, and the winter water temperature ranges from 72° to 80°.

Currency   The U.S. dollar is the coin of the realm here.

Customs   On arriving, you may bring in 1 quart of liquor, 200 cigarettes, 50 cigars, or 8 ounces of tobacco duty free. There are no restrictions on cameras, film, sports equipment, or personal items provided they aren't for resale. *Absolutely no spearguns are allowed,* and the importation of firearms without a permit is also prohibited. Illegal imported drugs bring heavy fines and lengthy terms of imprisonment.

Each U.S. citizen is eligible for a $400 duty-free exemption if he or she has been out of the country for at least 48 hours and if a period of 41 days has elapsed since that privilege was last exercised. This allowance may include 1 liter of liquor. In addition, you can mail home a number of unsolicited gifts to friends and relatives amounting to $50 or less per day and not to include more than 4 ounces of liquor or 1 ounce of perfume.

Dentist   See "Hospitals," below.

Doctors   See "Hospitals," below.

Drugstores   On Grand Turk, go to the Government Clinic, Grand Turk Hospital, Hospital Road (☎ **809/946-2040**). In Providenciales, go to the Providenciales Health Medical Center, Leeward Highway and Airport Road (☎ **809/946-4228**). Actually, it's best to arrive on the islands with whatever prescribed medication you think you will need.

Electricity   The electric current on the islands is 120 volts, 60 cycles, AC.

Emergencies   Most emergencies are handled by the police on the various islands (see "Police," below).

Entry Requirements   U.S. and Canadian citizens must have a birth certificate, a photo ID, and a return or ongoing ticket to enter the country. The photo ID could be an official driver's license with a photograph or a voter's registration card with a photograph. Of course, valid passports are always acceptable, and it's recommended that you carry one. Passports and visas are required for all aliens except nationals of certain countries, which include the United Kingdom, Commonwealth countries of the Caribbean, the Republic of Ireland, and EU countries. Visas for the Turks and Caicos Islands may be obtained from the British High Commission or various consulate offices in the United States.

Holidays   The actual dates of some of these observances may vary from year to year. If the date of a particular celebration falls on Saturday or Sunday, the actual observance may not take place until the following Monday. Holidays include New Year's Day, Commonwealth Day (March 11), Good Friday, Easter Sunday, Easter Monday, Birthday of Her Majesty the Queen (June 15), Emancipation Day (August 1), Columbus Day (October 12), International Human Rights Day (October 24), Christmas, and Boxing Day (December 26).

Hospitals   The islands are served by three medical practitioners and a qualified nursing staff. There is a 35-bed hospital on Grand Turk, Grand Turk Hospital, Hospital Road (☎ **809/946-2333**), with X-ray facilities, an operating theater, and a pathology laboratory. On Providenciales, there is the Providenciales Health Medical Center, Leeward Highway and Airport Road (☎ **809/946-4228**). There are clinics on South Caicos (☎ **809/946-3216**) and North Caicos (☎ **809/946-7194**). All the islands are served by one dentist, who can be reached at the Providenciales health center. Anyone critically ill is transferred to Grand Turk for hospital treatment or evacuated to Nassau, Miami, or Jamaica for specialist treatment. Should you become ill, your hotel will locate the nearest medical facility.

Information   The Turks & Caicos Sales and Information Office, Front Street, Cockburn Town, Grand Turk, BWI (☎ **800/241-0824** in the U.S., or 809/946-2321), is open Monday through Friday from 8am to 4:30pm.

Language   The official language is English.

Police   In Grand Turk, call ☎ **809/946-2299;** in Providenciales ☎ **809/946-4259;** and in South Caicos ☎ **809/946-3299.** On North Caicos, call ☎ **809/946-7116;** on Middle Caicos ☎ **809/946-6111.**

Post Office   The General Post Office is on Grand Turk (☎ **809/946-2801**). The second major post office is on Provo (☎ **809/946-4676**). There are suboffices on South Caicos, Salt Cay, Bottle Creek, and Middle Caicos. Offices are open Monday through Thursday from 8am to 1:30pm and from 2 to 4:30pm, Friday from 2 to 4pm. There is a Philatelic Bureau on Grand Turk, operated separately from the post office but keeping the same hours.

Safety   Although crime is minimal in the islands, petty theft does take place, so protect your valuables, money, and cameras. Don't leave luggage or parcels in an unattended car. Beaches are vulnerable to thievery, so don't take chances.

Taxes   There is a departure tax of $15, payable when you leave the islands. Also, the government collects an 8% occupancy tax, applicable to all hotels, guest houses, and restaurants in the 40-island chain.

Telephone, Telegram & Fax   It's not too difficult to keep in touch with the outside world, if you really want to. Cable and Wireless Ltd. provides a modern diversified international service via submarine cable and an earth station. There are automatic exchanges on Grand Turk, South Caicos, and Provo. Incoming direct dialing is available from the United States, the United Kingdom, and most countries in the world. Outgoing direct dialing is being introduced.

Most hotels in the country have fax machines. Your hotel's staff will offer to send and receive faxes for you. Telex service is fully automatic, operating 24 hours a day. The international-operator telephone service is available 24 hours a day and the telegraph service from 8am to 4:30pm Monday through Friday from the company's main office on Front Street, Cockburn Town, Grand Turk (☎ 809/946-2222).

Time   The islands are in the eastern time zone and daylight saving time is observed.

Tipping   Hotels usually add 10% to 15% automatically to handle service. If individual staff members perform various services for you, it is customary to tip them something extra. In restaurants, 10% to 15% is appropriate unless **service** has already been added. If in doubt, ask. Taxi drivers like at least a 10% tip.

Water   Don't drink from the tap and avoid ice in your drinks that was made from tap water. Don't even use tap water to brush your teeth. Remember that water is precious on the islands. Try to conserve it. Hotels provide safe drinking water.

1 Grand Turk

The most important of the island chain, Grand Turk (Cockburn Town), with its Government House, is the capital of the Turks and Caicos Islands. Cockburn (pronounced *Coburn*) Town is also the financial and business hub. The island has the largest population, 3,500 people, in the country.

Cockburn Town might remind you of New Plymouth on Green Turtle Cay in the Abacos, but there's more bustle here because of the larger number of inhabitants. The harbor road is called Front Street, like the one in Hamilton, the capital of Bermuda.

Grand Turk is rather barren and windswept. There is little vegetation; don't come here expecting to find a lush tropical island.

Once this was the teeming headquarters of a thriving salt industry. Today, there are those who want to restore the economy of the colony by making Grand Turk an offshore banking center like the Cayman Islands, but that may be difficult. There are many problems to face with both the British and the U.S. governments.

Grand Turk was in the limelight in 1962, when John Glenn, the first American astronaut to orbit the earth, alighted in the ocean about 40 miles offshore and was brought in by helicopter to the U.S. Air Force base here, where he was welcomed by Vice President Lyndon Johnson.

Chances are, if you come to the Turks and Caicos for your vacation, you'll land at Grand Turk. You'll find **Governor's Beach** near—you guessed it—the governor's residence on the west coast of the island. It's the best for swimming. If you are going on to another of the islands, at least take time to tour Cockburn Town's **historic section**, particularly Duke and Front streets, where three-story houses built of wood and limestone stand along the waterfront.

Many scholars believe that Grand Turk was the site of the first landfall of Columbus in 1492. They maintain he set foot on the western shores of the island late on the day of October 12. The native Arawaks were here to welcome him to their island of "Guanahani," although they were later to pay a terrible price for that hospitality, as they were sold into slavery in the Caribbean.

At the tourist office (see "Information" in "Fast Facts," above), the National Parks of Turks and Caicos produce a guide to the marine parks, nature reserves, sanctuaries, and historical sites of the island nation.

There are several protected historical buildings on the 7-square-mile island of Grand Turk, one of which is a hotel: Turks Head Inn. Other buildings include the police station and Government House.

GETTING AROUND   Many visitors walk where they are going, or else check with **Dutchie's Car Rental** (☎ 809/946-2244) if they need a car. Here rentals range from $40 to $65 per day, plus $10 government tax. Another way to get about is by scooter. Call **Kittina Scooter Rental** at ☎ 809/946-2232 to see if one is available. Rates range from $25 to $40 per day, plus $5 government tax. Taxis are available, but there is no central agency to call. Your hotel can call you one, or else you'll find them at the airport when you arrive. The fare is about $5 from the airport into town or from $6 to $11 (these are averages) if you're heading for a hotel outside town.

Another way to get around is by bike. Along Duke Street in Grand Turk, both the **Hotel Kittina** (☎ 809/946-2232) and the **Salt Raker Inn** (☎ 809/946-2260) will rent you bikes at about $10 per day, or else $40 per week.

Recently, a new public bus system was launched, but service is skimpy. The charge is only 50¢ one way to any scheduled stop.

SHOPPING   There isn't much. In Cockburn Town, **Blue Water Divers** (☎ 809/946-2432), found along Front Street, the main drag, has the island's best T-shirt selection. You'll find another collection of T-shirts at **Seaview Gift Shop** (no phone), also bordering Front Street. For the best souvenirs, seek out **Dot's Gifts,** Moxey's Folly (☎ 809/946-2324), lying east of Red Salina. Some of these handcrafted souvenirs are one of a kind. You can also pick up some books dealing with the history of the archipelago and its folklore traditions.

WHERE TO STAY

As mentioned, hotels add a 10% to 15% service charge, plus an 8% government occupancy tax, to the rates quoted below.

MODERATE

Coral Reef Beach Club. Lighthouse Rd., P.O. Box 156, Grand Turk, Turks & Caicos, BWI. Twelve minutes from the airport and 10 minutes from Cockburn Town. ☎ **809/946-2055.** Fax 809/946-2911. 15 rms, 4 suites. A/C TV TEL. Winter, $105 double; $235 suite. Off-season, $85 double; $115 suite. AE, MC, V.

Coral Reef Beach Club lies on a stretch of beachfront on the eastern coast and is the only hotel on the island with complete sports facilities. Even though the hotel is on a beachfront, the sea here is not ideal for swimming. It tends to be choppy and filled with weeds. Good beaches are just a short distance away, however. If you're a diver, this is your best deal for lodgings. As you negotiate the steep access road that winds down to it, a sweeping expanse of sea seems to surround the property. Stretched end to end along the beachfront, and interconnected with a sunny boardwalk, the ocean-view accommodations contain fully equipped kitchenettes and are designed like comfortably furnished studios and suites. Each was prefabricated in the United States, then constructed on the site. There is maid service.

An attractive dive package is offered for $665 per person, which includes 7 nights' accommodation, double occupancy, and 12 tank dives. The hotel works with two dive operators, Blue Water Divers and Sea Eye Diving, and there is daily transportation to the dive site. Guests can use a small freshwater pool and play on a floodlit tennis court. The hotel also has a beach bar and restaurant plus a gym and a Jacuzzi.

Guanahani Beach Resort. Pillory Beach, Grand Turk, Turks & Caicos, BWI. Twenty-five minutes north of Cockburn Town. ☎ **809/946-2135.** Fax 809/946-1460. 16 rms. A/C TV TEL. Winter, $150 double. Off-season, $130 double. Children under 12 free in parents' room. AE, MC, V.

Anthony Graham has remodeled and brightened up this place and now offers weekly packages. His is the finest inn on Grand Turk, a considerable improvement over The

Sitting Pretty Hotel, its main competitor. Composed of a handful of hip-roofed villas set directly on the sands of one of the finest beaches on the island (supposedly, according to local lore, where Columbus made one of his landfalls), this hotel is almost exclusively devoted to enjoyment of the sun, sand, and sea. It's a favorite with honeymooners. Only a decorative wooden railing separates its sandy grounds from unobstructed ocean views. Concrete walkways connect each of the accommodations to the hotel's pair of bars, its swimming pool, and its restaurant.

Each room has a private balcony and simple tropical furniture appropriate to the accommodation's beachside location. Laundry and baby-sitting are provided, and room service is offered daily from 9am to 9pm.

In the restaurant, The Shipwreck, three meals a day are served. The cuisine is Caribbean, and sometimes bands are brought in to entertain guests (see "Where to Dine," below).

The Sitting Pretty Hotel. Duke St., P.O. Box 42, Grand Turk, Turks & Caicos, BWI. ☎ **809/946-2232.** Fax 809/946-2877. 19 rms, 20 suites. A/C TEL. Winter, $100–$140 double; $160–$240 suite. Off-season, $90–$130 double; $150 suite. Extra person $15. Children under 2 free in parents' room. Children 2–12 sharing room $5. Dive packages available. AE, MC, V.

This is the largest hotel on Grand Turk. The hotel straddles two sides of the main street leading through the center of town. The older section is a low-slung building covered with trailing vines and bougainvillea. It contains a bar and restaurant (see "Where to Dine," below).

Across the street rise the modern two-story town houses with the newer and better accommodations. These rooms are not as noisy as the ones across the street. Each of these has a ceiling crafted from varnished pine, carpeting, a kitchen, a verandah with a view of the sea, and ceiling fans. The units on the upper floors benefit from high ceilings and more space.

You can snorkel or swim near the hotel's white-sand beach. If you're sailing, be sure to ask one of the staff members for instructions on the best places to moor your sailboat.

Salt Raker Inn. Duke St., P.O. Box 1, Grand Turk, Turks & Caicos, BWI. ☎ **809/946-2260.** Fax 809/946-2817. 10 rms, 3 suites. A/C. Year-round, $85–$135 double; $135 suite. AE, MC, V.

Lying a 1-mile taxi ride from the airport and a short walk from the island's busiest docks, the informal Salt Raker Inn occupies a clapboard house that was originally built in 1810 by a Bermudian shipwright. Its English-colonial style is visible in its front verandah that overlooks the ocean and a garden filled with bougainvillea. The main house, set close to the road paralleling the sea, contains a wide front hallway, a guest library, the establishment's office, and the three best accommodations. Each of the rooms has a private bath and a ceiling fan. Seven sea-facing rooms have a phone, and each has a minifridge. The two large upstairs suites have verandahs overlooking the sea. The downstairs accommodation has a large screened porch. Several others are in two motel units spread end to end on either side of the garden.

The Salt Raker Inn is also one of the most popular dining choices in town (see separate recommendation under "Where to Dine," below).

INEXPENSIVE

✪ **Turks Head Inn.** Duke St., P.O. Box 58, Grand Turk, Turks & Caicos, BWI. ☎ **809/946-2466.** Fax 809/946-2825. 7 rms. A/C TV. Year-round, $55–$95 double. MAP $35 per person extra. AE, MC, V.

As charming as anything you'll find on the island, this old-fashioned hotel was originally built in 1840 as a private home by Bermudian shipwrights. It has the most

---

😊 Family-Friendly Hotels

The Sitting Pretty Hotel *(see p. 303)*   A local landmark, this hotel is the family favorite on Grand Turk. Families prepare simple island meals in the units with kitchens.

Turquoise Reef Resort & Casino *(see p. 318)*   Provo's best choice for families, this resort on Grace Bay puts up an extra person in the room for $25 a night. A separate staff coordinates activities for children.

Le Deck Hotel & Beach Club *(see p. 318-319)*   Near one of Provo's best white sandy beaches, families like to rent these villalike condos. Kids delight in the freshwater swimming pool on the premises.

European flavor of any of the inns on the island. It was once the governor's private guest house and later the American consulate. Today, most of its business comes from its bar and restaurant (see "Where to Dine," below). However, a handful of bedrooms lie upstairs, behind a two-level verandah whose ornate balustrades are painted in bright tropical colors. Owned by French-born Xavier Tonneau (sometimes known to his friends as "Froggie"), the inn lies in a mature garden with towering trees and a shady terrace with outdoor tables. Be warned in advance that if you stay here, you'll basically occupy your room and be left alone by a management that's busy running its food and beverage facilities. For clients not interested in the facilities of a resort hotel, however, that might sound appealing. Two of the bedrooms have access to an open second-floor verandah in front, while four have access to the somewhat more private enclosed verandah overlooking the back. Each has a private bathroom, ceiling fan, high ceilings, and antique or period furnishings. All contain queen-size beds, two of which are four-posters.

WHERE TO DINE
MODERATE

The Pepper Pot. Front St. No phone. Visit to make arrangements for dinner. Meals $15–$25. No credit cards. Dining time (usually 7:30 or 8pm) to be arranged in advance. CARIBBEAN.

Guests are served on battered plastic tables amid crepe-paper streamers and the kind of decor that might have adorned a 1930s high-school prom. Despite its decor, diners retain happy memories of this place. It's the domain of a hardworking member of the island's Anglican church, Philistina Louise ("Peanuts") Butterfield. Born in North Caicos, she has attracted an ardent array of fans. Her conch fritters, carefully frozen and packaged, accompany diners back to the United States, where they've been served at receptions on Fifth Avenue.

To dine here, you must stop by on the evening of the day before you plan to eat, since there is no phone. Any taxi driver in town will conduct you to the clean but simple cement-sided house and pick you up at a prearranged time at the end of your meal. The menu depends on whatever Peanuts produced that day. It's likely to be lobster with all the fixings. Full meals are served only at dinner at a time mutually agreed upon.

In a pinch, try calling Ms. Butterfield's daughter, Vera Kennedy, at ☎ 809/946-1225. Although it's always better to speak directly to Ms. Butterfield, in some cases Ms. Kennedy might be able to establish contact for you.

Salt Raker Inn. Duke St. ☎ **809/946-2260.** Reservations recommended for dinner Wed and Sun only. Lunch platters $3.50–$8.50; dinner main courses $14.50–$23.60. AE, MC, V. Daily 7am–9pm (last order). CARIBBEAN/SEAFOOD.

Contained beneath the corrugated tin roof of the previously recommended hotel, this comfortably unpretentious restaurant remains open throughout the morning and afternoon for anyone who happens to wander in hungry from the nearby wharves and beaches. Many guests prefer to dine in the rear garden.

You can get lunch at virtually any time of the morning or afternoon, consisting of club sandwiches, cheeseburgers, fish-and-chips, or cracked conch. Evening meals are somewhat more elaborate, with grouper cooked island style (with onions and peppers), conch Creole, and the house favorite, broiled lobster with butter sauce. You might also try such specialties as an award-winning version of local Junkanoo-style (spicy) barbecued spareribs.

The Sitting Pretty Restaurant. In The Sitting Pretty Hotel, Duke St. ☎ **809/946-2232.** Reservations recommended. Main courses $10–$18. AE, MC, V. Daily 6:30–9:30pm. CARIBBEAN/AMERICAN.

Contained on the lobby level of the main (beachfront) building of the previously recommended hotel, this restaurant overlooks the ocean through sliding glass doors. It is simply decorated in white. This is one of the best-known restaurants on the island, offering a combination of American and local dishes with an emphasis on freshly caught seafood, such as lobster or red snapper. The conch chowder is invariably good. One specialty, conch steak, is a local delicacy. It is queen conch marinated in special herbs and spices, then deep-fried a golden brown and served with the house's spicy seafood sauce. We could find none better on the island. Other "fresh-from-the-sea" dishes include fresh filet of grouper and broiled lobster tail. If not fish, then you can try one of their down-home dishes such as southern fried chicken. Finish off with one of their homemade pies.

The Shipwreck Restaurant. In the Guanahani Beach Resort, Pillory Beach. ☎ **809/946-2135.** Reservations recommended. Breakfast $4.95–$8.95; lunch $4.95–$12.95; dinner $12.95–$24.95. AE, MC, V. Daily 7am–2:30pm and 6–10pm. INTERNATIONAL.

Contained within the most isolated hotel on the island, this restaurant lies on the north shore, about a 25-minute drive from Cockburn Town. It's justifiably the most consistently popular restaurant on the island.

Decorated in tones of off-white with large French windows, the restaurant offers sweeping views of the sea. On one side is the restaurant, and on the other is a lounge with a library and comfortable chairs. Here you can order rum punches and piña coladas. The menu features well-prepared seafood. Although steaks are offered, the most frequently requested dishes include grilled grouper served with tartar sauce, cracked conch, a succulent lobster with butter and bread crumbs, and any of the array of freshly caught fish that happen to have arrived that day from local fishing craft. If you plan an evening meal here, you might try to time your visit to catch the final rays of sundown, an event that is especially well framed from the restaurant's outdoor terrace.

Turks Head Inn. Duke St. ☎ **809/946-2466.** Reservations recommended on Fri night only. Lunch platters $6–$8; dinner main courses $12.50–$21. AE, MC, V. Daily 7am–10pm. INTERNATIONAL.

This is the island's oldest and busiest pub, a landmark to the many divers, dockworkers, writers, and eccentrics living on Grand Turk. Set within the previously recommended inn, it contains an indoor dining room, raffish and tropical, and a thatch-roofed annex that shelters outdoor diners from the sun and rain.

The well-flavored food is served informally, in large portions, according to whatever happens to have arrived from mainland suppliers that week. Specialties arerecited by a waitress and, depending on the mood of Xavier Tonneau, the

French-born chef and owner, might include baked grouper, steak, and lobster, or steak and lobster on the same platter. The food here has more continental overtones than the places previously recommended. The establishment's bar is open continuously every day throughout the afternoon until midnight, serving drinks to whatever dockworker or barefoot contessa happens to need one.

INEXPENSIVE

Regal Begal. Hospital St. ☎ **809/946-2274.** Soups and fritters $1.50–$3; sandwiches and salads $3.50–$7; platters $5.50–$17. No credit cards. Mon–Sat 10:30am–3pm and 7pm to midnight. CARIBBEAN.

Located beside the road, about a 3-minute drive from the center of Cockburn Town, this is one of the simplest and least pretentious restaurants on the island. There's a bar to quench your thirst, and a handful of plain tables where such dishes as lobster salad, several variations of conch, chicken or fish with chips, and pork are served.

WATER SPORTS & OTHER OUTDOOR ACTIVITIES

Blue Water Diver. P.O. Box 124, Front St., Grand Turk. ☎ **809/946-2432.**

This outfit offers single dives, PADI registration, and dive packages. These people are top rate and will tell you many legends about diving in their country. For example, the highest mountain in the Turks and Caicos is 8,000 feet tall. But only the top 140 feet are above sea level. Scuba divers flock here to enjoy panoramic "wall dives" on the vertical sides of the reefs surrounding them. A single-tank dive costs $30, with a two-tank dive going for $55. A night dive costs $35. A PADI instruction resort course is priced at $85.

Sea Eye Diving. Duke St., Grand Turk. ☎ **809/946-1407.**

This outfit is located near The Sitting Pretty and the Salt Raker Inn and is convenient to most other hotels, as well. It offers two-tank morning dives at $50 on a prepaid package, or $60 if purchased separately. An afternoon single-tank dive costs $30, and a single-tank night dive goes for $35. Rental equipment is also available. NAUI and PADI courses at all levels are offered. A full certification course goes for $350, including training equipment and boat checkout dives. Dive packages with accommodation are arranged at a hotel of your choice. Snorkeling and cay trips are available for nondivers. The owners and operators, Cecil Ingham and Connie Rus, are among the more experienced divers on the island, and they know where to guide you to see marine life in a kaleidoscope of colors.

In addition, tennis buffs will find one lighted court at the Coral Reef Resort.

EXPLORING THE ISLAND: SOAKING UP A BIT OF HISTORY

To enjoy swimming, snorkeling, scuba diving, and just doing nothing are the main reasons people go to Grand Turk. The island, however, does have one major sightseeing attraction, previewed below.

Turks & Caicos National Museum. Guinep House, Front St., Cockburn Town, Grand Turk. ☎ **809/946-2160.** Admission $5 nonresidents, $2 full-time island residents. Mon–Tues and Thurs–Fri 9am–4pm, Wed 9am–6pm, Sat 9am–1pm.

Established in 1991, this is the first (and only) museum in the country. It lies within a 150-year-old residence (Guinep House), which was originally built by Bermudian wreckers out of the salvaged timbers of ships that had been demolished on nearby reefs. Today, about half of its display areas are devoted to the remains of the most complete archaeological excavation ever performed in the West Indies, the wreck of a Spanish caravel (sailing ship) that sank in shallow offshore water sometime before

1513. Used for transporting members of the local Arawak tribe who were made slaves, it was designed solely for exploration purposes and is similar to types of vessels built in Spain and Portugal during the 1400s. The original finders of the wreck were treasure hunters who announced it as the *Pinta* of the fleet of Columbus to attract financial backers for their salvage and to guarantee a value to the otherwise valueless iron artifacts if there proved to be no gold. However, there is no proof that the *Pinta* ever came back to the New World after returning to Spain from the first voyage. Researchers from the Institute of Nautical Archeology at Texas A&M University began excavations in 1982, although staff members never assumed that the wreck was the *Pinta*. Today, the remains are referred to simply as the Wreck of Molasses Reef.

Today, although only 2% of the hull remains intact, the exhibits contain a rich legacy of the everyday (nonbiodegradable) objects used by the crews and officers.

The remainder of the museum is devoted to exhibits about the island's salt industries, its plantation economy, the pre-Columbian inhabitants of the island, and natural history. The natural history exhibit features an 8-by-20-foot, three-dimensional reproduction of a section of the Grand Turk Wall, the famous vertical reef. Also included are displays on the geology of the various types of ecological niches in the islands and information on the reef and coral growth.

GRAND TURK AFTER DARK   The scene is mainly hanging out and drinking rum or beer in bars. On most Wednesday and Sunday nights, you can hear pop or folk music at the **Salt Raker Inn** on Duke Street (☎ **809/946-2260**). Mr. X (actually Xavier Tonneau) often leads sing-alongs at his bar at the **Turk's Head Inn,** also on Duke Street (☎ **809/946-2466**). Still in search of action? At the former naval base, the not very aptly named **Lady** (no phone) offers occasional dancing. Live local bands or a DJ keeps the **Rack Room** at Back Salina (☎ **809/946-1802**) sometimes moving.

2 Salt Cay

Just 9 miles south of Grand Turk, this sparsely settled cay is named for its salt ponds, a once-flourishing industry that may be revived. In its day it was known for this "white gold," and some 100 vessels a year sailed from here and Grand Turk with their heavily laden cargoes bound for the United States. It is estimated that during the American Revolution more than 20 Bermudian privateers were running salt on a regular schedule from the Turks Islands past British blockades to Washington's battered armies. Salt was the chief preservative of meat for the colonial army.

In 1951 the government took control of the 300-year-old industry, and in 20 years managed to destroy it completely through bureaucratic mismanagement. Salt Cay fell into a long slumber until 1990, when chic guests began visiting the Windmills Plantation (see below).

The cay has a landmass of 3¹/₂ square miles, with a beautiful beach bordering the north coast. It has been designated as a historical site by the National Park Service of Turks and Caicos.

You can walk down to the salinas and see the windmills that once powered the salt business, and you can stroll past the 150-year-old "White House," built by a Bermudian salt raker. In addition, you can visit the ruins of an old whaling station and learn how fearless seamen caught whales in the early 19th century. It's also possible to drop in at the local school, where the children are likely to greet you with island calypso songs.

Essentially, Salt Cay is peaceful, quiet, and colorful—the perfect spot to get away from it all. Since there are only four automobiles on the island, traffic jams aren't a problem.

GETTING THERE   For a long time, residents of Salt Cay were dependent on their small sailboats for communication with the outside world, and the island is still often reached by private boat. But with the opening of a 3,000-foot airstrip, located 575 miles southwest of Miami, the island is connected to the wider world once again. Now you can fly direct from Miami to Provo on **American Airlines** and then on to Salt Cay via **Interisland Airways** (☎ **809/941-5481**). There are also six flights weekly Monday, Wednesday, and Friday on **Turks & Caicos Airways** (☎ **809/946-4255**).

WHERE TO STAY

✪ **Mount Pleasant Guest House.** Dockland, Salt Cay, Turks & Caicos, BWI. ☎ **809/ 946-6927.** Fax 809/946-6927. 10 rms. Year-round (EP), $85 double. All-inclusive weeklong dive packages, with lodging, meals, three daily boat dives, and unlimited beach dives, $895 per person double occupancy. MC, V.

Set across the street from the island's main docks, this friendly oasis of cost-conscious charm lies within the stone walls of what was originally built in the 1830s as the home of a salt merchant. It is a much simpler accommodation than the Windmills Plantation described below. Established in 1989 by Bryan and Emily Sheedy, refugees from New York City and Wyoming, respectively, the place caters mainly to divers who usually opt for the week-long, all-inclusive packages described above. Other guests come here for snorkeling, shelling, and bird-watching.

In addition to a likable restaurant (described below), the hotel maintains the only horseback-riding stables in the country, with four horses that guests of the hotel can ride for free, and which otherwise rent for around $20 for a half-day jaunt. Accommodations lie for the most part within a modern two-story annex built across the street. Rooms contain ceiling fans, comfortably unpretentious furniture, and simple accessories. Day-trippers or residents of other hotels are welcome to use the hotel's dive facilities. Dives cost $25 per tank, including the boat trip. A resort course for beginners goes for $75. Recently discovered by the Sheedys is one of the most celebrated dive sites in the region, the as-yet-unsalvaged wreck of a British warship that sank in 1790 in shallow waters far from shore. Still visible are 9-foot cannons and a quartet of massive anchors.

Visitors planning to stay here usually inform the hotel of their time of arrival in Grand Turk and are then ferried by the hotel's supply boat from a point near the airport to Salt Cay.

✪ **The Windmills Plantation at Salt Cay.** N. Beach Rd., Salt Cay, Turks & Caicos, BWI. ☎ **809/946-6962.** Fax 809/946-6930. (For reservations and information, contact Windmills Plantation at Salt Cay, P.O. Box 635, Easton, MD 21601. ☎ **410/819-0562.** Fax 410/ 820-9179.) 4 rms, 4 suites. Year-round (AP rates, including service, airport transfers, and all drinks), $495–$540 double; $650–$695 suite. AE, MC, V.

Set amid 17 acres of scrubland beside a white-sand beach on the north side of the island, this hotel was entirely built by local artisans using centuries-old building techniques.

Each of the dozen or so buildings within the compound has been designed in a different whimsical colonial style. The styles are influenced by French, English, Dutch, and Spanish plantations of 200 years ago. Their design by architect/owner Guy Lovelace was the culmination of years of research by a man who—until recently—made a career of designing other people's Caribbean resort hotels. The Windmills Plantation is the highly creative result of a dream come true. Its centerpiece is a trio of dramatically proportioned swimming pools, which include a 50-foot lap pool and a "fun pool" only 4 feet deep centered around a mermaid-shaped fountain.

Each of the resort's accommodations contains a tasteful selection of antique reproductions (mostly handmade in the Dominican Republic or in Haiti), a verandah, and a cathedral ceiling with a ceiling fan. Four of the accommodations are suites, two of which have their own plunge pools. All drinks are included in the rates (the hotel bar is open all the time for clients). Tax (but not service) is extra.

Dining/Entertainment: Meals feature a culinary tour of the Caribbean, with a visit to a different island for lunch and dinner every day.

Services: Laundry service.

Facilities: Swimming pool, lap pool, game room, 2-mile nature trail, mangrove trail, historic salt tour, bicycles, snorkeling on 2-mile reef.

WHERE TO DINE

Mount Pleasant Guest House. Dockland, Salt Cay. ☎ **809/946-6927.** Main courses $7–$18. MC, V. Daily 7:30–9am, noon–2pm, and 6–9pm. AMERICAN/BAHAMIAN.

Contained on a patio beside the previously recommended hotel, this is one of the most consistently popular and unpretentious restaurants on the island. Food is well prepared and served in large portions that are much appreciated by the establishment's clientele of serious scuba divers, as well as locals. Seafood is especially popular, much of it freshly caught several hours previous to its preparation. Don't overlook a before- or after-meal libation at the establishment's Gazebo Bar.

DINING AT THE WINDMILLS PLANTATION

You've got to be a guest of the hotel to dine here, but if you are, you'll be served your finest Caribbean meal in this island nation. Caribbean architects and interior designers Pat and Guy Lovelace spent some 25 years traveling the islands before settling down here. Along the way, Pat collected various recipes, often from restaurants serving an authentic cuisine that has now largely disappeared. She notes that these recipes were originally developed before the age of refrigeration and chemical tenderizers—meats were shredded, pounded, boiled, herbed, spiced, and blended with vegetables to achieve an exotic mélange. From the original Indians came corn and seafood, from Africa root vegetables and herbs, and from the Europeans beef and the many tropical fruits and spices carried from the East Indies. All of this produced a unique cuisine that is now almost lost. After years of researching and testing, Pat has married modern kitchen technology with traditional recipes.

3 North Caicos

North Caicos is the most northern of the major islands in the archipelago. This 41-square-mile island is strictly for people who want to get away from it all. If you're seeking deserted, soft white-sand beaches and crystal-clear water, then this is the place. No one dresses up here, so leave your jacket and tie at home. It contains miles and miles of uncrowded sandy beaches and is surrounded by a sea teeming with fish—an ideal place for scuba divers and snorkelers. Experienced guides can take you fishing for snapper, barracuda, or bonefish. Beach picnics, boating excursions, and fish cookouts on deserted cays are easily arranged. You can snorkel on a barrier reef or tour the island by taxi. Ask to be taken to **Flamingo Pond,** located south of Whitby, which is a nesting place for these elegant pink birds. You'll also be shown the ruins of old plantations and such tiny hamlets as Sandy Point and Kew.

But go now. North Caicos is a resort in the making, and the island is slated for development.

GETTING THERE & GETTING AROUND The local airline, **Turks & Caicos Airways** (☎ 809/946-4255), runs connecting flights to the island's terminal. If you disembark at Providenciales, the flight to North Caicos takes only 6 minutes. It is not necessary to prebook with TCA. When you clear Customs in Provo, you'll also find several reliable local pilots who fly continuously throughout the day from Provo to North Caicos at a price to be negotiated. No advance reservations are necessary.

The best way to see the island is to have your hotel arrange a taxi tour at a rate to be negotiated.

The most fun way to see the island is to rent a motor scooter at **Whitby Plaza** (☎ 809/946-7301), costing $25 per day.

WHERE TO STAY

Club Vacanze/Prospect of Whitby Hotel. Whitby, c/o Kew Post Office, North Caicos, Turks & Caicos, BWI. ☎ **809/946-7119.** Fax 809/946-7114. 24 rms, 4 suites. A/C. Dec–Apr and Aug–Sept (AP), $195 per person double occupancy. May–July and Oct–Nov (AP), $170 per person double occupancy. AE, MC, V.

Originally established in 1974, this beachside hotel was named after one of the most historic Thames-side pubs of London, the Prospect of Whitby. Repaired and renovated, the hotel is working hard to regain a niche in the tourist marketplace. It is surrounded by vegetation verdant for the Turks and Caicos Islands and is near the white sands of a highly desirable beach. Each of the half dozen buildings that compose this complex is painted a soft pink. The units contain a scattering of art, a ceiling fan, comfortable furnishings, and a view of the sea.

The establishment's bar and restaurant are popular with "yachties" who moor their sailing craft off the expansive north-coast beach on which the hotel sits. The hotel's Italian-born managers imbue the cuisine with a European flair.

The managers will help arrange excursions to nearby cays. Many different watersports activities, including scuba diving, windsurfing, snorkeling, and sailing, can also be organized by the staff.

✪ **JoAnne's Bed & Breakfast.** Villa Whitby Beach, North Caicos, Turks & Caicos, BWI. ☎ and fax **809/946-7301.** 3 rms. Year-round, $95 double. MC, V.

This home away from home is run by JoAnne Selver, the island's most gracious and helpful host. A former Peace Corps worker, she has established a beachhead right on the sands and will help you have a relaxing holiday while entertaining you with stories of island life. She'll also feed you well at Papa Grunts (see below). Her private villa shelters visitors from all over the world. Bedrooms are simply furnished but comfortable, with views of the water. Everything is informal and relaxed around here.

If you're interested, she can also rent you other accommodations, including basic motel rooms at Whitby Plaza with a shared bath, costing $60 in a double, or an executive suite room at $100 per night in a second-story location, with a restaurant and motor scooter rental outlet on the premises. The motel and executive suite accommodations are not on the beach, which is a short walk away.

Ocean Beach Hotel. Whitby, North Caicos, Turks & Caicos, BWI. ☎ **809/946-7113.** Fax 809/946-7386. (For information and reservations, write to RR no. 3, Campbellville, Ontario L0P 1B0. ☎ **800/710-5204** or 905/336-2876. Fax 905/336-9851.) 10 units. Year-round, $110 double; $140–$195 double suite; $155–$215 triple suite; $175–$255 quad suite. Extra person $40. Children under 12 free in parents' room. MAP $35 per person extra. MC, V.

This resort sits on a fine beach, a 6-mile taxi ride from the airport and 1 mile from the center (such as it is) of Whitby. A hotel condo, it features individual rooms or two- and three-bedroom suites. Each suite offers a fully equipped kitchen, full linen service, and safe drinking water. Sliding glass doors and picture windows open onto an ocean view, and the rooms are cooled by trade winds. Furnishings are in the typical Florida tropical style. Guests can purchase groceries and drinks at the commissary, or else patronize the dining room and lounge, which offer local and international dishes. Sometimes the place takes on a house-party atmosphere, with barbecues, patio dancing, or beach picnics.

Facilities include a pool and tennis court; fishing, scuba diving, and snorkeling can be arranged.

WHERE TO DINE

Papa Grunts. Whitby Plaza. ☎ **809/946-7301.** Reservations required for dinner. Main courses $15–$20.50; lunch from $10. MC, V. Daily 8:30–9:30am, 11am–3pm, and 5–7pm. AMERICAN.

The friendliest restaurant on the island, this is an operation directed by JoAnne Selver, who also operates JoAnne's Bed & Breakfast (see previous recommendation). Outside the hotels, it is the best place to eat on the island. Dining is indoors or on a screened verandah. The atmosphere is casual, friendly, and tranquil. Papa Grunts lies within walking distance of the Whiteby Beach area.

At lunch many visitors opt for the sandwiches made with fresh homemade bread or one of the homemade soups. You can also order conch, fried chicken, and the fish of the day, or else one of the local salads, most often made with conch or lobster. At dinner the choice is more varied, including the fish of the day or the inevitable conch (steamed or cracked). Chicken breast is also served, as are broiled steaks, and even vegetarian platters. Many guests prefer an old-fashioned banana split for dessert.

4 Middle Caicos

Called Grand Caicos by some islanders, Middle Caicos is the largest island in the archipelago, consisting of 48 square miles (it's 15 miles long). Secluded beaches and towering limestone cliffs that protrude into the sea along the north coast give Middle Caicos the most dramatic coastline of the islands. Conch Bar, on the north side of the island, offers cathedral-size **limestone caves** once used by the Lucayans. In the 1880s these caves were the site of a thriving guano (fertilizer) export industry. With their clear underground salt lakes, the caves have been called a "natural museum" of stalagmites and stalactites. Nearby wild cotton plants derive from the 18th century, when Loyalists from the former southern colonies in the new United States came to try their hand at establishing plantations.

Middle Caicos men were some of the most expert boat builders in the island nation. They made their vessels from pine taken from the middle island's pine groves. The boats were used by fishermen to work the waters around many of the cays and to gather conchs for shipment to Haiti.

Bring an insulated cooler packed with food and supplies, which you can procure on Provo. Pack whatever meats, milk, butter, bread, beer, staples, and more beer than you think you'll need. When you return home to Provo, use the cooler to pack whatever fish or lobster you catch offshore, or use it as an easy mode of carting conch shells back from Middle Caicos. The island has about a half dozen simple mom-and-pop food outlets, but their inventory is limited to dried or canned foods such as cornmeal, flour, sugar, salt, and powdered milk.

Big real-estate plans are slated, and there is wide speculation of major develop-ments in this now sleepy place, including a causeway linking its mangrove swamps and scrub-covered landscapes to the booming developments of nearby Provo.

GETTING THERE   Most visitors come to Middle Caicos on a private-boat tour for a 1-day visit to the caves. Ask at your hotel in North Caicos if any fishing or sup-ply boats will be going here during your stay. Larger boats usually avoid Middle Caicos because of the shallow waters that surround it.

The cheapest and easiest way to reach this largely undeveloped island is to fly to Provo any way you can and then transfer to one of two regional airlines. **Turks & Caicos Airlines** (☎ **809/946-4255**) stops at Middle Caicos several times a day as it island-hops between Provo and Grand Turk. The one-way cost (for the 15-minute flight) to Middle Caicos from Provo is $30.

WHERE TO STAY

Arthur's Guest House. Conch Bar, Middle Caicos, Turks & Caicos, BWI. ☎ **809/946-6122.** 2 rms. TV. Year-round, $60 double. No credit cards.

Stacia and Dolphus Arthur run this tiny, laid-back inn at the west end of the village. The rooms are basic but clean and pleasant, with private baths, tile floors, double beds, ceiling fans, and television sets. The house is only 100 feet from the beach, and Dolphus will take you fishing or snorkeling if you ask him. Stacia does the cooking upon request, but most of the guests prepare their own meals in the communal kitchen.

Eagles Rest Villas. Reality Subdivision, Bambarra Beach, Middle Caicos, Turks & Caicos, BWI. ☎ **809/946-6122.** (For reservations, call or write Eagle Enterprises, 240 Pebble Beach, Suite 712, Naples, FL 33962. ☎ 800/484-1882, code 7177. Fax 813/793-7157.) 2 two-bedroom villas. A/C TV. Winter, $900–$1,000 per week for up to six. Off-season, $750 per week for up to six. Cook and maid available for $35 extra per day. No credit cards.

This pair of seafront villas represents the only major overnight accommodations on Middle Caicos. Although they were originally built as part of a real-estate specula-tion by a Florida-based developer, their appeal has proven so successful that they will probably remain on the rental market for many years to come.

Both of them are the centerpiece of what's eventually intended as an upscale com-munity of about a hundred private homes whose building lots have been subdivided into parcels of about an acre each. Although only five homes have been built, it's one of the several developments on the Caicos Islands that will bear close attention as the island continues to develop. The island's only paved road is a 10-mile stretch that runs adjacent to the property.

Since developer Richard Zebo's initial interest, more than 30,000 plants have added touches of verdant growth to a landscape that is otherwise covered only in stunted trees, mangroves, and casuarinas.

Don't even think of coming here unless you want lots of seclusion, peace, and quiet. Rental cars and a quartet of fishing boats can be rented from an on-site man-ager, and a limited selection of scuba supplies is available. Other than that, however, there's very little to do except read, reflect, sunbathe, snorkel, and fish. Each of the villas is a white-walled, single-story structure with a red hip roof, its own fully equipped kitchen, two air-conditioned bedrooms, two bathrooms, a VCR-TV, ceil-ing fans, and summer-style rattan and wicker furnishings. A local resident from the nearby hamlet of Bambarra (about three-fourths of a mile to the south) can be employed on a daily basis as a cook and maid, but if you don't want to see anyone, this setting will provide the seclusion you need in ample amounts. Be warned that most of the provisions you consume will need to be imported, probably from Provo in a cooler.

Maria Taylor's Guest House. Conch Bar, Middle Caicos, Turks & Caicos, BWI. ☎ **809/ 946-6118.** 4 rms (1 with bath). Year-round, $45 double without bath; $50 double with bath. No credit cards.

The bare-bone rooms and general lack of ambience may be a disappointment to those expecting to stay in an old Bahamian-style home, but the price is the island's lowest. One room has a private bath whereas the other three share, and the only TV is in the living room. The nearest beach is about a 5-minute walk from the house. Maria can arrange snorkeling trips for anyone who's interested. Her neighbor (and sister-in-law) does all the cooking, fixing whatever is requested if one sticks to local dishes.

5 South Caicos

Some of the finest **diving** and **snorkeling** in the Bahamian archipelago are found on South Caicos, an $8^1/_2$-mile-long island with numerous secluded coves and panoramic coral reefs. Long Beach is a beachcomber's paradise. One visitor wrote, "This is like escaping to another era." There are always locals available to take you sailing, boating, or fishing for a small fee. Bonefishing here is the best in the country.

Some 600 miles southeast of Miami and 22 miles east of Grand Turk, South Caicos can be reached by **Turks & Caicos Airways** (☎ **809/946-4255**), which has daily flights. There is a 6,500-foot paved and lit jetport, where passengers disembark as they head for Cockburn Harbour, the best natural harbor of the island nation. It is the site of the annual **Commonwealth Regatta** in May.

Although the island may appear nearly deserted, there are 1,400 permanent residents and what one local described as "about 65 vehicles and a few wild horses and donkeys in the bush." Some of the residents use their cars as taxis and meet visitors at the airport.

WHERE TO STAY & DINE

Club Carib Harbour & Beach Resort. South Caicos, Turks & Caicos, BWI. ☎ **800/ 722-2582** in the U.S., 809/946-3444 or 305/258-1177. Fax 809/946-3446 or 305/257-2072. 24 rms, 12 suites. Winter, $75–$125 double; $140 suite. Off-season, $50–$100 double; $115 suite. Extra person $10; children 2–12 $5. Children under 2 free. MC, V.

This resort is comprised of two hotels: One is situated on the water at Cockburn Harbour, and the other is located about $1^1/_2$ miles to the east, on the beach. The isolated beachside hotel offers clean, no-frills accommodations for rest and relaxation. The rooms have private baths, kitchenettes, and ceiling fans, but no airconditioning.

The harbor hotel is located across the street from an old salt warehouse where salt shipments were weighed and loaded for the ocean-bound vessels anchored in the harbor. The rooms have private baths, air-conditioning, TV, and telephones. The harbor site offers guests great snorkeling, but for swimming it's best to stick to the pool. The Club Carib Café is also here, serving international fare.

Although room service is only available at the harbor site, both locations have daily maid service and can arrange for baby-sitting, laundry, and bicycle rentals. Water sports, such as paddle boats and windsurfing, are also available.

6 Providenciales

Affectionately known as Provo, this 38-square-mile island has white-sand beaches that stretch for 12 miles along the northeast coast. It also has peaceful rolling hills, clear water, a natural deep harbor, flowering cactus, and a barrier reef that attracts swimmers, divers, and boaters. The roads may not always be paved, but you'll still find some stores and two full-service banks. The island is served by an airport capable of handling wide-body jets and has good marina and diving facilities.

Provo is the most built-up island in the Turks and Caicos chain; its development began with the opening of the Club Med "Turkoise" (see below) at the cost of $27 million. Once known mainly to a group of millionaires headed by Dick du Pont, Provo has now developed a broader base of tourism.

It was first discovered by the rich back in the 1960s, but word just had to get out, and now the bulldozers are here in full force. Throughout most of the 1970s it was known as a "pedigreed playground." Other celebrities have arrived more recently, including Dick Clark, who liked the place so much he bought property.

Provo is the headquarters for PRIDE, a nonprofit organization for the Protection of Reefs and Islands from Degradation and Exploitation. PRIDE assists residents and visitors with conservation education and management.

To reach the island, see "Getting There," at the beginning of this chapter.

GETTING AROUND By Bus Executive Tours (☎ 809/946-4524) operates shuttle buses that run from the major hotels into town about every hour. Service is Monday through Saturday only from 9am to 6pm, a one-way fare costing $2.

By Bike & Scooter If you'd like a scooter rental, contact **Scooter Bob's** at ☎ 809/946-4684 or **Honda Shop** at ☎ 809/946-4397. Rentals range from $25 to $40 per day in general, plus a $5 government tax. Bikers will face a few steep grades, but little traffic. Rentals can be arranged at **Island Princess** (☎ 809/946-4260) for $10 per day. You can also try **Turtle Inn Divers** at Turtle Cove Inn (☎ 809/941-5389), with rentals costing $12 per day.

By Taxi Cabs are not metered, but government-controlled rates are posted in the taxi. Taxis meet arriving flights; otherwise, call ☎ 809/946-5481, the number for the **Provo Taxi Association.**

By Car Because the island is so large, and its hotels and restaurants so far-flung, you might find a car on Providenciales useful. There are some local outfits, but booking advance reservations with them, and settling disputes in the event of an accident, can be very difficult. The only U.S.–based car-rental agency with a franchise in the Turks and Caicos Islands is **Budget Rent-a-Car** on Providenciales. It's located in Butterfield Square, near the airport (☎ 800/527-0700 in the U.S., or 809/946-4079). A Suzuki Alto with automatic transmission rents for $234 per week, with unlimited mileage. A four-door Suzuki Swift, with automatic transmission and air-conditioning, costs $264 a week. This contract requires a 24-hour advance booking from the North American mainland and also requires that drivers be at least 25 years of age. Collision-damage insurance costs $10 to $11.95 a day. A slightly bigger vehicle, a Suzuki Baleno, also with air-conditioning and automatic transmission, costs $354 per week. The local government will collect a $10 tax for each rental contract, regardless of the number of days you keep the car.

Because the company's main office lies in the commercial center of the island, a short drive from the airport, a representative will come to meet your flight at the airport if you notify them in advance of your arrival.

If you'd like to try your chance with a local agency, try one of the following: **Turquoise Jeep Rentals** (☎ 809/946-2244), **Rent A Buggy** (☎ 809/946-4158), **Turks & Caicos National** (☎ 809/946-4701), or **Provo Rent-a-Car** (☎ 809/946-4404). Rates average from $40 to $65 per day, plus a $10 government tax.

Note: In the British tradition, cars throughout the country drive on the left.

WHERE TO STAY
EXPENSIVE

Club Med Turkoise. Grace Bay, Providenciales, Turks & Caicos, BWI. ☎ **800/CLUB-MED** in the U.S., or 809/946-5500. Fax 809/946-5501. 300 rms. A/C. Winter (AP), $910–$1,700 per person weekly. Off-season (AP), $910 per person weekly. AE, MC, V.

Set on 70 acres of sun-blasted scrubland, 11 miles from the airport, this resort was inaugurated in 1984 as the most widely publicized and upscale resort in the Club Med chain. Since then it has become one of the most popular and successful Club Meds in the Americas. However, if you're seeking a more secluded oasis, you might opt for the Club Med on San Salvador (see chapter 11).

Although its preeminence has been supplanted by more recent newcomers, such as Royal Bay Resort & Villas (see below), it remains an appealing oasis of verdant charm and communal diversion. Set on a bleached-white strip of beachfront overlooking Grace Bay, it was initially built for a total cost of $27 million. A self-contained irrigation system, with a built-in desalinization plant, keeps the arid landscape green. Unlike certain other Club Meds, this one does not particularly go out of its way to entertain children with a barrage of special programs—that is, it is not designated as a Club Med "Family Village." The ambience is among the most casual of any member of the Club Med chain, a fact that seems to appeal to the more laid-back members of its French and North American clientele.

The village-style cluster of two- and three-story, rather basic accommodations are painted a pastel pink and capped with cedar shingles imported from Sweden. All meals and most sports are included in the weekly package rates. Drinks, which cost extra, are paid for with bar tickets.

The resort contains 600 beds, each twin size, in ultrasimple rooms designed with beachfront lifestyles in mind.

Dining/Entertainment: Most meals are served buffet-style and consumed at long communal tables, in a system not unlike that of a summer camp. Table wine and beer are provided at mealtime for free. Two specialty restaurants have waiter/waitress service, and include a pizzeria and a beachfront eatery (the Grill) that specializes in late breakfasts, late lunches, and late suppers. A disco keeps residents active, if they wish, from 11:30pm to at least 3am nightly.

Facilities: Scuba diving, which is not included in the package price, is offered on a space-available basis. Activities that are part of the package include windsurfing, sailing, and waterskiing. Also at no extra charge are the introductory and intensive circus programs, which teach guests basic and advanced skills, such as aerial twists, somersaults, and spins. There are two Jacuzzis on the property and eight tennis courts, four of which are lit for night play.

✪ **Grace Bay Club.** Grace Bay Rd., P.O. Box 128, Providenciales, Turks & Caicos, BWI. ☎ **800/946-5757** in the U.S., or 809/946-5757. Fax 809/946-5758. 22 suites. A/C TV TEL. Winter, $455–$495 junior suite; $515–$755 one-bedroom suite; $895–$955 two-bedroom suite; $1,255 penthouse. Off-season, $355–$375 junior suite; $395–$565 one-bedroom suite; $675–$745 two-bedroom suite; $895 penthouse. Extra person $95 winter, $75 off-season. No children under 12. AE, MC, V.

Established late in 1992, this Swiss-owned and managed development is ringed with about 200 palm trees imported from Florida and Nevis. This place is the premier address on the island, far superior to once front-ranking Club Med. The hotel lies on 5 landscaped acres of what used to be sun-blasted and barren scrubland on Provo's North Shore.

Designed in the spirit of an Andalusian village at the edge of a white-sand beach, the hotel is mostly contained within a three-story building inspired by the Mediterranean traditions of Iberia. Capped with terra-cotta tiles and partially sheathed with sculpted coral stone, it was built around a courtyard in whose center stands a splashing fountain.

Each accommodation has an eclectic kind of elegance well suited to its water-loving clientele and can be configured as an individual room or as an extended suite simply by opening or closing inner doors. The bedrooms contain king-size beds with carved headboards imported from Mexico, carpets from Turkey or India, tables and armoires from Mexico or Guatemala, artwork from Haiti or Brazil, ceiling fans, safes, and cable TVs with VCRs. Suites and penthouses each have their own kitchens, washing machines, and dryers. Bathrooms throughout the resort contain hand-painted Mexican tiles and lots of mirrors.

Dining/Entertainment: The hotel's restaurant, the Anacaona (separately recommended in "Where to Dine," below) lies within three thatch-covered and interconnected satellites of the main building. The gracefully furnished bar area contains its own artificial waterfall and meandering stream and a wide selection of tropical drinks. Live music is presented several times a week. For other types of entertainment, guests usually walk for about 7 minutes along the beachfront to the casino and nightlife options at the Turquoise Reef.

Services: Room service, massage therapy, concierge, water-sports desk.

Facilities: Freshwater swimming pool; Jacuzzi; free use of equipment for Sunfish sailing, snorkeling, and windsurfing; two tennis courts lit for night play; availability of waterskiing, bonefishing and deep-sea fishing, boating excursions, and parasailing; and a small library with books and video games.

Ocean Club. P.O. Box 240, Grace Bay Beach, Providenciales, Turks & Caicos, BWI. ☎ **800/ 457-8787** or 809/946-5880. Fax 809/946-5845 or 302/369-1421. 84 suites. A/C TV TEL. Winter, $190–$210 studio suite; $265–$310 one-bedroom suite; $420 two-bedroom suite; $555 three-bedroom suite. Off season, $150–$160 studio suite; $175–$195 one-bedroom suite; $310 two-bedroom suite; $405 three-bedroom suite. AE, DISC, MC, V.

Across from the Provo Golf Club, this luxury condo—the best of its type on the island—opens onto Grace Bay, site of the finest beach. It bills itself as a place where you can go to "Escape the Stress of Success." Opened since 1992, the resort community has accommodations available for sale or rent—each spread across a 7-acre piece of landscaped property.

The resort consists of studio suites, deluxe studio suites, and one-, two-, or three-bedroom deluxe suites, all with ocean views and fully equipped kitchens, except for the studios, which have kitchenettes. Each suite is equipped with both ceiling fans and central air-conditioning. A series of buildings surround gardens and a courtyard. Except for the studio suite (the cheapest rental), accommodations are spacious and comfortable, with large screened balconies. Families or friends traveling together can opt for the two- or three-bedroom suites.

The hotel has a grill restaurant serving international food, plus a cabaña bar. In addition, there are two swimming pools, a fitness center, and a dive shop.

Ocean Point/Chalk Sound Villas. Between Sapodilla Bay and Taylor Bay, Providenciales, Turks & Caicos, BWI. (For information and reservations, write P.O. Box 550509, Atlanta, GA 30355. ☎ **404/351-2200.** Fax 404/351-2615.) 9 villas. TV TEL. Year-round, $1,800–$3,800 per week. AE, DC, MC, V.

Many visitors to Provo prefer to avoid accommodations in hotels in favor of the more private, and infinitely more isolated, pleasures that only a self-contained villa can afford. Between the early 1980s and around 1992, two villa compounds were developed on Provo's arid and windswept southern coast, midway between Sapodilla Bay and Taylor Bay. Each building within the compound is built of imported Canadian cedar, fir, glass, concrete, and (in one case) local stone; each blends into the rocky, scrub-covered landscape that surrounds it. Angled toward sweeping views over turquoise-colored waters, each features a verandah-ringed design based on West Indian or Créole models. Although their position on a half acre or more of seafront land transmits a sense of isolation, grocery stores lie within a 15-minute drive, and since each unit contains a kitchen, many visitors opt to prepare most of their meals on-site. Some of the villas boast their own piers, others have serpentine staircases that wind down to the water's edge. Each has a scattering of tasteful furniture and many of the amenities you'll need for an escapist vacation. All have ceiling fans, most also have air-conditioning, and some come with fax machines. Each has a satellite TV hookup with at least 32 channels to while away the moonlit nights when you're not otherwise occupied. All rental arrangements are made through the Atlanta address that is listed above, and the availability of any particular villa will vary with the schedule and priorities of each villa's individual owner.

Royal Bay Resort & Villas. Lower Bight Rd., P.O. Box 186, Providenciales, Turks & Caicos, BWI. ☎ **800/SANDALS** or 809/946-8000. Fax 809/946-8001 or 305/663-4369. 160 rms, 40 suites/villas. A/C MINIBAR TV TEL. Winter, $920–$1,010 double; $1,150 junior suite; $1,420–$1,740 one-bedroom suite. Off-season, $865–$980 double; $1,075 junior suite; $1,220–$1,530 one-bedroom suite. Rates all inclusive for three nights. AE, MC, V.

In April 1997, this complex converted to a Beaches Resort, which is part of the Sandals chain of all-inclusive hotels. The existing facilities were left alone, but there are new additions all over the property, including restaurants, a pool, a water-sports facility, and a fitness center. The hotel remains one of the most luxurious on the island, but it now caters to a broader selection of clientele than it did previously. The property opens onto the 12-mile-long Grace Bay Beach, the country's finest and among the top beaches in both The Bahamas and the Caribbean. The $30 million resort's Bermuda-style bungalows with lovely pink and white exteriors are a showcase of luxury.

Catering to travelers from Europe and North America, the property features mainly guest rooms, which, although finely decorated, could use more warmth. If you can afford it, the one- and two-bedroom villa suites are the pockets of posh in the Turks and Caicos. All these accommodations have panoramic ocean views from private balconies, king-size or double beds, individual climate control, in-room safes, coffee makers, hairdryers, and in-room fax capability. Villa suites also have a spacious living room, a kitchenette, and two baths (one with a Roman tub and separate shower).

Dining/Entertainment: For a review of the resort's showcase restaurant, Sapodilla's, see "Where to Dine," below. Reflections offers more casual fare, at breakfast, lunch, or dinner. Its weekend breakfast buffet is the island's best. Otherwise, it serves burgers and fries and all the standard fare of an international resort. Three new restaurants offer seafood, Southwestern cuisine, and Japanese food. The Turtles and

Iguanas is the spot for an after-dinner drink. There's another bar and lounge at poolside.

Services: Room service, laundry, baby-sitting, in-room massage.

Facilities: Professionally staffed children's club; free-form swimming pool with rock formations, waterfalls, and a swim-up bar; two tennis courts lit for night play; fitness center with full range of exercise equipment; game room; nearby championship 18-hole golf course; and a full array of water sports, including scuba diving, sailing, windsurfing, fishing, and snorkeling. Glass-bottom boat trips, parasailing, and kayaking can also be arranged.

Turquoise Reef Resort & Casino. Grace Bay, P.O. Box 205, Providenciales, Turks & Caicos, BWI. ☎ **800/223-6510** in the U.S., or 809/946-5555. Fax 809/946-5629. 230 rms. A/C TV TEL. Winter, $185–$230 double. Off-season, $125–$160 double. MAP $15 per person extra. AE, MC, V.

Set on 14 acres of flat, sandy land, with a 900-foot beachfront along the island's northeastern coast, this resort opened in 1990. Its prominence, however, has been overshadowed by the opening of Grace Bay Club and Royal Bay Resort & Villas. It was built with touches of style and offers fairly priced accommodations that seem even better during its seasonal promotions. It is the first of the island's properties to contain a casino, and it offers more glitter and flash than any of its competitors. The resort was designed with prominent balconies in a modern hip-roofed compound, the buildings of which are symmetrically arranged around a landscaped garden and central swimming pool.

Each of the resort's bedrooms contains clay-tile floors, wicker furniture, ceiling fans, and a private balcony or patio. The standard rooms are small.

Dining/Entertainment: The resort's most upscale restaurant, the Portofino, features grilled seafood and steaks, with an emphasis on Italian cuisine. Less formal dining and daytime drinks are available beside the pool and beach at Buddy's Bar. Especially convenient is the simple Coral Terrace Restaurant and Lounge, the resort's coffee shop. After dark, at 7pm, with live music beginning at 9pm Monday to Saturday, clients congregate in the Portofino Nightclub. It features musicians imported from the Caribbean and the U.S. mainland.

Services: Baby-sitting, massage, room service (7 to 10am and 6 to 10pm), guest-activities coordinators for adults and children, respectively.

Facilities: Health club with exercise machines and Jacuzzi, swimming pool, two tennis courts lit for night play, dive shop with facilities for underwater photography, tour desk, scooter and bicycle rental, in-house car rental, and duty-free shop for the purchase of perfumes, jewelry, and liquor. Entrance is free to the island's only casino (the Port Royale), which opens every night from 5:30pm to 2am.

MODERATE

Le Deck Hotel & Beach Club. P.O. Box 144, Grace Bay, Providenciales, Turks & Caicos, BWI. ☎ **809/946-5547.** Fax 809/946-5770. 23 rms, 2 suites, 1 one-bedroom condo. A/C TV TEL. Winter, $160–$185 double; $225 suite; $295 condo. Off-season, $110–$170 double; $170–$205 suite; from $210–$260 condo. AE, MC, V.

Set a few steps from the very white sands of the island's eastern beaches, this hotel opened in 1989. Its informal, laid-back West Indian style immediately attracted guests who preferred it to the more formal properties described above. The land on which it sits is rather modest when compared to the acreage of the bigger resorts. It benefits, however, from its location: a 10-minute walk from the larger and better-accessorized Turquoise Reef Resort & Casino. Guests frequently walk over to the bigger resort to patronize its facilities, including its restaurants and gambling casino.

Each accommodation has a ceiling fan, a private bathroom, and a comfortable but no-frills decor of beach-inspired furniture and Caribbean colors. There's also a villalike condominium that sits a short distance from the rest of the hotel.

Arranged in a U shape around a deck that serves as a social center (and gives the establishment its name), the two-story hotel is painted pink and white and contains on its premises a curve-sided freshwater swimming pool, a wood-trimmed clubhouse-bar-restaurant with big windows and sea views, and a full array of water-sports options.

Erebus Inn. Turtle Cove, Providenciales, P.O. Box 238, Turks & Caicos, BWI. ☎ **809/946-4240.** Fax 809/946-4704. 25 rms, 4 chalets. MINIBAR TV TEL. Winter, $140–$160 double; $165 chalet. Off-season, $105–$125 double; $130 chalet. MAP $45 per person extra. AE, DISC, MC, V.

One of Provo's oldest inns, Erebus Inn occupies a hillside above Turtle Cove on the northern shore of the island, near the airport. It's not on the beach, although a shuttle is available to take guests there. In its category, this inn is much preferred over a comparable property, Turtle Cove Inn (see below). Its 10 studio apartments face the marina at the bottom of the hill. Additional accommodations are in a long and narrow stone-sided annex whose breeze-filled central hallway evokes an enlarged version of an old Bahamian house. Twenty-two rooms are air-conditioned. Ringing both sections of the hotel are dry-weather plants such as cactus and carefully watered vines such as bougainvillea.

The social center is the big-windowed Spinnaker Bar, the perimeter of which offers a view of the marina and the gulf. There is also an open-air terrace surrounded by walls of chiseled stone. Facilities include two pools (one saltwater), two clay tennis courts, and a health club. The inn also operates a lively French restaurant.

Mariner Hotel. Sapodilla Point, Providenciales, Turks & Caicos, BWI. ☎ **809/946-4488.** Fax 809/946-4488. 25 rms. A/C. Winter, $95–$110 double. Off-season, $75–$85 double. AE, MC, V.

Uncluttered simplicity is the byword of this informal hotel, the principal decor of which are the sweeping sea vistas around it. It stands 3 miles southeast of the airport. The only object interrupting the panorama is a Shell Oil unloading dock, a concrete-and-steel giant jutting into the sea at the bottom of the slope supporting the hotel. Even the dock, however, has a form of isolated grandeur about it. The owners have worked hard to turn the locale into an oasis of flowering plants. These grow around the bases of the villas containing the accommodations. The social center is the swimming pool and the sundeck, where palms and parasols shade the planked boardwalks. The hotel also operates a simple restaurant.

Accommodations are basic and unfussy, with ceiling fans, bathrooms, and modern lines.

Turtle Cove Inn. Turtle Cove Marina, Suzie Turn Rd., Providenciales, Turks & Caicos, BWI. ☎ **800/887-0477** in the U.S., or 809/946-4203. Fax 809/946-4141. 28 rms, 2 suites. A/C TV TEL. Winter, $95–$115 double. Off-season, $85–$100 double; year-round, suite $115–$130. AE, MC, V.

Originally constructed of local stone and white stucco in 1983, and enlarged and upgraded in 1990, this two-story hotel is built in a U shape around a swimming pool. It's a favorite with divers and boaters. A few feet away, boats dock directly at the hotel's pier, which juts into Seller's Pond amid the many yachts floating at anchor. Near the pool lie the tables of the separately recommended Tiki Hut Cabaña Bar & Grill. Upstairs, open for dinner only, is the Terrace Restaurant. (See separate recommendations for restaurants.) The Tipsy Turtle liquor store is also on site. Each bedroom is simply but comfortably furnished, with views over either the pool or the marina.

Although it doesn't have a beach of its own, many guests don't consider this a problem because a shuttle carries them from the hotel's wharf to the sands of a nearby beach. There is a freshwater swimming pool. Dive packages are available.

WHERE TO DINE
EXPENSIVE

✪ **Alfred's Place.** Suzie Turn Rd., above the Turtle Cove Marina. ☎ **809/946-4679.** Reservations recommended. Lunch platters $6.25–$9; dinner main courses $12.50–$25. AE, MC, V. Daily noon–2pm and 7–10pm. FRENCH/INTERNATIONAL.

The most innovative restaurant on the island, this is the domain of Austrian-born Alfred Holzfeind, who worked for many years as a chef on an upscale cruise line. It occupies a pavilion-style building high on a hillside above the Turtle Cove Marina, with an outdoor terrace offering panoramic views.

Although the chef is firmly grounded in French culinary techniques, he also feels free to borrow from whatever international influences he cares to, even Thai, as re-flected by his fiery grilled swordfish or his Thai-style shrimp salad. The chef tries to use prime ingredients shipped to this remote outpost. Out of the freezer he transforms a roast rack of lamb by serving it with either blueberry sauce or goat cheese. His veal briard nestled in a bed of applesauce and melted Brie is worthy, as are any of his salads, especially the one with fresh tomatoes, fresh basil, and mozzarella. Our greatest praise is bestowed upon the grilled tuna in an anchovy and tomato sauce. Lunches are less complicated, featuring such dishes as prime rib or lobster sandwiches, chicken or fish in pita bread, and club sandwiches.

✪ **Anacaona.** In the Grace Bay Club, Grace Bay Rd. ☎ **809/946-5757.** Reservations recom-mended. Lunch salads, sandwiches, and platters $8–$13; dinner main courses $28–$38. AE, MC, V. Daily noon–3pm and 7–9:30pm. FRENCH/MEDITERRANEAN.

The unlikely name of this restaurant translates from a dialect of the native Lucayan tribe as either "feather of gold" or "flower," depending on its context. Set in three thatch-roofed and interconnected pods that serve as outbuildings of a previously rec-ommended resort, this place is lighthearted, fun, and elegant. It's as good as hotel restaurants get in Provo.

You might enjoy one of the frothy drinks in the bar before crossing over a foun-tain stream to the restaurant. French recipes are combined effectively with some of the produce of the Caribbean, not always an easy wedding. But here the effect is successful. At lunch you might prefer some of the dishes familiar to those who've visited the French Riviera, including a classic salade Niçoise. The grilled tuna is excellent. In the evening the atmosphere becomes more romantic, with the flicker-ing light of the torches and candlelight on the tables. The chef's grilled lobster is the island's finest dish, and it's worth the trip here just to sample it. But, to his credit, he also does fresh fish dishes extremely well. He's also grounded in the classics, of-fering such familiar fare as home-smoked salmon or a perfectly executed roast rack of lamb. His house dessert specialty deserves an award: crème brûlée topped with peaches.

Banana Boat Restaurant. Turtle Cove Marina. ☎ **809/941-5706.** Reservations recom-mended. Main courses $9.95–$16. AE, MC, V. Daily 11am–10pm. INTERNATIONAL.

Banana Boat Restaurant is the most popular independent restaurant on the island. That doesn't mean it's the best; it's not. But it's certainly the most convivial. It was established in 1981. Since then there's hardly been a "yachtie" on Providenciales who hasn't enjoyed at least one of the establishment's island meals and potent drinks, such as Wilbert's Wet and Wild Wonder. For a main course, you might try T-bone steak, cracked conch, or some freshly caught local fish. At lunch, favorites include lobster or tuna salads, along with half-pound burgers. Dessert might be carrot cake or key lime pie. No one in the kitchen fusses too much with these dishes, but they are good and flavorful. A choice seat is on the timber-and-plank verandah that juts on piers above the water of Turtle Cove.

Portofino. In the Turquoise Reef Resort & Casino, Grace Bay. ☎ **809/946-5555.** Reservations required. Main courses $15–$35. AE, MC, V. Mon–Sat 6–11pm. ITALIAN.

Inspired by the decor and cuisines of Italy, this is the most elegant Italian restaurant in Provo. Set adjacent to its own seafront terrace overlooking Grace Bay, in a previously recommended hotel, it sports modern furniture, subtle lighting, a formally dressed staff, and a soothing color scheme of turquoise and pale pink. Your meal might include any of about 10 varieties of pasta, including the chef's proposed pasta of the day, served either as a main course or as an appetizer. Main courses include strips of veal sautéed with morels and chanterelles in a vermouth sauce, roast pheasant with shiitake mushrooms and a mushroom sauce, a medley of shrimp and scallops with mushrooms and Italian seasonings served in a piquant béchamel sauce, and prime tenderloin of beef rubbed with fresh peppercorns and served in a cognac cream sauce. The chefs do an admirable job of turning out the flavorful and often zesty cuisine of Italy.

✪ Sapodilla's. Royal Bay Resort & Villas, Lower Bight Rd. ☎ **809/946-8000.** Main courses $29–$38. AE, MC, V. Reservations recommended. Mon–Sat 6–10pm. INTERNATIONAL/CARIBBEAN.

The only hotel restaurant that rivals Sapodilla's is Anacaona, in a neck-and-neck race. In an elegant setting, chef Sherman Gordon showcases his wares, adding a Caribbean emphasis to an international menu. His skills come into play in his selection of hot and cold appetizers, ranging from a peppery rare tuna with a miso and basil sauce to smoked duck and wild mushrooms in a fresh sage sauce. Who would need prodding to order his rack of lamb Sapodilla with an apple and scotch bonnet chutney with roast garlic, or his prawns and pasta in a red curry sauce with oriental rice noodles? This is a place worth searching out, and the setting and service match the first-rate cuisine.

MODERATE

Dora's Seafood Restaurant. Leeward Hwy. ☎ **809/946-4558.** Breakfast $4.50–$6; lunch $6.50–$7.50; main courses $10–$15. AE, MC, V. Daily 8am–3am. SEAFOOD.

This plain restaurant, contained within a single-story cement building beside the main highway, is the domain of Dora Lightbourne, born on remote South Caicos. This is a down-home eatery, patronized not only by locals but also by visitors bored with fancy hotel or continental fare. There's a bar area to quench your thirst, as well as a handful of tables where local and authentic dishes are served. Your meal might include conch fritters or conch chowder. Either of these is the best on the island. Other dishes include the famous and inevitable grouper fingers but also several different preparations of lobster or cracked conch. There's a seafood buffet served every Monday and Thursday night from 7 to 10pm, priced at $22 per person, which includes transportation to and from whatever hotel you happen to be staying in.

🧒 Family-Friendly Restaurants

Tiki Hut Cabaña Bar & Grill *(see p. 322)*   At Provo's Turtle Cove Inn, this cabaña-style restaurant places tables around the pool and offers children American breakfasts, sandwiches, or fresh pasta dinners.

Salt Raker Inn *(see p. 304)*   On Grand Turk, this simple family restaurant offers familiar fare at lunch (burgers, fish-and-chips, sandwiches), and at night grills the catch of the day for its largely boating crowd, many of whom are with their families.

Hey José Cantina *(see p. 323)*   Two Californians welcome the family trade at this Provo hotspot and feed their diners well on burritos, tacos, quesadillas, and the best pizzas on the island.

Hong Kong. Leeward Hwy., Grace Bay. ☎ 809/946-5678. Reservations recommended. Main courses $10–$18. AE, MC, V. Mon–Sat 11am–10pm, Sun 5–10pm. CANTONESE.

Contained within a white, cement-sided building on the highway, midway between the Turquoise Reef and Club Med, this simple hole-in-the-wall serves the best Chinese food on the island. But, remember, we're talking Provo here and not New York or San Francisco. Many of the cooks are immigrants from China. In one of a pair of dining rooms, you can enjoy a medley of Cantonese dishes served with such sauces as black bean, hot pepper, soya, sweet and sour, and lobster. A popular dish inspired by local culinary tastes includes sweet-and-sour conch.

The Terrace Restaurant. In the Turtle Cove Inn, Suzie Turn Rd., South Shore. ☎ 809/946-4763. Reservations recommended. Main courses $6.75–$24.50. AE, MC, V. Mon–Sat 11:30am–10pm. INTERNATIONAL.

Divers, boaters, and young couples, often guests at the Turtle Cove Inn (previously recommended), have turned this convivial place into Provo's trendiest spot. Trendy would mean little if the food weren't good. Fortunately, it is. The setting helps too: a covered outdoor terrace and an intimate dining room. Many guests still come here looking for Jimmy's, which became somewhat of a legend during its short reign. This is the same place, only different.

The old motto of "Eat, eat, eat—don't go away hungry," still prevails. The conch ravioli is one of the best we've ever sampled, and even Noël Coward's famous lobster mousse that he attempted to serve the Queen Mother (it melted before she could try it) surely didn't taste as smooth as this one. You can also enjoy a delectable home-smoked salmon to begin your meal. The local catch is invariably moist and tender, and grilled to perfection. The pasta dishes are also superb, but, alas, don't equal those of Portofino. For dessert, be sure to try one of their ice-cream creations. You'll find none finer in Provo.

Tiki Hut Cabaña Bar & Grill. In the Turtle Cove Inn, Turtle Cove Marina. ☎ 809/941-5341. American breakfast $4–$6; lunch platters $6–$11; dinner main courses $10.50–$15. AE, MC, V. Daily 7am–5pm and 6–10pm. AMERICAN/CARIBBEAN/PASTA.

This open-air, cabaña-style restaurant arranges its tables beside the pool of an informal inn that sits next to one of the island's biggest marinas. The restaurant was established in 1993 after its owner split away from the hugely successful Banana Boat Restaurant next door. The Tiki Hut serves full-fledged American-style breakfasts; lunches that include salads, fresh fish platters, and sandwiches; and dinners that consist almost completely of pasta and fresh fish. Culinary specialties include jerked grouper (slow-cooked with spices in the Jamaican style), panfried or grilled catch of the day served with fresh dill and caper-tartar sauce, and the traditional favorite, English-style fish-and-chips, prepared with your choice of wahoo, grouper, snapper, or dolphinfish. The house drink is a Banana Slammer. This place is a local favorite, serving solid, reliable fare. If you want a more refined cuisine, you can patronize the previously recommended Terrace Restaurant in the same hotel.

INEXPENSIVE

Hey José Cantina. Central Square, Leeward Hwy. ☎ **809/946-4812.** Lunch platters $6–$10; pizzas $6–$22; dinner main courses $8–$14. AE, MC, V. Mon–Sat noon–10pm. Bar Mon–Sat noon–midnight. MEXICAN/PIZZA/AMERICAN.

Set in the center of the island, as one of the focal points of a small shopping center, this lighthearted eatery was recently bought by Steve and Marilyn Mull. Within a decor of burnt orange, greens, and yellows, you can enjoy the best margaritas in Provo, as well as a wide array of tasty Mexican food. The parade of burritos, tacos, quesadillas, chimichangas, and a selection of grilled steaks and chicken will make you think you've been transplanted to some fiery little eatery along the Tex-Mex border. Also popular, especially with expatriate North Americans who have had their fill of grouper and cracked conch, are the richly topped pizzas. Available in three sizes, they culminate with a variety known as "the kitchen sink," where virtually everything you can think of is thrown on.

Tasty Temptations. In the Butterfield Square Shopping Center, Leeward Hwy. ☎ **809/946-4049.** Pastries and turnovers $1.50–$2; sandwiches $4.95–$6.95. No credit cards. Mon–Fri 6:30am–3pm; Sat 7:30am–1pm. Closed Sept. DELI.

No one would ever consider coming here for a full-fledged meal, but for a morning cup of espresso or cappuccino, bagels with smoked salmon and cream cheese, and any of about a dozen kinds of lunchtime sandwiches, this place is an excellent choice. It's arranged deli style, with prominent sandwich boards, oil paintings of nautical subjects from a nearby art gallery, and glass-fronted display cases where you collect your food on trays or in paper bags for take-out. If you opt to eat on the premises, there's an outdoor terrace. The place is popular with the office workers from Provo's administrative headquarters, and with anyone assembling the components of a picnic. "Tasty" sells cold cuts and deli foods by the pound. Run by an expatriate from French-speaking Canada, the establishment lies within a 10-minute drive west of Provo's airport.

BEACHES, WATER SPORTS & OTHER OUTDOOR ACTIVITIES

BEACHES

Provo Beach is a magnificent white sandy beach that goes on for a dozen or so miles along the northeast coast of Providenciales. **Sapodilla Bay Beach,** at the northwest point, is another gem of a beach.

FISHING

The best fishing excursions are offered by **Silver Deep** (☎ 809/941-5595), which features both half- and full-day fishing expeditions, usually bonefishing or bottom fishing. Tackle and bait are thrown in. For those who'd like to venture farther afield, and pay a lot more money, half- and full-day deep-sea fishing expeditions are arranged, with all equipment included. Catches turn up wahoo, tuna, kingfish, marlin, and even shark. Arranging virtually the same fishing tours is **Sakitumi** (☎ **809/946-4203**), at comparable prices.

GOLF

Provo Golf Club. Grace Bay Rd., Providenciales. ☎ **809/946-5991.**

Opened with much fanfare late in 1992, this is the only golf course in the country. Developed by the local water board, whose desalinization plants provide the water to irrigate it, the 6,560-yard, par-72, 18-hole course was designed by Karl Litten, of Boca Raton, Florida. Young palms and bougainvillea, as well as rocky outcroppings and powdery sand traps, help make the course a challenge to the serious golfer or a lovely day on the links for the beginner or novice. Four sets of tees allow golfers to tailor their game to their level of expertise. A driving range and putting greens are also available. The clubhouse contains a bar and a restaurant serving breakfast and lunch. Starting times are daily from 7:15am to 4pm. Greens fees are $95 per person for 18 holes. The price includes the use of a golf cart, which is mandatory. Golf clubs can be rented for $15 per set.

PARASAILING

This increasingly popular sport is presented by both **J&B Tours,** Leeward Marina (☎ **809/946-5047**), or at **Dive Provo,** Turquoise Reef Resort (☎ **809/946-5040**), costing around $45 for a 15-minute flight.

SAILING

Boating in the hard-to-reach islands has become a popular pastime. If you'd like to keep your vacation funds fairly intact, consider **Dive Provo,** Turquoise Reef Resort (☎ **809/946-5040**), which rents small sailboats for around $25 per hour. This outfitter will even provide beginning sailing instructions for $40 for up to 2 hours. You can also rent an open-cockpit ocean kayak here for $15 per hour for two adventurers. More expensive sailing craft, even with a private captain for half- or full-day excursions, are available from **J&B Tours** by calling ☎ **809/946-5047.**

If you'd like to join a group for sailing, consider **Ocean Outback** (☎ **809/946-4080**), a 70-foot motor cruiser. It touts its snorkel cruises to neighboring but uninhabited islands. A barbecue is part of the fun. **Tao** (☎ **809/946-5040**) has become a favorite for its sailing and snorkeling cruises. It's also known for its sunset cruises. A full day's cruise costs $60 per person, and that includes lunch and renting of snorkeling equipment.

SNORKELING & SCUBA DIVING

Art Pickering's Provo Turtle Divers Ltd. Turtle Cove. ☎ **800/833-1341** in the U.S., or 809/946-4232.

Provo Turtle Divers Ltd., with headquarters directly in front of Erebus Inn on the water, is the oldest and best dive operation in the islands. Dive experts, including Jacques Cousteau, have cited Provo as one of the 10 best sites in the world, because of a barrier reef that runs the full length of the island's 17-mile north coast. At Northwest Point there is a vertical drop-off to 7,000 feet.

Provo Turtle Divers offers personalized service. There are scuba tanks for rent, plus ample backpacks and weight belts. A single dive costs $40, a night dive goes for $45. A PADI open-water certification course is $350. Provo Turtle is a PADI training facility, with full instruction and resort courses. An open-water PADI referral course goes for $225. Snorkeling equipment is also available.

Dive Provo. In the Turquoise Reef Resort, Grace Bay. ☎ **800/234-7768** in the U.S., or 809/946-5029.

Diving Paradise

A reef system 65 miles across and 200 miles long, a great range of diving spots, playful dolphins who show up unexpectedly, countless varieties of fish and coral—these are the undersea attractions of the Turks and Caicos Islands.

The islands promise to be much more than the latest "hot dive spot." Dive operators can take visitors to spots popular with other divers or customize a trip of discovery to virgin territory.

For example, off the northwest corner of Providenciales, known locally as "Provo," is Smith's Reef, a walk-in dive to a seascape of brain and fan corals, purple gorgonias, anemones, and sea cucumbers, active with sergeant majors, green parrot fish, long-nosed trumpet fish, the odd, ominous-looking green moray, an occasional southern ray, and a visiting hawksbill turtle or two.

From the shore at Grace Bay, a sweep of powdery white beach that is graced by some of Provo's most highly regarded resorts, visitors can see where the sea breaks along 14 miles of barrier reef. But the reef is much more than the natural breakwater that makes this beach so accommodating, it is also the teeming undersea home of sea life ranging from swarms of colorful schools of fish to the singleton-feeding barracuda to large, rotund grouper.

Around Grand Turk, there are miles and miles of drop-off diving. Here you can enjoy one of the underwater world's great experiences: a night dive on a wall where the colors of the day become the phosphorescent illumination of the night.

Ledge and wall dives are the attractions around South Caicos. Here divers can literally select the level of their vertical descent, then glide horizontally among the multicolored, multishaped corals and drift through schools of trumpets, hamlets, basslets, and more.

Off Salt Cay, divers can explore the wreck of the HMS *Endymion,* which went down in a storm in 1790. Two centuries later, Brian Sheedy, a local diver and inn operator, discovered the wreck. Today, while the reef has reclaimed the hull and all else that was biodegradable, divers can nonetheless get a close-up look at its cannons and four huge anchors lying about.

But Salt Cay is more than the final resting place of a ghost ship. Between January and March each year, the humpback whales come here to play. Visitors can watch their antics from shore, boat out among them, or don dive equipment and go below.

To reach the underwater treasures of West Caicos, a handful of dive boats make hour-long transits (each way) from the southern tip of Provo (Sapodilla Bay) several times a week. Once they're below the water's surface, divers are usually awestruck at the more than 2 miles of sheer coral walls whose edges begin less than a quarter mile from the West Caicos shoreline. The most popular dive sites are Boat Cove, Sunday Service, and Isle's End.

Packages are available with international airlines serving the Turks and Caicos Islands and local hotels (with or without meals). Dive certification courses are also offered.

Dive Provo also has one of the best scuba programs on the island. You're taken to unspoiled spots where you see an extraordinary array of marine life. You can dive at the vertical walls of Northwest Point where sheer drop-offs begin at 50 to 60 feet. Here you'll discover a panoramic array of corals and vibrant gold and purple sponges. Its Grace Bay dive boat leaves the Turquoise Reef pier daily at 8:30am. It also offers PADI open-water certification courses, along with snorkeling trips, glass-bottom boat rides, equipment rental, Windsurfer or sailboat instruction, and sailing excursions. A two-tank scuba dive costs $65, with a PADI certification course going for $375. Snorkeling trips go for $20, and Windsurfers or sailboats can be rented for $20 per hour.

TENNIS

Many resorts have courts which are lit at night. Some of the best include **Turtle Cove Inn** (☎ **809/946-4203**), with two courts, both lit at night.

The best courts are at the all-inclusive **Club Med Turkoise** (see above), but these are usually set aside for guests. Nonguests can play at many other courts, however, including the two at **Turquoise Reef Resort** (☎ **809/946-5555**), and the two at **Erebus Inn** (☎ **809/946-4240**).

WATERSKIING

Provo with its calm seas and turquoise waters is ideal for this sport. The best outfitter is **Dive Provo** at the Turquoise Reef Resort (☎ **809/946-5040**), charging $35 for a 15-minute run.

WINDSURFING

Again **Dive Provo** (see "Waterskiing," above) is the best outfitter for this sport.

EXPLORING THE ISLAND: FROLICKING WITH JOJO THE DOLPHIN

The national treasure of Provo is a famous Atlantic bottle-nosed dolphin, **JoJo,** that has lived and played around these waters since 1983. What makes this wild dolphin unusual is that it chose to leave its pod and seek out the company of people. It cavorts and plays with the children of the residents of the town of Bight, on the northern shore of Provo, giving them rides out to the reef and back. Very few dolphins have ever adopted such a people-oriented lifestyle on their own. You can watch a video of JoJo at **Island Sea Center** (☎ **809/946-5849**), Monday through Saturday from 9am to 5pm.

This is also the site of the **Caicos Conch Farm** (see below).

Chalk Sound, a landlocked lagoon west of Five Cays Settlement, has been turned into a public park. The hamlet of Five Cays itself boasts a small harbor and a modern airport.

Caicos Conch Farm. Leeward Hwy. ☎ **809/946-5849.** Admission $6 adults, $3 children under 12. Mon–Fri 9am–3:30pm (last tour).

Located on the isolated eastern end of the island, amid a flat and sun-baked terrain of scrub and sand, this establishment was founded in 1984 by a consortium of investors from Miami and Canada. It is a pioneer (the only one of its kind in the West Indies) for the commercial production of the large edible mollusk, our faithful friend, the conch. Its techniques are not commercially viable, but this place could spark breeding techniques that could change the way conch is cultivated worldwide. Its staff will give visitors a walking tour of the breeding basins. For another $3, they give you a conch after the tour. Admission includes a tour of the hatchery and the laboratories. In the gift shop, you can buy rare conch pearls, shell jewelry, and commemorative T-shirts.

ORGANIZED TOURS

Executive Tours (☎ **809/946-4524** for information and reservations) is the largest and best ground-transport company on Provo. The company is responsible for transporting Club Med clients. However, when they are not busy with their Club Med obligations, they take visitors from all hotels on island tours in a 12-passenger minivan. Tours last half a day and cost $10 per person.

SHOPPING

Bamboo Gallery. Leeward Hwy., Providenciales. ☎ **809/946-4748.**

If shopping for paintings is one of the diversions you enjoy when you're on vacation, you might enjoy browsing through one of the leading art galleries of Provo. Its inventories include woodcarvings, ceramic sculptures, and the kinds of colorful oil paintings that, if they don't come directly from Haiti, were at least inspired by that island's traditions. The most unusual pieces—to look at if not to buy—are some of the locally made metal sculptures, sometimes created using oil drums or old car wrecks for material.

Greensleeves. Central Square, Providenciales. ☎ **809/946-4147.**

This is the leading craft and souvenir shop on Provo. Its merchandise features paintings and ceramics by local artists, as well as baskets, unusual jewelry, and sisal mats and bags. A collection of handmade soft toys is also sold.

Mama's Gifts. Ports of Call. ☎ **809/941-3338.**

This store is known for its collection of embroidered and hand-woven baskets. If you'd like a souvenir, it also sells jewelry made of shells and wood, along with handbags.

Paradise Gifts & Art. Central Square. ☎ **809/946-4343.**

This shop has an on-site ceramics studio where purchases can be made. Paintings by Provo artists are also for sale here. Some of them are really awful, but every now and then a gem turns up.

Royal Jewels. Leeward Hwy. ☎ **809/946-4885.**

For the best duty-free shopping, this is the place to go. It has good stocks in gold jewelry and designer watches, plus French and international perfumes, all the standard showcase stuff found on other islands in the Caribbean.

Tropical Fashions. Turtle Cove, Providenciales. ☎ **809/946-4343.**

This popular boutique sells well-made clothing, often inspired by the fashions you might expect to find in Miami's stylish South Beach neighborhood. Missing a sarong or a bathing suit, or did you leave your sandals on the beach during last week's midnight swim? T-shirts, sportswear, and designer clothing from California, as well as the store's own designs, are also sold.

PROVO AFTER DARK

Port Royale Casino. In the Turquoise Reef Resort & Casino, Grace Bay. ☎ **809/946-5555.**

The major center for after-dark diversion on Provo is this casino, which is the only one authorized to operate in any British Dependent Territory. It's generally packed every night, with resort visitors playing blackjack, craps, Caribbean stud, roulette, and poker. There are also about 100 slot machines. Casablanca-style fans whirl overhead, as waiters serve frosty drinks. Hours are daily from 6pm until 1 or 2am.

There are some other places for night-time diversion, and many hotels stage entertainment for their guests. If yours doesn't, you can seek some action at **Smokey's on the Beach,** near Le Deck Hotel (☎ **809/941-3466**), where the locals go to have fun—that is, when they're not serving guests in hotels. Right on the beach, it's the best place to sunset watch on the island. It is both a bar and a rather standard restaurant. **Bacchus,** across from the Turquoise Reef Resort (☎ **809/946-5214**), is open Thursday through Saturday nights, offering drinks and dancing. It's not special in any way, however. **Disco Elite,** Airport Rd. (☎ **809/946-4592**), is your typical disco with an elevated dance floor and strobe lighting. A much hotter spot, currently in fashion, is **Casablanca,** next to Club Med (☎ **809/946-5449**). Many Club Med residents flock here when they get bored with the diversions at their own resort. It's a Riviera-like club, with mirrors, music, drinks, and a lot of fun if the crowd's right.

7 Pine Cay

This exclusive territory, a private island in the West Indies, is owned and managed by members of the Meridian Club, who rightly praise its $2^1/_2$-mile talcum-powder beach, which is among the finest in all the islands.

Pine Cay is one of a chain of islets connecting Providenciales and North Caicos. Two miles long and 800 acres in area, it is a small residential community with a large area set aside for a park. It has its own 3,900-foot airstrip with scheduled local air service, as well as dock and harbor facilities. No cars are allowed, and transportation is by golf cart or bicycle. There is just enough fresh water, and the cay has its own generating plant.

Once a private club, Pine Cay still has members, but they now join the public guests for swimming, sunning, and shelling along the white-sand beach. Snorkeling and diving are possible in an unspoiled barrier reef. Explorers look for Arawak and British colonial remains. There is also a wide range of birds and plants.

The island's possibilities were recognized by Ferdinand Czernin, son of the last prime minister of the Austro-Hungarian Empire. It is said he was looking for an "intellectual Walden Pond" when he discovered this unspoiled, pristine retreat.

There is no place in Turks and Caicos—nor The Bahamas for that matter—that has the chic of the Meridian Club on Pine Cay. There are no newspapers, no TVs, no radios, no roads, and no cars, and that's how the people who visit here want to keep it. The island is the size of New York's Central Park, but much less dangerous. In fact, it's not dangerous at all. That's one of the many reasons the movers and shakers of the East Coast like to retreat here. They have enough trouble back home. When they arrive at Pine Cay, they like to leave "the world," as it's called here, behind. So far, club members have kept the developers at bay, watching in horror what happened to Provo. They even voted against adding more cabañas to their own club, even though they clearly need them. Once you leave the club, the pristine island is yours to explore. If you truly want to see what the islands looked like when Columbus made his landfall (wherever that was!), Pine Cay is the type of place he saw. Nothing has changed.

GETTING THERE   To reach Pine Cay, fly to Miami and then take another flight to Providenciales (see the "Getting There" section at the beginning of this chapter). There, an air taxi can be arranged to meet you for the 10-minute flight to Pine Cay.

WHERE TO STAY & DINE

✪ **The Meridian Club.** Pine Cay, Turks & Caicos, BWI. Fax 809/946-5128. (For reservations and information, contact the Meridian Club, c/o Resorts Management, Inc., $201^1/_2$ E. 29th St., New York, NY 10016. ☎ **800/331-9154,** or 212/696-4566 in the U.S.) 12 rms. Winter (AP), $525–$625 double. Off-season (AP), $425 double. No children under 12. No credit cards.

The Meridian Club is an environmentally sensitive resort that includes a main club-house that faces the beach and a freshwater pool. The club, barefoot elegance at its best, has a delightful dining room, a comfortable library, and an intimate bar with a panoramic terrace for sunset cocktails. A dozen motel-style units are offered, with bed- and sitting-room areas, dressing rooms, outdoor showers, and terraces facing the beach. You can easily walk the $2^1/2$ miles of the fine, white sand that stretches out from your back door. The rooms may not have phones or TVs or air-conditioning, but with a beach like this, who cares?

Dining/Entertainment: The Meridian Club has one dining room and two bars, one of which is poolside. The open-air dining room offers full American breakfasts, buffet-style lunches served poolside, and dinners by candlelight. The food is usually a Caribbean/continental cuisine. Local produce, especially lobster, conch, and snapper, is used whenever possible. Sometimes, though, the guests are treated to something different. The hotel participates in a visiting chef program, so you may be dining on the unexpected. Guests can enjoy poolside barbecues, a band once or twice weekly, and afternoon tea.

Services: Laundry, room service for breakfast only.

Facilities: One tennis court, large freshwater swimming pool, variety of nature trails. There are activities planned daily, such as offshore snorkeling trips or boat trips to neighboring islands. Boats, snorkeling gear, tennis rackets and balls, bicycles are provided; fishing guides and experienced boatmen are available.

Index

FROMMER'S COMPLETE TRAVEL GUIDES

*(Comprehensive guides to destinations around the world, with
selections in all price ranges—from deluxe to budget)*

Acapulco, Ixtapa & Zihuatenejo
Alaska
Amsterdam
Arizona
Atlanta
Australia
Austria
Bahamas
Barcelona, Madrid & Seville
Belgium, Holland & Luxembourg
Bermuda
Boston
Budapest & the Best of Hungary
California
Canada
Cancún, Cozumel & the Yucatán
Cape Cod, Nantucket & Martha's Vineyard
Caribbean
Caribbean Cruises & Ports of Call
Caribbean Ports of Call
Carolinas & Georgia
Chicago
Colorado
Costa Rica
Denver, Boulder & Colorado Springs
England
Europe
Florida
France
Germany
Greece
Hawaii
Hong Kong
Honolulu, Waikiki & Oahu
Ireland
Israel
Italy
Jamaica & Barbados
Japan
Las Vegas
London
Los Angeles
Maryland & Delaware
Maui

Mexico
Miami & the Keys
Montana & Wyoming
Montréal & Québec City
Munich & the Bavarian Alps
Nashville & Memphis
Nepal
New England
New Mexico
New Orleans
New York City
Northern New England
Nova Scotia, New Brunswick
    & Prince Edward Island
Paris
Philadelphia & the Amish Country
Portugal
Prague & the Best of the Czech Republic
Provence & the Riviera
Puerto Rico
Rome
San Antonio & Austin
San Diego
San Francisco
Santa Fe, Taos & Albuquerque
Scandinavia
Scotland
Seattle & Portland
South Pacific
Spain
Switzerland
Thailand
Tokyo
Toronto
Tuscany & Umbria
U.S.A.
Utah
Vancouver & Victoria
Vienna & the Danube Valley
Virgin Islands
Virginia
Walt Disney World & Orlando
Washington, D.C.
Washington & Oregon

FROMMER'S DOLLAR-A-DAY BUDGET GUIDES
(The ultimate guides to low-cost travel)

Australia from $50 a Day

Berlin from $50 a Day

California from $60 a Day

Caribbean from $60 a Day

Costa Rica & Belize from $35 a Day

England from $60 a Day

Europe from $50 a Day

Florida from $50 a Day

Greece from $50 a Day

Hawaii from $60 a Day

India from $40 a Day

Ireland from $45 a Day

Israel from $45 a Day

Italy from $50 a Day

London from $60 a Day

Mexico from $35 a Day

New York from $75 a Day

New Zealand from $50 a Day

Paris from $70 a Day

San Francisco from $60 a Day

Washington, D.C., from $50 a Day

FROMMER'S PORTABLE GUIDES
(Pocket-size guides for travelers who want everything in a nutshell)

Charleston & Savannah

Dublin

Las Vegas

Maine Coast

New Orleans

Puerto Vallarta, Manzanillo & Guadalajara

San Francisco

Venice

Washington, D.C.

FROMMER'S IRREVERENT GUIDES
(Wickedly honest guides for sophisticated travelers)

Amsterdam

Chicago

London

Manhattan

Miami

New Orleans

Paris

San Francisco

Santa Fe

U.S. Virgin Islands

Walt Disney World

Washington, D.C.

FROMMER'S AMERICA ON WHEELS
(Everything you need for a successful road trip, including full-color road maps and ratings for every hotel)

California & Nevada

Florida

Great Lakes States & Midwest

Mid-Atlantic

New England & New York

Northwest & Great Plains

South-Central States & Texas

Southeast

Southwest

FROMMER'S BY NIGHT GUIDES
(The series for those who know that life begins after dark)

Amsterdam

Chicago

Las Vegas

London

Los Angeles

Madrid & Barcelona

Manhattan

Miami

New Orleans

Paris

Prague

San Francisco

Washington, D.C.

WHEREVER YOU TRAVEL, *H*ELP IS NEVER FAR AWAY.

From planning your trip to providing travel assistance along the way, American Express® Travel Service Offices are always there to help.

Bahamas

Mundy Tours (R)
Suite 20, Regent Center 4
Freeport
809/352-4444

Playtours (R)
303 Shirley Street
Nassau
809/322-2931

Travel

http://www.americanexpress.com/travel